Embedded Controller FORTH

For the 8051 Family

Embedded Controller FORTH

For the 8051 Family

William H. Payne

Sandia National Laboratories
Albuquerque, New Mexico

ACADEMIC PRESS, INC.
Harcourt Brace Jovanovich, Publishers
Boston San Diego New York
London Sydney Tokyo Toronto

This book is printed on acid-free paper. ∞

ACADEMIC PRESS, INC.
1250 Sixth Avenue, San Diego, CA 92101

United Kingdom Edition published by
ACADEMIC PRESS LIMITED
24-28 Oval Road, London NW1 7DX

Library of Congress Cataloging-in-Publication Data

Payne, William H.
Embedded controller FORTH for the 8051 family / William H. Payne.
p. cm.
ISBN 0-12-547570-5 (alk. paper)
1. Intel 8051 (Computer) — Programming. 2. FORTH (Computer program language) I. Title.
QA76.8.I27P38 1990
005.4′465—dc20 89-18579
CIP

Printed in the United States of America
90 91 92 93 9 8 7 6 5 4 3 2 1

To the memory of Harriett B. Rigas
—1989

Contents

Preface xi

Chapter 1
The FORTH Embedded Controller Hardware/Software Development Strategy 1

A. 8051 Family Memory Models 1
B. Hardware Memory Signals 7
C. High-level and/or Assembler Coding Decisions 10
D. Hardware and Software Debugging Strategies 10

Chapter 2
8051 Family Hardware Systems Schematics 15

A. Memory and I/O Decode Methods 18
B. Combined Code/External Memory 25
C. Separate Code and External Data 27
D. Reset Circuitry 28
E. Single Board 8051 System Layout 30
F. Motherboard 8051 with Bus Layout 33
G. The 8051 Schematics 34
H. Addressing the National 82C50 Asynchronous Communications Element 47
References 51

Chapter 3
The IBM PC Compatible Four File FORTH Operating System 53

A. Bringing up FORTH on Your PC Using the Four File FORTH System 54
B. The Laxen Full Screen Editor 70
C. The PC/ASSEMBLER 8086 Family Table-Driven Assembler ...73
D. PC Hardware, BIOS, and PC/MS DOS References 75

Chapter 4
8051 FORTH Assembler Programming 77

A. The 8051 Family FORTH Assembler 78
B. Using the 8051 FORTH Assembler as a Cross Assembler 83
C. Transient Modules 88
D. Assembling 8051 Assembler Code on an 8051 93
E. Macro and Conditional Assembly 100
F. FORTH Assembler Conclusion 101

Chapter 5
Reverse Software Engineering Assembler Code 103

A. Disassembly of ROMs 103
B. Interactive 8051 Family Disassemblers 104

Chapter 6
The 8051 Family FORTH Operating System 109

A. 8051 FORTH Operating System Code Layout 109
B. Terminal and Disk PC Interface Protocol 112
C. 8051 FORTH Operating System Memory Layout 112

Chapter 7
The PC Terminal Emulator and Disk System 119

Chapter 8
The Nautilus Version 2 Metacompiler 123

A. Compiling the Nautilus Metacompiler with FORTH86 125
B. Compiling the 8086 Metaassembler 126
C. Metacompiling the 8086 Family FORTH, FORTH86 127
D. Compiling the 8051 Metaassembler 128
E. Metacompiling the 8051 FORTH Operating System 129
F. How to Write a Metacompiler 130

Chapter 9
FORTH Decompilers 133

A. The DIS FORTH Decompiler 134
B. The SEE Decompiler 135
C. Cross Decompilers 136

Chapter 10
Porting FORTH to Another FORTH Version or Processor 137

A. Converting Forth Interest Group FORTH to Another FORTH Version 137
B. Porting Fig FORTH to Another Processor 138
C. FORTH, Hardware, and Software 139

Appendix 1
Source Listing of the 8086 Family FORTH Nucleus 141

Appendix 2
ASCII Listing of the Binary of FORTH86 171

Appendix 3
FORTH86 System File: SYSTEM.SCR 179

Appendix 4
Nonassembler Version of the Laxen Full Screen FORTH Editor 191

Appendix 5
Assembler-Enhanced Version of Laxen's Full Screen Editor 221

Appendix 6
PC/ASSEMBLER 8086, 8087, and NEC V30 Family FORTH Assembler 229

Appendix 7
8051 FORTH Assembler in Cross Assembler Format 261

Appendix 8
"Examples" Syntax Tables for the 8051 FORTH Assembler 275

Appendix 9
8051 FORTH Operating System with ROMed Assembler and Mini-Full Screen Editor 285

Appendix 10
ASCII Listing of the 8051 FORTH Operating System 335

Appendix 11
Symbol Map of the Binary of the FORTH 8051 Operating System 347

Appendix 12
8051 Cross Disassembler to Screen 359

Appendix 13
The 8051 FORTH Operating System PC Terminal and Disk
Emulator..369

Appendix 14
Nautilus 2 Metacompiler Base 389

Appendix 15
The Nautilus Version 2 Metacompiler 399

Appendix 16
The 8086 Family Metaassembler 445

Appendix 17
8051 FORTH Metaassembler 479

Appendix 18
The DIS FORTH Decompiler..495

Appendix 19
The SEE FORTH Decompiler..499

Preface

Economic competition forces replacement of complicated mechanical or even some analog electrical systems with microcontrollers. We enter a new phase in the industrial revolution, in which microcontroller control of machines becomes the cheapest method. "Semiconductor companies," Intel customer engineer Mark Thompson has pointed out, "essentially sell sand."

Microcontroller-based systems offer greater control compared with rival technologies. Software implementation of control algorithms accounts for this difference. The selection of appropriate software implementation technology for embedded controllers must be viewed from the standpoint of economic competitiveness. FORTH is one of the major software technologies appropriate for embedded controller software development.

FORTH is an amalgamation of an operating system, a high level language system, compiler, assembler, linker, loader, editor, disassembler, decompiler. . . . All the software tools required to produce some software products are included in the FORTH environment.

FORTH is a tiny operating system. It occupies a position just above system development monitors. It is below BASICs, which are beneath MS-DOS, which is beneath the UNIXs.

FORTH has a limited range of hardware applicability. It is unsuited to the smallest microcontroller hosts such as the 8049 and HC05 families.

Assembler and token threaded technologies seem to work best on these machines. At the other extreme, it generally is unsuited to large computers such as Cray's or IBM mainframes, although there are implementations on the latter machine. FORTH is used to debug hardware at development time on the largest computers but it is not supplied to users.

FORTH's scope of software applicability is also limited. Writing payroll in FORTH is not advised. Mathematical software is better implemented in other languages. FORTH is not suited to projects requiring many programmers or huge codes.

FORTH is applicable to hardware intensive projects implemented by one, two, or three workers. Robots, computer numerical controlled machines, weapons programmers, cryptographic processors, engine controllers, unmanned observatories, computer hardware debuggers, laser printer graphics controllers, video games, work station device drivers, and BASICs writing are all candidates for FORTH software technology. FORTH is one of the top choices for embedded controller applications.

FORTH is unsurpassed in its ability to create minimal sized codes. For most applications 90% of the work is done in 10% of the code. Computation-intensive code sections are recoded in FORTH assembler to produce an application code that runs nearly as fast as one coded entirely in assembler. But the converted code was written with a fraction of the effort required to produce the all-assembler code.

FORTH's interactive environment permits the programmer to write extensive module testing routines easily. Subroutines can be exercised extensively to verify their correctness on the target machine.

FORTH brooks secrecy. Programmers must be able to reference the FORTH operating system source code to fix application bugs. FORTH's operation is intricate. Without the availability of a source code, FORTH's use is discouraged.

The 8051 microcontroller has emerged as the most popular of the 8-bit microcontrollers. It is second-sourced from a number of vendors. It comes in NMOS, CMOS, and radiation-hardened CMOS. It is used as a core processor to which is added many peripherals such as manchester or SLDC communications or analog-to-digital converters.

Process-stepping improvements to the 8051 family make it an electrically rugged computer. CMOS 8031s are nearly impossible to kill electrically. They tolerate incredible abuse.

The 8051 family is about the smallest processor on which one can implement FORTH. From a programmer's standpoint, making an 8051 do anything, especially bringing up FORTH, appears to be an unnatural act.

Several years ago Joseph Flores, Konrad Roeder, and the author were asked to implement quickly a cryptographic lock for missile launch control. We were required to use a radiation-hardened 8085. We evaluated our alternatives: assembler, PL/M, C, Pascal, Stoic, MAGIC/L, and FORTH. We wrote sample programs and dumped compiled code output. We looked at documentation, source code availability, support, applicability of the language to our project, and turnaround time for program revisions.

Joseph and I visited Ray Duncan in California, and he showed us 8085 FORTH. We were awestruck at how quickly Ray could develop software. Ray advised using a metacompiler as opposed to bringing up FORTH from assembler code. We returned to Albuquerque with the 8085 FORTH nucleus and a copy of the Nautilus metacompiler. Joseph and I added disk file and PC terminal emulation capability to the 8085 nucleus. This modification meant that we could compile, assemble, and edit 8085 programs on the 8085 using a PC as the only development tool.

We built a wire-wrapped back plane 8085 microcomputer to host our purchased FORTH operating system. We got FORTH working, but the hardware proved to be noisy. Konrad told Joseph and me we were building the hardware incorrectly and built an 8085 motherboard version of the hardware. Konrad's hardware worked much better.

Much to department manager Kent Parsons and our sponsor's surprise, we completed our hardware/software project ahead of schedule. Kent served as course advisor for several FORTH courses. He appeared surprised that more staff members did not use this software technology.

The 8051 microcontroller was just appearing in the market at that time. We decided to port our 8085 application to the 8051 for hardware real estate reasons. Ray Duncan was marketing the Nautilus metacompiler for its author, Jerry Boutelle. Sandia National Laboratory hired Jerry to port the 8085 nucleus to the 8051, using the Nautilus metacompiler. I wrote an 8051 disassembler to help Jerry with his work. Jerry wrote the nucleus by reading the manual without ever seeing a machine. I debugged the nucleus by using a loaned Arium logic analyzer. Sandia hired Jerry to rewrite the Nautilus metacompiler for its own use.

In 1986, Hal Pruett initiated a project to document all the system software we used. This multiperson, one-year effort, I believe, represents the most complete documentation ever undertaken on the internals of the 8086, 8085, and 8051 family FORTHs, or for that matter FORTH on any machine.

The original 8085 nucleus was written by members of the FORTH Interest Group. In June 1978, nine systems programmers decided to each develop a FORTH for a different microcomputer. These implementations would be distributed in the public domain by the FORTH Interest Group.

The 8051 FORTH included in this book uses fig-FORTH word definitions. We once converted to FORTH83 but converted back to fig-FORTH for various reasons. Lack of documentation was one principal reason. Pointers are given in the book on how to convert the code to other FORTH dialects. All of the code presented in this book is in the public domain.

We have a software Newton in our midst: Charles Moore, FORTH's inventor. Ray, Jerry, and anyone who studies FORTH's internals marvel at how Charles Moore thought up all that went into the FORTH operating system. Lots of hard work was one ingredient.

The software tools included in this book will help the user to complete appropriate 8051 hardware/software projects about 10 times as fast at about one hundredth the cost of other 8051 development technologies. All you need is an IBM PC compatible to use all the software in this book.

Listings of two binary files, one containing a FORTH for the IBM PC and the other an 8051 FORTH system, are included in this book. You can hand-enter the IBM PC FORTH, which allows you to use all of the cross-development tools including regenerating the binary you entered by hand from source. FORTH generates itself from source!

PROMing the 8051 binary accommodates your initial 8051 operating system to the 8051 hardware development system you built. From then on you can customize both your hardware and software to meet your requirements.

Disk copies of all the software included in this book and additional FORTH documentation are available from participating 8051 family hardware vendors. This includes FORTH encyclopedias of the 8051 and 8086 family systems.

Bill Payne
Albuquerque, NM

Acknowledgments

Baril, Don—RTX 2000 and VME bus
Barnhart, Joe—transient modules and 68000 address independent FORTH
Boutelle, Jerry—FORTH metacompilers, standards, and systems programmer
Duncan, Ray—FORTH and PC/MS-DOS course
Fierbach, Gary—FORTH courses
Flores, Joseph—FORTH applications programmer
Garner, Kim—PC board layout and artwork
Holloway, Bill—RTX 2000 and VME bus

Neugass, Henry—FORTH applications programmer, documentation, and courses
Parsons, Kent—FORTH course supervisor
Payne, Patty—FORTH assembler and book proofreader
Perry, Mike—FORTH decompilers, 68000, and systems programmer
Pruett, Hal—FORTH documentation project leader
Roeder, Konrad—FORTH hardware systems builder
Serna, Bob—PC board layout, artwork, schematics, and fab arrangements
Talbot, Ray—6800 series FORTH

Chapter 1

The FORTH Embedded Controller Hardware/Software Development Strategy

A. 8051 Family Memory Models

The 8051 family microcontroller's memory space is best thought of as looking like a tuning fork surrounded by two vertical bars. A diagram of the memory space is seen in Figure 1.1.

ROM means "read only memory." The generic term applies to genuine read only memory. Included in this broad term are EPROM (electrically programmable read only memory), EEPROM (electrically erasable programmable read only memory), One Time Programmable memory, and a host of other technologies. Basically, ROM means that when the power is turned off the contents do not disappear. Battery backed-up RAM also qualifies as ROM in this sense. Not being able to write to a memory technology does not qualify it as ROM, since it is possible to write single bytes to EEPROM.

The 8051 family all have decimal 128 bytes of internal RAM on board the chip. These are at locations hex 0 through 7F. These locations are seen as the base of the tuning fork in Figure 1.1.

The right-hand side of the tuning fork seen in Figure 1.1 is labeled "RAM" in quotations. This part of memory, present in all 8051 microcontrollers, is occupied by the Special Function Registers. All of the machine's registers are memory addressable.

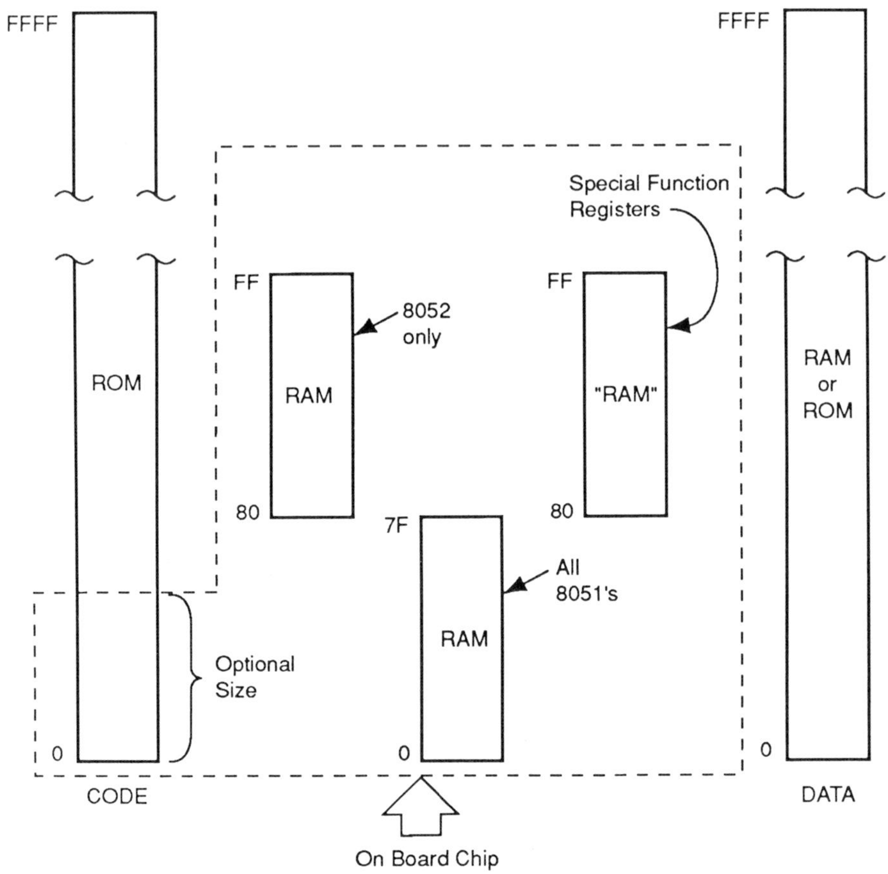

Figure 1.1. Memory space of an 8051 microcontroller family. The on-board chip memory includes hex locations 0 through 7F and the right part of the fork locations 80 through FF for all family members. The left part of the fork, locations 80 through FF, are included on the 8052 and some other members of the family. The CODE space is maximum decimal 64K bytes long and is usually occupied by ROM external to the processor. Some of this memory may be contained on board the chip. The 8031 has no on-board memory. The DATA memory is maximum decimal 64K bytes in length and can be populated with either ROM or RAM.

The left-hand side of the tuning fork is present on the 8052 and other variations of the 8051. These decimal-128 locations are addressed through indirect addressing.

CODE memory is seen as the left-hand bar in Figure 1.1. It has a maximum size of decimal 65536 bytes. CODE memory can only be read from, never written to. Its primary purpose is to contain program code. It can also contain tables of information intended only to be read from memory. CODE memory is occupied by ROM (used in the general sense).

DATA memory is seen as the right-hand bar in Figure 1.1. It has a maximum size of decimal 65536 bytes. It contains data that can be read or written to by the microcontroller. A hardware trick also allows it to contain program code.

The structure of internal RAM, hex addresses 0 through 7F, seen as the base of the tuning fork in Figure 1.1, is detailed in Figure 1.2. Locations hex 0 through 1F contain four banks of eight eight-bit registers. A particular bank is selected by setting bits 3 and 4 in the Program Status Word. Registers are symbolically labeled R0 through R7.

Locations hex 20 through 2F are bit addressable. Individual bits can be cleared, set, complemented, ORed, ANDed, moved to and from the carry bit, and tested to determine program flow.

Figure 1.3 shows how these locations are symbolically labeled in FORTH.

Observe that the high byte (H) is to the left of the low (L) byte. The reason is that the most significant byte is usually found to the left, in the memory of the high byte. The 8051 family is a true memory representation; it is not byte-swapped as in the case of the Intel 8086 family microcomputers. There is one exception to this pattern: the Data Pointer low value (DPL) is at location hex 82, whereas the Data Pointer high value (DPH) is at 83.

Locations hex 30 through 7F contain 7F − 30 + 1 = 50 hexadecimal bytes. In decimal this total is 80 bytes. The 8051 family hardware stack grows from low to high memory. It preincrements. The Stack Pointer (SP) is located in special function register 81. At hardware reset it is initialized by hardware to hex 07. At reset or cold start time it is a good idea to to initialize SP to hex 2F. In this case the first push to the stack goes into location hex 30.

Another view of locations hex 0 through 7F is given in Figure 1.4. Memory space allocation on the stack is frequently preferable to fixed location assignment. Space allocation and release become a matter of adjusting the stack pointer.

The right part of the tuning fork seen in Figure 1.1 contains the 8051's registers. Figure 1.5 shows the bit-addressable bits in the Special Function Registers.

Figure 1.6 shows an expanded layout of the Special Function Registers. Holes in the table are assigned uses in variations of the 8051 family.

Figure 1.7 shows all of the 8051/8052 family Special Function Registers' names and addresses, bit addressable and not.

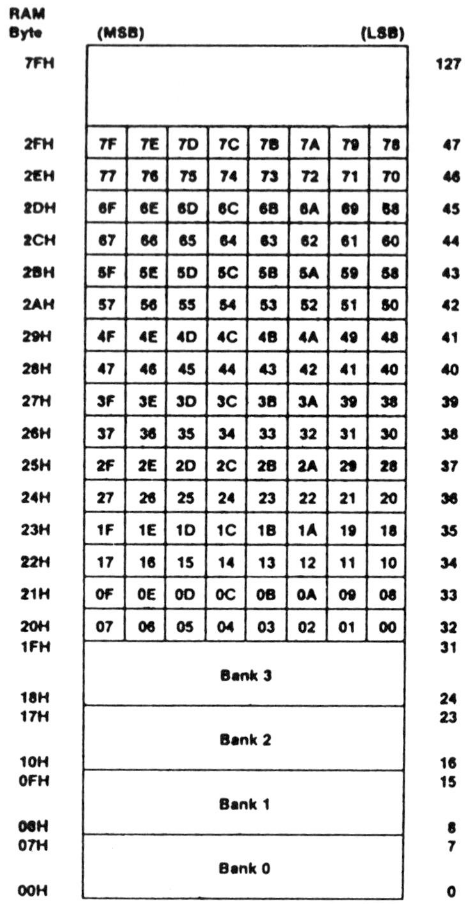

Figure 1.2. The internal RAM of all 8051 family members contains four banks of registers. Each bank contains eight bytes. The bytes are symbolically labeled R0, R1, R2, R3, R4, R5, R6, and R7. One of the four banks is selected by setting bits 3 and 4 in the Program Status Word. Locations hex 20 through 2F are bit addressable. The bit address is given in the boxes. Bits can be cleared, set, complemented, ORed, ANDed, and moved to and from the carry bit. The 80 bytes hex 30 through 7F are frequently reserved for the 8051s hardware stack, which advances from low to high memory.

X0H	20	X0L	21
X1H	22	X1L	23
X2H	24	X2L	25
X3H	26	X3L	27
X4H	28	X4L	29
X5H	2A	X5L	2B
X6H	2C	X6L	2D
X7H	2E	X7L	2F

Figure 1.3. Symbolic FORTH labels for the bit addressable internal RAM locations.

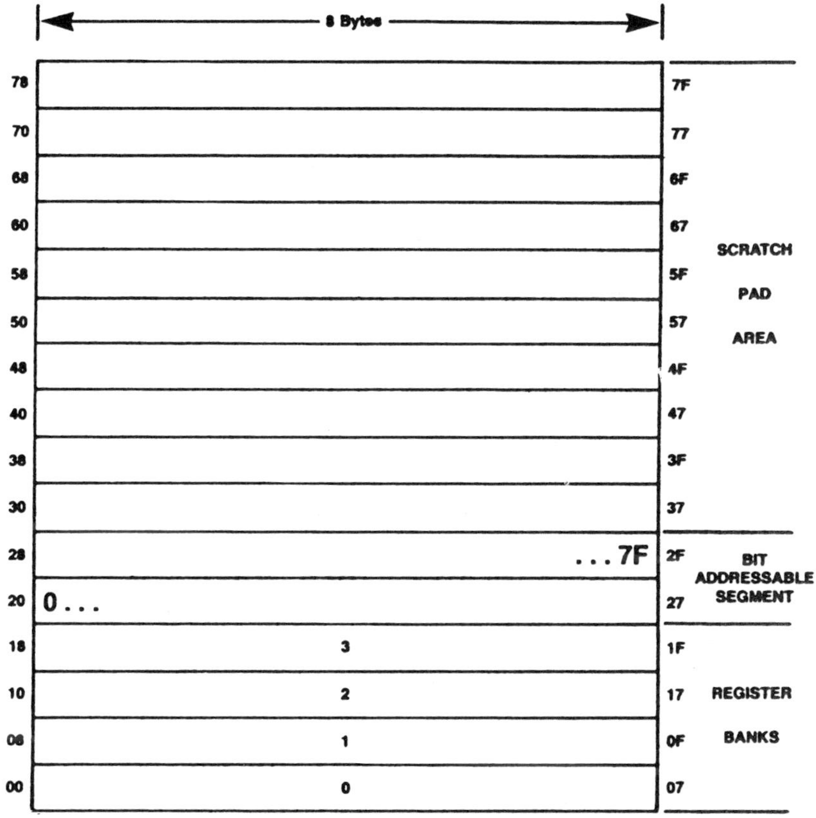

Figure 1.4. Expanded view of internal memory locations hex 0 through 7F. The Scratch Pad Area is well used as stack space by resetting the stack pointer from its power-on reset value of hex 07 to a value of 2F. This change causes the first pushed value to enter location hex 30.

Direct Byte Address	Bit Addresses (MSB)							(LSB)	Hardware Register Symbol
240	F7	F6	F5	F4	F3	F2	F1	F0	B
224	E7	E6	E5	E4	E3	E2	E1	E0	ACC
	CY	AC	F0	RS1	RS0	OV		P	
208	D7	D6	D5	D4	D3	D2	D1	D0	PSW
	TF2	EXF2	RCLK	TCLK	EXEN2	TR2	C/$\overline{T2}$	CP/$\overline{RL2}$	
200	CF	CE	CD	CC	CB	CA	C9	C8	T2CON
			PT2	PS	PT1	PX1	PT0	PX0	
184	—	—	BD	BC	BB	BA	B9	B8	IP
176	B7	B6	B5	B4	B3	B2	B1	B0	P3
	EA		ET2	ES	ET1	EX1	ET0	EX0	
168	AF	—	AD	AC	AB	AA	A9	A8	IE
160	A7	A6	A5	A4	A3	A2	A1	A0	P2
	SM0	SM1	SM2	REN	TB8	RB8	TI	RI	
152	9F	9E	9D	9C	9B	9A	99	98	SCON
144	97	96	95	94	93	92	91	90	P1
	TF1	TR1	TF0	TR0	IE1	IT1	IE0	IT0	
136	8F	8E	8D	8C	8B	8A	89	88	TCON
128	87	86	85	84	83	82	81	80	P0

Figure 1.5. The bit addresses for those bit-addressable locations are shown in this figure. Ports 0, 1, 2, and 3 are bit-addressable. Register B is used in division. The symbolic names are: ACC = accumulator, PSW = program status word, T2CON = 8052 timer 2 control register, IP = interrupt priority register, IE = interrupt enable register, SCON = serial control register, and TCON = timer control register.

In summary, the 8051 family can have a maximum of decimal 64K bytes of CODE memory, 64K bytes of DATA memory, decimal 128 bytes of internal RAM for the 8051 family, or 256 bytes for the 8052 family, and 128 bytes allocated to the Special Function Registers. CODE memory can only be read. Some of CODE memory may be internal to the 8051 family as EEPROM or masked ROM. DATA memory can be read and written.

8 Bytes

F8									FF
F0	B								F7
E8									EF
E0	ACC								E7
D8									DF
D0	PSW								D7
C8	T2CON		RCAP2L	RCAP2H	TL2	TH2			CF
C0									C7
B8	IP								BF
B0	P3								B7
A8	IE								AF
A0	P2								A7
98	SCON	SBUF							9F
90	P1								97
88	TCON	TMOD	TL0	TL1	TH0	TH1			8F
80	P0	SP	DPL	DPH				PCON	87

↑
Bit
Addressable

Figure 1.6. Memory map of the Special Function Registers for the 8051 family. Holes in the table are used in other versions of the 8051 family.

B. Hardware Memory Signals

There are three hardware signals associated with memory access. These are denoted −PSEN, −RD, and −WR. The "minus" in front of the mnemonic denotes an active low signal. "Active" means that these signals are normally high (about five volts in a normal system). When these signals are asserted, they go low to about 0 volts. The minus sign is sometimes replaced by a "\" or "/ " or a bar over the mnemonic. For the 80386 family a "#" following the mnemonic is used.

−PSEN stands for Program Store Enable. −PSEN is activated, or goes low, whenever an instruction or operand is fetched for execution. The MOVC instruction also activates it.

−RD stands for Read. −RD is activated any time a MOVX read from memory instruction is executed.

−WR stands for Write. −WR is activated anytime a MOVX write to memory instruction is executed.

A fourth pin, −EA, stands for External Address. When this pin is tied low (0 volts, grounded), all instructions are fetched from external CODE memory. If this pin is tied high (nominally 5 volts), −PSEN is directed to

Symbol	Name	Address
*ACC	Accumulator	0E0H
*B	B Register	0F0H
*PSW	Program Status Word	0D0H
SP	Stack Pointer	81H
DPTR	Data Pointer 2 Bytes	
DPL	Low Byte	82H
DPH	High Byte	83H
*P0	Port 0	80H
*P1	Port 1	90H
*P2	Port 2	0A0H
*P3	Port 3	0B0H
*IP	Interrupt Priority Control	0B8H
*IE	Interrupt Enable Control	0A8H
TMOD	Timer/Counter Mode Control	89H
*TCON	Timer/Counter Control	88H
*+T2CON	Timer/Counter 2 Control	0C8H
TH0	Timer/Counter 0 High Byte	8CH
TL0	Timer/Counter 0 Low Byte	8AH
TH1	Timer/Counter 1 High Byte	8DH
TL1	Timer/Counter 1 Low Byte	8BH
+TH2	Timer/Counter 2 High Byte	0CDH
+TL2	Timer/Counter 2 Low Byte	0CCH
+RCAP2H	T/C 2 Capture Reg. High Byte	0CBH
+RCAP2L	T/C 2 Capture Reg. Low Byte	0CAH
*SCON	Serial Control	98H
SBUF	Serial Data Buffer	99H
PCON	Power Control	87H

* = Bit addressable
\+ = 8052 only

Figure 1.7. Addresses of all of the 8051/8052 Special Function Registers. Only those registers seen in Figure 1.5 are bit-addressable.

the on-board CODE memory when the address is in range and to external memory when it exceeds the on-board maximum-address.

An addressing trick to overlap CODE and DATA memory is shown in Figure 1.8. −EA is tied low. −PSEN and −RD are ANDed together. This creates a "negative going OR" in the sense that if either −PSEN or −RD is an active low, a low is produced at the output. OUT is directed toward the overlapped CODE/DATA memory space. Observe the truth table in the figure. The situation wherein −RD and −PSEN are both low never occurs in the 8051.

This memory configuration usually has ROM at low addresses and RAM at high addresses. The total memory space is limited to decimal

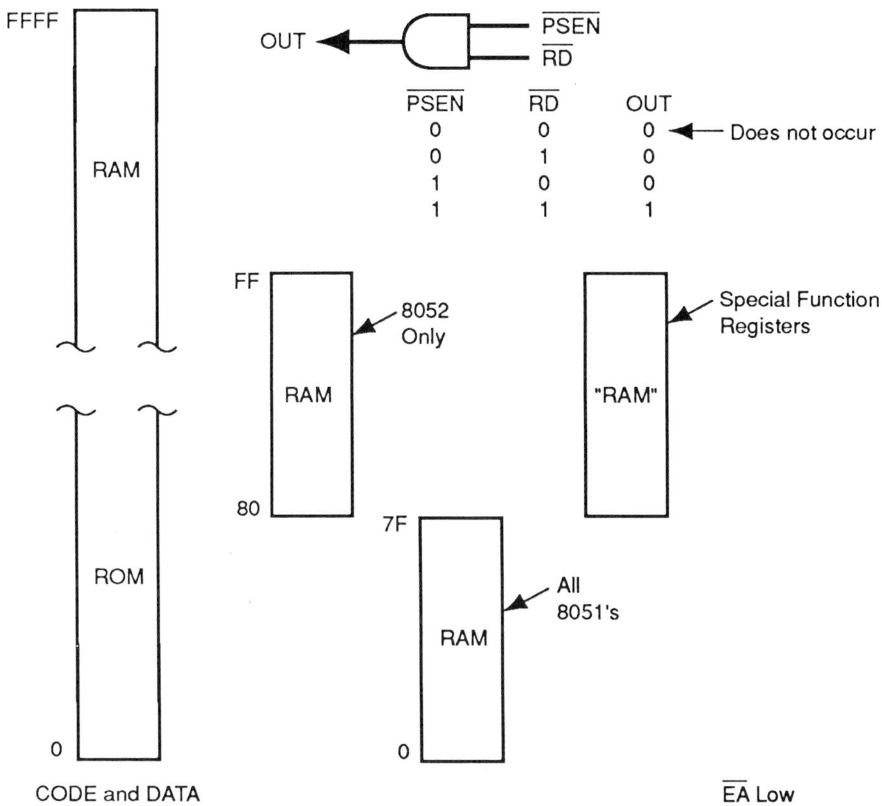

Figure 1.8. CODE and DATA memory are overlapped on an external memory 8051 family configuration. −EA is tied to indicate external addressing. ANDing −PSEN and −RD effectively ORs these to active low signals. ROM is usually placed below RAM on overlapped memory systems.

64K bytes of combined ROM and RAM. FORTH likes to see RAM directly above ROM, so this memory model is used to develop the code for all other memory models.

All of the FORTH operating system, compiled as ROMed assembler, mini-full screen editor, and terminal/disk communications software, for the 8051 family presented in this book occupies slightly more than decimal 17K bytes. More than 20 person-years were spent on its production. Respect the amount of time it takes to write and debug computer code. A good rule of thumb is about 5–10 lines per worker per day measured over the useful life of the code. This time includes only the code you write, not the code written by Charles Moore and the others who preceded you. Your programming effectiveness is increased by using as much of their code and ideas as possible.

C. High-Level and/or Assembler Coding Decisions

Choice of high level FORTH or assembler depends largely on the expected size of the code. Small-size codes generally are best coded in assembler.

Larger codes are best coded in high level FORTH initially to get the system working without regard to speed of execution. Once the code is working you should replace inner loops with assembler code. The rule "90% of the work is done in 10% of the code" applies. Coding routines in assembler that are executed once or only several times is wasteful of your time and accomplishes nothing.

FORTH is not recommended on large codes, say those that produce more than decimal 10K bytes of object code. FORTH is intricate, and it is possible to make some subtle and serious mistakes in that amount of code. It is not recommended for more than a two- or three-person effort, because FORTH gives the programmer total control over the machine. Multiple programmers' practices frequently conflict, making the software product a mess. FORTH does not have a linker and loader in the normal sense of a mainframe or minicomputer. Modules cannot easily be independently developed then linked and loaded at a later time. FORTH has an incremental compiler/assembler, linker, and loader. This software technology works well for quick turnaround debugging sessions but is relatively ineffective for producing large codes that require extensive linking, loading, and overlaying of code.

These are general guidelines based on conversations with experienced FORTH programmers. Much of the decision-making on how big a code can be handled and whether high level or assembler code should be used is based on your personal feeling. You do what you feel comfortable with. Determination of whether your decision was correct usually takes much time after you made it. Your experiences should make you wiser in the future.

D. Hardware and Software Debugging Strategies

Economics drives the hardware construction and debugging strategy. Hardware products must be made economically competitive, so the least expensive tools to get products working quickly must be used. "Quickly" is a key word. A logic analyzer is expensive but on some occasions can save much time. However, if you don't have the money, then you have to solve the problem without an expensive tool. You must be resourceful.

The minimum tools you need are

1. Hand-wire wrap and unwrap tools, 30 gauge
2. A voltmeter. Preferably a digital one that
   (a) beeps for continuity checks.
   (b) has a transistor checker.
   (c) has a capacitance measurer.
3. A logic probe that
   (a) is compatible with CMOS and NMOS parts.
   (b) indicates pulsing, low, and high signals.
   (c) does pulse or latched outputs.

Figure 1.9 shows the tools and debugging equipment that see use in low development-cost microcontroller hardware projects. The logic probe, seen at the left of the picture, detects pulses as short as 30 nanoseconds (17 MHz). This is sometimes too sensitive in that it detects "glitching," or unintended pulsing, instead of intended pulsing. In this case, an oscilloscope is required to determine if a pulse is caused by a glitch.

The digital multimeter is used to check voltage levels and continuity between points on the circuit board. The multimeter beeps for continuity and so permits you to concentrate on probe placement instead of visual meter inspection.

The wire wrap tool is used for initial system building. Later it is used in conjunction with the unwrap tool to edit. You can use the wire wrap tool to unwrap but you may find the additional time required to be uneconomical.

You will do enough wire stripping to justify the expense of a good wire stripper. A human-engineered tool will save you time and money.

For the paper and pencil design aspect you need

1. A logic template
2. Optionally, an electronic/logic symbols template
3. 8½ × 11 blank paper.

8½ × 11 paper use is particularly important. Larger sizes do not FAX well. If you get to the point of wanting to build printed circuit boards, then you will need to FAX your schematics to PC board layout people for bids. Most PC board layout individuals now use generic PCs hosting inexpensive layout tools such as AUTOCAD. They turn your 8½ × 11 pencil sche-

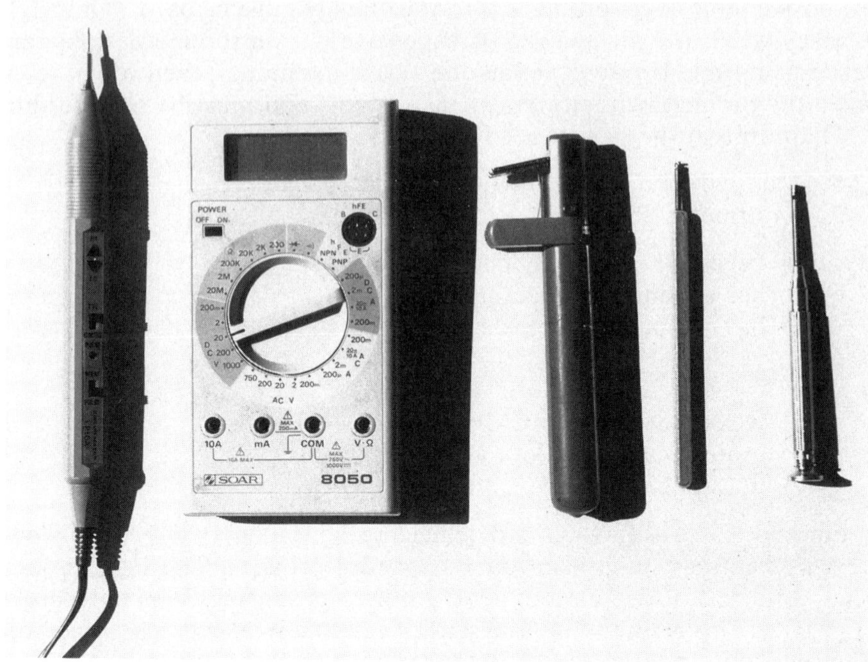

Figure 1.9. Minimal tools required for developing and debugging a microcontroller hardware system. Pictured from left to right are a logic probe, a digital multimeter, a human-engineered wire stripper, a wire unwrapper, and a wire wrap tool. All of the wire wrap tools are for 30-gauge wire. The wire wrap tool has a built-in stripper in the handle, but it is much harder to use than the human-engineered stripper.

matics into presentable formal schematics faster and cheaper than you can. Acceptable templates are seen in Figure 1.10.

You want to get your prototype boards back for debugging as soon as possible. Here are the steps.

1. Send in 8½ × 11 schematics.
2. Artwork is done from 8½ × 11 schematics.
3. You check artwork.
4. pc goes to fabrication (fab).
5. Formal schematic is entered into the computer by artwork layout people.
6. You debug prototype boards with 8½ × 11 and formal schematics. You check to insure that the formal schematics match your 8½ × 11 schematics and the board.

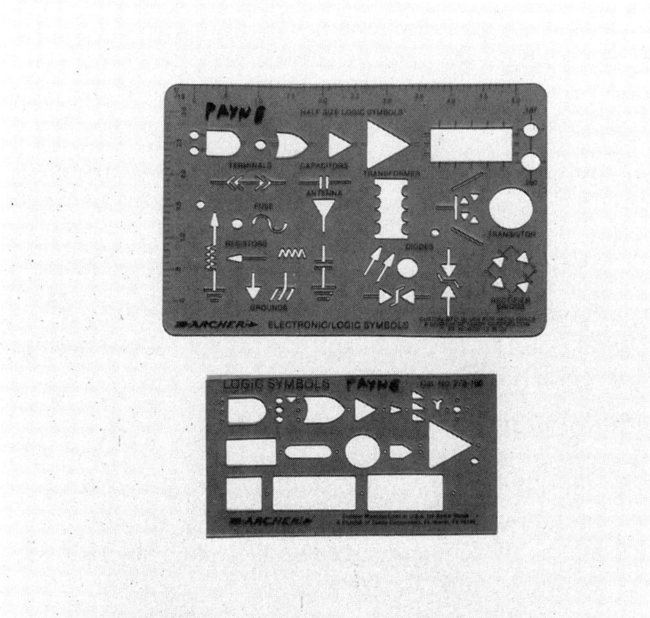

Figure 1.10. Acceptable logic and electronic templates used to compose hardware designs.

It is inadvisable to create the formal schematic at step two unless automatic placement, routing, and computer artwork is used. There is a "dead time" for the layout people when the boards go to fab. This dead time can be used to produce the formal schematics efficiently.

Soon all artwork will be produced from schematics by computers using inexpensive software tools. Some of you may wish to design your circuits directly from a computer. This is a matter of personal preference.

Hardware debugging strategy is split into two categories:

1. the microcontroller and associated central chips
2. peripherals

The strategy for debugging the microcontroller, reset circuit, clock circuit, decoding, and main ROM and RAM is to be as careful as possible in the software's design and construction. The main goal is to get the FORTH operating system running as soon as possible. FORTH then can be used to debug the remainder of the hardware.

Testability should be designed as part of peripheral hardware. For instance, what you write to a register you should be able to read back nondestructively. You should be able to write and read interactively from the keyboard. As another example, high-speed clocks should be multiplexed so single-step clocks can be supplied for a self-test.

The following rules were applied to the design of the software for the Boeing 767 airplane:

1. Each module performs a simple intended function,
2. Each module avoids performing adverse or benign unintended functions,
3. Each module provides adequate warning in event of failure.

This sage advice applies to hardware as well as software.

The software design and debugging strategy follows accepted software engineering guidelines:

1. Top-down design,
2. Bottom-up implementation,
3. Thorough individual testing of all software modules before they are included in the system. Interactive exercise of modules from the keyboard makes FORTH unsurpassed (though BASICs are as good) in the embedded controller world,
4. Adequate documentation.

FORTH produces perhaps the most memory-efficient code of any language. One reason for its efficiency is that when properly written it is nonredundant. Code a routine only once. Call it after that; don't recode it. Properly coded FORTH is composed of short subroutines. Neither the Intel 8051 family nor the 8086 family are particularly efficient at calling subroutines. Therefore, FORTH does not execute rapidly on them compared to other languages such as C. However, since 90% of the work is done in 10% of the code in most applications, FORTH can be made to approach the execution speed of other languages by recoding inner loops in assembler. Of course it does this recoding in a fraction of the memory space.

The Harris RTX 2000 microprocessor is designed for FORTH . It has FORTH-like machine language and separate data and return stack hardware, which reduce subroutine call overhead to near zero.

The development of ROMed applications or a change in the FORTH operating system requires an even more careful debugging strategy compared to bottom-up debugging each module. One mistake and the entire operating system or application stops working.

The debugging strategy is "one step at a time." Once the application is working, make one change at a time. When it all stops working, back up one step to see if the software still works. Correct the mistake and proceed: one step at a time.

Chapter 2

8051 Family Hardware Systems Schematics

The purpose of this chapter is to give you well-tested schematics that you can use to build your 8051 family FORTH development system.

In its simplest form, FORTH is a single-user operating system. It expects a keyboard for terminal input, a video screen for terminal output, and a mass storage device containing a single file.

Your IBM PC or clone furnishes FORTH's need for a keyboard, video screen, and mass storage device. A diagram of the system is seen in Figure 2.1. An asynchronous communications cable links the 8051 hardware development system and the PC. The link is run at 19.2K bits per second. The link has been run at 56K bits per second, but there was no overall improvement in performance. Moreover, the fact that our data line monitor would not run above 19.2K bps made it impossible to monitor communications traffic between the PC and the 8051 development system.

The first 8085 systems used a separate terminal for the keyboard and video screen.[1] After becoming more familiar with FORTH's internals, we discovered that terminal and disk I/O never occurred simultaneously. Disk and terminal I/O are multiplexed on the RS-232 transmit and data lines. The Ring Indicator is used to flag whether a character is bound for the disk or the terminal.

A design goal of the 8051 FORTH development system is to make the hardware required to run FORTH on the 8051 as unobtrusive as possible. A special point is made to use as little of the 8051's hardware as possible so as to leave it available for the microcontroller application.

Figure 2.1. Diagram of the 8051 family hardware development system. The PC communicates with the 8051 system over an asynchronous RS-232 link at 19.2K bps. The terminal\disk PC emulator source code is in a file called DS3.SCR (Development System—Revision 3). Its listing is included in this book's appendices.

The National Semiconductor 82C50A Asynchronous Communications Element is used to communicate to the PC. One reason for this choice is that it and its successor the (NS16C450A) are also used in PCs. The 8085 system used the Intel 8251 USART. This chip communicates both synchronously and asynchronously. The part comes with a no-part suffix and A and B suffixes. The B part is slower and does not work with the FORTH development system (It "sort of" works, which makes it difficult to find the "bug.")

CMOS is now the preferred technology. The switch was made from NMOS several years ago. Reduced power (about 20% of NMOS), cool operation, and improved CMOS part steppings prompted our switch.

8051s are not equal, despite the label on the package. As problems on the chip are uncovered, the parts undergo mask steppings. Early CMOS 8051s did not work well. Current CMOS parts are nearly impossible to kill. They tolerate incredible electrical abuse. By accident they have been plugged in backwards and continue to work when reinserted in the right direction.

Sometimes the power is left on before removing or inserting chips. This does not appear to harm them. Abused chips should not be used in fielded systems. These examples only show how well many chips are designed and constructed.

Most integrated circuits have been "ruggedized" to stand abuse. Protection diodes protect CMOS chips from over-voltages on their signal pins. These chips are suited for embedded controller applications.

The 8051 family microcontrollers are dynamic parts. Dynamic, as opposed to static, means that the part has a minimum oscillator frequency. The lower the frequency, the less power the chip consumes. However, the part stops working below a specified frequency.

The 8051 has its own internal clock circuit. A crystal and two capacitors are required externally to use the internal clock circuitry. A second option is to use an external crystal oscillator circuit to drive the 8051 clock circuit. Crystal oscillator circuits are available in both NMOS and CMOS technology. A crystal oscillator is connected to the XTAL1 pin for a NMOS part and to the XTAL2 pin for the CMOS part. Both methods work. Intel publishes an application note on selecting oscillators for microcontrollers.[2] CMOS crystal oscillators are preferable because of their simplicity and size. A 1.8432 MHz crystal used for the 82C50 is huge. Socketing a crystal oscillator allows you to switch oscillator frequencies without unsoldering parts.

The National 82C50A uses its own crystal or crystal oscillator circuit of 1.8432 MHz or 3.072 MHz. Sometimes you find an 8051 system that uses an 11.0592 MHz oscillator. The reason for using this frequency rather than the maximum of 12 or 16 MHz is that this oscillator frequency can be divided by six to produce the 1.8432 MHz needed by the 82C50. Separate CMOS oscillator circuit for each chip is perhaps best. Both ways work.

The next issue is whether to build a single-board microcontroller or a bussed system. Single-board systems are built on a single printed circuit or wire-wrap board. They are two-dimensional. The minimum number of lines and parts are all that are required to accomplish the task.

Bussed systems require that the microcontroller interface to a specified set of lines. This stipulation usually implies a connector such as the 62 pin connector in an IBM PC/XT or clone. Bussed systems can be modular. Each module is placed on a card, which is plugged into the bus. The modules usually incur an overhead penalty of separate decode for each board. But bussed systems are three-dimensional. They fill a volume efficiently with electronic components. Bussed systems are easier to modify and build efficiently than single-board computers. Several individuals can build and test the modules in parallel. Modifications require only a plug-in replacement board.

Single-board microcontroller systems are monolithic. Changes require removing hardware and wiring in the modifications. They can be made to contain the minimum number of parts and lines. Bussed systems, on the other hand, usually require a connector and additional decoding hardware and may include unused bus features. They are modular and fill a volume efficiently.

Your application dictates your choice of a bussed or single-board system, but because of modularity, favor should be given to a bussed system, particularly at hardware experimentation time.

A. Memory and I/O Decode Methods

Decoding is the selection of chip by the hardware system. Decode signals are active low (ground) in an 8051 system. Decode signals are connected to Chip Select inputs on individual chips.

Designing decode circuitry requires knowledge of the steps the 8051 takes to read and write data. The 8051 family has a sixteen-bit address labeled A0 through A15. A0 is the low bit. It has eight data bits labeled D0 through D7. D0 is the low bit.

A0 through A7 and D0 through D7 are multiplexed on port P0. That is, they share the same port pins. A signal called Address Latch Enable (ALE) indicates whether D0–D7 or A0–A7 appear on the pins. ALE's going low signals a valid address output on P0.

A8–A15 are output on port P2. They are not multiplexed.

The 8051 has two types of read cycles: one read from program memory (fetching the instructions to be executed) and the second from external data memory. The 8051 has a single write cycle to external memory.

The write cycle is as follows.

1. Address bits A0 through A15 appear at ports P0 and P2.
2. Address bits become valid addresses when ALE goes low. A0 through A8 are latched into a '373 chip at this time.
3. The write line −WR goes low, then data out becomes valid.
4. The −WR line goes high.
5. ALE goes high and data out is no longer valid.

The timing diagram for a data write is shown in Figure 2.2.[3] The time between ALE and −WR going low is very long. It is a minimum of 200 and a maximum of 300 nanoseconds for a 12 MHz 8051. Address glitching can occur during this time. It is manifested by a chip selects going low unintentionally. However, access to a peripheral chip is conditioned by both chip select going low and read or write going low. Thus an unintended chip read or write is prevented.

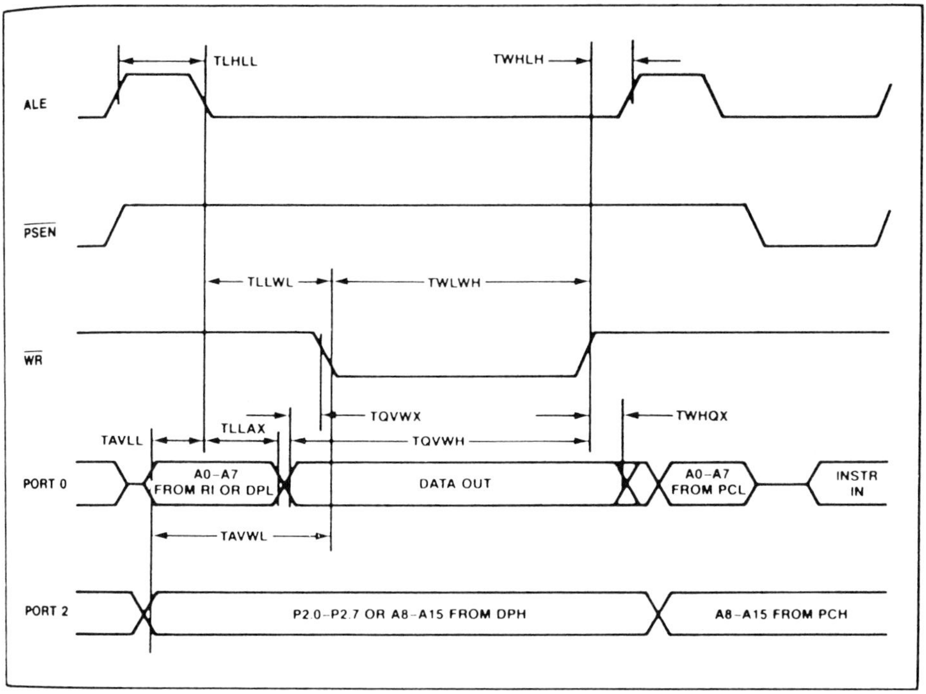

Figure 2.2. Timing diagram for an external data memory write cycle. While all timing limits must be met, observe that −WR goes high while the data is valid. −WR is used as a rising edge clock to latch the data into chips such as '374 latches.

An external memory read cycle is similar to a write cycle, but the data is sampled by the 8051 while −RD is low. This situation occurs in phase 1 of state 3. A external data memory read cycle timing diagram is seen in Figure 2.3.

In all of your designs you must be careful to observe minimum and maximum timings with both the processor and the external chips. This job is made easy for us in most cases by the chip designers. They are careful to make their chips compatible with the major microcontrollers. We must be careful when interfacing to more obscure chips such as analog-to-digital converters and liquid crystal display controllers.

The importance of address glitching to those of us who have only a logic probe for debugging prompts a detailed explanation of why your logic probe can deceive you.

Figure 2.4 shows a typical 16-bit decoding scheme mapping into eight chip selects. '682 chips match the P input with the Q inputs.[4] When they

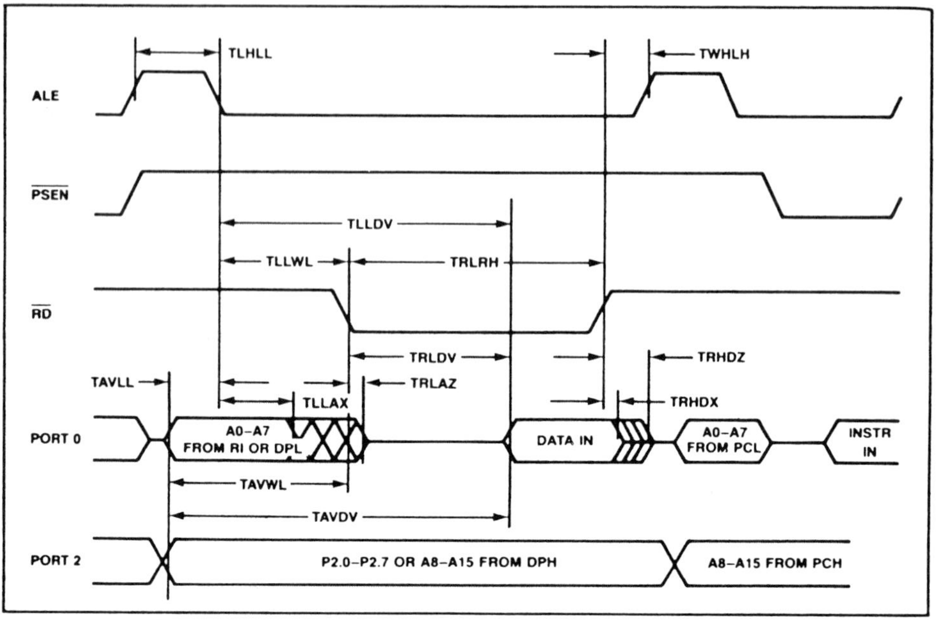

Figure 2.3. Timing diagram for an external data memory read cycle.

are equal, −(P=Q) goes low. These chips also have > comparison. They have internal pull-up resistors so an open input is a one. The '138 requires −G2A and G2B to be low and G1 high to have A, B, and C inputs cause an active low on Y0 through Y7. With their conditions met the '128 map is as follows.

C	B	A	Y0	Y1	Y2	Y3	Y4	Y5	Y6	Y7
0	0	0	0	1	1	1	1	1	1	1
0	0	1	1	0	1	1	1	1	1	1
0	1	0	1	1	0	1	1	1	1	1
0	1	1	1	1	1	0	1	1	1	1
1	0	0	1	1	1	1	0	1	1	1
1	0	1	1	1	1	1	1	0	1	1
1	1	0	1	1	1	1	1	1	0	1
1	1	1	1	1	1	1	1	1	1	0

Even though there is no software putting out addresses that match the Q's and A0, A1, and A2, the Y's may go low, making your logic probe blink when placed at test point A. The appearance is created of a wiring or address selection error. Actually it is the logic probe that is too sensitive and is picking up glitches. When you put the logic probe at point B or C, you do not see a low pulse. Some chips, such as memory chips, have two

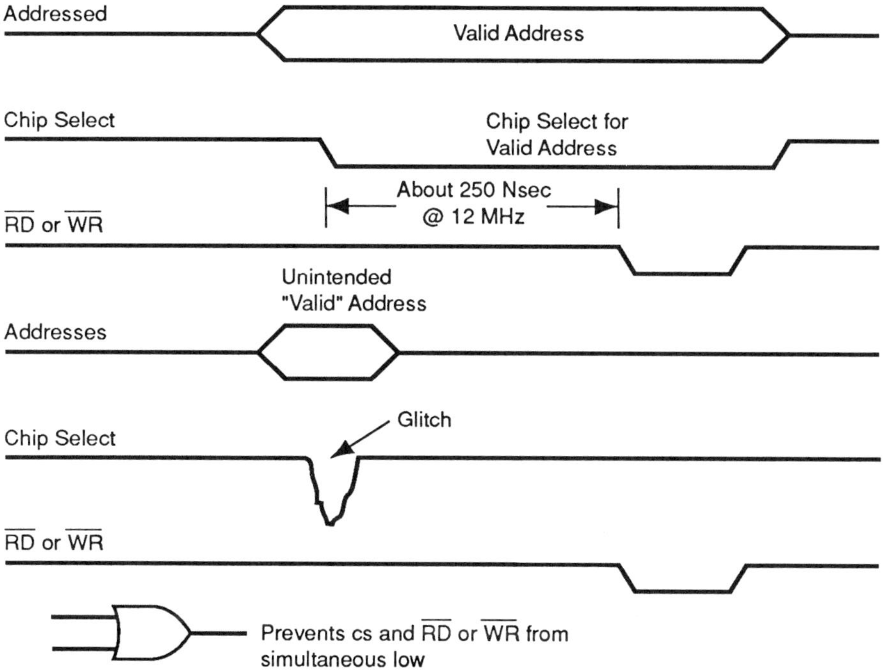

Figure 2.4. Typical 16-bit decoding scheme mapping into eight chip select addresses. A logic probe placed at point A may go low even though an address match should not have occurred. This "glitching" is defeated by requiring both the address match and −RD or −WR to go low simultaneously for a valid chip select.

OR gates for −RD and −WR inside the chip so you cannot observe test points B and C.

The top part of Figure 2.5 shows a sketch of a properly occurring peripheral chip reference. The top portion of this figure is a summary of Figures 2.2 and 2.3. The bottom portion of the figure shows what happens when an addressing glitch occurs. An unintended "valid" address is generated by the microcontroller or peripheral decoding chips. This "valid" address causes a spurious chip select early in the peripheral chip access cycle. ORing −RD or −WR with the chip select prevents an unintended chip access. Complex chips like memories, counter/timers, serial communications, or parallel I/O have the OR gate inside the chip. Your logic probe is sensitive enough to blink on glitches. You can easily see them with an oscilloscope. But if you do not have an oscilloscope, this can be a perplexing problem.

Two apparently identical wire-wrapped or printed circuit board systems can display different glitching behavior. The phenomenon may be due to the routing of the wire, differences in chips, or power supply.

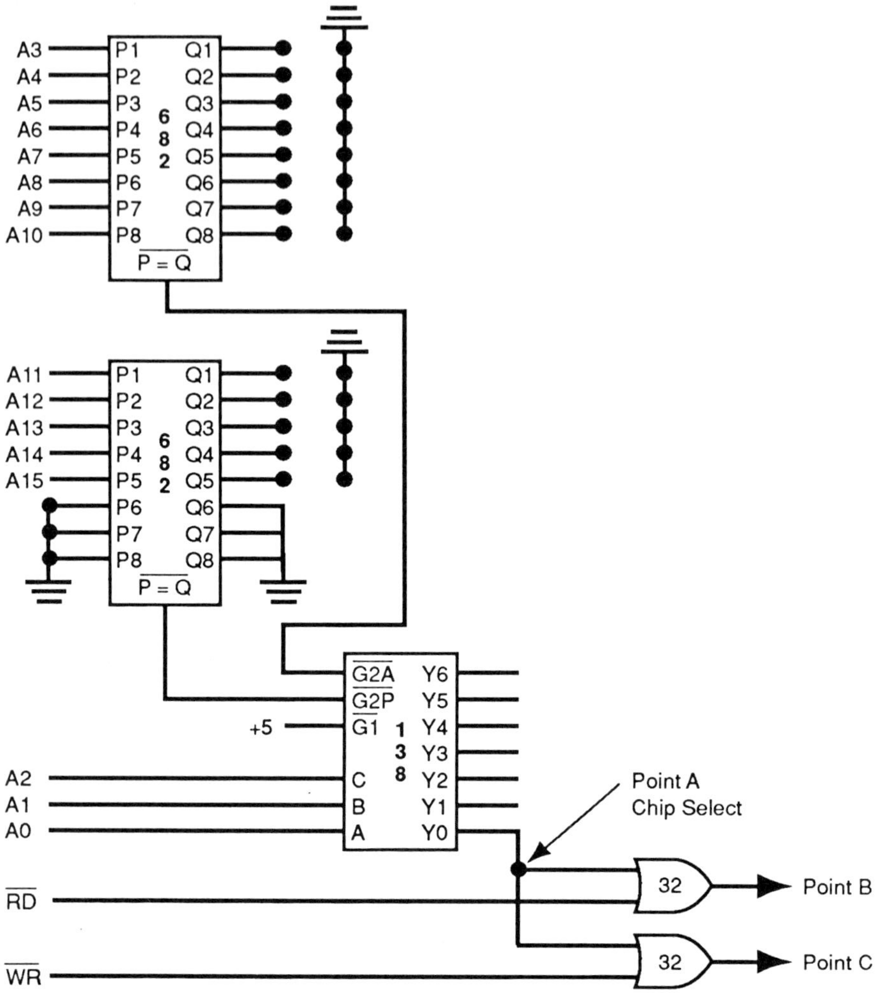

Figure 2.5. Sketch of what happens when an address glitch appears on a chip select. The top portion of the figure is a summary of what should happen during reads and writes. The bottom portion shows what happens when an unintended "valid" address appears. Address glitches appear early in the address cycle and disappear when −WR or −RD are active low. These glitches can trigger your logic probe making you mistakenly believe you made a wiring or address selection error.

An external program memory read cycle is used to read the instructions the microcontroller is to execute from memory. Figure 2.6. shows the time diagram. This code read memory cycle (−PSEN) occurs twice each machine cycle. Program memory speed needs to be selected on the basis of this timing specification. EPROMs of 250 nanoseconds work for a 12

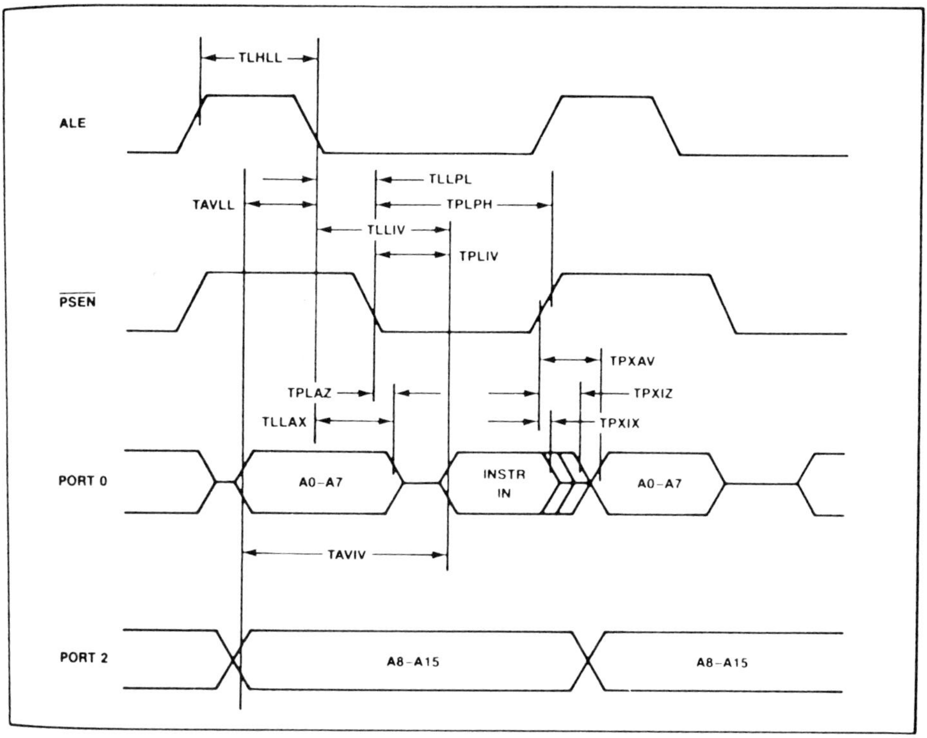

Figure 2.6. Timing diagram of internal program memory read cycle.

MHz 8051. RAMs of 32K×8 are usually 150 nanosecond access time or faster so they work.

The 8051 family microcontrollers, unlike the 8085 and 8086 family, do not have a separate I/O space. The I/O must be memory mapped or the internal I/O ports used. If external I/O is used, then some memory locations must be sacrificed to accommodate the I/O.

At the end of reset, an 8051 begins instruction execution at location 0. Therefore, some time of ROM (EPROM, EEPROM, etc.) at low memory is required. FORTH likes RAM directly above ROM. If external I/O space is required, then removing memory location at the end of RAM—in the data space, of course—is a good idea. Figure 2.7 shows a diagram of recommended data memory space allocation.

It is a good idea to use the largest capacity memory chips available within reasonable cost. The reasons are:

1. They are or soon will be the most cost effective.
2. Manufacturers drop smaller capacity chips from their production lines.

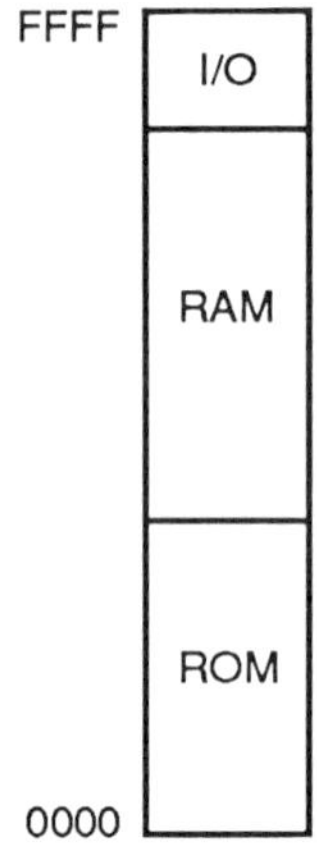

Figure 2.7. Diagram of recommended allocation of ROM, RAM, and I/O space to an 8051 family data memory system. I/O is allocated at the end of memory.

32K×8 byte RAMs, EPROMs, and EEPROMs are common. 64K×8 and 128K×8 EPROMs are available. For the 8051 we are limited to a maximum of 64K bytes of code space and 64K bytes of data space. 32K×8 chips are well suited to an external memory application system.

How much, if any, I/O space you allocate depends on your application. Giving up 16 or 256 bytes out of 32,868 bytes or more of RAM is inconsequential. Figure 2.8 pictures a simple decoding scheme which allocates 256 bytes of I/O space. Allocation of only 64 bytes may not be enough to warrant recovery of 256 − 64 = 192 bytes of additional memory. Allocation of more than 256 bytes of I/O space is probably unreasonable for most 8051 applications.

The chip selects −ROM, −RAM, and −I/O are active low. The reason for this is that A15 selects ROM or RAM. A15 = 0 selects ROM and A15 = 1 selects RAM. However, if A8 through A15 are all one, then the output of the eight input '30 NAND goes low, forcing the −ROM and −RAM output of the '138 decoder to one. The consequent forcing of G1 to zero disables all the Y outputs.

This decoding scheme is implemented with standard logic chips. It is preferable to implement decoding schemes using programmable logic devices or other similar technologies; the propagation delay is less, fewer parts are required, and the power is usually less. Programmable logic devices are generally more expensive.

Allocating more than 32K bytes of ROM is probably unreasonable in most applications. The 8051 FORTH given to you in source code in this book occupies slightly more than 17K bytes. This space includes the disk

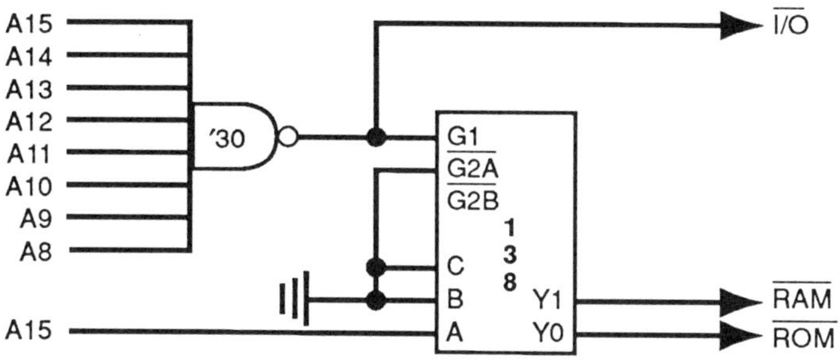

Address	$\overline{\text{ROM}}$	$\overline{\text{RAM}}$	$\overline{\text{I/O}}$
FFFF–F000	1	1	0
FFFF–8000	1	0	1
7FFF–0000	0	1	1

Figure 2.8. Recommended decoding scheme allocating 32,768 bytes of ROM, 32,768 − 256 = 32,512 bytes of RAM, and 256 bytes of I/O to external data memory.

operating system, compiler, interactive assembler, and mini-full screen editor. Perhaps more than 10 person-years went into its production.

Unless the application contains many ROM-based tables, few programmers can produce 32K bytes of application code. On the other hand, it is conceivable that more than 32,512 bytes of RAM is required. Figure 2.9 contains another decoding scheme that allows a variable fence to be placed between ROM and RAM.[5]

B. Combined Code/External Memory

Program store enable, −PSEN, is the read signal to external code memory. −RD is the read signal to external data memory. Both, of course, are active low signals. ANDing them produces a signal called −PSEN&−RD. This signal is used as the read signal to combine program and data memory.

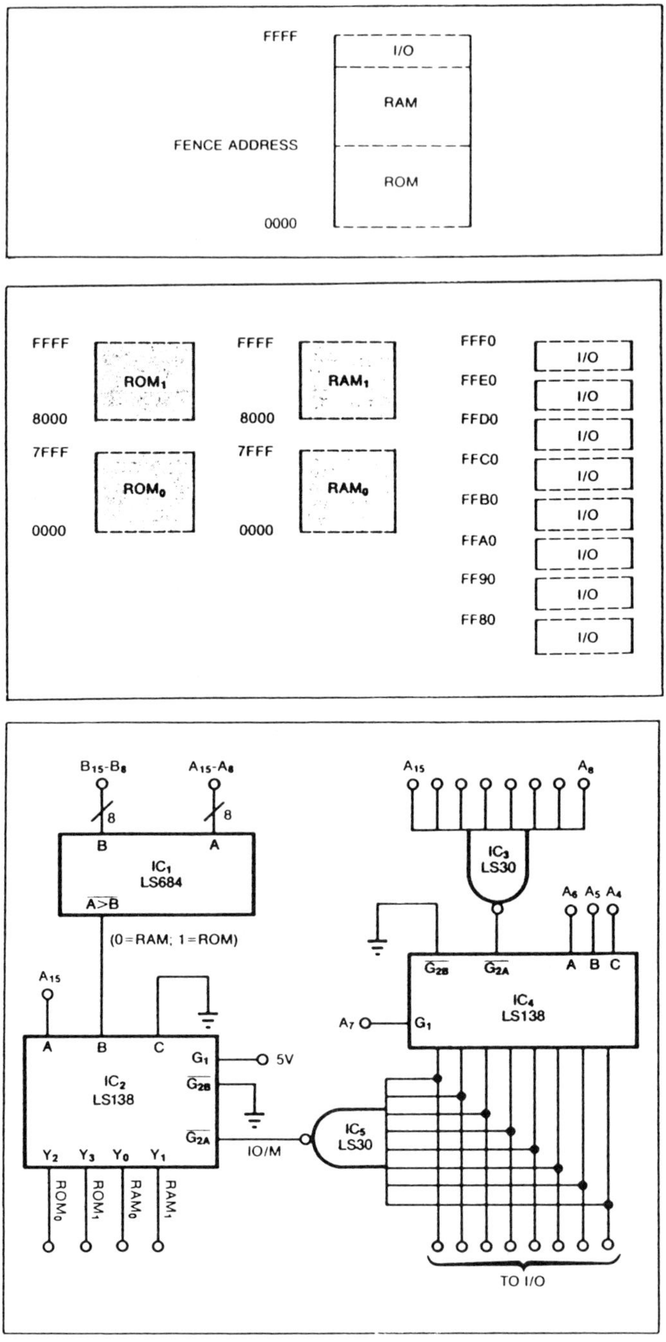

Figure 2.9. This more complicated decoding scheme allows a variable fence to be placed between ROM and RAM. Sixty four bytes are allocated for I/O.

−EA on the 8051 must be tied low to force the microcontroller to fetch instructions from external memory. If EA is tied high, then the 8051 fetches instructions from internal ROM (EPROM) until the address exceeds the physical memory on board the chip. −PSEN does not come out of the chip while the internal memory is accessed.

Figure 2.10 shows a diagram of a combined code and external memory layout emphasizing the three 8051 pins, −EA, −PSEN, and −RD, which must be correctly connected. The combined −PSEN&−RD are connected to the active low output enable (−OE) memory and other peripheral chips.

The truth table for −RD and −PSEN is shown at the bottom of the figure. −RD and −PSEN should never go low simultaneously.

C. Separate Code and External Data

Figure 2.11 shows the hookup of −EA, −RD, and −PSEN for two cases of separate code and external memory. The top portion of the figure shows −EA tied low, which causes the 8051 to fetch instructions from external code memory. The bottom portion shows −EA tied high, which causes the 8051 to fetch instructions from its internal ROM or EPROM.

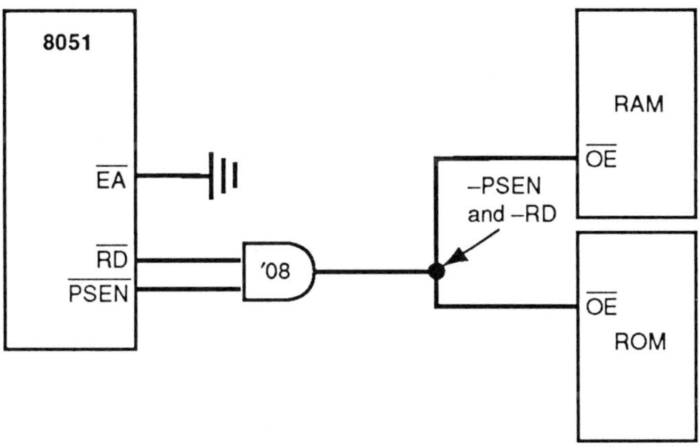

$\overline{\text{RD}}$	$\overline{\text{PSEN}}$	$\overline{\text{PSEN}}$ & $\overline{\text{RD}}$
0	0	Does not happen
0	1	0
1	0	0
1	1	1

Figure 2.10. Code and external memory are combined by tying −EA to ground and ANDing −PSEN and −RD to form a combined read signal.

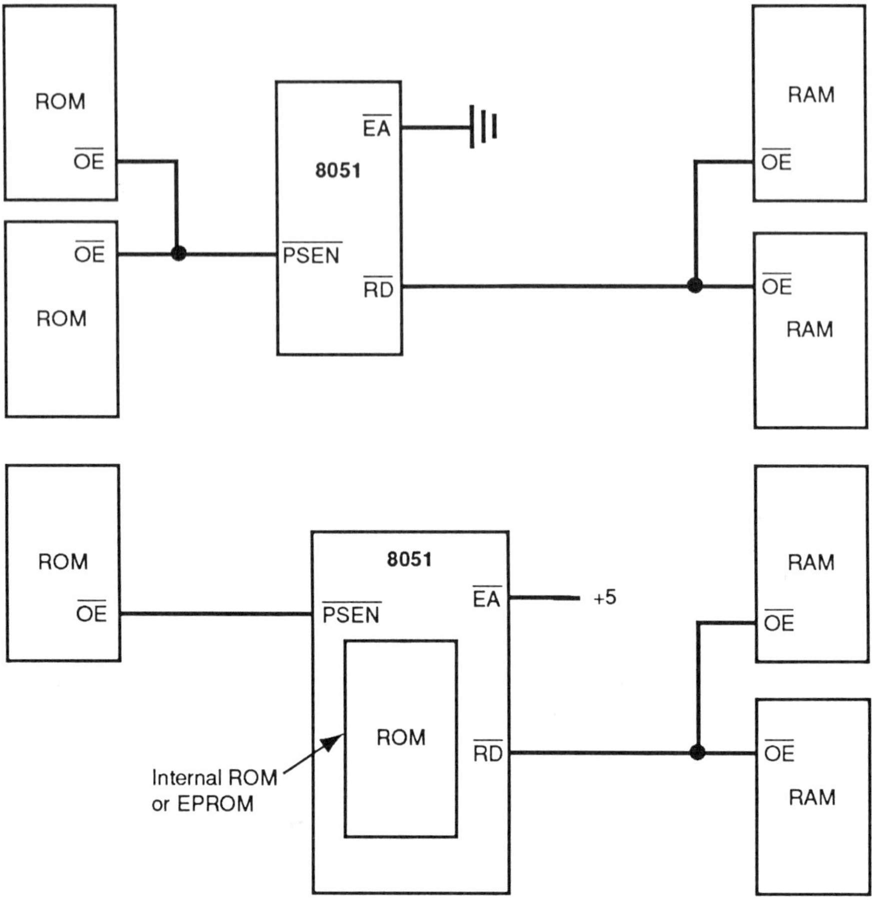

Figure 2.11. The top portion of this figure shows the hookup on −EA, −RD, and −PSEN to force the 8051 to fetch instructions from external code memory. The bottom portion shows the connections required for the microcontroller to fetch instructions from internal ROM or EPROM.

D. Reset Circuitry

The reset circuit for a microcontroller is important because microcontrollers can suffer transient software upsets (a software "crash"), which require a hardware reset to correct. A proper reset is required at power-up time for the microcontroller to begin properly executing code at location zero.

When the software crashes during the development process, the programmer must be able to push a button to reset the microcontroller. In a fielded embedded controller system, it is essential to have an activated watchdog circuit that, if not continually reset by software, invokes a hardware reset.[8]

Figure 2.12 shows a generalized reset circuit for an 8051. The Intel-suggested power-on reset circuit assumes that the Vcc risetime does not exceed a millisecond. The reset switch is current limited by the 10 ohm resistor.

The external reset must be buffered through a diode. The input to the buffer must be pulled low to permit the microcontroller's own power-on reset to function properly. The external reset driver must be able to overcome the pull-down resistor to invoke a reset. An unbuffered 8051 port pin is unable to overcome the resistor.

Figure 2.13 shows the state of the 8051 when reset is complete. As soon as reset is complete, the microcontroller begins program execution at location zero.

Advanced members of the 8051 family, notably the 83C152, have a low reset. Be careful with these processors when wiring reset with the schematics included in this book.

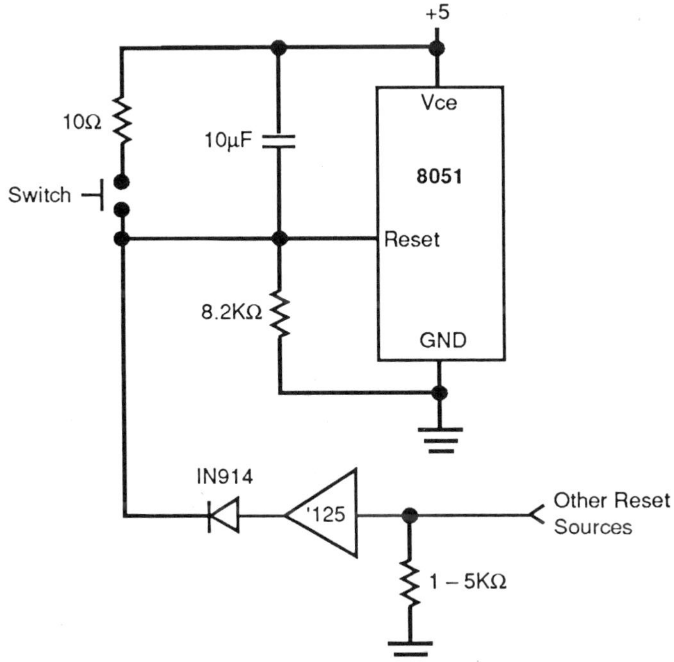

Figure 2.12. A generalized reset circuit for an 8051 microcontroller. This shows resets for power-on, programmer pushed switch, and some external reset, as from an external watchdog timer.

REGISTER	CONTENT
PC	0000H
ACC	00H
B	00H
PSW	00H
SP	07H
DPTR	0000H
P0–P3	0FFH
IP (8051)	XXX00000B
IP (8052)	XX000000B
IE (8051)	0XX00000B
IE (8052)	0X000000B
TMOD	00H
TCON	00H
T2CON (8052 only)	00H
TH0	00H
TL0	00H
TH1	00H
TL1	00H
TH2	00H
TL2	00H
RCAP2H (8052 only)	00H
RCAP2L (8052 only)	00H
SCON	00H
SBUF	Indeterminate
PCON (HMOS)	0XXXXXXXB
PCON (CHMOS)	0XXX0000B
X	Indeterminate

Figure 2.13. Internal state of the 8051 after reset is complete.

E. Single Board 8051 System Layout

The machine used to test the decoding idea seen in Figure 2.9 is seen in Figure 2.14. This machine is laid out as a single-board microcontroller system. It is compact but hard to change.

The '684 magnitude comparators were used in place of the superior '682's. Observe the pull-up resistors to the side of the fence selection switches. The '682 comparators have internal pull-up resistors. This machine has one 32K×8 EPROM and two 32K×8 RAM chips.

The machine uses a 12 MHz crystal for the 8051 and a 1.8432 Mhz crystal for the 8052 asynchronous communications element. Look how big the 1.8432 crystal is! Time and money are wasted by not using crystal oscillators. Wiring crystal oscillators is simpler than building a crystal-capacitor circuit.

There are additional possible problems with a crystal circuit. It may oscillate at some frequency other than the fundamental one. Fixing this variation can be time-consuming.

Placing a logic probe on the crystal-capacitor circuit of a 12 MHz 8051 system capacitively loads the circuits and stops the oscillator. Check ALE to see if the oscillator is working.

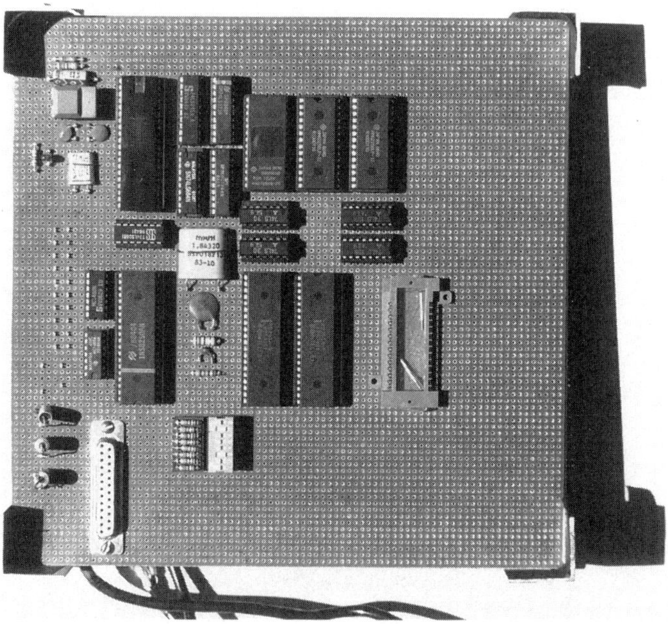

Figure 2.14. The 8051 system the author built to check the variable fence decoding scheme presented in Figure 2.9. Observe that both the 8051 microcontroller and the 8250 asynchronous communications elements have crystals opposed to crystal oscillators. The '684 magnitude comparators require external pull-up resistors. These are located next to the fence address selection registers. The machine contains one 32K×8 ROM, two 32K×8 RAMs, and two 8250 parallel I/O ports used for programming EPROMs. The zero insertion force socket holds an EPROM.

The machine is equipped with two 8255 parallel ports that are used to program EPROMs. The EPROMs are inserted into the zero insertion force socket.

The bottom side of the machine is seen in Figure 2.15. Plastic-wrap identification plates are placed on the bottom of the wire-wrap sockets to make pin identification easy. The machine pictured has red wire for power, black for ground, blue for data lines, yellow for address lines, and white for reset circuitry.

The power and ground lines are laid out in a tree structure. Everyone is advised to read the outstanding Intel Application Note, "Designing Microcontroller Systems for Electrically Noisy Environments.[7] The single-board system discussed here was built to many of the suggestions included in this note. However, it does not have on-board power regulation, which is recommended.

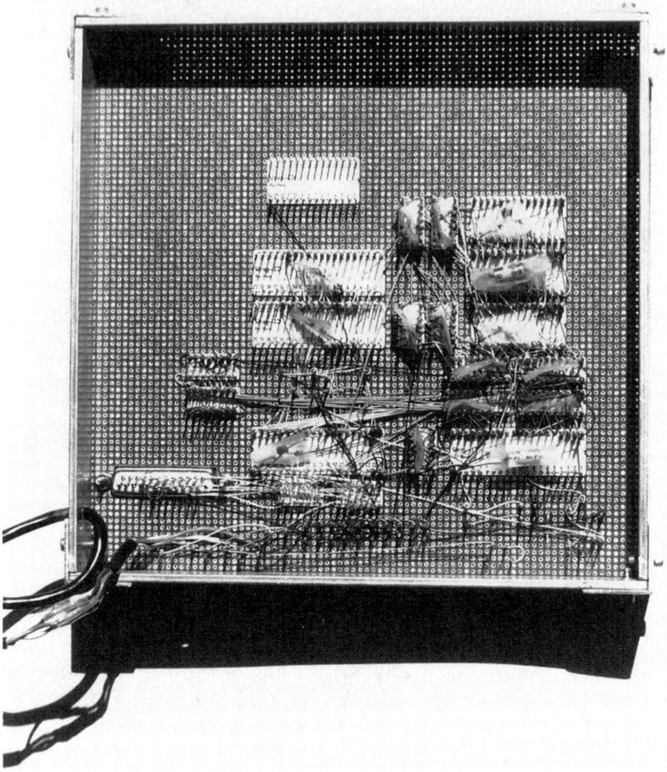

Figure 2.15. Bottom side of the single-board microcontroller system seen in Figure 2.14. Observe the bypass capacitors directly beneath the chips.

The bypass capacitors were made by soldering 30-gauge wire leads to capacitors. Transparent tape covers the capacitor and acts as insulation. The bypass capacitors are wire wrapped directly between Vcc and ground on the back side of the board. 4.7 μF capacitors bridge all memory chips.

Look inside a late-made Japanese car stereo. The chip capacitors (which are leadless) are soldered directly beneath chips on the solder side of the printed circuit board. Bypass capacitor effectiveness is diminished or lost if the capacitor is not equidistant between power and ground or if the leads are long.

The machine pictured in Figure 2.14 is very noise immune and does not exhibit address glitching despite the complicated decoding scheme. It unfortunately is limited in its development applicability because it is a single-board microcontroller.

F. Motherboard 8051 with Bus Layout

The necessary ingredients to make a computer system run include the clock circuit, reset circuit, address lines, data lines, and control signals. Most require some external ROM and RAM. The motherboard plan is to put the core of the computer on one board called the motherboard. The original IBM PC and most successors follow this plan. Some portables and industrial grade PC clones place the motherboard on a backplane. But the general plan is to keep the core machine on one board.

Peripheral IBM PC boards are inserted into a 62-pin connector that is organized as two rows of 31 pins (called a 31/2 connector). This connector is an edge connector as opposed to a two-piece pin connector. Two-piece connectors are used in the MAC II and VME bus, for example. IBM uses edge connectors in the PC/XT, PC/AT, Microchannel, and AS-400 machines. Edge connectors are less expensive than two-piece connectors.

Experts in connector technology cite studies by IBM and others to show that properly designed edge connectors equal the reliability of two-piece pin connectors. They say that connector reliability depends on only three things: the geometry, the mating force, and the connector material. Edge connectors should not be used in high vibration applications.

In their Technical Reference series for the XT and AT, IBM published detailed specifications and examples of interfacing to these busses. The IBM PC/XT pin assignments are shown in Figure 2.16. After-market vendors build almost any type of add-on board you need for these machines.

The IBM design allows the filling of a volume with electronic components. Single-board computers, on the other hand, fill an area.

The IBM PC/XT connector is used for a bussed 8051 microcontroller system. The pin assignments are given in Figure 2.17. The assignments are kept as close as possible to the IBM/XT assignments. This permits you to buy an IBM PC/XT prototyping card to develop your 8051 bussed microcontroller hardware ideas, or an XT extender card to troubleshoot a board.

As in the IBM PC/XT, the addresses are latched. −FF on pin A11 stands for I/O (address starting the FFxx where xx is "don't care"). Many of the microcontroller pins are jumpered. If you don't need these pins, then you can use them as user-assignable pins.

The idea behind the bussed system is to design and build the core once. The machine is transformed into an applications specific machine by changing the add-on cards on the bus. This idea worked well for IBM; it also works well for more complicated 8051 systems and parallel modular hardware development.

I/O Pin	Signal Name	I/O
A1	-I/O CH CK	I
A2	SD7	I/O
A3	SD6	I/O
A4	SD5	I/O
A5	SD4	I/O
A6	SD3	I/O
A7	SD2	I/O
A8	SD1	I/O
A9	SD0	I/O
A10	I/O CH RDY	I
A11	AEN	0
A12	SA19	I/O
A13	SA18	I/O
A14	SA17	I/O
A15	SA16	I/O
A16	SA15	I/O
A17	SA14	I/O
A18	SA13	I/O
A19	SA12	I/O
A20	SA11	I/O
A21	SA10	I/O
A22	SA9	I/O
A23	SA8	I/O
A24	SA7	I/O
A25	SA6	I/O
A26	SA5	I/O
A27	SA4	I/O
A28	SA3	I/O
A29	SA2	I/O
A30	SA1	I/O
A31	SA0	I/O

Side A

I/O Pin	Signal Name	I/O
B1	GND	Ground
B2	RESET DRV	0
B3	+5 Vdc	Power
B4	IRQ 2	I
B5	-5 Vdc	Power
B6	DRQ2	I
B7	-12 Vdc	Power
B8	-CARD SLCTD	I
B9	+12 Vdc	Power
B10	GND	Ground
B11	-MEMW	0
B12	-MEMR	0
B13	-IOW	I/O
B14	-IOR	I/O
B15	-DACK3	0
B16	DRQ3	I
B17	-DACK1	0
B18	DRQ1	I
B19	-DACK0	I/O
B20	CLK	0
B21	IRQ7	I
B22	IRQ6	I
B23	IRQ5	I
B24	IRQ4	I
B25	IRQ3	I
B26	-DACK2	0
B27	T/C	0
B28	ALE	0
B29	+5Vdc	Power
B30	OSC	0
B31	GND	Ground

Side B

Figure 2.16. IBM PC/XT bus pin assignments. Side A is the component side. B is the solder side.

G. The 8051 Schematics

The schematics for both single-board and bussed systems are combined. Also, external code, internal code, combined code, and external memory schematics are included on the same schematic. The reason for this inclusion is that the options are jumpered. The combined motherboard schematics are shown in Figure 2.18.

Warning! The processor is configured as a CMOS part with respect to the crystal oscillator. You will need to change the oscillator input if an NMOS part is used.

The power-on reset is included on the motherboard but the programmer reset switch is not. The HC373 (U1) is a flow-through latch that demultiplexes A0 through A7 from D0 through D7. ALE informs the HC373 to latch the address when it goes low.

The high order address lines A8 through A15 are buffered with an HC244 (U7), which gives additional drive to the address line output. The

8051 FAMILY BUS

i/o pin	signal name	i/o	i/o pin	signal name	i/o
A1	-RD&-PSEN	o	*B1		
A2	D7	i/o	B2	RESET	i/o
A3	D6	i/o	*B3		
A4	D5	i/o	+B4	-INT0 P3.2	i/o
A5	D4	i/o	+B5	P1.1	i/o
A6	D3	i/o	*B6		i/o
A7	D2	i/o	^B7	-12 Vdc	power
A8	D1	i/o	+B8	P1.4	i/o
A9	D0	i/o	^B9	+12 Vdc	power
A10	-PSEN	o	+B10	P1.6	i/o
A11	-FF	o	+B11	-WR P3.6	i/o
A12	P1.0	i/o	+B12	-RD P3.7	i/o
A13	P1.2	i/o	+B13	P3.0 RxD	i/o
A14	P1.3	i/o	+B14	P3.1 TxD	i/o
A15	P1.5	i/o	*B15		
A16	A15	o	*B16		
A17	A14	o	*B17		
A18	A13	o	*B18		
A19	A12	o	+B19	P1.7	i/o
A20	A11	o	+B20	P3.4 T0	i/o
A21	A10	o	*B21		
A22	A9	o	*B22		
A23	A8	o	*B23		
A24	A7	o	*B24		
A25	A6	o	+B25	-INT1 P3.3	i/o
A26	A5	o	+B26	-RAM	o
A27	A4	o	+B27	-ROM	o
A28	A3	o	B28	ALE	o
A29	A2	o	B29	+5 Vdc	power
A30	A1	o	+B30	P3.5 T1	i/o
A31	A0	o	B31	GND	ground

no termination on motherboard
jumpered on motherboard
not used on battery powered motherboard

Figure 2.17. 8051 family bussed system pin definitions. Side A is the component side. Side B is the solder side.

HC245 (U2) is a transceiver that buffers the data lines. Its direction is controlled by −RD. Its output is always enabled.

The decoding for I/O, the last 256 bytes of RAM substitution, is through the HC30 (U8). Notice that the inputs to the HC30 are taken from the processor rather than at the output of the HC244, in order to avoid gate propagation delay through the HC244.

The HC138 (U9), in combination with the HC30 (U8), implements the decoding scheme presented in Figure 2.8. ANDing −PSEN and −RD to

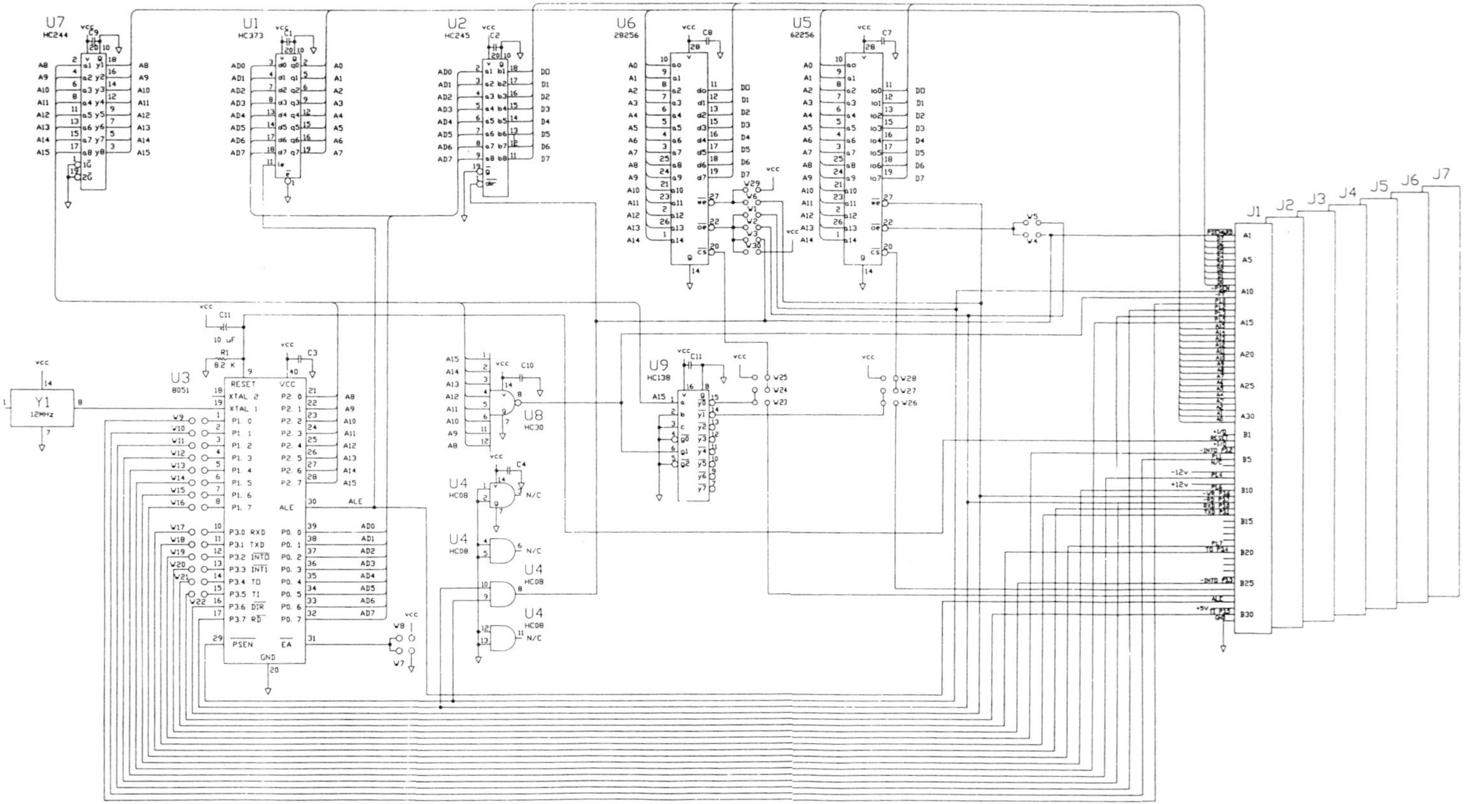

Figure 2.18. Combined schematics for the motherboard of the single board and bussed 8051 microcontroller system. Jumpers short all memory models.

form −PSEN&−RD is implemented in the HC08 (U4). Observe that all unused inputs are tied to ground.

Motherboard ROM (U6) is a 32K×8 EEPROM. It has extensive jumpers. Their functions are as follows.

Jumpers	Function
W6 open W7 closed	Disable write to the EEPROM
W6 closed W7 open	Allow write to the EEPROM

Other combinations of W6 and W7 are not permitted.

Jumpers	Function
W1 closed W2 open W3 open W8 open	Read strobe from −PSEN. Use memory external code.
W1 open W2 closed W3 open W8 open	Read strobe from −RD. Use memory external data.
W1 open W2 open W3 closed W8 open	Read strobe from −PSEN&−RD. Use memory as combined code and data.
W1 open W2 open W3 open W8 closed	Read strobe disabled. It is tied high to prevent all reads.

Other combinations of W1, W2, W3, and W8 are not permitted.

Jumpers	Function
W23 closed W24 open W25 closed	The −ROM signal goes out to the bus. This memory is disabled.
W23 open W24 closed W25 open	This memory is used for ROM.

W23 open W24 closed W25 closed	This memory is used for write-only or read-only.

Other combinations for W23, W24, and W25 are not permitted.

This EEPROM can be totally disabled. It can be enabled for reads using −PSEN, −RD, or −PSEN&−RD, or reads can be disabled. Writes can be either enabled or disabled.

The reason for implementing only EEPROM on the motherboard, as opposed to both EEPROM and EPROM, is that it may be preferable to solder the EEPROM to the board as opposed to socketing it.

The combination of jumpers not only allows configuration of all memory models but also makes it possible to reprogram the software without removing the part from the board. In fact, this 8051 system has the ability to reprogram itself, by disabling the read line to the EEPROM while enabling the write line.

To make this process clearer, a memory read in the space 0 through hex 7FFF accesses a memory chip on the bus. A write in this region accesses the EEPROM.

W26 closed W27 open W28 closed	The RAM is off-board on the bus.
W26 open W27 closed W28 open	The on-board RAM (U5) is used as RAM.

Other combinations of W26, W27, and W28 are not permitted.

W4 closed W5 open	Reads are combined code/data memory from −PSEN&−RD.
W4 open W5 closed	Reads are from data memory using −RD.

Other combinations of W4 and W5 are not permitted.

W7 closed W8 open	Instructions are fetched from internal code memory and possibly external code memory.

W7 open	Instructions are fetched from external
W8 closed	code memory.

Other combinations of W7 and W8 are not permitted.

Jumpers W9 through W22 jumper port pins. In case you run out of bus lines for your application, this arrangement permits you to use some of the port bus lines if you do not use the ports in your application.

If you decide to build a single board microcontroller system to run the FORTH development system included in this book, then configure your machine as an external code memory machine and overlap code and data memory. On a single board machine you probably will want to hard-wire your selections as opposed to jumpering them.

The schematic for the FORTH operations system EPROM or EEPROM and Asynchronous Communications Element is given in Figure 2.19. Jumpers W1 through W5 determine the base address of the National 82C50 Asynchronous Communications Element (ACE). The 82C50 uses eight addresses. Since the HC682 has internal pull-up resistors, closing no jumpers causes the ACE to have the base address FFF8. The FORTH operating system assigns the base address FFF0 to the ACE. Jumper W1 is closed and the remainder open. This assignment was made for the historical reason that two Intel 8051 USARTs were used with an Intel 8085. One was used for disk I/O and the other for terminal I/O. One had the address FFF0 and the other FFF8. Then it was discovered that disk and terminal I/O could be multiplexed so the disk address was equated to the terminal address of FFF0. It is possibly better to equate the terminal address to the disk address of FFF8. This assignment means that only the last eight bytes of I/O space are used for the operating system.

Some of the remaining jumper assignments involve selection of the memory as EPROM or EEPROM. For this reason the pin assignment for 32K×8 EPROMs, EEPROMs, and RAMs is given as in Figure 2.20.

Pin 1 on an EPROM is the programming voltage pin. It is held to Vcc when the chip is not being programmed. Pin 1 on an EEPROM is address line A14. Pin 27 on an EEPROM is −WE. Pin 27 on an EPROM is address line A14.

Therefore to configure the memory for an EPROM set the jumpers:

W6 closed	Vcc on pin 1
W7 open	
W8 open	
W9 closed	A14 on pin 27
W14 open	

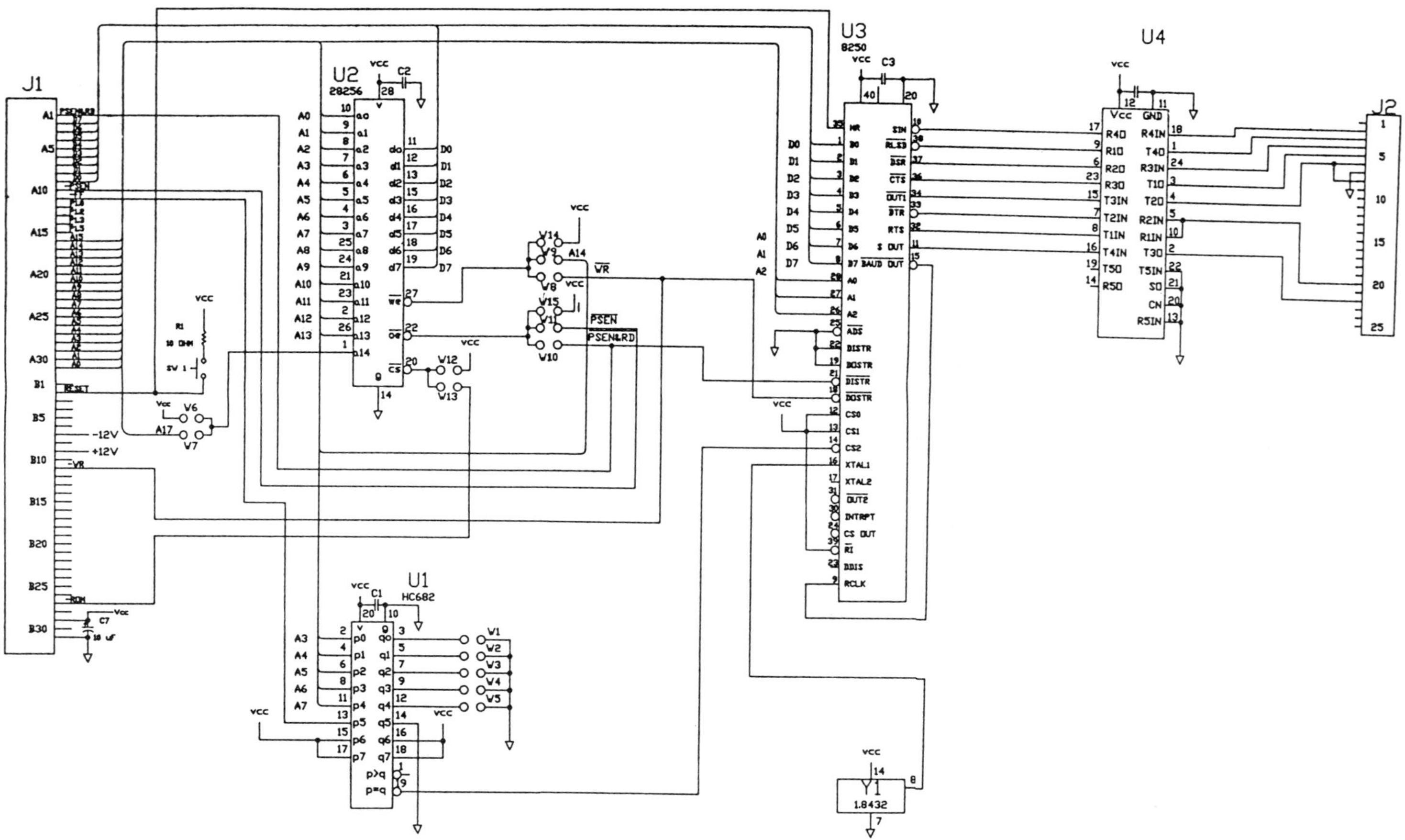

Figure 2.19. Combined schematics for the FORTH operating system and Asynchronous Communications Element (ACE) single-board and bussed 8051 microcontroller system. Jumpers support ACE addressing, FORTH operating system residing in EPROM or EEPROM, and assignment of this memory to either code or combined code/data address space.

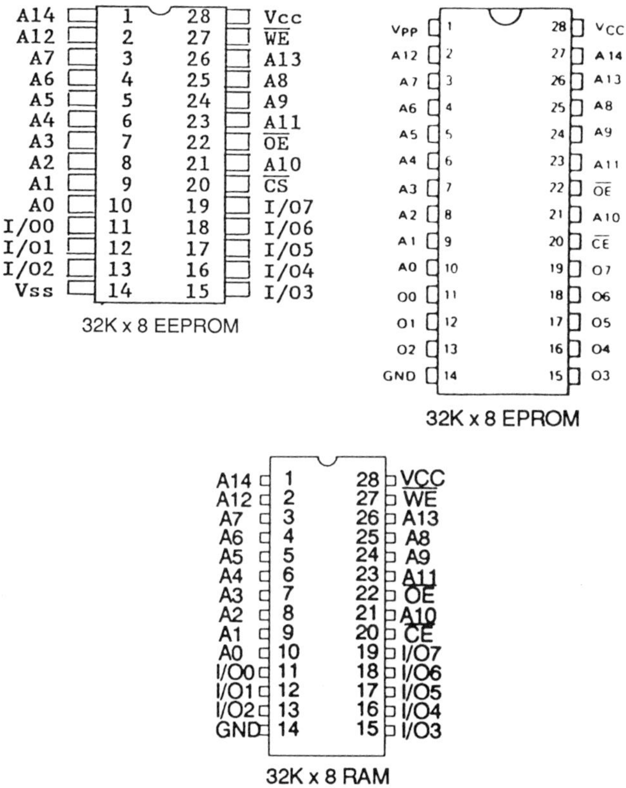

Figure 2.20. Pin assignment for 32K×8 EPROMs, EEPROMs, and RAMs.

To configure the memory for an EEPROM set the jumpers:

W6 open	
W7 closed	A14 on pin 1
W8 closed	−WR on pin 27
W9 open	
W14 open	

If you want to prevent writes to the EEPROM set:

W8 open	
W9 open	
W14 closed	−WR held to Vcc

The last option can be used to write to the EEPROM on the motherboard. Reads are directed to this chip while writes are directed to the EEPROM on the motherboard.

W10, W11, and W15 are used to control reads. The valid combinations are:

W10 closed	The memory is configured as combined code/data memory
W11 open	
W15 open	
W10 open	
W11 closed	The memory is configured as code memory.
W15 open	
W10 open	
W11 open	
W15 closed	Reads from this memory are inhibited.

This last option makes it possible to copy to this memory using the motherboard EEPROM to hold the executing code. Reads are directed to the motherboard EEPROM while writes are directed to this memory.

The primary function of this memory is to hold the FORTH operating system during software and hardware development. Once the application hardware/software is running, the software is copied to the motherboard EEPROM. At this time both this memory and ACE are eliminated, and it is even possible for FORTH to disappear.

Chip U4 in Figure 2.19 is a Maximum 235 line driver/receiver. It requires only a 5-volt input to produce the +12 and −12 output necessary for RS-232 communication. You can substitute 1488 and 1489 chips which require +12 and a maximum of −5 volts to meet RS 232 standards. A schematic for this substitution is shown in Figure 2.21.

These schematics apply to both single-board and bussed 8051 microcontroller development systems. For a single-board microcontroller system, wire directly to the chips and delete most of the jumpers. For a bussed system you probably want to include most of the jumpers. It is extra work, compared with a single-board system, to wire wrap the XT connectors. Printed circuit boards are used for the bussed system.

Figure 2.22 shows the silkscreen that is applied to the component side of a motherboard printed circuit board. Reduction of noise on a microcontroller system is the primary goal. Excessive noise can cause the hardware to malfunction, frequently leading to a software crash. One good way to reduce noise is to use multilayer printed circuit boards. One plane is allocated for power and another for ground.

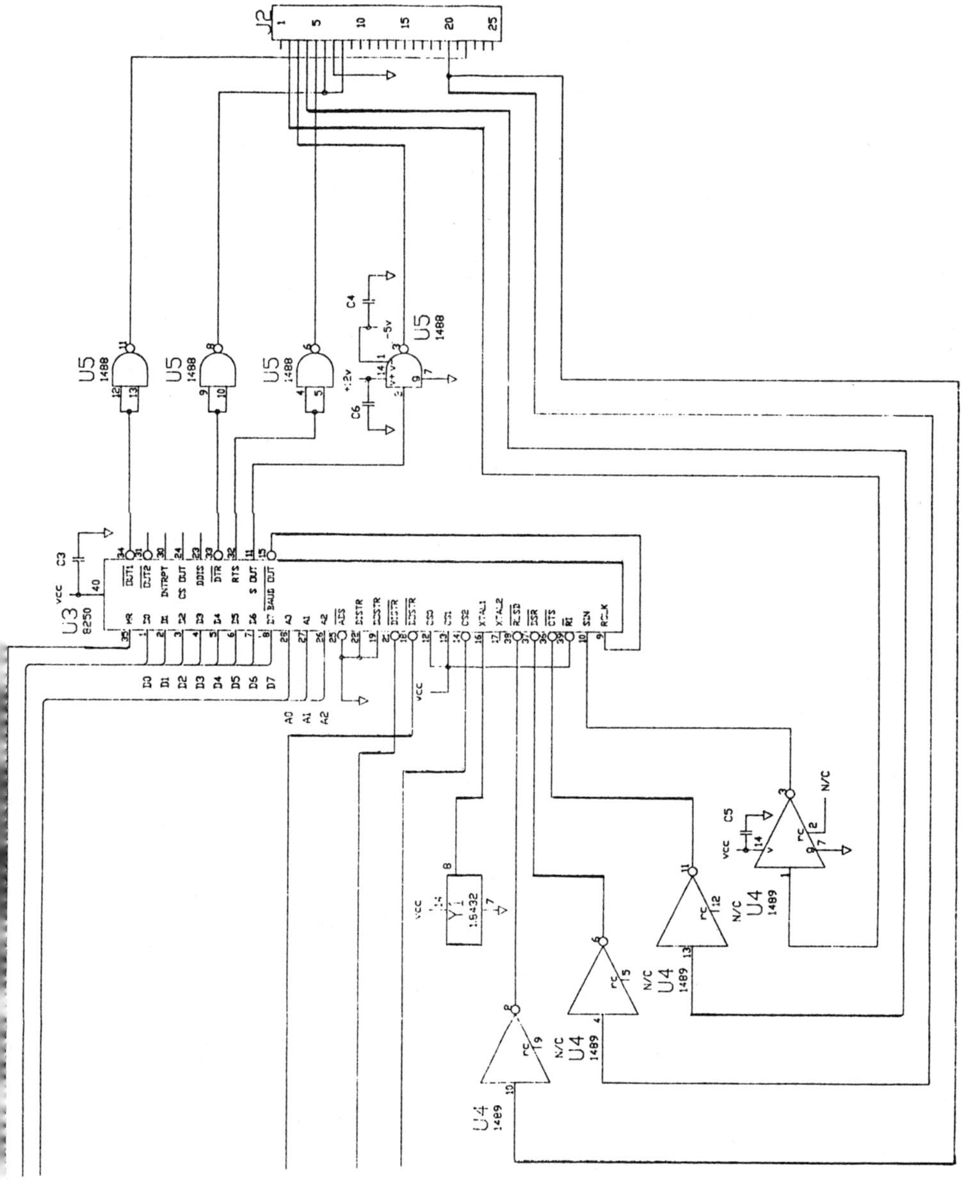

Figure 2.21. Schematic of 8250 ACE using a 1488 line driver and 1489 line receiver. +12 and a maximum of +5 volts are required for the 1488 chip to work properly.

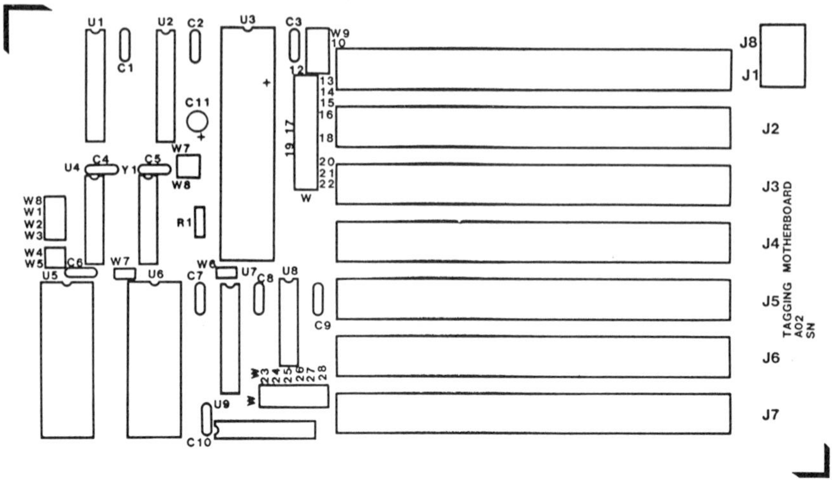

Figure 2.22. Silkscreen of motherboard printed circuit implementation.

Figure 2.23 shows the component side of a printed circuit layout of the motherboard schematic seen in Figure 2.18. Figure 2.24 shows the ground plane film. The ground plane is located directly beneath the component side. The +5V power plane film, located directly beneath the ground plane, is seen in Figure 2.25.

The bottom side of the board, the solder side, is seen in Figure 2.26. This revision of the motherboard includes chip capacitor pads beneath each integrated circuit. You can see the bars under the chips. The artwork for regular chip decoupling capacitors was not removed. It would cost money to change the artwork and there appeared no good electrical reason to remove it.

Finally, the pad master is seen in Figure 2.27. The pad master is used by the fabrication plant to show where the holes should be drilled through the board.

If you plan to build more than one or two systems, then you will probably find it cheaper to build a printed circuit board as opposed to wire-wrapping machines. Multilayer printed circuit boards are much more noise immune than two-layer boards. In Albuquerque, New Mexico, the relative humidity drops below 10%. Static electricity is a major problem. Multilayer printed circuit board 8051 microcontrollers practically eliminate software crashes resulting from static discharges.

A printed circuit version of the motherboard is pictured in Figure 2.28. The board measures 4 × 7 inches. External filter capacitors filter +5, +12, and −12 volts, which are fed into the board through the molex connector at the rear of the connectors.

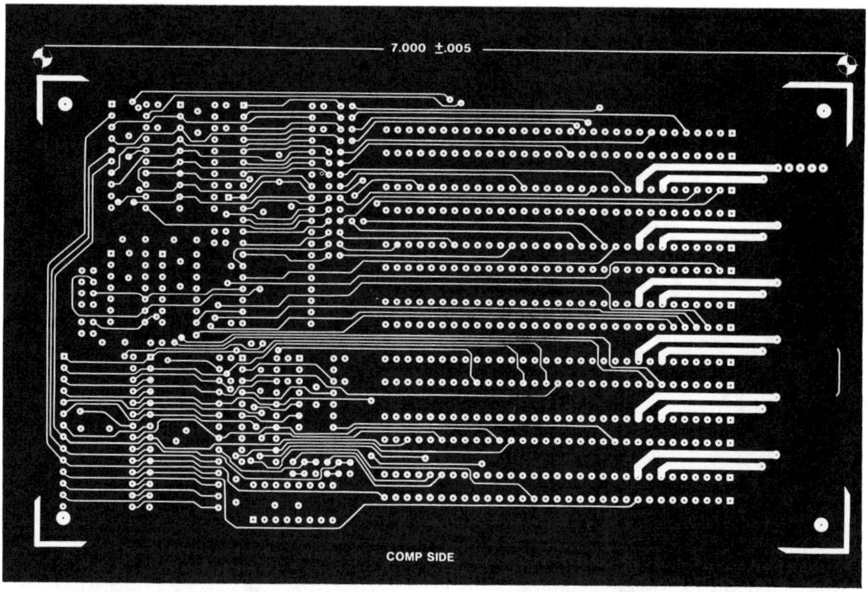

Figure 2.23. Component side of motherboard seen in Figure 2.18.

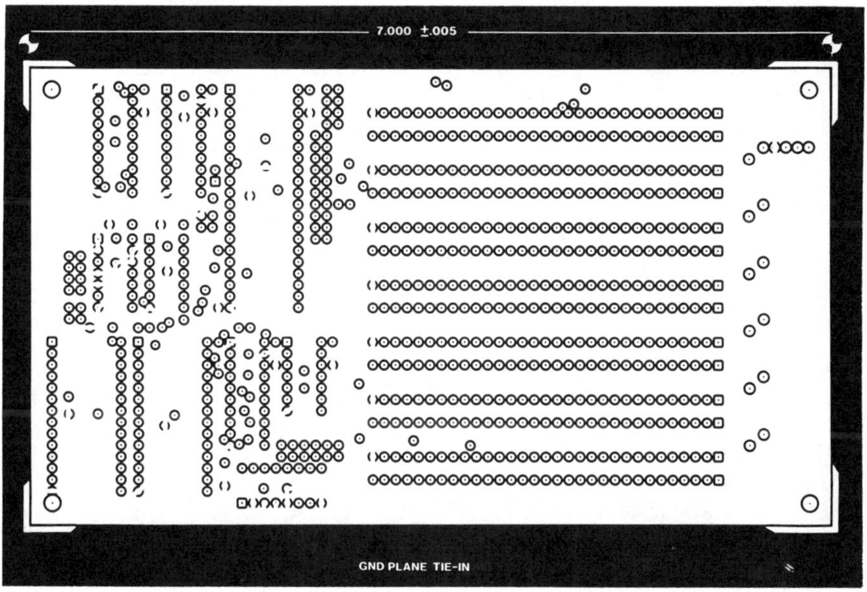

Figure 2.24. Ground plane film.

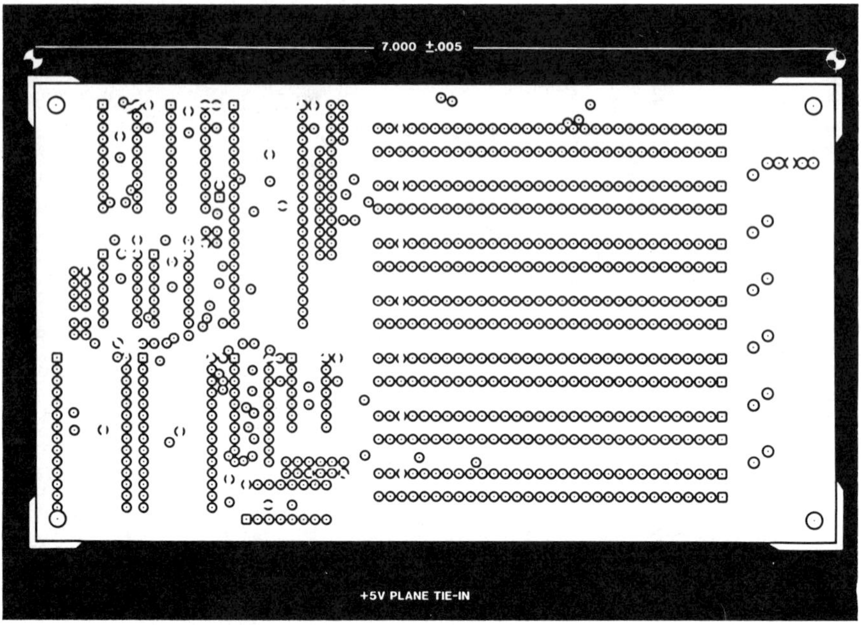

Figure 2.25. The +5V power plane film.

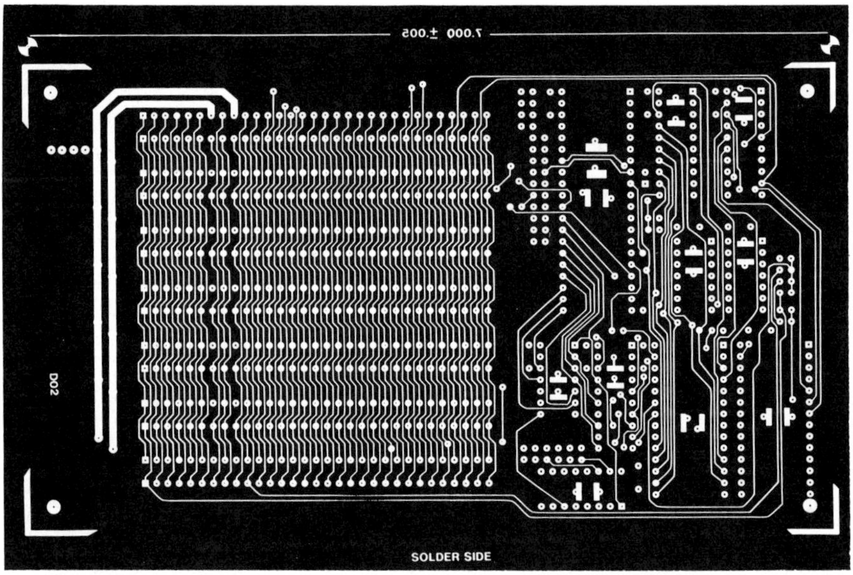

Figure 2.26. Solder side of motherboard seen in Figure 2.18. This motherboard revision includes pad for chip capacitors on the bottom of the board. These replace decoupling capacitors normally placed on the component side.

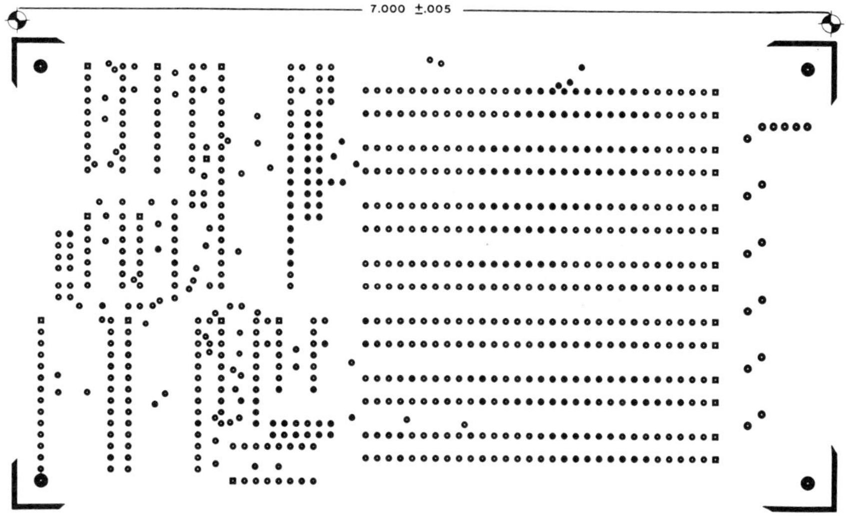

Figure 2.27. Pad master for the motherboard. It shows where the holes are to be drilled through the board.

The connectors are spaced ½ inch on center. This tight spacing accommodates components soldered to boards. Boards with socketed components barely fit.

A printed circuit version of the FORTH operating system memory and Asynchronous Communications Element diagrammed in Figure 2.19 is seen in Figure 2.29. The reset switch is located above the DB-25 connector. The board contains an EPROM rather than an EEPROM.

H. Addressing the National 82C50 Asynchronous Communications Element

The National 82C50 Asynchronous Communications Element (ACE) plays a critical role by providing terminal and disk communications between an 8051 microcontroller development system and a generic PC. Its decoding and addressing are typical of other, more complicated chips with multiple addresses. Therefore, its operation from a hardware and logical software standpoint is warranted at this time.

The register layout of the 80C52 is shown in Figure 2.30. The chip has eight internal addresses. These are offsets 0, 1, 2, 3, 4, 5, 6, and 7. The chip actually has 11 internal registers. Offset zero is three registers: the received is read from offset zero. The transmitted data is written to offset zero. When a bit called DLAB at offset 3, bit 7, is set to a one, then a write

Figure 2.28. Printed circuit version of the motherboard diagrammed in Figure 2.18.

Figure 2.29. Printed circuit version of a board containing the FORTH operating system memory and Asynchronous Communications Element diagrammed in Figure 2.19.

to offset zero stores the low byte of the divisor latch. The divisor latch is used to set the baud rate of the part. A write to offset one, with DLAB set, sets the high byte of the divisor latch.

If the jumpers are set to base address FFF0 (see Figure 2.19) then the ACE has the addresses:

```
FFF0    READ:  receive buffer register
        WRITE:  transmitter holding register
FFF1    READ and WRITE:  interrupt enable register
FFF2    READ only:  interrupt identification register
FFF3    READ and WRITE:  line control register
FFF4    READ and WRITE:  modem control register
FFF5    READ and WRITE:  line status register
FFF6    READ and WRITE:  model status register
FFF7    READ and WRITE:  scratch register
```

Bit No.	Register Address										
	0 DLAB=0	0 DLAB=0	1 DLAB=0	2	3	4	5	6	7	0 DLAB=1	1 DLAB=1
	Receiver Buffer Register (Read Only)	**Transmitter Holding Register (Write Only)**	**Interrupt Enable Register**	**Interrupt Ident. Register (Read Only)**	**Line Control Register**	**MODEM Control Register**	**Line Status Register**	**MODEM Status Register**	**Scratch Reg-ister**	**Divisor Latch (LS)**	**Divisor Latch (MS)**
	RBR	**THR**	**IER**	**IIR**	**LCR**	**MCR**	**LSR**	**MSR**	**SCR**	**DLL**	**DLM**
0	Data Bit 0 (Note 1)	Data Bit 0	Received Data Available	"0" if Interrupt Pending	Word Length Select Bit 0 (WLS0)	Data Terminal Ready (DTR)	Data Ready (DR)	Delta Clear to Send (DCTS)	Bit 0	Bit 0	Bit 8
1	Data Bit 1	Data Bit 1	Transmitter Holding Register Empty	Interrupt ID Bit (0)	Word Length Select Bit 1 (WLS1)	Request to Send (RTS)	Overrun Error (OE)	Delta Data Set Ready (DDSR)	Bit 1	Bit 1	Bit 9
2	Data Bit 2	Data Bit 2	Receiver Line Status	Interrupt ID Bit (1)	Number of Stop Bits (STB)	Out 1	Parity Error (PE)	Trailing Edge Ring Indicator (TERI)	Bit 2	Bit 2	Bit 10
3	Data Bit 3	Data Bit 3	MODEM Status	0	Parity Enable (PEN)	Out 2	Framing Error (FE)	Delta Data Carrier Detect (DDCD)	Bit 3	Bit 3	Bit 11
4	Data Bit 4	Data Bit 4	0	0	Even Parity Select (EPS)	Loop	Break Interrupt (BI)	Clear to Send (CTS)	Bit 4	Bit 4	Bit 12
5	Data Bit 5	Data Bit 5	0	0	Stick Parity	0	Transmitter Holding Register (THRE)	Data Set Ready (DSR)	Bit 5	Bit 5	Bit 13
6	Data Bit 6	Data Bit 6	0	0	Set Break	0	Transmitter Empty (TEMT)	Ring Indicator (RI)	Bit 6	Bit 6	Bit 14
7	Data Bit 7	Data Bit 7	0	0	Divisor Latch Access Bit (DLAB)	0	0	Data Carrier Detect (DCD)	Bit 7	Bit 7	Bit 15

Note 1: Bit 0 is the least significant bit. It is the first bit serially transmitted or received.

Figure 2.30. Register layout of the National 82C50.

The divisor latch contains the baud rate information. Figure 2.31 shows the divisor setting for a 1.8432 MHz crystal. The following is a high-level FORTH code to set the baud rate at 19,200 bits per second.

```
HEX
0FFF0             CONSTANT ACE

\ --- byte
: @LINECTRL   [ ACE 3 + ] LITERAL C@ ;   \ line control register

\ byte ---
: !LINECTRL   [ ACE 3 + ] LITERAL C! ;   \ store line control
                                          \  register
```

. Baud Rates Using 1.8432 MHz Crystal

Desired Baud Rate	Decimal Divisor Used to Generate 16 x Clock	Percent Error Difference Between Desired and Actual
50	2304	—
75	1536	—
110	1047	0.026
134.5	857	0.058
150	768	—
300	384	—
600	192	—
1200	96	—
1800	64	—
2000	58	0.69
2400	48	—
3600	32	—
4800	24	—
7200	16	—
9600	12	—
19200	6	—
38400	3	—
56000	2	2.86

Figure 2.31. Divisor latch settings to obtain baud rate for National 82C50 ACE.

```
\ divisor for baud rate ---
: >BAUD  @LINECTRL 80 OR !LINECTRL       \ set DLAB
         DUP ACE C!                      \  set low byte of divisor
         100 / [ ACE 1 + ] LITERAL C!    \  set high byte of divi-
                                         \  sor
         @LINECTRL 7F AND !LINECTROL ;   \ clear DLAB

6 >BAUD
```

This program is the introduction to this book's FORTH program conventions. Therefore, we shall explain its operation in some detail.

The base address is equated to the constant ACE. Always precede FORTH constants that do not begin with zero through nine with a zero. A FORTH word definition that consumes or leaves values on the parameter stack should be preceded by a stack diagram. The initial \ before the word definition @LINECTRL indicates that the remainder of the line is a comment.

The \ in the body of the comment is read "beneath." The comment arg1\arg2 is read "arg1 is beneath arg2 on the stack." The three dashes, ---, are read as "before" and "after" pictures of the stack.

In the definition "fetch line control," @LINECTRL, [ACE 3 +] LITERAL could be replaced by ACE 3 +. This command is executed each time @LINECTRL is invoked, whereas the LITERAL is evaluated only during compilation.

Redundant code in FORTH is undesirable. Therefore, @LINECTRL and !LINECTRL ("store line control") are defined as separate routines because they are invoked twice.

Isolating the high byte of a word by hexadecimal 100 / works, but it is better to define "byte swap" >< in assembler to accomplish this task.

The divisor of six sets the ACE's baud rate at 19,200 bits per second. This value is found in Figure 2.31. >BAUD is invoked from the FORTH interpreter.

The 82C50 requires inputs of −RD, −WR, −CS, A0, A1, and A2. −CS comes from the HC682 comparator. The 82C50 has the equivalent of an HC138 decoder and the HC32 OR gates internally. Most of the larger chips such as the Intel 8255 parallel port, 8253 or 8254 counter/timers, or clock/calendar chips also have decoding internally, with the exception of −CS.

The code for a complete initialization and handling under operation of this part is given in both the 8086 family and 8051 systems.

References

1. Payne, W. H., "ROMable FORTH applications code development." IEEE Software, October 1984, 100–102.
2. Williamson, T., "Oscillators for Microcontrollers." Intel Applications Note AP-155.
3. Intel, *Embedded Controller Handbook,* Volume **1**:8-bit. 1984–1989. *Note:* Each year Intel publishes an updated microcontroller handbook. Material is deleted and added. Some older handbooks have valuable tables that were deleted in recent additions. For example, the ordered op code table is missing from recent editions.
4. Texas Instruments, *High-speed CMOS Logic.* 1988. *Note:* Texas Instruments and other semiconductor manufacturers publish technical specifications for their products. Texas Instruments' multi-volume series includes most logic families. High-speed CMOS may be replaced by the faster advanced CMOS technology or by Bi-CMOS, which is used for the Intel 386 family.
5. Payne, W. H., "Decode overlapped EPROM, RAM, and I/O." EDN, May 14, 1987.
6. Intel, *Embedded Controller Applications.* 1988.
7. Williamson, T., "Designing Microcontroller Systems for Electrically Noisy Environments." Intel Applications Note 125, November 1986.

Chapter 3

The IBM PC Compatible Four File FORTH Operating System

The goal of this chapter is to get you up and running on a FORTH operating system hosted on a generic IBM PC system. You can start the system using only the contents of this book, if necessary.

By the end of this book, you will be in complete control of all your embedded controller software, including both the 8086 family and 8051 family. You can use the tools included in this book to bring up the generic operating system on hosts other than the 8051 family.

Distribution disks containing all the source code included in this book are in the possession of cooperating 8051 family hardware vendors. You are advised to get copies of the software from them on disk, from their bulletin boards, or from friends. Not only do you get this software from them, but cooperating vendors also distribute disks documenting each of the FORTH words in FORTH encyclopedia style.

Obtaining copies of the distribution disks is the easiest way to get up and running, although you can use just this book to do the same thing. Unfortunately, there is not room here to publish the 8086 and 8051 family FORTH encyclopedias. You must obtain them from a cooperating 8051 hardware vendor or from someone else who has a copy.

There may be a reader in some remote place with only an IBM PC clone who wants to run this software. All you need to do is enter a binary file slightly greater than 12K bytes in length. An ASCII listing of this binary file, with checksums, is given in this book. Once you enter it correctly, with the aid of the source code presented in this book, you can generate the binary file you entered from source.

That FORTH generates itself from source is an awesome feat. The cross assembly and cross compilation tools hosted on the generic IBM PC FORTH extend FORTH to the 8051 family. Moreover, you can extend it to other families of processors and microcontrollers.

The text of this book is its least important aspect. The code presented in this book warrants your greatest study. Charles Moore's genius is brought to you by members of the FORTH interest group. Jerry Boutelle's genius with metacompilers allows us to generate FORTH from source. You can figure out what Charles Moore had in mind fairly easily. Understanding what Jerry is doing in the metacompiler baffles the best programmers. Henry Laxen's expertise at writing editors makes you want to add features. Our expertise at writing table driven assemblers makes you want to tackle new processors. The code in this book is exciting. Learning it can be profitable if you use the tools to bring up embedded controller applications fast.

All individuals familiar with FORTH realize that FORTH is like calculus. It is an intellectual treasure to be appreciated and used by those who spend the time to learn it. Newton and Leibnitz didn't quit their jobs to attempt to make a fortune selling calculus. Instead, they published their results.

A. Bringing up FORTH on Your PC Using the Four File FORTH System

FORTH is an operating system. FORTH takes over PC/MS DOS. FORTH uses BIOS and DOS function calls to eliminate the need to write disk drivers and other complicated system software. Although one FORTH software vendor wrote all FORTH needed on a PC from scratch, this approach is not recommended.

Our IBM PC FORTH nucleus is stored in a PC/MS DOS file named IMAGE.COM. A program takes IMAGE.COM and formats it in ASCII, so you can enter it even if you are unable to get a copy of IMAGE.COM for your IBM/PC in binary form.

The program is compiled with IMAGE.COM. Care must be taken to select a good method to debug a program that writes to a disk, especially a hard disk. Debugging takes place in three steps. First, output is written to the screen. Second, screen write is replaced with disk writes directed to a floppy disk. Finally, the output is directed to a hard disk.

Following is the program. Borland's Sidekick, through its "cut and paste" (Ctrl KE), is used to import the FORTH program from its screen file into a WordStar book file.

```
DECIMAL
32          CONSTANT LINESIZE
0           VARIABLE ASCIIBUFFER -2 ALLOT LINESIZE ALLOT
: 0>ASCIIBUFFER ASCIIBUFFER LINESIZE ERASE ;

\--- bytes read
: READLINE          0>ASCIIBUFFER
                    PRIF HANDLE ASCIIBUFFER LINESIZE READ
                    IF CR ." Read file error # " U. SP! QUIT
                    THEN ;

\ line length --- checksum
: CHECKSUM          0 SWAP 0
                    DO ASCIIBUFFER I + C@ +
                    LOOP ;

\line length---
: WRITELINE         DUP 0
                    DO ASCIIBUFFER I + C@
                      BASE @ >R HEX 0 <# # # #> TYPE R> BASE !
                    LOOP SPACE CHECKSUM 0 < # # # # # #> TYPE CR ;
                    DECIMAL

\line number---
: .HEADING          0 16 U/ SWAP 0=
                    IF 0 <# # # #> TYPE CR
                    ELSE DROP
                    THEN ;

: BTOASCII          -1
                    BEGIN 1+ READLINE DUP
                      IF OVER .HEADING THEN
                      DUP LINESIZE =
                    WHILE WRITELINE
                    REPEAT DUP
                    IF WRITELINE
                    ELSE DROP THEN DROP ;
```

A 32-byte buffer is allocated to contain a line to be read from disk. The FORTH word VARIABLE allots two bytes so the dictionary pointer, DP, is moved back two positions with −2 ALLOT. The contents of the buffer translates into a 64-byte ASCII output line. "Zero to asciibuffer," 0>ASCIIBUFFER, zeros the contents of ASCIIBUFFER.

For those new at FORTH, ":" is read "begin procedure," and ";" is read "end procedure."

READLINE reads 32 bytes from the primary file. Here is the major difference with the FORTH we use for software development. The primary file has four screen files. These four files are called the Primary, Secondary, Auxiliary, and System files.

FORTH normally has one open file called the screen file. This file contains a maximum of 32,768 1024-byte blocks, or 33,554,432 bytes! This is an absurdly big file.

Copying information from one FORTH screen file to another used to be an unpleasant task because of FORTH's single screen file. Solutions usually involved writing a program in FORTH that read one file and copied it into another. Here, FORTH has been modified by splitting the single screen file into four files, each containing 33,554,432 ÷ 4 = 8,388,608 bytes. Bits 13 and 14 of the block number indicated that file reads and writes are directed to different files. Here is the format of a FORTH block number.

```
High order bit  15  FORTH UPDATE bit
                14  Assigned to file number
                13  Assigned to file number
                12  Highest bit of block number
                11
                10
                 9
                 8
                 7
                 6
                 5
                 4
                 3
                 2
                 1
Low order bit    0  Lowest bit of block number
```

The following is the file number assignment.

```
Bit 14 13
     0  0         Primary file
     0  1         Secondary file
     1  0         Auxiliary file
     1  1         System file
```

The FORTH update bit is set by UPDATE to tell that a block has been modified.

This modification to FORTH has greatly speeded software development. This FORTH is kept as close as possible to the FORTH Interest Group's model, but this feature is indispensable. It is named FORTH86 because it is hosted on 8086 family machines. The source code is in Appendix 1.

FORTH86 supports file pathnames. Four buffers named PRIF, SECF, AUXF, and SYSF contain pathnames of declared files. At cold start SYSF contains the name SYSTEM.SCR. The data structure of these buffers are:

```
bute 0      count of characters
     1      first character of file pathname
     2      second character of file pathname
     3
     n      last character of file pathname
     n+1    file handle if file opened.
```

The file pathname is formatted in the buffer as a counted string. If the file is open, its UNIX-like handle is stored in the byte following the last character in the name. FORTH86 supports the UNIX-like file handling included in PC/MS DOS. The CPM-like interface is not supported.

Four commands, PFILE, SFILE, AFILE, and SYSFILE, read a filename and either open or ask you if you want to create a file by the specified name (interpreting only). Interactively entering the command

```
PFILE IMAGE.COM
```

opens the file IMAGE.COM as the primary file and points the read/write pointer to the first byte of the file.

READLINE zeros ASCIIBUFFER. The sequence of FORTH words

```
PRIF HANDLE ASCIIBUFFER LINESIZE
```

sets up the arguments for a UNIX-like read from the primary file. These are

```
handle\buffer address\number of bytes to read ---
```

READ reads the contents of the file into the buffer. It attempts to read the number of bytes specified. It may read fewer bytes. READ returns

```
--- \error #\1
```

if an error occurred. Or it returns

```
--- \number of bytes read\0
```

if the read was successful. In the event that the read failed, READLINE prints the error number, restores the parameter stack pointer with SP!, and returns to the operating system with QUIT.

If READLINE executes successfully, then it returns the number of bytes read on the parameter stack. When the end of the file is reached, some number less than LINESIZE bytes is read. This value can be zero.

CHECKSUM computes the sum of the bytes of line length long. This value gives you a negative indication if you entered a line incorrectly. Just because the checksum is correct does not mean you did not make a mistake entering a line.

WRITELINE is the debug routine that writes the contents of ASCIIBUFFER line length long and the checksum to the screen.

The word .HEADING (“.” in FORTH is pronounced “print”) prints the block number of the 64-character × 16-line block of ASCII characters plus checksum.

BTOASCII (binary to ASCII) is the main program that reads the primary file and prints the ASCII-formatted file to the screen. After some debugging and enhancement, it works. The program is changed to write the output to the screen. ASCII files should be terminated with “Ctrl Z.” This is a decimal 26. All of the strings to be written to the file have the arguments address\length --- for a common interface. Following is the modified program.

```
DECIMAL
32          CONSTANT LINESIZE
0           VARIABLE ASCIIBUFFER -2 ALLOT LINESIZE ALLOT
0           VARIABLE CRLF -2 ALLOT 2 C, 13 C, 10 C,
0           VARIABLE ASPACE -2 ALLOT 1 C, 32 C,
0           VARIABLE CTRLZ -2 ALLOT 1 C, 26 C,

: 0>ASCIIBUFFER ASCIIBUFFER LINESIZE ERASE ;


\ address\length ---
: >SFILE             >R >R SECF HANDLE R> R WRITE
                     IF CR ."Write file error # " U. R> SP! QUIT
                     THEN R> <>
                     IF CR ." File full" SP! QUIT THEN ;


\ line number ---
: .HEADING           0 16 U/ SWAP 0=
                     IF 0 <# # # #> >SFILE CRLF COUNT >SFILE
                     ELSE DROP
                     THEN ;


\ --- bytes read
: READLINE           0>ASCIIBUFFER
                     PRIF HANDLE ASCIIBUFFER LINESIZE READ
                     IF CR ." Read file error # " U. SP! QUIT
                     THEN ;
```

```
\ line length --- checksum
: CHECKSUM          0 SWAP 0
                    DO ASCIIBUFFER I + C@ +
                    LOOP ;

\ line length ---
: WRITELINE         BASE @ >R DUP 0
                    DO ASCIIBUFFER I + C@
                      HEX 0 <# # # #> >SFILE
                    LOOP ASPACE COUNT >SFILE
                    CHECKSUM 0 <# # # # # #> >SFILE
                    CRLF COUNT >SFILE R> BASE ! ;

: BTOASCII          -1
                    BEGIN 1+ READLINE OVER .HEADING
                      DUP WRITELINE LINESIZE <>
                    UNTIL CTRLZ COUNT >SFILE
                    SECF CLOSEHANDLE DROP ;
```

SECF CLOSEHANDLE closes the secondary file.

If any additional FORTH words in this program confuse you, then study their definitions in Appendix 1. There are no secrets in this book.

The use of "To R," >R, " R," and "R from" (R> in >SFILE) illustrate how useful the return stack can be to store values temporarily.

The program may be run with the interactive commands

```
PFILE IMAGE.COM
SFILE A:IMAGE.DOC
BTOASCII
```

The SFILE command prompts a response as to whether the file IMAGE.DOC is to be created. The response is "yes." The file is converted. The command, TYPE IMAGE.DOC, shows that the file is apparently correctly converted. The file view from WordStar still looks correct. But is it? A hard copy of this file is located in Appendix 2.

The next step is to write a BASIC program that converts IMAGE.DOC to a second copy of IMAGE.COM. Comparison of the two versions of the binary IMAGE.COM will convince us that the program above worked correctly. You can use the BASIC program to bring up your FORTH86. There are other ways, but, discounting the time you spend creating the ASCII file IMAGE.DOC in Appendix 2, using BASIC is a relatively easy way of bringing up FORTH86.

Before programming in BASIC, examine the following program, which converts the FORTH screen file containing FORTH86 (FORTH86.SCR) to an ASCII file. FORTH screen files contain blocks of 1024 bytes.

```
DECIMAL
16          CONSTANT LINES/SCR

0           VARIABLE PBLS \ previous blank lines
0           VARIABLE CRLF -2 ALLOT 2 C, 13 C, 10 C,
0           VARIABLE CTRLZ -2 ALLOT 1 C, 26 C,

\ address\length ---
: >SFILE             >R >R SECF HANDLE R> R WRITE
                     IF CR ." Write file error # " U. R> SP! QUIT
                     THEN R> <>
                     IF CR ." File full" SP! QUIT THEN ;

\ screen number ---
: .SCR#              0 <# #S #> >SFILE CRLF COUNT >SFILE ;

: .CRLF              PBLS @ IF CRLF COUNT >SFILE THEN ;

\ screen number ---
: SCR>ASCII          LINES/SCR 0
                     DO DUP I SWAP (LINE) -TRAILING DUP
                       IF >SFILE 1 PBLS ! .CRLF
                       ELSE DROP DROP .CRLF 0 PBLS !
                       THEN
                     LOOP DROP ;

\ start screen\end screen ---
: SCRTOASCII         DEPTH 2 <>
                     IF CR ." Check # of arguments" QUIT THEN
                     1+ SWAP
                     DO 0 PBLS ! I .SCR# I SCR>ASCII
                     LOOP
                     CTRLZ COUNT >SFILE
                     SECF CLOSEHANDLE ;
```

There are no carriage returns (hex 0D), line feeds (hex 0A), or other delimiters separating blocks. If you read a FORTH screen file with a standard word processor such a WordStar or PC Write, the file looks like one long sentence.

The FORTH word "#S" is used to suppress leading blanks in .SCR#. Multiple blank lines are compressed into a single blank line. "Screen to ASCII," SCRTOASCII, checks the number of arguments on the stack. The possibility of creating a large output file exists, so it is best to run a check.

IMAGE.DOC, seen in Appendix 2, contains an ASCII file of the binary object code of the 8086 family FORTH. This file needs to be converted to a binary file so that it is executable on a PC. Microsoft or IBM BASICs can be a problem. They frequently won't run on some clone PCs. Several versions crashed on a PC clone or reported "Wrong DOS version" on 80286 and 80386 systems. A copy of Microsoft's GWBASIC worked on all machines.

Here is the BASIC program to convert IMAGE.DOC to IMAGE.COM.

```
0    REM C$ is list of hexadecimal digits. A0% = low order digit of
     byte.
1    REM A1% high order digit of byte. A% = decimal or hex byte
     value.
2    REM D% = checksum. AA% = computed checksum. B% = location of
     blank
3    REM separating data and checksum. A% = ASCII representation of
4    REM then block number. E$ = binary representation of ASCII
     byte.
10   FSTBLK=0
20   LSTBLK=24
30   C$="0123456789ABCDEF"
40   OPEN "IMAGE.DOC" FOR INPUT AS #1
50   OPEN "IMAGE.COM" FOR OUTPUT AS #2
60   GOTO 290
70   LINE INPUT #1,A$: PRINT A$: RETURN
80   AA%=0: FOR I=1 TO B%-1 STEP 2: GOSUB 90: GOSUB 110:
     AA%=AA%+A%: NEXT I: RETURN
90   A0%=INSTR (C$,MID$(A$,I,1))-1
100  A1%=INSTR(C$,MID$(A$,I+1,1))-1: RETURN
110  A%=16*A0%+A1%: RETURN
120  A%=10*A0%+A1%: RETURN
130  B%=INSTR(A$," "): RETURN
140  D0%=INSTR(C$,MID$(A$,B%+1,1))-1
150  D1%=INSTR(C$,MID$(A$,B%+2,1))-1
160  D2%=INSTR(C$,MID$(A$,B%+3,1))-1
170  D3%=INSTR(C$,MID$(A$,B%+4,1))-1
180  D%=((D0%*16+D1%)*16+D2%)*16+D3%
190  IF D%<>AA% THEN PRINT JJ, "CHECKSUM FAIL": STOP: ELSE RETURN
200  FOR I=1 TO B%-1 STEP 2: GOSUB 90: GOSUB 110: E$=MKI$(A%)
210  PRINT #2,MID$(E$,1,1);: NEXT I: RETURN
220  CLOSE #2: CLOSE #1: PRINT " FILES CLOSED": JJ=17:RETURN
230  IF LEN(A$)<>2 THEN PRINT "WRONG SCR# LEN": STOP ELSE RETURN
240  I=1: GOSUB 90: GOSUB 120
250  IF A%<>J THEN PRINT A%,J,"WRONG BLK #": STOP ELSE RETURN
```

```
260  FOR JJ=1 TO 16: GOSUB 70: GOSUB 130: GOSUB 80: GOSUB 140: GOSUB
     200
270  IF B%<>65 THEN GOSUB 220
280  NEXT JJ:RETURN
290  FOR J=FSTBLK TO LSTBLK: GOSUB 70: GOSUB 230: GOSUB 240
300  GOSUB 260: NEXT J
310  END
```

Conversion from ASCII to hexadecimal does not appear easy using Microsoft's BASIC. The checksum is written in hexadecimal and the block number in decimal. This discrepancy is the reason for the two base conversion statements located at 110 and 120. Microsoft's BASIC includes the verb MKI$, which converts a binary integer to a string. The verb writes the binary values to the file.

A programmer is able to write about 10 lines of debugged code per day. The time required to get this program running was in line with the estimate. The program checks for valid block number and length and for correct checksum.

A DIR of the original IMAGE.COM is:

```
IMAGE    COM    12555    10-15-89    1:33p
```

and the DIR of IMAGE.COM produced by the BASIC program is:

```
IMAGE    COM    12556    10-15-89    2:11p
```

The one-byte discrepancy in length results from BASIC's adding a Ctrl Z, hex 1A, to the end of the file with the CLOSE statement. BASIC assumes ASCII files are written. The additional 1A has no bad effect on a .COM file. However, using the DOS COMP utility to compare the original binary file with the binary file produced by BASIC is impractical because it does not compare files of unequal length.

IMAGE.COM took about eight minutes running on an 8 MHz 8088 to produce from the BASIC program. It works.

Embedded controller programmers frequently must work at the bit level. It is necessary to compare binary files to discover the differences between an image that works properly and one that crashes. These differences are then related to the source code that produced them.

Most programmers can't, or probably shouldn't, spend lots of time writing elegant and user-friendly software tools, but should get the applications code working. Spending too much time on software tools takes time away from the applications software. FORTH intrigues some programmers so much that they spend most of their time modifying or enhancing FORTH, rather than spending time on the applications software.

Perhaps the previous paragraph gives insight to the image-compare program, COMP. It was written and tested in about 15 minutes. It does the job, depending on your viewpoint, either with elegant simplicity or inelegantly.

```
FORTH DEFINITIONS DECIMAL
: TASK ;
: CASE          ?COMP CSP @ !CSP 4 ; IMMEDIATE
: OF            4 ?PAIRS COMPILE OVER COMPILE = COMPILE
                0BRANCH HERE 0 , COMPILE DROP 5 ; IMMEDIATE
: ENDOF         5 ?PAIRS COMPILE BRANCH HERE 0 ,
                SWAP 2 [COMPILE] THEN 4 ; IMMEDIATE
: ENDCASE       4 ?PAIRS COMPILE DROP BEGIN SP@
                CSP @ = 0= WHILE 2 [COMPILE]
                THEN REPEAT CSP ! ; IMMEDIATE

HEX
\ character
: PAB DROP BL EMIT ;
\ character
: PAC 0 <# # # #> TYPE ;
: BEEP 7 EMIT ;

\ character
: PIT     DUP CASE
          0C OF PAB ENDOF
          0A OF PAB ENDOF
          07 OF PAB ENDOF
          0D OF PAB ENDOF
          00 OF PAB ENDOF
          08 OF PAB ENDOF
          EMIT ENDCASE ;
HEX
SFILE IMAGE.COM
AFILE \GWBASIC\IMAGE.COM
\ start address\end address ---
: COMP          SWAP DO I CR DUP 4 .R 4 SPACES
                0 400 U/ OVER OVER SBLOCK + C@ DUP PIT SPACE
                DUP PAC 2 SPACES >R ABLOCK + C@
                DUP PAC 2 SPACES R> =
                IF ." ="
                ELSE ." <>" BEEP KEY DROP THEN
                LOOP CR ;
```

```
DECIMAL
CLS .FILES KEY DROP -CURSOR 0 12555 COMP CURSOR
\ HEX
\ CLS PRINTER .FILES KEY DROP 42E0 4340 COMP CONSOLE
```

The FORTH CASE statement was written by Jay Eacker and published in *FORTH Dimensions*. You can learn much about FORTH by studying it to discover how it works. You should compare it to ONGOSUB and ENDGOSUB, defined in FORTH86 on screen 36 in Appendix 1. COMP is a FORTH version of the BASIC ONGOSUB construct. Jerry Boutelle wrote ?GOSUBW seen on screen 102 to speed ENDGOSUB.

PAB stands for "print a blank," PAC for "print a character," and PIT for "print it." The purpose of PIT is to remove those characters that cause printing to go awry. The FORTH word names were selected because they were fast to type.

The files to be compared are assigned to the secondary and auxiliary files. The primary file is thus free to point to the COMP program. COMP is designed to be changed and recompiled rapidly for custom requirements.

The BASIC-produced image file, when compared, proved equal to its successor except for the last byte. COMP is invoked with

```
DECIMAL 12550 12555 COMP
```

to see

```
DECIMAL 12550 12556 COMP
12550     1 49  49   =
12551     4 52  52   =
12552       09  09   =
12553     6 54  54   =
12554       08  08   =
12555       00  26   <>
ok
```

You see the Ctrl Z, a hex 1A or decimal 26, in location 12555. This is the Ctrl Z added by BASIC with the CLOSE statement.

If you successfully created the file IMAGE.COM from the contents of Appendix 2 and the BASIC program, then you have the version of FORTH whose source code is listed in Appendix 1 and is working.

If you type IMAGE.COM, and FORTH can't find a file called SYSTEM.SCR, then FORTH resorts to numbered messages by setting a variable called WARNING to zero. The logon message for this case is shown in Appendix 3 along with an ASCII listing of SYSTEM.SCR. This ASCII listing of SYSTEM.SCR is called SYSTEM.DOC.

FORTH needs SYSTEM.SCR to print warning or error messages to the screen. SYSTEM.SCR is also used as a type of AUTOEXEC.BAT for FORTH. FORTH loads screen 1 of SYSTEM.SCR (if it is present) after it boots up. We need to create SYSTEM.SCR, but all we have, if there is no disk copy, is the ASCII listing of SYSTEM.SCR, SYSTEM.DOC, seen in Appendix 3. Instructions on creating SYSTEM.SCR this way are as follows.

Use your word processor in the nondocument form to enter SYSTEM.DOC into a file called SYSTEM.DOC. Some word processors mask characters with hex 80. Use spaces, not tabs.

Now you have SYSTEM.DOC. Following is a program to convert the .DOC file created by SCRTOASCII back to screen format files.

```
DECIMAL
65          CONSTANT BUFFERSIZE
0           VARIABLE INBUFFER -1 ALLOT
0           VARIABLE ASCIIBUFFER -2 ALLOT BUFFERSIZE ALLOT
0           VARIABLE SCR#            0        VARIABLE LINE#
0           VARIABLE START           0        VARIABLE EOF
0           VARIABLE SCRNUMBER

: CLOSEFILES FLUSH PRIF CLOSEHANDLE SECF CLOSEHANDLE ;

\ --- character
: READCHR   SECF HANDLE INBUFFER 1 READ
            IF CR ." File read err #" U. SP! QUIT THEN 1 <
            IF CR ." End of file" THEN
            INBUFFER C@ DUP 26 =
            IF CLOSEFILES SP! QUIT THEN ;

: READLINE   ASCIIBUFFER BUFFERSIZE ERASE 0
             BEGIN READCHR DUP 13 <>
             WHILE OVER [ ASCIIBUFFER 1+ ] LITERAL + C! 1+
             REPEAT DROP READCHR DROP
             ASCIIBUFFER C! ;

\ --- number\number of digits
\ --- 0 none
: SCR#?  0 0 ASCIIBUFFER (NUMBER)
         ASCIIBUFFER - 1- DUP 0>
         IF SWAP DROP
         ELSE DROP DROP DROP 0
         THEN ;
```

```
\ primary file screen # ---
: BLANKSCR       BLOCK 1024 BLANKS UPDATE ;

\ screen # ---
: NEXTSCREEN     DUP BLANKSCR SCR# ! 0 LINE# ! ;

\ start screen ---
: INITSCRS       DUP 0>
                 IF DUP 0 DO I BLANKSCR LOOP THEN
                 SCR# ! 0 LINE# ! 1 START ! ;

: ISSCR#         SCR#?
                 IF START @ 0=
                   IF INITSCRS 0 SCRNUMBER !
                   ELSE SCR# @ 1+ =
                     IF SCR# @ 1+ NEXTSCREEN 0 SCRNUMBER !
                       ELSE CR ." Scr # " SCR# @ 1+ U.
                       ." expected. Scr # " SCR#?
                       DROP U. ." found." SP! QUIT
                     THEN
                   THEN
                 THEN ;

\ line length ---
: >LINE          ASCIIBUFFER COUNT DUP 0>
                 IF >R LINE# @ SCR# @ (LINE) DROP
                   R> CMOVE UPDATE
                 ELSE DROP DROP
                 HEN ;

: NEXTLINE       LINE# @ 1+ 15 MIN LINE# ! ;

: NEWSCREEN      1 SCRNUMBER !
                 ASCIIBUFFER C@ 4 < ASCIIBUFFER C@ 0> AND
                 IF ISSCR# THEN ;

: .ASCIILINE     CR ASCIIBUFFER COUNT TYPE ;

: ASCIITOSCR     0 EOF ! 0 START ! 0 SCR# ! 0 LINE# !
                 BEGIN READLINE .ASCIILINE NEWSCREEN
                   SCRNUMBER @
                   IF >LINE NEXTLINE THEN
                 AGAIN ;
```

You need to enter this program manually from the keyboard.

When this is done, then you type "enter" at the end of the string

```
PFILE SYSTEM.SCR
```

and

```
SFILE SYSTEM.DOC.
```

Now type

```
ASCIITOSCR
```

The text is listed on the screen as it is converted to a screen file. Now when you reboot FORTH, you have SYSTEM.SCR and verbal warning messages. A .DOC version of this code is given in Appendix 3. You will need it to load other .DOC files listed in the Appendices. Most important you need Laxen's editor.

If you have the misfortune to have some high bits set, hex 80's ORed, in your .DOC file, then you will need to write a CLEAN utility that reads each character from the .DOC file and ANDs hex 7F with each character. You need to write the characters back to another file. This task is easy to do from the keyboard with code presented in this chapter. Or you can modify READLINE to

```
WHILE 127 AND OVER [ ASCIIBUFFER 1+ ] LITERAL + C! 1+,
```

which accomplishes the same task.

ASCIITOSCR was complicated by the paper-saving feature of SCRTOASCII. (NUMBER) converts a string to the specified base to a double number. It starts one byte after the starting address. It stops on the first nonconvertible byte. ASCIIBUFFER was zeroized to guarantee a nonconvertible byte. ASCIITOSCR is all decimal. Be careful about changing the base before invoking the routine since the conversion base also changes.

General routines take time to write and may not be necessary in some applications. ASCIITOSCR was tested by converting all of the .DOC files in this book back to screen files. SYSTEM.DOC contained 89 alone on screen 12, line 9. This amount stopped ASCIITOSCR so RESERVED was added. Be careful about writing routines that do everything but may not do a specific task well. They take a long time to write and occupy more memory than a specific routine.

The word-by-word details of ASCIITOSCR are not covered in detail. It was designed top down, more or less, and debugged bottom up. ISSCR#—"Is it a screen number?"—probably is too complicated for

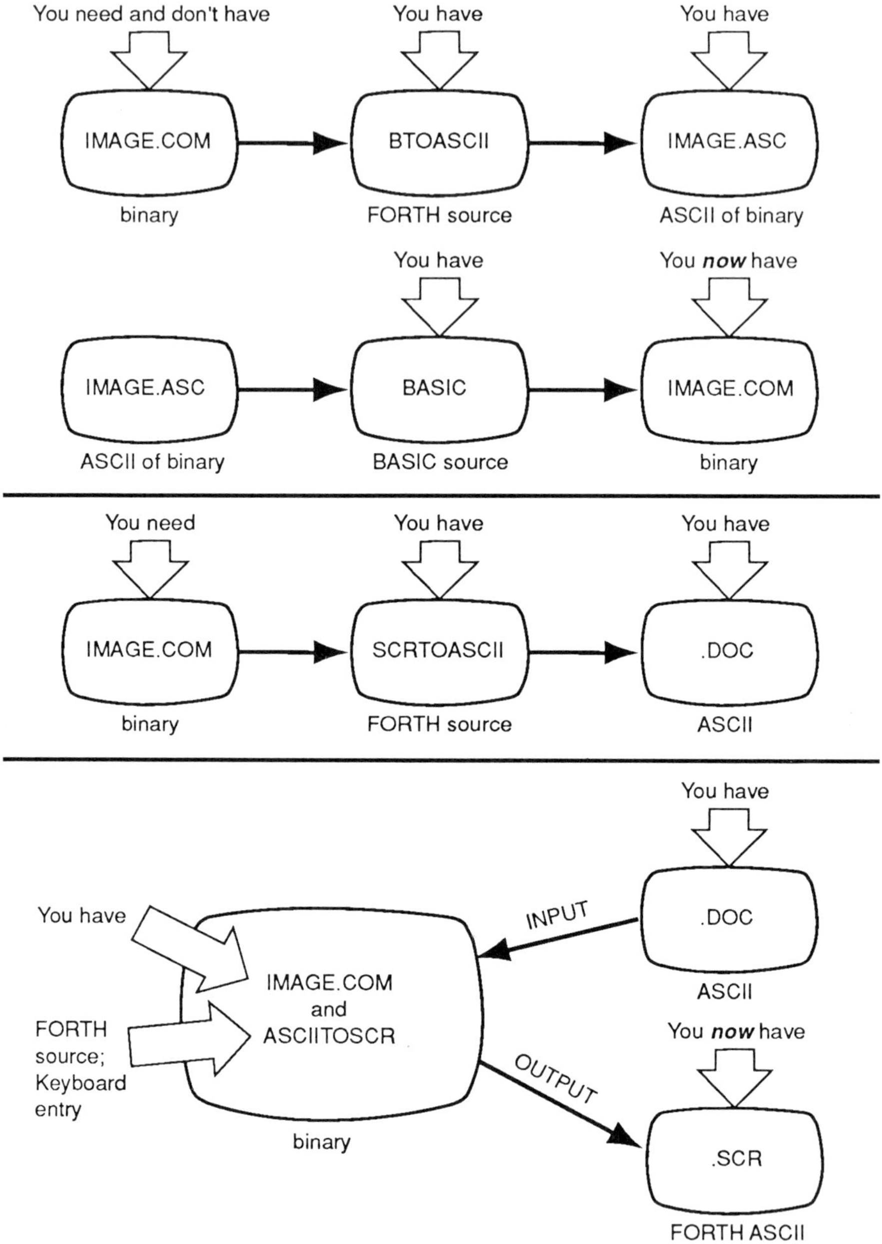

Figure 3.1. Diagram of "where you were and where you are." The process was started with a binary copy of FORTH source, called IMAGE.COM, for the 8086 family. A program called SCRTOASCII converts binary to an ASCII file, which is compiled by IMAGE.COM. SCRTOASCII converted IMAGE.COM to an

good FORTH. As a result, the routine took a long time to debug and revise. Good FORTH is composed of short nonredundant subroutines.

The word READCHR may appear to you to be inefficient because only one byte is read as opposed to a line. PC/MS DOS and the disk device drivers appear to do multiple layers of buffering. Reading a single character as opposed to a line does not appear to slow this routine.

You may need a FORTH encyclopedia to help understand the FORTH words. Mitch Derick and Linda Baker wrote an excellent encyclopedia detailing the Forth Interest Group FORTH for the 8080 family.[1] The nucleus for the 8086 family seen in Appendix 1 and for the forthcoming 8051 nucleus are derived from Forth Interest Group nucleus. Encyclopedias for the 8086 and 8051 family FORTH written in the Derick and Baker format are available from participating vendors.

Here is a quick review. Figure 3.1 diagrams the steps taken to get from source to either binary or FORTH screen file formats. FORTH gets these formats into ASCII format files. You use BASIC to build a binary of the FORTH nucleus seen in Appendix 1. From then on, you use FORTH.

The easiest way to get to this position is to get a disk copy of the code from a participating 8051 family hardware vendor. If you can't obtain a disk copy, then you need to follow the steps given in this chapter. Even though you may not hand-enter the file, it is worth your reading about the steps needed to develop operating systems from source. Reading helps you understand the procedure for nonFORTH operating systems.

You now have:

1. The ASCII version of IMAGE.COM, IMAGE.ASC, seen in Appendix 2.
2. The BASIC program for converting .ASC files to binary in .BAS format.
3. A working copy of Microsoft BASIC.
4. A working FORTH nucleus, IMAGE.COM.
5. SYSTEM.DOC in ASCII format
6. ASCIITOSCR.DOC in ASCII format
7. FORTH.SCR for FORTH warning messages
8. ASCIITOSCR in .SCR format

---

ascii format a file called IMAGE.ASC. IMAGE.ASC is entered into a file with a nondocument word processor. It is converted to your binary file, IMAGE.COM, by a BASIC program. IMAGE.COM compiles a program called SCRTOASCII to produce the listing given in the appendices in this book. You convert ASCII .DOC format files to screen files with the keyboard-entered program SCRTOASCII. SCRTOASCII entered from the keyboard converts the version of itself into a screen format file.

B. The Laxen Full Screen Editor

The next step is to add an editor. Studies show that programmers spend more than 90% of their time on a computer in the editor. There are two versions of the editor. One is coded solely in high-level FORTH. The other is speeded with some assembler.

Here is the plan. Bring up the editor written in high level by entering its source. Use a word processor running in the nondocument mode. Then use ASCIITOSCR to convert it to the FORTH.SCR file format. Compile the editor using IMAGE.COM, and save the combined image using the routine in screen 3 of SYSTEM.COM.

Now you are free of .DOC files! Enter the remainder of the code given in this book using Laxen's FORTH editor. The next step is to enter the 8086 family assembler in .SCR format in order to compile the assembler spiced version of Laxen's editor.

The nonassembler version of the editor is listed in Appendix 4. The global character string search written in high-level FORTH is unacceptably slow. Therefore, the assembler search, MATCH, and its associated words in screen 94 through 96 are commented out so the editor compiles successfully.

The nonassembler version of the editor does not write directly to the PC video memory. The assembler version may not work with some video cards, but this version has a good chance of working with all video cards.

The editor listed in Appendix 4 is compiled using IMAGE.COM. The editor occupies 8,515 bytes. FORTH uses about one order of magnitude less memory space to accomplish the same task as most other languages. Its nonredundancy accounts for most of this saving.

ASCIITOSCR successfully converts the program text in Appendix 4 from the file SLAX.DOC ("slow Laxen editor") to SLAX.SCR. A summary of the editor commands is given in screens 17 through 20 of the file SYSTEM.SCR. These commands are seen in the .DOC listing in Appendix 3.

The IBM PC/XT or AT keyboard lends itself to the editor definition of the special function keys F1 through F10. This is the keyboard with the special function keys located in two columns at the left of the keyboard. If you have a Keytronics-style keyboard with the special function keys located in a row along the top of the keyboard, then you probably want to change the definition of F1 through F10 and ^F1 through ^F10. These current definitions are not a good human engineering match for the Keytronics-style keyboard.

The assembler screens and recently updated screens for the assembler version are given in Appendix 5. You can use your .SCR version of the nonassembler editor to build an assembler version. Of course you can't assemble and compile it until the assembler is written.

The slow version of the editor was compiled with the commands:

```
PFILE SLAX
2 LOAD
```

The following information appeared on the screen.

```
Compiling editor
CURSOR is redefined
END is redefined
Editor size 8515 ok
```

Type 3 SYSLOAD and then SAVE SP.COM. Respond with "Y" when the following appears.

```
3 SYSLOAD ok
SAVE PS.COM

PS.COM File not found
Do you wish to create it (Y/N)? Y
21091 bytes were written to file PS.COM
PS.COM was closed
ok
```

FORTH prompts to allow you to create the file PS.COM. These two commands save IMAGE.COM and the editor in the file PC.COM. This sequence is an example of FORTH's extensibility.

SAVE writes the FORTH image to a .COM file. Its source code is given in screen 89 in Appendix 1.

The instructions on screen 3 of SYSTEM.SCR are so important to FORTH that they appear here. The following four locations must be modified so FORTH remembers the additional code which has been added to the system.

```
HEX
LATEST       0C +ORIGIN !   \ top NFA
HERE         1C +ORIGIN !   \ FENCE
HERE         1E +ORIGIN !   \ DP
VOC-LINK @   20 +ORIGIN !   \ vocabulary list
```

These locations are defined by the Forth Interest Group model. A full listing of the start-up parameters for the fig-FORTH 8080 model follows.

Offset	Parameter	Description
0	S0	Initial parameter stack pointer address
2	R0	Initial return stack pointer address
4	TIB	Terminal input buffer address
6	WIDTH	Number of characters saved in a Name Field
8	WARNING	Flag specify error message status
0A	FENCE	Address below which the dictionary cannot be forgotten
OC	VOC-LINK	Pointer to the last chronological added vocabulary

Observe that the locations differ slightly for our 8086 family FORTH, but the purpose is the same.

Screens 3 and 4 of the source code listing of FORTH86 are seen in Appendix 1. They detail the assignments in the 8086 family nucleus.

FORTH is an implementation of a pseudo-machine on a particular processor. FORTH requires the implementation of four 16-bit FORTH registers, as follows.

W	work register
IP	interpreter pointer
RP	return stack pointer
SP	parameter or data stack pointer

Following are register assignments for 8086 family FORTH:

BX	W
SI	IP
BP	RP
SP	SP
SS	base of FORTH
CS	base of FORTH
DS	base of FORTH
direction flag	set

FORTH86 hosts both the terminal and disk I/O for the 8051 system. You may wish to make modifications both to the 8086 family FORTH nucleus or 8051 terminal and to the disk I/O system. You need to know the register assignments for FORTH86 to make such modifications.

C. The PC/ASSEMBLER 8086 Family Table-Driven Assembler

The PC/ASSEMBLER FORTH assembler code holds three points of interest:

1. The assembler-enhanced Laxen editor needs this code to assemble and compile.
2. The 8051 terminal and disk I/O emulator software is partially written in it.
3. The 8051 syntax-checking assembler is PC/ASSEMBLER-adapted to the 8051.

The assembler listed in Appendix 6 is table-driven 8086/186/286, 8087/287, and NEC V20/30 interactive FORTH assembler. It selects the shortest form of equivalent instructions. You can set the D bit and it will assemble most of the 80386 instructions.

You should build a .SCR file, if you do not have a disk containing it, with the slow Laxen editor. You need to enter the assembler code into an .SCR file called AMS86.SCR. When you have done so, enter IMAGE.COM and type

```
PFILE ASM86
```

Then type

```
1 LOAD
```

This routine compiles the assembler. You see:

```
PC/ASSEMBLER TM
Intel 8086/87/88/186/188/286/287
NEC V20/30 uPD70108/70116 processors
Copyright 1985, 1986, 1987 by Computer Systems Documentation

Loading syntax tables
247
# is redefined
WORD is redefined
ST0 is redefined
ST1 is redefined
BL is redefined
AND is redefined
CLRB is redefined
IN is redefined
```

```
LEAVE is redefined
LOOP is redefined
NOT is redefined
NOTB is redefined
OR is redefined
OUT is redefined
SETB is redefined
TESTB is redefined
XOR is redefined
FLD is redefined
0= is redefined
<> is redefined
= is redefined
U< is redefined
U> is redefined
> is redefined
< is redefined
SIGN is redefined
IF is redefined
ELSE is redefined
THEN is redefined
BEGIN is redefined
UNTIL is redefined
WHILE is redefined
REPEAT is redefined
12769 Kbytes assembler size
ok
```

Next type:

```
PFILE LAXED 2 LOAD
```

This step causes assembly and compilation of the editor. You see:

```
Compiling editor
CURSOR is redefined
END is redefined
Editor size 9752 ok
```

The image is saved by typing:

```
3 SYSLOAD SAVE P.COM
```

You see:

```
P.COM File not found
Do you wish to create it (Y/N)? Y
35097 bytes were written to file P.COM
P.COM was closed
ok
```

The assembler and editor are saved in the file P.COM. The size of memory space remaining for program development is determined by typing:

```
SP@ HERE - DECIMAL . 27901 ok
```

If this is not enough space, then you can use advanced FORTH programming techniques to load the assembler as a transient module. The editor is then assembled and compiled, and the assembler is discarded. Transient modules are covered in a later chapter. This FORTH and assembler are used to host 8051 family cross-development tools.

D. PC Hardware, BIOS, and PC/MS DOS References

FORTH86 takes over the PC/MS DOS operating system. It borrows as much of the Basic Input Output System and Disk Operating System as possible. The exception is writing to the screen for video operation speed.

You need to understand the operating of your PC, BIOS, and PC/MS DOS to understand the internals of FORTH86. PC/MS DOS is certainly the most understood and documented operating system ever. Here are some references that will help you.

IBM, *DOS,* versions 1 through 4.
IBM, *Technical Reference.* Listings of IBM BIOS are included.
IBM, *Disk Operating System Version 3.30 Technical Reference.*

Norton, P., *Inside the IBM PC.* Brady.
Duncan, R., *The MS-DOS Encyclopedia.* Microsoft Press.
Microsoft, *Microsoft MS-DOS Operating System Programmers Reference Manual.*

The Microsoft and IBM books are both outstanding technical manuals describing the interface to PC/MS DOS. They are essentially the same manuals written by different companies. Earlier versions of the DOS manual had some of the same information.

Most computer manufacturers either write or purchase their versions of BIOS. A C language version is available. BIOS is composed of a ROM resident portion and a transient portion. Some manufacturers distribute the IBM transient portion with their ROM BIOS. All BIOSes are not the same. Many have "features" not included in others. MCT BIOS V3.1 won't format a particular model TEAC FB55 drives. Diskcopy must be used to format disks. But this inconvenience is minor compared to the advantage of a less than $100 8MHz motherboard.

The Ctrl Break interrupt takes over in FORTH86 as seen in screen 76, SETINTS, of Appendix 1. Ctrl Break gives many BIOS writers difficulty. If your system crashes when you hit Ctrl Break while executing FORTH, then the BIOS authors probably made a mistake. The problem is probably not in FORTH86. Ctrl Break crashed early versions of Hewlett-Packard and Radio Shack PC compatibles. It works fine on later versions. After keying Ctrl Break eight times, Toshiba machines crash with the message "internal stack failure." On most PC clones, including MCT BIOS, Ctrol Break works properly.

Chapter 4

8051 FORTH Assembler Programming

Assembler is perhaps the top choice computer language for small applications or when maximum speed is required. Fortunately, the rule "90% of the work is done in 10% of the code" applies in most applications. Not much assembler is required in large applications.

FORTH assemblers are used interactively on a host system. The 8051 family assembles its own code. If the host is an 8051, then testing assembler subroutines are quicker. If the host is an 8086 family machine, then the FORTH operating system's interactivity helps to resolve syntactic mistakes quickly.

FORTH assemblers for the 8051 family are used in cross assembler mode on the 8086 family. The debugging strategy here is to write short subroutines and test them interactively on an 8051 system. Once they appear to work they are imported into the cross assembly file for batch cross assembly. Debugging cross assembled code is difficult because code can crash the target machine. Using this strategy, most of the code is debugged before it is cross assembled.

FORTH assemblers require traditional assembler programmers to change their thinking about assemblers. FORTH assemblers interpret operands and opcodes. They are invoked directly from the operating system.

FORTH assemblers go against what nearly all software students are taught. Nonetheless, even to these individuals, their interactivity makes them immediately appealing. Compared with the traditional assembler, the speed at which code is written and debugged, particularly on microcontrollers, makes their importance apparent.

A. The 8051 Family FORTH Assembler

The 8051 family FORTH assembler, unlike many FORTH assemblers, checks syntax. Other assemblers produce "garbage" code if syntactic mistakes are made, and they can be written in several screens of code. The time spent tracking bugs produced from executing "garbage" code prompted writing both the 8086 family PC/ASSEMBLER and the 8051 assembler. The 8051 syntax-checking assembler is the 8086 PC/ ASSEMBLER adapted for the 8051.

Source code for the assembler, in cross assembler form that runs on the 8086 family, is given in Appendix 7. The 8086 family stores a 16-bit number in a "byte swapped" format. The low byte precedes the high byte. The advantage to this set-up is that single-byte data are expanded to 16-bit data by extending the sign. The FORTH words "," , "!", and "@", to mention just three, work differently on a byte-swapped machine compared to a nonbyte-swapped machine such as the 8051.

The assembler is "table driven." Tables are searched to determine what code is to be executed.

FORTH assemblers differ from traditional assemblers in that the operation code mnemonic follows the operand. There is a simple reason for this sequence: Operation codes are determined by the operands in many cases.

The 8051 assembler and PC/ASSEMBLER use two stacks. One stack contains the values of the operands. The second stack contains, in one-to-one correspondence, attributes of the operands. When the operand is encountered, then the assembler searches tables of valid operand formats for a match. If a match is found, then the code generator is invoked. If no match is found, then the assembler terminates execution with an error message.

Some individuals think that good computer programming resembles mathematics. This notion may be true. Good systems programming resembles accounting, in that exhaustive searches cover all possibilities.

Generic assembler syntax forms are given below. "Syntax by example" tables are given in Appendix 8. If these forms are not met, then the assembler signals an error.

```
A Rn ADD
A direct ADD
A @Ri ADD
A # data ADD

A Rn ADDC
A direct ADDC
```

```
A @Ri ADDC
A # data ADDC

A Rn SUBB
A direct SUBB
A @Ri SUBB
A # data SUBB

A INC
Rn INC
direct INC
@Ri INC
DPTR INC

A DEC
Rn DEC
direct DEC
@Ri DEC

AB MUL
AB DIV
A DA

A Rn ANL
A direct ANL
A @Ri ANL
A # data ANL
direct A ANL
direct # data ANL

A Rn XRL
A direct XRL
A @Ri ORL
A # data ORL
direct A ORL
direct # data ORL

A Rn XRL
A direct XRL
A @Ri XRL
A # data XRL
direct A XRL
direct # data XRL
```

```
A CLR
A CPL
A RL
A RLC
A RR
A RRC
A SWAP

A Rn MOV
A direct MOV
A @Ri MOV
A # data MOV
Rn A MOV
Rn direct MOV
Rn # data MOV
direct A MOV
direct Rn MOV
direct direct MOV
direct @ Ri MOV
direct # data MOV

@Ri A MOV
@Ri direct MOV
@Ri # data MOV
DPTR # data 16 MOV
A @A+DPTR MOVC
A @A+PC MOVC
A @Ri MOVX
A @DPTR MOVX
@Ri A MOVX
@DPTR A MOVX

direct PUSH
direct POP
A Rn XCH
A direct SCH
A @Ri SCH
A @Ri SCHD

C CLR
bit CLR
C SETB
bit SETB
C CPL
bit CPL
C bit ANL
```

```
C bit ANL/      \ or complement of bit
C bit ORL
C bit ORL/      \ or complement of bit
C bit MOV
bit C MOV

addr11 ACALL
addr16 LCALL
RET
RETI
addr11 AJMP
addr16 LJMP
rel SJMP
@A+DPR JMP
rel JZ
rel JNZ
rel JC
rel JNC
bit rel JB
bit rel JNB
bit rel JBC
A direct rel CJNE
A # data rel CJNE
@Ri # data rel CJNE
Rn rel DJNZ
direct rel DJNZ
NOP
```

The assembler supports local labels. Local labels of the form "number $:" are referenced by relative jumps of "number $." Following are several examples.

```
   1 $ JC    \ forward jump if carry is set
       NOP
1 $:   NOP

1 $:   NOP
       NOP
       1 $ JC\ backward jump if carry is set
```

The variable MAX#$, seen in the listing in Appendix 7, defines the maximum number of local labels plus the number of unresolved forward references. MAX#$ is set at decimal 32.

The word BEGIN$ clears the local label table. BEGIN$ is invoked by CODE. END$ checks to see that all local labels have been resolved. END$ is invoked by END-CODE. If you use local labels in code fragments, then you should initialize the local label tables with BEGIN$ and call END$ to check for label resolution.

The assembler understands the following conditionals:

```
0=              \ A is zero
0<>             \ A is not zero
CARRY           \ carry is set
NOCARRY         \ carry is not set
BIT             \ bit is set
NOBIT           \ bit is not set
```

These conditionals are used with the following high-level constructs:

```
condition IF true condition THEN
condition IF true condition ELSE false condition THEN

BEGIN . . . condition UNTIL
BEGIN . . . condition WHILE . . . REPEAT
```

Branch addresses and the location of branch addresses are kept on the stack. A balanced stack is checked when THEN, ELSE, UNTIL, and REPEAT are invoked. Following are examples of the use of each of the high-level constructions.

```
0=              \ is a zero?
IF              \ no, jump to nop
  A # 1 MOV     \ yes, set a=1
THEN
NOP

0<>             \ is not zero?
IF
  A CLR         \ yes, clr a
ELSE
  A # 1 MOV     \ no, set a=1
THEN

BEGIN
  A DEC         \ continued decrementing a
  0=            \ until it is zero
UNTIL

BEGIN
  A INC         \ increment a
  NOCARRY       \ is carry set?
WHILE           \ while carry is not set
  20 DEC        \ decrement 20
```

```
REPEAT          \ jump to NOP when carry is set
NOP
```

B. Using the 8051 FORTH Assembler as a Cross Assembler

One important advantage of writing an assembler in high-level FORTH is that the assembler becomes reasonably portable. It can be compiled on almost any machine running FORTH and made to work with only minor modifications.

One alternative is to build the target assembler image in the host memory. The 8051 assembler seen in Appendix 7 needed modification to compensate for byte swapping in the FORTH word "," on screen 26 in the word T22. The word "><" is pronounced "byte swap."

Observe that part of some screens have been "commented out." These "commented out" screens contain words that relate to use of the assembler on an 8051 system running FORTH.

The 8051 FORTH assembler can be used as a stand-alone assembler. The assembler image is built in the 8086 family memory and then written to a disk file for ROMing.

FORTH assemblers are more primitive, yet more powerful, than traditional assemblers. They are "one pass" assemblers; that is, FORTH processes the assembler code only once to finish the assembly. Traditional assemblers frequently make multiple passes through the assembler code to complete the code generation part of the assembler. Conditional assembly, macro assembly, and forward reference are frequently handled on separate passes through the assembler source code.

Forward references are difficult for assemblers. Here is an example:

```
          JMP AHEAD
          NOP NOP NOP NOP NOP
AHEAD:    NOP
```

The 8086 family traditional syntax is used. The 8086 family has five forms of jump. Two of these are intra-segment direct jumps. A direct short jump spans at most 127 bytes ahead. A direct jump spans at most 32,767 bytes ahead. An assembler processing a forward reference JMP does not know which form of the JMP to use. Microsoft's MASM assembles a three-byte direct jump. If MASM discovers a short jump instruction, two bytes in length, it can be used when it encounters the forward reference; then it NOP's the first byte of the three-byte direct jump and assembles a short jump in the last two bytes! Other assemblers back up to the point of a presumed short jump and begin reassembly with a long jump. Forward references in FORTH assembler also cause problems and are handled manually.

When used as a cross assembler, FORTH assembler requires you to construct a symbol table for all except local labels. Following are the code fragments demonstrating the conditionals in a screen file.

```
7
\                                                    14:19 09/25/89
HEX
0 VARIABLE STARTASM ASSEMBLER RESET BEGIN$
HERE STARTASM !
            1 $ JC
            NOP
  1 $:      NOP END$
BEGIN$
  1 $:      NOP
            NOP
            1 $ JC

            0=
            IF A CLR THEN
-->

8
\                                                    14:33 09/25/89
HEX
            0<>
            IF A CLR
            ELSE A # 1 MOV
            THEN

            BEGIN A DEC 0=
            UNTIL

            BEGIN A INC NOCARRY
            WHILE 20 DEC
            REPEAT NOP
END$ FORTH
DECIMAL
STARTASM @ HERE OVER - COMSAVE EXAMPLE.ASM
```

The cross assembler version of the 8051 FORTH assembler is compiled first. This version is the code seen in Appendix 7.

Laxen's editor is used to create the code fragment file. The variable STARTASM is used to contain the start address of the 8051 assembler object code. ASSEMBLER selects the 8051 FORTH assembler vocabulary. RESET resets the assembler's syntax checker. $BEGIN initializes the local label facility. HERE is the 8086 family FORTH's location counter. The start of assembly location is stored in the variable STARTASM.

The END$ and BEGIN$ located at the end of the first conditional are required because 1 $ is used again. END$ checks for unresolved local references.

FORTH86, seen in Appendix 1, contains the word COMSAVE. COMSAVE saves memory with a specified starting address and length in a file. Following are the results of typing 7 LOAD.

```
EXAMPLE.ASM File not found
Do you wish to create it (Y/N)? Y
33 bytes were written to file EXAMPLE.ASMok
```

The object file contents are dumped with:

```
PFILE EXAMPLE.ASM
ok
0 BLOCK HEX DUP U. 40 DUMP F7F8

      0  1  2  3  4  5  6  7  8  9  A  B  C  D  E  F 0123456789ABCDEF

F7F0 5A E9 1F 01 BB 47 00 00 40 01 00 00 04 00 00 00 Z....G..@.......
F800 40 FC 70 01 E4 60 03 E4 80 02 74 01 14 70 FD 04 @.p..`....t..p..
F810 40 04 15 20 80 F9 00 04 00 00 00 00 00 00 00 00 @..............
F820 00 00 00 00 00 00 00 00 00 00 00 00 00 00 00 00 ................
F830 00 00 00 00 00 00 00 00 00 00 00 00 00 00 00 00 ................
ok
HEX F7F8 DECIMAL 30 + HEX U. F816 ok
```

DUMP, whose definition is seen near the end of Appendix 1, starts on a paragraph boundary. BLOCK, on the other hand, starts at address F7F8. The dump of the program starts at location F7F8 and ends at location F816. These computations are interactively made in FORTH at the end of the dump.

The last code fragment, BEGIN A INC NOCARRY WHILE 20 DEC REPEAT NOP starts at dump location F88F and ends at dump location F816. The 04 at the program start is A INC. The 4004 is a JC to the NOP listed at F816. The 1520 is the 20 DEC and 80F9 is a SJMP to A INC. The file EXAMPLE.ASM is used as input to a ROM burner.

We have thus seen a simple example of the 8051 FORTH assembler used as a stand-alone cross assembler.

The next sample demonstrates handling forward and backward jump references. The assembler program is as follows:

```
HEX
: COMPUTEVALUE    40 2 / ;
0 VARIABLE STARTASM
0 VARIABLE SUB1
0 VARIABLE SUB2
0 VARIABLE SUB2REF
HERE STARTASM ! ASSEMBLER RESET BEGIN$
         NOP
         A # 2 3 * MOV
         A # COMPUTEVALUE MOV
         1 $ SJMP
\ subroutine 1
         HERE SUB1 !
         NOP  NOP  A # 1 MOV RET
  1 $: NOP  NOP  NOP
         SUB1 @ STARTASM @ - LCALL
         HERE 1+ SUB2REF ! 0 LCALL
         NOP  NOP  NOP  NOP
  2 $: 2 $ SJMP
\ subroutine 2
         HERE SUB2 !
         A # 11 MOV
         A # 22 MOV
         RET  END$ FORTH
SUB2 @ STARTASM @ - >< SUB2REF @ !
CR ." SUB1 address " SUB1 @ STARTASM @ - U.
CR ." SUB2 address " SUB2 @ STARTASM @ - U.
STARTASM @ HERE OVER - COMSAVE FORREF.ASM
```

The address to be patched with the forward reference must be kept in a table until it can be resolved. The byte swap, ><, is seen just after the value of the forward reference was computed and is required to compensate for the 8086 family byte swapping. The value in SUB2REF is a pointer that points to the forward reference value to be patched.

Here is what is printed to the screen:

```
SUB1 address 7
SUB2 address 1B
34  bytes were written to file FORREF.ASMok
```

Here is a memory dump of the output file FORREF.ASM:

```
HEX  ok
0 BLOCK DUP U. 30 DUMP F7F8

      0  1  2  3  4  5  6  7  8  9  A  B  C  D  E F   0123456789ABCDEF

F7F0 00 00 00 00 00 00 00 00 00 74 06 74 20 80 05 00  .........t.t ...
F800 00 74 01 22 00 00 00 12 00 07 12 00 1B 00 00 00  .t." ...........
F810 00 80 FE 74 11 74 22 22 08 00 00 00 00 00 00 00  ...t.t"".......
F820 00 00 00 00 00 00 00 00 00 00 00 00 00 00 00 00  ................
ok
F7F8 7 + U. F7FF ok
F7F8 1B + U. F813 ok
```

The file ends at dump location F817. The 22 in this location is a RET. The start-dump addresses of SUB1 and SUB2 are computed interactively so the code starts are easily located.

This example shows FORTH invoked to compute operand values of COMPUTEVALUE and 2 3 *. The feature to invoke FORTH within the assembler makes a FORTH assembler one of the most powerful types of cross assemblers. The methods of a FORTH assembler are alien to most traditional assembler programmers.

Although assembler code for the 8051 is written with the 8051 FORTH cross assembler and lies in memory, it cannot be executed without crashing the 8086 family processor. Storage of the target image limits the size of the target code to the memory available in FORTH86. An alternative to host memory construction is to build the assembler object image in a disk file. This image fills the entire 64-K byte code and/or data space. The ","s and "C,"s in the code generator portion of the 8051 FORTH cross assembler must be replaced with disk writes.

The basic idea is as follows. A variable called IMAGEDP, "image dictionary pointer," is defined. The value of IMAGEDP points into the secondary file, which is opened to hold the 8051 assembler object code. SEEK+, whose definition is seen in Appendix 1, positions the file read/write pointer at a random location within a file. FORTH words similar to , C, ! C! ALLOT and +!, but operating on the secondary file, are defined. The 8051 FORTH assembler target image is built in the secondary file. Following is some sample, but undebugged, initial code.

```
0 VARIABLE IMAGEDP
0 VARIABLE IMAGEHERE

:IMAGEHERE    IMAGEDP @ ;
```

```
\ address ---
: SEEK! SECF HANDLE SWAP 0 SEEK+
       IF CR ." Seek err " U. SP! QUIT THEN ;

\ handle\buffer address\# byte to write ---
: !WRITE DUP >R WRITE
        IF R> DROP CR ." write err " U. SP! QUIT THEN R> <>
        IF CR ." file end " SP! QUIT THEN ;
\ word\address ---
: IMAGE!  SEEK! >< BWBUFFER ! SECF HANDLE BWBUFFER 2 !WRITE ;

\ byte\address ---
: IMAGEC! SEEK! >< BWBUFFER C! SECF HANDLE BWBUFFER 1 !WRITE ;

\ value\address ---
: IMAGE+!    DUP @ SWAP + SWAP ! ;

\ word ---
: IMAGEALLOT  IMAGEDP IMAGE+! ;

\ word ---
: IMAGE,  IMAGE! 2 IMAGEALLOT ;

\ byte ---
: IMAGEC, IMAGEC! 1 IMAGEALLOT ;
```

With a FORTH assembler, a programmer is limited only by his or her imagination.

EPROMs and EEPROMs contain all hex FFs when they are erased. An FF is a R7 A MOV in 8051 machine language. It is a good idea to program all unused locations in an embedded controller application code memory with a LJMP to 0 or some other error recovery location. Programming unused locations with hex 00, an NOP, also works since the 8051 eventually NOP's itself back to locations 0.

You can initialize the contents of a file to all zeros by writing 64 Kbytes of zeros to it before using COMSAVE to save the image. Alternatively you can first fill the file with hex 020000, a LJMP to 0, or whatever you need. With a FORTH assembler this procedure is a simple task. It may not be with other assemblers.

C. Transient Modules

A transient module is program code that is loaded into computer memory, executed, then discarded. An overlay like that supported by BASIC,

FORTRAN, COBOL, and other languages is a type of transient module. Another type of transient module is one that is assembled or compiled, used, and then discarded.

FORTH expands from low to high memory. The variable DP—dictionary pointer—is incremented by ALLOT. Once a code is included in a FORTH operating system, it cannot easily be discarded without destroying all of the code compiled after it.

The Laxen editor with the assembler speed enhancements could not be loaded until after the assembler was loaded in Chapter 3. The assembler resided in memory at lower addresses than the editor. Any attempt to discard the assembler with FORGET also discarded the editor.

But there is a way around this difficulty, a way to load, execute, and discard a transient module. An assembler is a good example of a transient module in that once it assembles application code, it is no longer required to be in memory.

The following code loads the 8086 family assembler listed in Appendix 6 as a transient module. The assembler version of the Laxen editor seen in Appendices 4 and 5 is assembled using the transient module and is compiled by the FORTH operating system, FORTH86, seen in Appendix 1. This code warrants a detailed explanation because of its complexity.

```
DECIMAL
LATEST HERE VOC-LINK @ SP@  \ save \latest\dp\voc-link and sp
10000 ALLOT        \ reserve enough space for tm by adding to dp
                   \ begin transient module
AFILE\PCA\ASM86 1 ALOAD\ load assembler as a transient module
SP@ 2+ ?PAIRS      \ check for balanced stack
VOC-LINK !         \ restore voc-link
DUP DP ! SP@       \ restore dp and save a copy of it, save sp
                   \ end of transient module
SFILE\PCA\LAXED 2 SLOAD\ editor assembled and compiled
SP@ 2+ ?PAIRS      \ check for balanced stack
PFA LFA !          \ link new definitions defined by transient
                   \ module
                   \ to old LATEST. This move discards the transient
                   \ module.
```

Words in a FORTH dictionary residing in RAM can be reordered by replacing link fields. The FORTH Forth Interest Group module has the following header data structure:

```
Name Field          NFA   variable length
Link Field          LFA   2-byte address pointer
Code Field          CFA   2-byte address pointer
Parameter Field     PFA   variable length
```

The Name Field is decomposed into:

Bit position	Meaning
80	Set to denote start of name field.
40	Immediate bit. Indicates immediate execution even when compiling.
20	SMUDGE bit. Set when compilation begun. Cleared when compilation finished without error. Not cleared when error found.
10	Length of name in binary. Name
08	is a maximum of 32 bytes long.
04	
02	
01	

The last letter in the Name Field is ORed with hex 80. Study TRAVERSE in Appendix 1 to see how the Link Field should be located. The variable WIDTH is disregarded in both the FORTH86 seen in Appendix 1 and the 8051 FORTH operating system listed in Appendix 9. The reason for disregarding it is that (FIND) works much faster if the NFA length points to the LFA. A search is replaced by an addition.

FORTH was originally designed to store shorter versions of a name. The maximum length is determined by the user variable WIDTH. Changing either version of FORTH back to recognize WIDTH is not a simple matter. Several complicated changes to FORTH are required. Expert FORTH programmer, Jerry Boutelle, author of the Nautilus Metacompiler, started this task with FORTH86 and gave up because of all the work involved. With today's large memories, there is little reason to make WIDTH functional again.

The first word in the first line of the transient module code is LATEST. LATEST is the NFA of the last word defined. Here is an example:

```
: WXYZ ; ok
VLIST

8A19 WXYZ          8A0A SYSE         89FD AE        89F0 SE
89E6 E             63EE EDITOR       63D1 CODE      63B1 ;CODE
320D ASSEMBLER     3202 TASK         31C5 ?DEF

ok
HEX ok
' WXYZ U. 8A22 ok
' WXYZ NFA U. 8A19 ok
```

```
' WXYZ NAF ID. WXYZ ok
LATEST U. 8A19 ok
LATEST ID. WXYZ ok
HERE U. 8A24 ok
DP @ U. 8A24 ok
CURRENT @ @ U. 8A19 ok
CONTEXT @ @ U. 8A19 ok
```

WXYZ is compiled. VLIST shows the Name Field Address followed by the name. The NFA of WXYZ is 8A19. The PFA of WXYZ is 8A22. The Name field is 4 + 1 = 5 bytes long. The LFA is two bytes. The CFA is two bytes. Therefore, 8A19 + 5 + 2 + 2 = 8A22. The CFA points to the run time portion of

```
: - DOCOL, do colon -
```

while the PFA points to the run time portion of

```
; - ;S, semicolon S -
```

For this example the code is "begin procedure" at the CFA and "end procedure" at the PFA. NFA finds the NFA from the PFA. ID. prints the name knowing the NFA. LATEST is the NFA of the last word compiled.

HERE points to the next location in memory available to compile a definition. Words in the input stream are copied from the Terminal Input Buffer (TIB) to HERE. Study the code from QUERY by following it on down, as is done in Appendix 1. You can then explain why the following occurs in FORTH when a carriage return is keyed just after the first TYPE.

```
HERE COUNT TYPE TYPE ok
```

HERE is defined as DP @.

CONTEXT is a variable that contains a pointer to a pointer, which points to where FORTH is going to search in an attempt to locate a word. CURRENT is a variable that contains a pointer to a pointer that points to where FORTH is going to append the next word.

VOC-LINK is a variable that contains a pointer linking the FORTH vocabularies in the chronological order in which they were created. The data structure of a vocabulary creation, like VOCABULARY EDITOR IMMEDIATE, is as follows.

Name Field	Name of vocabulary, EDITOR for example.
Link Field	Link to next definition.
Code Field	Pointer to run time portion of >DOES.
CFA	Pointer to run time portion of VOCABULARY.

Pseudo Name Field	81A0. A single blank. 80 is ORed with the hex 20 to get the hex A0 because hex 20 is the last character in the field.
Chronological Link Field	Pointer to previous created vocabulary via VOC-LINK. Pointer is 0 when there are no more vocabularies.

VOC-LINK points to the chronological Link Field. Most FORTH programmers are just as confused by all this as you probably are. Observe that the CFA is normally where the PFA is—that is, six bytes behind the pointer. The author wrote the program SHOWVOCS as

```
: SHOWVOCS        VOC-LINK @
                  BEGIN DUP
                  WHILE DUP 6 - NFA CR ID. @
                  REPEAT DROP ;
```

which executes to produce

```
EDITOR
ASSEMBLER
FORTH ok
```

to avoid a likely incomprehensible explanation of what VOC-LINK is doing. The program was run on FORTH86, with the assembler and editor saved with the FORTH nucleus.

FORTH has a known problem with FORGET. Most FORGETs do not unravel VOC-LINK when FORGETTING through multiple vocabularies. The FORGET in the FORTHs presented in this book are no exception.

VOC-LINK needs to be saved because the transient module might create a vocabulary. The 8086 FORTH assembler creates an assembler vocabulary.

You must know the size of the transient module in order to leave room for it in the hole created in the dictionary. SP@ saves a copy of the current stack pointer on the stack. This copy is used to check for a balanced stack after the transient module is loaded.

The assembler is opened as the auxiliary file and compiled. The stack is checked with ?PAIRS to see whether it is pointing to the same place. VOC-LINK is restored. The code that is compiled with the transient module may create a new vocabulary, which must be linked through VOC-LINK. Observe that the assembler changed VOC-LINK. The dictionary pointer is restored and a new copy of the stack pointer is stored on the stack for a later balance test. A copy of the old dictionary pointer is kept on the stack. This arrangement is effectively the NFA of the first word that appears in the code compiled by the transient module. The LFA of this word is replaced by the NFA, saved from LATEST, of the last word defined before the transient module was compiled.

The EDITOR is compiled and assembled by loading it from the secondary file. The stack is checked to see if it is still balanced. The HERE saved on the stack points to the first word defined in the module to be compiled with the help of the transient module. In this example it is the editor, LAXED. PFA finds the Parameter Field Address from the NFA, which is the same as the saved HERE. LFA finds the Link Field Address, and ! saves the NFA of the word defined just previous to loading the transient module at the link field address. This process effectively eliminates the transient module of the pointer (to the transient module with the pointer) to the Name Field of the word defined just previous to loading the transient module. A diagram of what happens is given in Figure 4.1.

The following printout is seen when assembling and compiling the editor using the assembler as a transient module. The assembler has already been loaded. You can see by the VLIST that the assembler is missing.

```
Compiling editor
CURSOR is redefined
END is redefined
Editor size 9752 ok
VLIST

5829 SYSE            581C AE            580F SE            5805 E
320D EDITOR          3202 TASK          31C5 ?DEF          317D IIF
```

Suppose you wanted to speed assembler execution by writing portions of the assembler in assembler. The all high-level FORTH version of the assembler is loaded as a transient module and is used to assemble and compile the assembler-enhanced version of the assembler.

D. Assembling 8051 Assembler Code on an 8051

When the 8051 hardware shown in Chapter 2 is built and the binary of the 8051 FORTH operating system listed in Appendices 9 and 10 is ROMed, and the terminal emulator listed in Appendix 13 is installed, then you can interactively, write, assemble, and debug 8051 assembler code on the 8051.

The FORTH operating system uses some of the resources of the 8051. You must avoid destroying the contents of the registers FORTH uses.

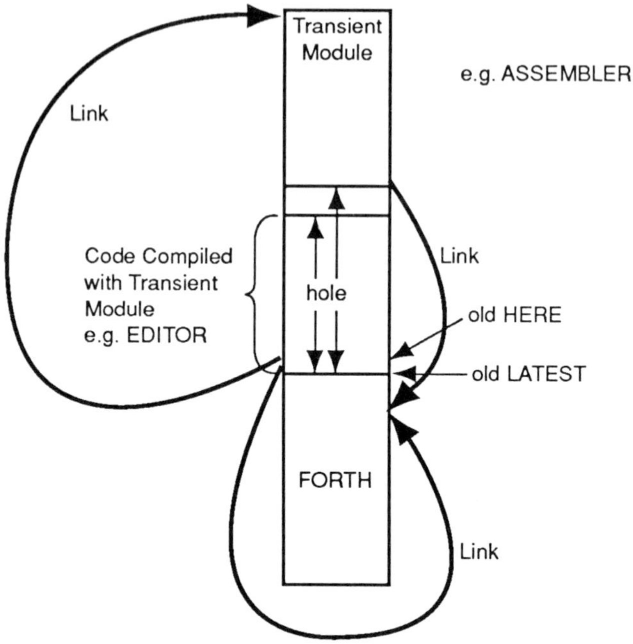

Figure 4.1. This figure diagrams loading, using, and discarding a transient module. In this diagram the transient module is loaded on top of FORTH. The old LATEST points to the Name Field at the end of FORTH. The old HERE points to the Name Field in the module to be compiled with the help of the transient module. A hole is created in the dictionary with use of ALLOT to hold the code compiled with the help of the transient module. The transient module is compiled, and DP is set back to the old HERE.

The code to be compiled or assembled with the help of the transient module is compiled. The transient module is discarded by replacing the Link Field Address in the first word of the module assembled or compiled by the transient module with the Name Field Address of the last word defined in FORTH.

The 8051 FORTH operating systems uses the registers in bank 0,

```
Register          FORTH use

R0,R1             W
R2,R3             IP
R4,R5             Parameter stack
R6,R7             Return stack
```

and the following locations:

Locations	FORTH use
20,21	X0H,X0L \work locations
22,23	X1H,X1L
24,25	X2H,X2L
26,27	X3H,X2L

Register bank 1 is used for U, U/, and (FIND).

The next available byte in the parameter stack is pointed to by R4,R5. This convention is different from the hardware predecrement of the stack before a push on the 8085/86 family microcomputers.

The assembler includes several ROMed utility macros that call subroutines. These macros relieve you of repeating commonly used subroutine linkage code. These are:

```
NEXT,          returns control to the FORTH operating system
               by calling NEXT.

A0PUSH,        pushes a 0 high byte on the stack, then pushes
               register a on the stack, then calls NEXT.

APUSH,         pushes a on the stack and calls NEXT;
               decrements the stack pointer first.

-DPTR,         decrements the data pointer.

GETX0,         moves R4,R5 to the data pointer, then moves the
               top of stack to locations 20,21. 20 is the
               high byte.

GETX1,         moves the top of stack to locations 22,23.
               Assumes that GETX0, was previously called to set the
               data pointer.

GETX2,         moves the top of stack to locations 24,25.
               Assumes that GETX0, was previously called to set the
               data pointer.

GETX3,         moves the top of stack to locations 26,27.
               Assumes that GETX0, was previously called to set the
               data pointer.
```

GETSP, moves the contents of register R4,R5 to the data pointer.

SAVESP, decrements the data pointer to point to the next available location on the stack, then saves it to register R4,R5.

GETRP, moves the contents of R6,R7 to the data pointer.

SAVERP, moves the data pointer to R6,R7.

GETIP, places ip in the data pointer.

SAVEIP, places the data pointer in register R2,R3.

Following is some 8051 FORTH nucleus, listed in Appendix 9, which applies to FORTH assembler language programming:

```
20 EQU S0H  21 EQU S0L  ( temp storage for S0 i.e. top of stk )
22 EQU S1H  23 EQU S1L
24 EQU S2H  25 EQU S2L  ( etc. )
26 EQU S3H  27 EQU S3L
```

These storage locations are accessed by the following macros:

```
: X0L          S0L ;          : X0H          S0H ;
: X1L          S1L ;          : X1H          S1H ;
: X2L          S2L ;          : X2H          S2H ;
: X3L          S3L ;          : X3H          S3H ;
```

The macros that transfer the top of stack into the memory locations X0H=20, X0L=21, . . . X3L = 27 are defined as follows:

```
: GETX0,        (S0)        12 C, , ;
: GETX1,        (S1)        12 C, , ;
: GETX2,        (S2)        12 C, , ;
: GETX3,        (S3)        12 C, , ;
^!
```

The 12 is the LCALL opcode and expands into a long call to one of the following routines:

```
L: (S0)
   GET_SP ABSOLUTE ( ACALL ) LCALL
   DPTR INC
   A @DPTR MOVX     S0H  A MOV
   DPTR INC
```

```
    A @DPTR MOVX     S0L  A MOV
    RET

L: (S1)
    DPTR INC
    A @DPTR MOVX     S1H  A MOV
    DPTR INC
    A @DPTR MOVX     S1L  A MOV
    RET
```

Subroutines (S2) and (S3) have definitions similar to (S1). (S0) must be called before calling (S1), (S2), or (S3) or you must set the data pointer by some other code. L: specifies that a metacompiler symbolic label follows.

Macros that get and save the parameter stack pointer, return stack pointer, and interpreter pointer and decrement the data pointer all expand into long calls to subroutines. Their definitions are as follows:

```
: GETSP,         GET_SP  12 C, , ;
: SAVESP,        SAVE_SP 12 C, , ;
: GETRP,         GET_RP  12 C, , ;
: SAVERP,        SAVE_RP 12 C, , ;

: GETIP,         GET_IP  12 C, , ;
: SAVEIP,        SAVE_IP 12 C, , ;
: -DPTR,         -DPTR   12 C, , ;
```

Following is the code invoked by them:

```
L: GET_SP
    DPL  R5 MOV    DPH  R4 MOV
    RET

L: SAVE_SP
    -DPTR ( ACALL ) LCALL    R5  DPL MOV    R4  DPH MOV
    RET ^!

L: GET_RP
    DPL  R7 MOV    DPH  R6 MOV
    RET

L: SAVE_RP
    -DPTR ( ACALL ) LCALL    R7  DPL MOV    R6  DPH MOV
    RET

L: GET_IP
    DPL  R3 MOV    DPH  R2 MOV
    RET
```

```
L: SAVE_IP
   DPTR INC   R3   DPL MOV     R2   DPH MOV
   RET
L: -DPTR
   A   DPL XCH      0 =
   IF   DPH DEC THEN   A DPL XCH
   DPL DEC
   RET
```

Macros that generate code to return to the FORTH operating system expand into long jumps to the FORTH address interpreter. Following are their definitions:

```
: NEXT,             NEXT      02 C, , ;
: A0PUSH,           A0PUSH    02 C, , ;
: APUSH,            APUSH     02 C, , ;
```

The code they call is as follows:

```
L: A0PUSH
   @DPTR A MOVX   -DPTR ( ACALL ) LCALL
   A CLR   @DPTR A MOVX
   -DPTR ( ACALL ) LCALL   R5 DPL MOV     R4 DPH MOV
   NEXT REL8 SJMP

L: APUSH
   -DPTR ( ACALL ) LCALL
   @DPTR A MOVX
   -DPTR ( ACALL ) LCALL
   R5   DPL MOV     R4   DPH MOV   ( fall thru to NEXT)

L: NEXT DPL   R3 MOV   DPH   R2 MOV   A @DPTR MOVX   R0 A MOV
        DPTR INC   A @DPTR MOVX   R1 A MOV   DPTR INC
        R3   DPL MOV   R2   DPH MOV

L: NEXT1
        DPL   R1 MOV   DPH   R0 MOV
        A @DPTR MOVX   S0H   A MOV   DPTR INC   A @DPTR MOVX
        DPL   A MOV   DPH S0H MOV   A CLR     @A+DPTR JMP
```

Following is an example of using the 8051 FORTH assembler on the 8051.

```
CODE X GETSP, A # 7 MOV A0PUSH, END-CODE X . 7 ok
```

This routine was entered from the PC 8051 terminal emulator and the results of the assembly printed on the screen by the 8051. The 8051 assembled and loaded the code, linked it, ran the program, and printed out the result in about one second.

Following is an assembler program composed with a full screen editor. It adds the two numbers at the top of the stack and returns the sum on the stack.

```
Screen # 1
  0\                                            15:27 07/22/86
  1\ value 1\ value2 --- sum
  2 CODE ADD        GETX0,          \ 20=X0H, 21=X0L value 2
  3                 GETX1,          \ 22=X1L, 23=X1H value 1
  4                 A X0L MOV       \ value 2 low to A
  5                 A X1L ADD       \ add value 1 low to A
  6                 X0L A MOV       \ put low byte sum in X0L
  7                 A X0H MOV       \ value 2 high to A
  8                 A X1H ADDC      \ add value 1 high to A
  9                 X0H A MOV       \ put sum in X0H
 10                 A X0L MOV       \ low byte sum to A
 11 ->

Screen # 2
  0\                                            15:37 07/22/86
  1
  2                 @DPTR A MOVX    \ push it on the stack
  3                 A X0H MOV       \ high byte of sum to A
  4                 APUSH,          \ push it, save stack pointer
  5                                 \ back to forth.
  6                 END-CODE        \ End of assembler code
  7
  8 2 3 ADD CR .
```

The source assembler code is transferred from the PC disk to the 8051 at 19.2 Kbits. The code is assembled, loaded, linked, and run with the command 1 LOAD. Following is the screen listing of the outcome:

```
1 LOAD
5 ok
```

This process took less than five seconds.

When the MOVX command on line 2 of screen 2 is changed to MOV, it creates an invalid syntax form. Following is an example of the assembler's syntax checking:

```
1 LOAD Error: "MOV"  invalid opcode/operand form
at screen 2 line 2
                @DPTR A MOV  \ push it on the stack
                          ^
 ok
```

The basic idea is to write and debug all of your application code on the 8051 itself. You do not need a development system or emulator.

Assembler code can be written and debugged about 10 times as fast using these methods as using the traditional edit/assemble/link/load/run assembler technology.

It is a good strategy not to rewrite code that is already in the FORTH nucleus. For example, call FILL to fill memory with a constant value rather than recode it.

Once all your assembler code appears to work, you have two choices for building a ROMable minimum-sized application. The first alternative is to cross assemble the code using the cross assembly techniques described in section A of this chapter. The second alternative is to add your code to the 8051 FORTH operating system seen in Appendix 9. This choice is especially wise if your assembler calls routines in the FORTH nucleus. You then metacompile all of the code, including the FORTH operating system and your application.

You then begin eliminating words, one at a time, in the FORTH operating system not referenced by your assembler application code, and re-metacompile. Eventually you reach a minimum-sized application code.

E. Macro and Conditional Assembly

FORTH is the macro and conditional assembly language for the 8051 FORTH assembler. Following is an example of macro ADDMAC, which expands into:

```
A CLR
A # 0 ADD
A # 1 ADD
A # 2 ADD
A # 3 ADD
A # 4 ADD
A # 5 ADD
```

```
55 LIST
Screen # 55
\                                                  10:00 09/04/86
FORTH DEFINITIONS
\ number + 1 ---
: ADDMAC,        ASSEMBLER           \ assembler vocabulary
                 RESET               \ reset syntax checker
                 A CLR               \ clear A
```

```
                   0 DO               \ do number times
                   RESET              \ reset syntax checker
                   A # I ADD          \ expand add code
                   LOOP ;
\ --- sum
CODE ADDS          GETSP,             \ get sp to data pointer
                   6 ADDMAC,          \ invoke add macro
                   A0PUSH,            \ push 0 high byte a low byte
                   END-CODE
ADDS . \ execute the code
ok
55 LOAD 15 ok
```

Care must be taken to reset the syntax checker, which also checks stack balancing, before assembling code fragments.

Conditional assembly is also processed by FORTH. Constructs of if . . . then and if . . . then . . . else are used conditionally to direct assembler code expansion.

You can load the macro as a transient module using the technique explained in section C of this chapter. A macro definition is useless after its invocation.

F. FORTH Assembler Conclusion

The contents of this chapter are sure to leave readers who have not used a FORTH assembler puzzled about the merits of what was written.

FORTH assemblers are incredibly powerful compared to traditional assemblers. You can write an assembler program that executes immediately to evaluate an expression for an operand in an assembler statement. Following is an example using the 8086 family listed in Appendix 6: The expression evaluation module, X, is used as a transient module, executed, then discarded before the assembler subprogram, Y, is invoked.

```
3 LIST 3 LOAD
Screen # 3
\                                                08:08 09/28/89
DECIMAL
LATEST HERE VOC-LINK @ SP@  \ save\latest\dp\voc-link and sp
100    ALLOT           \reserve enough space for tm by adding to dp
                       \ begin transient module
CODE X AX # 7 MOV AX PUSH NEXT, END-CODE\ transient module
SP@ 2+ ?PAIRS          \ check for balanced stack
VOC-LINK !             \ restore voc-link
```

```
DUP DP ! SP@           \ restore dp and save a copy of it, save sp
                       \ end of transient module
CODE Y AX # X MOV  AX PUSH NEXT, END-CODE \ wow! awesome!
SP@ 2+ ?PAIRS          \ check for balanced stack
PFA LFA !              \ link new definitions defined by
                       \ transient module
                       \ to old LATEST. This discards the transient
                       \ module.
Y .
7 ok
```

FORTH assemblers are implemented with little memory compared to Microsoft's MASM or Borland's Turbo Assembler. In fact, FORTH assembler is a radically different viewpoint on how assembly language programming should be done. Short subroutines and minimizing the amount of assembler that should be written in an application are emphasized in FORTH assembler. High-level language programming is the best way to program larger embedded controller applications. Some assembler is surely necessary. The approach we have described is the least painful way of getting assembler programming done quickly and inexpensively.

Chapter 5
Reverse Software Engineering Assembler Code

"Plagiarize, let no one's work evade your eyes . . . but be sure to call it research," sang Tom Lehr about a quarter-century ago.

Reverse software engineering is the science of reconstructing source code from binary machine object code. Embedded controller programmers must sometimes reconstruct source code from object code to uncover bugs in compilers or assemblers. Or sometimes they must research the work of other programmers.

A central principle in this book is invertibility of processes. Binary files were converted to ASCII files. A BASIC program converted them back to a binary file again. Screen files were converted to ASCII files and back again with FORTH programs. In Chapter 4, assembler source code was converted to binary machine object code. In this chapter binary machine code is converted to source code for the 8051 microcontroller.

A. Disassembly of ROMs

If the code to be researched is in ROM, the first step is to remove it from the ROM and place it in a disk file.

If you either bought or built your own EPROM programmer, then you are able to read the ROM and write the contents to a disk file.

If you look inside your PC clone, then you may see vacant sockets for 32K×8 byte EPROMs used for BIOS extensions or ROMed BASIC. You can modify a chip carrier to fit the ROM to be researched into the PC. You need to discover the segment address of the chip. When you have done so, you can read the ROM contents directly to disk.

Following is a FORTH program that uploads MCT 2.2 and 3.0 BIOS to disk. The author broke a pin on a BIOS EEPROM. A wire was jerry-rigged to the broken chip so that it could be inserted in a PC. A disk copy of the BIOS was made, and a replacement EPROM was successfully burned from the disk file image. The following program was used to create this disk file.

```
HEX
AFILE MCT30.BAK
\byte\offset ---
: !FB             400 /MOD ABLOCK + C! UPDATE ;
: @I              FFFF BEGIN DUP CR U. F000 OVER C@L SPACE U.
                  1- DUP 0= UNTIL DROP ;
: !IMAGE          0000
                  BEGIN F000 OVER 8000 +
                    C@L OVER !FB 1+ DUP 8000 =
                  UNTIL FLUSH AUXF CLOSEHANDLE DROP ;
```

The FORTH word C@L—C fetch long—does an intersegment byte fetch. Its assembler source is seen in Appendix 1. @I stands for "fetch image" and was used to look at the image.

!IMAGE is perhaps too simple. The file should probably have been read back and compared with the ROM. This was a rushed job, but the ROM works.

The next step is to get the disk file into a source format so that it can be reassembled. The goal is to create an identical copy of the original object file from source code. Programmers modify this source to give the researched code their original signature.

B. Interactive 8051 Family Disassemblers

Disassembly of mostly unknown code requires you to be a sleuth. The first problem is that tables of data are sometimes difficult to distinguish from code.

FORTH is incomprehensible to most traditional programmers since memory is, for the most part, filled with tables of addresses. FORTH is a table-driven code.

The second problem in reverse software engineering is discovering what is done by systems call or calls to run time libraries. If the operating system is PC/MS DOS or UNIX, then the calls are fairly well known. But even in PC/MS DOS there are "secret" system calls and obscure variables. Proprietary operating systems can present formidable obstacles.

One strategy is to begin where execution begins and interactively disassemble the code trail. Paranoid programmers, perhaps rightfully so after they read this chapter, may attempt to hide the code trail by writing over previously executed code. This means that you want a nonexecuting code copy, if at all possible, to research.

You want an interactive disassembler that disassembles to screen only for forays onto possible code trails. This is sometimes called the "browse mode." Once you are sure you have picked up a trail, then you want to store the code to disk.

FORTH assemblers place the operation code, or opcode, after the operands. This is almost an essential requirement, because the form of the opcode is unknown until the operands are known. Opcodes usually appear before the operands in machine code for most microcomputers. There are some exceptions. Traditional assembler format with the operations code preceding the operands is the easiest presentation format for disassemblers. In this case the opcodes are completely defined and may determine the operand forms when they are assembled.

Some additional work is required to disassemble into FORTH assembler format where the opcode follows the operand. This step is not a major programming task.

The source code for an 8051 cross disassembler is listed in Appendix 12. The code runs on FORTH86, whose source is listed in Appendix 1. The 8051 object code is read from secondary file.

The 8051 cross disassembler is compiled on FORTH86. The secondary file is opened to the binary of the ASCII listing of the 8051 FORTH operating system seen in Appendix 10. The FORTH word 0= contains branch instructions. The symbol table of the 8051 FORTH operating system in Appendix 11 shows the Code Field Address of 0= to be at location hex 4B5 in the FORTH vocabulary. The Parameter Field Address is two bytes beyond the CFA. The PFA is at hex 4B7. This is the start location of the assembler subroutine. This disassembler produced:

```
HEX ok
4B7 DIS
Key space to proceed; esc to stop
04B7      1200CA              LCALL    00CA
04BA      A3                  INC      DPTR
04BB      E0                  MOVX     A,@DPTR
04BC      A3                  INC      DPTR
04BD      F520                MOV      20,A
04BF      E0                  MOVX     A,@DPTR
```

```
04C0      4520                ORL     A,20
04C2      7003                JNZ     04C7
04C4      04                  INC     A
04C5      8001                SJMP    04C8
04C7      E4                  CLR     A
04C8      0200E2              LJMP    00E2
```

The source code is seen in screen number 42 of Appendix 9. Observe that the disassembler computed the address of the short jump and jump not zero. Computing absolute addresses from relative offsets is best left to a computer.

This program disassembles only to screen. Not much work is required to have it write the screen output to the auxiliary file when a >DISK flag variable is set.

As mentioned, the FORTH disassembler is a table-driven code. The general principle to write table-driven code is: Make the data smart and the code dumb.

The format of FORTH CODE words is given in the following example.

```
0100 0102          \ Code Filed Address
0102 beginning of machine object code
```

The CFA contains an address pointer to the parameter field address. The FORTH word " ' "—tick—locates the PFA of a FORTH word. If the disassembler is modified to run on the 8051 FORTH operating system, then

```
' 0= DIS
```

is required to disassemble 0= on the 8051 microcontroller.

This program is disassembling in traditional Intel format, because the assembler code is developed using FORTH. FORTH assembler code can be written and debugged about 10 times as fast as assembler code written with traditional cross assemblers debugged on development systems. It is disassembled into Intel format and reassembled with a Intel format assembler. The code is then delivered to individuals who continue to remain unaware of the economic importance of FORTH assemblers.

Once the disassembly is on disk, the editor is used to replace absolute locations and jump addresses with symbolic names. The 8051 FORTH assembler is used to reassemble the code once a programmer has added a proprietary signature. The capability of assembling 8051 assembler code and inverting the binary object code to source means that invertibility is achieved with assembler.

Spite Software markets snOOp II interactive disassembler for the 8086 family of microprocessors.[1] It is more sophisticated than a FORTH disassembler. It also occupies much more memory, took longer to write than a FORTH disassembler, and is not user-modifiable because the source code is not distributed. It recognizes DOS calls and automatically comments some disassembly. snOOp II is designed for serious PC code research.

References

McCullough, R. *snOOp II.* Spite Software, TriDos Software Publishers, Portland, OR.

Chapter 6

The 8051 Family FORTH Operating System

The 8051 family FORTH operating system is listed in Appendix 9. The listing is in a format processed by the Nautilus metacompiler. The source code for the metacompiler is included in this book.

A. 8051 FORTH Operating System Code Layout

The FORTH operating system is split into several distinct functional parts.

Screens 2-4 contain the equates. These set many parameters of the operating system into symbols.

Screen 5 contains the interrupt vectors. These vectors are initially set to a LJMP to 0, but they are patched in screen 199 to point to the variables in this screen. The reason for doing this is that the interrupt vectors lie in the low portion of memory, which is ROMed. Pointing to the variables in screen 199 gives you a method to write and debug interrupt routines without burning ROMs. Handling interrupts this way has been used extensively and works well.

Screen 6 contains the FORTH start-up variables. The layout is similar to the beginning of the FORTH86 system. These variables reside in ROM on screen 3 of SYSTEM.SCR, and, while applicable in principle, cannot be used to update them. These variables are set by the metacompiler.

Screen 7 contains the jump to high-level FORTH. The contents of the screen are important to you if you need to jump from assembler to high-level FORTH. Interrupts are unexpected machine language subprogram calls. Interrupt handlers can be written in high-level FORTH. In the equivalent to this code, which must invoke a high-level FORTH word, you will jump to the handler rather than COLD.

Screen 8 contains undebugged code to field the 8051 external interrupt, and has that code perform a FORTH warm start. Cold start destroys everything—including, perhaps, your application program. Warm start leaves all of the pointers as they are and just branches to WARM. A similar feature on the 8085 version of this operating system saved much time when the application software got into an infinite loop. The basic idea is to push the address of the jump to WARM on the stack and then do a RETI.

Screens 9 through 19 contain basic routines that FORTH requires for efficient implementation. Those experienced at bringing up FORTH on new machines implement these in the most efficient hardware way.

Screen 20 contains the FORTH address interpreter, NEXT. This routine effectively calls (or actually jumps) lists of subroutines. Rather than having a jump or call redundantly preceding each address, NEXT effectively generates calls. A FORTH which does include the jump or call is called "subroutine threaded": no NEXT.

The efficiency of high-level FORTH is largely determined by how efficiently NEXT is executed. On the 8051 it is fairly inefficient. Experience shows that a 12MHz 8051 FORTH keeps up with or outruns a 5MHz 8085.

The Harris RTX 2000 chip implements NEXT in hardware. Moreover, it has separate address and data lines for this return and parameter stack. As a result it runs FORTH extremely fast.

Look at NEXT for the 8086 family in Appendix 1. The 8086 with its autoincrementing SI does a fairly efficient job running FORTH.

Screens 21 through 73 contain the FORTH operating system nucleus CODE word. The equivalent of each of these needs to be implemented on any host to run FORTH. FORTH runs on a virtual machine. The closer the virtual machine architecture is to the host hardware architecture, the better FORTH works. The 8051 is probably the smallest microcontroller on which FORTH can be implemented. FORTH experts say that the Intel 8048/49 and Motorola HC05 are too small for FORTH. A FORTH cross assembler, of course, can be used to program them.

Screens 52 through 55 contain code for port fetches. These port fetches and stores are both character and word wide. There are two types of port stores and fetches. PC@, P@, PC!, and P! apply to the first 128 bytes of internal RAM and to the special function registers. IC@, I@, IC!, and I! apply to the same first 128 bytes of RAM. Fetches and stores to address 128 through 255 access the additional 128 bytes of RAM of 8052 type processors. These instructions use R0 in bank 0.

Variable address loads and stores, which are also a ROMed system, are not built into 8051 instructions. A way to implement a variable address is to build an instruction on the parameter stack and execute it off the stack. This tactic is an extreme example of self-modifying code, but it works well.

Screens 73 through 82 contain standard FORTH arithmetic high-level words. Programmers should not attempt to duplicate their functions in assembler. The cleverness of these routines is unparalleled. They were written by Charles Moore.

Screens 83 through 88 contain terminal I/O routines. While they can be written in high-level FORTH, it is best to convert some of them to assembler for performance. This version of FORTH uses Request to Send and Clear to Send for flow control. These hardware lines need to be connected. The 8051 FORTH operating system does not send characters to the PC if Clear to Send (CTS) is not asserted.

Screens 89 through 99 contain the disk I/O routines. Assertion of Ring Indicator (RI) indicates that characters are destined to be sent the disk. This instruction is transmitted through OUT1 on the 80C52. Otherwise characters are destined for the PC terminal. The disk I/O routines call serial communications routines. You should compare these routines to the 8086 family PC/MS calls seen in Appendix 1.

Screens 100 through 113 contain FORTH compiler words. They are complicated but eventually comprehensible. Again, you are studying what is in the mind of a software genius, so the way the code works is not immediately obvious.

Screens 114 through 121 contain FORTH utility programs. These are relatively easy to understand and are, in their current form or in modified form, useful in application code development.

Screens 123 through 141 contain the disk communications protocol. Some of the screens are commented out. Communications protocol code is some of the most difficult to get working over a wide variety of situations. Communications protocols frequently contain 1) the message types, 2) retry counts, and 3) timeout values. The timeout values, especially for slow floppy disks, were originally troublesome and have been modified every several years. What you see is the current version—with the code that worked fairly well, but not well enough, still included but commented out.

Screen 142 contains the BASIC motivated ONGOSUB—ENDGOSUB construct. It is even more informative than Eaker's CASE—OF—ENDCASE for discovering how such words as COMPILE, [COMPILE], and IMMEDIATE work.

Screens 143 through 190 contain the ROM version of the FORTH assembler listed in Appendix 7. The original Nautilus metacompiler could not process <BUILDS, DOES>, and IMMEDIATE FORTH words. The interpreted table building is particularly troublesome to a metacompiler. There is approximately a five-year history, starting in England, of the evolution of the Nautilus metacompiler, which has made metacompilation of the assembler possible.

The Ragsdale mini-full screen editor is contained in screens 191 through 199. Some find this editor useful for development of code on the 8051. The control keys have been adapted to the PC. Both Laxen's and Ragsdale's editors show how much can be done in a short amount of FORTH code. When it comes to manipulating tables and character strings, FORTH is unparalleled.

Last, screen 200 is the destination of the interrupts for a ROMed system.

FORTH is amazing in that once the code words work, then the entire systems comes to life. All of the high-level constructs are, from an installation labor standpoint, effectively free.

B. Terminal and Disk PC Interface Protocol

The communications protocol between the 8051 FORTH operating system and a PC has always been somewhat of a problem on account of the increasing PC speeds. The protocol relies on ACKs and NAKs given in the right time frame. The "right" time frame changes as PCs run faster.

"If it's not broken, don't fix it" applies. The communications software does not appear to be broken until a faster PC comes along. Compounding the problem is the fact that floppy disks still run slowly. Turning on the motor appears to take a long time. These speed differences are accentuated with a 25 or 33 MHz 80386. Every two years or so someone resolves to fix the problem once and for all.

Understanding the terminal and disk protocol requires that you comprehend both the contents of screen 131–149 and the terminal and disk emulation PC software listed in Appendix 13. You, of course, are welcome to solve the problem once and for all.

There is a good reason for each of the ACKs and NAKs in the protocol. However, some reasons escape even the authors' memory on reinspection of their own code. Their removal, nonetheless, reminds the authors why they were required.

C. 8051 FORTH Operating System Memory Layout

The 8051 FORTH operating system compiles with the FORTH Interest Group Standard Memory Map. The top of the figure is high memory.

```
LIMIT                                          USE
                       DISK BUFFERS

FIRST                                          PREV

                       USER AREA

UP

R0                     RETURN STACK
                       grows down              IN

RP                     TERMINAL BUFFER         TIB
                       grows up

S0                     PARAMETER STACK
                       grows down
SP

                       TEXT BUFFER             PAD

                       ''WORD'' BUFFER

DP                     DICTIONARY

                       BOOT-UP LITERALS        0+ORIGIN
```

The Return Stack and Terminal Input Buffer share the same area. IN is the variable that contains the offset of the present character being read into TIB. When carriage return is keyed, the line is converted to a counted string and copied to the word buffer.

The equates in screens 1 and 2 of Appendix 9 give the assignment. They are reproduced here so that you can look at them as they are explained.

```
0000 ( 6000 ) 0 ORG/DB            ( beginning of ROM )
8000 ( B000 ) 0100 ROM/RAM        ( start RAM, length init RAM)
FEFE ( BFFE ) EQU EM              ( end of RAM memory )

400 EQU BPS          ( bytes per physical disk sector)
  2 EQU DBH          ( bytes at head of disk buffer)
  2 EQU DBT          ( null bytes at tail of disk buffer)
400 EQU KBBUF        ( length of data in disk buffer)
  2 EQU NSCR -->     ( number of SCREENS to buffer in RAM )

DBH DBT KBBUF + + EQU HDBT        ( total memory per disk buffer)
NSCR 400 * KBBUF / EQU NBUF       ( total disk buffers allocated)
EM HDBT NBUF * -   EQU BUF1       ( addr of first disk buffer)
```

```
040 EQU US                        ( length of user var area)
100 EQU RTS                       ( depth of return stack and )
                                  ( terminal buffer combined)

BUF1 US -      EQU INIT-RO        ( base of return stack )
INIT-RO RTS -  EQU INIT-SO        ( base of data stack )
```

Some of the parameter settings are specific to the Nautilus Metacompiler. ORG/DB tells where ROM begins. Here it is zero. The second zero on the stack is not used but is left for backward metacompiler compatibility. The commented out values—the ( )— are left from a previous configuration so that they would not be forgotten.

ROM/RAM tells where RAM starts. Here it is at hex 8000. The second number 100 is the number of bytes reserved for ROM-defined variables in RAM. It is presently not used but is kept for backward metacompiler compatibility.

EM stands for "end of memory." The 8051 hardware memory decoding scheme seen in Chapter 2 allocated all addresses above hex FF00 to I/O space. Therefore, the last value RAM address is hex FEFF. See Figures 2.7 and 2.8 for diagrams. One or two bytes less than this is usually specified.

Each disk buffer, BPS, contains decimal 1024 bytes, which is hex 400. Two bytes, DBH, are allocated to the front of each disk buffer. These two bytes hold the block number and update bit. Two bytes at the end of the disk buffer contain nulls, hex 00's. Nulls are very important in FORTH. They execute. The word that defines null is called X. You see the metacompiler word IS-X on screen 104 of Appendix 9. This instruction changes X to null. You also see the definition of null.

Be careful in the Laxen editor to blank a screen from all nulls, hex 00's, to blanks, hex 20's. This blanking is done by keying special function key F9. Nulls embedded in a screen with FORTH text do terrible things to you. The nulls at the end of a buffer terminate loading of the buffer.

KBBUF specifies the number of bytes of data in the buffer. The reason for this parameter is obscure.

NSCR specifies the number of disk buffers. The number two is selected from experimentation. Increasing the number does not appear to make the 8051 FORTH operating system run faster. More memory is used without any apparent benefit by increasing this number.

The total amount of storage for one disk buffer is hex 404 bytes, including the head and tail words. The number of buffers is computed in a round about way to 2 = NBUF.

The address of the first disk buffer including head and tail bytes, BUF1, is hex FEFE − 404 * 2 = F8F6.

Forty hex bytes are reserved for user variables. The user variable list seen on screen 74 is copied here:

```
06 USER S0          08 USER R0           0A USER TIB
0C USER WIDTH       0E USER WARNING      10 USER FENCE
12 USER DP          14 USER VOC-LINK     16 USER BLK
18 USER IN          1A USER OUT          1C USER SCR
20 USER CONTEXT     22 USER CURRENT
24 USER STATE       26 USER BASE         28 USER DPL
2A USER FLD         2C USER CSP          2E USER R#
30 USER HLD
```

You can modify FORTH to handle multiple users. Each user must have a set of user variables. Still, while a multiple user FORTH is possible, it probably is not a good idea. Each user can crash all of the other users.

The author implemented a multitasking FORTH received indirectly from a Mr. Wong at IBM on an 8085 FORTH system with a round robin task invocation. Several tasks produced some interesting screen output. The scheme involved making a copy of the parameter stack for each task. While multitasking is possible in high-level FORTH, it may not be practical for real-world tasks.

The Return Stack and terminal buffer occupy the same space. One hundred hex bytes are allocated to this combined area. The return stack usually does not have much on it when input from the terminal is required. FORTH usually does not have much on the Return Stack when input is requested. Look at QUIT on screen 108 of Appendix 9. The Return Stack is reset to the RP! just prior to the invocation of QUERY, which waits for terminal input.

The data or parameter stack is located just below the Return Stack/ Terminal Input Buffer. This configuration is exactly what is specified in the Forth Interest Group Standard Memory Map.

There is one important, but obscure modification to this map required to build a ROMed FORTH operating system. Variables must reside in RAM. Forth Interest Group FORTH also allows initialized variables.

The Nautilus metacompiler realizes that variables must be allocated space in RAM. ALLOT could refer to either ROM or RAM. Therefore, normal ALLOT refers to ROM and a new construct called ALLOT-RAM allots space in RAM. Use of this construct is seen on screens 6, 143, and 200 in Appendix 9. The word THERE on screen 200 is just like HERE but applies to the target image HERE.

The problem of initializing ROM variable in RAM is solved by creating a data structure just behind the last word defined in ROM which contains the initialized variables. The structure is:

```
bytes 0,1          word count
bytes 2 -          values
```

Following is the information obtained from the 8051 operating system running on the hardware described in Chapter 2.

```
8051 series microcontroller
ROMed DOS MC 2.2
19.2 kbs, rts, cts flow control
Version 1.4 03/03/89 10:00

 ok
HEX HERE U. 8053 ok

VLIST
43EE TASK            43E3 SINT            43D6 TIMER1            43CA

HEX 43EE 50 DUMP

      0  1  2  3  4  5  6  7  8  9  A  B  C  D  E  F  0123456789ABCDEF

43E0 45 80 4D 84 53 49 4E D4 43 D6 0C 45 80 50 84 54  E.M.SIN.C..E.P.T
43F0 41 53 CB 43 E3 0C 72 0A 69 00 53 00 00 81 A0 43  AS.C..r.i.S....C
4400 EE F6 F6 F6 F6 00 00 00 00 81 A0 29 55 00 00 FF  ...........)U...
4410 FF 81 A0 43 67 00 00 00 00 00 00 00 00 00 00 00  ...Cg...........
4420 00 00 00 00 00 00 00 00 00 00 00 00 00 00 00 00  ................
4430 00 00 00 00 00 00 00 00 00 00 00 00 00 00 00 00  ................
ok
8000 30 DUMP

      0  1  2  3  4  5  6  7  8  9  A  B  C  D  E  F  0123456789ABCDEF

8000 F6 B6 81 A0 43 EE F6 F6 F6 F6 00 00 00 00 81 A0  ....C...........
8010 29 55 00 00 FF FF 81 A0 43 67 00 00 00 00 00 00  )U......Cg......
8020 00 00 00 00 00 00 00 00 00 00 00 00 00 00 00 00  ................
```

VLIST located the last word, TASK, in ROM. 43EE is the NFA of task. 43E3 is the LFA which points to the NFA of SINT. The CFA is 0672 which is the run time code of :. 0A69 is the run time code of ;S, which ends the definition of TASK.

The 0053 is the byte count of the variable and other structure initializations. HERE starts are 8053. This location is the first in RAM following the ROM variables.

The copies in RAM are dumped by typing 8000 30 DUMP. Look at the ALLOT-RAM on screen 6 of Appendix 9 for the Return Stack Pointer. The Return Stack pointer initial value is hex 40 beneath the first disk buffer. This is F6F6 − 40 = F6BF and that is in location 8000 where it should be. The 81A0's indicate the bogus name used in vocabularies to chaining via links back to the last defined vocabularies through VOC-LINK.

The FORTH word COLD is modified to copy these variables to RAM. Following is the source code copied from screen 119 of Appendix 9!

```
: COLD           INIT-R0 RAM-START !
                 INIT-RAM DUP >R 4 +
                   RAM-START 2+ R> @ 2 - CMOVE
                 INIT-USERV S0 10 CMOVE
                 INIT-FORTH @ ' FORTH 2+ @ 2+ !
                 EMPTY-BUFFERS
                 FIRST PREV !  FIRST USE !
                 1 WARNING ! PINIT
                 ABORT ;
```

Following is a dump of the object code:

```
' COLD DUP U. 50 DUMP 234E

      0  1  2  3  4  5  6  7  8  9  A  B  C  D  E  F  0123456789ABCDEF

2340 55 06 B2 0A 69 84 43 4F 4C C4 23 29 0C 72 01 20  U...i.COL.#).r.
2350 F6 B6 01 20 80 00 07 7D 01 20 43 F9 06 C7 05 F3  ... ...}.C.....
2360 01 20 00 04 04 54 01 20 80 00 0B 06 06 11 07 56  . ...T. .......V
2370 0A BF 04 6A 04 0C 01 20 00 38 0D 68 01 20 00 10  ...j... .8.h. ..
2380 04 0C 01 20 00 32 07 56 01 20 0D 4A 0B 06 07 56  ... .2.V. .J...V
2390 0B 06 07 7D 15 FE 13 F7 14 18 07 7D 13 F7 14 0D  ...}.......}....
```

The Return Stack initial address is seen at 2350. It is placed on the stack by LIT, 0120. It is stored at 8000.

INIT-RAM is 43F9. This location is the start of the 0053 located just after TASK in the previous dump. The INIT-RAM through the CMOVE code gets the initialized variables copied to RAM. Observe that Boutelle has to avoid overwriting RPP at location 8000.

The user variables are initialized next. Finally, the INIT-FORTH line of code sets the FORTH vocabulary pointer pointing back to RAM. Following is a dump, using the 8051 FORTH operating system listed in Appendix 10, of the RAM locations initialized by this code.

```
HEX ok
CURRENT U. F6D8 ok
CURRENT @ U. 8004 ok
CURRENT @ @ U. 43EE ok
' TASK NFA U. 43EE ok
CONTEXT U. F6D6 ok
CONTEXT @ U. 8004 ok
ASSEMBLER ok
CURRENT @ @ U. 43EE ok
CONTEXT @ @ U. 4367 ok
ASSEMBLER DEFINITIONS ok
CURRENT @ @ U. 4367 ok
```

If you have trouble understanding vocabularies, the examples following the ' TASK line will clear up any confusion. Typing the vocabulary name sets CONTEXT to point to the latest defined word NFA. CURRENT is set by DEFINITIONS. DEFINITIONS defines the vocabulary to which newly defined words are to be added.

This particular section of the 8051 FORTH operating system is specific to the binary image generated by the Nautilus metacompiler.

If you consult the symbol map in Appendix 11, then you can easily decompile the FORTH seen in the dump. For embedded controller FORTH, or any type of embedded controller language, a programmer becomes proficient at reading dumps quickly. The image dump program located at screen 204 in Appendix 9 is used to look at a target image. With the cross disassembler described in Chapter 5 any code can be converted to source code.

Chapter 7

The PC Terminal Emulator and Disk System

FORTH is a one-file disk operating system. An IBM PC or clone serves as the 8051 FORTH's terminal, and its open primary file is the 8051's disk file.

The cable connecting the National 82C50 Asynchronous Communications Element to the PC must have TXD, RXD, RTS, CTS, and RI and be ground wired straight through. The crossings for a null modem are done at the 8051 end.

The source code for the 8051 terminal and disk emulator is given in Appendix 13. You need to assemble and compile this program using FORTH86 on top of the LAXEN editor. You need the assembler to load this program. You can either include the assembler or load it as a transient module to compile the emulator.

The emulator is configured for COM1. This configuration can be changed by replacing COM1 with COM2 in line 4 of screen 3 and recompiling the emulator.

BEGINIDS—Begin Initialize Development System—sets the video mode and prints the emulator logo. The start-up word is best placed on screen 2 of the system file, SYSTEM.SCR. Here is an example:

```
PFILE MY8051AP    BEGINIDS
```

BEGINIDS prints the following information at the top of the screen:

```
Televideo 910 terminal emulator, 01/29/88 14:17
Type IDS to run emulator
```

```
Type ^A to return to Forth 86
Forth 86

ok
IDS
```

At this point you are still in the PC environment. IDS is typed to enter the 8051 environment. IDS sets the interrupt vectors if they have not previously been set. The screen is cleared and you see:

```
8051 televideo 910 terminal emulator

8051 series microcontroller
ROMed DOS MC 2.2
19.2 kbs, rts, cts flow control
Version 1.4 03/03/89 10:00

 ok
```

At this point you are on the 8051 hardware/software development system. The screen file is the primary file.

To get back to the PC, type Ctrl A. This command clears the screen and prints:

```
Forth 86

 ok
```

All of FORTH86 is available to you.

You type 1 LOAD to load the emulator. Load the code on screen 3 of SYSTEM.SCR, then you can save the emulator with FORTH86, the Laxen editor, and the 8086 family assembler. The command

```
3 SYSLOAD SAVE PCF.COM
```

saves the emulator in the file PCF.COM.

The disk input/output routines have at least three layers of buffering. A screen is stored at the top of the 8051 system RAM memory. The same screen is also in the PC RAM. It is also on the PC's disk. Depending on the disk's buffering scheme, it may be located in some disk buffer in the PC's RAM.

The 8051 FORTH words UPDATE FLUSH flushes only the 8051's disk buffers to the PC RAM. Therefore, a new FORTH word, BYE, on the 8051 system flushes the PC's disk buffers to disk. Physically, this move may be made only when you BYE off FORTH86 and all the files are closed.

If you edit on the 8051 with the Ragsdale mini-full screen editor, then you need to issue the series of FORTH commands

```
UPDATE FLUSH BYE
```

to insure that your changes got to the PC's disk. Following is screen 0 edited with the Ragsdale mini-full screen editor.

```
Screen # 0
  0 \                                                  12:46 09/30/90
  1
  2 This is the Ragsdale mini full screen editor ROMed on the 8051
  3
  4
  5
  6
  7
  8
  9
 10
 11
 12
 13
 14
 15
  cursor up           cursor left           DY start of next line
  cursor down         Home start of screen  Del backspace and de-
                                            lete
  cursor right        Home restore screen   PgDn next screen
PgUp  previous screen tab right             Esc exit editor
End  erase screen
UPDATE FLUSH BYE Started . . . completed.
ok
```

The PC 25 × 80 graphics do not appear on this printout. They appear on the PC screen, however. When BYE is typed, "Started . . . " appears. When the disk buffers serial transfer is complete, "completed." appears on the screen.

When the PC editor is used to make changes on an 8051 program screen file and you log back onto the 8051 system, then you must type EMPTY-BUFFERS to insure that the 8051 uses the new screen copy received from the PC rather than the stale 8051 buffers.

The disk and terminal protocol uses Esc, hex 1B, decimal 26. If you inadvertently key Esc, then it confuses the terminal emulator software. The way out of this problem is to key Ctrl Break and then IDS.

The interrupt routine in the terminal emulator program is long by good interrupt routine standards. BIOS authors, each with their own variations so as not to be sued by IBM or one another, sometimes spend too long in their system interrupt routines. With some BIOSes, notably the Toshiba family, some serial interrupts are lost, which results in lost characters.

The 8051 is capable of outrunning a 12 MHz 80286 with respect to printing characters. The terminal I/O routines signal the 8051 by dropping CTS when the buffer is almost filled. The flow control is an essential feature to this system.

The terminal and disk I/O routines have been used heavily for almost five years. No one can remember seeing a checksum failure! Nonetheless, its removal is not recommended.

Chapter 8

The Nautilus Version 2 Metacompiler

To bring up all of the FORTH utility programs listed in this book, a binary of FORTH running on a PC was required. This binary was built by reading the ASCII file in Appendix 2 and converting it to a binary file using a BASIC program.

The Forth Interest Group distributes assembler listings of the FORTH nucleus. It is through these listings that they build the portion of FORTH required to load and save the remainder. The "save" code on screen 3 of the system file SYSTEM.SCR is used for the "save." This process is probably more painful than typing Appendix 2.

A second approach is to use a metacompiler. A FORTH metacompiler is a FORTH source code program that assembles and compiles the FORTH operating system and FORTH compiler. It can even compile a FORTH assembler and editor. The 8051 family FORTH operating system code compiled by the metacompiler is listed in Appendix 10. The 8051 FORTH operating system source code compiled by the metacompiler is listed in Appendix 9.

A diagram of the process wherein FORTH generates itself from source with a metacompiler is shown in Figure 8.1. The caption of this figure tells the story. UNIX, OCCAM, NEON, and some other operating systems follow a similar process, perhaps not as complete as that of FORTH, to generate their operating systems.

The Intel corporation has released source code for the 8052 BASIC. It was written entirely in assembler. A second file distributed by Intel contains a floating point package that is included with the 8052 BASIC. Using this package is a painful way to write an operating system. The FORTH metacompiler method is much more advanced.

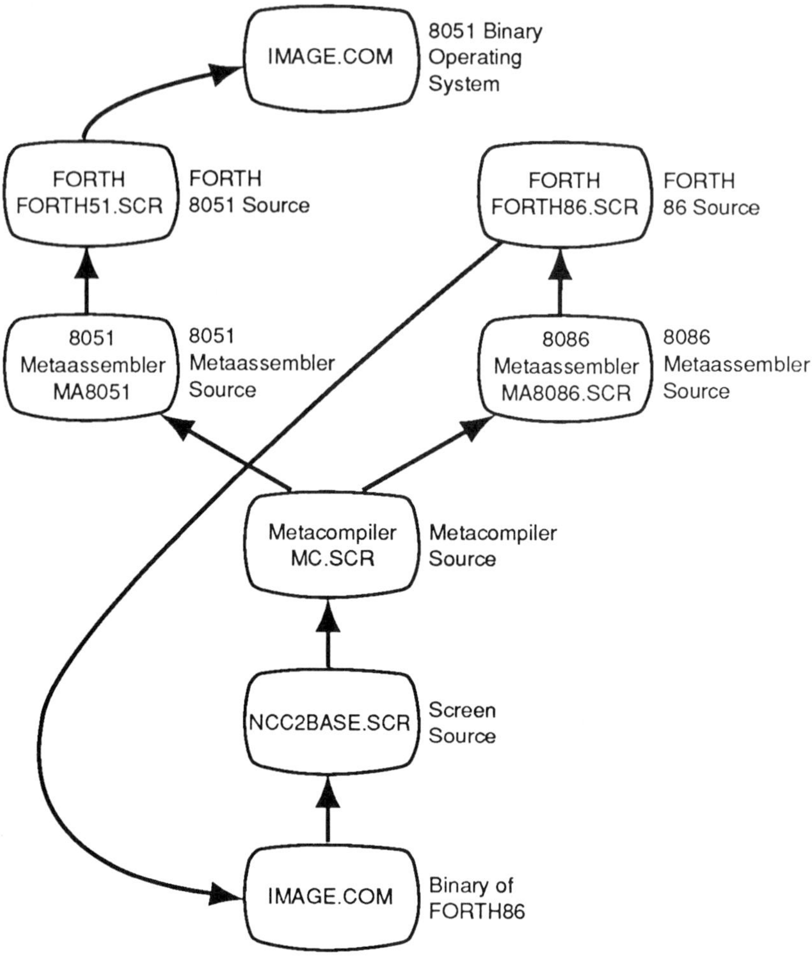

Figure 8.1. An ASCII listing of the FORTH 8086 family operating system is listed in Appendix 2. Its binary, IMAGE.COM, compiles a set of base routines required by the metacompiler. NCC2BASE.SCR is listed in Appendix 14. The metacompiler is compiled next. Its source is listed in Appendix 15. For generation of an 8086, a FORTH 8086 metaassembler is compiled next. The 8086 family metaassembler is listed in Appendix 16. It contains minor variations on the 8086 assembler, also listed in Appendix 6. The program is used to compile the FORTH 8086 family operating system, FORTH86. FORTH86 is listed in Appendix 1. The output from the metacompiler is IMAGE.COM for the 8086.

An 8051 family cross metaassembler, listed in Appendix 17, is compiled on top of the metacompiler. This metaassembler is a minor variation of the 8051 cross assembler listed in Appendix 7. The metacompiler then processes the FORTH 8051 operating system listed in Appendix 9. This is the binary of the ASCII listing in Appendix 10.

A. Compiling the Nautilus Metacompiler with FORTH86

The first step to loading the Nautilus 2 metacompiler is to load the base code. The base code is in file NCC2BASE and listed in Appendix 14. The base code is written partially in assembler, so the 8086 family FORTH assembler listed in Appendix 6 must be loaded as a transient module prior to assembling and compiling it. FORTH86 with no editor or assembler must be used because of the size of the metacompiler.

When you type

```
PFILE NCC2BASE 1 LOAD
```

you see, omitting some of the early assembler messages,

```
BEGIN is redefined
UNTIL is redefined
WHILE is redefined
REPEAT is redefined
12769 Kbytes assembler size

NOT is redefined
NCC2BASE.COM File not found
Do you wish to create it (Y/N)? Y
15544 bytes were written to file NCC2BASE.COM
For Nautilus Meta-compiler version 2.5 10/12/89 07:24
ok
```

NCC2BASE.COM is used to compile the Nautilus Version 2 metacompiler. The metacompiler is now loaded by typing PFILE MC and 1 LOAD. The screen dialog is seen below.

```
PFILE MC ok
1 LOAD
Loading Nautilus Forth Meta-compiler Version 2.5 10/12/89 07:24

--> is redefined    2 3 4 5 6 7 8 9 10 11 12 13 14 15 16 17 18 19
20 21 22 23 24 2
5 26 27 28 29 30 31 32 33 34 35 36 37 38 39 40 41 42 43 44 45 46
47 48 49 50 51
52 53 54 55 56 57 58 59 60 61 62 63 64 65 66 67 68 69 70 71 72 73
74 75 76 77 78
 79 80 81 82 83 84 85 86 87 88 89 90 91 92 93 94 95 96 97 98 99
100 101 102 103
104 105 106 107 108 109 110 111 112 113 114 115 116 117 118 119
120 121 122 123
124 125 126 127 128 129 130 131 132 133 134 135 136 137 138 139
140 141 142 143
144 145 146 147 148 149 150 151 152 153 154 155 156 157 158 159
```

```
160 161 162 163
164 165 166 167 168 169 170 171 172 173 174 175 176 177 178 179
180 181 182 183
184 185 186 187 188 189 190 191 192 193 194 195 196 197 198 199
200 201 202 203
204 205 206 207 208 209 210
Nautilus Forth Meta-compiler 2.5 10/12/89 07:24 loaded
25632 bytes sued

MCNOASM.COM File not found
Do you wish to create it (Y/N)? Y
41176 bytes were written to file MCNOASM.COM
ok
```

The metacompiler, minus any metaassembler, is placed in the files MCNOASM.COM. You now need to add a target metaassembler.

B. Compiling the 8086 Metaassembler

The next step prior to metacompiling the FORTH86 source listed in Appendix 1 is to compile the 8086 family metaassembler. Following is the screen dialog needed if you are proceeding from section A of this chapter. If not, then you must first type MCNOASM.

```
PFILE MA8086
ok

1 LOAD
```

You finally see:

```
BEGIN is redefined
UNTIL is redefined
WHILE is redefined
REPEAT is redefined    131
13595 bytes used by meta-assembler
ok
3 SYSLOAD SAVE MC86.COM
MC86.COM File not found
Do you wish to create it (Y/N)? Y
54780  bytes were written to file MC86.COM
MC86.COM was closed
ok
```

The early assembler messages are not shown. When the 8086 family metaassembler is loaded, you can type SYMBOL.TABLE to generate a symbol table for the metacompiler. The table the metacompiler generates is called DEFAULT.SYM. If you do not generate a symbol table, then the metacompiler automatically creates DEFAULT.SYM when the metacompiler is invoked.

The dialog starting with 3 SYSLOAD shows a copy of the metacompiler being saved with the 8086 metaassembler. This program is ready to metacompile FORTH86, seen in Appendix 1.

When you invoke the metacompiler, it prompts you to respond in which file you wish the compiler to be saved. Respond with MC86.COM at that time.

Keep the 8051 and 8086 metacompiler files in separate directories. The metacompiler cannot distinguish between 8051 and 8086 symbol tables.

C. Metacompiling the 8086 Family FORTH, FORTH86

The metacompiler is ready to metacompile the FORTH86 source listed in Appendix 1. If you are proceeding from section B of this chapter, you type

```
PFILE FORTH86 1 LOAD
```

Otherwise you must first type MC86. The screen at this point reads

```
---------------- Nautilus Forth Metacompiler ----------------
 Compiler version: 2.5 10/12/89 07:24
 Assembler version: 2.1 01/05/89 15:29
 Target: 8086
 File: FORTH86.SCR
 Screen:    5  Line:    8
 State: Compiling
 Undefined references:    3
-------------------------------------------------------------
Generating default symbol table, please wait
Enter the file name for the compiler: MC86
Compiler placed in file: MC86.COM
-------------------------------------------------------------
 < message window >

-------------------------------------------------------------
```

The metacompiler displays the screen and line number being metacompiled. The states of the metacompiler are assembling, compiling, and interpreting. The state is also displayed on the screen.

Messages from either the metacompiler or the target source are displayed in the window below the “Undefined references” line. The target source can contain ." in the interpreted state, and these messages appear here. They may be interlaced with FORTH messages such as "is redefined."

The number of undefined references is also displayed. These, of course, are forward references. There should be no undefined references at the end of metacompilation.

When the metacompiler is done, type

```
.TARGET-RESOLVE IMAGE
```

to check for unresolved references. Any found are placed in a file called IMAGE.RES.

The command

```
.TARGET-MAP IMAGE
```

invokes a program that generates a symbol table, similar to the 8051 symbol table seen in Appendix 11. The file is in WordStar nondocument format.

BYE returns you to PC/MS DOS.

D. Compiling the 8051 Metaassembler

MCNOASM.COM is run on a PC. This program contains the compiled metacompiler base and metacompiler. You type:

```
PFILE MA8051 1 LOAD
```

Deleting early assembler messages, you see the screen dialog:

```
PC/ASSEMBLER technology assembler
Intel 8051 family processors
14 15 16 17 18 19 20 21 22 23 24 25 26 Loading syntax tables
27 28 29 30 31 32 33 34 35 36 37 38 39 40 41 42 43 44 45 46 47 48
49 50 51 52 53
 54
DPL is redefined  55
R0 is redefined
R1 is redefined
R2 is redefined
R3 is redefined
R4 is redefined
R5 is redefined
# is redefined  56 57 58 59 60
SWAP is redefined  61
0= is redefined
IF is redefined
```

```
ELSE is redefined
THEN is redefined  62
BEGIN is redefined
UNTIL is redefined
WHILE is redefined
REPEAT is redefined  63 64
5647 bytes used by meta-assembler
ok
3 SYSLOAD SAVE MC51.COM
MC51.COM File not found
Do you wish to create it (Y/N)? Y
46865 bytes were written to file MC51.COM
MC51.COM was closed
ok
```

You could type SYMBOL.TABLE just before # SYSLOAD to create DEFAULT.SYM for the 8051 metacompiler version. If you do not type SYMBOL.TABLE, then the metacompiler automatically generates DEFAULT.SYM. Remember to keep the 8086 and 8051 metacompiler files in separate directories.

The metacompiler, ready to metacompile an 8051 system, is saved in file MC51.COM with the 3 SYSLOAD SAVE MC51.COM. If you proceed to the next step, the metacompiler asks you the file name to store the metacompiler. The response is MC51.COM.

E. Metacompiling the 8051 FORTH Operating System

The 8051 FORTH metacompiler is invoked by typing:

```
MC51
```

You then type:

```
FORTH51 1 LOAD
```

The following screen dialog shows the 8051 FORTH operating system source listed in Appendix 9 being metacompiled.

```
---------------- Nautilus Forth Metacompiler ----------------
 Compiler version: 2.5 10/12/89 07:24
 Assembler version: 10/12/89 07:39
 Target: 8051
 File: FORTH51.SCR
 Screen:    1  Line:    2
 State: Interpreting
 Undefined references:    0
-------------------------------------------------------------
```

```
 Generating default symbol table, please wait
 Enter the file name for the compiler: MC51

< compiler and target messages appear here >
------------------------------------------------------------
```

When the metacompilation is done, then execute the following dialog:

```
Resolve map placed in file: IMAGE.RES ok
Map placed in file: IMAGE.MAP ok
```

F. How to Write a Metacompiler

The principle behind writing a metacompiler is reasonably simple. Think of the 8051 FORTH operating system source listed in Appendix 9. The source is composed of assembler and high-level FORTH code.

FORTH has two states determined by the variable STATE. FORTH is either compiling or interpreting. The FORTH word "]" puts FORTH into the compiling state, and "[" puts it into the interpreting state. IMMEDIATE words are executed even though FORTH is compiling.

A metacompiler must compile the FORTH words and assemble code definitions in the target. Since FORTH interprets, the metacompiler must interpret as well. Further complication results from metacompiling a definition that was compiled in the target image and then executed. Look at the 8051 assembler in Appendix 9. 1MI—one machine instruction—on screen 184 is a <BUILD DOES> construct that is first compiled. This code is then executed to build some of the assembler tables.

The metacompiler should be able to execute code out of the target image. The Nautilus 2 metacompiler does so.

The metacompiler must emulate, to the greatest degree possible, what the target is doing. Some words like BLOCK and CODe are practically impossible to emulate. The clever metacompiler writer is able to emulation most FORTH words.

An apparently impossible task is to have a metacompiler process an image that first compiles and assembles a <BUILDS ;CODE definition then executes it to build more of the target. But even this task may not be impossible. The 8051 FORTH operating system could host a metacompiler. Here the 8051 can execute code definitions after they are defined in the target, and patch the generated code into the EEPROM memory on the motherboard shown in Chapter 2. With FORTH the programmer is only limited by his or her imagination.

FORTH metacompilers come in various forms of complexity. The more complex ones process <BUILDS, DOES> and IMMEDIATE words. Even a simple metacompiler can save you much time.

FORTH an be used, once running, to patch the IMAGE.COM file.

Chapter 9

FORTH Decompilers

Assembler language is invertible, as is seen in Chapter 5. The object code from many languages is not.

Prospective embedded controller language users need to inspect the object code of compilers before committing to their use. Some compilers for microcontrollers and microprocessors are nearly FORTH-like in that the compiler produces a series of calls to the run-time compiler library or operating system. Microsoft's new BASIC compiler does this. This type of compiler implementation is not a "true" compiler implementation in the sense of an optimizing FORTRAN, COBOL, or C compiler.

Quality of the code output of compilers, viewed from the standpoint of "clean" and efficient code, varies considerably. Some C compilers for the 8051 suffer from "code bloat." Much generated code and run-time libraries are required for even the smallest task.

A Forth Interest Group FORTH compiler is perhaps unique, in that all versions produce the same high-level compiled code independent of the host computer. This is not surprising since FORTH compiled code is nothing more than a list of Code Field Addresses and perhaps some data.

The memory map and names of the symbols are stored in memory in the Forth Interest Group's FORTH. Some FORTH programmers, as well as the Nautilus metacompiler, produce "headerless" code, but it is the exception in FORTH.

VLIST, seen in either Appendix 1 or 9, chains back through links printing word names. It is not hard to imagine traversing a list of FORTH CFAs and printing out their names. Data consisting of character strings, numbers, and branch offset must be identified and listed. This task belongs to a FORTH decompiler.

Ray Duncan's decompiler is listed in Appendix 18. Mike Perry's SEE decompiler is listed in Appendix 19.

A. The DIS FORTH Decompiler

The DIS FORTH decompiler, listed in Appendix 18, is loaded on the 8051 FORTH operating system exercised by the commands:

```
8051 series microcontroller
ROMed DOS MC 2.2
19.2 kbs, rts, cts flow control
Version 1.4 03/03/89 10:00

 ok
7 LOAD
Wait . . . loading Decompiler
TASK is redefined
  Decompiler loaded. 28984 bytes left.
To decompile word xxx type: DIS xxx <return>
ok

DIS -TRAILING

121E     :
1220     DUP
1222     0
1224     (DO)
1226     OVER
1228     OVER
122A     +
122C     1
122E     -
1230     C@
1232     BL
1234     -
1236     Branch if zero to 1240
123A     LEAVE
123C     Branch to 1244
1240     1
1242     -
1244     Loop to 1226
1248     ;S

ok
```

DIS does not load on the 8086 FORTH because this FORTH does not understand C/L—characters per line. C/L is 64, so you can modify the code, if you wish, so it works on the 8086 machines.

B. The SEE Decompiler

The SEE FORTH decompiler, listed in Appendix 19, is loaded on the 8051 FORTH operating system and exercised with the commands:

```
8051 series microcontroller
ROMed DOS MC 2.2
19.2 kbs, rts, cts flow control
Version 1.4 03/03/89 10:00


 ok
7 LOAD CR is redefined
  ok
SEE -TRAILING
: -TRAILING  DUP 0 (DO) OVER OVER + 1 - C@ BL - 0BRANCH 8 LEAVE
BRANCH 6
1 - (LOOP) 65504 ; ok
```

SEE works without change on the 8051 FORTH operating system. Following are commands loading and exercising it.

```
FORTH86 01/05/89
PC/ASSEMBLER 02/27/87 09:02
Space available:  27760 bytes
System file:  SYSTEM.SCR
Primary file:  SEE.SCR


 OK
7 LOAD
CR is redefined  ok
SEE -TRAILING
: -TRAILING  DUP 0 (DO) OVER OVER + 1- C@ BL - 0BRANCH 8 LEAVE
BRANCH 4
1- (LOOP) 65508 ; ok
```

Mike Perry's comments about decompilers, seen on screen 1 of Appendix 19, confirm the author's opinions on code produced by other high-level languages.

C. Cross Decompilers

Serious software researchers need to modify a decompiler to decompile from a FORTH disk image. The screen output should also be sent to disk on command. This task is not a hard one.

FORTH programmers, who realize that FORTH is like calculus, give you the source code. Decompilation is not required.

If you decide to modify a decompiler, then you can debug your code using the binary of the FORTH 8051 operating system whose ASCII version is listed in Appendix 10. You can compare its output to the source listed in Appendix 9.

If the FORTH word to be decompiled is a code word, the SEE prints, for example:

```
SEE 0=
0= is code ok
```

If you feel ambitious, you can modify SEE at this point to invoke the cross disassembler listed in Appendix 12 and thus disassemble the code.

Chapter 10

Porting FORTH to Another FORTH Version or Processor

The FORTH in this book can be transported to other microprocessors, microcontrollers, or versions of FORTH. The task of porting this code to another version of FORTH should be covered first.

A. Converting Forth Interest Group FORTH to Another FORTH Version

Two versions of FORTH immediately come to mind. First is FORTH-79. FORTH-79 appears to be dead. There is no advantage in converting to this FORTH version.

FORTH-83 is used considerably. Its SKIP and SCAN, which replace ENCLOSE, are an improvement. BLANKS is changed to BLANK—an example of many changes that are only changes, not improvements.

One serious mistake in FORTH-83 was dropping "state smart" words. Following is an example run on the 8051 FORTH system.

```
: SSWORD CR ." dot quote is a state smart word" ; ok
SSWORD
dot quote is a state smart wordok
CR ." dot quote is a state smart word"
dot quote is a state smart wordok
```

Because FORTH-83 dropped state smart words, you now have to use ." when compiling and .(when interpreting. Following is the definition of Forth Interest Group ." :

```
: ."            22 STATE @
                IF COMPILE (.") WORD HERE C@ 1+ ALLOT
                ELSE WORD HERE COUNT TYPE THEN   ; IMMEDIATE
```

Hex 22 is the quote. STATE is hex C0 if FORTH is compiling and zero if it is interpreting. Now there are two definitions. You can't give interpreted code a name and enclose the code in : and ; and have it work.

There is no documentation of FORTH-83 equivalent to Derick and Baker's *FORTH encyclopedia.* The documentation of FORTH-83 internals is inferior to Forth Interest Group FORTH.

FORTH-83 implementations are regarded as proprietary by many FORTH vendors. Source code is no longer forthcoming.

FORTH is designed to help you write applications code quickly. The merit of spending time converting from one dialect to another is questionable, since there are no apparent advantages and several major disadvantages.

An ANSII standards committee is apparently considering a standard version of FORTH. If this happens and the result is reasonable, then it may be worthwhile to spend time with a conversion.

Meanwhile, it probably takes a month or so, perhaps less, to convert the code in this book to some other dialect. This time could be spent writing applications code rather than playing with FORTH.

B. Porting Fig FORTH to Another Processor

If the other processor is an 8086 family microprocessor used as a microcontroller, such as the Intel 80C186/187, then porting the 8051 system takes about a week or so.

Here is what you should do to make a port of this code.

1. Modify the assembler given in this book to handle the target's instruction set in cross assembler format.
2. Write a cross disassembler by modifying the 8051's cross disassembler.
3. Make a file of all possible opcode/operand formats, and test the assembler and disassembler against these. See the list at the end of Appendix 6 for an example.

4. Modify the assembler into metaassembler by studying the examples in Appendices 16 and 17.
5. Determine how best to implement W, IP, SP, and RP on the target hardware. Do research into what others have done if an existing FORTH is available. Your cross disassembler helps. See Chapter 5.
6. Write the code words for the nucleus. Or see Chapter 5 for research techniques.
7. Metacompile a target image. Dump the image with the cross disassembler.
8. Build some hardware that includes the National 82C50 ACE.
9. Debug the code.

You can write simple 82C50 I/O routines that can be used to single step FORTH. Modify NEXT to send debugging information to your PC screen.

Code words of ENCLOSE and (FIND) are difficult to write because of their complexity and the number of cases that have to be debugged. U/ is complicated on an 8-bit processor but simple on a 16-bit processor with a hardware divide. The run time portion of DOES> is intricate. All the remaining routines are relatively simple. Look at the 8051 code words in Appendix 9. The 8051 is one of the more difficult machines on which to implement FORTH.

Experienced FORTH programmers take about a month to port an operating system to a new machine. This can be an exciting and enjoyable task.

Unlike many other operating systems, when FORTH comes up, it does so fast. The reason for this speed is that all of the high-level language definitions are, so to speak, free.

C. FORTH, Hardware, and Software

The C language is the current computer language in favor. C is not an operating system. Applications software of any complexity requires an operating system of some sort. If an operating system is not available, then the applications programmer reinvents, recodes, and debugs again many operating system functions.

High-level languages cannot replace assembler or microcode required for parts of application software.

FORTH is an operating system. It is a high-level language. It supports interactive program development in both assembler or microcode and high-level language. It is a software development environment. It is nearly the most memory efficient software technology known.

FORTH is transportable to most microprocessors and microcontrollers. It is a virtual operating system. Your knowledge about FORTH moves from system to system and accompanies you through time. Your FORTH knowledge and experience do not become obsolescent, but become more valuable with time.

FORTH is a medium in which to express your software thoughts. When applied to the right task, it is used to produce software quickly with little cost.

FORTH is so intriguing that some programmers focus only on its internal operation. FORTH's interface with hardware makes it one of the most useful software tools for hardware debugging.

FORTH should be studied by all programmers. It embodies all aspects of software but in a simple framework. Charles Moore's brilliance warrants the scrutiny provided only by the source code detailing it. His expertise helps you bring up carefully selected hardware/software applications at a fraction of the cost of other technologies.

Appendix 1

Source Listing of the 8086 Family FORTH Nucleus

FORTH source code for the 8086 family nucleus is included in this Appendix. This FORTH is called FORTH86 after the Intel 8086 family processors. It runs under PC/MS DOS on all members of the 8086 family. This includes the 80386.

A FORTH screen contains 1024 bytes. Screen numbers are given above each screen. Multiple blank lines are compressed into a single blank line. The program SCRTOASCII, printed in Chapter 3, running on the binary of this source code, produced this ASCII version of the screen file.

An ASCII listing of the binary of this program, called the FORTH nucleus, is given in Appendix 2. If you want to reassemble and recompile this program, then you need to get it into a FORTH screen file. You have two choices. Get a copy on diskette from a cooperating 8051 microcontroller hardware vendor or someone else. The second choice is to use your word processor in nondocument form to enter the code in this appendix into an ASCII file.

```
0
\ forth86                                          JFB 21:05 05/30/88
The target code in this file has been adapted from the Forth
Interest Group 8086 family code.  This code is public domain.
It is extended with assembler calls to PC-DOS/MS-DOS version 2
and above operating systems.  This operating system code was
produced with the NAUTILUS metacompiler using PC/ASSEMBLER
in cross assembler form.

NAUTILUS META-COMPILER:
  Jerry Boutelle, 542 Blackjack Lane, Santa Cruz, Ca. 95062
  408-462-9461
PC/ASSEMBLER:
  Computer System Documentation, pob 5478, Albuquerque,NM 87115
MS-DOS and BIOS calls and 4 file system:
  Sandia Labs, pob 5800 KAFB,NM 87185

1
\ load screen for cross compilation                JFB 19:16 06/04/88
DECIMAL       \ NCC V2
CROSS-COMPILE
2 LOAD

2
\ equates                                        \ JFB 15:11 01/05/89
HEX
0100 0 ORG/DB  FFFE   MEM-END
0400 EQU BPS         5C EQU DOSFCB    80 EQU DOSBUFF    DECIMAL
  01 EQU FIG-REL     05 EQU FIG-VER   89 EQU FIG-REV    HEX
  20 EQU ABL         0D EQU ACR       2E EQU ADOT
  07 EQU BELL        08 EQU BSIN      08 EQU BSOUT
  10 EQU DLE         0A EQU LF        0C EQU FFEED
  02 EQU NSCR      0400 EQU KBBUF     02 EQU DBH
  02 EQU DBT         40 EQU US         0A0 EQU RTS
DBH KBBUF DBT + +       EQU HDBT
NSCR 400 * KBBUF /      EQU NBUF
EM HDBT NBUF * -        EQU BUF1
BUF1 US -               EQU INIT-R0
INIT-R0 RTS -           EQU INIT-S0 -->

3
\ initialization                                 \      15:00 01/27/86
HEX
ASSEMBLER RESET
NOP  NOP  ECLD REL8 JMP \ 00 +origin   jump to cold
NOP  NOP  EWRM REL8 JMP \ 04 +origin   jump to warm

FORTH

FIG-REL      C, \ 08 +origin  release
FIG-VER      C, \ 09 +origin  version
FIG-REV      C, \ 0A +origin  revision
0E           C, \ 0B +origin  implementation attributes
HERE LABEL
INIT-FORTH 0  , \ 0C +origin  nfa of topmost forth word
BSIN          , \ 0E +origin  backspace character received
-->
4
\ initialization                                 \      15:00 01/27/86
INIT-R0           ,  \ 10 +origin  initial user area pointer
INIT-S0           ,  \ 12 +origin  initial parameter stack pointer
INIT-R0           ,  \ 14 +origin  initial return stack pointer
INIT-S0           ,  \ 16 +origin  initial tib pointer
```

```
01F             ,  \ 18 +origin  width of nfa
0               ,  \ 1A +origin  error warning mode
HERE LABEL
INIT-FENCE    0 ,  \ 1C +origin  nfa dictionary forgetting limit
HERE LABEL
INIT-DP       0 ,  \ 1E +origin  initial dictionary pointer
HERE LABEL
INIT-VOC-LINK 0 ,  \ 20 +origin  initial vocabulary link
BASE-36 80XXX. , , \ 22 +origin  base 36 cpu number
HERE LABEL
UP       INIT-R0 , --> \ storage for up
5
\ cold start warm start                          JFB 22:05 03/05/88
HEX
ASSEMBLER RESET
HERE LABEL ECLD
                AX CS MOV  SS AX MOV  ES AX MOV  DS AX MOV
                SI # CLD1 ABSOLUTE MOV  SP 0112 MOV  BP 0114 MOV
                CLD  NEXT REL8 JMP

HERE LABEL CLD1 ] COLD [
ASSEMBLER RESET
HERE LABEL EWRM
                SI # WRM1 ABSOLUTE MOV  NEXT REL8 JMP

HERE LABEL WRM1 ] WARM [ -->

6
\ ctrl-break control                             \     15:00 01/27/86
ASSEMBLER RESET
HERE LABEL BRKEY
                AX CS MOV DS AX MOV  ES AX MOV  SS AX MOV
                AL # 20 MOV  20  AL OUT  STI
                SP 0112 MOV  BP 0114 MOV  EWRM JMP

ASSEMBLER RESET
HERE LABEL 0DIV
                AX CS MOV  SS AX MOV  ES AX MOV  DS AX MOV
                SI # ZDIV ABSOLUTE MOV
                SP 0112 MOV  BP 0114 MOV
                CLD  NEXT REL8 JMP
HERE LABEL ZDIV ] 0DIVMESS [ -->

7
\ inner interpreter                              \     15:00 01/27/86
ASSEMBLER RESET

HERE LABEL DPUSH        DX PUSH
HERE LABEL APUSH        AX PUSH
HERE LABEL NEXT         WORD LODS  BX AX MOV
HERE LABEL NEXT1        [BX] JMP
-->

8
\ enclose                                        \     09:59 03/25/86
FORTH   DEFINITIONS
HEX -->
CODE ENCLOSE    AX POP BX POP  BX PUSH  AH # 0 MOV
                DX # -1 MOV  BX DEC
           1 $: BX INC  DX INC  AL [BX] CMP  1 $ JZ
                DX PUSH  AH [BX] CMP  2 $ JNZ
                AX DX MOV  DX INC  DPUSH JMP
      3 $: 2 $: BX INC  DX INC  AL [BX] CMP  4 $ JZ
                AH [BX] CMP  3 $ JNZ
```

```
                AX DX MOV   DPUSH JMP
           4 $: AX DX MOV   AX INC   DPUSH JMP   END-CODE
-->

9
\ enclose                                           07:56 06/27/86
HEX
CODE ENCLOSE    AX DS MOV                 \ set up es:di addressing
                ES AX MOV                 \ for scas
                AX POP                    \ delimiter
                DI POP                    \ start address of string
                DI PUSH                   \ start address of string
                AH AH SUB                 \ null in ah
                CX # -1 MOV               \ maximum repeat count
                REPE BYTE SCAS            \ look for 1st nondelimiter
                DX # -2 MOV               \ start to calculate offset
                DX CX SUB                 \ offset to 1st nondelimite
                DX PUSH                   \ offset of string start
                AH -1 [DI] CMP            \ is it a null?
                2 $ JNZ                   \ jump if it is not
-->
10
\ enclose                                      \    09:59 03/25/86

                AX DX MOV        \ offset of unexamined character
                AX INC AX PUSH   \ push offset of null
                DX PUSH
                NEXT,
          2 $:  SI DI XCHG       \ save forth ip
                BX AX MOV        \ null and delimiter to bx
          4 $:  BYTE LODS        \ character to examine
                AL BL CMP        \ is it a delimiter?
                3 $ JZ           \ jump if it is
                AL BH CMP        \ is it a null?
                4 $ LOOPNZ       \ jump if it is not
-->

11
\ enclose                                      \    09:59 03/25/86

                DX # -2 MOV
                DX CX SUB     \ offset to null
                DX PUSH
                DX PUSH
                SI DI XCHG    \ restore forth ip
                NEXT,
          3 $:  DX # -1 MOV
                DX CX SUB     \ offset to delimiter
                DX PUSH
                DX INC        \ offset of unexamined charater
                DX PUSH
                SI DI XCHG    \ restore forth ip
                NEXT,
                END-CODE -->
12
\ digit toggle                                  JFB 14:49 05/28/88
HEX
CODE DIGIT      DX POP  AX POP  AL # 30 SUB  2 $ JB
                AL # 09 CMP 1 $ JBE
                AL # 07 SUB  AL # 0A CMP 2 $ JB
          1 $:  AL DL CMP  2 $ JAE  DX DX SUB
                DL AL MOV  AL # 1 MOV  DPUSH JMP
          2 $:  AX AX SUB  APUSH JMP  END-CODE
```

```
CODE TOGGLE      AX POP  BX POP  [BX] AL XOR
                 NEXT JMP  END-CODE
-->

13
\ find                                             \      09:36 03/18/86
HEX -->
CODE (FIND)      AX DS MOV  ES AX MOV  BX POP  CX POP
          1 $:   DI CX MOV  AL [BX] MOV  DL AL MOV
                 AL [DI] XOR  AL # 03F AND  5 $ JNZ
          2 $:   BX INC  DI INC  AL [BX] MOV AL [DI] XOR
                 AL AL ADD  5 $ JNZ  2 $ JNB
                 BX # 5 ADD  BX PUSH  AX # 1 MOV
                 DH DH SUB DPUSH JMP
          5 $:   BX INC  6 $ JB  AL [BX] MOV
                 AL AL ADD  5 $ JMP
          6 $:   BX [BX] MOV  BX BX OR  1 $ JNZ
                 AX # 0 MOV  APUSH JMP  END-CODE -->
\ This is the original (find) definition.  The (find) following
\ this screen speeds compilation about 50%.

14
\ find                                             \      09:36 03/18/86
HEX
CODE (FIND)      AX DS MOV   \ set es=ds for di addressing
                 ES AX MOV   \
                 AX SI MOV   \ forth ip to ax
                 SI POP      \ nfa pointer
                 BX POP      \ save string count address
                 AX PUSH     \ save forth ip
         20 $:   DL [SI] MOV \ save nfa count
                 DI BX MOV   \ di points to string count
-->
\ 8086 family fast (find).  This (find) combined with changing
\ the definition of -find, more than doubles compilation and
\ interpretation speed over the original definitions.

15
\ find                                             \      09:36 03/18/86

                 BYTE LODS       \ nfa count byte to al
                 AL # 3F AND     \ leave only smudge and count
                 BYTE SCAS       \ compare to string count
                 1 $ JNZ         \ <> jump
                 AX # 1F AND     \ leave count byte in ax
                 AX DEC          \ only search n-1 bytes
                 CX AX MOV       \ cx is the scan count
                 2 $ JCXZ        \ jump if count is zero
                 REPE BYTE CMPS  \ are the first n-1 bytes =
                 2 $ JZ          \ jump =
                 SI CX ADD       \ <>, then point si to lfa
                 SI INC          \ jump over last byte
                 30 $ JMP        \ report <>
-->
16
\ find                                             \      09:36 03/18/86

          2 $:   BYTE LODS       \ last byte
                 AL # 7F AND     \ nfa byte - 80
                 BYTE SCAS       \ is it = last string byte?
                 4 $ JZ          \ jump if =
                 30 $ JMP        \ report <>
          4 $:   AX POP          \ forth ip to ax & report =
                 SI # 4 ADD      \ point at pfa
```

```
                  SI PUSH          \ return pfa
                  SI AX MOV        \ forth ip to si
                  DX # 00FF AND    \ mask off first character
                  DX PUSH          \ return nfa count byte
                  AX # 01 MOV      \ set true flag
                  AX PUSH          \ return true flag
                  NEXT, -->
17
\ find                                         \      09:36 03/18/86

            1 $:  AX # 1F AND \ leave count
                  SI AX ADD   \ move to lfa & report <>
           30 $:  SI [SI] MOV \ move from lfa to nfa
                  SI # 0 CMP  \ compare lfa to zero
                  20 $ JNE    \ jump if lfa <> 0, try again
                  SI POP      \ restore forth ip
                  AX AX SUB   \ false flag
                  AX PUSH     \ return false flag
                  NEXT, END-CODE -->

18
\ + - u/ u* <> * m*                            \      15:00 01/27/86

CODE +      AX POP  BX POP  AX BX ADD  APUSH JMP  END-CODE
CODE -      DX POP  AX POP  AX DX SUB  APUSH JMP  END-CODE
CODE U/     BX POP  DX POP  AX POP  DX BX CMP  1 $ JNB
            BX DIV DPUSH JMP  1 $:
            AX # -1 MOV  DX AX MOV  DPUSH JMP  END-CODE
CODE U*     AX POP  BX POP  BX MUL  AX DX XCHG  DPUSH JMP
            END-CODE
CODE <>     AX POP  BX POP  AX BX CMP  AX # 0 MOV  1 $ JZ
            AX INC  1 $: APUSH JMP  END-CODE
CODE *      AX POP  BX POP  BX IMUL
            APUSH JMP  END-CODE
CODE M*     AX POP  BX POP  BX IMUL  AX DX XCHG
            DPUSH JMP END-CODE
-->
19
\ 1+ 2+ 1- 2- 2* 2/ D2/ 1 2 3 -1 -2            \      13:07 03/06/86
CODE 1+   AX POP  AX INC            APUSH JMP  END-CODE
CODE 2+   AX POP  AX INC  AX INC    APUSH JMP  END-CODE
CODE 1-   AX POP  AX DEC            APUSH JMP  END-CODE
CODE 2-   AX POP  AX DEC  AX DEC    APUSH JMP  END-CODE
CODE 2*   AX POP  AX 1 SAL          APUSH JMP  END-CODE
CODE 2/   AX POP  AX 1 SAR          APUSH JMP  END-CODE
CODE D2/  DX POP  AX POP  DX 1 SAR  AX 1 RCR  AX PUSH
          DX PUSH  NEXT JMP  END-CODE
CODE 0    AX AX SUB  APUSH JMP  END-CODE
CODE 1    AX #  1 MOV  APUSH JMP  END-CODE
CODE 2    AX #  2 MOV  APUSH JMP  END-CODE
CODE 3    AX #  3 MOV  APUSH JMP  END-CODE
CODE -1   AX # -1 MOV  APUSH JMP  END-CODE
CODE -2   AX # -2 MOV  APUSH JMP  END-CODE
CODE -3   AX # -3 MOV  APUSH JMP  END-CODE -->
20
\ d+ d- s->d and or xor not                    \      15:01 01/27/86

CODE D+     AX POP  DX POP  BX POP  CX POP  DX CX ADD
            AX BX ADC  DPUSH JMP  END-CODE
CODE D-     BX POP  CX POP  AX POP  DX POP  DX CX SUB
            AX BX SBB  DPUSH JMP  END-CODE
CODE S->D   AX POP  CWD  AX PUSH
            DX PUSH  NEXT JMP END-CODE
CODE AND    AX POP  BX POP  AX BX AND
```

```
                APUSH JMP END-CODE
CODE OR         AX POP  BX POP  AX BX OR
                APUSH JMP  END-CODE
CODE XOR        AX POP  BX POP  AX BX XOR
                APUSH JMP  END-CODE
CODE NOT        AX POP  AX NOT
                APUSH JMP  END-CODE -->
21
\ = < >  0< 0= 0> U<                              \      15:01 01/27/86

CODE =      AX POP   BX POP   AX BX CMP   AX # 1 MOV   1 $ JZ
            AX DEC   1 $:   APUSH JMP   END-CODE
CODE <      BX POP   AX POP   AX BX SUB   AX # 1 MOV   1 $ JL
            AX DEC   1 $: APUSH JMP   END-CODE
CODE >      AX POP   BX POP   AX BX SUB   AX # 1 MOV   1 $ JL
            AX DEC   1 $:   APUSH JMP   END-CODE
CODE 0<     AX POP   AX AX OR   AX # 1 MOV   1 $ JS
            AX DEC   1 $:   APUSH JMP   END-CODE
CODE 0>     AX POP   AX AX OR   AX # 1 MOV   1 $ JG
            AX DEC   1 $:   APUSH JMP   END-CODE
CODE 0=     AX POP   AX AX OR   AX # 1 MOV   1 $ JZ
            AX DEC   1 $:   APUSH JMP   END-CODE
CODE U<     AX POP   DX POP   DX AX SUB   AX # 1 MOV   1 $ JB
            AX DEC   1 $:   APUSH JMP   END-CODE -->
22
\ U> D< D> D=                                     \      15:01 01/27/86

CODE U>           DX POP   AX POP   DX AX SUB   AX # 1 MOV 1 $ JB
                  AX DEC   1 $:   APUSH JMP   END-CODE
CODE D<           BX POP   CX POP   AX POP   DX POP   DX CX SUB
                  AX BX SBB   AX # 1 MOV 1 $ JL
                  AX DEC   1 $:   APUSH JMP   END-CODE
CODE D>           AX POP   DX POP   BX POP   CX POP   DX CX SUB
                  AX BX SBB   AX # 1 MOV 1 $ JL
                  AX DEC   1 $:   APUSH JMP   END-CODE
CODE D=           BX POP   CX POP   AX POP   DX POP   DX CX CMP
                  1 $ JNZ   AX BX CMP   2 $ JNZ
                  AX # 1 MOV   APUSH JMP
                  1 $: 2 $:    AX AX XOR   APUSH JMP   END-CODE
-->

23
\ sp@ sp! rp@ >r r> i j r execute                 \      15:01 01/27/86

CODE SP@     AX SP MOV   APUSH JMP   END-CODE
CODE SP!     BX UP MOV   SP 6 [BX] MOV   NEXT JMP   END-CODE
CODE RP!     BX UP MOV   BP 8 [BX] MOV   NEXT JMP   END-CODE
CODE RP@     AX BP MOV   APUSH JMP   END-CODE
CODE >R      BX POP   BP DEC BP DEC   [BP] BX MOV
             NEXT JMP END-CODE
CODE R>      AX [BP] MOV   BP INC   BP INC APUSH JMP   END-CODE
CODE I       AX [BP] MOV   APUSH JMP   END-CODE
CODE J       AX 4 [BP] MOV   APUSH JMP   END-CODE
CODE R       AX [BP] MOV   APUSH JMP   END-CODE
CODE EXECUTE    BX POP   NEXT1 JMP   END-CODE
-->

24
\ swap over drop dup -dup rot 2dup 2drop    \      15:01 01/27/86
CODE SWAP    DX POP AX POP DPUSH JMP   END-CODE
CODE OVER    BX SP MOV SS: 2 [BX] PUSH NEXT JMP   END-CODE
CODE DROP    AX POP   NEXT JMP   END-CODE
CODE DUP     BX SP MOV   SS: [BX] PUSH   NEXT JMP   END-CODE
CODE -DUP    AX POP   AX AX OR    AX PUSH    1 $ JZ
```

```
            AX PUSH  1 $:  NEXT JMP  END-CODE
CODE ROT    DX POP  BX POP  AX POP  BX PUSH
            DPUSH JMP  END-CODE
CODE 2DUP   AX POP  DX POP  DX PUSH  AX PUSH
            DPUSH JMP  END-CODE
CODE 2DROP  AX POP  AX POP  NEXT JMP  END-CODE
CODE PICK   BX POP  BX DEC  BX BX ADD  BX SP ADD
            SS: [BX] PUSH  NEXT JMP  END-CODE
CODE DEPTH  BX UP MOV  AX 6 [BX] MOV  AX SP SUB
            AX 1 SAR  APUSH JMP  END-CODE -->
25
\ ! @ c! c@ 2@ 2! +! ><                    \     15:01 01/27/86

CODE @      BX POP  AX [BX] MOV  APUSH JMP END-CODE
CODE !      BX POP  AX POP  [BX] AX MOV  NEXT JMP END-CODE
CODE 2!     BX POP  AX POP  [BX] AX MOV  AX POP
            2 [BX] AX MOV  NEXT JMP END-CODE
CODE 2@     BX POP  AX [BX] MOV  DX 2 [BX] MOV
            DPUSH JMP END-CODE
CODE C@     BX POP  AL [BX] MOV  AH # 0 MOV  APUSH JMP
            END-CODE
CODE C!     BX POP  AX POP  [BX] AL MOV  NEXT JMP END-CODE
CODE +!     BX POP  AX POP  [BX] AX ADD  NEXT JMP  END-CODE
CODE ><     AX POP  AH AL XCHG  AX PUSH  NEXT JMP END-CODE
-->

26
\ minus dminus +- d+- abs dabs             \     15:01 01/27/86

CODE MINUS   HERE LABEL MINUS1
             AX POP AX NEG APUSH JMP  END-CODE
CODE DMINUS  HERE LABEL DMINUS1
             BX POP  CX POP  BX NOT  CX NOT  CX # 1 ADD
             BX # 0 ADC  CX PUSH  BX PUSH  NEXT JMP  END-CODE
CODE +-      AX POP  AX AX OR  MINUS1 JS  NEXT JMP  END-CODE
CODE D+-     AX POP  AX AX OR  DMINUS1 JS  NEXT JMP  END-CODE
CODE ABS     AX POP  AX AX OR  1 $ JNS  AX NEG 1 $:
             AX PUSH  NEXT JMP  END-CODE
CODE DABS    AX POP  AX PUSH  AX AX OR  DMINUS1 JS
             NEXT JMP  END-CODE
-->

27
\ max min fill erase blanks                \     15:01 01/27/86

CODE MAX        AX POP  BX POP  CX AX MOV  AX BX SUB 1 $ JL
                CX PUSH  NEXT JMP  1 $:
                BX PUSH  NEXT JMP  END-CODE

CODE MIN        AX POP  BX POP  CX AX MOV  AX BX SUB 1 $ JL
                BX PUSH  NEXT JMP  1 $:
                CX PUSH  NEXT JMP  END-CODE

CODE FILL       AX POP  HERE LABEL FILL1
                CX POP  DI POP  BX DS MOV  ES BX MOV
                CLD  REP BYTE STOS  NEXT JMP  END-CODE
CODE ERASE      AX # 0 MOV  FILL1 JMP  END-CODE
CODE BLANKS     AX # 0020 MOV  FILL1 JMP  END-CODE
-->
28
\ cmove traverse cmove>                    \     15:01 01/27/86

CODE CMOVE      CLD  BX SI MOV  CX POP  DI POP  SI POP
                CX CX OR  CMOVE1 REL8 JZ  AX DS MOV  ES AX MOV
```

```
                REP BYTE MOVS
     HERE LABEL CMOVE1  SI BX MOV NEXT JMP END-CODE

CODE CMOVE>     BX SI MOV  CX POP  DI POP  SI POP
                CX CX OR  CMOVE1 JZ  AX CX MOV  AX DEC
                DI AX ADD  SI AX ADD  AX DS MOV  ES AX MOV
                STD  REP  BYTE  MOVS  CLD  SI BX MOV  NEXT JMP
                END-CODE

CODE TRAVERSE   CX POP  BX POP
                1 $:  BX CX ADD  AL [BX] MOV  AL AL OR  1 $ JNS
                BX PUSH  NEXT JMP  END-CODE -->
29
\ p@ p! pc@ pc! lit do ;s leave             \     15:01 01/27/86

CODE P@     DX POP  AX DX IN  APUSH JMP  END-CODE
CODE PC@    DX POP  AL DX IN  AH # 0 MOV  APUSH JMP  END-CODE
CODE P!     DX POP  AX POP  DX AX OUT  NEXT JMP  END-CODE
CODE PC!    DX POP  AX POP  DX AL OUT  NEXT JMP  END-CODE
CODE LIT    WORD LODS APUSH JMP  END-CODE

CODE (DO)     DX POP  AX POP  BP SP XCHG  AX PUSH  DX PUSH
              BP SP XCHG  NEXT JMP  END-CODE
CODE ;S       SI [BP] MOV  BP INC  BP INC  NEXT JMP  END-CODE
CODE LEAVE    AX [BP] MOV  2 [BP] AX MOV  NEXT JMP  END-CODE
-->

30
\ branch (loop (+loop                       \     15:01 01/27/86

CODE BRANCH   HERE LABEL BRAN1
              SI [SI] ADD  NEXT JMP  END-CODE
CODE 0BRANCH  AX POP  AX AX OR  BRAN1 JZ
              SI INC  SI INC  NEXT JMP  END-CODE
CODE (LOOP)   \ increment value ---
              BX # 1 MOV  [BP] BX ADD  AX [BP] MOV
              AX 2 [BP] SUB  AX BX XOR  HERE LABEL (LOOP)'
              BRAN1 JS  BP # 4 ADD  SI INC  SI INC
              NEXT JMP  END-CODE
CODE (+LOOP)  BX POP  [BP] BX ADD  AX [BP] MOV  DX 2 [BP] MOV
              BX BX TEST  (+LOOP)' REL8 JNS  AX DX XCHG
              HERE LABEL (+LOOP)'  AX DX SUB
              (LOOP)' JMP  END-CODE -->

31
\ 21INT2                                   JFB 08:32 03/05/88

CODE 21INT5 ( ds \ dx \ cx \ bx \ ax - ax \ dx \ truth flag )
            AX CS MOV  ES AX MOV
            AX POP  BX POP  CX POP  DX POP  DS POP  21 INT
            AX PUSH  DX PUSH  AX CS MOV  DS AX MOV  1 $ JB
            AX AX XOR  APUSH JMP
            1 $: AX # 1 MOV  APUSH JMP  END-CODE
  -->

32
\ constant user :                           \     14:01 03/21/86

: CONSTANT      CREATE SMUDGE ,
                ;CODE BX INC  BX INC   AX [BX] MOV
                APUSH JMP  END-CODE

: USER          CONSTANT
                ;CODE  BX INC  BX INC   BL [BX] MOV
```

```
                BH BH SUB  DI UP MOV  AX [BX+DI] LEA
                APUSH JMP  END-CODE

: :             ?EXEC !CSP CURRENT @ CONTEXT ! CREATE
                [COMPILE] ]
                ;CODE BX INC BX INC BP DEC BP DEC [BP] SI MOV
                SI BX MOV  NEXT JMP  END-CODE -->

33
\ does> variable vocabulary                    JFB 16:52 06/04/88

: DOES>         R> LATEST PFA !
                ;CODE BP SP XCHG  SI PUSH
                BP SP XCHG  BX INC  BX INC  SI [BX] MOV
                BX INC  BX INC  BX PUSH  NEXT JMP END-CODE

: VARIABLE      CONSTANT
                ;CODE  BX INC BX INC BX PUSH NEXT JMP END-CODE

: VOCABULARY    <BUILDS  A081 , CURRENT @ CFA ,
                HERE VOC-LINK @ , VOC-LINK !
                DOES> 2+ CONTEXT ! ;

VOCABULARY FORTH IMMEDIATE
-->
34
\ user variables  errors messages              plp 12:43 06/07/86

06 USER S0          08 USER R0          0A USER TIB
0C USER WIDTH       0E USER WARNING     10 USER FENCE
12 USER DP          14 USER VOC-LINK    16 USER BLK
18 USER IN          1A USER OUT         1C USER SCR
20 USER CONTEXT     22 USER CURRENT     24 USER STATE
26 USER BASE        28 USER DPL         2A USER FLD
2C USER CSP         2E USER R#          30 USER HLD

6004 CONSTANT SYSERR
600C CONSTANT SYSMESS
-->

35
\ +origin here allot , c, nfa lfa cfa          JFB 18:55 06/04/88

: +ORIGIN       ORIGIN + ;
: HERE          DP @ ;
: ALLOT         DP +! ;
: ,             HERE ! 2 ALLOT ;
: C,            HERE C! 1 ALLOT ;
: NFA           5 - -1 TRAVERSE ;
: LFA           4 - ;
: CFA           2- ;
: PFA           1 TRAVERSE 5 + ;

: DECIMAL       0A BASE ! ;
: HEX           10 BASE ! ;
-->

36
\  ongosub endgosub                            \     15:02 01/27/86

( 0, 1, 2, ..., n <- n is else case --- )
: ONGOSUB       ?COMP COMPILE 2* COMPILE LIT HERE 0 ,
                COMPILE 2DUP COMPILE OVER COMPILE 0<
                COMPILE 0BRANCH HERE 0 , COMPILE SWAP
```

```
                HERE OVER - SWAP ! COMPILE >
                COMPILE 0BRANCH HERE 0 , COMPILE SWAP
                HERE OVER - SWAP ! COMPILE DROP
                COMPILE LIT HERE 0 , COMPILE + COMPILE @
                COMPILE EXECUTE COMPILE BRANCH HERE 0 , SWAP
                HERE SWAP ! HERE 6 ; IMMEDIATE

: ENDGOSUB      6 ?PAIRS HERE SWAP -  DUP 2 <
                13 ?ERROR DUP 2+ ROT ! 2- SWAP ! ; IMMEDIATE
-->
37
\ lpflag setcursor cursor -cursor bwcursor  \ JFB 08:16 01/06/89
HEX
0 VARIABLE LPFLAG   \ 0=console 1=printer
\ start line\end line ---
CODE SETCURSOR  AX POP  CL AL MOV  AX POP  CH AL MOV  AH # 1 MOV
                10 INT  NEXT JMP END-CODE
: BWCURSOR      0C 0D SETCURSOR ;
: COLORCURSOR   06 07 SETCURSOR ;
: (CURSOR) ?MODE ONGOSUB BWCURSOR     COLORCURSOR  COLORCURSOR
                         COLORCURSOR  COLORCURSOR  COLORCURSOR
                         COLORCURSOR  BWCURSOR     COLORCURSOR
                      ENDGOSUB 2DROP ;
: CURSOR (CURSOR) ;
: (-CURSOR)       20 20 SETCURSOR ;
: -CURSOR (-CURSOR) ;
-->
38
\ video attributes                              \     15:30 03/17/86
HEX
7 VARIABLE VIDEO    \ video attribute
\ ---
CODE BLINK      AL VIDEO MOV  AL # 80 OR
HERE LABEL !VIDEO  VIDEO AL MOV  NEXT JMP  END-CODE
CODE -BLINK     AL VIDEO MOV  AL # 7F AND !VIDEO JMP  END-CODE
CODE INTENSITY  AL VIDEO MOV  AL # 08 OR  !VIDEO JMP  END-CODE
CODE -INTENSITY AL VIDEO MOV  AL # F7 AND !VIDEO JMP  END-CODE
CODE UNDERLINE  AL VIDEO MOV  AL # 88 AND
                AL # 01 OR                !VIDEO JMP  END-CODE
CODE -UNDERLINE AL VIDEO MOV  AL # 07 OR  !VIDEO JMP  END-CODE
-->

39
\ color routines and constants                  \     15:21 03/17/86

CODE REVERSE    AL VIDEO MOV  AL # F8 AND  AL # 70 OR
                !VIDEO JMP  END-CODE
CODE -REVERSE   AL VIDEO MOV  AL # 8F AND  AL # 07 OR
                !VIDEO JMP  END-CODE
\ ---
CODE BW80       AX # 02 MOV  HERE LABEL SETVIDEO
                             SI PUSH  BP PUSH  10 INT
                BP POP  SI POP  NEXT JMP  END-CODE
CODE CO80       AX # 03 MOV  SETVIDEO JMP  END-CODE
CODE BW40       AX AX SUB    SETVIDEO JMP  END-CODE
CODE CO40       AX # 01 MOV  SETVIDEO JMP  END-CODE
CODE CO320      AX # 04 MOV  SETVIDEO JMP  END-CODE
CODE BW320      AX # 05 MOV  SETVIDEO JMP  END-CODE
CODE BW640      AX # 06 MOV  SETVIDEO JMP  END-CODE -->
40
\ color routines and constants                  \     15:19 03/17/86
\ --- active display page\# char cols on screen\video mode
CODE ?MODE      AH # 0F MOV  SI PUSH  BP PUSH  10 INT
                BP POP  SI POP  BL BH MOV  BH BH SUB  BX PUSH
```

```
                BL AH MOV  BX PUSH  BL AL MOV  BX PUSH
                NEXT JMP  END-CODE
\ ---
0 CONSTANT BLACK                8 CONSTANT GRAY
1 CONSTANT BLUE                 9 CONSTANT LIGHTBLUE
2 CONSTANT GREEN               0A CONSTANT LIGHTGREEN
3 CONSTANT CYAN                0B CONSTANT LIGHTCYAN
4 CONSTANT RED                 0C CONSTANT LIGHTRED
5 CONSTANT MAGENTA             0D CONSTANT LIGHTMAGENTA
6 CONSTANT BROWN               0E CONSTANT YELLOW
7 CONSTANT LIGHTGRAY           0F CONSTANT WHITE
-->
41
\ color routines and constants                JFB 17:42 05/07/88
HEX
\ color code between 0 and 7 ---
CODE (BORDER)    BX POP  BL # 07 AND  BH BH SUB  AH # 0B MOV
                SI PUSH  BP PUSH  10 INT
                BP POP  SI POP  NEXT JMP  END-CODE
: BORDER (BORDER) ;

\ color code between 0 and 7 ---
CODE BACKGROUND AX POP  AL # 07 AND  CL # 04 MOV  AL CL SHL
                BL VIDEO MOV  BL # 8F AND  AL BL OR
                VIDEO AL MOV  NEXT JMP  END-CODE
\ color code between 0 and f ---
CODE FOREGROUND AX POP  AL # F AND  BL VIDEO MOV  BL # F0 AND
                AL BL OR  VIDEO AL MOV  NEXT JMP  END-CODE
-->
42
\ print a character                               09:57 07/14/86
ASSEMBLER RESET BEGIN$
  5 $:  DL AL MOV  AX # 0600 MOV
        21 INT  RET \ ms-dos handles bell
\ character ---
HERE LABEL PCA                  \ print character and attribute
        AL # 07 CMP  5 $ JE     \ let ms-dos a bell
        AX PUSH
        BH BH SUB  AH # 3 MOV  10 INT     \ get cursor position
        AX POP
        AL # 08 CMP  1 $ JNE       \ backspace
          DX # 0 CMP 4 $ JE        \ cursor home?
            DX DEC                 \ back cursor up
            DL # FF CMP 4 $ JNE    \ is cursor at bol?
            DL # 4F MOV            \ put it at eol
  4 $: 6 $ JMP -->
43
\ print a character                               09:52 07/14/86

1 $:    AL # 0A CMP  2 $ JNE              \ line feed
        DL # 50 MOV  6 $ JMP
2 $:    AL # 0D CMP  3 $ JNE              \ carriage return
        DL DL SUB  6 $ JMP

3 $:    BL VIDEO MOV
        CX # 1 MOV  AH # 9 MOV  10 INT  \ write char/attribute
        BH BH SUB AH # 3 MOV  10 INT    \ get cursor position
        DL INC                          \ advance cursor
-->

44
\ print a character                               09:58 07/14/86

  6 $:  DL # 4F CMP U>                       \ line end?
```

```
        IF DL DL SUB  DH INC  DH # 18 CMP U> \ page end?
          IF
            AX # 601 MOV  CX # 0 MOV
            DX # 184F MOV BH VIDEO MOV  10 INT \ scroll up
            DX # 1800 MOV                      \ set cursor
          THEN
        THEN  BH BH SUB  AH # 2 MOV  10 INT     \ save cursor
        RET                                     \ position
END$
FORTH
-->

45
\ (type type                                       09:53 07/14/86
CODE (TYPE) \ address\count ---
                CX POP  DX POP  CX>0
                IF  AX LPFLAG MOV  AX # 0 CMP  =
                  IF    BX # 1 MOV            \ console output
                  ELSE  BX # 4 MOV  2 $ JMP   \ printer
                  THEN  SI PUSH   BP PUSH   SI DX MOV
          1 $:      BYTE LODS  CX PUSH  PCA CALL  CX POP
                    1 $ LOOP  BP POP  SI POP  \ bdos write
                THEN  NEXT JMP

          2 $:  AX # 4000 MOV  21 INT  NEXT JMP  END-CODE
: TYPE \ address\count ---
                DUP OUT +! (TYPE) ;
-->

46
\ count type <# ("  (>"  pad #> hold sign   \     08:10 02/18/86

: COUNT         DUP 1+ SWAP C@ ;
\  : TYPE          -DUP IF OVER + SWAP DO I C@ EMIT LOOP
\                  ELSE DROP THEN ;
: (")           R DUP C@ 1+ R> + >R ;
: (.")          R COUNT DUP 1+ R> + >R TYPE ;
: PAD           HERE 44 + ;
: #>            DROP DROP HLD @ PAD OVER - ;
: HOLD          -1 HLD +! HLD @ C! ;
: SIGN          ROT 0< IF 2D HOLD THEN ;
: #             BASE @ M/MOD ROT 9 OVER < IF 7 + THEN
                30 + HOLD ;
: #S            BEGIN # 2DUP OR 0= UNTIL ;
: <#            PAD HLD ! ;
-->
47
\ .cpu d.r d. . u. .r ? pckey               \     15:01 01/27/86

: .CPU          BASE @ 24 BASE ! 22 +ORIGIN 2@ D. BASE ! ;
: D.R           >R SWAP OVER DABS <# #S SIGN #> R>
                OVER - SPACES TYPE ;
: D.            0 D.R SPACE ;
: .             S->D D. ;
: U.            0 D. ;
: .R            >R S->D R> D.R ;
: ?             @ . ;
-->

48
\ space -trailing (line .line  id. 21int    JFB 22:44 05/07/88

: SPACE         BL EMIT ;
: SPACES        0 MAX -DUP IF 0 DO SPACE LOOP THEN ;
```

```
: -TRAILING     DUP 0 DO OVER OVER + 1- C@ BL -
                IF LEAVE ELSE 1- THEN LOOP ;
: (LINE)        >R 40 B/BUF */MOD R> B/SCR *  + BLOCK + 40 ;
: .LINE         (LINE) -TRAILING TYPE ;
: ID.           DUP 1+ SWAP C@ 01F AND OVER + SWAP DO
                I C@ 07F AND EMIT LOOP SPACE ;

CODE 21INT \ ax \ dx  - ax \ dx
                 DX POP  AX POP  21 INT  AX PUSH  BX PUSH
                 NEXT JMP  END-CODE
-->

49
\ interface variables                          \     15:01 01/27/86
HEX
NBUF            CONSTANT #BUFF
KBBUF BPS /     CONSTANT SEC/BLK
400 KBBUF /     CONSTANT B/SCR
BUF1            CONSTANT FIRST
EM              CONSTANT LIMIT
FIRST           VARIABLE USE
FIRST           VARIABLE PREV
0               VARIABLE REC
0               VARIABLE DISK-ERROR
KBBUF           CONSTANT B/BUF
20              CONSTANT BL
-->

50
\ scrollu scrolld                              \     15:01 01/27/86
HERE LABEL SCROLLE ASSEMBLER RESET
        SI PUSH  BP PUSH  10 INT  BP POP  SI POP
        NEXT JMP
CODE SCROLLU  \ # lines to scroll\xu\yu\xl\yl ---
        BH VIDEO MOV  AX POP  DH AL MOV  AX POP  DL AL MOV
        AX POP  CH AL MOV  AX POP  CL AL MOV  AX POP
        AH # 6 MOV  SCROLLE JMP  END-CODE
CODE SCROLLD  \ # lines to scroll\xu\yu\xl\yl ---
        BH VIDEO MOV  AX POP  DH AL MOV  AX POP  DL AL MOV
        AX POP  CH AL MOV  AX POP  CL AL MOV  AX POP
        AH # 7 MOV  SCROLLE JMP  END-CODE
-->
\ specifying 0 for the number of line to scroll up or down
\ clears the window specifiled by the x,y coordinates to the
\ attribute contained in the variable VIDEO
51
\ gotoxy cls (cls cls                          JFB 12:44 05/07/88
HEX
CODE (GOTOXY) \ x coordinate\y coordinate ---
        DX POP  DH DL MOV  AX POP  DL AL MOV
        AX # 200 MOV  BX # 0 MOV
        SI PUSH  BP PUSH  10 INT
        BP POP  SI POP  NEXT JMP  END-CODE
: GOTOXY (GOTOXY) ;

CODE (CLS) \ ---
        AX # 600 MOV  BH VIDEO MOV
        DX # 184F MOV  CX CX SUB  SI PUSH  BP PUSH
        10 INT  BP POP  SI POP  NEXT JMP  END-CODE
\ ---
: CLS          (CLS) VIDEO @ 10 / BORDER 0 0 GOTOXY ;
-->
52
\ cr ?terminal key printer console          \ JFB 10:04 01/05/89
```

```
: CR          0D EMIT 0A EMIT ;
: ?TERMINAL       0B00 0 21INT DROP 0FF AND IF 1 ELSE 0 THEN ;
: PCKEY       0700 0 21INT DROP 0FF AND ;
: ?KEY        0B00 0 21INT DROP 0FF AND DUP
              IF DROP (KEY) THEN ;
: (KEY)       PCKEY DUP 0= IF DROP PCKEY 0100 OR THEN ;
: KEY (KEY) ;
: PRINTER     1 LPFLAG ! ;
: CONSOLE     0 LPFLAG ! ;
  -->

53
\ emit                                            JFB 10:57 05/08/88
: EMIT        (EMIT) 1 OUT +! ;
CODE (EMIT) AX POP  BX LPFLAG MOV  BX # 0 CMP =
            IF  SI PUSH  BP PUSH
              PCA CALL  BP POP  SI POP
            ELSE DL AL MOV  AX # 500 MOV  21 INT
            THEN  NEXT JMP  END-CODE
-->

54
\ seek+                                           WHP 10:39 06/07/86
\ handle\low offset\high offset --- 0 okay or error #\1
CODE SEEK+        AX # 4200 MOV  CX POP  DX POP  BX POP  21 INT
                  1 $ JNC  AX PUSH
                  1 $:  URET REL16 JMP END-CODE

\ handle\low offset\high offset ---
\ low offset\high offset\ 0 or err #\1 error
CODE SEEK-        AX # 4202 MOV  CX POP  DX POP  BX POP  21 INT
                  1 $ JNC  AX PUSH  AX # 1 MOV  AX PUSH  NEXT,
          1 $:    AX PUSH  DX PUSH  AX AX SUB  AX PUSH NEXT,
                  END-CODE

\ handle\low offset\high offset ---
\ low offset\high offset\ 0 or err #\1 error
CODE SEEK+-       AX # 4201 MOV  ' SEEK- 3 + JMP  END-CODE -->
55
\ read write                                      WHP 10:38 06/07/86
\ handle\buffer\bytes --- #bytes read\0 or err #\1
CODE READ         AX # 3F00 MOV
HERE LABEL RandW
                  CX POP DX POP  BX POP  21 INT
                  AX PUSH  URET REL16 JMP  END-CODE

\ handle\buffer\bytes --- #bytes witten\0 or err #\1
CODE WRITE        AX # 4000 MOV  RandW JMP  END-CODE
-->

56
\ gethandle set-io                            \     15:01 01/27/86
30 CONSTANT DOSERR

\ block # --- handle or 0 if file not opened
: GETHANDLE       2000 / ONGOSUB PRI SEC AUX SYS QUIT ENDGOSUB
                  DUP 0=
                  IF 7FFF USE @ 2- ! FIRST USE !
                     [ DOSERR 5F + ] LITERAL MESSAGE SP! QUIT
                  THEN ;

\ ---
: SET-IO          REC @ DUP GETHANDLE SWAP 1FFF AND 400 M*
                  SEEK+ -DUP
```

```
                IF CR ." Seek error " . QUIT THEN ;
-->

57
\ sec-read sec-write                              \     15:01 01/27/86
HEX
\ ---
: SEC-READ      REC @ GETHANDLE USE @ 400 READ
                IF DUP DISK-ERROR !
                  ." Disk read error # " . QUIT
                THEN DUP 400 <>
                IF DUP USE @ + OVER 400 SWAP - ERASE
                THEN DROP ;

\ ---
: SEC-WRITE     REC @ GETHANDLE USE @ 400 WRITE
                IF DUP DISK-ERROR !
                  ." Disk write error # " . QUIT
                THEN 400 <>
                IF  ." Disk full" QUIT THEN ; -->
58
\ +buf empty-buff update flush                    \     13:43 04/21/86

: +BUF          B/BUF 4 + + DUP LIMIT =
                IF DROP FIRST THEN DUP PREV @ - ;

: EMPTY-BUFFERS FIRST LIMIT OVER - ERASE
                LIMIT FIRST DO 07FFF I ! HDBT +LOOP ;

: UPDATE        PREV @ @ 08000 OR PREV @ ! ;

: FLUSH         LIMIT FIRST
                DO I @ 08000 AND
                  IF I @ 07FFF AND DUP I !
                    I 2+ SWAP 0 R/W
                  THEN B/BUF 4 +
                +LOOP ; -->
59
\ block                                           \     15:01 01/27/86

: BLOCK         0 DISK-ERROR !
                >R PREV @ DUP @ R - DUP +
                IF BEGIN +BUF 0=
                   IF DROP R BUFFER DUP R
                      0 DISK-ERROR !
                      1 R/W 2 -
                   THEN
                DUP @ R - DUP + 0= UNTIL
                DUP PREV !
                DISK-ERROR @ IF UPDATE THEN
                THEN
                R> DROP 2+ ;
-->

60
\ buffer r/w                                      \     15:01 01/27/86

: BUFFER        USE @ DUP >R BEGIN +BUF UNTIL
                USE ! R @ 0<
                IF R 2+ R @ 7FFF AND 0 R/W THEN
                R ! R PREV ! R> 2+ ;

: R/W           USE @ >R SWAP SEC/BLK * ROT USE !
                SEC/BLK 0 DO
```

```
                  OVER OVER REC ! SET-IO
                  IF SEC-READ ELSE SEC-WRITE THEN
                  1+ BPS USE +!
                  LOOP
                2DROP R> USE ! ;
-->

61
\ show-error ?depth                              \      11:11 03/10/86
HEX
: ?DEPTH \ number ---
        DEPTH 1- SWAP < 9 ?ERROR ;

: SHOW-ERROR \ ---
                BLK @
                IF IN @ 2- 40 / BLK @ 2DUP
                ." at screen " 01FFF AND . ." line " . CR
                .LINE CR IN @ 2- 40 MOD SPACES 18 EMIT CR CR
                THEN QUIT ;
-->

62
\ error handling                                   JFB 09:21 05/07/88
: MESSAGE       WARNING @ IF -DUP IF SYSERR .LINE
                SPACE THEN ELSE ."  Msg # " . THEN ;
: ERROR         DECIMAL WARNING @ 0< IF (ABORT) THEN HERE COUNT
                CR ." Error: " 22 EMIT TYPE 22 EMIT 2 SPACES
                MESSAGE SP! SHOW-ERROR ;
: ?ERROR        SWAP IF ERROR ELSE DROP THEN ;
: ?COMP         STATE @ 0= 11 ?ERROR ;
: ?STACK        SP@ S0 @ SWAP U< 1 ?ERROR
                SP@ HERE 80 + U< 7 ?ERROR ;
: ?EXEC         STATE @ 12 ?ERROR ;
: ?PAIRS        - 13 ?ERROR ;
: ?CSP          SP@ CSP @ - 14 ?ERROR ;
: ?LOADING      BLK @ 0= 16 ?ERROR ;
: (ABORT)       ABORT ;
-->
63
\  roll                                          \      15:01 01/27/86

CODE ROLL \ number ---
                AX SS MOV  ES AX MOV  DX SI MOV
                CX POP  DI CX MOV  DI DEC
                DI 1 SHL  DI SP ADD
                SI DI MOV  SI # 2 SUB
                SS: [DI] PUSH  STD
                CLI SS: REP WORD MOVS  STI  CLD
                SI DX MOV  SP # 2 ADD  NEXT JMP  END-CODE
-->

: ROLL \ number ---
                DUP >R PICK R> 0 SWAP DO
                SP@ I DUP + + DUP 2- @ SWAP ! -1 +LOOP DROP ;

64
\ m/mod m/ /mod / mod */mod */ \                 \      15:01 01/27/86

: M/MOD         >R 0 R U/ R> SWAP >R U/ R> ;
: M/            OVER >R >R DABS R ABS U/ R> R XOR +-
                SWAP R> +- SWAP ;
: /MOD          >R S->D R> M/ ;
: /             /MOD SWAP DROP ;
: MOD           /MOD DROP ;
```

```
: */MOD         >R M* R> M/ ;
: */            */MOD SWAP DROP ;
: \             IN @ 40 / 1+ 40 * IN ! ; IMMEDIATE
-->

65
\ (number number                            \     15:01 01/27/86

: (NUMBER)      BEGIN   1+ DUP >R C@ BASE @ DIGIT
                WHILE   SWAP BASE @ U* DROP ROT BASE @ U* D+
                        DPL @ 1+
                        IF   1 DPL +!
                        THEN R>
                REPEAT  R> ;

: NUMBER        0 0 ROT DUP 1+ C@ 2D = DUP >R + -1
                BEGIN   DPL ! (NUMBER) DUP C@ BL -
                WHILE   DUP C@  2E - 5 ?ERROR 0 ( is undefined)
                REPEAT  DROP R> IF DMINUS THEN ;
-->

66
\ expect word -find                         \     15:01 01/27/86

: EXPECT        OVER + OVER DO KEY DUP 0E +ORIGIN @ =
                IF DROP DUP I = DUP R> 2- + >R
                  IF BELL ELSE BSOUT EMIT BL EMIT BSOUT
                  THEN
                ELSE DUP 0D =
                  IF LEAVE DROP BL 0
                  ELSE DUP
                  THEN R C! 0 R 1+ !
                THEN EMIT LOOP DROP ;

: WORD          BLK @ IF BLK @ BLOCK ELSE TIB @ THEN IN @ +
                SWAP ENCLOSE HERE 22 BLANKS IN +! OVER - >R
                R HERE C! + HERE 1+ R> CMOVE ;
-->
67
\ -find x create                            \     10:13 03/26/86

: -FIND         BL WORD HERE CONTEXT @ @ (FIND) DUP 0=
                IF DROP HERE LATEST CONTEXT @ @ OVER -
                  IF (FIND) ELSE 2DROP 0 THEN THEN ;
: X             BLK @
                IF 1 BLK +! 0 IN ! BLK @ B/SCR 1- AND 0=
                  IF ?EXEC R> DROP THEN
                ELSE R> DROP
                THEN ;  IMMEDIATE  IS-X
: CREATE        -FIND
                IF   DROP NFA CR ID. 4 MESSAGE SPACE
                THEN HERE DUP C@ WIDTH @ MIN 1+ ALLOT
                DUP 0A0 TOGGLE HERE 1- 80 TOGGLE
                LATEST , CURRENT @ ! HERE 2+ , ; -->

68
\ interpret                                 \     15:02 01/27/86

: INTERPRET     BEGIN -FIND
                  IF STATE @ <
                    IF CFA ,
                    ELSE CFA EXECUTE
                    THEN ?STACK
                  ELSE HERE NUMBER DPL @ 1+
```

```
                    IF [COMPILE] DLITERAL
                    ELSE DROP [COMPILE] LITERAL
                    THEN ?STACK
                  THEN
                AGAIN ;
-->

69
\ !csp [ ] definitions query quit <builds   \     15:02 01/27/86

: !CSP           SP@ CSP ! ;
: QUERY          TIB @ 50 EXPECT 0 IN ! ;
: [              0 STATE ! ; IMMEDIATE
: ]              0C0 STATE ! ;
: DEFINITIONS    CONTEXT @ CURRENT ! ;
: <BUILDS        0 CONSTANT ;

: QUIT           0 BLK ! [COMPILE] [ ." ok"
                 BEGIN CR RP! QUERY INTERPRET
                   STATE @ 0=
                   IF ." ok" THEN
                 AGAIN ;
-->

70
\ begin then do loop literal                 \     14:18 04/14/86

: BACK           HERE - , ;
: BEGIN          ?COMP HERE 1 ; IMMEDIATE
: THEN           ?COMP 2 ?PAIRS HERE OVER - SWAP ! ; IMMEDIATE
: DO             COMPILE (DO) HERE 3 ; IMMEDIATE
: LOOP           3 ?PAIRS COMPILE (LOOP) BACK ; IMMEDIATE
: +LOOP          3 ?PAIRS COMPILE (+LOOP) BACK ; IMMEDIATE
: EXIT           R> DROP ;
: COMPILE        ?COMP R> DUP 2+ >R @ , ;
: [COMPILE]      -FIND 0= 0 ?ERROR DROP CFA , ; IMMEDIATE
: LITERAL        STATE @ IF COMPILE LIT , THEN ; IMMEDIATE
: DLITERAL       STATE @ IF SWAP [COMPILE] LITERAL
                 [COMPILE] LITERAL THEN ; IMMEDIATE
: UNTIL          1 ?PAIRS COMPILE 0BRANCH BACK ; IMMEDIATE -->

71
\ end again repeat if else while             \     12:17 04/17/86

: END            [COMPILE] UNTIL ; IMMEDIATE
: AGAIN          1 ?PAIRS COMPILE BRANCH BACK ; IMMEDIATE
: REPEAT         >R >R [COMPILE] AGAIN R> R> 2-
                 [COMPILE] THEN ; IMMEDIATE
: IF             COMPILE 0BRANCH HERE 0 , 2 ; IMMEDIATE
: ELSE           2 ?PAIRS COMPILE BRANCH HERE 0 , SWAP 2
                 [COMPILE] THEN 2 ; IMMEDIATE
: WHILE          [COMPILE] IF 2+ ; IMMEDIATE
: ;              ?CSP COMPILE ;S SMUDGE [COMPILE] [ ; IMMEDIATE
: (;CODE)        R> LATEST PFA CFA ! ;
: ."             22 STATE @ IF COMPILE (.") WORD HERE C@ 1+ ALLOT
                 ELSE WORD HERE COUNT TYPE THEN ; IMMEDIATE
: "              22 STATE @ IF COMPILE (") THEN WORD HERE
                 C@ 1+ ALLOT ; IMMEDIATE -->
72
\ immediate smudge ' load --> forget               12:47 07/09/86

: IMMEDIATE      LATEST 40 TOGGLE ;
: SMUDGE         LATEST 20 TOGGLE ;
: LATEST         CURRENT @ @ ;
```

```
: (               29 WORD ; IMMEDIATE
: '               -FIND 0= 05 ?ERROR DROP
                  [COMPILE] LITERAL ; IMMEDIATE
: LOAD            BLK @ >R IN @ >R 0 IN ! B/SCR * BLK !
                  INTERPRET R> IN ! R> BLK ! ;
: -->             ?LOADING 0 IN ! B/SCR BLK @ OVER
                  MOD - BLK +! ; IMMEDIATE
: FORGET          CURRENT @ CONTEXT @ - 18 ?ERROR [COMPILE] '
                  DUP FENCE @ U< 15 ?ERROR DUP NFA DP !
                  LFA @ CURRENT @ ! ;
-->
73
\ sstate file area                              \     15:02 01/27/86
HEX
\ save area offsets: 0 cap locks  2 int 00  6 int 1b  A int 23
0 VARIABLE SSTATE 0C ALLOT \ ms-dos system state

0 VARIABLE SYSF  -2 ALLOT " SYSTEM.SCR" 0 C, 0 ,

0 VARIABLE PRIF -2 ALLOT 40 ALLOT
0 VARIABLE SECF -2 ALLOT 40 ALLOT
0 VARIABLE AUXF -2 ALLOT 40 ALLOT
-->

74
\ entry messages                                \     15:02 01/27/86

\ can't open system file
: BM              ." Undefined error code" DUP U. ;
: R1              ." Invalid function code" ;
: R2              ." File not found" ;
: R3              ." Path not found" ;
: R4              ." Too many open files" ;
: R5              ." Access denied" ;
: R12             ." Invalid access" ;
-->

75
\ adios dosver                                  \     15:02 01/27/86
HEX
\ byte return code ---
CODE ADIOS        AX POP  AH # 4C MOV  21 INT  END-CODE

\ --- minor version\major version
CODE DOSVER       AH # 30 MOV  21 INT  BL AH MOV  BH BH SUB
                  BX PUSH  AH AH SUB  AX PUSH  NEXT JMP END-CODE
-->

76
\ fig 2+ forth entry                               JFB 11:33 03/06/88

CODE SETINTS      AX AX XOR  DS AX MOV      \ 0 ds
                  AL 417 MOV
                  CS: SSTATE AL MOV         \ save key board flag
                  AL # 40 MOV 417 AL MOV    \ caps lock (ONLY) on
                  AX CS MOV  DS AX MOV      \ restore forth ds
                  AX # 3500 MOV  21 INT     \ save 0div
                  BX PUSH  SSTATE 02 + POP
                  ES PUSH  SSTATE 04 + POP
                  AX # 351B MOV  21 INT     \ save ctrl break
                  BX PUSH  SSTATE 06 + POP
                  ES PUSH  SSTATE 08 + POP
                  AX # 3523 MOV  21 INT     \ save critical error
                  BX PUSH  SSTATE 0A + POP
```

```
                ES PUSH  SSTATE 0C + POP -->
77
\ fig 2+ forth entry                             \     12:35 03/11/86
                DX # 0DIV  MOV  AX # 2500 MOV  21 INT \ set 0div
                DX # BRKEY MOV  AX # 251B MOV  21 INT \ set ctrl
                DX # BRKEY MOV  AX # 2523 MOV  21 INT \ set crit
                BX # 0001 MOV              \ raw output
                AX # 4400 MOV  21 INT  DX # 20 OR
                AX # 4401 MOV  21 INT
                NEXT JMP  END-CODE
-->

78
\ fig 2+ forth exit                              \ JFB 10:18 11/04/88
CODE RESINTS AX AX XOR  DS AX MOV              \ address 0 ds
             CS: AL SSTATE MOV
             AL # 0F0 AND                      \ mask off "down" bits
             AH 417 MOV                        \ get kbd flags
             AH # 0F AND                       \ save down bits
             AL AH OR                          \ combine flags
             417 AL MOV                        \ restore keyboard
             CS: SSTATE 02 + PUSH   0 POP \ 0div offset
             CS: SSTATE 04 + PUSH  02 POP \ cs
             CS: SSTATE 06 + PUSH  6C POP \ ctrl brk offset
             CS: SSTATE 08 + PUSH  6E POP \ cs
             CS: SSTATE 0A + PUSH  8C POP \ ctrl brk offset
             CS: SSTATE 0C + PUSH  8E POP \ cs
             AX CS MOV  DS AX MOV              \ restore forth ds
             NEXT JMP END-CODE  -->
79
\ doserr openh closeh                             WHP 10:41 06/07/86
HEX

HERE LABEL URET ASSEMBLER RESET \ unix-like function call ret
                AX # 0 MOV  1 $ JNC
                AX INC  1 $:  APUSH JMP

\ path name\int 21 function --- ax\0=okay, 1=error
CODE OPENH      AX CS MOV  DS AX MOV  CX CX SUB  AX POP  DX POP
                21 INT  AX PUSH  URET JMP  END-CODE

\ bx\ax --- ax\0=okay ,1 error
CODE CLOSEH     AX POP  BX POP  21 INT  1 $ JNC  AX PUSH
                1 $:  URET  JMP END-CODE
-->

80
\ handle closehandle createhandle                 plp 12:44 06/07/86
\ filename buffer address --- handle
: HANDLE        COUNT + 1+ @ ;
\ file name buffer address ---
: CLOSEMESS     COUNT DUP 0> BLK @ 0= AND
                IF CR TYPE 0E SYSMESS .LINE CR
                ELSE 2DROP
                THEN ;
\ file name buffer address ---
: CLOSEHANDLE   FLUSH EMPTY-BUFFERS DUP HANDLE -DUP
                IF ABS 3E00 CLOSEH -DUP
                  IF SWAP DOSERR + ?ERROR THEN
                THEN DUP CLOSEMESS DUP C@ 4 + ERASE ;
\ file name buffer address --- handle
: CREATEHANDLE  1+ 3C00 OPENH IF DOSERR + ERROR THEN ;
-->
81
```

```
\ y/n ?.SCR                                        08:01 06/27/86
HEX
\ --- 0=no, 0>=yes
: Y/N           ." (Y/N)? N" 08 EMIT KEY 59 AND 59 =
                IF 59 EMIT 1 ELSE 4E EMIT 0 THEN SPACE ;

\ filename buffer address ---
: ?.SCR         DUP C@ 3D <
                IF 1 OVER COUNT OVER + SWAP
                  DO I C@ 2E =
                    IF DROP 0 LEAVE THEN
                  LOOP
                  IF DUP COUNT + " .SCR" COUNT ROT SWAP CMOVE
                    DUP DUP C@ 4 + SWAP C! THEN
                DROP THEN ;
-->
82
\ using                                      \     15:02 01/27/86
HEX
\ WARNING! USING transfers up to decimal 68 bytes to
\          file name buffer address
\ file name buffer address ---
: USING         DUP CLOSEHANDLE DUP BL WORD HERE SWAP
                OVER C@ 1+ DUP 40 > 1A ?ERROR
                CMOVE DUP ?.SCR
                DUP COUNT + 03 ERASE OPENHANDLE ;
-->

83
\ openhandle                                   JFB 16:45 05/30/88
\ file name buffer address ---
: OPENHANDLE    DUP 1+ 3D02 OPENH
                IF DUP 2 =
                  IF CR -CURSOR DROP DUP COUNT TYPE SPACE R2
                    CR ." Do you wish to create it " CURSOR Y/N
                    IF DUP CREATEHANDLE
                    ELSE 4 ERASE QUIT
                    THEN
                  ELSE SWAP 4 ERASE DOSERR + ERROR
                  THEN
                THEN SWAP COUNT + 1+ ! ;
-->

84
\ prifile primary sys                        \     15:02 01/27/86
\ creates a file such as PFILE MYFILE.SCR
: PFILE       PRIF USING ;
: SFILE       SECF USING ;
: AFILE       AUXF USING ;
\ forth buffer identifier for MS-DOS files
\ ---
: SECONDARY     2000 OR ;
: AUXILIARY     4000 OR ;
: SYSTEM        6000 OR ;
\ --- handle or 0 if no handle
: SYS           SYSF HANDLE ;
: PRI           PRIF HANDLE ;
: SEC           SECF HANDLE ;
: AUX           AUXF HANDLE ;
-->
85
\ Modify Memory Allocation                     JFB 17:43 05/07/88
\ ---
: ModMemAloc ?CS: 0 0 [ EM 0 10 U/ 1+ SWAP DROP ] LITERAL
```

```
             4A00 21INT5 \ increase allocation to MEM-END
             IF CR ." Not enough contigeous memory" CR
                ?CS: 0 0 0 0 21INT5 \ exit
             THEN 2DROP ;
  -->

86
\ cold1                                          JFB 17:43 05/07/88
HEX
\ ---
: COLD1         ModMemAloc SETINTS DOSVER DUP 2 <
                IF ." DOS " . . ." found. DOS > 2 required"
                   01 ADIOS
                THEN SYSF 1+ 3D02 OPENH
                IF CLS ." Can't open SYSTEM.SCR " DUP
                  ONGOSUB BM R1 R2 R3 R4 R5  BM
                          BM BM BM BM BM R12 BM ENDGOSUB DROP
                  CR ." Fig MS-DOS Forth "
                  CR ." Numbered messages!" 0 WARNING !
                  SYSF 4 ERASE
                ELSE SYSF COUNT + 1+ !
                THEN PRIF 4 ERASE SECF 4 ERASE AUXF 4 ERASE
                ; -->
87
\ cold warm  0divide mess                        JFB 22:04 03/05/88

: COLD          EMPTY-BUFFERS
                FIRST PREV !
                FIRST USE !
                12 +ORIGIN UP @ 6 + 10 CMOVE 0 R# !
                0C +ORIGIN @ ' FORTH 4 + !
                DECIMAL COLD1 ABORT ;

: WARM          EMPTY-BUFFERS SP! ?STACK
                CR ." Ready" QUIT ;

: 0DIVMESS      EMPTY-BUFFERS SP! ?STACK
                CR ." Divide overflow" QUIT ;
-->

88
\ abort                                               10:42 06/27/86
HEX
: ABORT         SP! DECIMAL ?STACK
                [COMPILE] FORTH DEFINITIONS
                SYSF HANDLE
                IF 1 WARNING ! RP! 0 IN ! 0 BLK ! [COMPILE] [
                  01 SYSLOAD
                THEN QUIT ;

: BYE           BLACK BACKGROUND LIGHTGRAY FOREGROUND CLS
                CR ." Goodbye "DECIMAL .TIME SPACE .DATE CR
                CURSOR RESINTS FLUSH EMPTY-BUFFERS 00 ADIOS ;
-->

89
\ save memory image                                   09:56 07/01/86

\ SAVE myforth.com
: SAVE          SAVE0 100 HERE OVER - SAVE1 SAVE3 ;

\ SAVE0 filename :  --- handle
: SAVE0         AFILE AUX DUP 0 0 SEEK+ SAVE4 ;
```

```
\ handle\buffer\length --- length written
: SAVE1          DUP >R WRITE SAVE4
                 R <> [ DOSERR 5B + ] LITERAL ?ERROR R> ;

\ address\length  filename
: SAVE2          2 ?DEPTH SAVE0 ;
-->

90
\ save memory image                            plp 12:44 06/07/86

\ length ---
: SAVE3          CR DECIMAL U. 0A SYSMESS .LINE SPACE AUXF
                 COUNT TYPE AUXF CLOSEHANDLE ;

\ err #\1 or 0 ---
: SAVE4          DUP
                 IF SWAP DOSERR + SWAP
                 ELSE 0
                 THEN SWAP ?ERROR ;
-->

91
\ comsave and blosave                              09:56 07/01/86
HEX

\ address\length COMSAVE mycom.com
: COMSAVE        SAVE2 ROT ROT SAVE1 SAVE3 ;

\ address\length BLOSAVE myblo.blo
: BLOSAVE        SAVE2 >R 0FD PAD ! ?CS: PAD 1+ ! OVER PAD 3 + !
                 DUP PAD 5 + ! R PAD 7 SAVE1 DROP
                 R ROT ROT SAVE1
                 01A PAD C! R> PAD 1 SAVE1 DROP 8 + SAVE3 ;
-->

92
\ .files list                                  \    08:40 02/04/86

: .FILES    -CURSOR
            SYSF HANDLE
            IF CR ." System file:    " SYSF COUNT TYPE THEN
            PRIF HANDLE
            IF CR ." Primary file:   " PRIF COUNT TYPE THEN
            SECF HANDLE
            IF CR ." Secondary file: " SECF COUNT TYPE THEN
            AUXF HANDLE
            IF CR ." Auxiliary file: " AUXF COUNT TYPE THEN
            CURSOR CR ;

: LIST           -CURSOR CR DUP SCR ! ." Screen # " 1FFF AND .
                 10 0 DO CR R 3 .R SPACE R SCR @ .LINE
                 LOOP CR CURSOR ; -->
93
\ primary secondary auxiliary files            \    15:02 01/27/86

: SYSBLOCK       SYSTEM    BLOCK ;
: SBLOCK         SECONDARY BLOCK ;
: ABLOCK         AUXILIARY BLOCK ;

: SYSLOAD        SYSTEM    LOAD ;
: SLOAD          SECONDARY LOAD ;
: ALOAD          AUXILIARY LOAD ;
```

```
: SYSLIST        SYSTEM    LIST ;
: SLIST          SECONDARY LIST ;
: ALIST          AUXILIARY LIST ;
-->

94
\ triad show                                   \ JFB 10:06 01/05/89
HEX
: TRIAD          DUP 3 + SWAP DO CR I LIST
                 LOOP CR CR 0 OUT !
                 ." MS-DOS fig Forth " 2 SPACES
                 .DATE 2 SPACES .TIME 2 SPACES CR
                 LPFLAG @ IF FFEED EMIT THEN ;

: SHOW           PRINTER 1+ SWAP DO I TRIAD ?TERMINAL
                 IF KEY DROP LEAVE THEN 3 +LOOP CONSOLE ;
-->

95
\ vlist                                        \ JFB 10:05 01/05/89
HEX
: VLIST          -CURSOR BASE @ >R HEX CR CR 0 OUT ! CONTEXT @ @
                 BEGIN DUP DUP 0 <# # # # # #> TYPE
                     SPACE ID.
                     OUT @ 3C >
                     IF   CR 0 OUT !
                     ELSE 14 OUT @ OVER MOD - SPACES
                     THEN PFA LFA @ DUP 0=
                     ?TERMINAL DUP IF KEY DROP THEN OR
                 UNTIL
                 DROP CR CR R> BASE ! CURSOR ;
-->

96
\ Memory dump, byte format                     \     14:25 04/14/86
HEX
: DUMP    ( addr  n  ---  )
  -CURSOR BASE @ >R HEX CR CR 5 SPACES
  10 0 DO I 3 .R LOOP 2 SPACES
  10 0 DO I 0 <# # #> TYPE LOOP CR
  OVER + SWAP DUP 0F AND XOR DO
  CR I 0 4 D.R SPACE
  I 10 + I 2DUP
    DO I C@ SPACE 0 <# # # #> TYPE LOOP
    2 SPACES
    DO I C@ DUP 20 < OVER 07E > OR IF DROP 02E THEN
    EMIT LOOP
  10 +LOOP CR R> BASE ! CURSOR ;
-->

97
\ Display stack                                \     15:02 01/27/86

: .S             BASE @ >R SP@ S0 @ =
                 IF CR ." <empty stack> "
                 ELSE SP@ S0 @ SWAP
                   DO CR I @ DUP DECIMAL 4 .R
                     HEX ."  (" 0 4 D.R ."  h)"
                   2 +LOOP CR
                 THEN  R> BASE ! ;
-->

98
\ 2@l 2!l                                      \     15:02 01/27/86
```

```
\ segment\offset --- low word\high word
CODE 2@L         BX POP  ES POP  ES: 2 [BX] PUSH  ES: [BX] PUSH
                 NEXT JMP  END-CODE

\ low word\high word\ segment\offset ---
CODE 2!L         BX POP  ES POP  ES: [BX] POP  ES: 2 [BX] POP
                 NEXT JMP  END-CODE

\ --- cs:
CODE ?CS:        CS PUSH  NEXT JMP END-CODE
-->

99
\ @L !L C@L C!L                              \      15:02 01/27/86

( segment\offset --- n )
CODE @L          BX POP  DS POP  AX [BX] MOV
                 BX CS MOV  DS BX MOV  APUSH JMP  END-CODE

( n\segment\offset --- )
CODE !L          BX POP  DS POP  AX POP  [BX] AX MOV
                 BX CS MOV  DS BX MOV  NEXT JMP  END-CODE

( segment\offset --- b )
CODE C@L         BX POP  DS POP  AL [BX] MOV  AH AH SUB
                 BX CS MOV  DS BX MOV  APUSH JMP  END-CODE
( b\segment\offset --- )
CODE C!L         BX POP  DS POP  AX POP  [BX] AL MOV
                 BX CS MOV  DS BX MOV  NEXT JMP  END-CODE -->
100
\ cmovel s=                                  \      15:02 01/27/86

( from-seg\from-address\to-seg\to-address\length --- )
CODE CMOVEL      BX SI MOV  CX POP  DI POP  ES POP
                 SI POP  DS POP  CX>0  IF  REP BYTE MOVS  THEN
                 AX CX MOV  DS AX MOV  ES AX MOV
                 SI BX MOV  NEXT JMP  END-CODE

( address1\address2\length --- flag )
CODE S=          BX SI MOV  AX DS MOV  ES AX MOV
                 CX POP  DI POP  SI POP  AX AX XOR  CX>0
                 IF  REPZ BYTE CMPS THEN
                 SI BX MOV  0=  IF  AX INC  THEN
                 APUSH JMP  END-CODE
-->

101
\ @date !date @time !time .time .date        \      15:02 01/27/86
HEX
CODE @DATE       AH # 2A MOV  21 INT  CX PUSH
                 DX PUSH  NEXT JMP END-CODE
CODE !DATE       DX POP  CX POP  AH # 2B MOV  21 INT
                 NEXT JMP END-CODE
CODE @TIME       AH # 2C MOV  21 INT  CX PUSH
                 DX PUSH  NEXT JMP  END-CODE
CODE !TIME       DX POP  CX POP  AH # 2D MOV  21 INT
                 NEXT JMP END-CODE
: .TD            0 <# # # #> TYPE ;
: .TIME          @TIME DROP 0 100 U/ .TD 3A EMIT .TD ;
: .DATE          @DATE 0 100 U/ .TD 2F EMIT .TD
                 2F EMIT 076C - .TD ;
-->
```

```
102
\ ?gosubw                                      \      09:00 03/21/86
HEX
\ table\value --- index if found, -1 not found
CODE ?GOSUBW     AX POP                 \ word to possibly locate
                 BX POP                 \ address of table
                 CX [BX] MOV            \ count of # of table values
                 DI BX MOV  DI INC  DI INC
                 DX CS MOV  ES DX MOV
                 REPNE WORD SCAS        \ try to find word
                 AX # -01 MOV           \ not found flag
                 1 $ JNZ                \ was it found?
                 AX [BX] MOV            \ get # table entries
                 AX CX SUB  AX DEC      \ compute offset
           1 $:  AX PUSH                \ push offset or -1
                 NEXT, END-CODE
-->
103
\ interpreter: if, else & then; match name          07:03 10/12/89

: NFA= ( nfa - bool )
  1                                 \ assume they are equal
  SWAP 1+ HERE C@ WIDTH @ MIN  \ get min of head and width
  HERE 1+ SWAP                   \ stk: truth, nfa+1, here+1, count
  0
  DO OVER I + C@ 07F AND OVER I + C@ <>
    IF ROT DROP 0 ROT ROT          \ place false
       LEAVE
    THEN
  LOOP 2DROP ;                      \ rid addresses
-->
match word at here with the given dictionary header

104
\ interpreter: if, else & then                  JFB 09:32 05/21/89

: #THEN ( - ) ; IMMEDIATE

: #ELSE ( - )
   BEGIN  BL WORD HERE C@ 5 =
      IF [ ' #THEN NFA ] LITERAL NFA=
      ELSE HERE 1+ C@ 0= 013 ?ERROR 0 \ error on null
      THEN
   UNTIL ; IMMEDIATE
  -->

105
\ interpreter: if, else & then                  JFB 09:33 05/21/89

: #IF ( bool - )
   0=
   IF BEGIN  BL WORD HERE C@ 5 =
         IF [ ' #ELSE NFA ] LITERAL NFA=
            [ ' #THEN NFA ] LITERAL NFA= OR
         ELSE HERE 1+ C@ 0= 013 ?ERROR 0 \ error on null
         THEN
      UNTIL
   THEN ; IMMEDIATE
  -->

106
\ ?DEF                                          \ JFB 12:08 01/05/89

: ?DEF ( - bool )
```

```
  BL WORD HERE CONTEXT @ @ (FIND)
  IF 2DROP 1
  ELSE HERE CURRENT @ @ (FIND)
      IF 2DROP 1
      ELSE 0
      THEN
  THEN ; IMMEDIATE
  -->

107
\ Cross compiler finish                            JFB 19:16 06/04/88

: TASK          ; IS-FENCE
FINIS

108
\ revision history                                      19:18 08/11/86
Revsym              Revision history
03/17/86        Initial formal release date.  Preliminary
                versions in limited use since the summer of
                1985.

03/20/86        Dump changed to start on paragraph boundary,
                whp

04/14/86        endif removed from target, whp

06/07/86        Constants SYSMESS and SYSERR added to make
                offsets into system file variable numbers, whp

109
\ revision history                                      19:19 08/11/86
Revsym              Revision history
06/27/86        Make sure es loaded with ds contents in enclose,
                Jerry Boutelle.

                SPACE in Y/N, hdn

                QUIT relocation in ABORT, hdn

                SYSF 4 ERASE if SYSTEM.SCR not found, hdn

07/01/86        SAV2, COMSAVE, BLOSAVE included, whp

07/09/86        ' error message changed from 0 to 05, whp

110
\ revision history                                 JFB 11:36 03/06/88
Revsym              Revision history

07/14/86        Local labels replace gobals in PCA and TYPE0,
                BEGIN$, END$, and FORTH placed in PCA, whp

03/05/87        Modified COLD sequence to permit forth to
                initialize before doing machine specific
                code in COLD1. jfb

03/05/87        Added ModMemAloc to request the memory forth
                uses ( memory above limit of .com file )
                from DOS. jfb

111
\ revision history                               \ JFB 10:03 01/05/89
Revsym              Revision history
```

```
03/06/88         Modified SETINTS and RESINTS to fetch/store
                 the keyboard flags byte (0000:0417) as a byte
                 not a word. Modified RESINTS to clear all "down"
                 bits (Ctrl, Alt and shift keys) before
                 restoring keyboard flags byte.

05/07/88         Made GOTOXY,BORDER and CLS vectored. Modified
                 COLD to initialize the user variable R#.
                 Added ?KEY.

5/30/88          Vectored KEY, CURSOR and -CURSOR

112
\ revision history                              \ JFB 08:18 01/06/89

6/5/88           Modified RESINTS to restore keboard flags with
                 the current state of the down bits (Ctrl, Alt
                 and shift keys)

11/04/88         Corrected invalid hex number on scr 78,
                 #0F -> # 0F

01/05/89         Added interpretive if for use in system.scr.
                 Removed extra screens from end of file.

01/06/89         Made mode 2 a color mode in (CURSOR)

113
\ revision history                                    07:05 10/12/89

10/12/89         Made spelling correction in comment of NFA=
                 Assme -> Assume
```

Appendix 2

ASCII Listing of the Binary of FORTH86

The ASCII listing of the binary of FORTH86 source code is given in this appendix. A decimal block number followed by a carriage return and line feed (hex 0D0A) precedes a block. The ASCII of the binary is given by 32 hex characters terminated by a blank. A four byte hexadecimal checksum formed by adding the 32 bytes is appended after the blank. The checksum is followed by a carriage return and a line feed.

A BASIC program printed in Chapter 3 is used to convert this file to an executable finary .COM file. You can enter just the program text using DEBUG. But this is not advised because you may have a hard time finding keyboard entry errors.

This file, when converted to a binary .COM file, hosts most of the software included in this book. The exception, of course, is the software running on the 8051 microcontroller family.

```
00
9090EB249090EB380105590E00320800B6F716F7B6F716F71F00000000320B32 0B1
BF09CD00D5B3B6F78CC88ED08EC08ED8BE3E018B2612018B2E1401FCEB3A2E29 0F3
BE4501EB337F298CC88ED88EC08ED0B020E620FB8B2612018B2E1401EBE28CC8 0FB
8ED08EC08ED8BE74018B2612018B2E1401FCEB04A0295250AD8BD8FF2787454E 0E7
434C4F53C5000089018CD88EC0585F572AE4B9FFFFF3AEBAFEFF2BD1523A65FF 114
750A8BC2405052AD8BD8FF2787F78BD8AC3AC374123AC7E0F7BAFEFF2BD15252 122
87F7AD8BD8FF27BAFFFF2BD152425287F7AD8BD8FF278544494749D47D01E001 11D
5A582C3072173C0976062C073C0A720D3AC273092BD28AD0B001E979FF2BC0E9 0C0
75FF86544F47474CC5D6010D02585B3007E964FF862846494E44A902021F028C 0B8
D88EC08BC65E5B508A148BFBAC243FAE752E251F00488BC8E309F3A6740503F1 0ED
46EB22AC247FAE7402EB1A5883C604568BF081E2FF0052B8010050AD8BD8FF27 0F3
251F0003F08B3483FE0075BC5E2BC050AD8BD8FF2781AB14027B02585B03C3E9 0D9
F5FE81AD750288025A582BC2E9E8FE8255AF820296025B5A583BD37305F7F3E9 109
D4FEB8FFFF8BD0E9CCFE8255AA8F02B102585BF7E392E9BDFE823CBEAA02C002 140
585B3BC3B80000740140E9AAFE81AAB902D302585BF7EBE99DFE824DAACD02E1 10A
02585BF7EB92E98DFE8231ABDA02F0025840E982FE8232ABE902FC02584040E9 10D
01
75FE8231ADF50209035848E969FE8232AD02031503584848E95CFE8232AA0E03 0CD
220358D1E0E94FFE8232AF1B032F0358D1F8E942FE834432AF28033D035A58D1 0DF
FAD1D85052E930FE81B035034E032BC0E924FE81B148035903B80100E918FE81 0F1
B253036503B80200E90CFE81B35F037103B80300E900FE822DB16B037E03B8FF 0CC
FFE9F3FD822DB277038B03B8FEFFE9E6FD822DB384039803B8FDFFE9D9FD8244 147
AB9103A503585A5B5903D113C3E9C6FD8244AD9E03B7035B59585A2BD11BC3E9 0E9
B4FD84532D3EC4B003CB0358995052E9A6FD83414EC4C203DA03585B23C3E996 0FE
FD824FD2D203E803585B0BC3E988FD83584FD2E103F703585B33C3E979FD834E 110
4FD4EF03060458F7D0E96BFD81BDFE031204585B3BC3B80100740148E958FD81 0EC
BC0C0425045B582BC3B801007C0148E945FD81BE1F043804585B2BC3B801007C 0AB
0148E932FD8230BC32044C04580BC0B80100780148E91FFD8230BE45045F0458 0B6
0BC0B801007F0148E90CFD8230BD58047204580BC0B80100740148E9F9FC8255 0CC
BC6B048504585A2BD0B80100720148E9E5FC8255BE7E0499045A582BD0B80100 0CB
720148E9D1FC8244BC9204AD045B59585A2BD11BC3B801007C0148E9B9FC8244 0E5
BEA604C504585A5B592BD11BC3B801007C0148E9A1FC8244BDBE04DD045B5958 0DA
5A3BD1750A3BC37506B80100E988FC33C0E983FC835350C0D604FC048BC4E976 104
02
FC835350A1F40409058B1E26018B6706E965FC835250A101051B058B1E26018B 0B2
6F08E953FC835250C013052D058BC5E945FC823ED2250539055B4D4D895E00E9 0D1
36FC8252BE320549058B46004545E926FC81C9420557058B4600E91AFC81CA51 0D0
0563058B4604E90EFC81D25D056F058B4600E902FC87455845435554C5690581 0C1
055BE9F6FB84535741D075058E055A58E9E3FB844F5645D285059C058BDC36FF 100
7702E9D3FB8444524FD09305AE0558E9C6FB834455D0A505BA058BDC36FF37E9 10C
B6FB842D4455D0B205CB05580BC050740150E9A3FB83524FD4C205DD055A5B58 0EB
53E992FB84324455D0D505ED05585A5250E982FB853244524FD0E405FE055858 0F7
E975FB84504943CBF4050C065B4B03DB03DC36FF37E960FB8544455054C80306 0E2
22068B1E26018B47062BC4D1F8E947FB81C0180636065B8B07E93BFB81A13006 0CB
42065B588907E92FFB8232A13C0650065B58890758894702E91DFB8232C04906 0BB
62065B8B078B5702E90BFB8243C05B0672065B8A07B400E9FDFA8243A16B0681 0D5
065B588807E9F0FA822BA17A068F065B580107E9E2FA823EBC88069D065886E0 0E6
50E9D4FA854D494E55D39606AE0658F7D8E9C3FA86444D494E55D3A406BF065B 105
59F7D3F7D183C10183D3005153E9A8FA822BADB406D706580BC078D2E999FA83 121
442BADD006E706580BC078D3E989FA834142D3DF06F706580BC07902F7D850E9 101
03
76FA84444142D3EF060B0758500BC078AEE964FA834D41D802071C07585B8BC8 0D9
2BC37C0451E950FA53E94CFA834D49CE14073407585B8BC82BC37C0453E938FA 0E9
51E934FA8446494CCC2C074D0758595F8CDB8EC3FCF2AAE91EFA8545524153C5 0FF
44076407B80000EBE586424C414E4BD35A077407B82000EBD585434D4F56C569 0C5
078307FC8BDE595F5E0BC974068CD88EC0F2A48BF3E9E0F986434D4F5645BE79 111
07A3078BDE595F5E0BC974E78BC14803F803F08CD88EC0FDF2A4FC8BF3E9B8F9 133
8854524156455253C59807CD07595B03D98A070AC079F853E99DF98250C0C007 0E6
E2075AEDE990F9835043C0DB07EF075AECB400E981F98250A1E707FD075A58EF 11B
E975F9835043A1F6070B085A58EEE967F9834C49D403081908ADE95AF9842844 0EF
4FA9110826085A5887EC505287ECE947F9823BD31D0838088B76004545E938F9 0D3
```

```
54C454156C531084A088B4600894602E925F9864252414E43C840085E080334 0A3F
915F987304252414E43C853086F08580BC074EA4646E9FFF886284C4F4F50A9 0E2C
3088408BB0100015E008B46002B460233C378CA83C5044646E9DCF887282B4C 0B49
F4F50A97908A8085B015E008B46008B560285DB7901922BC2EBD7863231494E 0BD1
4B59C08C6088CC88EC0585B595A1FCD2150528CC88ED8720533C0E999F8B801 0F89
0E993F888434F4E5354414ED4BB083409831DFB20F80A7B2043438B07E977F8 0DAE
4
4555345D2E4083409EF087B2043438A1F2AFF8B3E26018D01E95BF881BA0009 0C54
4093E1A261E5A0A34064C0A4006831D5E1E7B2043434D4D8976008BF3E938F8 0980
5444F4553BE1C09340947051O214B0B40067B2087EC5687EC43438B37434353 09E1
915F888564152494142 4CC540093409EF087B20434353E9FEF78A564F434142 0D08
54C4152D9630934098E1E170881A0F80A5A0A34063F0BF80ADC0A170A3406F8 09C7
A170A40064809FA024C0A40063608C5464F5254C87A095409A70981A0003200 0843
08253B0AF090D0906008252B0C1090D090800835449C2CA090D090A00855749 08BF
454C8D3090D090C00875741524E494EC7DD090D090E008546454E43C5E9090D 09EA
910008244D0F7090D09120088564F432D4C494ECB030A0D09140083424CCB0C 0841
A0D0916008249CE1B0A0D091800834F55D4250A0D091A00835343D22E0A0D09 06B5
C0087434F4E544558D4380A0D09200087435552524 54ED4420A0D0922008553 0846
44154C5500A0D09240084424153C55E0A0D09260083445 0CC6A0A0D09280083 081D
64CC4750A0D092A00834353D07F0A0D092C008252A3890A0D092E0083484CC4 08F2
30A0D09300086535953455 2D29C0AF908046087535953 4D4553D3A60AF9080C 0AD7
0872B4F52494749CEB30A3409170800017902360884484552C5C10A3409080A 086F
406360885414C4C4FD4D50A3409080A8D06360881ACE40A3409DC0A40066303 08E2
5
C0A36088243ACF40A3409DC0A7F065703EC0A3608834E46C1040B3409170805 0921
086027C03CB073608834C46C1150B3409170804008602360883434 6C1290B34 0768
913033608835046C1390B34095703CB0717080500790236088744454 3494D41 06EB
C450B340917080A00710A40063608834845D8590B340917081000710A400636 0630
8C74F4E474F5355C26F0B3409F9195D1F20035D1F1708DC0A4C03F80A5D1FEB 0A0D
55D1F9A055D1F4A045D1F6D08DC0A4C03F80A5D1F8C05DC0A9A0586028C0540 08FD
65D1F36045D1F6D08DC0A4C03F80A5D1F8C05DC0A9A0586028C0540065D1FAC 08FD
055D1F1708DC0A4C03F80A5D1F79025D1F34065D1F7F055D1F5C08DC0A4C03F8 0891
A8C05DC0A8C054006DC0A170806003608C8454E44474F5355C2810B34091708 0828
0600551ADC0A8C058602B805630323041708130 0DF19B805FA02DB0540061303 07DD
3C054006360886 4C50464C41C7110C7409000089534554435552534FD2460C61 08F1
C588AC8588AE8B401CD10E90AF58842574355525 34FD2530C340917080C0017 0B57
80D005F0C36088B434F4C4F52435552534FD26E0C34091708060017080700 5F 0687
0C360888284355525 34F52A9870C3409560E200317081000EB059A054A046D08 0759
4008C0536046D0804008C05AC051708DC0C790234067F055C081400790C950C 0668
950C950C950C950C950C790C950CFC05360886435552534FD2A30C3409AE0C36 0A4A
06
889282D435552534F52A9F20C34091708200017082000 5F0C3608872D435552 076D
534FD2010D34090D0D3608855649444 5CF1B0D7409070085424C494ECB2B0D41 082D
0DA0350D0C80A2350DE92CF4862D424C494ECB370D570DA0350D247FEBE88949 0BDD
4E54454E534954D94C0D6C0DA0350D0C08EBD38A2D494E54454E534954D95E0D 0AED
320DA0350D24F7EBBD89554E4445524C494EC5730D970DA0350D24880C01EBA6 0C33
8A2D554E4445524C494EC5890DAF0DA0350D0C07EB90875245564552 53C5A00D 0B6F
C20DA0350D24F80C70E97AFF882D524556455253C5B60DD90DA0350D248F0C07 0C4D
E963FF84425738B0CC0DEC0DB802005655CD105D5EE980F384434F38B0E30D01 0E6A
0EB80300EBE984425734B0F80D0F0E2BC0EBDC84434F34B0060E1C0EB80100EB 0C4E
CE85434F3332B0130E2B0EB80400EBBF854257333 2B0210E3A0EB80500EBB085 0B41
42573634B0300E490EB80600EBA1853F4D4F44C53F0E580EB40F5655CD105D5E 0AB4
8ADF2AFF538ADC538AD853E90AF385424C4143CB4E0EF908000084475241D96E 0E9D
0EF90808008442 4C55C57A0EF9080100894C49474854424C55C5850EF9080900 0A13
8547524545CE900EF90802008A4C494748544 7524545CEA00EF9080A00844359 0AE3
41CEAC0EF9080300894C4947485443 5941CEBD0EF9080B00835245C4C80EF908 0C05
0400884C494748545245C4D80EF9080C00874D4147454E54C1E20EF90805008C 0AD8
07
4C494748544D4147454E54C1F10EF9080D008542524F57CEFF0EF90806008659 0B82
454C4C4FD7120FF9080E00894C494748544 75241D91E0FF90807008557484954 09DD
C52B0FF9080F008828424F52444552A93B0F540F5B82E3072AFFB40B5655CD10 0B0A
5D5EE913F286424F524445D2470F3409520F36088A4241434B47524F554EC465 0AEE
0F830F582407B104D2E08A1E350D82E38F0AC3A2350DE9DFF18A464F52454752 0D22
4F554EC4740FA80F58240F8A1E350D82E3F00AC3A2350DE9BEF18AD0B80006CD 0DE8
```

```
21C33C0774F4502AFFB403CD10583C08750F83FA0074084A82FAFF7502B24FEB 0DDD
233C0A7504B250EB1B3C0D75042AD2EB138A1E350DB90100B409CD102AFFB403 0AC4
CD10FEC282FA4F761B2AD2FEC682FE187612B80106B90000BA4F188A3E350DCD 0E49
10BA00182AFFB402CD10C3862854595045A9990F3610595AE320A1510C3D0000 0AD9
7505BB0100EB05BB0400EB1156558BF2AC51E86DFF59E2F85D5EE91BF1B80040 0F35
CD21E913F184545950C52B103409B805340A8D063410360885434F554ED46510 0AAC
3409B805EE028C0570063608832822A9781034096D05B8057006EE0247057902 08C6
3705360884282E22A98C1034096D058010B805EE024705790237056C10360883 07E7
5041C4A4103409DC0A17084400790236088223BEBF103409AC05AC05A20A3406 08FF
C5109A058602360884484F4CC4D11034097C03A20A8D06A20A34067F06360884 096E
08
534947CEE8103409DB054A046D08080017082D00EF10360881A3FF103409710A 0905
3406DB1ADB05170809009A0523046D080800170807007902170830007902EF10 05E4
36088223D3181134091C11EB05E60370046D08F6FF3608823CA342113409C510 0A04
A20A40063608842E4350D557113409710A340617082400710A400617082200CB 06B4
0A6006B411710A4006360883442ED26611340937058C059A0509075C11471106 06F6
11D61047059A0586020D126C1036088244AE8B1134094C039111FC11360881AE 08FB
AF113409C903B41136088255AEBE1134094C03B4113608822ED2CA1134093705 0985
C90347059111360881BFD71134093406C21136088553504143C5E81134095613 09B8
F0143608865350414345D3F41134094C031A07C9056D080C004C032408FC1182 0912
08FCFF3608892D545241494C494EC704123409B8054C0324089A059A05790207 091C
037006561386026D08080048085C08040007038208E4FF360886284C494E45A9 07D3
251234093705170840004D134F1B4705F912D1027902DE177902170840003608 068B
852E4C494EC559123409621231126C103608834944AE80123409B805EE028C05 093F
700617081F00D8039A0579028C0524085505700617087F00D803F0148208F2FF 092E
FC113608853231494ED49212CE125A58CD215053E9A1EE8523425546C6C412F9 0DF7
080200875345432F424CCBD712F908010085422F5343D2E312F9080100854649 0A48
09
5253D4F112F908F6F7854C494D49D4FD12F908FEFF835553C509137409F6F784 10F5
505245D615137409F6F7835245C31F13740900008A4449534B2D4552524FD22A 0AF1
137409000085422F4255C63413F90800048242CC4513F90820005655CD105D5E 097B
E915EE875343524F4C4CD551136F138A3E350D588AF0588AD0588AE8588AC858 0E57
B406EBD6875343524F4C4CC4631390138A3E350D588AF0588AD0588AE8588AC8 0EB0
58B407EBB58828474F544F5859A98413B2135A8AF2588AD0B80002BB00005655 0CFA
CD105D5EE9B1ED86474F544F58D9A5133409B01336088528434C53A9C713E013 0D0A
B800068A3E350DBA4F182BC95655CD105D5EE983ED83434CD3D6133409DE1333 0CA8
0D3406170810002F1B6E0F4C034C03D01336088243D2F513340917080D00F014 0708
17080A00F0143608893F5445524D494E41CC131434091708000B4C03CC12AC05 077B
1708FF00D8036D08080057035C0804004C0336088550434B45D9281434091708 06DE
00074C03CC12AC051708FF00D8033608843F4B45D9541434091708000B4C03CC 0832
12AC051708FF00D803B8056D080600AC059D14360885284B4559A9701434095C 08F0
14B80570046D080C00AC055C1417080001E6033608834B45D9951434099D1436 07E7
08875052494E5445D2B514340957034F0C4006360887434F4E534F4CC5C11434 0995
094C034F0C4006360884454D49D4D514340905155703340A8D0636088628454D 0753
10
4954A9E9140715588B1E510C83FB0075095655E8ACFA5D5EEB078AD0B80005CD 0D83
21E954EC855345454BABFC142E15B80042595A5BCD21730150E96E0F85534545 0C77
4BAD24154615B80242595A5BCD21730A50B8010050AD8BD8FF2750522BC050AD 0C1A
8BD8FF27865345454B2BAD3C156F15B80142EBD584524541C464157D15B8003F 0CC1
595A5BCD2150E9210F8557524954C574159315B80040EBE886444F534552D289 0D4F
15F90830008947455448414E444CC598153409170800202F1B200317080800EB 0783
059A054A046D0804008C0536046D0804008C05AC051708E315790234067F055C 069D
080C009227A027AE2784279D1EB80570046D081E001708FF7F1B133406130340 07EE
0605131B13400617088F006C1907059D1E3608865345542D49CFA51534093013 06BB
3406B805B1158C051708FF1FD80317080004DF022C15C9056D0816001814AB10 07EB
0B5365656B206572726F7220C2119D1E3608885345432D524541C41316340930 098B
133406B1151B133406170800047B156D082100B80541134006AB10124469736B 0673
2072656164206572726F72202320C2119D1EB80517080004BE026D081600B805 08DF
1B13340679029A05170800048C0586026207AC053608895345432D57524954C5 07B2
5216340930133406B1151B1334061708000491156D082200B80541134006AB10 05C2
134469736B207772697465206572726F72202320C2119D1E17080004BE026D08 097C
11
1000AB10094469736B2066756C6C9D1E3608842B4255C6B61634094D13170804 08C3
0079027902B805111310046D080600AC050513B80526133406860236088D454D 0644
```

```
054592D425546464552D312173409051311139A058602620711130513240817 0668
8FF7F5505400617080404A608F2FF3608865550444154C53D17340926133406 08F7
40617080080E603261334064006360885464C5553C871173409111305132408 066D
505340617080080D8036D081C00550534061708FF7FD803B805550540065505 0762
A028C054C0395184D13170804007902A608CEFF360885424C4F43CB90173409 0994
C0341134006370526133406B80534066D058602B80579026D08440019177004 061E
D081A00AC056D054F18B8056D054C03411340065703951863038602B8053406 071D
D058602B805790270046D08D0FFB80526134006411334066D0804007A174705 080A
C05FA023608864255464645D2D61734091B133406B805370519176D08FCFF1B 09F1
340066D0534064A046D0814006D05FA026D0534061708FF7FD8034C0395186D 07D7
540066D05261340064705FA02360883522FD7461834091B13340637058C05ED 075A
2D102DB051B134006ED124C0324089A059A05301340061C166D0808005D165C 06F8
80400C216EE02170800041B138D068208DEFFFC0547051B1340063608863F44 0827
55054C88F183409200607038C05230417080900DF1936088A53484F572D4552 076A
12
24FD2DD183409210A34066D0851002A0A34061303170840002F1B210A3406EB 064D
5AB100A61742073637265656E201708FF1FD803C211AB10056C696E6520C211 0AA5
814881218142A0A34061303170840003F1B0D1217081800F014181418149D1E 049C
608874D4553534147C5F8183409F30934066D081200C9056D080800AF0A8812 08F2
C115C080E00AB1007204D7367202320C2113608854552524FD262193409630B 08B1
30934064A046D0804009F1ADC0A80101814AB10074572726F723A2017082200 07BF
0146C1017082200F01463030D126C19070505193608863F4552524FD2941934 07E7
98C056D0808009C195C080400AC053608853F434F4DD0D6193409660A340670 07DC
417081100DF193608863F53544143CBF1193409FA04C60934068C0583045703 08E5
F19FA04DC0A170880007902830417080700DF193608853F455845C3091A3409 08A2
60A340617081200DF193608863F50414952D3361A3409860217081300DF1936 074A
8843F4353D04C1A3409FA048F0A3406860217081400DF193608883F4C4F4144 087D
94EC7611A3409210A3406700417081600DF193608872841424F5254A97A1A34 07F2
9C829360884524F4CCC951AAE1A8CD08EC08BD6598BF94FD1E703FC8BF783EE 10CD
236FF35FDFA36F2A5FBFC8BF283C402E9A5E6854D2F4D4FC4A51A340937054C 1046
36D05940247058C053705940247053608824DAFD31A34099A05370537050907 0713
13
D05F506940247056D05F503D5068C054705D5068C053608842F4D4FC4F11A34 0A6D
93705C9034705F61A360881AF181B34091F1B8C05AC053608834D4FC42B1B34 0862
91F1BAC053608852A2F4D4FC4391B34093705DF024705F61A3608822AAF471B 0875
4094F1B8C05AC053608C1DC5B1B34092A0A3406170840002F1BEE0217084000 06DD
1022A0A4006360888284E554D424552A96A1B3409EE02B80537057006710A34 087D
6DE016D082C008C05710A3406AF02AC05DB05710A3406AF02A3037B0A3406EE 08C7
26D08080057037B0A8D0647055C08C6FF47053608864E554D4245D2881B3409 089F
C034C03DB05B805EE02700617082D001004B805370579027C037B0A4006931B 076D
8057006561386026D081800B805700617082E00860217080500DF194C035C08 0688
AFFAC0547056D080400BD063608864558504543D4D51B34099A0579029A0524 0A29
8BB14B80517080E00CB0A340610046D083200AC05B80555051004B805470513 0683
3790237056D080A00170807005C08100017080800F0145613F014170808005C 04EE
82800B80517080D0010046D080E004808AC0556134C035C080400B8056D057F 057F
64C036D05EE024006F014820894FFAC05360884574F52C42E1C3409210A3406 0939
D080C00210A3406DE175C080600D90934062A0A340679028C058701DC0A1708 0668
20072072A0A8D069A05860237056D05DC0A7F067902DC0AEE02470581073608 0805
14
52D46494EC4B31C34095613BA1CDC0A4C0A340634061D02B80570046D082000 0833
C05DC0A10214C0A340634069A0586026D0808001D025C080600FC054C033608 064D
180001D3409210A34066D0828005703210A8D064C032A0A4006210A3406F912 05EE
703D80370046D0808003E1A4705AC055C0806004705AC053608864352454154 06C5
5401D3409081D6D081200AC051B0B18149812170804006C19FC11DC0AB80570 0780
6E50934063207EE02EC0AB8051708A0000B02DC0A0703170880000B021021F8 079B
A5A0A34064006DC0AFA02F80A360889494E544552505245D47A1D3409081D6D 093C
81E00660A340623046D080A003F0BF80A5C0806003F0B7F05121A5C081C00DC 0582
ADE1B7B0A3406EE026D080800B41F5C080600AC05971F121A5C08C2FF360884 08E6
214353D0CF1D3409FA048F0A400636088551554552D91F1E3409D90934061708 091B
000371C4C032A0A40063608C1DB301E34094C03660A4006360881DD4C1E3409 0719
1708C000660A400636088B44546494E4954494F4ED35A1E34094C0A34065A0A 07C3
40063608873C4255494C44D36A1E34094C03EF08360884515549D4841E34094C 0945
3210A4006501EAB1003206F6B18141905381EDB1D660A340670046D080700AB 0677
10026F6B5C08E7FF360884424143CB961E3409DC0A8602F80A3608C542454749 0B04
```

```
CECA1E3409F919DC0A57033608C4544845CEDB1E3409F9196303551ADC0A9A05 0B9
15
86028C0540063608C244CFED1E34095D1F2408DC0A6F033608C44C4F4FD0081F 099
34096F03551A5D1F8208D11E3608C52B4C4F4FD0191F34096F03551A5D1FA608 087
D11E36088445584 9D42E1F34094705AC0536088 7434F4D50494CC5441F3409F9 09D
194705B805FA0237053406F80A3608C95B434F4D50494C45DD531F3409081D70 092
044C03DF19AC053F0BF80A3608C74C4954455241CC6F1F3409660A34066D0808 08C
005D1F1708F80A3608C8444C4954455241CC8D1F3409660A34066D0808008C05 081
971F971F3608C5554E5449CCA91F34095703551A5D1F6D08D11E3608C3454EC4 0A8
C61F3409CE1F3608C541474149CEDC1F34095703551A5D1F5C08D11E3608C652 0A1
45504541D4E81F340937053705F01F470547051303F41E3608C249C6FE1F3409 09E
5D1F6D08DC0A4C03F80A63033608C4454C53C519203409630355 1A5D1F5C08DC 094
0A4C03F80A8C056303F41E63033608C55748494CC52E2034091E20FA023608C1 098
BB4F203409681A5D1F3608FB20501E36088 7283B434F4445A95F203409470510 083
214B0B3F0B40063608C22EA2712034091708220 0660A34066D0814005D1FAB10 065
BA1CDC0A7006EE02EC0A5C080A00BA1CDC0A80106C103608C1A2892034091708 09F
2200660A34066D0806005D1F9210BA1CDC0A7006EE02EC0A360889494D4D4544 08B
494154C5B82034091021170840000B02360886534D554447C5DA203409102117 07D
16
0820000B023608864C41544553D4F22034095A0A340634063608C1A807213409 077
17082900BA1C3608C1A71A213409081D70041708 0500DF19AC05971F3608844C 076
4F41C42821340921 0A340637052A0A340637054C032A0A4006F912D102210A40 063
06DB1D47052A0A40064705210A40063608C32D2DBE3E213409851A4C032A0A40 069
06F912210A34069A053F1B8602210A8D06360886464F524745D4712134095A0A 07F
34064C0A34068602170818 00DF192C21B805FF093406830417081500DF19B805 073
1B0B080A40062F0B34065A0A34064006360886535354415 4C593217409000005 062
414C4C4F5420202020202084535953C6D22174090A53595354454D2E53435200 08F
000084505249C6EB21740905414C4C4F54202020202020202020202020202020 071
2020202020202020202020202020749CA0C61DA2BB1D8B1E3B1DE84D037453 08E
3C2C75F7E84403744A9A1F84534543C60222740905414C4C4F54202020202020 098
202020202020202020202020202020202020202020202020202018740E9AB06DFD18 066
74079A41FBFD1875EB9AA46DFD189AD26DFD18E984415558C64B22740905414C 0F1
4C4F5420202020202020202020202020202020202020202020202020202020202020 048
20B8F2E877F775F3EBE28A079A0CDEFD1874C0E9F400803E41190074B68242CD 116
94223409AB1014556E646566696E6564206572726F7220636F6465B805CF1136 0B2
17
088252B1DD223409AB1015496E76616C69642066756E6374696F6E20636F6465 0BA
36088252B201233409AB100E46696C65206E6F7420666F756E6436088252B322 0A0
233409AB100E50617468206E6F7420666F756E6436088252B43C233409AB1013 099
546F6F206D616E79206F70656E2066696C657336088252B556233409AB100D41 0A9
63636573732064656E69656436088 35231B275233409AB100E496E76616C6964 0AF
2061636365737336088541 44494FD38E23B32358B44CCD2186444F535645D2A9 0C9
23C323B430CD218ADC2AFF532AE450E9A6DD87534554494E54D3B823DE2333C0 0F8
8ED8A017042EA2DD21B040A217048CC88ED8B80035CD21538F06DF21068F06E1 0D9
21B81B35CD21538F06E321068F06E521B82335CD21538F06E721068F06E921BA 0BF
5E01B80025CD21BA4701B81B25CD21BA4701B82325CD21BB0100B80044CD2181 0B2
CA2000B80144CD21E92DDD87524553494E54D3D223572433C08ED82EA0DD2124 0DB
F08A26170482E40F0AC4A217042EFF36DF218F0600002EFF36E1218F0602002E 0AD
FF36E3218F066C002EFF36E5218F066E002EFF36E7218F068C002EFF36E9218F 0D2
068E008CC88ED8E9CEDCB80000730140E9C4DC854F50454EC84B24BD248CC88E 0F8
D82BC9585ACD2150EBE086434C4F5345C8B324D524585BCD21730150EBCC8648 0F0
414E444CC5CA24340980107902EE02340636088 9434C4F53454D4553D3DE2434 0A6
18
098010B8055D04210A34067004D8036D08140018146C1017080E00BD0A881218 064
145C080400FC0536088B434C4F534548414E444CC5F324340998174D17B805E7 09F
24C9056D081800F5061708003ED324C9056D080A008C05A1157902DF19B805FF 099
24B805700617080400790262073608 8C435245415445 48414E444CC529253409 079
EE021708003CBB246D080800A11579029C19360883592FCE6F253409AB100828 086
592F4E293F204E17080800F014BB1417085900D80317085900100 46D080E0017 061
085900F01457035C080A0017084E00F0144C03FC113608853F2E5343D2942534 087
09B80570061708 3D0023046D08530057039A0580109A0579028C052408550570 06B
0617082E0010046D080800AC054C0348088208EAFF6D082700B8058010790292 079
10042E5343528010DB058C058107B805B80570061708040079028C057F06AC05 080
3608855553494EC7D7253409B8053725B8055613BA1CDC0A8C059A057006EE02 0A9
```

```
8051708400036041708 1A00DF198107B805DF25B8058010790217080300 6207 0723
12636088A4F50454E48414E444CC542263409B805EE021708023DBB246D0864 0945
0B805630310046D084C001814250DAC05B80580106C10FC1127231814AB1019 0727
46F20796F7520776973682074 6F2063726561746520697420FB0C9A256D080A 0B04
0B8057E255C080A0017080400620 79D1E5C0810008C05170804006207A11579 05D5
.9
29C198C0580107902EE024006360885504 6494CC5842634090 9224A26360885 0881
346494CC50F27340952224A26360885414 6494CC51F2734099B224A26360889 0865
345434F4E444152D92F2734091708002 0E603360889415558494C494152D93F 0921
7340917080040E6033608886535953544 5CD5527340917080060E60336088353 080A
9D36B273409F221E7243608835052C97E2734090922E72436088353 45C38C27 0B2C
4095222E7243608834155D89A2734099B22E72436088A4D6F644D656D416C6F 0AD4
3A8273409712F4C034C031708001017080 04AC4086D0831001814AB101C4E6F 06F7
420656E6F75676820636F6E746967656F7573206D656D6F72791814712F4C03 0B4E
C034C034C03C408FC05360885434F4C44B1B6273409C327DC23C123B8056303 0A5A
3046D082D00AB1004444F5320C211C211AB1017666F756E642E20444F53203E 08B4
03220726571756972656417080100B123F221EE021708023DBB246D08A600FB 0A1D
3AB101643616E2774206F70656E2053595354454D2E53435220B80520031708 089D
A00EB059A054A046D0804008C0536046D0804008C05AC051708A62879023406 0698
F055C081E00E222062327234123 5B237A23E222E222E222E222E222E2229423 0ACB
222AC051814AB101146696720 4D532D444F5320466F727468201814AB10124E 0920
56D6265726564206D6573736167657321 4C03F3094006F22117080400620 75C 0A09
0
80C00F22180107902EE02400609221708040062075222170804006207 9B2217 05F3
804006207360884434F4CC40C2834094D17051326134006051 31B1340061708 04F0
200CB0A170826013406170806007902170810008107 4C03980A400617080C00 0420
B0A34061708B909170804007902400663 0B1428C829360884574152CD272934 076C
94D170705121A1814AB10055265616479 9D1E36088830444956 4D4553D37829 0873
4094D170705121A1814AB100F446976696465206F766572666C6F779D1E3608 08B1
541424F52D4952934090705630B121AB709781EF221E7246D081E005703F309 097B
00619054C032A0A40064C03210A4006501E170801008D2C9D1E3608834259C5 0610
0293409760E810F370FA60FFB131814AB1008476F6F646279652063 0B6E30FC 0A23
190301814FB0C552498174D1717080000B12336088453415 6C5FC293409582A 08D8
7080001DC0A9A058602722AA42A36088553415645B0352A34093727AE27B805 08C5
C034C032C15CA2A36088553415645B1502A3409B80537059115CA2A6D05BE02 08F2
7088B00DF1947053608855341564 5B26A2A34096303E618582A360885534156 08F6
5B38A2A34091814630BCF1117080A00BD0A8812FC119B2280106C109B223725 08DC
6088553415645B49C2A3409B8056D080E008C05A11579028C055C0804004C03 07F3
C05DF19360887434F4D534156C5C22A3409922ADB05DB05722AA42A36088742 0AF2
1
C4F534156C5E62A3409922A37051708FD00C5104006712FC510EE0240069A05 0A10
5106F0379024006B805C510170805007902400 66D05C51017080700722AAC05 0739
D05DB05DB05722A17081A00C5107F064705C5105703722AAC05170808007902 07CB
42A3608862E46494C45D3FE2A3409250DF221E7246D081D001814AB10105379 09BD
374656D2066696C653A20202020F22180106C100922E7246D081D001814AB10 0901
05072696D61727920666 96C653A20202009228010 6C105222E7246D081D0018 08AE
4AB10105365636F6E646172792066696C653A20522280106C109B22E7246D08 0A5E
D001814AB1010417578696C69617279206669 6C653A209B2280106C10FB0C18 09CE
43608844C4953D4642B3409250D1814B8053E0A4006AB100953637265656E20 084B
3201708FF1FD803C211170810004C03240818146D056F03DC11FC116D053E0A 079C
40688128208ECFF1814FB0C3608885359534 24C4F43CB032C34097427DE1736 0A5E
88653424C4F43CB4E2C34094B27DE1736088641424C4F43CB612C34096127DE 0A0A
73608875359534C4F41C4722C340974274521360885534C4F41C4832C34094B 0944
745213608854 14C4F41C4952C34096127452136088753595 34C4953D4A52C34 09A2
974270A2C36088553 4C4953D4B52C34094B270A2C360885414C4953D4C72C34 0959
961270A2C3608855452 4941C4D72C3409B8056F0379028C052408181455050A 07B5
2
C8208F8FF181418144C03340A4006AB10114D532D444F532066696720466F72 08F4
4682063030D12903063030D126E3063030D1218144F0C34066D08080017080C 0552
0F01436088453484FD7E72C3409CB14EE028C0524085505EF2C34146D080800 099D
B14AC0548086F03A608ECFFDF14360885564C4953D4452D3409250D710A3406 0A39
705750B181418144C03340A40064C0A34063406B805B8054C035C111C111C11 0541
C111C11D6106C10FC119812340A340617083C0036046D080E0018144C03340A 05BC
0065C0812001708140034 0A34069A053F1B86020D124B0B2F0B3406B8057004 0502
```

```
3414B8056D080600BB14AC05E6036D08A4FFAC05181418144705710A4006FB0C 091
36088444554DD0702D3409250D710A34063705750B181418141708050000D1217 05A
0810004C03240855056F03DC118208F8FF63030D12170810004C03240855054C 06A
035C111C11D6106C108208F2FF18149A0579028C05B80517080F00D803F50324 093
08181455054C03170804009111FC11550517081000079025505EB052408550570 05F
06FC114C035C111C111C11D6106C108208ECFF63030D1224085505700 6B80517 085
08200023049A0517087E003604E6036D080800AC0517082E00F0148208DCFF17 07A
081000A6089CFF18144705710A4006FB0C3608822ED3022E3409710A34063705 07C
FA04C609340610046D0819001814AB100E3C656D707479207374616 36B3E205C 08F
23
083900FA04C60934068C0524081814550534 06B805630B17080400DC11750BAB 072
100220284C031708040091 11AB1003206829630 3A608D7FF18144705710A4006 070
3608833240CCD32E4A2F5B0726FF770226FF37E922D2833221CC422F5E2F5B07 0BB
268F07268F4702E90ED2843F4353BA562F732F0EE901D28240CC6A2F7E2F5B1F 0BD
8B078CCB8EDBE9EED18221CC772F902F5B1F5889078CCB8EDBE9DCD1834340CC 115
892FA42F5B1F8A072AE48CCB8EDBE9C6D1834321CC9C2FB92F5B1F5888078CCB 0F0
8EDBE9B3D186434D4F5645CCB12FD02F8BDE595F075E1FE302F2A48BC18ED88E 10E
C08BF3E992D18253BDC52FED2F8BDE8CD88EC0595F5E33C0E302F3A68BF37501 12C
40E973D18540444154C5E62F0E30B42ACD215152E961D18521444154C5043021 0D4
305A59B42BCD21E94ED1854054494DC517303430B42CCD215152E93BD1852154 0D3
494DC52A3047305A59B42DCD21E928D1832E54C43D3034094C035C111C111C11 0A1
D6106C103608852E54494DC5503034093230AC054C031708000194025630170 8 077
3A00F014563036088 52E444154C5663034090C304C0317080001940256301708 070
2F00F014563017082F00F01417086C0786025630360887 3F474F535542D78830 08B
C230585B8B0F8BFB47478CCA8EC2F2AFB8FFFF75058B072BC14850AD8BD8FF27 111
844E4641BDB630340957038C05EE02DC0A7006E50934063207DC0AEE028C054C 0A8
24
0324089A0555057902700617087F00D8039A0555057902700 6BE026D080E00DB 079
05AC054C03DB05DB0548088208D6FFFC053608C523544845CEE03034093608C5 0B9
23454C53C5333134095613BA1CDC0A70061708050010046D080C0017083331E7 072
305C081200DC0AEE02700670041708130 0DF194C036D08D2FF3608C32349C63F 099
31340970046D083A005613BA1CDC0A70061708050010046D08140017083F31E7 066
3017083331E730E6035C081200DC0AEE02700670041708130 0DF194C036D08CA 08A
FF3608C43F4445C67B3134095613BA1CDC0A4C0A340634061D026D080A00FC05 090
57035C081A00DC0A5A0A340634061D026D080A00FC0557035C0804004C033608 058
84544153CBC33134093608 03A6
```

Appendix 3

FORTH86 System File: SYSTEM.SCR

The binary file, IMAGE.COM, that you either created from the BASIC program in Chapter 3 or obtained in binary form uses a file called SYSTEM.SCR for boot-up, error message, and for the editor.

If this file is not present, FORTH86 still comes up but with the warning:

```
Can't open SYSTEM.SCR File not found
Fig MS-DOS Forth
Numbered messages! ok
```

The FORTH variable WARNING is set to zero. This causes FORTH to print numbered messages. You want readable messages. In this case WARNING must be set to 1. These are included in SYSTEM.SCR.

If SYSTEM.SCR is present, FORTH loads screen 1 with a 1 SYSLOAD. Screen 1 is similar to DOS running AUTOEXEC.BAT if it is present. Jerry Boutelle recently added an interpreted IF. He had trouble with FORTH using the wrong video mode with a COMPAQ machine so he made the modifications you see in screens 1 and 2.

If you have FORTH86 running, then you need the file SYSTEM.SCR for full FORTH functionality. If you don't have a disk containing all of this software, then you need to create SYSTEM.SCR from the listing in this appendix.

We assume you have FORTH86 running. You did this by typing in the ASCII version of the binary of FORTH86 and converting it to binary with the BASIC program given in Chapter 3. You still have no easy way of entering a FORTH format .SCR file. You must type in the ASCII version of SYSTEM.SCR. Call this file SYSTEM.DOC. Use your word processor in the nondocument form so that hex 80 is not sometimes ORed with characters.

Chapter 3 gives a program that is entered manually. This program converts an ASCII .DOC file to a FORTH .SCR screen file format. Now you have SYSTEM.SCR from SYSTEM.DOC.

Here is the file SYSTEM.DOC. This is the ASCII version of SYSTEM.SCR.

```
0
\                                                   10:46 07/08/86
The screens in this file are for FORTH86 boots, error messages,
and editor.  They may be modified for your customized
application packages.

Screen 3 is loaded to save memory images.  This is FORTH's
language extensibility --- adding your code it its language
system.  If you make a mistake in subroutine X, then type
        ' X NFA FENCE ! FORGET X 3 SYSLOAD
to restore your FORTH system to its previous state forgetting
all subroutines after and including X.

Don't recompile or reassemble unchanged code.  Use FORTH's
extensibilty to speed compilation and assembly time.

1
\ system start up                                   17:44 10/11/89
-CURSOR
: %?VIDEO ?MODE
  ONGOSUB 0 1 1 1 1 1 1 0 1 ENDGOSUB >R 2DROP R> ;
%?VIDEO CONSTANT %?COLOR
%?COLOR
#IF CO80 BLACK BACKGROUND  YELLOW FOREGROUND
#ELSE BW80 INTENSITY
#THEN CLS
264 CONSTANT %MON 265 CONSTANT %DAY 266 CONSTANT %YEAR
10 CONSTANT %TEN
#IF ." 0" 1 .R #ELSE 2 .R #THEN ." /" %DAY C@ DUP %TEN <
#IF ." 0" 1 .R #ELSE 2 .R #THEN ." /" %YEAR C@ 2 .R
2 SYSLOAD

2
\ system start up                                   13:47 10/15/89

?DEF ASSEMBLER
#IF ASSEMBLER ?DEF REVSYM
   #IF CR ." PC/ASSEMBLER  " ASSEMBLER REVSYM COUNT TYPE
   #THEN #THEN FORTH
%?COLOR
#IF RED FOREGROUND #THEN
CR ." Space available: " SP@ HERE - U. ." bytes" %?COLOR
#IF GREEN FOREGROUND #THEN %?COLOR
#IF BLACK BACKGROUND YELLOW FOREGROUND
#ELSE -INTENSITY
#THEN FORGET %?VIDEO
( PFILE - select your files ) .FILES
CR CURSOR
\ You can change your start up logo
3
\ save system                                 \ JFB 13:19 01/05/89
HEX
LATEST     0C +ORIGIN !  \ top NFA
HERE       1C +ORIGIN !  \ FENCE
HERE       1E +ORIGIN !  \ DP
VOC-LINK @ 20 +ORIGIN !  \ vocabulary list

\ SAVE MYFILE.COM \ or whatever filename you select

4
\ FORTH86 messages  hex 00 +                        10:49 07/08/86
empty stack
```

```
dictionary full
has incorrect address mode
is redefined
is undefined
disk address out of range
stack overflow
disk error
incorrect number of arguments on stack
Fig MS-DOS Forth error 0A
Fig MS-DOS Forth error 0B
Fig MS-DOS Forth error 0C
BASE must be DECIMAL
missing decimal point
PC/ASSEMBLER FORTH
5
\ FORTH86 messages  hex 10 +                        10:49 07/08/86
compilation only, use in definition
execution only
conditionals not paired
definition not finished
in protected dictionary
use only when loading
off current editing screen
declare vocabulary
no case body
directory pathname more than 64 characters
Fig MS-DOS Forth error 1B
Fig MS-DOS Forth error 1C
Fig MS-DOS Forth error 1D
Fig MS-DOS Forth error 1E
Fig MS-DOS Forth error 1F
6
\ PC/ASSEMBLER messages  hex 20 +                   09:37 02/04/88
relative address out of range
illegal label
duplicate local label
too many operands
invalid opcode/operand form
cs illegal
local label table full
unresolved local label
PC/ASSEMBLER error 27
PC/ASSEMBLER error 28
PC/ASSEMBLER error 29
PC/ASSEMBLER error 2A
PC/ASSEMBLER error 2B
PC/ASSEMBLER error 2C
PC/ASSEMBLER error 2D
7
\ MS-DOS errors DOSERR=30                           10:49 07/08/86
1  Invalid function code
2  File not found
3  Path not found
4  Too many open files (no open handles left)
5  Access denied
6  Invalid handle
7  Memory control blocks destroyed
8  Insufficient memory
9  Invalid memory block address
10  Invalid environment
11  Invalid format
12  Invalid access code
13  Invalid data
14  RESERVED
```

```
15  Invalid drive
8
16  Attempt to remove the current directory
17  Not same device
18  No more files
19  Disk is write-protected
20  Bad disk unit
21  Drive not ready
22  Invalid disk command
23  CRC error
24  Invalid length (disk operation)
25  Seek error
26  Not an MS-DOS disk
27  Sector not found
28  Out of paper
29  Write fault
30  Read fault
31  General failure
9
32  Sharing violation
33  Lock violation
34  Wrong disk
35  FCB unavailable
36  RESERVED
37  RESERVED
38  RESERVED
39  RESERVED
40  RESERVED
41  RESERVED
42  RESERVED
43  RESERVED
44  RESERVED
45  RESERVED
46  RESERVED
47  RESERVED
10
48  RESERVED
49  RESERVED
50  Network not supported
51  Remote computer not listening
52  Duplicate name on network
53  Network name not found
54  Network busy
55  Network device no longer exists
56  Net BIOS command limit exceeded
57  Network adapter hardware error
58  Incorrect response from network
59  Unexpected network error
60  Incompatible remote adapt
61  Print queue full
62  Queue not full
63  Not enough space for print file
11
64  Network name was deleted
65  Access denied
66  Network device type incorrect
67  Network name not found
68  Network name limit exceeded
69  Net BIOS session limit exceeded
70  Temporarily paused
71  Network request not accpeted
72  Print or disk redirection is paused
73  RESERVED
74  RESERVED
```

```
75  RESERVED
76  RESERVED
77  RESERVED
78  RESERVED
79  RESERVED
12
\   File exists                                         15:13 09/22/89
81  RESERVED
82  Cannot make
83  Interrupt 24 failure
84  Out of structures
85  Already assigned
86  Invalid password
87  Invalid parameter
88  Net write fault
89  RESEVED
 bytes were written to file
91 Disk containing auxiliary file full

 was closed
No handle - file was not opened
13
\                                                       10:47 07/08/86

\ this screen intentionally left blank.

14
\                                                       10:48 07/08/86

\ this screen intentionally left blank.

15
\                                                       10:48 07/08/86

\ this screen intentionally left blank.

16
\                                               \ JFB 17:25 01/05/89

\ this screen intentionally left blank.

17
FORGET Z                                        \     08:31 12/12/85
CLS -CURSOR
CYAN FOREGROUND ." Cursor control" YELLOW FOREGROUND
CR 24 EMIT ."       cursor up"
CR 25 EMIT ."       cursor down"
CR 26 EMIT ."       cursor right"
CR 27 EMIT ."       cursor left"
CR 94 EMIT 26 EMIT ."      word right"
CR 94 EMIT 27 EMIT ."      word left"
CR 26 EMIT 221 EMIT ."      tab right"
CR 222 EMIT 27 EMIT ."      tab left"
CR ." F7     vertical tab up"
CR ." F8     vertical tab down"
CR ." Home   start of screen"
CR ." ^Home  end of screen text"
-->
18
                                                \     15:13 12/11/85
CR 17 EMIT 196 EMIT 217 EMIT ."     start of next line"
CR ." End    end of line"
CR ." ^End   beginning of line"
CR CYAN FOREGROUND ." Insert" YELLOW FOREGROUND
```

```
CR ." Ins    insert mode, word wrap"
CR ." space  insert space"
CR ." ^N     insert line at cursor"
CR ." ^F1    insert blank screen into file"
30 0 GOTOXY CYAN FOREGROUND ." Delete" YELLOW FOREGROUND
30 1 GOTOXY ." ^G     delete charcter or rest of blank line"
30 2 GOTOXY ." ^T     delete word right or rest of blank line"
30 3 GOTOXY ." ^Y     delete line"
30 4 GOTOXY ." ^QY    delete from cursor to line end"
-->

19
\                                                08:47 09/26/86
30  5 GOTOXY ." Del    backspace and delete"
30  6 GOTOXY 17 EMIT 196 EMIT ."      backspace"
30  7 GOTOXY ." F9     blank screen"
30  8 GOTOXY ." F10 "GREEN FOREGROUND
             ."    restore " YELLOW FOREGROUND
             ." screen contents"

30  9 GOTOXY ." ^F2    remove screen from file"
30 10 GOTOXY ." ^F3    truncate file"
-->

20
                                             \      09:00 03/12/86
30 11 GOTOXY CYAN FOREGROUND ." Exit editor" YELLOW FOREGROUND
30 12 GOTOXY ." Esc     exit and save"
30 13 GOTOXY ." ^KQ     abandon edit, text unchanged"
30 14 GOTOXY ." ^Break  abandon edit, possibly lose changes"

40 15 GOTOXY CYAN FOREGROUND ." Page control" YELLOW FOREGROUND
40 16 GOTOXY ." PgDn    next screen"
40 17 GOTOXY ." ^PgDn   last screen"
40 18 GOTOXY ." PgUp    previous screen"
40 19 GOTOXY ." ^PgUp   first screen"
00 21 GOTOXY CYAN FOREGROUND ." Configuration Management"
             YELLOW FOREGROUND
00 22 GOTOXY ." Type EDITOR MYID, enter your initials, then 3 SY
SLOAD"-->

21
                                             \      14:26 01/24/86
20 24 GOTOXY RED FOREGROUND
      ." Hit a key to continue" YELLOW FOREGROUND KEY DROP
CLS
CYAN FOREGROUND ." Line stack" YELLOW FOREGROUND
CR ." F3   push line and cursor down"
CR ." F4   push line and delete"
CR ." F5   pop line and cursor up"
CR ." F6   pop line and insert"
CR ." ^F4  reclaim top of line stack"
CR ." ^F5  discard top of line stack"
-->

22
                                             \      10:53 04/11/86
CR CYAN FOREGROUND ." Search and replace" YELLOW FOREGROUND
CR ." ^QF  enter search string"
CR ." ^L   continue search"
CR ." ^QA  enter replacement string"
CR ." ^F8  replace found string"

CR CYAN FOREGROUND ." Block commands" YELLOW FOREGROUND
```

```
CR ." ^KB  mark block begin"
CR ." ^KK  mark block end"
CR ." ^KC  move block"
CR ." ^KI  insert blanks in block"
CR ." ^KY  delete block"
-->

23
                                                   \     16:02 03/18/86
CR CYAN FOREGROUND ." Edit" YELLOW FOREGROUND
CR ." E    primary file"
CR ." SE   secondary file"
CR ." AE   auxiliary file"
CR ." SYSE system file"

20 24 GOTOXY RED FOREGROUND

R> DROP R> DROP R> DROP R> DROP R> DROP R> DROP
R> DROP R> DROP R> DROP R> DROP E  CURSOR QUIT

24
\                                                        15:18 09/22/89

\ this screen intentionally left blank.

25
FORGET Z                                           \     09:52 03/11/86
CLS -CURSOR
INTENSITY ." Cursor control" -INTENSITY
CR 24 EMIT ."        cursor up"
CR 25 EMIT ."        cursor down"
CR 26 EMIT ."        cursor right"
CR 27 EMIT ."        cursor left"
CR 94 EMIT 26 EMIT ."      word right"
CR 94 EMIT 27 EMIT ."      word left"
CR 26 EMIT 221 EMIT ."      tab right"
CR 222 EMIT 27 EMIT ."      tab left"
CR ." F7     vertical tab up"
CR ." F8     vertical tab down"
CR ." Home   start of screen"
CR ." ^Home  end of screen text"
-->
26
                                                   \     15:13 12/11/85
CR 17 EMIT 196 EMIT 217 EMIT ."     start of next line"
CR ." End    end of line"
CR ." ^End   beginning of line"
CR INTENSITY ." Insert" -INTENSITY
CR ." Ins    insert mode, word wrap"
CR ." space  insert space"
CR ." ^N     insert line at cursor"
CR ." ^F1    insert blank screen into file"
30 0 GOTOXY INTENSITY ." Delete" -INTENSITY
30 1 GOTOXY ." ^G     delete charcter or rest of blank line"
30 2 GOTOXY ." ^T     delete word right or rest of blank line"
30 3 GOTOXY ." ^Y     delete line"
30 4 GOTOXY ." ^QY    delete from cursor to line end"
-->

27
\                                                        08:47 09/26/86
30 5 GOTOXY ." Del    backspace and delete"
30 6 GOTOXY 17 EMIT 196 EMIT ."      backspace"
30 7 GOTOXY ." F9     blank screen"
```

```
30 8 GOTOXY ." F10 " INTENSITY
            ."    restore " -INTENSITY
            ." screen contents"

30 9 GOTOXY ." ^F2    remove screen from file"
30 10 GOTOXY ." ^F3    truncate file"
-->

28
                                                \     10:56 04/11/86
30 11 GOTOXY INTENSITY ." Exit editor" -INTENSITY
30 12 GOTOXY ." Esc      exit and save"
30 13 GOTOXY ." ^KQ      abandon edit, text unchanged"
30 14 GOTOXY ." ^Break   abandon edit, possibly lose changes"

40 15 GOTOXY INTENSITY ." Page control" -INTENSITY
40 16 GOTOXY ." PgDn     next screen"
40 17 GOTOXY ." ^PgDn    last screen"
40 18 GOTOXY ." PgUp     previous screen"
40 19 GOTOXY ." ^PgUp    first screen"
00 21 GOTOXY INTENSITY ." Configuration Management" -INTENSITY
00 22 GOTOXY ." Type EDITOR MYID, enter your initials, then 3 SY
SLOAD"
-->

29
                                                \     10:55 04/11/86
20 24 GOTOXY INTENSITY ." Hit a key to continue" KEY DROP
-INTENSITY
CLS
INTENSITY ." Line stack" -INTENSITY
CR ." F3   push line and cursor down"
CR ." F4   push line and delete"
CR ." F5   pop line and cursor up"
CR ." F6   pop line and insert"
CR ." ^F4  reclaim top of line stack"
CR ." ^F5  discard top of line stack"
-->

30
                                                \     10:53 04/11/86

CR INTENSITY ." Search and replace" -INTENSITY
CR ." ^QF  enter search string"
CR ." ^L   continue search"
CR ." ^QA  enter replacement string"
CR ." ^F8  replace found string"

CR INTENSITY ." Block commands" -INTENSITY
CR ." ^KB  mark block begin"
CR ." ^KK  mark block end"
CR ." ^KC  move block"
CR ." ^KI  insert blanks in block"
CR ." ^KY  delete block"
-->

31
                                                \     10:55 04/11/86

CR INTENSITY ." Edit" -INTENSITY
CR ." E     primary file"
CR ." SE    secondary file"
CR ." AE    auxiliary file"
CR ." SYSE  system file"
```

```
20 24 GOTOXY INTENSITY ." Hit a key to continue" KEY DROP
-INTENSITY
R> DROP R> DROP R> DROP R> DROP R> DROP R> DROP
R> DROP R> DROP R> DROP R> DROP E  CURSOR QUIT
```

Here is DOCTOSCR.DOC which converts one of the .DOC files in these appendices to .SCR format in .DOC format.

```
1
\                                                  15:00 09/22/89
DECIMAL
65      CONSTANT BUFFERSIZE
0       VARIABLE INBUFFER -1 ALLOT
0       VARIABLE ASCIIBUFFER -2 ALLOT BUFFERSIZE ALLOT
0       VARIABLE SCR#           0       VARIABLE LINE#
0       VARIABLE START          0       VARIABLE EOF
0       VARIABLE SCRNUMBER

: CLOSEFILES FLUSH PRIF CLOSEHANDLE SECF CLOSEHANDLE ;
\ --- character
: READCHR   SECF HANDLE INBUFFER 1 READ
            IF CR ." File read err #" U. SP! QUIT THEN 1 <
            IF CR ." End of file" THEN
            INBUFFER C@ DUP 26 =
            IF CLOSEFILES SP! QUIT THEN ; -->
2
\                                                  00:23 01/01/80
DECIMAL
: READLINE ASCIIBUFFER BUFFERSIZE ERASE 0
           BEGIN READCHR DUP 13 <>
           WHILE OVER [ ASCIIBUFFER 1+ ] LITERAL + C! 1+
           REPEAT DROP READCHR DROP
           ASCIIBUFFER C! ;

\ --- number\number of digits
\ --- 0 none
: SCR#? 0 0 ASCIIBUFFER (NUMBER)
        ASCIIBUFFER - 1- DUP 0>
        IF SWAP DROP
        ELSE DROP DROP DROP 0
        THEN ; -->

3
\                                                  00:40 01/01/80

\ primary file screen # ---
: BLANKSCR      BLOCK 1024 BLANKS UPDATE ;

\ screen # ---
: NEXTSCREEN    DUP BLANKSCR SCR# ! 0 LINE# ! ;

\ start screen ---
: INITSCRS      DUP 0>
                IF DUP 0 DO I BLANKSCR LOOP THEN
                SCR# ! 0 LINE# ! 1 START ! ;
-->

4
\                                                  00:41 01/01/80
```

```
DECIMAL
: ISSCR#          SCR#?
                  IF START @ 0=
                    IF INITSCRS 0 SCRNUMBER !
                    ELSE SCR# @ 1+ =
                      IF SCR# @ 1+ NEXTSCREEN 0 SCRNUMBER !
                      ELSE CR ." Scr # " SCR# @ 1+ U.
                        ." expected.  Scr # "  SCR#?
                        DROP U. ."  found." SP! QUIT
                      THEN
                    THEN
                  THEN ; -->

5
\                                                    14:54 09/22/89
DECIMAL

\ line length ---
: >LINE           ASCIIBUFFER COUNT DUP 0>
                  IF >R LINE# @ SCR# @ (LINE) DROP
                    R> CMOVE UPDATE
                  ELSE DROP DROP
                  THEN ;

: NEXTLINE        LINE# @ 1+ 15 MIN LINE# ! ;

: NEWSCREEN       1 SCRNUMBER !
                  ASCIIBUFFER C@ 4 < ASCIIBUFFER C@ 0> AND
                  IF ISSCR# THEN ; -->

6
\                                                    15:29 09/22/89
DECIMAL
: .ASCIILINE      CR ASCIIBUFFER COUNT TYPE ;

: ASCIITOSCR      0 EOF ! 0 START ! 0 SCR# ! 0 LINE# !
                  BEGIN READLINE .ASCIILINE NEWSCREEN
                    SCRNUMBER @
                    IF >LINE NEXTLINE THEN
                  AGAIN ;
;S
Primary file contains the .SCR output.
Secondary file contains the .DOC input.
Auxiliary file contains this program.

Load it with AFILE DOCTOSCR.SCR and 1 ALOAD after you converted
it with the keyboard entered version seen in Chapter 3.
```

Appendix 4

Nonassembler Version of the Laxen Full Screen FORTH Editor

Henry Laxen's modified full screen editor listed in this appendix has any assembler replaced by high-level FORTH. Screens 88 through 96 are commented out because a high-level FORTH version of the assembler MATCH is impossibly slow. The WordStar-like commands ^QA (Ctrl QA), ^QF, and ^QL and the "search and replace" ^F8 were nullified by enclosing them in the FORTH "begin procedure", :, and "end procedure", ;.

The file is called SLAX.DOC for "slow Laxen editor". You must enter it with a word processor in the nondocument mode and use ASCIITOSCR listed in Chapter 3 to convert it to a screen file, or get a disk copy of it in a screen file.

This version of the editor uses BIOS and PC MS DOS calls to write to the screen. The assembler-enhanced version given in Appendix 5 writes directly to the screen. This version of the editor works with nearly all video cards. The assembler version may need some modifications to work with unusual video cards.

The editor commands are summarized in screen 17-20 in file SYSTEM.SCR. Its listing is given in Appendix 3.

```
0
\  acknowledgments                                   14:16 06/24/86

This full screen editor was published in the september 1981
issue of Dr. Dobb's Journal. It was originally written by

Henry Laxen                  This editor is in the public
1259 Cornell Ave.            domain, and may be distributed
Berkeley, CA 94704           further with the inclusion
(415) 525-8582               of this notice.

and modified for ms-dos compatible computers running F86 by

Nautilus Systems 408-688-8121  \ And these notices.
Sandia Labs  Albq, NM 87185
Computer Systems Documentation  pob 5478  kafb,nm 87115

1
\ acknowledgments                                    12:44 09/26/86
\ this screen to be filled by contributors

' EDITOR FENCE ! FORGET EDITOR 2 LOAD 3 SYSLOAD SAVE SP.COM

2
\ BEEP cursor sizes                                  12:39 09/26/86
-CURSOR VOCABULARY EDITOR IMMEDIATE
EDITOR DEFINITIONS -CURSOR
CLS ." Compiling editor"
HEX HERE \ size editor
0 VARIABLE REVSYM -2 ALLOT " 09/26/86"
: BEEP          07 EMIT ;
: BIGBWCURSOR   00 0D SETCURSOR ; \ black and white big cursor
: BIGCOCURSOR   00 07 SETCURSOR ; \ color big cursor
: BIGCURSOR     ?MODE ONGOSUB BIGBWCURSOR BIGCOCURSOR
                              BIGBWCURSOR BIGCOCURSOR
                              BIGCOCURSOR BIGCOCURSOR
                              BIGCOCURSOR BIGBWCURSOR
                              BIGCOCURSOR
                        ENDGOSUB 2DROP ; -->
\ RING THE BELL ON THE TERMINAL. USUALLY AFTER AN ERROR.
3
( BOUNDS          DO LOOP SETUP                   10:32 12/01/85 )
DECIMAL
\ ADDR LEN - ADDR+LEN ADDR
: BOUNDS          OVER + SWAP ;
-->
\ BOUNDS IS A COMMON DO LOOP SETUP WORD. IT ASSUMES THERE IS
\ AN ADDRESS AND A LENGTH ON THE STACK. BOUNDS CONVERTS THIS
\ INTO A HIGH ADDRESS AND A LOW ADDRESS. THE I INDEX OF A DO
\ LOOP WILL THEN RUN THROUGH THIS RANGE OF VALUES WHILE
\ EXECUTING.

4
\ MOVE     WORKS IN EITHER DIRECTION                     25APR81HHL

: MOVE     \ FROM TO LEN -
   ROT ROT 2DUP U< IF
     ROT CMOVE>
   ELSE
     ROT CMOVE
   THEN ;
-->
```

```
\ MOVE WILL MOVE LEN BYTES FROM ADDRESS FROM TO ADDRESS TO
\ AND WILL NOT OVERLAP THEM, NO MATTER WHAT THE RELATIVE VALUES
\ OF FROM TO AND LEN ARE. MOVE SHOULD ALWAYS BE USED WHENEVER
\ THERE IS DANGER OF OVERLAPPING FIELDS.

5
( -TIDY                                        20:19 11/26/85 )
HEX
: -TIDY    \ ADDR LEN -
   BOUNDS DO          \ RUN THROUGH THE STRING
    I C@ DUP 0FF > SWAP BL < OR
    IF                \ is it a control character?
     BL I C!          \ YES, REPLACE IT WITH A BLANK
    THEN
   LOOP ;
DECIMAL -->
\ -TIDY REPLACES ALL CONTROL CHARACTERS IN A SPECIFIED
\ RANGE WITH BLANKS

6
\ VARIABLE AND CONSTANT DEFINITIONS          \     11:32 05/06/86
HEX
 0 VARIABLE &MODE           \ CURRENT MODE ( OVERSTRIKE OR INSERT
 0 VARIABLE &WRAP 2 ALLOT    \ wrap mode
 0 VARIABLE &LS              \ line stack pointer
 0 VARIABLE &SEARCH          \ search update flag
 0 VARIABLE REPLACE          \ replace update flag
 0 VARIABLE &CURSOR          \ CURSOR POSITION
 0 VARIABLE &OLD-MODE        \ PREVIOUS MODE
 0 VARIABLE &UPDATE          \ UPDATE FLAG
 0 VARIABLE &BUF-ADR         \ ADDRESS OF CURRENT BUFFER
 0 VARIABLE &E-ID 012 ALLOT \ DATE AND USER ID LAST MODIFIED
   &E-ID 014 BLANKS          \ INITIALIZE TO BLANKS
-->

7
\ VARIABLE AND CONSTANT DEFINITIONS           WHP 13:32 06/07/86

0  VARIABLE &VMODE      \ video mode
-1 VARIABLE &KB         \ block start screen
-1 VARIABLE &KK         \ block end screen

05  CONSTANT %X-OFF     \ X OFFSET FOR CURSOR POSITIONING
03  CONSTANT %Y-OFF     \ Y OFFSET FOR CURSOR POSITIONING

040 CONSTANT C/L

B/SCR B/BUF *  CONSTANT C/SCR       \ CHARACTER PER SCREEN
C/SCR C/L   /  CONSTANT L/SCR       \ LINES PER SCREEN

10 CONSTANT EDHELP      \ help starts on this screen
20 CONSTANT EDLS -->    \ line stack starts on this screen
8
\ CURSOR POSITIONING VECTORS                   \     15:13 02/03/86

0 VARIABLE 'CRTXY         \ CFA OF ROUTINE THAT MOVES CURSOR
0 VARIABLE 'CRTCLR-SCR    \ CFA OF ROUTINE THAT CLEARS SCREEN
0 VARIABLE 'CLEAR-TO-EOL \ CFA OF ROUTINE CLEARS TO EOL

: CRTXY      \ X Y -
   'CRTXY @ EXECUTE ;

: CRTCLR-SCR    \ -
   'CRTCLR-SCR @ EXECUTE ;
```

```
: CLEAR-TO-EOL      \ -
   'CLEAR-TO-EOL @ EXECUTE ;
: CURSOR &MODE @ IF BIGCURSOR ELSE CURSOR THEN ; -->

9
\ print edit file name                          \     09:17 02/24/86
HEX
: .SYSF          ." System file: "    SYSF COUNT TYPE ;
: .PF            ." Primary file: "   PRIF COUNT TYPE ;
: .SF            ." Secondary file: " SECF COUNT TYPE ;
: .AF            ." Auxiliary file: " AUXF COUNT TYPE ;

: .EF            -CURSOR 0 0 0 4F 0 SCROLLU 5 0 CRTXY
                 SCR @ 0 2000 U/ SWAP DROP ONGOSUB
                 .PF .SF .AF .SYSF BEEP ENDGOSUB CURSOR ;
-->
\ prints the current edit file name

10
\ CURPOS +CURPOS      MOVE-CURSOR                     12:39 09/26/86

: CURPOS      \ - POS
   &CURSOR @ ;           \ RETURN CURRENT CURSOR POSITION
: +CURPOS       \ N -
   &CURSOR +!
   CURPOS 0 MAX          \ AND DO BOUNDS CHECKING
   [ C/SCR 1- ] LITERAL \ CHAR PER SCREEN - 1
   MIN &CURSOR ! ;       \ ALWAYS VALID
: MOVE-CURSOR      \ N -
   -CURSOR +CURPOS       \ MOVE THE CURSOR
   CURPOS C/L /MOD       \ RAW X Y
   %Y-OFF + SWAP         \ ADD IN Y OFFSET
   %X-OFF + SWAP         \ ADD IN X OFFSET
   CRTXY CURSOR ;  -->   \ AND MOVE THERE

11
\ fast curpos and +curpos                             12:39 09/26/86
-->
CODE CURPOS      AX &CURSOR MOV
                 AX PUSH NEXT, END-CODE

CODE +CURPOS     AX POP                   \ relative cursor move
                 &CURSOR AX ADD           \ add it to the cursor
                 AX &CURSOR MOV           \ get the sum
                 AX # 0 CMP               \ compare it to zero
                 < IF &CURSOR # 0 MOV THEN        \ 0
                 AX # C/SCR 1- CMP        \ compare it to end of scr
                 > IF &CURSOR # C/SCR 1- MOV THEN \ c/scr
                 NEXT, END-CODE
-->

12
\  fast move-cursor                                   12:39 09/26/86
-->
CODE M-C         AX POP                   \ relative cursor move
                 &CURSOR AX ADD           \ add it to the cursor
                 AX &CURSOR MOV           \ get the sum
                 AX # 0 CMP <             \ compare it to zero
                 IF &CURSOR # 0 MOV THEN          \ 0
                 AX # C/SCR 1- CMP >      \ compare it to end of scr
                 IF &CURSOR # C/SCR 1- MOV THEN \ c/scr
                 BX AX MOV                \ move curpos to bx
                 CL # 6 MOV BX CL SAR     \ bx contains line #
```

```
                BX # %Y-OFF ADD       \ add in editor offset
-->

13
\  fast move-cursor                                   12:39 09/26/86
-->
                AX # C/L 1- AND     \ get raw x coordinate
                AX # %X-OFF ADD     \ add in editor offset
                AX PUSH             \ return x coordinate
                BX PUSH             \ return y coordinate
                NEXT, END-CODE

: MOVE-CURSOR -CURSOR M-C CRTXY CURSOR ;  \ AND MOVE THERE
-->
pc/assembler code to speed editor

14
\ BUF-ADR    BUFPOS                                         25APR81HHL

: BUF-ADR    \ POS - ADR
   &BUF-ADR @ + ;

\ BUF-ADR CONVERTS THE CURSOR POSITION IT IS CALLED WITH
\ TO THE ADDRESS WITHIN THE DISK BUFFER WHICH CORRESPONDS
\ TO THAT POSITION

: BUFPOS    \ - ADDR
   CURPOS BUF-ADR ;
-->
\ BUFPOS RETURNS THE ADDRESS IN THE DISK BUFFER OF THE
\ CURRENT CHARACTER

15
\ E-UPDATE                                     \     16:19 02/16/86
HEX
\ ---
: E-DT          &E-ID 06 + @DATE SWAP <# 076C - 0 # #
                2DROP 02F HOLD DUP 100 MOD 0
                # # 2DROP 02F HOLD 100 / 0 # #
                2DROP BL HOLD @TIME DROP DUP 100 MOD
                0 # # 2DROP
                3A HOLD 100 / 0 # # #> >R SWAP R> CMOVE ;
: CLRM          0 5 14 4F 14 SCROLLU CURSOR ;
: MODM          05 14 GOTOXY ." Screen modified" ;
: E-UPDATE      UPDATE 1 &UPDATE ! ;
-->
\ E-UPDATE IS CALLED WHENEVER THE CONTENTS OF THE BUFFER
\ HAS CHANGED. IT SETS THE UPDATE FLAG.
\ E-DT is date and time stamp for changed screens
16
\ BUF-MOVE                                     \     18:50 01/01/86
DECIMAL
: GETSCR        SCR @ BLOCK &BUF-ADR ! ;

: EPURGE        UPDATE FLUSH EMPTY-BUFFERS GETSCR ;

: BUF-MOVE     \ FROM TO LEN -
   ROT BUF-ADR
   ROT BUF-ADR
   ROT MOVE
   E-UPDATE ;
-->
\ BUF-MOVE PERFORMS A MOVE OPERATION ON THE CHARACTERS IN THE
\ DISK BUFFERS CORRESPONDING TO THE GIVEN CURSOR POSITION
```

```
17
\ ?PRINTABLE                                        \      12:48 02/15/86

: ?PRINTABLE     \ CHAR - BOOL
   DUP 32 <
   SWAP 126 >
   OR 0= ;
-->
\ ?PRINTABLE RETURNS A TRUE FLAG IF THE CHARACTER IS PRINTABLE.
\ OTHERWISE IT RETURNS A FALSE FLAG

18
\ >LINE# LINE#>                                            12:40 09/26/86

: >LINE#        \ POS - LINE#
   C/L / ;

\ CONVERT A CHARACTER POSITION TO A LINE NUMBER

: LINE#>        \ LINE# - POS
   C/L * ;
-->
CODE >LINE#      AX POP  CL # 6 MOV  AX CL SAR
                 AX PUSH  NEXT, END-CODE
CODE LINE#>      AX POP  CL # 6 MOV  AX CL SAL
                 AX PUSH  NEXT, END-CODE
-->
\ CONVERT A LINE NUMBER TO A CHARACTER POSITION
19
\ CHARS-TO-EOL                                             12:40 09/26/86
HEX
: CHARS-TO-EOL       \ POS - N
   C/L MOD
   C/L SWAP - ;
-->
CODE CHARS-TO-EOL BX POP  BX # C/L 1- AND
                   AX # C/L MOV
                   AX BX SUB
                   AX PUSH  NEXT, END-CODE
-->
\ CHARS-TO-EOL RETURNS THE NUMBER OF CHARACTERS LEFT ON THE
\ LINE GIVEN THE CURRENT CHARACTER POSITION

20
\ fast typet                                               12:41 09/26/86
-->
\ address\length ---
CODE ETYPE       CX POP              \ length
                 DI POP              \ start address
                 1 $ JCXZ            \ jump if zero length
                 SI PUSH             \ save forth ip
                 AX &VMODE MOV       \ video mode
                 AX # 0 CMP =        \ is it zero?
-->
```

Substitute AH VIDEO MOV 2 $: BYTE LODS WORD STOS 2 $ LOOP if you do not have a IBM color adapter for 2 $: --- 2 $. Only the IBM video color adapter (not ibm ega) produces snow when writing directly to the adapter memory.

```
21
\ fast typet                                               12:41 09/26/86
-->
```

```
                IF DX # 3B4 MOV              \ black and white
                  AL # 0E MOV  DX AL OUT
                  DX # 3B5 MOV AL DX IN    \ cursor high
                  AH AL MOV
                  DX # 3B4 MOV
                  AL # 0F MOV  DX AL OUT
                  DX # 3B5 MOV  AL DX IN \ cursor low
                  AX 1 SHL  SI AX MOV      \ print position in si
                  SI DI XCHG
                  AX # B000 MOV \ bw80
                  ES AX MOV
-->

22
\ fast typet                                          12:41 09/26/86
-->
                ELSE DX # 3D4 MOV             \ color
                  AL # 0E MOV  DX AL OUT
                  DX # 3D5 MOV  AL DX IN    \ cursor high
                  AH AL MOV
                  DX # 3D4 MOV
                  AL # 0F MOV  DX AL OUT
                  DX # 3D5 MOV  AL DX IN    \ cursor low
                  AX 1 SHL  SI AX MOV       \ print position in si
                  SI DI XCHG
                  AX # B800 MOV              \ co80 segment
                  ES AX MOV
                THEN
-->

23
\ fast typet                                          12:41 09/26/86
-->
                AX &VMODE MOV          \ video mode
                AX # 0 CMP =           \ is it zero?
              IF
                AH VIDEO MOV           \ black and white video write
          4 $:  BYTE LODS
                WORD STOS
                4 $ LOOP
-->

24
\ fast typet                                          12:41 09/26/86
-->           ELSE
          2 $:  BYTE LODS              \ get byte to write
                BL AL MOV              \ save byte in bl
                DX # 3DA MOV           \ video adapter status
                CLI                    \ interrupts off
          3 $:  AL DX IN AL # 1 AND    \ snow?
                3 $ JZ                 \ wait for snow to clear
                AL BL MOV  BYTE STOS \ write character
                STI                    \ interrupts on
                DI INC                 \ point to next write
                2 $ LOOP               \
              THEN
                SI POP                 \ restore forth ip
          1 $:  NEXT, END-CODE -->

25
\ DISPLAY-TO-EOL                                      12:41 09/26/86
DECIMAL
: DISPLAY-TO-EOL       \ POS -
   -CURSOR DUP BUF-ADR           \ GET ADDRESS IN BUFFER
```

```
   OVER CHARS-TO-EOL             \ REST OF LINE
   -TRAILING                     \ IGNORE BLANKS
   ROT OVER + >R                 \ SAVE RESULTANT CURSOR POSITION
    TYPE                         \ DISPLAY WHAT'S THERE
   R> DUP >LINE# CURPOS >LINE# =   \ same line?
   IF CLEAR-TO-EOL               \ only if cursor is on same line
   ELSE DROP                     \ discard curpos
   THEN CURSOR ;                 \ AND REMOVE THE REST
-->
\ DISPLAY-TO-EOL DISPLAYS THE REST OF THE LINE STARTING FROM
\ THE CURRENT CURSOR POSITION.

26
\ ?EMPTY-LINE                                  \      12:51 03/07/86
HEX
: ?EMPTY-LINE       \ LINE# - BOOL
   LINE#> BUF-ADR C/L      \ ADDR LEN
   -TRAILING               \ REMOVE TRAILING BLANKS
   SWAP DROP 0= ;          \ REPORT SUCCESS IF ALL BLANKS

: FULL          05 14 GOTOXY ." Screen full" BEEP ;

-->
\ ?EMPTY-LINE RETURNS TRUE IF THE SPECIFIED LINE NUMBER IS
\ COMPLETELY BLANK. OTHERWISE IT RETURNS FALSE.

27
\ DISPLAY-TO-EOS                                      12:41 09/26/86

: DISPLAY-TO-EOS               \ LINE# -
   -CURSOR CURPOS SWAP         \ SAVE CURRENT CURSOR POSITION
   L/SCR SWAP DO               \ RUN THROUGH REST OF SCREEN
    I LINE#>
    DUP &CURSOR !              \ SET CURSOR POSITION
    0 MOVE-CURSOR
    DISPLAY-TO-EOL             \ AND DISPLAY LINE FROM THERE
   LOOP
   &CURSOR !                   \ RESTORE CURSOR POSITION
   0 MOVE-CURSOR CURSOR ;
-->
\ DISPLAY THE ENTIRE SCREEN FROM THE GIVEN LINE NUMBER TO
\ THE END OF THE SCREEN. THIS IS USED WHEN A LINE IS
\ INSERTED OR DELETED FROM THE MIDDLE OF THE SCREEN.
28
\ fast display-to-eos                                 12:42 09/26/86
--> CODE DISPLAY-TO-EOS
                BX POP            \ line #
                CX # L/SCR MOV    \ lines per screen
                CX BX SUB         \ number of lines to show
                SI PUSH           \ save forth ip
                SI &BUF-ADR MOV   \ point si at screen buffer
                AL # C/L MOV      \ characters per line
                BL MUL            \ offset to line #
                SI AX ADD         \ buffer offset to line #
                BL # %Y-OFF ADD   \ lines above screen display
                AL # 50 MOV       \ 80 characters per line
                BL MUL            \ lines 80 *
                DI AX MOV         \ byte offset into video buffer
                DI # %X-OFF ADD   \ move to left hand side
-->
29
\ fast display-to-eos                                 12:42 09/26/86
-->
                DI 1 SAL               \ adjust for attribute byte
```

```
             AX &VMODE MOV         \ video mode
             AX # 0 CMP =          \ is it zero?
             IF   AX # B000 MOV    \ bw
             ELSE AX # B800 MOV    \ color
             THEN  ES AX MOV       \ video segment in es
-->

30
\ fast display-to-eos                                  12:42 09/26/86
-->
        1 $:  CX PUSH             \ save line count index
              AX &VMODE MOV       \ video mode
              CX # C/L MOV        \ characters per line
              AX # 0 CMP =        \ is it zero?
            IF
              AH VIDEO MOV        \ black and white video write
        4 $:  BYTE LODS
              WORD STOS
              4 $ LOOP
-->

31
\ fast display-to-eos                                  12:42 09/26/86
-->
            ELSE
        2 $:  BYTE LODS              \ get byte to write
              BL AL MOV              \ save byte in bl
              DX # 3DA MOV           \ video adapter status
              CLI                    \ interrupts off
        3 $:  AL DX IN AL # 1 AND    \ snow?
              3 $ JZ                 \ wait for snow to clear
              AL BL MOV  BYTE STOS   \ write character
              STI                    \ interrupts on
              DI INC                 \ point to next write
              2 $ LOOP
            THEN
-->

32
\ fast display-to-eos                                  12:42 09/26/86
-->
              DI # 50 C/L - 2* ADD \ point video line
              CX POP               \ restore line count index
              1 $ LOOP             \ do until done
              SI POP               \ restore forth ip
              NEXT, END-CODE -->
```

Substitute AH VIDEO MOV 2 $: BYTE LODS WORD STOS 2 $ LOOP if you do not have a IBM color adapter for 2 $: --- 2 $. Only the IBM video color adapter (not ibm ega) produces snow when writing directly to the adapter memory.

```
33
\ EXPAND                                        \      16:14 02/16/86

: EXPAND                      \ POS -
     DUP DUP                  \ P P P
     C/L +                    \ P FROM TO
     C/SCR OVER -             \ P FROM TO LEN
     BUF-MOVE                 \ TEXT MOVED IN BUFFER
     BUF-ADR C/L BLANKS ;     \ INSERT BLANK LINE
-->
\ EXPAND MOVES ALL OF THE LINES DOWN BY ONE AND INSERTS A BLANK
LINE AT THE SPECIFIED POSITION
```

```
34
\ SHRINK                                                  25APR81HHL

: SHRINK      \ POS - )
   DUP                            \ POS POS
   C/L + SWAP                     \ FROM TO
   OVER C/SCR SWAP -              \ FROM TO LEN
   BUF-MOVE                       \ MOVE IT
   [ L/SCR 1- ] LITERAL           \ INSERT A BLANK LINE
   LINE#> BUF-ADR C/L BLANKS ;    \ AT THE BOTTOM OF THE SCREEN
-->
\ SHRINK DELETES THE SPECIFIED LINE IN THE DISK BUFFER AND
\ REPLACES THE LAST LINE OF THE SCREEN WITH A BLANK LINE.

35
 \                                                   11:41 05/06/86

: ?FLUSH          &UPDATE @ IF -CURSOR MODM E-DT &E-ID
                  [ C/L 14 - ] LITERAL BUF-ADR 14 CMOVE
                  205C 0 BUF-ADR ! UPDATE CURSOR
                  0 &UPDATE ! THEN FLUSH CLRM ;

\ screen # --- last screen #
: LASTSCR         2000 / ONGOSUB PRI SEC AUX SYS -1 ENDGOSUB
                  0 0 SEEK- IF 1 SWAP DOSERR + THEN
                  400 U/ SWAP DROP 1- 0 MAX ;
: 1FFFM           1FFF AND ;
\ screen # ---
: MMESS           05 14 GOTOXY ." Moving screen " 1FFFM 4 .R ;
\ screen # ---
: TMESS           ."  to " 1FFFM 4 .R ; -->
36
\ insert screen  blank screen                  \     11:12 03/07/86
\ # screens to insert ---
: INSSCR          SCR @ 1FFFM 1- SCR @ LASTSCR
                  DO I DUP MMESS SCR @ E000 AND OR
                  BLOCK 2- DUP @ 3 PICK +
                  8000 OR DUP TMESS SWAP ! -1 +LOOP DROP
                  FLUSH EMPTY-BUFFERS ;
\ screen # ---
: BMESS           05 14 GOTOXY ." Blanking screen "
                  1FFFM 4 .R ;
\ # screens to blank ---
: BLANKSCR        DUP 0>
                  IF 0 DO SCR @ I + DUP BMESS BLOCK
                    400 BLANKS UPDATE LOOP
                  ELSE DROP
                  THEN FLUSH EMPTY-BUFFERS ; -->
37
\ INSERT-LINE                                  \     09:01 03/11/86
DECIMAL
: (IL)    \ POS - 0=expanded,1=last line not empty
   [ L/SCR 1- ] LITERAL               \ LAST LINE NUMBER
   ?EMPTY-LINE                        \ IS IT EMPTY?
  IF EXPAND 0                         \ YES, EXPAND THE BUFFER
  ELSE DROP 1                         \ if last line report
  THEN ;
\ pos ---
: INSERT-LINE     -CURSOR DUP (IL) IF FULL THEN
                  >LINE# DISPLAY-TO-EOS ; -->
\ INSERT-LINE CHECK TO SEE THAT THERE IS NO TEXT ON THE
\ LAST LINE OF THE SCREEN. IF THERE IS NONE, IT EXPANDS THE
\ SCREEN AT THE GIVEN CURSOR POSITION AND RE-DISPLAYS THE
```

```
\ ALTERED SCREEN and reports whether or not it was expanded.

38
\ DELETE-LINE                                        \     13:30 02/16/86

: DELETE-LINE       \ POS -
   >LINE# DUP LINE#> SHRINK
   -CURSOR DISPLAY-TO-EOS CURSOR ;
-->
\ DELETE-LINE REMOVES THE LINE THE CURSOR IS ON AND RE-DISPLAYS
\ THE RESULTING SCREEN

39
\ DEL-CHAR                                                  25APR81HHL

: DEL-CHAR     \ POS -
   DUP DUP 1+ SWAP                      \ POS FROM TO
   OVER CHARS-TO-EOL                    \ POS FROM TO LEN
   BUF-MOVE                             \ MOVE IT
   DUP CHARS-TO-EOL + 1-                \ POSITON AT EOL
   BUF-ADR BL SWAP C! ;                 \ AND STICK IN A BLANK
-->
\ DEL-CHAR DELETES THE CHARACTER AT THE SPECIFIED CURSOR
\ POSITION

40
\ ARROW COMMANDS                                            25APR81HHL

: R-ARROW       \ -
   1 +CURPOS ;                  \ MOVE RIGHT BY ONE

: L-ARROW       \ -
   -1 +CURPOS ;                 \ MOVE LEFT BY ONE

: U-ARROW       \ -
   C/L MINUS +CURPOS ;          \ MOVE UP BY ONE

: D-ARROW       \ -
   C/L +CURPOS ;                \ MOVE DOWN BY ONE
-->

41
\ I-LINE D-LINE D-CHAR INSERT-MODE                   \     12:08 02/03/86

: I-LINE    \ -
    CURPOS INSERT-LINE 0 MOVE-CURSOR ;

: D-LINE    \ -
    -CURSOR CURPOS DELETE-LINE CURSOR ;

: INSERT-MODE    \ -
   &MODE 1 TOGGLE CURSOR ;
-->

42
\ RETURN EXIT-EDIT                                   \     12:56 03/20/86

: RETURN        \ -
   CURPOS >LINE#                 \ GET LINE NUMBER OF CURRENT LINE
   1+                            \ INCREMENT BY ONE
   [ L/SCR 1- ] LITERAL MIN      \ DON'T MOVE BELOW BOTTOM
   LINE#> &CURSOR ! ;            \ AND MOVE THERE
\ RETURN IS EXECUTED WHENEVER THE CARRIAGE RETURN KEY
\ IS PRESSED. IT MOVES THE CURSOR TO THE BEGINNING OF THE
```

```
\ NEXT LINE. IF THE CURSOR IS AT THE BOTTOM OF THE SCREEN,
\ IT REMAINS THERE.
\ ---
: EXIT-EDIT CLS SCR @ LIST
            R> DROP R> DROP R> DROP R> DROP R> DROP ; -->
\ GET OUT OF THE EDITOR AND RETURN TO PREVIOUS ACTIVITY

43
\ EXIT-UPDATE                                    \     13:01 03/20/86
HEX
: EXIT-UPDATE    \ -
                -CURSOR ?FLUSH       \ show user screen
                CURSOR EXIT-EDIT ;   \ GET OUT OF EDITOR
-->
\ EXIT-UPDATE LEAVES THE EDITOR AND RETURNS TO FORTH. IF
\ THE SCREEN HAS BEEN MODIFIED, THE USER ID IS INSERTED ON LINE
\ 0 IN THE RIGHT HAND CORNER

44
\ EXIT-SCRATCH                                         25APR81HHL
HEX
: EXIT-SCRATCH      \ -
                -CURSOR CLS
                CURSOR EXIT-EDIT ;  \ GET OUT OF EDITOR
-->
\ EXIT-SCRATCH WILL LEAVE THE EDITOR and leave the screen
\ as it was before beginnign the edit.  Just like WORDSTAR
\ ^K^Q or ^KQ.  You can type either.

45
\ E-TAB                                                25APR81HHL
DECIMAL
: E-TAB       \ -
   8 CURPOS 8 MOD -
   +CURPOS ;

: L-TAB       \ -
   8 CURPOS 8 MOD - MINUS
   +CURPOS ;
-->
\ MOVE THE CURSOR TO THE NEXT TAB STOP. TABS ARE CURRENTLY
\ DEFINED AS BEING 8 APART, THEY CAN BE REDEFINED BY SIMPLY
\ ALTERING E-TAB

46
\ SCAN+=                                               25APR81HHL
: SCAN+=                \ CHAR ADR1 ADR2 --- N
   2DUP = IF                \ RETUEN ZERO IF THERE
     DROP 2DROP 0           \ IS NOTHING TO SEARCH
   ELSE
     0 ROT ROT DO           \ OTHERWISE RUN THRU MEMORY
       OVER I C@ = IF       \ FROM LOW TO HIGH
         LEAVE              \ LOOKING FOR THE SPECIFIED CHARACTER
       ELSE 1+ THEN
     LOOP
     SWAP DROP              \ RETURN RESULTS
   THEN ; -->
\ SCANS THROUGH MEMORY STARTING AT ADR2 TO ADR1 AND
\ INCREMENTING BY +1 LOOKING FOR THE SPECIFIED CHARACTER.
\ RETURNS THE NUMBER OF CHARACTERS SCANNED UNTIL SUCCESS

47
\ SCAN+<>                                        \     13:34 01/30/86
: SCAN+<>               \ CHAR ADR1 ADR2 --- N
```

```
   2DUP = IF                  \ RETURN ZERO IF THERE
     DROP 2DROP 0             \ IS NOTHING TO SEARCH
   ELSE
     0 ROT ROT DO             \ OTHERWISE RUN THRU MEMORY
       OVER I C@ <> IF        \ FROM LOW TO HIGH
         LEAVE                \ LOOKING FOR THE SPECIFIED CHARACTER
       ELSE 1+ THEN
     LOOP
     SWAP DROP                \ RETURN RESULTS
   THEN ;    -->
\ SCANS THROUGH MEMORY STARTING AT ADR2 TO ADR1 AND
\ INCREMENTING BY +1 UNTIL ANY CHARACTER NOT MATCHING THE ONE
\ SPECIFIED IS FOUND.  RETURNS COUNT OF CHARACTERS SCANNED

48
\ SCAN-=                                                25APR81HHL
: SCAN-=                \ CHAR ADR1 ADR2 --- N
   2DUP = IF                  \ RETUEN ZERO IF THERE
     DROP 2DROP 0             \ IS NOTHING TO SEARCH
   ELSE
     0 ROT ROT DO             \ OTHERWISE RUN THRU MEMORY
       OVER I C@ = IF         \ FROM HIGH TO LOW
         LEAVE                \ LOOKING FOR THE SPECIFIED CHARACTER
       ELSE 1- THEN
     -1 +LOOP
     SWAP DROP                \ RETURN RESULTS
   THEN ;       -->
\ SCANS THROUGH MEMORY STARTING AT ADR2 TO ADR1 AND
\ DECREMENTING BY -1 LOOKING FOR THE SPECIFIED CHARACTER.
\ RETURNS THE NUMBER OF CHARACTERS SCANNED UNTIL SUCCESS

49
\ SCAN-<>                                               25APR81HHL
: SCAN-<>               \ CHAR ADR1 ADR2 --- N
   2DUP = IF                  \ RETUEN ZERO IF THERE
     DROP 2DROP 0             \ IS NOTHING TO SEARCH
   ELSE
     0 ROT ROT DO             \ OTHERWISE RUN THRU MEMORY
       OVER I C@ <> IF        \ FROM HIGH TO LOW
         LEAVE                \ LOOKING FOR THE SPECIFIED CHARACTER
       ELSE 1- THEN
     -1 +LOOP
     SWAP DROP                \ RETURN RESULTS
   THEN ;          -->
\ SCANS THROUGH MEMORY STARTING AT ADR2 TO ADR1 AND
\ DECREMENTING BY -1 UNTIL ANY CHARACTER NOT MATCHING THE
\ SPECIFIED ONE IS FOUND. RETURNS COUNT OF CHARACTERS SCANNED

50
\ MOVE-LEFT-WORD                                \     10:14 12/06/85
HEX
: MOVE-LEFT-WORD     \ - N
    BUFPOS DUP 1- C@ BL =        \ middle of word?
    SWAP C@ BL = OR              \
    IF BL 0 BUF-ADR BUFPOS       \ SCAN BACKWARDS FOR THE
      SCAN-= >R                  \ FIRST BLANK
      BL 0 BUF-ADR BUFPOS R +    \ NOW SCAN BACKWARDS FOR THE
      SCAN-<> R> + >R            \ FIRST NON BLANK
    ELSE 0 >R                    \ middle of word
    THEN
    BL 0 BUF-ADR BUFPOS R +      \ scan backward to look for
    SCAN-= R> +                  \ first blank
    DUP CURPOS +                 \ correct for start of screen
    IF 1+ THEN ;
```

```
-->
51
\ MOVE-RIGHT-WORD                                       25APR81HHL

: MOVE-RIGHT-WORD   \ - N
   BL [ C/SCR 1- ] LITERAL BUF-ADR
   BUFPOS SCAN+= >R
   BL [ C/SCR 1- ] LITERAL BUF-ADR
   BUFPOS R +
   SCAN+<> R> + ;
-->
\ RETURNS THE NUMBER OF CHARACTERS THAT MUST BE SKIPPED TO
\ MOVE TO THE BEGINNING OF THE NEXT WORD RELATIVE TO THE CURRENT
\ CURSOR POSITION.

52
\ R-WORD L-WORD                                         25APR81HHL

: R-WORD      \ -
   MOVE-RIGHT-WORD                \ MOVE FORWARD ONE WORD
   DUP CURPOS + [ C/SCR 1- ] LITERAL <> \ end of screen?
   IF +CURPOS ELSE DROP THEN ; \ AND UPDATE CURSOR
\ R-WORD MOVES THE CURSOR RIGHT 1 WORD. THE CURSOR IS LEFT
\ AT THE BEGINNING OF THE WORD. IF THERE ISN'T ANY, THE CURSOR
\ MOVES TO THE END OF THE SCREEN

: L-WORD      \ -
   MOVE-LEFT-WORD                 \ MOVE BACKWARDS ONE WORD
   +CURPOS ; -->                  \ AND UPDATE CURSOR
\ L-WORD MOVES THE CURSOR LEFT 1 WORD. THE CURSOR IS LEFT
\ AT THE END OF THE PREVIOUS WORD. IF THERE ISN'T ANY, THE
\ CURSOR MOVES TO THE BEGINNING OF THE SCREEN
53
\ DEL-CHARS                                   \     17:03 02/04/86

: DEL-CHARS      \ N POS -
   2DUP + OVER                  \ N P FROM P
   DUP CHARS-TO-EOL             \ N P F L
   BUF-MOVE                     \ N P
   DUP CHARS-TO-EOL +           \ N EOL
   OVER - BUF-ADR               \ N EOL-N
   SWAP BLANKS ;                \ FILL END WITH BLANKS
-->
\ DEL-CHARS DELETES N CHARACTERS STARTING AT POSITION POS.
\ THIS IS USED MAINLY FOR DELETING ENTIRE WORDS AT ONE TIME.
\ IT IS MUCH FASTER THAN CALLING DEL-CHAR N TIMES FOR MOST
\ WORDS

54
\ shrinkup
HEX
\ pos ---
: SHRINKLINE    >R BL R BUF-ADR DUP C/L + SWAP
                SCAN+<> R> DEL-CHARS ;

\ --- :
: SHRINKUP      CURPOS >LINE# 1+ LINE#> DUP SHRINKLINE >R
                R BUF-ADR BUFPOS CURPOS CHARS-TO-EOL CMOVE>
                CURPOS CHARS-TO-EOL R DEL-CHARS
                R >LINE# ?EMPTY-LINE IF R SHRINK THEN
                R> DROP CURPOS >LINE#
                -CURSOR DISPLAY-TO-EOS CURSOR ;
-->
\ SHRINKLINE removes leading blanks from a line
```

```
\ SHRINKUP moves the next line to the cursor
55
\                                              \     18:11 02/03/86
: D-CHAR    \ -
   BUFPOS CURPOS CHARS-TO-EOL      \ ON THE CURRENT LINE
   -TRAILING SWAP DROP 0=          \ trailing blanks?
   CURPOS >LINE#
   [ L/SCR 1- ] LITERAL < AND      \ and not line 15?
   IF SHRINKUP                     \ overwrite blank line
   ELSE CURPOS DEL-CHAR
   THEN CURPOS DISPLAY-TO-EOL ;
-->

56
\ wrapon wrapoff wraptonext                    \     17:09 02/08/86
\ ---
: WRAPON        1 &WRAP ! CURPOS 1+ &WRAP 2+ ! ; \ begin wrap

: WRAPOFF       1 &WRAP 2+ +!               \ update wrap cursor
                CURPOS 1+ &WRAP 2+ @ <>     \ wrap cursor=cursor?
                CURPOS C/L MOD 0=           \ start of new line?
                &WRAP @ AND                 \ is wrap on also?
                OR                          \ is either true?
                IF &WRAP 4 ERASE THEN ;     \ wrap off
\ eol pos ---
: WRAPTONEXT    DUP BUF-ADR
                DUP 1+ 3F CMOVE> \ wrap a character
                1+ DUP CURPOS - DUP >R MOVE-CURSOR
                DISPLAY-TO-EOL R> MINUS MOVE-CURSOR ; -->

57
\ wrap                                         \     13:01 02/16/86
\ eol pos --- 0=successful,1=screen full
: WRAP  &WRAP @
        IF DUP BUF-ADR 40 +         \ buffer address of next eol
          C@ BL =                   \ nonblank at next line end?
          IF WRAPTONEXT 0           \ wrap to next line
          ELSE DUP 1+ (IL)          \ try to blank next line
            IF DROP 1               \ last line not empty
            ELSE DUP >LINE#
              -CURSOR DISPLAY-TO-EOS
              WRAPTONEXT 0          \ wrap to blank line
            THEN
          THEN
        ELSE DROP 0                 \ don't need to wrap
        THEN ;
-->
58
\ ?wrap swrap                                  \     13:01 02/16/86
\ pos --- eol pos\0=successful,1=screen full
: SWRAP WRAPOFF                   \ turn wrap off?
        >LINE# 1+ LINE#>          \ pos of start of next line
        1- DUP BUF-ADR            \ pos of eol
        C@ BL <>                  \ nonblank at eol?
        &WRAP @ 0= AND
        IF WRAPON DUP 1+ (IL) DUP >LINE# -CURSOR
          DISPLAY-TO-EOS CURSOR \ open a blank line for wrap
        ELSE 0
        THEN ;
\ pos --- 0=successful,1=screenfull
: ?WRAP SWRAP                     \ start wrap sequence
        IF DROP 1                 \ screen full
        ELSE WRAP                 \ try to wrap
        THEN ; -->
```

```
59
\ INS-CHAR                                          \     16:15 02/16/86

: INS-CHAR       \ CHAR POS -  0=successful,1=screen full
   DUP ?WRAP                        \ wrap?
   IF 2DROP 1                       \ screen is full
   ELSE DUP DUP 1+                  \ CHAR POS FROM TO
     OVER CHARS-TO-EOL 1-           \ CHAR POS FROM TO LEN
     BUF-MOVE                       \ MOVE IT
     BUF-ADR C! 0                   \ AND STICK IN CHAR
   THEN ;
-->
\ INS-CHR INSERTS THE GIVEN CHARACTER INTO THE DISK BUFFER.
\ NOTE THAT CHARACTERS FALLING OFF THE RIGHT END OF THE LINE
\ ARE not lost but wrapped onto next line if possible.  If the
\ screen is full, then the insert character is discarded and the
\ user warned with a beep.
60
\ D-WORD                                                   25APR81HHL
DECIMAL
: D-WORD      \ -
   MOVE-RIGHT-WORD                   \ MOVE OVER 1 WORD
   CURPOS BUF-ADR                    \ BUT LESS THAN LAST BLANK
   CURPOS CHARS-TO-EOL               \ ON THE CURRENT LINE
   -TRAILING SWAP DROP               \ FOR SPEED
   MIN DUP 0=                        \ blank line?
   CURPOS >LINE# [ L/SCR 1- ] LITERAL < AND \ and not line 15?
   IF DROP SHRINKUP                  \ overwrite blank line
   ELSE CURPOS DEL-CHARS             \ AND DELETE TEXT
   CURPOS DISPLAY-TO-EOL             \ AND SHOW RESULT
   THEN ;
-->
\ D-WORD DELETES THE NEXT WORD IN THE INPUT STREAM or remaining
\ blanks on the line
61
\ U-TAB D-TAB CRL-SCREEN                            \     12:27 02/03/86
DECIMAL
: F7 \ U-TAB    \ -
   4 C/L *                      \ MOVE UP 4 LINES
   MINUS +CURPOS ;

: F8 \ D-TAB    \ -
   4 C/L *                      \ MOVE DOWN 4 LINES
   +CURPOS ;

: CLR-SCREEN     \ -
   -CURSOR 0 &CURSOR !                \ RESET CURSOR
   CURPOS BUF-ADR                     \ GET BUFFER ADDRESS
   C/SCR BLANKS                       \ AND SET ALL TO BLANKS
   0 DISPLAY-TO-EOS                   \ AND RE DISPLAY
   E-UPDATE CURSOR ; -->              \ INDICATE SCREEN CHANGED
62
\ DISPLAY-STATUS                                    \     17:13 02/09/86
DECIMAL
: DISPLAY-STATUS     \ -
   &MODE @ &OLD-MODE @ <> IF              \ HAS MODE CHANGED?
    -CURSOR 38 1 CRTXY                    \ MOVE CURSOR
    &MODE @ IF                            \ 1=INSERT 0=OVERSTRIKE
     ." Insert"                           \ DISPLAY MESSAGE ON THE
    ELSE                                  \ STATUS LINE
     06 SPACES
    THEN
    &MODE @ &OLD-MODE !                   \ RESET OLD-MODE
   THEN
```

```
   CURPOS C/L /MOD -CURSOR                  \ CHAR POS, LINE#
   34 1 CRTXY 2 .R                          \ DISPLAY LINE#
   28 1 CRTXY 2 .R CURSOR ;                 \ DISPLAY CHAR#
-->
63
\ CLR-LINE                                                25APR81HHL

: CLR-LINE     \ -
   -CURSOR CURPOS DUP               \ SAVE CURRENT CURSOR POSITION
   >LINE# LINE#> &CURSOR !          \ GET TO BEGINNING OF LINE
   CURPOS BUF-ADR                   \ BUFFER ADDRESS OF BOL
   C/L BLANKS                       \ BLANK IT OUT
   E-UPDATE                         \ INDICATE TEXT HAS CHANGED
   0 MOVE-CURSOR                    \ GET TO BEGINNING
   CURPOS CLEAR-TO-EOL              \ AND CLEAR THE LINE
   &CURSOR ! CURSOR ;               \ RESTORE THE CURSOR
-->
\ CLR-LINE SETS THE CURRENT LINE TO BLANKS

64
\ control character table                       \      11:21 02/09/86
HEX      0 VARIABLE CCTABLE
         147 , 177 ,        \ 0 home  1 ^home
         14B , 173 ,        \ 2 left arrow  3 ^ left arrow
         14F , 175 ,        \ 4 end  5 ^end
         150 , 151 , 176 , \ 6 down arrow  7 PgDn  8 ^PgDn
         14D , 174 ,        \ 9 right arrow  10 ^right arrow
         149 , 184 , 148 , \ 11 PgUp  12 ^PgUp  13 up arrow
         153 ,  08 ,  7F , \ 14 delete  15 backspace 16 rubout
         152 , 13B , 13C , \ 17 Ins  18 F1  19 F2
         13D , 13E , 13F , \ 20 F3  21 F4  22 F5
         140 , 141 , 142 , \ 23 F6  24 F7  25 F8
         143 , 144 , 014 , \ 26 F9  27 F10  28 ^T
         019 , 007 , 00B , \ 29 ^Y  30 ^G  31 ^K
-->

65
\ control character table                       \      08:54 02/18/86

         011 , 009 , 10F , \ 32 ^Q  33 Tab right  34 Tab left
         00E , 01B , 00D , \ 35 ^N  36 Esc  37 return
         15E , 15F , 160 , \ 38 ^F1 39 ^F2  40 ^F3
         161 , 162 , 00C , \ 41 ^F4 42 ^F5  43 ^L
         165 ,              \ 44 ^F8
         HERE CCTABLE 2 + - 2/ CCTABLE !

         0 VARIABLE KTABLE
          02 ,  03 ,  04 , \ 00 ^B  01 ^C  02 ^D
          0B ,  11 ,  12 , \ 03 ^K  04 ^Q  05 ^R
          16 ,  17 ,  18 , \ 06 ^V  07 ^W  08 ^X
          19 ,  09 ,        \ 09 ^Y  0A ^I
         HERE KTABLE 2 + - 2/ KTABLE !
-->
66
\ control character table home ^home            \      15:03 03/10/86

         0 VARIABLE QTABLE
          01 ,  06 ,  19 , \ 00 ^A  01 ^F  02 ^Y
         HERE QTABLE 2 + - 2/ QTABLE !

: HOME           0 &CURSOR ! ;

: ^HOME          HOME CURPOS BUF-ADR C/SCR -TRAILING
                 SWAP DROP 01023 MIN +CURPOS 0 MOVE-CURSOR ;
```

```
: LINEBEG        CURPOS >LINE# LINE#> ; \ curpos of line begin
-->

67
\ end ^end del bs                          \     11:16 03/17/86
DECIMAL
: END            LINEBEG DUP &CURSOR !
                 BUF-ADR C/L -TRAILING SWAP DROP
                 063 MIN +CURPOS 0 MOVE-CURSOR ;

: ^END           LINEBEG &CURSOR !
                 0 MOVE-CURSOR ;

: DEL            CURPOS C/L MOD 0>
                 IF L-ARROW 0 MOVE-CURSOR D-CHAR 0 MOVE-CURSOR
                 THEN ;

: BS             L-ARROW ;
-->

68
\ display scr#  showscreen newscreen       \     11:12 03/07/86
HEX

: DISPLAY-SCR#   -CURSOR 14 1 CRTXY SCR @ 1FFFM 4 .R CURSOR ;

: SHOW-SCREEN    0 -CURSOR DISPLAY-TO-EOS CURSOR ;

: NEW-SCR        -CURSOR SCR @ BLOCK SCR @ LASTSCR
                 SCR @ 1FFFM <
                 IF DUP 400 BLANKS THEN \ blanks if doesn't exit
                 &BUF-ADR ! DISPLAY-SCR#
                 SHOW-SCREEN ; \ SAVE BUFFER ADDRESS
-->

69
\ pagedown pageup ^pagedown                \     12:59 03/20/86
HEX
: PGDN           1 SCR +! ?FLUSH NEW-SCR ;

: PGUP           SCR @ DUP 1- SWAP
                 6000 AND MAX SCR ! ?FLUSH NEW-SCR ;

: ^PGDN          SCR @ LASTSCR  SCR @ 6000 AND OR SCR !
                 ?FLUSH NEW-SCR ;

: ^PGUP          SCR @ 6000 AND SCR ! ?FLUSH NEW-SCR ;
-->

70
\ wordstar ^kx ^kd ^kq and ^pageup         \     12:10 02/16/86
HEX
: ^KX            FLUSH BYE ;
: ^KD            R> DROP R> DROP R> DROP EXIT-UPDATE ;
: ^KQ            R> DROP R> DROP R> DROP EXIT-SCRATCH ;

: KMESS1         05 14 GOTOXY ." Invalid ^KB ^KK markers" BEEP ;

: .KP            ."  PRI" ;
: .KS            ."  SEC" ;
: .KA            ."  AUX" ;
: .KSYS          ."  SYS" ;
: .3B            4 SPACES ;
```

```
: .KF             &KB @ 0 2000 U/ SWAP DROP ONGOSUB
                  .KP .KS .KA .KSYS .3B ENDGOSUB CURSOR ;
-->
71
\ ^kb ^kk status information                      \     11:12 03/07/86
HEX
: INITKBKK        -1 &KB ! -1 &KK ! ;
: KBKKMESS        -CURSOR
                  2F 1 CRTXY &KB @ DUP 0<
                  IF DROP 8 SPACES
                  ELSE ." ^KB=" 1FFFM  4 .R
                  THEN
                  39 1 CRTXY &KK @ DUP 0<
                  IF DROP 8 SPACES
                  ELSE ." ^KK=" 1FFFM 4 .R
                  THEN .KF CURSOR ;
\ --1=yes,0=no
: ?SURE           ."  Are you sure " Y/N ;
-->

72
\ ^kb ^kk and bounds check                        \     13:12 03/11/86

\ --- 1=yes,0=no
: ?KBKKOK         1 &KK @ E000 AND &KB @ E000 AND <>
                  IF DROP 0 THEN
                  &KB @ -1 = &KK @ -1 = OR
                  IF DROP 0 THEN KBKKMESS ;

\ --- 1=yes,0=no
: ?SSCR           SCR @ E000 AND &KB @ E000 AND = ?KBKKOK AND ;
\ same screen file?
-->

73
\ ^kb and ^kk                                     \     11:06 02/10/86

: ^KB             SCR @ DUP &KB !                 \ set begin screen
                  6000 AND &KK @ 6000 AND <>      \ same file?
                  IF &KK @ -1 <>                  \ initial value?
                    IF KMESS1 THEN -1 &KK !       \ beep if not init
                  THEN                            \ no, reset ^kk
                  KBKKMESS ;                      \ show results

: ^KK             SCR @ DUP &KK !                 \ set end screen
                  6000 AND &KB @ 6000 AND <>      \ same file?
                  IF &KB @ -1 <>                  \ initial value?
                    IF KMESS1 THEN -1 &KB !       \ beep if not init
                  THEN                            \ no, reset ^kb
                  KBKKMESS ;                      \ show results
-->
74
\ restore  blank screen  insert blank scree \     11:13 03/07/86
HEX
: F10             EMPTY-BUFFERS NEW-SCR ;

: F9              &BUF-ADR @ 400 BLANKS 0 MOVE-CURSOR E-UPDATE
                  SHOW-SCREEN ;

: F2              E-UPDATE ?FLUSH SHOW-SCREEN ;
\ # of 41 + pad neeeded ---
: ?PAD            41 * SP@ PAD ROT + - 52 <
                  IF 05 14 GOTOXY ." Not enough room for edit
 operation"       R> R> 2DROP BEEP THEN ;
```

```
\ --- # of screens
: ^KRANGE       &KK @ 1FFFM &KB @ 1FFFM - 1+ ;
-->
75
\ insm ^ki ^f1                                \     11:13 03/07/86
: IMESS         05 14 GOTOXY ." Inserting blank screens " ;
\ screen # --- 1=yes,0=no
: INSM          IMESS &KB @ 1FFFM U. ." thru "
                &KK @ 1FFFM U. ?SURE CLRM ;
: ^KI           ?SSCR ^KRANGE 0> AND        \ ^kb and ^kk okay
                IF INSM -CURSOR
                  IF ^KRANGE DUP
                    &KB @ SCR ! INSSCR      \ insert screens
                    CLRM BLANKSCR           \ and blank them
                    NEW-SCR                 \ show ^kb screen
                  THEN
                ELSE KMESS1
                THEN INITKBKK KBKKMESS CLRM ;
: ^F1           SCR @ DUP &KB ! &KK ! ^KI ; \ ins 1 blank screen
-->
76
\ which cursor  chop file  truncate file    \     09:35 03/07/86
\ --- handle
: CURSCR#       SCR @ 2000 /
                ONGOSUB PRI SEC AUX SYS -1 ENDGOSUB
                DUP 0 0 SEEK+- >R 2DROP R>
                IF 1 SWAP DOSERR + THEN ;
\ --- 0=no,1=yes
: ?CHOP         05 14 GOTOXY ." Truncate file. " ?SURE CLRM ;

: CHOP          CURSCR# PAD 0 SAVE1 DROP EMPTY-BUFFERS ;

: ^F3           EPURGE ?CHOP
                IF CHOP NEW-SCR THEN ;
-->

77
\ delete screen                               \     11:13 03/07/86

\ # screens to delete ---
: DELSCR        SCR @ LASTSCR 1+
                SCR @ 1FFFM 3 PICK +
                DO I DUP MMESS SCR @ E000 AND OR
                  BLOCK 2- DUP @ 3 PICK - 8000 OR
                  DUP TMESS SWAP ! FLUSH
                LOOP CHOP DROP ;

\ --- 1=yes,0=no
: ?DEL          05 14 GOTOXY
                ." Delete screens " &KB @ 1FFFM U. ."  thru "
                &KK @ 1FFFM U. ?SURE CLRM ;
-->

78
\ ^krange ^ky ^f2                             \     09:54 03/11/86

: ^KY             ?SSCR ^KRANGE 0> AND      \ ^kb and ^kk okay?
                  IF ?DEL -CURSOR           \ are you sure?
                    IF ^KRANGE              \ # screens to process
                      &KB @ SCR ! GETSCR    \ make sure its there
                      DELSCR                \ delete the screens
                      NEW-SCR               \ display ^kb screen
                    THEN
```

```
                ELSE KMESS1
                THEN INITKBKK KBKKMESS CLRM ;

: ^F2           SCR @ DUP &KB ! &KK ! ^KY ; \ delete 1 screen
-->

79
\ move screens                                  \     11:13 03/07/86

: CLRS          0 0 16 4F 17 SCROLLU ;

: .MOVEF        05 16 GOTOXY &KB @ 0 2000 U/ SWAP DROP ONGOSUB
                .PF .SF .AF .SYSF BEEP ENDGOSUB CURSOR ;
\ --- 1=yes,0=no
: ?MOVE         .MOVEF 05 14 GOTOXY
                ." Move screens " &KB @ 1FFFM U. ."  thru "
                &KK @ 1FFFM U. ?SURE ;
-->

80
                                                \     13:09 03/11/86

\ --- 0=invalid,1=okay
: ?KBKKSCR      0 ?SSCR 0= OR
                SCR @ &KK @ > IF 1 OR THEN
                SCR @ &KB @ > 0= IF 1 OR THEN ;

\ ^krange ---
: +KBKK         SCR @ &KB @ < ?SSCR AND
                IF DUP &KB @ + &KB ! &KK @ + &KK !
                ELSE DROP
                THEN ;
-->
\ ?kbkkscr checks whether destination screen is between ^kb
\ and kk in the same file
\ +kbkk compensates for hole made in the same file.
81
\ move screens                                  \     10:28 03/07/86
HEX
\ # of screens ---
: MOVESCREENS   CLRM 0 -CURSOR      \
                DO I &KB @ +        \
                DUP MMESS BLOCK     \ get source screen
                SCR @ I             \
                + DUP TMESS         \ find destination block
                8000 OR             \ update block
                SWAP 2- !           \ change block #
                LOOP ;              \
-->

82
\ ^kc move screens                              \     10:39 03/11/86

: ^KC           ?KBKKOK ?KBKKSCR AND    \ ^kb and ^kk okay?
                ^KRANGE 0> AND
                IF ?MOVE                \ are you sure?
                  IF ^KRANGE DUP CLRM   \ # screens to move
                    -CURSOR INSSCR      \ make a hole in file
                    DUP +KBKK           \ adjust ^kb and ^kk?
                    MOVESCREENS         \ move screens to hole
                  THEN
                  FLUSH EMPTY-BUFFERS
                  NEW-SCR
                ELSE KMESS1
```

```
                THEN INITKBKK KBKKMESS CLRS CLRM ;
-->

83
\ wordstar ^k commands                          \     10:50 02/09/86
HEX
: ^K            -CURSOR 05 1 CRTXY ." ^K" CURSOR
                KTABLE KEY 3F AND DUP 40 OR -CURSOR 07 1 CRTXY
                EMIT CURSOR ?GOSUBW ONGOSUB
                \ 00 ^KB  01 ^KC  02 ^KD
                  ^KB     ^KC     ^KD
                \ 03 ^KK  04 ^KQ  05 ^KR
                  ^KK     ^KQ     BEEP
                \ 06 ^KV  07 ^KW  08 ^KX  09 ^KY   0A ^KI
                  BEEP    BEEP    ^KX     ^KY      ^KI
                \ illegal
                  BEEP
                ENDGOSUB -CURSOR 05 1 CRTXY ."    ";
-->

84
\ line stack                                          12:44 09/26/86
HEX
\ ---    show top line on line stack
: SHOWLS  &LS @ -DUP                      \ line stack empty?
          IF DUP 0 15 GOTOXY 3 .R         \ print line stack number
            2 SPACES                      \ ahead two spaces
            40 M* 400 U/ EDLS + SYSBLOCK +  \ no, get top line
            40 -CURSOR  TYPE CURSOR       \ print line
          ELSE 0 0 15 4F 15  SCROLLU      \ yes, blank stack window
          THEN GETSCR ;

\ --- pop line stack and discard top line
: ^F5    &LS @ -DUP IF -1 &LS +! SHOWLS THEN ;
\ --- reconstruct top lines of stack
: ^F4    1 &LS +! SHOWLS ; -->

85
\ line stack                                      plp 12:50 06/07/86
HEX
\ ---
: F34     1 ?PAD GETSCR LINEBEG         \ address of bol
          BUF-ADR PAD 40 CMOVE 0 &SEARCH !      \ line to pad
          1 &LS +! &LS @ 40 M*        \ byte offset into line stack
          400 U/ EDLS + SYSBLOCK + \ top of line stack
          PAD SWAP 40 CMOVE UPDATE    \ pad to top line
          SHOWLS ;                    \ show line stack

\ ---    push line and move cursor down
: F3      F34 CURPOS >LINE# 0F =      \ line 15?
          IF PGDN HOME                \ yes, on to next page
          ELSE D-ARROW                \ no cursor down one line
          THEN ;
-->
86
\ line stack                                    \     14:33 04/14/86
HEX
\ ---    push and delete line
: F4         E-UPDATE F34 GETSCR                \ push line
             LINEBEG DELETE-LINE ;              \ delete line
\ ls pointer # ---
: F56        E-UPDATE 1 ?PAD -1 &LS +!          \ pop line stack
             40 M* 400 U/ EDLS + SYSBLOCK +     \ top of line stack
             PAD 40 CMOVE 0 &SEARCH !           \ line to pad
```

```
            PAD GETSCR LINEBEG BUF-ADR
            40 CMOVE E-UPDATE               \ pad to edit screen
            SHOWLS                          \ show line stack
            SHOW-SCREEN ;                   \ show screen
-->

87
\ line stack                               \     09:08 03/11/86
\ ---      pop line and move cursor up
: F5        &LS @ DUP                      \ line stack >0?
            IF F56 CURPOS >LINE# 0=        \ warn user?
              IF FULL THEN
              U-ARROW 0 MOVE-CURSOR
            ELSE DROP BEEP
            THEN ;
\ ---      insert blank line then pop line
: F6        &LS @ DUP
            IF LINEBEG (IL)                \ find line start
              IF DROP FULL
              ELSE F56
              THEN
            ELSE DROP BEEP
            THEN ; -->
88
\ match+                                         09:21 09/23/89
--> \ adr string to find\length\adr string to search\length ---
\ 0 not found or count of remaining characters\1 found
CODE MATCH       CX POP          \ length of search string
                 DI POP          \ start address of search string
                 DX POP  DX DEC \ length of find string -1
                 BX POP          \ start address of find string
                 CX DX CMP  U>= \ search longer or = to find?
                 IF  CX DX SUB          \ yes,  search possibles
                   SI PUSH              \ save forth ip
                   AX DS MOV  ES AX MOV \ establish es addressing
            3 $:   SI BX MOV  BYTE LODS \ 1st find char in al
                   1 $ JCXZ             \ anything to search?
                   REPNE BYTE SCAS      \ yes, look for match
                   1 $ JNZ              \ no matches, exit
-->
89
\ match+                                         09:21 09/23/89
-->                CX PUSH     \ save search string count
                   DI PUSH     \ save pointer to next search char
                   CX DX MOV   \ find count of remaining n-1
                   2 $ JCXZ    \ jump if find string 1 character
                   REPE BYTE CMPS \ compare remaining chars
                   DI POP      \ restore pointer to next search ch
                   CX POP      \ restore search string count
                   3 $ JNZ     \ no match
            4 $:   SI POP      \ match, restore forth ip
                   CX DX ADD   \ characters following 1st found
                   CX PUSH     \ count of remaining characters
                   AX AX SUB  AX INC   \ true flag
                   AX PUSH NEXT, -->   \ return true flag

90
\ match+                                         09:21 09/23/89
-->
            2 $:   DI POP      \ restore pointer to next search ch
                   CX POP      \ restore search string count
                   4 $ JMP
            1 $:   SI POP         \ restore forth ip
                 THEN  AX AX SUB \ false flag
```

```
                AX PUSH NEXT,    \ return false flag
                END-CODE
-->

91
\ ^QF and ^L support                                  09:22 09/23/89
HEX -->
\ count position of buffer address ---
: COUNTEDSTR    >R 0
                BEGIN 1+ R OVER + C@ 0= \ locate null
                UNTIL 1- R> C! ;    \ store count in 1st position
\ ---
: GETSRCH       1 ?PAD CLRS
                0 16 GOTOXY ." Enter search string: "
                PAD 1+ 30 EXPECT PAD COUNTEDSTR PAD C@
                IF 0 REPLACE ! 1 ELSE 0 THEN &SEARCH ! ;

\ # remaining characters---
: SHOWMATCH     3FF SWAP - &CURSOR ! DISPLAY-SCR# SHOW-SCREEN ;
-->

92
\ ^QF and ^L support                                  09:22 09/23/89
-->
\ ---
: SEARCHM       05 14 GOTOXY ." Searching for "
                PAD COUNT TYPE ;

\ ---
: CANTFIND      05 14 GOTOXY ."    Can't find " ;

\ ---
: NOSEARCH      05 14 GOTOXY ." No search string" ;

\ --- remaining characters\1 or 0
: ?MATCH          PAD COUNT CURPOS
                  BUF-ADR 400 CURPOS - SEARCHM MATCH ;
-->
93
\ ^L continue global search                           09:23 09/23/89
-->
: LOOK -CURSOR &SEARCH @ \ --- 0=not found,1=found
       IF SEARCHM SCR @ >R  CURPOS >R SCR @ LASTSCR 1+ >R
        BEGIN ?TERMINAL
          IF KEY DROP R SCR ! R> R> 1+ >R >R 0 ELSE ?MATCH THEN
          IF CURSOR SHOWMATCH R> R> R> 2DROP DROP 1 1
          ELSE SCR @ 1FFFM R <
              IF 1 SCR +! GETSCR 0 &CURSOR ! 0
              ELSE R> DROP R> 1- &CURSOR ! R> SCR !
                GETSCR CANTFIND BEEP 0 1
              THEN
          THEN
        UNTIL
      ELSE NOSEARCH BEEP 0 \ no search string
      THEN CLRS CLRM CURSOR ; -->
94
\ ^qf global search ^qa enter replace                 09:35 09/23/89
HEX
: KILLS         0 &SEARCH ! 0 REPLACE ! ; : ^QF ; : ^L ; \ **
-->
\ ---
: ^L            1 +CURPOS LOOK DROP ;
\ ---
: ^QF           GETSRCH LOOK DROP ;
```

```
\ ---
: NOREPLACE     05 14 GOTOXY ." No search/replace pair" BEEP ;

\ ---
: REPLACING     05 14 GOTOXY ." Replacing string with "
                PAD 41 + COUNT TYPE ;
-->
95
\ repl replace a string                          09:23 09/23/89
-->
: REPL  -CURSOR                       \ turn off cursor
        &SEARCH @ REPLACE @ AND       \ search\replace string
        IF REPLACING                  \ yes, show message
          PAD C@ CURPOS DEL-CHARS     \ discard old chars
          PAD 41 + C@ DUP             \ replace length
          IF PAD 42 + DUP ROT + SWAP \ replace buffer if not 0
            DO I C@ CURPOS INS-CHAR  \ insert characters
            IF CLRM FULL LEAVE        \ full screen
            ELSE 1 +CURPOS            \ advance cursor
            THEN LOOP E-UPDATE        \ date and time stamp
          THEN 0 DISPLAY-TO-EOS       \ show screen
          PAD C@ 1- +CURPOS           \ update cursor
        ELSE NOREPLACE                \ no search\replace
        THEN ; -->
96
\ ^qa search and replace ^f8 s & r again         09:37 09/23/89
: ^QA ; : ^F8 ; --> \ **
: GETREPL       2 ?PAD CLRS
                0 16 GOTOXY ." Enter replace string: "
                PAD 42 + 30 EXPECT PAD 41 + COUNTEDSTR
                1 REPLACE ! CLRS ;

: ?REPL         IF REPL PAD C@ MINUS 1+ +CURPOS
                ELSE KILLS
                THEN ;

: ^QA           GETSRCH GETREPL LOOK ?REPL ;

: ^F8           LOOK ?REPL ;
-->

97
\ ^q  delete to eol                          plp 12:49 06/07/86
HEX
\ ---
: F1            KILLS EPURGE EDHELP SYSLOAD ;  \ help

\ ---
: ^QY           BUFPOS CURPOS CHARS-TO-EOL BLANKS E-UPDATE
                CURPOS DISPLAY-TO-EOL ;
\ ---
: ^Q            -CURSOR 05 1 CRTXY ." ^Q" CURSOR
                QTABLE KEY 3F AND DUP 40 OR -CURSOR 07 1 CRTXY
                EMIT CURSOR ?GOSUBW ONGOSUB
                \ 00 ^QA  01 ^QF  02 ^QY  illegal
                  ^QA     ^QF     ^QY     BEEP
                ENDGOSUB -CURSOR 05 1 CRTXY ."    ";
-->
98
\ control character vector                 \     12:55 02/15/86

\ 'key' value ---
: (CONTROL-CHAR)  CCTABLE SWAP ?GOSUBW ONGOSUB
```

```
        \   0    1     2        3       4    5    6        7
            HOME ^HOME L-ARROW L-WORD END ^END D-ARROW PGDN
        \   8     9        10      11    12      13       14  15
            ^PGDN R-ARROW R-WORD PGUP ^PGUP U-ARROW DEL BS
        \   16 17           18 19 20 21 22 23 24 25 26
            BS INSERT-MODE F1 F2 F3 F4 F5 F6 F7 F8 F9
        \   27  28      29      30      31 32
            F10 D-WORD D-LINE D-CHAR ^K ^Q
-->

99
\ control character vector                        \     08:55 02/18/86

        \   33    34    35     36            37     38
            E-TAB L-TAB I-LINE EXIT-UPDATE RETURN ^F1

        \   39    40    41    42    43   44
            ^F2   ^F3   ^F4   ^F5   ^L   ^F8

        \   ELSE
            BEEP ENDGOSUB ;
-->

100
\ CONTROL-CHAR                                    \     12:50 02/25/86
HEX
: CONTROL-CHAR   \ CHAR -
   DUP DUP 1C < SWAP 07F > OR \ <= than esc or > 7f
   IF                               \ MIGHT IT BE VALID ?
     (CONTROL-CHAR)                 \ YES, SO GO DO IT
   ELSE
     BEEP                           \ NO, COMPLAIN
   THEN ;
-->
\ PROCESS A CONTROL CHARACTER. IF IT LESS THAN OR EQUAL TO
\ AN ESCAPE or an ibm pc special character , IT IS EXECUTED,
\ OTHERWISE WE BEEP.

101
\ E-OVERSTRIKE                                    \     16:27 02/16/86

: E-OVERSTRIKE    \ -
   KEY DUP                     \ GET NEXT KEYSTROKE
   ?PRINTABLE IF               \ IF ITS PRINTABLE
    DUP -CURSOR EMIT CURSOR    \ SHOW IT ON THE SCREEN
    BUFPOS C!                  \ STICK IT IN THE BUFFER
    E-UPDATE                   \ BUFFER HAS CHANGED
    1 +CURPOS                  \ AND MOVE THE CURSOR
   ELSE
    CONTROL-CHAR               \ ELSE PROCESS IT AS A COMMAND
   THEN ; -->
\ E-OVERSTRIKE IS CALLED WHENEVER THE EDITOR IS IN
\ OVERSTRIKE MODE. NOTE THAT ONLY A SINGLE CHARACTER IS
\ PROCESSED, AND CONTROL IS ALWAYS RETURNED TO THE MAIN
\ PROCESSING LOOP
102
\   INSERT                                        \     13:40 03/07/86
: E-INSERT    \ -
   KEY DUP                     \ GET THE NEXT CHARACTER
   ?PRINTABLE                  \ CHECK IF ITS PRINTABLE
   IF CURPOS INS-CHAR          \ IF SO, try to INSERT IT HERE
     IF FULL                   \ screen full
     ELSE                      \ insert it
     CURPOS DISPLAY-TO-EOL     \ RE-DISPLAY THE LINE
```

```
     1 +CURPOS                    \ AND MOVE OVER 1
     THEN
   ELSE
    CONTROL-CHAR                  \ ELSE PROCESS THE COMMAND
   THEN ;
-->
\ E-INSERT IS CALLED WHENEVER THE EDITOR IS IN INSERT MODE.

103
\ border  help                                  \     08:58 02/16/86
DECIMAL
: E-HELP         0 24 GOTOXY ." F1 Help" ;

: .VER           2 SPACES REVSYM COUNT TYPE ;

: PBORDER        0 03 02 69 02 SCROLLU
                 0 03 19 69 19 SCROLLU
                 0 03 02 03 18 SCROLLU
                 0 69 02 69 18 SCROLLU ;

: ?DECIMAL       BASE @ 10 <>
                 IF CR ." Edit in decimal" QUIT
                 THEN ;
-->

104
\ border  help                                  \     16:06 03/10/86
DECIMAL

: BWBORDER       0 &VMODE ! REVERSE PBORDER E-HELP
                 -REVERSE .VER -INTENSITY ;

: COBORDER       1 &VMODE ! CYAN BACKGROUND PBORDER
                 BLACK FOREGROUND E-HELP CYAN FOREGROUND
                 BLACK BACKGROUND .VER YELLOW FOREGROUND ;

: E-BORDER       ?MODE ONGOSUB BWBORDER    COBORDER
                               BWBORDER    COBORDER
                               COBORDER    COBORDER
                               COBORDER    BWBORDER
                               COBORDER
                       ENDGOSUB 2DROP ; -->
105
\ E-INIT                                        \     11:13 03/07/86
HEX
: E-INIT       \ [N] -
   DEPTH IF SCR ! THEN          \ EDIT LAST SCREEN IF STACK EMPTY
   SCR @ BLOCK &BUF-ADR !       \ SAVE THE BUFFER ADDRESS
   ( MYID )     CRTCLR-SCR      \ get user id & CLEAR SCREEN
   E-BORDER                     \ make border
   0 &MODE ! 0 &CURSOR ! 0 &WRAP !      \ INIT VARIABLES
   0 &UPDATE !                  \ NOT MODIFIED
   0 %Y-OFF -CURSOR CRTXY       \ MOVE CURSOR TO START
   L/SCR 0 DO                   \ DISPLAY LINE NUMBERS FOR USER
    I 3 .R CR
   LOOP
   0A 1 CRTXY ." Screen # " SCR @ 1FFFM 4 .R 3
   SPACES ." x=     y=" CURSOR
   .EF SHOW-SCREEN SHOWLS KBKKMESS ; -->       \ show the screen
106
\ EDIT                                          \     19:48 02/08/86
DECIMAL \ [N] -
: EDIT ?DECIMAL
   E-INIT             \ INITIALIZE THE SCREEN
```

```
   BEGIN               \ THIS IS THE ONLY LOOP IN THE EDITOR
    DISPLAY-STATUS     \ DISPLAY THE STATUS ON LINE 0
    0 MOVE-CURSOR      \ MOVE THE CURSOR TO WHERE IT SHOULD BE
    &MODE @ IF         \ CHECK THE MODE, 1=INSERT 0=OVERSTRIKE
     E-INSERT
    ELSE
     E-OVERSTRIKE
    THEN
   AGAIN ;
--> \ USED TO ENVOKE THE EDITOR. SCREEN NUMBER SHOULD BE ON THE
\ STACK.

107
\ vector to machine dependent code                \     19:36 02/03/86
DECIMAL
' GOTOXY CFA 'CRTXY !

' CLS CFA 'CRTCLR-SCR !

: IBM-CRTCLR-EOL DUP C/SCR <
                 IF 0 SWAP C/L /MOD %Y-OFF + SWAP %X-OFF +
                 SWAP C/L 4 + OVER SCROLLU
                 ELSE DROP THEN ;

' IBM-CRTCLR-EOL CFA 'CLEAR-TO-EOL !
-->

108
\ configuration management                           WHP11:49 05/06/86
HEX
\ see EDITOR MYID in help, you have no choice with date and time
\ ---
: MYID          -CURSOR CR ." Enter your ID: " \ PROMPT USER
                03 0 DO 2E EMIT LOOP     \ DISPLAY DOTS
                03 0 DO 08 EMIT LOOP     \ AND BACKUP
                BIGCURSOR
                PAD 03 EXPECT
                PAD &E-ID 02 + 03 CMOVE
                &E-ID 02 + 03 -TIDY CURSOR ;
-->
\ you can enter three letters identifying who changed a screen

109
\ editor entry                                    \     08:28 02/16/86
FORTH DEFINITIONS
DECIMAL
\ screen # ---
: E                       EDITOR EDIT ;
: SE            SECONDARY EDITOR EDIT ;
: AE            AUXILIARY EDITOR EDIT ;
: SYSE          SYSTEM    EDITOR EDIT ;

\ EDITOR ' REVSYM ' MYID LFA !
FORTH DECIMAL
HERE SWAP - CR ." Editor size " U. CURSOR

110
\ showc  compressed show                          \     10:16 03/14/86
HEX
: BOLD          1B EMIT 45 EMIT ;
: -BOLD         1B EMIT 46 EMIT ;
: .PF           PRIF COUNT TYPE ;
: .SF           SECF COUNT TYPE ;
: .AF           AUXF COUNT TYPE ;
```

```
: .SYSF         SYSF COUNT TYPE ;
: .FILENAME     SCR @ 0 2000 U/ SWAP DROP EDITOR
                ONGOSUB .PF .SF .AF .SYSF BEEP ENDGOSUB ;
: .BANNER       BOLD CR 06 SPACES .FILENAME
                2B OUT @ - SPACES .TIME 2 SPACES .DATE 2 SPACES
                -BOLD ;
-->

111
\ showc  compressed show                        \     10:16 03/14/86

: ."SCR#"       ." Screen # " ;
: .BLK# ( n -- )     ( prints block#'s )
                1FFFF AND 0 OUT ! CR CR 06 SPACES
                BOLD ."SCR#" DUP . 32 OUT @ - SPACES
                ."SCR#" 1+ . -BOLD CR ;
-->

112
\ showc  compressed show                        \     10:16 03/14/86

\ from\to ---
: SHOWC  2 ?DEPTH 0 ROT ROT
   PRINTER 1+ SWAP
   DO I .BLK# 400 0
     DO OF EMIT 0B SPACES
        J    SCR @ E000 AND OR BLOCK I + 40 TYPE 3 SPACES
        J 1+ SCR @ E000 AND OR BLOCK I + 40 TYPE CR
     40 +LOOP 12 EMIT
     1+ DUP 3 = IF DROP 0 .BANNER 0C EMIT THEN
     2 +LOOP -DUP
   IF 3 SWAP - 13 * 0 DO  CR  LOOP .BANNER THEN
   0C EMIT CONSOLE FORTH ;
  DECIMAL

113
\ revision history                              \     11:27 05/06/86

REVSYM                  Revision history
03/20/86        Formal release of editor modifications begun
                in November 1985.

04/04/86        Added GETSCR in F34 after SHOWLS to correct
                seeing wrong screen. whp

04/14/86        04/04/86 didn't always work.  Removed and
                GETSCR added to SHOWLS. whp

05/06/86        \ moved from two characters before initials on
                line 0 to home position.  whp
```

Appendix 5
Assembler-Enhanced Version of Laxen's Full Screen Editor

Those screens that have been modified and those containing assembler of Laxen's full screen editor are included in the listing in this Appendix.

Use the full screen editor in Appendix 4 to update a copy of the Laxen editor. You need to compile the assembler before you assemble and compile this version of the editor.

```
0
\  acknowledgments                                  \ JFB 15:35 01/05/89

This full screen editor was published in the september 1981
issue of Dr. Dobb's Journal. It was originally written by

Henry Laxen                 This editor is in the public
1259 Cornell Ave.           domain, and may be distributed
Berkeley, CA 94704          further with the inclusion
(415) 525-8582              of this notice.

and modified for ms-dos compatible computers running F86 by

Jerry Boutelle 408-462-9461
Sandia Labs  Albq, NM 87185
Computer Systems Documentation  pob 5478  kafb,nm 87115

1
\ acknowledgments                                   \ JFB 15:37 01/05/89
\ this screen to be filled by contributors

?DEF EDITOR
IIF ' EDITOR FENCE ! FORGET EDITOR
ITHEN 2 LOAD

2
\ BEEP cursor sizes                                       10:46 09/23/89
-CURSOR VOCABULARY EDITOR IMMEDIATE
EDITOR DEFINITIONS -CURSOR
CLS ." Compiling editor"
HEX HERE \ size editor
0 VARIABLE REVSYM -2 ALLOT " 01/06/89"
: BEEP            07 EMIT ;
: BIGBWCURSOR     00 0D SETCURSOR ; \ black and white big cursor
: BIGCOCURSOR     00 07 SETCURSOR ; \ color big cursor
: BIGCURSOR       ?MODE ONGOSUB BIGBWCURSOR BIGCOCURSOR
                                BIGCOCURSOR BIGCOCURSOR
                                BIGCOCURSOR BIGCOCURSOR
                                BIGCOCURSOR BIGBWCURSOR
                                BIGCOCURSOR
                        ENDGOSUB 2DROP ; -->
\ RING THE BELL ON THE TERMINAL. USUALLY AFTER AN ERROR.

11
\ fast curpos and +curpos                                 11:44 05/06/86

CODE CURPOS       AX &CURSOR MOV
                  AX PUSH NEXT, END-CODE

CODE +CURPOS      AX POP                  \ relative cursor move
                  &CURSOR AX ADD          \ add it to the cursor
                  AX &CURSOR MOV          \ get the sum
                  AX # 0 CMP              \ compare it to zero
                  < IF &CURSOR # 0 MOV THEN        \ 0
                  AX # C/SCR 1- CMP      \ compare it to end of scr
                  > IF &CURSOR # C/SCR 1- MOV THEN \ c/scr
                  NEXT, END-CODE
-->

12
\  fast move-cursor                                 \     16:05 02/16/86
```

```
CODE M-C          AX POP                  \ relative cursor move
                  &CURSOR AX ADD          \ add it to the cursor
                  AX &CURSOR MOV          \ get the sum
                  AX # 0 CMP <            \ compare it to zero
                  IF &CURSOR # 0 MOV THEN         \ 0
                  AX # C/SCR 1- CMP >     \ compare it to end of scr
                  IF &CURSOR # C/SCR 1- MOV THEN \ c/scr
                  BX AX MOV               \ move curpos to bx
                  CL # 6 MOV BX CL SAR    \ bx contains line #
                  BX # %Y-OFF ADD         \ add in editor offset
-->

13
\  fast move-cursor                               \      18:56 02/17/86

                  AX # C/L 1- AND       \ get raw x coordinate
                  AX # %X-OFF ADD       \ add in editor offset
                  AX PUSH               \ return x coordinate
                  BX PUSH               \ return y coordinate
                  NEXT, END-CODE

: MOVE-CURSOR -CURSOR M-C CRTXY CURSOR ;  \ AND MOVE THERE
-->
pc/assembler code to speed editor


18
\ >LINE# LINE#>                                   \      08:29 02/16/86

CODE >LINE#       AX POP  CL # 6 MOV  AX CL SAR
                  AX PUSH  NEXT, END-CODE
CODE LINE#>       AX POP  CL # 6 MOV  AX CL SAL
                  AX PUSH  NEXT, END-CODE
-->
: >LINE#       \ POS - LINE#
   C/L / ;

\ CONVERT A CHARACTER POSITION TO A LINE NUMBER

: LINE#>       \ LINE# - POS
   C/L * ;
-->
\ CONVERT A LINE NUMBER TO A CHARACTER POSITION
19
\ CHARS-TO-EOL                                    \      08:29 02/16/86
HEX
CODE CHARS-TO-EOL BX POP  BX # C/L 1- AND
                    AX # C/L MOV
                    AX BX SUB
                    AX PUSH  NEXT, END-CODE
-->
: CHARS-TO-EOL       \ POS - N
   C/L MOD
   C/L SWAP - ;
-->
\ CHARS-TO-EOL RETURNS THE NUMBER OF CHARACTERS LEFT ON THE
\ LINE GIVEN THE CURRENT CHARACTER POSITION

20
\ fast typet                                      \      16:12 03/10/86
\ address\length ---
CODE ETYPE        CX POP              \ length
                  DI POP              \ start address
                  1 $ JCXZ            \ jump if zero length
```

```
                SI PUSH                 \ save forth ip
                AX &VMODE MOV           \ video mode
                AX # 0 CMP =            \ is it zero?
-->
```

Substitute AH VIDEO MOV 2 $: BYTE LODS WORD STOS 2 $ LOOP if you do not have a IBM color adapter for 2 $: --- 2 $. Only the IBM video color adapter (not ibm ega) produces snow when writing directly to the adapter memory.

```
21
\ fast typet                                    \      18:34 02/17/86

                IF DX # 3B4 MOV             \ black and white
                  AL # 0E MOV  DX AL OUT
                  DX # 3B5 MOV AL DX IN     \ cursor high
                  AH AL MOV
                  DX # 3B4 MOV
                  AL # 0F MOV  DX AL OUT
                  DX # 3B5 MOV  AL DX IN    \ cursor low
                  AX 1 SHL  SI AX MOV       \ print position in si
                  SI DI XCHG
                  AX # B000 MOV \ bw80
                  ES AX MOV
-->

22
\ fast typet                                    \      11:03 03/17/86

                ELSE DX # 3D4 MOV            \ color
                  AL # 0E MOV  DX AL OUT
                  DX # 3D5 MOV  AL DX IN     \ cursor high
                  AH AL MOV
                  DX # 3D4 MOV
                  AL # 0F MOV  DX AL OUT
                  DX # 3D5 MOV  AL DX IN     \ cursor low
                  AX 1 SHL  SI AX MOV        \ print position in si
                  SI DI XCHG
                  AX # B800 MOV              \ co80 segment
                  ES AX MOV
                THEN
-->

23
\ fast typet                                    \      11:12 03/17/86

                AX &VMODE MOV           \ video mode
                AX # 0 CMP =            \ is it zero?
              IF
                AH VIDEO MOV            \ black and white video write
          4 $:  BYTE LODS
                WORD STOS
                4 $ LOOP
-->

24
\ fast typet                                    \      11:02 03/17/86
              ELSE
          2 $:  BYTE LODS                  \ get byte to write
                BL AL MOV                  \ save byte in bl
                DX # 3DA MOV               \ video adapter status
                CLI                        \ interrupts off
          3 $:  AL DX IN AL # 1 AND        \ snow?
                3 $ JZ                     \ wait for snow to clear
```

```
              AL BL MOV  BYTE STOS \ write character
              STI                  \ interrupts on
              DI INC               \ point to next write
              2 $ LOOP             \
            THEN
              SI POP               \ restore forth ip
        1 $:  NEXT, END-CODE -->

28
HEX \ fast display-to-eos                       \     08:05 02/16/86
CODE DISPLAY-TO-EOS
              BX POP           \ line #
              CX # L/SCR MOV   \ lines per screen
              CX BX SUB        \ number of lines to show
              SI PUSH          \ save forth ip
              SI &BUF-ADR MOV  \ point si at screen buffer
              AL # C/L MOV     \ characters per line
              BL MUL           \ offset to line #
              SI AX ADD        \ buffer offset to line #
              BL # %Y-OFF ADD  \ lines above screen display
              AL # 50 MOV      \ 80 characters per line
              BL MUL           \ lines 80 *
              DI AX MOV        \ byte offset into video buffer
              DI # %X-OFF ADD  \ move to left hand side
-->
29
\ fast display-to-eos                           \     11:11 03/17/86

              DI 1 SAL             \ adjust for attribute byte
              AX &VMODE MOV        \ video mode
              AX # 0 CMP =         \ is it zero?
              IF   AX # B000 MOV   \ bw
              ELSE AX # B800 MOV   \ color
              THEN  ES AX MOV      \ video segment in es
-->

30
\ fast display-to-eos                           \     11:12 03/17/86

        1 $:  CX PUSH              \ save line count index
              AX &VMODE MOV        \ video mode
              CX # C/L MOV         \ characters per line
              AX # 0 CMP =         \ is it zero?
            IF
              AH VIDEO MOV         \ black and white video write
        4 $:  BYTE LODS
              WORD STOS
              4 $ LOOP
-->

31
\ fast display-to-eos                           \     11:11 03/17/86

            ELSE
        2 $:  BYTE LODS            \ get byte to write
              BL AL MOV            \ save byte in bl
              DX # 3DA MOV         \ video adapter status
              CLI                  \ interrupts off
        3 $:  AL DX IN AL # 1 AND  \ snow?
              3 $ JZ               \ wait for snow to clear
              AL BL MOV  BYTE STOS \ write character
              STI                  \ interrupts on
              DI INC               \ point to next write
              2 $ LOOP
```

```
              THEN
-->

32
\ fast display-to-eos                              \ JFB 20:02 01/05/89

                DI # 50 C/L - 2* ADD \ point video line
                CX POP               \ restore line count index
                1 $ LOOP             \ do until done
                SI POP               \ restore forth ip
                NEXT, END-CODE -->
```

Substitute AH VIDEO MOV 2 $: BYTE LODS WORD STOS 2 $ LOOP if you do not have a IBM color adapter for 2 $: --- 2 $. Only the IBM video color adapter (not ibm ega) produces snow when writing directly to the adapter memory.

```
88
\ match+                                          plp 12:50 06/07/86
\ adr string to find\length\adr string to search\length ---
\ 0 not found or count of remaining characters\1 found
CODE MATCH      CX POP          \ length of search string
                DI POP          \ start address of search string
                DX POP  DX DEC  \ length of find string -1
                BX POP          \ start address of find string
                CX DX CMP  U>=  \ search longer or = to find?
                IF  CX DX SUB           \ yes,  search possibles
                  SI PUSH               \ save forth ip
                  AX DS MOV  ES AX MOV  \ establish es addressing
            3 $:  SI BX MOV  BYTE LODS  \ 1st find char in al
                  1 $ JCXZ              \ anything to search?
                  REPNE BYTE SCAS       \ yes, look for match
                  1 $ JNZ               \ no matches, exit
-->
89
\ match+                                     \     19:59 02/17/86
                  CX PUSH     \ save search string count
                  DI PUSH     \ save pointer to next search char
                  CX DX MOV   \ find count of remaining n-1
                  2 $ JCXZ    \ jump if find string 1 character
                  REPE BYTE CMPS \ compare remaining chars
                  DI POP      \ restore pointer to next search ch
                  CX POP      \ restore search string count
                  3 $ JNZ     \ no match
            4 $:  SI POP      \ match, restore forth ip
                  CX DX ADD   \ characters following 1st found
                  CX PUSH     \ count of remaining characters
                  AX AX SUB  AX INC  \ true flag
                  AX PUSH NEXT, -->  \ return true flag

90
\ match+                                     \     11:57 02/16/86

            2 $:  DI POP      \ restore pointer to next search ch
                  CX POP      \ restore search string count
                  4 $ JMP
            1 $:  SI POP         \ restore forth ip
                THEN  AX AX SUB \ false flag
                AX PUSH NEXT,   \ return false flag
                END-CODE
-->

91
```

```
\ ^QF and ^L support                          \     08:59 02/18/86
HEX
\ count position of buffer address ---
: COUNTEDSTR     >R 0
                 BEGIN 1+ R OVER + C@ 0= \ locate null
                 UNTIL 1- R> C! ;   \ store count in 1st position
\ ---
: GETSRCH        1 ?PAD CLRS
                 0 16 GOTOXY ." Enter search string: "
                 PAD 1+ 30 EXPECT PAD COUNTEDSTR PAD C@
                 IF 0 REPLACE ! 1 ELSE 0 THEN &SEARCH ! ;

\ # remaining characters---
: SHOWMATCH      3FF SWAP - &CURSOR ! DISPLAY-SCR# SHOW-SCREEN ;
-->

92
\ ^QF and ^L support                          \     21:17 02/17/86

\ ---
: SEARCHM        05 14 GOTOXY ." Searching for "
                 PAD COUNT TYPE ;

\ ---
: CANTFIND       05 14 GOTOXY ."    Can't find " ;

\ ---
: NOSEARCH       05 14 GOTOXY ." No search string" ;

\ --- remaining characters\1 or 0
: ?MATCH           PAD COUNT CURPOS
                   BUF-ADR 400 CURPOS - SEARCHM MATCH ;
-->
93
\ ^L continue global search                   \     09:51 03/15/86
: LOOK -CURSOR &SEARCH @ \ --- 0=not found,1=found
       IF SEARCHM SCR @ >R  CURPOS >R SCR @ LASTSCR 1+ >R
        BEGIN ?TERMINAL
          IF KEY DROP R SCR ! R> R> 1+ >R >R 0 ELSE ?MATCH THEN
          IF CURSOR SHOWMATCH R> R> R> 2DROP DROP 1 1
          ELSE SCR @ 1FFFM R <
              IF 1 SCR +! GETSCR 0 &CURSOR ! 0
              ELSE R> DROP R> 1- &CURSOR ! R> SCR !
                GETSCR CANTFIND BEEP 0 1
              THEN
          THEN
        UNTIL
      ELSE NOSEARCH BEEP 0 \ no search string
      THEN CLRS CLRM CURSOR ; -->

94
\ ^qf global search ^qa enter replace         \     21:44 02/17/86
HEX
\ ---
: ^L             1 +CURPOS LOOK DROP ;
\ ---
: ^QF            GETSRCH LOOK DROP ;

\ ---
: NOREPLACE      05 14 GOTOXY ." No search/replace pair" BEEP ;

\ ---
: REPLACING      05 14 GOTOXY ." Replacing string with "
                 PAD 41 + COUNT TYPE ;
```

```
: KILLS          0 &SEARCH ! 0 REPLACE ! ;
-->
95
\ repl replace a string                      \     09:34 03/11/86
: REPL  -CURSOR                            \ turn off cursor
        &SEARCH @ REPLACE @ AND            \ search\replace string
        IF REPLACING                       \ yes, show message
          PAD C@ CURPOS DEL-CHARS          \ discard old chars
          PAD 41 + C@ DUP                  \ replace length
          IF PAD 42 + DUP ROT + SWAP       \ replace buffer if not 0
            DO I C@ CURPOS INS-CHAR        \ insert characters
            IF CLRM FULL LEAVE             \ full screen
            ELSE 1 +CURPOS                 \ advance cursor
            THEN LOOP E-UPDATE             \ date and time stamp
          THEN 0 DISPLAY-TO-EOS            \ show screen
          PAD C@ 1- +CURPOS                \ update cursor
        ELSE NOREPLACE                     \ no search\replace
        THEN ; -->

96
\ ^qa search and replace ^f8 s & r again    \     22:47 02/17/86

: GETREPL        2 ?PAD CLRS
                 0 16 GOTOXY ." Enter replace string: "
                 PAD 42 + 30 EXPECT PAD 41 + COUNTEDSTR
                 1 REPLACE ! CLRS ;

: ?REPL          IF REPL PAD C@ MINUS 1+ +CURPOS
                 ELSE KILLS
                 THEN ;

: ^QA            GETSRCH GETREPL LOOK ?REPL ;

: ^F8            LOOK ?REPL ;
-->


104
\ border  help                               \ JFB 08:17 01/06/89
DECIMAL

: BWBORDER       0 &VMODE ! REVERSE PBORDER E-HELP
                 -REVERSE .VER -INTENSITY ;

: COBORDER       1 &VMODE ! CYAN BACKGROUND PBORDER
                 BLACK FOREGROUND E-HELP CYAN FOREGROUND
                 BLACK BACKGROUND .VER YELLOW FOREGROUND ;

: E-BORDER       ?MODE ONGOSUB BWBORDER    COBORDER
                               COBORDER    COBORDER
                               COBORDER    COBORDER
                               COBORDER    BWBORDER
                               COBORDER
                       ENDGOSUB 2DROP ; -->

114
\ revision history                           \ JFB 08:19 01/06/89

06/07/86         Made start of line stack and help screen
                 constants EDLS and EDHELP plp

01/06/89         Make mode 2 a color mode in BIGCURSOR and
                 E-BORDER
```

Appendix 6

PC/ASSEMBLER 8086, 8087, and NEC V30 Family FORTH Assembler

PC/ASSEMBLER was copyrighted. Permission is given to use it in any way.

Instructions on how to load and save it are given in Chapter 3.

```
0
\ PC/ASSEMBLER copyright notice                       10:05 01/15/87

PC/ASSEMBLER (TM)
IBM PC implementation
COPYRIGHT 1985, 1896, 1987
                     Computer Systems Documentation
                     PO Box 5478
                     Albuquerque, NM 87115

The software technology used to implement this assembler is
protected as a trade secret by Computer Systems Documentation.

1
\ product logo copyright notice                       15:13 01/21/87
FORTH DEFINITIONS
-CURSOR
CLS ." PC/ASSEMBLER " ." TM "
CR ." Intel 8086/87/88/186/188/286/287"
CR ." NEC   V20/30 uPD70108/70116  processors"
CR ." Copyright 1985, 1986, 1987 by Computer Systems Documentati
on"
CR HERE \ size information
-->

2
\ Assembler variables                                 09:38 04/13/88
HEX
VOCABULARY ASSEMBLER IMMEDIATE
ASSEMBLER DEFINITIONS

     0  VARIABLE REVSYM -2 ALLOT " 04/13/88 10:34"
     " Copyright, P. L. Payne, CSD, 1985,86,87"
     0  VARIABLE T0 3 ALLOT
     0  VARIABLE TOP
     0  VARIABLE CSP0
     0  VARIABLE #$
    20  CONSTANT MAX#$
     0  VARIABLE $A -2 ALLOT MAX#$ 4 * ALLOT
-->

3
\                                                     09:02 09/25/86
-->
REVSYM  Revision symbol of release
T0      Operand attribute stack
TOP     Pointer to top of operand stack
CSP0    Assembler compiler stack pointer used to detect numbers
        placed on the parameter stack not by the assembler.
#$      Number of local labels or forward references times 4.
MAX#$   Maximum number of local labels plus forward references
        permitted.
$A      Array containing the local labels, forward references,
        and their addresses.

4
\ reset  relative jumps                               08:47 09/25/86
HEX
\ ---
: RESET          T0 4 ERASE       \ zero attribute stack
                 0 TOP !          \ zero attributer stack pointer
                 DEPTH CSP0 !     \ store assembler compiler stack
;                                 \ pointer
```

```
\ address --- relative address\0=range okay,1=out of range
: ?R0           HERE 2+ - DUP DUP 07F > SWAP 0FF80 < OR ;
-->
```

Check whether short jump is within +127 to -128 bytes and return relative address.

```
5
\ reset  relative jumps                               08:44 09/25/86
HEX
\ 0=range okay,1=out of range ---
: ?R1           21 ?ERROR       \ error 21 if relative address
                                \ out of range.
;
\ branch address --- relative address
: ?R            ?R0 ?R1 ;
-->
```

```
6
\ Assembler local labels                              08:59 09/25/86

\ label --- label
: $R            DUP 7FFC > OVER 0 < OR 22 ?ERROR ;
-->
```

Check whether local label value is greater than 0 and less than 32764. Zero indicates that there is no local label stored in the table. The local label table has the structure

```
        0 offset 2 offset
        label    address
```

Local labels (like 1 $:) are stored as a negative value. Forward references (like 1 $) are stored as a positive value. Local label code checks for forward references, immediately resolve them, and deletes the entry from the table. Backward references are immediately resolved.

```
7
\ Assembler local labels                              09:14 09/25/86
\ label ---
: !$            DUP     \ make a copy of label
                #$ @    \ get number of labels * 4.
                IF      \ if there are any labels
                  $A #$ @ + $A  \ scan table
                  DO I @ 0=     \ look for a vacant space
                    IF          \ space is found
                      I !       \ store the label
                      HERE I 2+ !  \ and its address
                      DROP 0 LEAVE  \ discard label and leave 0
                    THEN
                  4 +LOOP  \ keep scanning or leave
                THEN  \ 0 indicates label is stored, >0 no space
                      \ available to reclaim
-->
8
\ Assembler local labels                              09:27 09/25/86
                IF \ space not reclaimed, try to in new space
                  #$ @ DUP \ get number of labels * 4
                  4 /      \ number of labels
                  MAX#$ <  \ is there room?
                  IF               \ yes,
                    $A +           \ get table address
                    HERE OVER 2+ ! \ store address
                    !              \ store label
                    4 #$ +!        \ more label space used
                  ELSE 27 ?ERROR   \ table size exceeded
                  THEN
```

```
                THEN ; -->
```

"Store label" stores a local label in the local label table. Error 27 is issued if no space remains in local label table.

```
9
\ syntax tokens                                     09:54 09/25/86
HEX
    00 CONSTANT NUL               \ null token
    01 CONSTANT DISP=LO           \ eight bit displacement
    02 CONSTANT DISP=LOHI         \ 16 bit displacement
    03 CONSTANT DATA8             \ eight bit data
    04 CONSTANT DATA16            \ 16 bit data
    05 CONSTANT ALREG             \ AL register
    06 CONSTANT AXREG             \ AX register
    07 CONSTANT BREG              \ byte register
    08 CONSTANT WREG              \ word register
    09 CONSTANT SREG              \ segment register
    0A CONSTANT R/M               \ r/m memory reference
    0B CONSTANT BYT8              \ BYTE modifier
-->

10
\ syntax tokens                                     09:56 09/25/86
HEX
    0C CONSTANT WO16              \ WORD modifier
    0D CONSTANT STX               \ ST0 ... ST7
    0E CONSTANT ST0               \ ST0
    0F CONSTANT ST1               \ ST1
    10 CONSTANT FI/R              \ SHORTREAL, SHORTINTEGER, ...
    11 CONSTANT FQTB              \ TEMPORARYREAL, LONGINTEGER, ..
    12 CONSTANT CLREG             \ CL register
    13 CONSTANT ONE               \ 1
    14 CONSTANT PT                \ PTR modifier
    15 CONSTANT FR                \ FAR modifier
    16 CONSTANT DXREG             \ DX register
    17 CONSTANT PKD               \ BCD modifier
-->

11
\ syntax table builder                              10:34 09/25/86
DECIMAL
     58 CONSTANT #VFS   \ number of valid forms
      0 VARIABLE VFS    \ Number of syntax types and boundaries
                        \ to the attribute forms
        #VFS 2* ALLOT   \ space for the boundary pointers
        0 VFS !         \ number of syntax types

\ transient module load
LATEST            \ save latest
HERE              \ save dp
SP@               \ check for balanced stack
10000 ALLOT       \ make room for tables
-->
```

The code on the following screen is discarded once the syntax tables are loaded.

```
12
\ transient module code                             10:34 09/25/86

\ # processed\type0\type1\type2\type3 --- # proceesed + 1
: VF,             >< OR ROT ROT >< OR , ,
                  DUP 0 6 GOTOXY U. 1+ ;

\ cummulative #\form # --- cummulative #
: !VF#            VFS + OVER SWAP ! ;
```

```
-->
```

VF, compiles valid operand form attrbiute tables into memory. The boundaries of each set of valid operand is stored into VFS. The attribute stack, T0, is compared to each valid operand form to check syntax for an opcode. If attribute stack does not match any of the valid syntax forms, then the operand for that opcode is invalid.

```
13
\ transient module code                              10:36 09/25/86

SP@ 2+ ?PAIRS    \ stack balanced?
DUP DP !         \ point to old here, end transient module
SP@              \ check for balanced stack
-->
```

The following syntax tables are attributes of valid operand forms for selected opcodes. The documentation is by example of the operand attributes and an example opcode.

```
14
( syntax tables                                  WHP 15:21 08/21/85 )
DECIMAL
0 5 GOTOXY ." Loading syntax tables "

      0 VARIABLE VF -2 ALLOT
( register to register 2 hex 2 )
0 ( start cumulative count of forms)
BREG BREG NUL NUL VF, \ 1  CL DL MOV
WREG WREG NUL NUL VF, \ 2  CX DX MOV
2 !VF# -->

15
( syntax tables                                  PLP 19:04 03/10/85 )

( memory to register 4 hex 4 )
BREG DISP=LO    NUL NUL VF, \  3   CL 12 MOV
BREG DISP=LO    R/M NUL VF, \  4   CL 12 [BX] MOV
BREG DISP=LOHI  NUL NUL VF, \  5   CL 1234 MOV
BREG DISP=LOHI  R/M NUL VF, \  6   CL 1234 [BX] MOV
BREG R/M        NUL NUL VF, \  7   CL [BX] MOV
WREG DISP=LO    NUL NUL VF, \  8   CX 12 MOV
WREG DISP=LO    R/M NUL VF, \  9   CX 12 [BX] MOV
WREG DISP=LOHI  NUL NUL VF, \ 10   CX 1234 MOV
WREG DISP=LOHI  R/M NUL VF, \ 11   CX 1234 [BX] MOV
WREG R/M        NUL NUL VF, \ 12   CX [BX] MOV
4 !VF# -->

16
( syntax tables                                  PLP 19:04 03/10/85 )

( register to memory 6 hex 6 )
DISP=LO   BREG NUL  NUL VF, \ 13  12 CL MOV
DISP=LO   R/M  BREG NUL VF, \ 14  12 [BX] CL MOV
DISP=LOHI BREG NUL  NUL VF, \ 15  1234 CL MOV
DISP=LOHI R/M  BREG NUL VF, \ 16  1234 [BX] CL MOV
R/M       BREG NUL  NUL VF, \ 17  [BX] CL MOV
DISP=LO   WREG NUL  NUL VF, \ 18  12 CX MOV
DISP=LO   R/M  WREG NUL VF, \ 19  12 [BX] CX MOV
DISP=LOHI WREG NUL  NUL VF, \ 20  1234 CX MOV
DISP=LOHI R/M  WREG NUL VF, \ 21  1234 [BX] CX MOV
R/M       WREG NUL  NUL VF, \ 22  [BX] CX MOV
6 !VF#  -->

17
```

```
\ syntax tables                                   \     20:09 02/15/86

( data to reg 8 hex 8 )
BREG DATA8  NUL  NUL  VF,       \ 23  CL # 12 ADC
WREG DATA8  NUL  NUL  VF,       \ 24  CX # 12 ADC
WREG DATA16 NUL  NUL  VF,       \ 25  CX # 1234 ADC
8 !VF#

( data to memory 10 hex A )
DISP=LO   DATA8  BYT8  NUL  VF, \ 26  12 # 34 BYTE ADC
DISP=LOHI DATA8  BYT8  NUL  VF, \ 27  1234 # 56 BYTE ADC
DISP=LO   DATA8  NUL   NUL  VF, \ 28  12 # 34 ADC
DISP=LOHI DATA8  NUL   NUL  VF, \ 29  1234 # 56 ADC
DISP=LO   DATA16 NUL   NUL  VF, \ 30  12 # 3456 ADC
DISP=LOHI DATA16 NUL   NUL  VF, \ 31  1234 # 5678 ADC
-->
18
\ syntax tables                                   \     20:09 02/15/86

( data to memory, continued )
DISP=LO   R/M    DATA8  BYT8 VF, \ 32  12 [BX] # 34 BYTE ADC
DISP=LOHI R/M    DATA8  BYT8 VF, \ 33  1234 [BX] # 56 BYTE ADC
DISP=LO   R/M    DATA8  NUL  VF, \ 34  12 [BX] # 34 ADC
DISP=LOHI R/M    DATA8  NUL  VF, \ 35  1234 [BX] # 56 ADC
DISP=LO   R/M    DATA16 NUL  VF, \ 36  12 [BX] # 3456 ADC
DISP=LOHI R/M    DATA16 NUL  VF, \ 37  1234 [BX] # 5678 ADC
R/M       DATA8  BYT8   NUL  VF, \ 38  [BX] # 12 BYTE ADC
R/M       DATA8  NUL    NUL  VF, \ 39  [BX] # 12 ADC
R/M       DATA16 NUL    NUL  VF, \ 40  [BX] # 1234 ADC
10 !VF# -->

19
( syntax tables                               PLP 21:55 06/23/85 )

( accumulator to memory 12 hex C )
DISP=LO   ALREG NUL NUL VF,     \ 41  12 AL MOV
DISP=LOHI ALREG NUL NUL VF,     \ 42  1234 AL MOV
DISP=LO   AXREG NUL NUL VF,     \ 43  12 AX MOV
DISP=LOHI AXREG NUL NUL VF,     \ 44  1234 AX MOV
12 !VF#

( memory to accumulator 14  hex E )
ALREG DISP=LO   NUL NUL VF,     \ 45  AL 12 MOV
ALREG DISP=LOHI NUL NUL VF,     \ 46  AL 1234 MOV
AXREG DISP=LO   NUL NUL VF,     \ 47  AX 12 MOV
AXREG DISP=LOHI NUL NUL VF,     \ 48  AX 1234 MOV
14 !VF#
-->
20
( syntax tables                               PLP 21:34 06/23/85 )

( data to accumulator 16  hex 10 )
ALREG DATA8  NUL  NUL  VF, \ 49  AL # 12 ADD
AXREG DATA8  NUL  NUL  VF, \ 50  AX # 12 ADD
AXREG DATA16 NUL  NUL  VF, \ 51  AX # 1234 ADD
16 !VF# -->

21
(                                             PLP 21:34 06/23/85 )

( memory or register to segment register not cs 18 hex 12 )
SREG WREG      NUL NUL VF, \ 52  ES AX MOV
SREG DISP=LO   NUL NUL VF, \ 53  ES 12 MOV
SREG DISP=LOHI NUL NUL VF, \ 54  ES 1234 MOV
```

```
SREG DISP=LO    R/M NUL VF, \ 55  ES 12 [BX] MOV
SREG DISP=LOHI R/M NUL VF, \ 56  ES 1234 [BX] MOV
SREG R/M        NUL NUL VF, \ 57  ES [BX] MOV
18 !VF# -->

22
(                                            PLP 21:34 06/23/85 )

( segment register to memory or register 20 hex 14 )
WREG       SREG NUL NUL VF, \ 58  CX ES MOV
DISP=LO    SREG NUL NUL VF, \ 59  12 ES MOV
DISP=LOHI SREG NUL NUL VF, \ 60  1234 ES MOV
DISP=LO    R/M SREG NUL VF, \ 61  12 [BX] ES MOV
DISP=LOHI R/M SREG NUL VF, \ 62  1234 [BX] ES MOV
R/M        SREG NUL NUL VF, \ 63  [BX] ES MOV
20 !VF# -->

23
(                                            PLP 10:36 06/24/85 )

( cl rotates 22 hex 16 )
BREG       CLREG NUL    NUL    VF, \ 64  BL CL RCL
WREG       CLREG NUL    NUL    VF, \ 65  BX CL RCL
DISP=LO    CLREG BYT8   NUL    VF, \ 66  12 CL BYTE RCL
DISP=LO    R/M   CLREG  BYT8   VF, \ 67  12 [BX] CL BYTE RCL
DISP=LOHI CLREG BYT8   NUL    VF, \ 68  1234 CL BYTE RCL
DISP=LOHI R/M   CLREG  BYT8   VF, \ 69  1234 [BX] CL BYTE RCL
R/M        CLREG BYT8   NUL    VF, \ 70  [BX] CL BYTE RCL
DISP=LO    CLREG WO16   NUL    VF, \ 71  12 CL WORD RCL
DISP=LOHI CLREG WO16   NUL    VF, \ 72  1234 CL WORD RCL
DISP=LO    R/M   CLREG  WO16   VF, \ 73  12 [BX] CL WORD RCL
DISP=LOHI R/M   CLREG  WO16   VF, \ 74  1234 [BX] CL WORD RCL
R/M        CLREG WO16   NUL    VF, \ 75  [BX] CL WORD RCL
22 !VF# -->
24
(                                            PLP 13:46 06/24/85 )

( 1 rotates 24 hex 18 )
BREG       ONE  NUL  NUL  VF, \ 76  BL 1 RCL
WREG       ONE  NUL  NUL  VF, \ 77  BX 1 RCL
DISP=LO    ONE  BYT8 NUL  VF, \ 78  12 1 BYTE RCL
DISP=LO    R/M  ONE  BYT8 VF, \ 79  12 [BX] 1 BYTE RCL
DISP=LOHI ONE  BYT8 NUL  VF, \ 80  1234 1 BYTE RCL
DISP=LOHI R/M  ONE  BYT8 VF, \ 81  1234 [BX] 1 BYTE RCL
R/M        ONE  BYT8 NUL  VF, \ 82  [BX] 1 BYTE RCL
DISP=LO    ONE  WO16 NUL  VF, \ 83  12 1 WORD RCL
DISP=LOHI ONE  WO16 NUL  VF, \ 84  1234 1 WORD RCL
DISP=LO    R/M  ONE  WO16 VF, \ 85  12 [BX] 1 WORD RCL
DISP=LOHI R/M  ONE  WO16 VF, \ 86  1234 [BX] 1 WORD RCL
R/M        ONE  WO16 NUL  VF, \ 87  [BX] 1 WORD RCL
24 !VF# -->
25
(                                            PLP 10:36 06/24/85 )
( segment register, not cs 26 hex 1A )
SREG NUL NUL NUL VF,      \ 88  SS POP
26 !VF#

( segment register, 28 hex 1C )
SREG NUL NUL NUL VF,      \ 89  CS PUSH
28 !VF#

( memory word operand  30 hex 1E )
DISP=LO   NUL NUL NUL VF, \ 90  12 PUSH
DISP=LO   R/M NUL NUL VF, \ 91  12 [BX] PUSH
```

```
DISP=LOHI NUL NUL NUL VF, \ 92  1234 PUSH
DISP=LOHI R/M NUL NUL VF, \ 93  1234 [BX] PUSH
R/M       NUL NUL NUL VF, \ 94  [BX] PUSH
30 !VF# -->
26
( syntax tables                           PLP 10:37 06/24/85 )

( indirect 32 hex 20 )
DISP=LO   PT  NUL NUL VF, \ 95  12 PTR JMP
DISP=LOHI PT  NUL NUL VF, \ 96  1234 PTR JMP
DISP=LO   R/M NUL NUL VF, \ 97  12 [BX] JMP
DISP=LOHI R/M NUL NUL VF, \ 98  1234 [BX] JMP
R/M       NUL NUL NUL VF, \ 99  [BX] JMP
WREG      NUL NUL NUL VF, \ 100 CX JMP
32 !VF# -->

27
( syntax tables                           PLP 10:37 06/24/85 )

( far indirect 34 hex 22 )
DISP=LO   PT  FR  NUL VF, \ 101  12 PTR FAR JMP
DISP=LOHI PT  FR  NUL VF, \ 102  1234 PTR FAR JMP
DISP=LO   R/M FR  NUL VF, \ 103  12 [BX] FAR JMP
DISP=LOHI R/M FR  NUL VF, \ 104  1234 [BX] FAR JMP
R/M       FR  NUL NUL VF, \ 105  [BX] FAR JMP
WREG      FR  NUL NUL VF, \ 106  CX FAR JMP
34 !VF#

( data to register 36 hex 24 )
BREG DATA8  NUL NUL VF,   \ 107  BL # 12 MOV
WREG DATA8  NUL NUL VF,   \ 108  BX # 12 MOV
WREG DATA16 NUL NUL VF,   \ 109  BX # 1234 MOV
36 !VF# -->
28
( syntax tables                           PLP 10:37 06/24/85 )

( word or byte 38 hex 26 )
NUL  NUL NUL NUL VF,     \ 110  LODS
BYT8 NUL NUL NUL VF,     \ 111  BYTE LODS
WO16 NUL NUL NUL VF,     \ 112  WORD LODS
38 !VF#

( word register only 40 hex 28 )
WREG NUL NUL NUL VF,     \ 113  BX DEC or AX PUSH
40 !VF# -->

29
( syntax tables                           PLP 18:45 07/03/85 )

( intrasegment relative or direct 42 hex 2A )
DISP=LO   NUL NUL NUL VF,       \ 114  012 JMP
DISP=LOHI NUL NUL NUL VF,       \ 115  1234 JMP
42 !VF#

( intersegment direct 44 hex 2C )
DISP=LO   DISP=LO   FR  NUL VF, \ 116  12 34 FAR CALL
DISP=LO   DISP=LOHI FR  NUL VF, \ 117  12 3456 FAR CALL
DISP=LOHI DISP=LO   FR  NUL VF, \ 118  1234 56 FAR CALL
DISP=LOHI DISP=LOHI FR  NUL VF, \ 119  1234 5678 FAR CALL
44 !VF#
-->

30
( syntax tables                           WHP 08:43 09/02/85 )
```

```
( relative jump 46 hex 2E )
DISP=LO   NUL NUL NUL VF,    \ 120  12 JNE
DISP=LOHI NUL NUL NUL VF,    \ 121  1234 JNE
46 !VF#

( fixed input port 48 hex 30 )
ALREG DISP=LO NUL NUL VF,    \ 122  AL 12 IN
AXREG DISP=LO NUL NUL VF,    \ 123  AX 12 IN
48 !VF#
-->

31
( syntax tables                            PLP 10:19 08/20/85 )

( variable port 50 hex 32 )
BREG DXREG NUL NUL VF,      \ 124  AL DX IN
WREG DXREG NUL NUL VF,      \ 125  AX DX IN
50 !VF#

( interrupts 52 hex 34 )
DISP=LO NUL NUL NUL VF,     \ 126  67 INT or 3 INT
52 !VF#
-->

32
( syntax tables                            PLP 15:44 07/05/85 )

( byte or word memory operand 54 hex 36 )
DISP=LO   BYT8 NUL  NUL VF, \ 127  12 BYTE DEC
DISP=LO   R/M  BYT8 NUL VF, \ 128  12 [BX] BYTE DEC
DISP=LOHI BYT8 NUL  NUL VF, \ 129  1234 BYTE DEC
DISP=LOHI R/M  BYT8 NUL VF, \ 130  1234 [BX] BYTE DEC
R/M       BYT8 NUL  NUL VF, \ 131  [BX] BYTE DEC
DISP=LO   WO16 NUL  NUL VF, \ 132  12 WORD DEC
DISP=LO   R/M  WO16 NUL VF, \ 133  12 [BX] WORD DEC
DISP=LOHI WO16 NUL  NUL VF, \ 134  1234 WORD DEC
DISP=LOHI R/M  WO16 NUL VF, \ 135  1234 [BX] WORD DEC
R/M       WO16 NUL  NUL VF, \ 136  [BX] WORD DEC
BREG      NUL  NUL  NUL VF, \ 137  BL DEC
WREG      NUL  NUL  NUL VF, \ 138  BX DEC
54 !VF#  -->
33
( syntax tables                            PLP 15:44 07/05/85 )
( mod reg r/m not mod=11 56 hex 38 )
WREG DISP=LO   NUL NUL VF, \ 139  CX 12 LES
WREG DISP=LO   R/M NUL VF, \ 140  CX 12 [BX] LES
WREG DISP=LOHI NUL NUL VF, \ 141  CX 1234 LES
WREG DISP=LOHI R/M NUL VF, \ 142  CX 1234 [BX] LES
WREG R/M       NUL NUL VF, \ 143  CX [BX] LES
56 !VF#
( returns 58 hex 3A )
NUL       NUL NUL NUL VF,  \ 144  RET
DISP=LO   NUL NUL NUL VF,  \ 145  12 RET
DISP=LOHI NUL NUL NUL VF,  \ 146  1234 RET
FR        NUL NUL NUL VF,  \ 147  FAR RET
DISP=LO   FR  NUL NUL VF,  \ 148  12 FAR RET
DISP=LOHI FR  NUL NUL VF,  \ 149  1234 FAR RET
58 !VF# -->
34
( syntax tables                            PLP 18:45 07/03/85 )
( intrasegment direct 60 hex 3C )
DISP=LO   NUL NUL NUL VF, \ 150  12 CALL
DISP=LOHI NUL NUL NUL VF, \ 151  1234 CALL
```

```
60 !VF#

( null byte 62 hex 3E )
NUL NUL NUL NUL VF,        \ 152  AAA
62 !VF#

( null word 64 hex 40 )
NUL NUL NUL NUL VF,        \ 153  AAD
64 !VF#
-->

35
( 8087 syntax tables                          PLP 15:44 07/05/85 )
( stx to st0 66 hex 42 )
ST0 STX NUL NUL VF,  \ 154  ST0 ST2 FLD
66 !VF#

( st0 to stx 68  hex 44 )
STX ST0 NUL NUL VF,  \ 155  ST2 ST0 FST
68 !VF#

( st0 70 hex 46 )
ST0 NUL NUL NUL VF,  \ 156  ST0 FTST
70 !VF#

( st0 and st1 72 hex 48 )
ST0 ST1 NUL NUL VF,  \ 157  ST0 ST1 FCOMPP
72 !VF# -->
36
\ 8087 syntax tables                          P      09:48 09/25/86

( integer/real memory to st0 74 hex 4A )
ST0 DISP=LO   FI/R NUL  VF, \ 158  ST0 12 SHORTREAL FLD
ST0 DISP=LO   R/M  FI/R VF, \ 159  ST0 12 [BX] SHORTREAL FLD
ST0 DISP=LOHI FI/R NUL  VF, \ 160  ST0 1234 SHORTREAL FLD
ST0 DISP=LOHI R/M  FI/R VF, \ 161  ST0 1234 [BX] SHORTREAL FLD
ST0 R/M       FI/R NUL  VF, \ 162  ST0 [BX] SHORTREAL FLD
ST0 WREG      FI/R NUL  VF, \ 163  ST0 AX SHORTREAL FLD
74 !VF# -->

37
( 8087 syntax tables                          PLP 15:43 07/05/85 )

( integer/real st0 to memory 76 hex 4C )
DISP=LO   ST0  FI/R NUL  VF, \ 164  12 ST0 SHORTREAL FST
DISP=LO   R/M  ST0  FI/R VF, \ 165  12 [BX] ST0 SHORTREAL FST
DISP=LOHI ST0  FI/R NUL  VF, \ 166  1234 ST0 SHORTREAL FST
DISP=LOHI R/M  ST0  FI/R VF, \ 167  1234 [BX] ST SHORTREAL FST
R/M       ST0  FI/R NUL  VF, \ 168  [BX] ST0 SHORTREAL FST
WREG      ST0  FI/R NUL  VF, \ 169  AX ST0 SHORTREAL FLD
76 !VF# -->

38
\ 8087 syntax tables                          P      09:50 09/25/86

( other ftype memory to st0 78 hex 4E )
ST0 DISP=LO   FQTB NUL  VF, \ 170  ST0 12 PACKED FLD
ST0 DISP=LO   R/M  FQTB VF, \ 171  ST0 12 [BX] PACKED FLD
ST0 DISP=LOHI FQTB NUL  VF, \ 172  ST0 1234 PACKED FLD
ST0 DISP=LOHI R/M  FQTB VF, \ 173  ST0 1234 [BX] PACKED FLD
ST0 R/M       FQTB NUL  VF, \ 174  ST0 [BX] PACKED FLD
ST0 WREG      FQTB NUL  VF, \ 175  ST0 AX PACKED FLD
78 !VF#
-->
```

```
39
( 8087 syntax tables                           PLP 15:43 07/05/85 )

( integer/real st0 to memory 80 hex 50 )
DISP=LO    STO  FQTB NUL  VF, \ 176  12 STO PACKED FSTP
DISP=LO    R/M  STO  FQTB VF, \ 177  12 [BX] STO PACKED FSTP
DISP=LOHI  STO  FQTB NUL  VF, \ 178  1234 STO PACKED FSTP
DISP=LOHI  R/M  STO  FQTB VF, \ 179  1234 [BX] STO PACKED FSTP
R/M        STO  FQTB NUL  VF, \ 180  [BX] STO PACKED FSTP
WREG       STO  FQTB NUL  VF, \ 181  AX STO PACKED FSTP
80 !VF#

( stx 82 hex 52 )
STX        NUL  NUL  NUL  VF, \ 182  ST2 FFREE
82 !VF#
-->

40
( 8087 syntax tables                           PLP 18:46 07/03/85 )

( to/from  memory 84 hex 54 )
DISP=LO    NUL NUL NUL  VF, \ 183  12 FSTENV
DISP=LO    R/M NUL NUL  VF, \ 184  12 [BX] FSTENV
DISP=LOHI  NUL NUL NUL  VF, \ 185  1234 FSTEVN
DISP=LOHI  R/M NUL NUL  VF, \ 186  1234 [BX] FSTENV
R/M        NUL NUL NUL  VF, \ 187  [BX] FSTENV
WREG       NUL NUL NUL  VF, \ 188  AX FSTENV
84 !VF#
-->

41
( 80186/80286 insructions                      PLP 11:03 07/03/85 )

( push immediate 86  hex 56 )
DATA8  NUL NUL  NUL  VF,         \ 189   # 12 PUSH
DATA16 NUL NUL  NUL  VF,         \ 190   # 1234 PUSH
86 !VF#

( immediate data word 88 hex 58 )
WREG  WREG       DATA8  NUL  VF, \ 191   CX DX # 12 IMUL
WREG  WREG       DATA16 NUL  VF, \ 192   CX DX # 1234 IMUL
WREG  DISP=LO    DATA8  NUL  VF, \ 193   CX 12 # 34 IMUL
WREG  DISP=LOHI  DATA8  NUL  VF, \ 194   CX 1234 # 56 IMUL
-->

42
( 80186/80286 insructions                      PLP 15:39 07/05/85 )

( immediate data word continued )
WREG DISP=LO   DATA16 NUL    VF, \ 195   CX 12 # 3456 IMUL
WREG DISP=LOHI DATA16 NUL    VF, \ 196   CX 1234 # 5678 IMUL
WREG DISP=LO   R/M    DATA8  VF, \ 197   CX 12 [BX] # 34 IMUL
WREG DISP=LOHI R/M    DATA8  VF, \ 198   CX 1234 [BX] # 56 IMUL
WREG DISP=LO   R/M    DATA16 VF, \ 199   CX 12 [BX] # 3456 IMUL
WREG DISP=LOHI R/M    DATA16 VF, \ 200   CX 1234 [BX] # 5678 IMUL
WREG R/M       DATA8  NUL    VF, \ 201   CX [BX] # 12 IMUL
WREG R/M       DATA16 NUL    VF, \ 202   CX [BX] # 1234 IMUL
88 !VF# -->

43
( 80186/80286 insructions                      PLP 13:12 07/03/85 )

( immediate rotates 90 hex 5A )
```

```
BREG       DISP=LO NUL      NUL     VF, \ 203  BL 7 RCL
WREG       DISP=LO NUL      NUL     VF, \ 204  BX 7 RCL
DISP=LO    DISP=LO BYT8     NUL     VF, \ 205  12 7 BYTE RCL
DISP=LO    R/M     DISP=LO  BYT8    VF, \ 206  12 [BX] 7 BYTE RCL
DISP=LOHI  DISP=LO BYT8     NUL     VF, \ 207  1234 7 BYTE RCL
DISP=LOHI  R/M     DISP=LO  BYT8    VF, \ 208  1234 [BX] 7 BYTE RCL
R/M        DISP=LO BYT8     NUL     VF, \ 209  [BX] 7 BYTE RCL
DISP=LO    DISP=LO WO16     NUL     VF, \ 210  12 7 WORD RCL
DISP=LOHI  DISP=LO WO16     NUL     VF, \ 211  1234 7 WORD RCL
DISP=LO    R/M     DISP=LO  WO16    VF, \ 212  12 [BX] 7 WORD RCL
DISP=LOHI  R/M     DISP=LO  WO16    VF, \ 213  1234 [BX] 7 WORD RCL
R/M        DISP=LO WO16     NUL     VF, \ 214  [BX] 7 WORD RCL
90 !VF# -->
44
( 80186/80286 insructions                   PLP 14:37 07/03/85 )

( enter 92 hex 5C )
DISP=LO    DISP=LO NUL NUL  VF, \ 215  12 34 ENTER
DISP=LOHI  DISP=LO NUL NUL  VF, \ 216  1234 56 ENTER
92 !VF#

( word register to register 94 hex 5E )
WREG NUL NUL NUL VF,             \ 217  CX DX LTR
94 !VF# -->

45
( 80186/80286 insructions                   PLP 18:46 07/03/85 )

( memory to word register 96 hex 60 )
WREG DISP=LO    NUL NUL VF, \ 218  CX 12 or 1234 BOUND
WREG DISP=LO    R/M NUL VF, \ 219  CX 12 [BX] BOUND
WREG DISP=LOHI  NUL NUL VF, \ 220  CX 1234 BOUND
WREG DISP=LOHI  R/M NUL VF, \ 221  CX 1234 [BX] BOUND
WREG R/M        NUL NUL VF, \ 222  CX [BX] BOUND
96 !VF# -->

46
( 80186/80286 insructions                   PLP 18:47 07/03/85 )

( memory or word register to word register 98 hex 62 )
WREG WREG       NUL NUL VF, \ 223  CX DX LTR
WREG DISP=LO    NUL NUL VF, \ 224  CX 12 LTR
WREG DISP=LO    R/M NUL VF, \ 225  CX 12 [BX] LTR
WREG DISP=LOHI  NUL NUL VF, \ 226  CX 1234 LTR
WREG DISP=LOHI  R/M NUL VF, \ 227  CX 1234 [BX] LTR
WREG R/M        NUL NUL VF, \ 228  CX [BX] LTR
98 !VF# -->

47
( 80186/80286 insructions                   PLP 10:05 08/20/85 )

( memory operand protection 100  hex 64 )
DISP=LO    NUL NUL NUL VF,  \ 229  12 LGDT
DISP=LO    R/M NUL NUL VF,  \ 230  12 [BX] LGDT
DISP=LOHI  NUL NUL NUL VF,  \ 231  1234 LGDT
DISP=LOHI  R/M NUL NUL VF,  \ 232  1234 [BX] LGDT
R/M        NUL NUL NUL VF,  \ 233  [BX] LGDT
100 !VF#

( xchg ax with register 102 hex 66 )
AXREG WREG NUL NUL VF,      \ 234  AX BX XCHG
102 !VF#
-->
```

```
48
\                                                  plp 08:06 06/05/86

( fixed output port 104 hex 68 )
DISP=LO ALREG NUL NUL VF,     \ 235  # 12 AL OUT
DISP=LO AXREG NUL NUL VF,     \ 236  # 12 AX OUT
104 !VF#

( variable output port 106 hex 6A )
DXREG BREG NUL NUL VF,      \ 237  DX AL OUT
DXREG WREG NUL NUL VF,      \ 238  DX AX OUT
106 !VF#
-->

49
\                                                      07:03 06/11/86

( NEC V20/30 lods stos 108 hex 6C )
BREG BREG    NUL NUL VF,      \ 239  DL CL LODS     V20/30
108 !VF#

( NEC V20/30 lods stos 110 hex 6E )
BREG DISP=LO NUL NUL VF,      \ 240  DL 3 LODS      V20/30
110 !VF#

( NEC V20/30 bcd add sub cmp 112 hex 70 )
PKD  NUL     NUL NUL VF,      \ 241  BCD CMP        V20/30
112 !VF#
-->

50
\                                                      10:37 09/25/86
( NEC V20/30 bcd rotates 114 hex 72 )
BREG      PKD NUL NUL VF, \ 242  BL BCD ROL         V20/30
DISP=LO   PKD NUL NUL VF, \ 243  12 BCD ROL
DISP=LO   R/M PKD NUL VF, \ 244  12 [BX] BCD ROL
DISP=LOHI PKD NUL NUL VF, \ 245  1234 BCD ROL
DISP=LOHI R/M PKD NUL VF, \ 246  1234 [BX] BCD ROL
R/M       PKD NUL NUL VF, \ 247  [BX] BCD ROL
114 !VF#

( NEC V20/30 brkem 116 hex 74 )
DISP=LO,  NUL NUL NUL VF, \ 248  12 BRKEM           V20/30
116 !VF# DROP    \ drop the cumulative count
SP@ 2+ ?PAIRS    \ check for balanced stack
PFA LFA !        \ discard transient module
-->
51
\ attribute vector                                     16:06 09/25/86
HEX
( number ---  )
: ?TOP           3 > 24 ?ERROR ; \ too many operands?
( --- )
: 1+TOP          TOP DUP @ DUP ?TOP 1+ SWAP ! ; \ increment TOP

( opcode or operand type --- )
: !TOP           TO TOP @ + C!     \ push the attribute on the
                 1+TOP             \ stack.  Increment stack ptr
                 DEPTH CSP0 !      \ reset assembler compiler
;                                  \ stack pointer
-->
\ diagnostic for printing the attribute stack
: .T             TO TOP @ 0 ?DO DUP I + C@ U. SPACE LOOP DROP ;
```

```
52
\ stack check                                          15:57 09/25/86
HEX
: ?DISP          DEPTH CSP0 @ - -DUP 0>
                 IF MINUS 0 SWAP
                   DO I ABS PICK DUP 0FF > SWAP FF00 < OR
                   IF 02 ELSE 01 THEN TO TOP @ 1- + C@ DATA16 =
                     IF 2+ TOP DUP @ 1- SWAP ! THEN !TOP
                   LOOP
                 THEN ;
-->
```

?DISP checks to see if any number has been palced on the stack since the last opcode or operand was processed. If one or more number appeared, then their attributes are correctly added to the attribute stack. Eight or 16 bit displacements are distinguished from 8 and 16 bit data.

```
53
\ object code print                                    10:55 09/25/86
-->
\ put --> here to stop printing to screen also change 79
: ,              DUP , BASE @ >R HEX >< 0 <# # # # # #> TYPE
                 R> BASE ! ;
: C,             DUP C, BASE @ HEX >R 0 <# # # #> TYPE
                 R> BASE ! ;
-->
```

Redifintions of , and C, print the object code to the screen. This used for debugging.

```
54
\ ssembler code generator                              10:49 09/25/86
-->
```

The assembler code generator is documented by example of representative instructions processed by each routine.

```
55
( assembler code generator                         WHP 15:26 09/26/85 )
HEX
: INVALID        25 ERROR ;

: L0             0100 OR ; \ set word operands
: L7             0200 OR ; \ set sign extended data
: PL             0006 OR ; \ effective address = disp-high:low
: PM             0040 OR ; \ disp-low sign extended
: PN             0080 OR ; \ disp-high:disp-low
: PO             00C0 OR ; \ r/m treated as "reg" field

: LV             >< , ;
: PK             OR LV ;      \ [BX]
: L3             OR C, ;      \  BX POP or CX INC
: QO             LV C, ;      \ 12 BRKEM
-->
56
( assembler code generator                         PLP 09:10 12/27/85 )
HEX
: L4             SWAP 8 * PK ;
: JT             OR L4 ;
: L1             PO JT ;    \ DL CL
: L2             L0 L1 ;    \ CX DX

: PQ             C, C, ;
: NZ             C, , ;     \ 1234 RET
: PJ             01 OR ;
: KC             02 OR ;
```

```
-->

57
( assembler code generator                    WHP 13:17 09/26/85 )
HEX
: L5            PL L4 , ;            \ 12 or 1234 CL
: L6            PM ROT JT C, ;       \ 12 [BX] CL
: L8            PN ROT JT , ;        \ 1234 [BX] CL
: L9            ROT DUP 06 =
                IF PM JT 0 C,        \ 0 [BP] CL
                ELSE JT
                THEN ;               \ [BX] CL

: LA            L0 L5 ;              \ 12 or 1234 CX
: LB            L0 L6 ;              \ 12 [BX] LX
: LD            L0 L8 ;              \ 1234 [BX] CX
: LE            L0 L9 ;              \ [BX] CX
-->

58
( assembler code generator                    PLP 08:15 09/24/85 )
HEX
: LF            >R SWAP R> ;
: LG            >R ROT R> ;
: JU            OR LF ;

: LH            LF L5 ;    \ CL 12 or 1234
: LI            LG L6 ;    \ CL 12 [BX]
: LK            LG L8 ;    \ CL 1234 [BX]
: LL            LF L9 ;    \ CL [BX]

: LM            L0 LF LA ; \ CX 12 or 1234
: LN            L0 LG LB ; \ CX 12 [BX]
: LP            L0 LG LD ; \ CX 1234 [BX]
: LQ            L0 LF LE ; \ CX [BX]
-->
59
\ assembler code generator                         14:39 07/15/86
HEX
: PF            OR ROT PK ;

: LS            02C0 PF C, ;          \ CL # 12 ADC
: QF            03C0 PF C, ;          \ CX # 12 ADC
: PE            01C0 PF , ;           \ CX # 1234 ADC
: LT            DUP C000 U>
                IF PE                 \ TEST or MOV
                ELSE DUP 038 AND 8 /  \ is sign extended?
                  ONGOSUB QF PE QF QF \ or an AND, OR,or XOR
                          PE QF PE QF \ which cannot be sign
                  ENDGOSUB            \ extended.
                THEN ;
-->

60
\ assembler code generator                    \    10:02 02/16/86
HEX
: PH            SWAP DROP ;
: PR            , C, ;
: PS            , , ;
: LX            PH PL LF LV PR ;   \ 1234 # 56 BYTE 12 # 34 BYTE
: LY            0306 JU LV PR ;      \ 12 # 34 ADC
: LZ            0106 JU LV PS ;      \ 1234 # 56 AND
: LW            DUP C000 U>
                IF LZ                \ TEST or MOV
```

```
                ELSE DUP 038 AND 8 /  \ is sign extended?
                  ONGOSUB LY LZ LY LY \ or an AND, OR,or XOR
                          LZ LY LZ LY \ which cannot be sign
                ENDGOSUB              \ extended.
                THEN ;
-->
61
\ assembler code generator                  \     10:03 02/16/86
HEX
: PI            >R ROT ROT R> ;
: PG            PI OR LV ;

: M2            PH PM PG PQ ;         \ 12 [BX] # 34 BYTE
: M3            PH PN PG PR ;         \ 1234 [BX] # 56 BYTE
: QA            0140 OR PG NZ ;       \ 12 [BX] # 34 AND
: M4            0340 OR PG PQ ;       \ 12 [BX] # 34 ADC
: Q9            DUP C000 U>
                IF QA                   \ TEST or MOV
                ELSE DUP 038 AND 8 /    \ is sign extended?
                  ONGOSUB M4 QA M4 M4   \ or an AND, OR,or XOR
                          QA M4 QA M4   \ which cannot be sign
                  ENDGOSUB              \ extended.
                THEN ; -->
62
\ assembler code generator                  \     10:02 02/16/86
HEX

: QB            0180 OR PG PS ;         \ 1234 [BX] # 56 AND
: M5            0380 OR PG PR ;         \ 1234 [BX] # 56 ADC
: QC            DUP C000 >
                IF QB                   \ MOV or TEST
                ELSE DUP 038 AND 8 /    \ is sign extended?
                  ONGOSUB M5 QB M5 M5   \ or an AND, OR,or XOR
                          QB M5 QB M5   \ which cannot be sign
                  ENDGOSUB              \ extended.
                THEN ;
: M6            0140 OR PI OR LV NZ ;   \ 12   [BX] # 3456
: M7            0180 OR PI OR LV PS   ; \ 1234 [BX] # 5678
: M8            PH LF OR QO ;           \ [BX] # 12 BYTE
-->
63
\ assembler code generator                      plp 12:05 06/06/86
HEX
: QE            0100 JU OR LV , ;        \ [BX] # 12 AND
: M9            0300 JU OR QO ;          \ [BX] # 12 ADC
: QD            DUP C000 >
                IF QE                    \ MOV or TEST
                ELSE DUP 038 AND 8 /     \ is sign extended?
                  ONGOSUB M9 QE M9 M9    \ or an AND, OR,or XOR
                          QE M9 QE M9    \ which cannot be sign
                  ENDGOSUB               \ extended.
                THEN ;

: MA            LO LF OR LV , ;         \ [BX] # 1234
-->

64
\ assembler code generator                  \     20:22 02/15/86
HEX
: MB            C, PH , ;        \ AL 1234
: MC            PJ MB ;          \ AX 1234
: MD            C, DROP , ;      \ 1234 AL
: ME            PJ MD ;          \ 1234 AX
```

```
: MK              PQ DROP ;         \ AL # 12
: ML              PJ NZ DROP ;      \ AX # 1234

: MN              0006 PK , ;       \ 12 or 1234
: MP              PM PK C, ;        \ 12 [BX]
: MQ              PN PK , ;         \ 1234 [BX]
: MR              PO PK ;           \ CL or CX
-->

65
( assembler code generator                    WHP 13:18 09/26/85 )
HEX
: MS              PH PH ;
: MT              MS 0006 PK , ;    \ 12 or 1234 1 BYTE RCL
: MU              L0 MT ;           \ 12 or 1234 1 WORD RCL
: MV              MS PK ;           \ [BX] 1 BYTE RCL
: MW              L0 MV ;           \ [BX] 1 WORD RCL
: MX              MS PM PK C, ;     \ 12 [BX] 1 BYTE RCL
: MY              L0 MX ;           \ 12 [BX] 1 WORD RCL
: MZ              MS PN PK , ;      \ 1234 [BX] 1 BYTE RCL
: N0              L0 MZ ;           \ 1234 [BX] 1 WORD RCL
: N1              PH PO PK ;        \ CL 1 RCL
: N3              L0 N1 ;           \ CX 1 RCL
-->

66
\ assembler code generator                     \     18:30 02/15/86
HEX
: N2              26 ?ERROR ;
: N4              SWAP 08 * L3 ;          \ CS PUSH
: N5              OVER 01 = N2 N4 ;       \ SS POP
: N6              LF L3 ;
: N7              N6 C, ;                 \ DL # 12 MOV
: N8              08 OR N6 , ;            \ DX # 1234 MOV
: N9              C, DROP ;               \ BYTE LODS
: NA              01 L3 ;                 \ LODS
: LJ              PH NA ;                 \ WORD LODS
: NB              PH C, SWAP PS  ;        \ OFFSET SEGAD FAR JMP
-->

67
\ assembler code generator                           16:47 01/20/87
HEX
: NE              SWAP ?R SWAP PQ ;                  \ 1$ JZ
: NF              PQ DROP ;                          \ AL 12 IN
: NG              1 OR NF ;                          \ AX 12 IN
: NH              C, 2DROP ;                         \ AL DX IN
: NI              PJ NH ;                            \ AX DX IN
: Q4              LF NF ;                            \ 12 AL OUT
: Q5              LF NG ;                            \ 12 AX OUT
: Q6              LF NH ;                            \ DX AL OUT
: Q7              LF NI ;                            \ DX AX OUT

: NJ              SWAP DUP 3 =
                  IF DROP C, ELSE SWAP PJ PQ THEN ; \ 67 INT
-->

68
( assembler code generator                    WHP 13:19 09/26/85 )
HEX
: NK              PH 0006 PK , ;       \ 12 or 1234 BYTE DEC
: NL              PH PM SWAP PK C, ; \ 12 [BX] BYTE DEC
: NM              PH PN SWAP PK , ;  \ 1234 [BX]
: NO              PH PK ;            \ [BX]
```

```
: NP            LO NK ;             \ 12 WORD DEC
: NQ            LO NL ;             \ 12 [BX] WORD DEC
: NR            LO NM ;             \ 1234 [BX] WORD DEC
: NS            LO NO ;             \ [BX] WORD DEC
: NT            PO PK ;             \ BL DEC
: NU            LO NT ;             \ BX DIV
-->

69
( assembler code generator                    PLP 09:19 12/27/85 )

: NV            PL ROT 8 * PK , ;      \ CX 12 or 1234 LES
: NW            PM OR ROT 8 * PK C, ; \ CX 12 [BX] LES
: NX            PN OR ROT 8 * PK , ;  \ CX 12 [BX] LES
: NY            OR L4 ;                \ CX [BX] LES

: O0            PJ  C, ;               \ RET
: O1            PH 08 OR O0 ;          \ FAR RET
: O2            PH 08 OR NZ ;          \ 1234 FAR RET
-->

70
\ assembler code generator                          09:01 02/27/87

: O4            PICK 01 = N2 ;
: O5            3 O4 L1 ;  \ ES CX MOV
: O6            3 O4 LH ;  \ ES 12 CX MOV
: O7            3 O4 LH ;  \ ES 1234 CX MOV
: O8            4 O4 LI ;  \ ES 12 [BX] MOV
: O9            4 O4 LK ;  \ ES 1234 [BX] MOV
: OA            3 O4 LL ;  \ ES [BX] MOV
: OB            LF L1 ;    \ CX ES MOV
-->

71
( assembler code generator                    WHP 13:19 09/26/85 )
HEX
: OI            OR C, DROP ;        \  AX DX XCHG

: OJ            PH MN ;             \ 12 or 1234 PTR JMP
: OK            PH MP ;             \ 12 [BX] FAR JMP
: OL            PH MQ ;             \ 1234 [BX] FAR JMP
: OM            PH PK ;             \ [BX] FAR JMP
: PC            PH MR ;             \ CX FAR JMP
: OO            MS MN ;             \ 12 or 1234 PTR FAR JMP

: OP            SWAP ?R0
                IF SWAP C, 1- ,
                ELSE SWAP KC PQ
                THEN ;              \ 1$ JMP
-->
72
( assembler code generator                    WHP 13:20 09/26/85 )
HEX
: OQ            PK DROP ;           \ ST ST(2) FLD
: OS            LV DROP ;           \ ST FTST
: OT            PH PK ;             \ ST(2) ST FST
: OV            LV 2DROP ;          \ ST ST(1) FTST
: OW            >R LF R> ;
: OX            >R PI R> ;
: OY            PL OR >< PS DROP ; \ ST 12 or 1234 SHORTREAL
: OZ            PM OR PK C, DROP ; \ ST 12 [BX] SHORTREAL
: P0            PN OR PK , DROP ;  \ ST 1234 [BX] SHORTREAL
: P1            OR PK DROP ;       \ ST [BX] SHORTREAL
```

```
-->

73
( assembler code generator                     WHP 13:20 09/26/85 )
HEX
: P2           OR P0 OR OS ;       \ ST AX SHORTREAL
: P3           OW OY ;             \ ST 12 SHORTREAL
: P4           OX OZ ;             \ ST 12 [BX] SHORTREAL
: P5           OX P0 ;             \ ST 1234 [BX] SHORTREAL
: P6           OW P1 ;             \ ST [BX] SHORTREAL
: P7           OW P2 ;             \ ST AX SHORTREAL

: K0           KC PQ ;             \ # 12 PUSH

: K1           PI OR PO L4 ;
: K2           L7 K1 C, ;          \ CX DX # 12 IMUL
: K3           K1 , ;              \ CX DX # 1234 IMUL
-->

74
( assembler code generator                     WHP 13:21 09/26/85 )

: K4           L7 PL LG L4 SWAP PR ; \ CX 12 or 1234 # 56 IMUL
: K5           PL LG L4 SWAP PS ;   \ CX 12 or 1234 # 5678 IMUL
: K6           L7 PM SWAP >R JU
               L4 C, R> C, ;        \ CX 12 [BX] # 34 IMUL
: K7           L7 PN SWAP >R JU
               L4 , R> C, ;         \ CX 1234 [BX] # 56 IMUL
: K8           PM SWAP >R JU
               L4 C, R> , ;         \ CX 12 [BX] # 3456 IMUL
: K9           PN SWAP >R JU
               L4 , R> , ;          \ CX 1234 [BX] # 5678 IMU
: KA           L7 PI JT C, ;        \ CX [BX] # 12 IMUL
: KB           PI JT , ;            \ CX [BX] # 1234 IMUL
-->

75
( assembler code generator                     WHP 13:21 09/26/85 )

: J9           03 PICK ;

: KD           02 PICK >R N1 R> C,  ; \ BL 7 RCL
: KE           L0 KD ;                \ BX 7 RCL
: KF           J9 >R MT R> C, ;    \ 12 or 1234 7 BYTE RCL
: KH           J9 >R MX R> C, ;      \ 12 [BX] 7 BYTE RCL
: KI           J9 >R MZ R> C, ;      \ 1234 [BX] 7 BYTE RCL
: KK           J9 >R MV R> C, ;      \ [BX] 7 BYTE RCL
: KL           L0 KF ;               \ 12 or 1234 7 WORD RCL
: KM           L0 KH ;               \ 12 [BX] 7 WORD RCL
: KN           L0 KI ;               \ 1234 [BX] 7 WORD RCL
: KO           L0 KK ;               \ [BX] 7 WORD RCL
-->

76
( assembler code generator                     WHP 13:21 09/26/85 )

: KR           PL LF L4 , ;  \  CX 12 or 1234 BOUND
: KS           PM JU L4 C, ; \  CX 12 [BX] BOUND
: KT           PN JU L4 , ;  \  CX 1234 [BX] BOUND

: J0           0F C, ;
: J1           DUP 6300 <>
               IF J0 THEN ;
: KV           J1 P0 JT ;    \  CX DX LAR
```

```
: KW             J1 KR ;         \  CX 12 or 1234 LAR
: KX             J1 KS ;         \  CX 12 [BX] LAR
: KY             J1 KT ;         \  CX 1234 [BX] LAR
: KZ             J1 JT ;         \  CX [BX] LAR
-->

77
\ assembler code generator                              21:34 08/11/86

: KQ             J0 PO PK ;         \ CX LTR

: J2             J0 PL LV , ;       \ 12 or 1234 LGDT
: J3             J0 PM PK C, ;      \ 12 [BX] LGDT
: J5             J0 PN PK , ;       \ 1234 [BX] LGDT
: J6             J0 PK ;            \ [BX] LGDT

: PD             C, HERE 2+ - , ;   \ FREESUB CALL
: Q3             C, ;               \ for printing

: QN             LV 8 * 0C0
                 OR OR C, ;         \ DL CL LODS or STOS V20/30
-->

78
\                                                       16:05 01/20/87

: QG             LV SWAP 0C0       \ DL 9 LODS           V20/30
                 OR C, C, ;

: QI             OS C0 OR C, ;     \ DL BCD ROL          V20/30
: QJ             OS 06 C, , ;      \ 12 or 1234 BCD ROL
: QK             OS 40 OR C, C, ; \ 12 [BX] BCD ROL
: QL             OS 80 OR C, ,  ; \ 1234 [BX] BCD ROL
: QM             OS C, ;           \ [BX] BCD ROL
: QR             C, SWAP , C, ;    \ 1234 56 ENTER
-->

79
\ assembler code generator                              10:55 09/25/86
HEX
0 VARIABLE WF                        \ ndp wait flag
: ?WAIT          0F800 AND 0D800 = \ need an ndp wait?
                 IF WF @            \ yes, is wait flag set
                   IF 09B C,        \ assemble a wait
                   THEN 1 WF !      \ set wait flag
                 THEN ;
-->
\ put --> to stop printing, also change screen 53
'    , NFA DUP C@ 20 OR SWAP C!
'   C, NFA DUP C@ 20 OR SWAP C!
-->

80
\ attribute analyzer                                    11:02 09/25/86
-->
The attribute analyzer compares each value on the attribute
stack to each value in the valid operand syntax table.

81
\ attribute analyzer                                    08:51 09/26/86
HEX
( index --- type )
: T0@            T0 + C@ ;
```

```
( index --- true or false )
: PNUL          TO@ NUL       = ;
: PDISP=LO      TO@ DISP=LO   = ;
: PDISP=LOHI    TO@ DISP=LOHI = ;
: PDATA8        TO@ DATA8     = ;
: PDATA16       TO@ DATA16    = ;
: ?REG          = SWAP TOP @ 1- SWAP - DEPTH CSP0 @ - SWAP +
                   PICK ;
-->

82
\ attribute analyzer                                     08:51 09/26/86
HEX
: JV            ?REG 0 = AND ;
: JW            ?REG 1 = AND ;
: PALREG        DUP TO@ BREG JV ;
: PAXREG        DUP TO@ WREG JV ;
: PBREG         TO@ BREG = ;
: PWREG         TO@ WREG = ;
: PSREG         TO@ SREG = ;
: PR/M          TO@ R/M  = ;
: PBYTE         TO@ BYT8 = ;
: PWORD         TO@ WO16 = ;
: PSTX          TO@ STX  = ;
: PST0          DUP TO@ STX JV ;
-->

83
\ attribute analyzer                                     16:14 09/25/86
HEX
: PST1          DUP TO@ STX JW ;
: PFI/R         TO@ FI/R = ;
: PFQTB         TO@ FQTB = ;
: PCLREG        DUP TO@ BREG JW ;
: PONE          DUP TO@ DISP=LO JW ;
: PPT           TO@ PT = ;
: PFR           TO@ FR = ;
: PDXREG        DUP TO@ WREG ?REG 2 = AND ;
: PBCD          TO@ PKD = ;
: PINVALID      0 ;
-->

84
\ attribute analyzer                                     20:00 06/05/86
HEX
( attribute table address --- true or false )
: ?=            FFFF SWAP 4 0
                DO DUP I DUP ROT + C@ ONGOSUB
                   PNUL     PDISP=LO    PDISP=LOHI PDATA8
                   PDATA16  PALREG      PAXREG     PBREG
                   PWREG    PSREG       PR/M       PBYTE
                   PWORD    PSTX        PST0       PST1
                   PFI/R    PFQTB       PCLREG     PONE
                   PPT      PFR         PDXREG     PBCD
                   PINVALID
                   ENDGOSUB 0=
                IF SWAP DROP 0 SWAP LEAVE THEN
                LOOP DROP ; -->

85
\ attribute analyzer                                     13:57 09/25/86

( form # --- 0=no match otherwise processing type )
: ?VF           0 SWAP VFS + DUP 2-
```

```
                @ 4 * SWAP @ 4 * OVER - OVER + SWAP
                DO VF I + ?=
                  IF DROP I 4 / 1+ LEAVE THEN
                4 +LOOP ;
-->
Main loop of attribute analyzer.

86
\ code generator vector                               10:03 01/15/87
HEX
: ASM,          OVER ?WAIT ONGOSUB
                INVALID L1      L2      LH      LI      \ 0
                LH      LK      LL      LM      LN      \ 5
                LM      LP      LQ      L5      L6      \ 10
                L5      L8      L9      LA      LB      \ 15
                LA      LD      LE      LS      LT      \ 20
                PE      LX      LX      LW      LW      \ 25
                LZ      LZ      M2      M3      Q9      \ 30
                QC      M6      M7      M8      QD      \ 35
                MA      MD      MD      ME      ME      \ 40
                MB      MB      MC      MC      MK      \ 45
                ML      ML      O5      O6      O7      \ 50
                O8      O9      OA      OB      L5      \ 55
-->
87
( code generator vector                        PLP 15:32 07/05/85 )

                L5      L6      L8      L9      N1      \  60
                N3      MT      MX      MT      MZ      \  65
                MV      MU      MU      MY      N0      \  70
                MW      N1      N3      MT      MX      \  75
                MT      MZ      MV      MU      MU      \  80
                MY      N0      MW      N5      N4      \  85
                MN      MP      MN      MQ      PK      \  90
                OJ      OJ      MP      MQ      PK      \  95
                MR      OO      OO      OK      OL      \ 100
                OM      PC      N7      N8      N8      \ 105

-->

88
( code generator vector                        PLP 11:33 08/18/85 )

                NA      N9      LJ      L3      OP      \ 110
                OP      NB      NB      NB      NB      \ 115
                NE      NE      NF      NG      NH      \ 120
                NI      NJ      NK      NL      NK      \ 125
                NM      NO      NP      NQ      NP      \ 130
                NR      NS      NT      NU      NV      \ 135
                NW      NV      NX      NY      O0      \ 140
                NZ      NZ      O1      O2      O2      \ 145
                PD      PD      Q3      LV      OQ      \ 150
-->

89
( code generator vector                        PLP 15:32 07/05/85 )

                OT      OS      OV      OY      OZ      \ 155
                OY      P0      P1      P2      P3      \ 160
                P4      P3      P5      P6      P7      \ 165
                OY      OZ      OY      P0      P1      \ 170
                P2      P3      P4      P3      P5      \ 175
                P6      P7      PK      MN      MP      \ 180
                MN      MQ      PK      MR      K0      \ 185
```

```
-->

90
\ code generator vector                                  16:07 01/20/87
                NZ      K2      K3      K4      K4      \ 190
                K5      K5      K6      K7      K8      \ 195
                K9      KA      KB      KD      KE      \ 200
                KF      KH      KF      KI      KK      \ 205
                KL      KL      KM      KN      KO      \ 210
                QR      QR      KQ      KR      KS      \ 215
                KR      KT      JT      KV      KW      \ 220
                KX      KW      KY      KZ      J2      \ 225
                J3      J2      J5      J6      OI      \ 230
                Q4      Q5      Q6      Q7      QN      \ 235
                QG      OS      QI      QJ      QK      \ 240
                QJ      QL      QM      QO              \ 245
                ENDGOSUB RESET ;
-->

91
\ opcode forms                                           14:05 09/25/86
-->
```

1MI compiles in the valid form types of each instruction and the generic opcode for each valid form. The opcodes execute 1MI to search the syntax tables for the first encountered valid form. 1MI returns the code generation index if a match of the attribute stack and syntax tables is found. Otherwise a 0 is returned. The code generation index is passed to the code generator. The code generator issues the invalid opcode/operand error message if it receives a zero index.

```
92
\ opcode forms                                           19:57 06/05/86
HEX
( form1\opcode1\...\formn\opcoden\2*n --- ;compile )
( --- word opcode\form # found, 0 not found ;execute )
: 1MI           <BUILDS DUP C, 0 DO , C, LOOP
                DOES> >R ?DISP 0 R> DUP 1+ SWAP C@ 3 * OVER +
                DO I 1- C@         \          DUP CR ." VF " .
                  ?VF -DUP
                  IF SWAP DROP I 3 - @ SWAP LEAVE THEN -3
                +LOOP ASM, ;

: JX            STX !TOP ;
: JY            BREG !TOP ;
: Q8            WREG !TOP ;
: Q0            R/M !TOP ; -->

93
\ attribute vector modifiers                             14:09 09/25/86
-->
```

The attribute stack or vector modifiers are invoked by operand execution. The operand attribute is placed on the attribute stack while its value is placed on the parameter. ?DISP is invoked to check whether a number or numbers where placed on the parameter stack since a last operand or opcode executed.

```
94
\ attribute vector modifiers                             14:47 09/26/86
HEX
( --- )
: #             ?DISP DATA16  !TOP ;
: BYTE          ?DISP 0 BYT8 !TOP ;
: WORD          ?DISP 0 WO16 !TOP ;
```

```
: PTR           ?DISP 0 PT   !TOP ;
: FAR           ?DISP 0 FR   !TOP ;
: BCD           ?DISP 0 PKD  !TOP ;
: SHORTREAL     ?DISP    0 FI/R !TOP ;
: SHORTINTEGER  ?DISP 0200 FI/R !TOP ;
: LONGREAL      ?DISP 0400 FI/R !TOP ;
: WORDINTEGER   ?DISP 0600 FI/R !TOP ;
: TEMPORARYREAL ?DISP 0228 FQTB !TOP ;
: LONGINTEGER   ?DISP 0628 FQTB !TOP ;
: PACKED        ?DISP 0620 FQTB !TOP ; -->
95
\ operand execution                                   08:54 09/26/86
HEX
: ST        ?DISP 0 JX ;
: ST0       ?DISP 0 JX ;
: ST1       ?DISP 1 JX ;
: ST2       ?DISP 2 JX ;
: ST3       ?DISP 3 JX ;
: ST4       ?DISP 4 JX ;
: ST5       ?DISP 5 JX ;
: ST6       ?DISP 6 JX ;
: ST7       ?DISP 7 JX ;
-->

96
\ operand execution                                   08:53 09/26/86
HEX

: AL    ?DISP 0 JY ;      : CL    ?DISP 1 JY ;
: DL    ?DISP 2 JY ;      : BL    ?DISP 3 JY ;
: AH    ?DISP 4 JY ;      : CH    ?DISP 5 JY ;
: DH    ?DISP 6 JY ;      : BH    ?DISP 7 JY ;

: AX    ?DISP 0 Q8 ;      : CX    ?DISP 1 Q8 ;
: DX    ?DISP 2 Q8 ;      : BX    ?DISP 3 Q8 ;
: SP    ?DISP 4 Q8 ;      : BP    ?DISP 5 Q8 ;
: SI    ?DISP 6 Q8 ;      : DI    ?DISP 7 Q8 ;
-->

97
\ operand execution                                   08:53 09/26/86
HEX

: [BX+SI]   ?DISP 0 Q0 ; : [BX+DI]   ?DISP 1 Q0 ;
: [BP+SI]   ?DISP 2 Q0 ; : [BP+DI]   ?DISP 3 Q0 ;
: [SI]      ?DISP 4 Q0 ; : [DI]      ?DISP 5 Q0 ;
: [BP]      ?DISP 6 Q0 ; : [BX]      ?DISP 7 Q0 ;

: ES        ?DISP 0 SREG !TOP ;
: CS        ?DISP 1 SREG !TOP ;
: SS        ?DISP 2 SREG !TOP ;
: DS        ?DISP 3 SREG !TOP ;
-->

98
\ syntax forms                                        14:11 09/25/86
-->
Syntax forms given in the following screens define the search
order within each generic opcode.  The form is followed by a
generic opcode.

99
\ syntax forms                                    plp 09:21 06/05/86
HEX
```

```
                    3E 0037 01 1MI AAA
                    40 D50A 01 1MI AAD
                    40 D40A 01 1MI AAM
                    3E 003F 01 1MI AAS
 02 1200  04 1200   06 1000
 10 0014  08 8010   0A 8010 06 1MI ADC
                    02 0200
 04 0200  06 0000   10 0004
 08 8000  0A 8000   70 0F20 07 1MI ADD
 02 2200  04 2200   06 2000
 10 0024  08 8020   0A 8020 06 1MI AND
 3C 00E8  20 FF10   2C 009A
                    22 FF18 04 1MI CALL
                    60 6200 01 1MI BOUND -->
100
\ syntax forms                                    PLP 10:50 06/08/86
HEX
                    74 0FFF 01 1MI BRKEM
                    3E 0098 01 1MI CBW
                    3E 00F8 01 1MI CLC
                    3E 00FC 01 1MI CLD
                    3E 00FA 01 1MI CLI
          16 1200   5A 1A00 02 1MI CLRB
: CLRB 0F C, CLRB ; ' CLI NFA ' CLRB LFA !
                    3E 00F5 01 1MI CMC
                    02 3A00
 04 3A00  06 3800   10 003C
 08 8038  0A 8038   70 0F26 07 1MI CMP
                    26 00A6 01 1MI CMPS
                    3E 0099 01 1MI CWD
                    3E 0027 01 1MI DAA -->
101
\ syntax forms                                        15:58 01/20/87
HEX
                    3E 002F 01 1MI DAS
          28 0048   36 FE08 02 1MI DEC
                    36 F630 01 1MI DIV
                    5C 00C8 01 1MI ENTER
                    3E 00F4 01 1MI HLT
                    36 F638 01 1MI IDIV
          36 F628   58 6900 02 1MI IMUL
          30 00E4   32 00EC 02 1MI IN
          28 0040   36 FE00 02 1MI INC
                    26 006C 01 1MI INS
                    34 00CC 01 1MI INT
                    3E 00CE 01 1MI INTO
                    3E 00CF 01 1MI IRET
-->
102
( syntax forms                                 PLP 19:16 07/03/85 )
HEX
 2E 0077 01 1MI JA
 2E 0077 01 1MI JNBE
 2E 0073 01 1MI JAE
 2E 0073 01 1MI JNB
 2E 0072 01 1MI JB
 2E 0072 01 1MI JNAE
 2E 0076 01 1MI JBE
 2E 0076 01 1MI JNA
 2E 0072 01 1MI JC
 2E 00E3 01 1MI JCXZ
 2E 0074 01 1MI JE
 2E 0074 01 1MI JZ
 2E 007F 01 1MI JG
```

```
-->
103
( syntax forms                                     PLP 19:16 07/03/85 )
HEX
                    2E 007F 01 1MI JNLE
                    2E 007D 01 1MI JGE
                    2E 007D 01 1MI JNL
                    2E 007C 01 1MI JL
                    2E 007C 01 1MI JNGE
                    2E 007E 01 1MI JLE
                    2E 007E 01 1MI JNG
  2A 00E9  20 FF20  2C 00EA
                    22 FF28 04 1MI JMP
                    2E 0073 01 1MI JNC
                    2E 0075 01 1MI JNE
                    2E 0075 01 1MI JNZ
-->

104
( syntax forms                                     PLP 19:16 07/03/85 )
HEX
 2E 0071 01 1MI JNO
 2E 0079 01 1MI JNS
 2E 007B 01 1MI JNP
 2E 007B 01 1MI JPO
 2E 0070 01 1MI JO
 2E 007A 01 1MI JP
 2E 007A 01 1MI JPE
 2E 0078 01 1MI JS
 3E 009F 01 1MI LAHF
 38 C500 01 1MI LDS
 38 8D00 01 1MI LEA
 3E 00C9 01 1MI LEAVE
 38 C400 01 1MI LES
-->
105
\ syntax forms                                          08:00 06/11/86
HEX
                    3E 00F0 01 1MI LOCK
 26 00AC  6C 0F33   6E 0F3B 03 1MI LODS
                    2E 00E2 01 1MI LOOP
                    2E 00E1 01 1MI LOOPE
                    2E 00E1 01 1MI LOOPZ
                    2E 00E0 01 1MI LOOPNZ
                    2E 00E0 01 1MI LOOPNE
 02 8A00  24 00B0   0E 00A0
 0C 00A2  04 8A00   06 8800
 0A C600  12 8E00   14 8C00 09 1MI MOV
                    26 00A4 01 1MI MOVS
                    36 F620 01 1MI MUL
                    36 F618 01 1MI NEG
                    3E 0090 01 1MI NOP -->
106
\ syntax forms                                      PLP 10:50 06/08/86
HEX
                    36 F610 01 1MI NOT
          16 1600   5A 1E00 02 1MI NOTB
: NOTB OF C, NOTB ; ' NOT NFA ' NOTB LFA !
 02 0A00  04 0A00   06 0800
 10 000C  08 8008   0A 8008 06 1MI OR
          68 00E6   6A 00EE 02 1MI OUT
                    26 006E 01 1MI OUTS
 28 0058  1A 0007   1E 8F00 03 1MI POP
                    3E 0061 01 1MI POPA
```

```
                    3E 009D 01 1MI POPF
 28 0050   1C 0006  1E FF30
                    56 0068 04 1MI PUSH
                    3E 0060 01 1MI PUSHA
                    3E 009C 01 1MI PUSHF -->
107
\ syntax forms                                 09:38 04/13/88
HEX
 18 D010   16 D210  5A C010 03 1MI RCL
 18 D018   16 D218  5A C018 03 1MI RCR
                    3E 00F3 01 1MI REP
                    3E 0065 01 1MI REPC
                    3E 00F3 01 1MI REPE
                    3E 00F3 01 1MI REPZ
                    3E 0064 01 1MI REPNC
                    3E 00F2 01 1MI REPNE
                    3E 00F2 01 1MI REPNZ
                    3A 00C2 01 1MI RET
                    18 D000
 16 D200   5A C000  72 0F28 04 1MI ROL
                    18 D008
 16 D208   5A C008  72 0F2A 04 1MI ROR -->
108
\ syntax forms                             PLP 10:50 06/08/86
HEX
                    3E 009E 01 1MI SAHF
 18 D020   16 D220  5A C020 03 1MI SAL
 18 D020   16 D220  5A C020 03 1MI SHL
 18 D038   16 D238  5A C038 03 1MI SAR
 02 1A00   04 1A00  06 1800
 10 001C   08 8018  0A 8018 06 1MI SBB
                    26 00AE 01 1MI SCAS
           16 1400  5A 1C00 02 1MI SETB
: SETB 0F C, SETB ; ' SCAS NFA ' SETB LFA !
 18 D028   16 D228  5A C028 03 1MI SHR
                    3E 00F9 01 1MI STC
                    3E 00FD 01 1MI STD
                    3E 00FB 01 1MI STI -->

109
\                                              08:00 06/11/86
HEX
 26 00AA   6C 0F31  6E 0F39 03 1MI STOS
                    02 2A00
 04 2A00   06 2800  10 002C
 08 8028   0A 8028  70 0F22 07 1MI SUB
 02 8400   04 8400  06 8400
 10 00A8   08 F600  0A F600 06 1MI TEST
           16 1000  5A 1800 02 1MI TESTB
: TESTB 0F C, TESTB ; ' TEST NFA ' TESTB LFA !
-->

110
\ syntax forms                             plp 11:47 06/06/86
HEX
                    3E 009B 01 1MI WAIT
 66 0090
 02 8600   04 8600 06 8600  04 1MI XCHG
                    3E 00D7 01 1MI XLAT
 02 3200   04 3200  06 3000
 10 0034   08 8030  0A 8030 06 1MI XOR
                    3E 0036 01 1MI SS:
                    3E 0026 01 1MI ES:
                    3E 003E 01 1MI DS:
```

```
                    3E 002E 01 1MI CS:   -->

111
( 8087 syntax forms                         PLP 19:17 07/03/85 )
HEX
                    46 D9E1 01 1MI FABS
 42 D8C0  44 DCC0   4A D800 03 1MI FADD
          44 DEC0   42 DAC0 02 1MI FADDP
                    46 D9E0 01 1MI FCHS
                    40 DBE2 01 1MI FCLEX
                                 ( FNCLEX )
          42 D8D0   4A D810 02 1MI FCOM
          42 D8D8   4A D818 02 1MI FCOMP
                    48 DED9 01 1MI FCOMPP
                    40 D9F6 01 1MI FDECSTP
                    40 DBE1 01 1MI FDISI
                                 ( FNDISI )
-->

112
( 8087 syntax forms                         PLP 19:17 07/03/85 )
HEX
 42 D8F0  44 DCF0   4A D830 03 1MI FDIV
          44 DEF0   42 DAF0 02 1MI FDIVP
 42 D8F8  44 DCF8   4A D838 03 1MI FDIVR
          42 DAF8   44 DEF8 02 1MI FDIVRP
                    40 DBE0 01 1MI FENI
                                 ( FNENI )
                    52 DDC0 01 1MI FFREE
                    40 D9F7 01 1MI FINCSTP
                    40 DBE3 01 1MI FINIT
                                 ( FNINIT )
 42 D9C0  4A D900   4E D900 03 1MI FLD
                    54 D928 01 1MI FLDCW
-->

113
\ 8087 syntax forms                         P      10:18 01/01/80
HEX
                    54 D920 01 1MI FLDENV
                    46 D9EC 01 1MI FLDLG2
                    46 D9ED 01 1MI FLDLN2
                    46 D9EA 01 1MI FLDL2E
                    46 D9E9 01 1MI FLDL2T
                    46 D9EB 01 1MI FLDPI
                    46 D9EE 01 1MI FLDZ
                    46 D9E8 01 1MI FLD1
 42 D8C8  44 DCC8   4A D808 03 1MI FMUL
          44 DEC8   42 DAC8 02 1MI FMULP
                    40 D9D0 01 1MI FNOP
                    48 D9F3 01 1MI FPATAN
-->

114
( 8087 syntax forms                         PLP 19:17 07/03/85 )
HEX
          48 D9F8 01 1MI FPREM
          46 D9F2 01 1MI FPTAN
          46 D9FC 01 1MI FRNDINT
          54 DD20 01 1MI FRSTOR
          54 DD30 01 1MI FSAVE
                       ( FNSAVE )
          48 D9FD 01 1MI FSCALE
          46 D9FA 01 1MI FSQRT
```

```
 44 DDD0   4C D910  02 1MI FST
           54 D938  01 1MI FSTCW
                         ( FNSTCW )
-->

115
\ 8087 syntax forms                              P      15:58 01/01/80
HEX
                    54 D930   1 1MI FSTENV
                                  ( FNSTENV )
 44 DDD8   4C D918  50 D910  03 1MI FSTP
                    54 DD38  01 1MI FSTSW
                                  ( FNSTSW )
 42 D8E0   44 DCE0  4A D820  03 1MI FSUB
           44 DEE0  42 DAE0  02 1MI FSUBP
 42 D8E8   44 DCE8  4A D828  03 1MI FSUBR
           42 DAE8  44 DEE8  02 1MI FSUBRP
                    46 D9E4  01 1MI FTST
                 (  40 009B  01 1MI FWAIT )
                    46 D9E5  01 1MI FXAM
-->

116
( 8087 syntax forms and 80286 priviledged  PLP 09:11 07/06/85 )
HEX
 42 D9C8 01 1MI FXCH
 46 D9F4 01 1MI FXTRACT
 48 D9F1 01 1MI FYL2X
 48 D9F9 01 1MI FYL2XP1
 46 D9F0 01 1MI F2XM1

 64 0110 01 1MI LGDT
 64 0100 01 1MI SGDT
 64 0118 01 1MI LIDT
 64 0108 01 1MI SIDT
-->

117
( 80286 priviledged                        PLP 09:11 07/06/85 )
HEX

 5E 0010 64 0010 02 1MI LLDT
 5E 0000 64 0000 02 1MI SLDT
 5E 0018 64 0018 02 1MI LTR
 5E 0008 64 0008 02 1MI STR
 5E 0130 64 0130 02 1MI LMSW
 5E 0120 64 0120 02 1MI SMSW
 5E 0020 64 0020 02 1MI VERR
 5E 0028 64 0028 02 1MI VERW
         62 0200 01 1MI LAR
         62 0300 01 1MI LSL
         62 6300 01 1MI ARPL
         40 0F06 01 1MI CLTS
-->
118
( macros                                   WHP 08:57 08/08/85 )

: NEXT,          WORD LODS  BX AX MOV  [BX] JMP ;

: NOWAIT         0 WF ! ;

: FNCLEX         NOWAIT FCLEX  ;
: FNDISI         NOWAIT FDISI  ;
: FNENI          NOWAIT FENI   ;
```

```
: FNINIT        NOWAIT FINIT  ;
: FNSAVE        NOWAIT FSAVE  ;
: FNSTCW        NOWAIT FSTCW  ;
: FNSTENV       NOWAIT FSTENV ;
: FNSTSW        NOWAIT FSTSW  ;
-->

119
\  structured assembler constructs                    14:12 09/25/86
HEX ASSEMBLER DEFINITIONS
74 CONSTANT 0<>            75 CONSTANT 0=
74 CONSTANT <>             75 CONSTANT =
73 CONSTANT U<             72 CONSTANT U>=
77 CONSTANT U<=            76 CONSTANT U>
7E CONSTANT >              7F CONSTANT <=
7D CONSTANT <              7C CONSTANT >=
79 CONSTANT SIGN           78 CONSTANT NOSIGN
72 CONSTANT NOCARRY        73 CONSTANT CARRY
71 CONSTANT OVERFLOW       70 CONSTANT NOOVERFLOW
7B CONSTANT EVENPARITY     7A CONSTANT ODDPARITY
E3 CONSTANT CX>0           E2 CONSTANT CX=0
-->
```

The opcodes opcodes for the high-level constructs are defined by these constants

```
120
\ Assembler local labels                              14:15 09/25/86

\ ---
: BEGIN$        0 #$ ! ;

\ ---
: END$          #$ @ IF $A #$ @ + $A DO I @ 0< 28 ?ERROR
                4 +LOOP THEN ;
-->
```

BEGIN$ initializes the local label facility by asserting that there are no local labels in the table.

END$ searches the table for unresolved forward reference located by a negative label. If one is found, then an unresolved label message is issued.

```
121
\ Assembler local labels                              14:19 09/25/86
\ label --- address of backward reference
: $             FORTH $R DUP #$ @
                IF $A #$ @ + $A DO DUP I @ =
                  IF 2DROP I 2+ @ 0 LEAVE THEN
                  4 +LOOP
                THEN
                IF HERE SWAP MINUS !$ THEN ;
-->
```

The local label table is searched for a label matching the candidate forward or backward reference. If the label is found, then the reference is backward and it is resolved by placing the address on the stack. If the label is not found, then it is an unresolved forward reference. The label is negated and placed in the local label table.

```
122
\ Assembler local labels                              14:22 09/25/86

\ label ---
: $:            FORTH $R #$ @
                IF $A #$ @ + $A DO DUP I @ OVER OVER =
```

```
          23 ?ERROR MINUS =
          IF I DUP 0 SWAP ! 2+ @ DUP ?R MINUS DUP 0>
            IF 4 - SWAP 1+ C! THEN
          THEN 4 +LOOP
        THEN !$ ;
-->
```

The local label table is searched to check for a duplicate label. If one is found, then error message 23 is issued. The local label table is searched to resolve any forward references to it. It is then stored in the table.

```
123
\  structured assembler constructs                 14:23 09/25/86
HEX
: IF             RESET C, HERE
                 0 C, HERE 2+ 7FFE RESET ;
: ELSE           7FFE ?PAIRS 0EB C, 0 C, ?R MINUS SWAP
                 C! HERE 1- HERE 2+ 7FFE RESET ;
: THEN           7FFE ?PAIRS ?R MINUS SWAP C! RESET ;
: BEGIN          HERE 7FFF RESET ;
: UNTIL          SWAP 7FFF ?PAIRS C, ?R 1+ C, RESET ;
: WHILE          SWAP 7FFF ?PAIRS C, HERE
                 DUP 0 C, 7FFD RESET ;
: REPEAT         7FFD ?PAIRS 0EB C, ?R 2+ MINUS SWAP C!
                 ?R 1+ C, RESET ;
-->
```

These are the standard assembler high level constructs adapated to the 8086 short conditional jumps.

```
124
( assembler prologues and epilog            PLP 10:33 01/01/86 )

ASSEMBLER DEFINITIONS

: END-CODE       ASSEMBLER FORTH ?EXEC ?CSP END$
                 SMUDGE [COMPILE] FORTH ; IMMEDIATE

FORTH DEFINITIONS

: ;CODE          FORTH ?CSP COMPILE (;CODE) [COMPILE] [
                 [COMPILE] ASSEMBLER  ASSEMBLER RESET
                 -1 WF ! BEGIN$ ; IMMEDIATE

: CODE           FORTH ?EXEC !CSP CREATE [COMPILE]
                 ASSEMBLER ASSEMBLER
                 RESET -1 WF ! BEGIN$ ; IMMEDIATE -->
125
\ assembler search reduction                       13:22 02/18/87

ASSEMBLER ' RESET  NFA ' #     LFA !
ASSEMBLER ' REVSYM NFA ' RESET LFA !
\  Words not directedly used by the assembler are hidden.

DECIMAL
HERE SWAP - CR U.
CURSOR

126
\ Revsion history                                  08:52 09/26/86
Revsym                 Revision history

07/15/86 14:40  SUB did not sign extend.  Constant C000 changed
                from 8000 to correct in : LT , plp

08/11/86 21:32  NEC V20/30 manual wrong on format of EXT (LODS)
```

```
                  Code generator NQ changed not to swap operands,
                  plp

                  Local label table full error message # 27 issued
                  with more than 8 local labels and unresolved
                  forward references.  Local label array dimension
                  and limit check code corrected to hold 32 labels
                  and unresolved forward references. plp

127
\ Revsion history                                      15:08 01/21/87

                  Ndp wait flag set changed from -1 to 1, whp

                  Simplified attribute analyzer by removing TOF,
                  whp.

01/15/87 08:32    PC/Assembler checked against PC/Disassembler.

                  Syntax form 12 # 3456 ADC gave syntax error.
                  Code generator word PK corrected to LZ for
                  syntax form # 30, plp.

                  Syntax table for enter wrong.  Changed from
                  1234 ENTER to 1234 56 ENTER.  Code generator
                  form QR replaces NZ for 215 and 216, plp
128
\ Revsion history                                      09:08 02/27/87

                  Code generator for AX 12 IN generated AL 12 IN
                  NG changed to or 1 rather than 100, plp

                  Opcode for REP changed from F3 to F2, plp

                  FSUBPR opcode changed to FSUBRP, plp

                  ST FPATAN syntax changed to ST ST1 FPATAN, plp

02/27/87 09:02    SS CX MOV gave syntax error.  PICK arguments on
                  code generation forms 05, 06, 07, 08, 09, 0A
                  increased by 1 to correctly flag CS destination
                  register, plp.

129
\ Revsion history                                      09:39 04/13/88

04/13/88 10:34    Opcode for REP changed from F2 back to F3, whp
```

Appendix 7

8051 FORTH Assembler in Cross Assembler Format

The 8051 assembler in this appendix is in cross assembler format. This means that it compensates for the 8086 family byte swapping.

```
0
\                                                    13:11 08/27/86

8051 interpreting assembler in cross assembler form

Bill Payne

host is a pc compatible.  Byte swapping corrected.

1
\ Assembler local labels                             13:08 08/27/86
CLS -CURSOR HERE
VOCABULARY ASSEMBLER IMMEDIATE
ASSEMBLER DEFINITIONS

0       VARIABLE REVSYM " 08/27/86"
0       VARIABLE TO 2 ALLOT
0       VARIABLE TOP
0       VARIABLE CSP0
0       VARIABLE #$
20      CONSTANT MAX#$
0       VARIABLE $A MAX#$ 2- ALLOT

\ ---
: RESET          TO 4 ERASE 0 TOP ! DEPTH CSP0 ! ;
-->
2
\ assembler syntax tokens                    \      15:20 02/20/86
HEX
    00 CONSTANT NUL                  01 CONSTANT DIRCT
    02 CONSTANT ADR16                03 CONSTANT DATA8
    04 CONSTANT DATA16               05 CONSTANT AREG
    06 CONSTANT RREG                 07 CONSTANT @REG
    08 CONSTANT DPR                  09 CONSTANT ABREG
    0A CONSTANT A+DPTR               0B CONSTANT @DP
    0C CONSTANT CBIT                 0D CONSTANT BADDR
    0E CONSTANT A+PC                 0F CONSTANT ADR11
    10 CONSTANT RELAD
: ?R0            HERE 2+ - DUP DUP 07F > SWAP 0FF80 < OR ;
: ?R1            21 ?ERROR ;
: ?R             ?R0 ?R1 ;
-->

3
\ Assembler local labels                     \      08:37 04/01/86

\ label --- label
: $R             DUP 7FFC > OVER 0 < OR 22 ?ERROR ;
\ label\here --- adusted here
: $8051          SWAP 0<
                 IF TOP @ 1 >
                   IF 1+
                   ELSE TOP @
                     IF 1+ THEN
                     TO C@ RREG =
                     IF 1- THEN
                   THEN
                 THEN ; -->

4
\ local labels                               \      12:54 02/20/86
```

```
\ label ---
: !$            DUP #$ @
                IF $A #$ @ + $A
                  DO I @ 0=
                    IF DUP I ! HERE $8051 I 2+ !
                    DROP 0 LEAVE THEN
                  4 +LOOP
                THEN
                IF #$ @ DUP MAX#$ <
                  IF $A + OVER HERE $8051 OVER 2+ ! ! 4 #$ +!
                  ELSE 27 ?ERROR
                  THEN
                THEN ; -->

5
\ syntax table builder                              13:01 08/27/86
DECIMAL
             ( VF = valid format )
             ( <destination>  <source> VF  )
        3 CONSTANT #VF

( # processed\type0\type1\type2\type3 --- # processed + 1 )
: VF,           #VF 0 DO C, LOOP
                DUP 0 6 GOTOXY U. 1+ ;
41      CONSTANT #VFS
0       VARIABLE VFS #VFS 2* ALLOT 0 VFS !

( cummulative #\form # --- cummulative # )
: !VF#          VFS + OVER SWAP ! ;
-->

6
\ syntax tables                                     12:47 08/27/86
DECIMAL
0 5 GOTOXY ." Loading syntax tables"

0       CONSTANT VF HERE DUP 2- !

0 ( start cumulative count of forms)
( A 2 hex 2 )
AREG  NUL NUL VF, \  1  A INC
2  !VF#

( direct 4 hex 4 )
DIRCT NUL NUL VF, \  2  17 DEC
4  !VF#
-->

7
\ syntax tables                               \     09:15 01/28/86

( @Ri 6 hex 6 )
@REG NUL NUL VF,      \  3  @R0 DEC
6  !VF#

( Rn 8 hex 8 )
RREG NUL NUL VF,      \  4  R0 DEC
8  !VF#

( addr16 10 hex A )
ADR16 NUL NUL VF,     \  5  DEST LJMP
10  !VF#
-->
```

```
8
\ syntax tables                                  \      14:40 02/19/86

( bit,rel 12 hex C )
BADDR RELAD NUL VF, \ 6  17 1$ JBC
12  !VF#

( A,#data 14  hex E )
AREG DATA8 NUL VF,  \ 7  A # 51 ADD
14  !VF#

( A,Rn 16  hex 10 )
AREG RREG NUL VF,   \ 8  A @R0 ADD
16  !VF#
-->

9
\                                                \      09:15 01/28/86

( no operands 18 hex 12 )
NUL NUL NUL VF,          \  9  RETI
18  !VF#

( A,direct 20 hex 14 )
AREG DIRCT NUL VF,       \ 10  17 A ORL
20  !VF#

( direct,#data 22 hex 16 )
DIRCT DATA8 NUL VF,      \ 11  17 # 07 ORL
22  !VF#
-->

10
\                                                \      09:15 01/28/86
( bit,direct 24 hex 18 )
CBIT DIRCT NUL VF, \ 12  C 17 ORL
24  !VF#

( @A+DPTR 26 hex 1A )
A+DPTR NUL NUL VF, \ 13  @A+DPTR JMP
26  !VF#

( @Ri,#data 28 hex 1C )
@REG DATA8 NUL VF, \ 14  @R0 17 MOV
28  !VF#

( AB 30 hex 1E )
ABREG NUL NUL VF,  \ 15  AB MUL
30  !VF# -->
11
\ syntax tables                                  \      09:15 01/28/86

( Rn,#data 32 hex 20 )
RREG DATA8 NUL VF,  \ 16  R0 # 17 MOV
32  !VF#

( A,@A+PC 34 hex 22 )
AREG A+PC NUL VF,   \ 17  A @A+PC MOVC
34  !VF#

( direct,direct 36 hex 24 )
DIRCT DIRCT NUL VF, \ 18  17 S0 MOV
36  !VF#
-->
```

```
12
\ syntax tables                                   \      09:15 01/28/86

( direct,@Ri 38 hex 26 )
DIRCT @REG NUL VF,  \ 19  17 @R0 MOV
38  !VF#

( direct,C 40 hex 28 )
DIRCT CBIT NUL VF,  \ 20  2E C MOV
40  !VF#

( A,@A+DPTR 42 hex 2A )
AREG A+DPTR NUL VF, \ 21  A @A+DPTR MOVC
42  !VF#
-->

13
\                                                 \      09:16 01/28/86

( DPTR 44 hex 2C )
DPR NUL NUL VF,     \ 22  DPTR INC
44  !VF#

( @Ri,direct 46 hex 2E )
@REG DIRCT NUL VF, \ 23  @R0 # 17 MOV
46  !VF#

( bit 48 hex 30 )
BADDR NUL NUL VF,  \ 24  2E CLR
48  !VF#
-->

14
\                                                 \      09:16 01/28/86

( C 50 hex 32 )
CBIT NUL NUL VF,     \ 25  C CLR
50  !VF#

( CJNE operand forms 52 hex 34 )
AREG DATA8 RELAD VF, \ 26  A # 17 1 $ CJNE
AREG DIRCT RELAD VF, \ 27  A 17 1 $ CJNE
@REG DATA8 RELAD VF, \ 28  @R0 # 17 1 $ CJNE
RREG DATA8 RELAD VF, \ 29  R0 # 17 1 $ CJNE
52  !VF#
-->

15
\                                                 \      12:28 02/19/86

( direct,rel or Rn,rel DJNZ 54 hex 36 )
DIRCT RELAD NUL VF,   \ 30  17 1 $ DJNZ
RREG  RELAD NUL VF,   \ 31  R0 1 $ DJNZ
54  !VF#

( A,@Ri 56 hex 38 )
AREG @REG NUL VF,     \ 32  A @R0 XCHD
56  !VF#
-->

16
\                                                 \      09:16 01/28/86
```

```
( rel 58 hex 3A )
RELAD NUL NUL VF,     \ 33  1$ JC
58  !VF#

( A,@DPTR 60 hex 3C )
AREG @DP NUL VF,      \ 34  A @DPTR MOVX
60  !VF#

( DPTR,#data16 58 hex 3E )
DPR DATA8  NUL VF,    \ 35  DPTR # 12 MOV
DPR DATA16 NUL VF,    \ 36  DPTR # 1234 MOV
62  !VF#
-->

17
\                                          \      09:16 01/28/86

( addr11 64  hex 40 )
ADR11 NUL NUL VF,    \ 37  MYSUB ACALL
64  !VF#

( direct,A 66 hex 42 )
DIRCT AREG NUL VF,  \ 38  023 A ANL
66  !VF#

( C,bit 68 hex 44 )
CBIT BADDR NUL VF,  \ 39  C 023 ANL
68  !VF#
-->

18
\                                          \      09:16 01/28/86

( Rn,A 70 hex 46 )
RREG AREG NUL VF,  \ 40  R0 A MOV
70  !VF#

( @Ri,A 72 hex 48 )
@REG AREG NUL VF,  \ 41  @R0 A MOV
72  !VF#

( direct,Rn 74 hex 4A )
DIRCT RREG NUL VF, \ 42  17 R0 MOV
74  !VF#
-->

19
\                                          \      09:16 01/28/86

( Rn,direct 76 hex 4C )
RREG DIRCT NUL VF, \ 43  R0 # 17 MOV
76  !VF#

( @DPTR,A 78 hex 4E )
@DP AREG NUL VF,    \ 44  @DPTR A MOVX
78  !VF#
-->

20
\                                                 13:05 08/27/86

( @Ri,#data 80 hex 50 )
@REG DATA8 NUL VF,     \ 45  @R0 # 017 MOV
80  !VF#
```

```
( bit,C 82 hex 52 )
BADDR CBIT NUL VF,      \ 46  2E C MOV
82  !VF#
DROP
-->

21
\ attribute stack                              \     13:08 02/19/86
HEX
( number ---  )
: ?TOP           3 > 24 ?ERROR ;
( --- )
: 1+TOP          TOP DUP @ DUP ?TOP 1+ SWAP ! ;

( opcode or operand type --- )
: !TOP           TO TOP @ + C! 1+TOP DEPTH CSP0 ! ;
-->

( stack attribute print diagnostic )
: .T             TO TOP @ DUP IF
                 0 DO DUP I + C@ U. SPACE LOOP THEN DROP ;

22
\ stack check                                  \     09:16 01/28/86
HEX
: ?DISP          DEPTH CSP0 @ - -DUP 0>
                 IF MINUS 0 SWAP
                   DO I ABS PICK DUP 0FF > SWAP FF00 < OR
                   IF 02 ELSE 01 THEN TO TOP @ 1- + C@ DATA16 =
                     IF 2+ TOP DUP @ 1- SWAP ! THEN !TOP
                       01 +LOOP
                 THEN ;
-->

23
\ assembler code generator                     \     20:15 04/15/86
HEX
( diagnostic screen print of assembly )
: NDY            2A ERROR ;
-->
: ,              DUP , 0 <# # # # # #> TYPE ;
: C,             DUP C, 0 <# # # #> TYPE ;

24
\ code generation                              \     11:16 02/05/86
HEX
: INVALID        25 ERROR ;

: T1             C, DROP ;        \  A INC
: T2             C, C, ;          \  17 DEC
: T3             OR C, ;          \  R0 DEC
: T4             C, T2 ;          \  17 19 MOV
: T5             OR C, DROP ;     \  A R0 ADD
: T6             C, SWAP T2 ;     \  17 # 07 ORL
: T7             T2 DROP ;        \  A # 51 ADD
: T8             T2 C, ;          \  17 19 MOV
: T9             C, DROP C, ;     \  17 A MOV
: T10            ROT OR T2 ;      \  R0 17 MOV
: T11            C, 2DROP ;       \  A @A+DPTR
-->
25
\ code generation                              \     14:40 03/14/86
HEX
```

```
: ?7F           DUP DUP 07F > SWAP FF80 < OR 21 ?ERROR ;
: REL,          HERE 1+ - ?7F C, ;

: T12           SWAP >R SWAP >R OR C,
                R> R> SWAP C, REL, ;
: T13           C, SWAP C, REL, ;            \ 17 1 $ JB
: T14           OR T2 ;                      \ 17 R0 MOV
: T15           04 OR T13 DROP ;             \ A # 17 1 $ CJNE
: T16           05 OR T13 DROP ;             \ A 17 1 $ CJNE
-->

26
\ code generation                              13:10 08/27/86
HEX
: T17           08 OR T12 ;                  \ R0 # 17 1 $ CJNE
: T18           06 OR T12 ;                  \ @R0 # 17 1 $ CJNE
: T19           08 OR ROT OR C, REL, ;       \ R0 1 $ DJNZ
: T20           05 OR T13 ;                  \ 17 1 $ DJNZ
: T21           C, REL, ;                    \ 1 $ JC
: T22           C, >< , ;                    \ MYSUB LJMP
: T23           T22 DROP ;                   \ DPTR # 1234 MOV
: T24           SWAP DROP OR C, ;            \ @R0 A MOV
: T25           >R DUP HERE 2+ - ABS 800 /
                26 ?ERROR
                DUP 07FF AND 100 / 20 *
                R> OR T2 ;                   \ MYSUB AJMP
-->

27
\                                            \    15:13 02/25/86
HEX
( index --- type )
: T0@           T0 + C@ ;
( attribute\table value --- true or false )
: TOF           = IF FFFF ELSE 0 THEN ;
( index --- true or false )
: PNUL          T0@ NUL    TOF ;
: PDIRCT        T0@ DIRCT  TOF ;
: PADR16        T0@ DUP DIRCT TOF SWAP ADR16 TOF OR ;
: PDATA8        T0@ DATA8  TOF ;
: PDATA16       T0@ DATA16 TOF ;
-->

28
\                                            \    09:17 01/28/86
HEX
: PAREG         T0@ AREG   TOF ;
: PRREG         T0@ RREG   TOF ;
: P@REG         T0@ @REG   TOF ;
: PDP           T0@ DPR    TOF ;
: PABREG        T0@ ABREG  TOF ;
: PA+DPTR       T0@ A+DPTR TOF ;
: P@DP          T0@ @DP    TOF ;
: PCBIT         T0@ CBIT   TOF ;
: PBADDR        T0@ DIRCT  TOF ;
: PA+PC         T0@ A+PC   TOF ;
-->

29
\                                            \    13:26 04/04/86
HEX
: PADR11        T0@ DUP DIRCT TOF SWAP ADR16 TOF OR ;
: PRELAD        T0@ DUP RELAD TOF SWAP
                DUP ADR16 TOF SWAP DIRCT TOF OR OR ;
```

```
: PINVALID      0 ;
-->

30
\                                              \     09:17 01/28/86
HEX
( attribute table address --- true or false )
: ?=            FFFF SWAP #VF DUP
                  IF 0 DO DUP I DUP #VF SWAP - 1- ROT + C@
                    ONGOSUB
                    PNUL    PDIRCT     PADR16     PDATA8
                    PDATA16 PAREG      PRREG      P@REG
                    PDP     PABREG     PA+DPTR    P@DP
                    PCBIT   PBADDR     PA+PC      PADR11
                    PRELAD  PINVALID
                   ENDGOSUB ( ."   OUT OF ?= " DUP .)  0=
                   IF SWAP DROP 0 SWAP LEAVE THEN LOOP
                  THEN DROP ;
-->

31
\                                              \     09:18 01/28/86

( form # --- 0=no match otherwise processing type )
: ?VF           0 SWAP VFS + DUP 2- @ #VF * SWAP @
                #VF * OVER - OVER + SWAP
                DO VF I + ?=
                IF DROP I #VF / 1+ LEAVE THEN
                #VF +LOOP ;
-->

32
\ valid operand forms                          \     11:16 02/05/86
HEX
: ASM,        (  .S KEY DROP) ONGOSUB INVALID
              (  1   2   3   4   5   6   7   8   9   10 )
                 T1  T2  T3  T3  T22 T13 T7  T5  C,  T7
              (  11  12  13  14  15  16  17  18  19  20 )
                 T6  T7  T1  T10 T1  T10 T11 T4  T14 T9
              (  21  22  23  24  25  26  27  28  29  30 )
                 T11 T1  T10 T2  T1  T15 T16 T18 T17 T20
              (  31  32  33  34  35  36  37  38  39  40 )
                 T19 T5  T21 T11 T23 T23 T25 T9  T7  T24
              (  41  42  43  44  45  46  47             )
                 T24 T14 T10 T11 T11 T9  T9 NDY
                 ENDGOSUB RESET ;
-->

33
\ opcode forms                                 \     09:51 04/28/86
HEX
( form1\opcode1\...\formn\opcoden\2*n --- ;compile )
( --- byte opcode\form # found, 0 not found ;execute )
: 1MI           <BUILDS DUP C, 0 DO C, C, LOOP
                DOES> >R ?DISP 0 R> DUP 1+ SWAP C@ 2 * OVER +
                DO I 1- C@       \ DUP CR ." vf " .
                  ?VF -DUP
                IF SWAP DROP I 2- C@ SWAP LEAVE THEN -2
                +LOOP ASM, ;

: #     ?DISP  DATA16 !TOP ;
-->

34
```

```
\ symbolic bit addresses                                    10:24 09/09/86
HEX
0E0 CONSTANT ACC                  0F0 CONSTANT B
0D0 CONSTANT PSW                  080 CONSTANT P0
090 CONSTANT P1                   0A0 CONSTANT P2
0B0 CONSTANT P3                   088 CONSTANT TCON
089 CONSTANT TMOD
0C8 CONSTANT T2CON                098 CONSTANT SCON
0B8 CONSTANT IP                   0A8 CONSTANT IE
087 CONSTANT PCON                 099 CONSTANT SBUF
08A CONSTANT TL0                  08C CONSTANT TH0
08B CONSTANT TL1                  08D CONSTANT TH1
0CC CONSTANT TL2                  0CD CONSTANT TH2
0CA CONSTANT RCAP2L               0CB CONSTANT RCAP2H
083 CONSTANT DPH                  082 CONSTANT DPL
-->
35
\ operand execution                                 \      15:31 02/07/86
HEX
: R0     ?DISP 0 RREG !TOP ;       : R1     ?DISP 1 RREG !TOP ;
: R2     ?DISP 2 RREG !TOP ;       : R3     ?DISP 3 RREG !TOP ;
: R4     ?DISP 4 RREG !TOP ;       : R5     ?DISP 5 RREG !TOP ;
: R6     ?DISP 6 RREG !TOP ;       : R7     ?DISP 7 RREG !TOP ;

: @R0    ?DISP 0 @REG !TOP ;       : @R1    ?DISP 1 @REG !TOP ;

: DPTR   ?DISP 0 DPR  !TOP ;       : @DPTR ?DISP 0 @DP  !TOP ;
: A      ?DISP 0 AREG !TOP ;       : C      ?DISP 0 CBIT !TOP ;
: @A+PC ?DISP 0 A+PC !TOP ;

: AB     ?DISP 0 ABREG !TOP ;      : @A+DPTR ?DISP 0 A+DPTR !TOP ;

-->
36
\                                                   \      09:18 01/28/86

                                     040 011   01 1MI ACALL
010 028   014 025   038 026   00E 024   04 1MI ADD
010 038   014 035   038 036   00E 034   04 1MI ADDC
                                     040 001   01 1MI AJMP
010 058   014 055   038 056   00E 054
          042 052   016 053   044 082   07 1MI ANL
                                     044 0B0   01 1MI ANL/
                                     034 0B0   01 1MI CJNE
          002 0E4   032 0C3   030 0C2   03 1MI CLR
          002 0F4   032 0B3   030 0B2   03 1MI CPL
                                     002 0D4   01 1MI DA
 002 014 008 018   004 015   006 016   04 1MI DEC
-->

37
\                                                   \      09:18 01/28/86
                                               01E 084   01 1MI DIV
                                               036 0D0   01 1MI DJNZ
002 004   008 08   004 05   006 006   02C 0A3   05 1MI INC
                                               00C 020   01 1MI JB
                                               00C 010   01 1MI JBC
                                               03A 040   01 1MI JC
                                               01A 073   01 1MI JMP
                                               00C 030   01 1MI JNB
                                               03A 050   01 1MI JNC
                                               03A 070   01 1MI JNZ
                                               03A 060   01 1MI JZ
                                               00A 012   01 1MI LCALL
```

```
                                          00A 002  01 1MI LJMP
-->

38
\                                                   \      09:18 01/28/86

010 0E8   014 0E5   038 0E6
00E 074   046 0F8   04C 0A8
020 078   042 0F5   04A 088
024 085   026 086   016 075
048 0F6   02E 0A6   01C 076
044 0A2   052 092   03E 090  012 1MI MOV
-->

39
\                                                   \      09:18 01/28/86
                    02A 093   022 083   02 1MI MOVC
038 0E2   03C 0E0   048 0F2   04E 0F0   04 1MI MOVX
                              01E 0A4   01 1MI MUL
                              012 000   01 1MI NOP
010 048   014 045   038 046   00E 044
          042 042   016 043   044 072   07 1MI ORL
                              044 0A0   01 1MI ORL/
                              004 0D0   01 1MI POP
                              004 0C0   01 1MI PUSH
                              012 022   01 1MI RET
                              012 032   01 1MI RETI
                              002 023   01 1MI RL
                              002 033   01 1MI RLC
                              002 003   01 1MI RR
-->
40
\                                                   \      09:19 01/28/86

                              002 013   01 1MI RRC
                    030 0D2   032 0D3   02 1MI SETB
                              03A 080   01 1MI SJMP
010 098   014 095   038 096   00E 094   04 1MI SUBB
                              002 0C4   01 1MI SWAP
          010 0C8   014 0C5   038 0C6   03 1MI XCH
                              038 0D6   01 1MI XCHD
010 068   014 065   038 066   00E 064
                    042 062   016 063   06 1MI XRL
-->

41
\ 8051 asm high level control constructs    \      09:19 01/28/86
HEX
070   CONSTANT 0=         060     CONSTANT 0<>
050   CONSTANT CARRY      040     CONSTANT NOCARRY

: BIT             030 C, ;
: NOBIT           020 C, ;

: IF              C, HERE 00 C, DUP 1+ 07FFE RESET ;

: ELSE            07FFE ?PAIRS 080 C, HERE 0 C, ROT ROT
                  HERE FORTH SWAP ASSEMBLER - ?7F
                  FORTH SWAP ASSEMBLER C! DUP 1+ 07FFE RESET ;

: THEN            07FFE ?PAIRS HERE FORTH SWAP ASSEMBLER - ?7F
                  FORTH SWAP ASSEMBLER C! RESET ; -->
42
\ 8051 asm high level control constructs    \      12:27 01/29/86
```

```
HEX
: BEGIN          HERE 07FFF RESET ;

: UNTIL          FORTH SWAP 07FFF ?PAIRS C,
                 HERE 1+ - ?7F C, RESET ;

: WHILE          FORTH SWAP 07FFF ?PAIRS C, HERE 00 C,
                 07FFD RESET ;

: REPEAT         FORTH 07FFD ?PAIRS 080 C, SWAP
                 HERE 1+ - ?7F C, DUP HERE 1- SWAP
                 - ?7F SWAP C! RESET ;
-->

43
\ Assembler local labels                    \      09:19 01/28/86

\ ---
: BEGIN$        0 #$ ! ;

\ ---
: END$           #$ @ IF $A #$ @ + $A DO I @ 0< 28 ?ERROR
                 4 +LOOP THEN ;
-->

44
\ Assembler local labels                    \      08:24 04/04/86
\ label --- address of backward reference
: $              >R ?DISP R> FORTH $R DUP #$ @
                 IF $A #$ @ + $A DO DUP I @ =
                   IF 2DROP I 2+ @ 0 LEAVE THEN
                   4 +LOOP
                 THEN
                 IF HERE SWAP MINUS !$ THEN RELAD !TOP ;
\ label ---
: $:             FORTH $R #$ @
                 IF $A #$ @ + $A DO DUP I @ OVER OVER =
                   23 ?ERROR MINUS =
                   IF I DUP 0 SWAP ! 2+ @ DUP ?R MINUS DUP 0>
                     IF 4 - SWAP 1+ C! THEN
                   THEN 4 +LOOP
                 THEN !$ RESET ; -->
45
\                                                  13:06 08/27/86
-->
: X0L            S0L ;                       : X0H           S0H ;
: X1L            S1L ;                       : X1H           S1H ;
: X2L            S2L ;                       : X2H           S2H ;
: X3L            S3L ;                       : X3H           S3H ;

: GETSP,         GET_SP  12 C, , ;
: SAVESP,        SAVE_SP 12 C, , ;
: GETRP,         GET_RP  12 C, , ;
: SAVERP,        SAVE_RP 12 C, , ;
-->

46
\ macros                                           13:06 08/27/86
HEX
: END-CODE       ASSEMBLER END$ FORTH
                 ?EXEC ?CSP SMUDGE [COMPILE] FORTH ; IMMEDIATE
-->
: GETIP,         GET_IP  12 C, , ;
: SAVEIP,        SAVE_IP 12 C, , ;
```

```
: NEXT,         NEXT    02 C, , ;
: A0PUSH,       A0PUSH  02 C, , ;
: APUSH,        APUSH   02 C, , ;
: -DPTR,        -DPTR   12 C, , ;
: GETX0,        (S0)    12 C, , ;
: GETX1,        (S1)    12 C, , ;
: GETX2,        (S2)    12 C, , ;
: GETX3,        (S3)    12 C, , ;

47
\ CODE | ;CODE | END-CODE                          13:08 08/27/86

ASSEMBLER ' RESET  NFA ' #     LFA !
ASSEMBLER ' REVSYM NFA ' RESET LFA !
FORTH DEFINITIONS

: CODE          ?EXEC !CSP CREATE [COMPILE] ASSEMBLER
                ASSEMBLER RESET BEGIN$ FORTH ; IMMEDIATE

: ;CODE         ?CSP COMPILE (;CODE)
                [COMPILE] [ [COMPILE] ASSEMBLER
                ASSEMBLER RESET BEGIN$ FORTH ; IMMEDIATE

HERE SWAP - DECIMAL U. ."  bytes used by assembler"
CURSOR
```

Appendix 8

"Examples" Syntax Tables for the 8051 FORTH Assembler

You may find this "syntax by example" listing easier to understand than the generic form syntax tables given in Chapter 4. This table, listed in numeric operation order, is useful for manual program disassembly.

H. D. Neugass, author of the FORTH encyclopedias for the 8086 family source code seen in Appendix 1 and the 8051 family code seen in Appendix 9, believed that the 8051 assembler was working improperly. The assembler assembled these instructions and a disassembler verified the correctness. No problems were found with this assembler. He apparently used improper syntax structures. This type of syntax-checking FORTH assembler demands exact compliance to syntax forms.

Screen #3 repeats the code to save a FORTH image on 8086 family system. This time it is presented in decimal. This code is so important to you that it is repeated, in decimal.

8051 family FORTH uses screens 4, 5, and 6 of the screen file for an error message when WARNING is set to 1. They are included for your study.

```
0
\                                                   14:11 04/18/88

Syntax tables for the 8051 family interpreting assembler

Numbers such as 12 and 34 are generic examples of a one byte
numbers
1234 is a generic example of a two byte number
1 $: is a generic local label
1 $  is a generic reference to a local label

Bill Payne

1
2
3
( Write system image )
FORTH DEFINITIONS DECIMAL
LATEST 12 +ORIGIN !                ( top NFA )
HERE 28 +ORIGIN !                  ( FENCE )
HERE 30 +ORIGIN !                  ( DP )
VOC-LINK @ 32 +ORIGIN !            ( vocabulary list )
SAVE FORTH
;S

4
( System messages )                         \      09:47 02/19/86
empty stack
dictionary full
has incorrect address mode
is redefined
is undefined
disk address out of range
stack overflow
disk error
line 4 09
line 4 10
line 4 11
line 4 12
BASE must be DECIMAL
missing decimal point
line 4 15
5
( System messages )                         \      09:48 02/19/86
compilation only, use in definition
execution only
conditionals not paired
definition not finished
in protected dictionary
use only when loading
off current editing screen
declare vocabulary
no case body
line 5 10
line 5 11
line 5 12
line 5 13
line 5 14
line 5 15
6
( 8051 assembler messages )                 \      13:15 02/19/86
relative address out of range
```

```
illegal label
duplicate label
too many operands
invalid opcode/operand form
11 bit address out of range
local label table full
unresolved local label
illegal bit address designation
command form not implemented
line 6 12
line 6 13
line 6 14
line 6 15
line 6 16
7
\                                                   08:54 06/10/88

0 VARIABLE SYNTAX -2 ALLOT
HEX ASSEMBLER RESET
        NOP                                         \ 00
        012 AJMP                                    \ 01
        12 LJMP  1234 LJMP                          \ 02
        A RR                                        \ 03
        A INC                                       \ 04
        12 INC                                      \ 05
        @R0 INC                                     \ 06
        @R1 INC                                     \ 07
-->

8
\                                                   11:04 06/08/88
HEX ASSEMBLER RESET

        R0 INC                                      \ 08
        R1 INC                                      \ 09
        R2 INC                                      \ 0A
        R3 INC                                      \ 0B
        R4 INC                                      \ 0C
        R5 INC                                      \ 0D
        R6 INC                                      \ 0E
        R7 INC                                      \ 0F
-->

9
\                                                   13:58 06/09/88
HEX ASSEMBLER RESET

        12 34 JBC                                   \ 10
        012 ACALL                                   \ 11
        A RRC                                       \ 12
        A DEC                                       \ 13
        12 DEC                                      \ 14
        @R0 DEC                                     \ 15
        @R1 DEC                                     \ 16
-->                                                 \ 17

10
\                                                   11:04 06/08/88
HEX ASSEMBLER RESET

        R0 DEC                                      \ 18
        R1 DEC                                      \ 19
        R2 DEC                                      \ 1A
        R3 DEC                                      \ 1B
```

```
        R4 DEC                                          \ 1C
        R5 DEC                                          \ 1D
        R6 DEC                                          \ 1E
        R7 DEC                                          \ 1F
-->

11
\                                                       13:58 06/09/88
HEX ASSEMBLER RESET

        12 34 JB                                        \ 20
        123 AJMP                                        \ 21
        RET                                             \ 22
        A RL                                            \ 23
        A # 12 ADD                                      \ 24
        A 12 ADD                                        \ 25
        A @R0 ADD                                       \ 26
        A @R1 ADD                                       \ 27
-->

12
\                                                       11:04 06/08/88
HEX ASSEMBLER RESET

        A R0 ADD                                        \ 28
        A R1 ADD                                        \ 29
        A R2 ADD                                        \ 2A
        A R3 ADD                                        \ 2B
        A R4 ADD                                        \ 2C
        A R5 ADD                                        \ 2D
        A R6 ADD                                        \ 2E
        A R7 ADD                                        \ 2F
-->

13
\                                                       13:58 06/09/88
HEX ASSEMBLER RESET

        12 34 JNB                                       \ 30
        123 ACALL                                       \ 31
        RETI                                            \ 32
        A RLC                                           \ 33
        A # 12 ADDC                                     \ 34
        A 12 ADDC                                       \ 35
        A @R0 ADDC                                      \ 36
        A @R1 ADDC                                      \ 37
-->

14
\                                                       11:04 06/08/88
HEX ASSEMBLER RESET

        A R0 ADDC                                       \ 38
        A R1 ADDC                                       \ 39
        A R2 ADDC                                       \ 3A
        A R3 ADDC                                       \ 3B
        A R4 ADDC                                       \ 3C
        A R5 ADDC                                       \ 3D
        A R6 ADDC                                       \ 3E
        A R7 ADDC                                       \ 3F
-->

15
\                                                       14:57 06/09/88
```

```
HEX ASSEMBLER RESET

        7F JC -80 JC                              \ 40
        234 AJMP                                  \ 41
        12 A ORL                                  \ 42
        12 # 34 ORL                               \ 43
        A # 12 ORL                                \ 44
        A 12 ORL                                  \ 45
        A @R0 ORL                                 \ 46
        A @R1 ORL                                 \ 47
-->

16
\                                                 11:04 06/08/88
HEX ASSEMBLER RESET

        A R0 ORL                                  \ 48
        A R1 ORL                                  \ 49
        A R2 ORL                                  \ 4A
        A R3 ORL                                  \ 4B
        A R4 ORL                                  \ 4C
        A R5 ORL                                  \ 4D
        A R6 ORL                                  \ 4E
        A R7 ORL                                  \ 4F
-->

17
\                                                 15:01 06/09/88
HEX ASSEMBLER RESET

        7F JNC  -80 JNC                           \ 50
        234 AJMP                                  \ 51
        12 A ANL                                  \ 52
        12 # 34 ANL                               \ 53
        A # 12 ANL                                \ 54
        A 12 ANL                                  \ 55
        A @R0 ANL                                 \ 56
        A @R1 ANL                                 \ 57
-->

18
\                                                 11:04 06/08/88
HEX ASSEMBLER RESET

        A R0 ANL                                  \ 58
        A R1 ANL                                  \ 59
        A R2 ANL                                  \ 5A
        A R3 ANL                                  \ 5B
        A R4 ANL                                  \ 5C
        A R5 ANL                                  \ 5D
        A R6 ANL                                  \ 5E
        A R7 ANL                                  \ 5F
-->

19
\                                                 15:01 06/09/88
HEX ASSEMBLER RESET

        7F JZ  -80 JZ                             \ 60
        345 AJMP                                  \ 61
        12 A XRL                                  \ 62
        12 # 34 XRL                               \ 63
        A # 12 XRL                                \ 64
        A 12 XRL                                  \ 65
```

```
        A @R0 XRL                                          \ 66
        A @R1 XRL                                          \ 67
-->

20
\                                                           11:04 06/08/88
HEX ASSEMBLER RESET

        A R0 XRL                                           \ 68
        A R1 XRL                                           \ 69
        A R2 XRL                                           \ 6A
        A R3 XRL                                           \ 6B
        A R4 XRL                                           \ 6C
        A R5 XRL                                           \ 6D
        A R6 XRL                                           \ 6E
        A R7 XRL                                           \ 6F
-->

21
\                                                           15:02 06/09/88
HEX ASSEMBLER RESET

        7F JNZ  -80 JNZ                                    \ 70
        345 ACALL                                          \ 71
        C 12 ORL                                           \ 72
        @A+DPTR JMP                                        \ 73
        A # 12 MOV                                         \ 74
        12 # 34 MOV                                        \ 75
        @R0 # 12 MOV                                       \ 76
        @R1 # 12 MOV                                       \ 77
-->

22
\                                                           13:09 06/08/88
HEX ASSEMBLER RESET

        R0 # 12 MOV                                        \ 78
        R1 # 12 MOV                                        \ 79
        R3 # 12 MOV                                        \ 7A
        R4 # 12 MOV                                        \ 7B
        R4 # 12 MOV                                        \ 7C
        R5 # 12 MOV                                        \ 7D
        R6 # 12 MOV                                        \ 7E
        R7 # 12 MOV                                        \ 7F
-->

23
\                                                           14:58 06/09/88
HEX ASSEMBLER RESET

        7F SJMP  -80 SJMP                                  \ 80
        456 AJMP                                           \ 81
        C 12 ANL                                           \ 82
        A @A+PC MOVC                                       \ 83
        AB DIV                                             \ 84
        12 34 MOV                                          \ 85
        12 @R0 MOV                                         \ 86
        12 @R1 MOV                                         \ 87
-->

24
\                                                           11:05 06/08/88
HEX ASSEMBLER RESET
```

```
        12 R0 MOV                                  \ 88
        12 R1 MOV                                  \ 89
        12 R2 MOV                                  \ 8A
        12 R3 MOV                                  \ 8B
        12 R4 MOV                                  \ 8C
        12 R5 MOV                                  \ 8D
        12 R6 MOV                                  \ 8E
        12 R7 MOV                                  \ 8F
-->

25
\                                                  13:59 06/09/88
HEX ASSEMBLER RESET

        DPTR # 12 MOV  DPTR # 1234 MOV             \ 90
        456 ACALL                                  \ 91
        12 C MOV                                   \ 92
        A @A+DPTR MOVC                             \ 93
        A # 12 SUBB                                \ 94
        A 12 SUBB                                  \ 95
        A @R0 SUBB                                 \ 96
        A @R1 SUBB                                 \ 97
-->

26
\                                                  11:05 06/08/88
HEX ASSEMBLER RESET

        A R0 SUBB                                  \ 98
        A R1 SUBB                                  \ 99
        A R2 SUBB                                  \ 9A
        A R3 SUBB                                  \ 9B
        A R4 SUBB                                  \ 9C
        A R5 SUBB                                  \ 9D
        A R6 SUBB                                  \ 9E
        A R7 SUBB                                  \ 9F
-->

27
\                                                  14:00 06/09/88
HEX ASSEMBLER RESET

        C 12 ORL/                                  \ A0
        567 AJMP                                   \ A1
        C 12 MOV                                   \ A2
        DPTR INC                                   \ A3
        AB MUL                                     \ A4
\ reserved                                         \ A5
        @R0 12 MOV                                 \ A6
        @R1 12 MOV                                 \ A7
-->

28
\                                                  11:05 06/08/88
HEX ASSEMBLER RESET

        R0 12 MOV                                  \ A8
        R1 12 MOV                                  \ A9
        R2 12 MOV                                  \ AA
        R3 12 MOV                                  \ AB
        R4 12 MOV                                  \ AC
        R5 12 MOV                                  \ AD
        R6 12 MOV                                  \ AE
        R7 12 MOV                                  \ AF
```

```
-->

29
\                                                15:05 06/09/88
HEX ASSEMBLER RESET BEGIN$

        C 12 ANL/                               \ B0
        567 ACALL                               \ B1
        12 CPL                                  \ B2
        C CPL                                   \ B3
1 $:    A # 12 1 $ CJNE                         \ B4
        A 12 1 $ CJNE                           \ B5
        @R0 # 12 1 $ CJNE                       \ B6
        @R1 # 12 1 $ CJNE                       \ B7
-->

30
\                                                15:06 06/09/88
HEX ASSEMBLER RESET

        R0 # 12 1 $ CJNE                        \ B8
        R1 # 12 1 $ CJNE                        \ B9
        R2 # 12 1 $ CJNE                        \ BA
        R3 # 12 1 $ CJNE                        \ BB
        R4 # 12 1 $ CJNE                        \ BC
        R5 # 12 1 $ CJNE                        \ BD
        R6 # 12 1 $ CJNE                        \ BE
        R7 # 12 1 $ CJNE                        \ BF
END$
-->

31
\                                                14:00 06/09/88
HEX ASSEMBLER RESET

        12 PUSH                                 \ C0
        678 AJMP                                \ C1
        12 CLR                                  \ C2
        C CLR                                   \ C3
        A SWAP                                  \ C4
        A 12 XCH                                \ C5
        A @R0 XCH                               \ C6
        A @R1 XCH                               \ C7
-->

32
\                                                11:05 06/08/88
HEX ASSEMBLER RESET

        A R0 XCH                                \ C8
        A R1 XCH                                \ C9
        A R2 XCH                                \ CA
        A R3 XCH                                \ CB
        A R4 XCH                                \ CC
        A R5 XCH                                \ CD
        A R6 XCH                                \ CE
        A R7 XCH                                \ CF
-->

33
\                                                14:00 06/09/88
HEX ASSEMBLER RESET

        12 POP                                  \ D0
```

```
        678 ACALL                                   \ D1
        12 SETB                                     \ D2
        C SETB                                      \ D3
        A DA                                        \ D4
        12 1 $ DJNZ                                 \ D5
        A @R0 XCHD                                  \ D6
        A @R1 XCHD                                  \ D7
-->

34
\                                            15:06 06/09/88
HEX ASSEMBLER RESET BEGIN$

1 $:    R0 1 $ DJNZ                                 \ D8
        R1 1 $ DJNZ                                 \ D9
        R2 1 $ DJNZ                                 \ DA
        R3 1 $ DJNZ                                 \ DB
        R4 1 $ DJNZ                                 \ DC
        R5 1 $ DJNZ                                 \ DD
        R6 1 $ DJNZ                                 \ DE
        R7 1 $ DJNZ                                 \ DF
END$
-->

35
\                                            14:00 06/09/88
HEX ASSEMBLER RESET

        A @DPTR MOVX                                \ E0
        789 AJMP                                    \ E1
        A @R0 MOVX                                  \ E2
        A @R1 MOVX                                  \ E3
        A CLR                                       \ E4
        A 12 MOV                                    \ E5
        A @R0 MOV                                   \ E6
        A @R1 MOV                                   \ E7
-->

36
\                                            11:05 06/08/88
HEX ASSEMBLER RESET

        A R0 MOV                                    \ E8
        A R1 MOV                                    \ E9
        A R2 MOV                                    \ EA
        A R3 MOV                                    \ EB
        A R4 MOV                                    \ EC
        A R5 MOV                                    \ ED
        A R6 MOV                                    \ EE
        A R7 MOV                                    \ EF
-->

37
\                                            14:00 06/09/88
HEX ASSEMBLER RESET

        @DPTR A MOVX                                \ F0
        789 ACALL                                   \ F1
        @R0 A MOVX                                  \ F2
        @R1 A MOVX                                  \ F3
        A CPL                                       \ F4
        12 A MOV                                    \ F5
        @R0 A MOV                                   \ F6
        @R1 A MOV                                   \ F7
```

```
-->

38
\                                                       09:38 06/10/88
HEX ASSEMBLER RESET

        R0 A MOV                                       \ F8
        R1 A MOV                                       \ F9
        R2 A MOV                                       \ FA
        R3 A MOV                                       \ FB
        R4 A MOV                                       \ FC
        R5 A MOV                                       \ FD
        R6 A MOV                                       \ FE
        R7 A MOV                                       \ FF
-->

39
\                                                       15:53 06/10/88
HEX ASSEMBLER RESET BEGIN$
1 $:    NOP NOP NOP NOP NOP NOP NOP NOP NOP NOP NOP NOP NOP NOP
        NOP NOP NOP NOP NOP NOP NOP NOP NOP NOP NOP NOP NOP NOP
        NOP NOP NOP NOP NOP NOP NOP NOP NOP NOP NOP NOP NOP NOP
        NOP NOP NOP NOP NOP NOP NOP NOP NOP NOP NOP NOP NOP NOP
        NOP NOP NOP NOP NOP NOP NOP NOP NOP NOP NOP NOP NOP NOP
        NOP NOP NOP NOP NOP NOP NOP NOP NOP NOP NOP NOP NOP NOP
        NOP NOP NOP NOP NOP NOP NOP NOP NOP NOP NOP NOP NOP NOP
        NOP NOP NOP NOP NOP NOP NOP NOP NOP NOP NOP NOP NOP NOP
        NOP NOP NOP NOP NOP NOP NOP NOP NOP NOP NOP NOP NOP NOP
\       NOP \ adding this opcode creates relative address
        1 $ JC \ out of range
-->

40
\                                                       15:53 06/10/88
HEX ASSEMBLER RESET BEGIN$
1 $     JC
        NOP NOP NOP NOP NOP NOP NOP NOP NOP NOP NOP NOP NOP NOP
        NOP NOP NOP NOP NOP NOP NOP NOP NOP NOP NOP NOP NOP NOP
        NOP NOP NOP NOP NOP NOP NOP NOP NOP NOP NOP NOP NOP NOP
        NOP NOP NOP NOP NOP NOP NOP NOP NOP NOP NOP NOP NOP NOP
        NOP NOP NOP NOP NOP NOP NOP NOP NOP NOP NOP NOP NOP NOP
        NOP NOP NOP NOP NOP NOP NOP NOP NOP NOP NOP NOP NOP NOP
        NOP NOP NOP NOP NOP NOP NOP NOP NOP NOP NOP NOP NOP NOP
        NOP NOP NOP NOP NOP NOP NOP NOP NOP NOP NOP NOP NOP NOP
        NOP NOP NOP NOP NOP NOP NOP NOP NOP NOP NOP NOP NOP NOP
        NOP       \ one more nop results in "relative address
1 $:    R7 A MOV  \ out of range"
DECIMAL
CR CR ." Done assembling syntax tables" CR
```

Appendix 9

8051 FORTH Operating System with ROMed Assembler and Mini-Full Screen Editor

The source code of the 8051 FORTH operating system is listed here. This is compiled and assembled by the Nautilus 2.5 metacompiler. The source for the metacompiler and 8051 cross assembler used to process this source is given in these appendices.

Screen 204 contains a version of DUMP modified to dump an IMAGE.COM opened as the primary file.

```
0
  8051 FORTH ROMable disk operating system        20:14 10/15/88

Intel 8051 series disk based operating system FORTH source code

             1985 by Plexicon
POB 1098
Santa Cruz, CA 95061     (408) 475-7461

             1985 by Sandia National Laboratories
Division 2311
POB 5800
Albuquerque, NM 87185    (505) 844-4734

8051 code nucleus written by Jerry Boutelle of Plexicon.
Code nucleus debugged and enhanced by Bill Payne of SNLA.

1
\ Compile ROMable 8051 target image               20:44 10/17/88

CROSS-COMPILE
DECIMAL 2 LOAD
;S

2
\ equates                                         12:17 01/26/89
HEX
SWAP-BYTES                        ( 8051 h,l)
0000 ( 6000 ) 0 ORG/DB            ( beginning of ROM )
8000 ( B000 ) 0100 ROM/RAM        ( start RAM, length init RAM)
FEFE ( BFFE ) EQU EM              ( end of RAM memory )

 1 EQU FIGREL    3 EQU FIGVER    0 EQU USRVER    20 EQU ABL
0D EQU ACR      2E EQU ADOT     07 EQU BELL      8 EQU BSIN
 8 EQU BSOUT    10 EQU DLE      0A EQU LF       0C EQU FFEED

400 EQU BPS      ( bytes per physical disk sector )
  2 EQU DBH      ( bytes at head of disk buffer)
  2 EQU DBT      ( null bytes at tail of disk buffer)
400 EQU KBBUF    ( length of data in disk buffer)
  2 EQU NSCR -->   ( number of SCREENS to buffer in RAM )
3
\ equates                                  \      13:12 04/21/86

DBH DBT KBBUF + +  EQU HDBT       ( total memory per disk buffer)
NSCR 400 * KBBUF / EQU NBUF       ( total disk buffers allocated)
EM HDBT NBUF * -   EQU BUF1       ( addr of first disk buffer)

040 EQU US                        ( length of user var area)
100 EQU RTS                       ( depth of return stack and )
                                  ( terminal buffer combined)

BUF1 US -     EQU INIT-R0         ( base of return stack )
INIT-R0 RTS - EQU INIT-S0         ( base of data stack )
-->

4
\ Equates for serial controller                   19:43 10/17/88

HEX
FFF0 EQU TERMINAL    ( control and status of terminal )
FFF0 EQU DISK        ( control and status of disk )
```

```
01   EQU DR          ( bit set when receive data available )
20   EQU THRE        ( bit set when transmit buffer is ready )
40   EQU TSRE        ( bit set when transmitter is empty )
10   EQU CTS         ( bit set when cts is asserted )
01   EQU DTR         ( bit set to assert dtr )
02   EQU RTS         ( bit set to assert rts )
04   EQU OUT1        ( bit set to assert ring indicator )
-->

5
\ initialization                                        13:24 10/12/86
ASSEMBLER
CLD LJMP                    \ start 0
0 LJMP  NOP  NOP  0 LJMP \       3 EXTI0
0 LJMP  NOP  NOP  0 LJMP \       b TIMER0
0 LJMP  NOP  NOP  0 LJMP \      13 EXTI1
0 LJMP  NOP  NOP  0 LJMP \      1b TIMER1
0 LJMP  NOP  NOP  0 LJMP \      23 SINT
WRM LJMP                  \      2b
                          \      2e

-->
6
\ initialization                                 \      12:43 04/24/86

FORTH FIGREL C, FIGVER C, USRVER C, 0E C,
L: INIT-FORTH 0 ,
BSIN , INIT-R0 ,
L: INIT-USERV    INIT-S0 , INIT-R0 , INIT-S0 1+ , 01F ,
L: INIT-WARNING  0 ,      ( initial value of WARNING )
L: INIT-FENCE 0 ,
L: INIT-DP 0 ,
L: INIT-VOC-LINK 0 ,
L: CPU BASE-36 8051. , , HEX
HERE LABEL SPP INIT-S0 ,
HERE LABEL RPP INIT-R0 ,
HERE LABEL UP  INIT-R0 , 2 ALLOT-RAM
-->

7
\ cold start                                     \      09:30 01/28/86
HEX
L: CLD1 ] COLD [

ASSEMBLER

L: CLD 81 # 2F MOV
       DPTR # SPP MOV  A @DPTR MOVX  R4 A MOV  DPTR INC
       A @DPTR MOVX  R5 A MOV  ( init sp)
       DPTR # RPP MOV  A @DPTR MOVX  R6 A MOV  DPTR INC
       A @DPTR MOVX  R7 A MOV  ( init rp)
       DPTR # CLD1 MOV  A  DPL MOV   R3 A MOV
       A  DPH MOV  R2 A MOV  ( init ip)
       NEXT LJMP
FORTH -->
\  NOTE: SPP, RPP, & CLD1 cannot be forward referenced.
8
\ warm start                                     \      08:48 01/28/86

L: WRM1   ] WARM1 [

ASSEMBLER

L: WRM DPTR # WRM1 MOV   A  DPL MOV   R3 A MOV   A  DPH MOV
```

```
       R2 A MOV   NEXT LJMP

L: FORTHINT 81  # 31 MOV   30  # WRM 100 MOD MOV
                           31  # WRM 100 /   MOV   RETI

FORTH
-->

9
\ decrement dptr subroutine                        \     08:48 01/28/86
ASSEMBLER

L: -DPTR
    A  DPL XCH    0=
    IF  DPH DEC THEN  A DPL XCH
    DPL DEC
    RET

FORTH
-->

10
\ s0h&l-s3h&l                                      \     08:48 01/28/86

20 EQU S0H  21 EQU S0L  ( temp storage for s0 i.e. top of stk )
22 EQU S1H  23 EQU S1L
24 EQU S2H  25 EQU S2L  ( ect. )
26 EQU S3H  27 EQU S3L
-->

11
\ (S0 subroutine                                         09:10 03/03/89
ASSEMBLER

L: (S0)
   GET_SP ( ACALL ) LCALL
   DPTR INC
   A @DPTR MOVX   S0H  A MOV
   DPTR INC
   A @DPTR MOVX   S0L  A MOV
   RET

FORTH
-->
move the top of stack ( as indexed by (dptr) ) to a temp loc
NOTE: the stack ptr is not updated

12
\ (S1 subroutine                                   \     08:49 01/28/86

ASSEMBLER

L: (S1)
   DPTR INC
   A @DPTR MOVX   S1H  A MOV
   DPTR INC
   A @DPTR MOVX   S1L  A MOV
   RET

FORTH

-->
move the top of stack ( as indexed by (dptr) ) to a temp loc
NOTE: the stack ptr is not updated
```

```
13
\ (S2 subroutine                                \     08:49 01/28/86

ASSEMBLER

L: (S2)
   DPTR INC
   A @DPTR MOVX    S2H  A MOV
   DPTR INC
   A @DPTR MOVX    S2L  A MOV
   RET

FORTH
-->
```

move the top of stack (as indexed by (dptr)) to a temp loc
NOTE: the stack ptr is not updated

```
14
\ (S3 subroutine                                \     08:49 01/28/86

ASSEMBLER

L: (S3)
   DPTR INC
   A @DPTR MOVX    S3H  A MOV
   DPTR INC
   A @DPTR MOVX    S3L  A MOV
   RET

FORTH
-->
```

move the top of stack (as indexed by (dptr)) to a temp loc
NOTE: the stack ptr is not updated

```
15
\ get and save rp subroutines                   \     08:49 01/28/86

ASSEMBLER

L: GET_RP
   DPL  R7 MOV   DPH  R6 MOV
   RET

L: SAVE_RP
   -DPTR ( ACALL ) LCALL   R7  DPL MOV   R6  DPH MOV
   RET

FORTH
-->

16
\ get and save sp subroutines                   \     08:49 01/28/86

ASSEMBLER

L: GET_SP
   DPL  R5 MOV   DPH  R4 MOV
   RET

L: SAVE_SP
   -DPTR ( ACALL ) LCALL   R5  DPL MOV   R4  DPH MOV
   RET

FORTH
```

```
-->

17
\ get and save ip subroutines                    \     08:49 01/28/86

ASSEMBLER

L: GET_IP
   DPL  R3 MOV   DPH  R2 MOV
   RET

L: SAVE_IP
   DPTR INC  R3  DPL MOV   R2  DPH MOV
   RET

FORTH
-->

18
\ a0push subroutine                                    13:25 10/12/86

ASSEMBLER

L: A0PUSH
   @DPTR A MOVX  -DPTR ( ACALL ) LCALL
   A CLR  @DPTR A MOVX
   -DPTR ( ACALL ) LCALL   R5 DPL MOV   R4 DPH MOV
   NEXT SJMP
FORTH
-->

save the a reg on the stack as the low byte followed by a 0.
saves the value of sp from dptr

19
\ apush subroutine                               \     08:50 01/28/86

ASSEMBLER

L: APUSH
   -DPTR ( ACALL ) LCALL
   @DPTR A MOVX
   -DPTR ( ACALL ) LCALL
   R5  DPL MOV   R4  DPH MOV  ( fall thru to NEXT)
FORTH
-->

save the a reg on the stack, assumes the low byte of the
stack has already been pushed.
saves the value of sp from dptr

20
\ inner interpreter                              \     08:50 01/28/86

ASSEMBLER

L: NEXT DPL  R3 MOV  DPH  R2 MOV  A @DPTR MOVX  R0 A MOV
        DPTR INC  A @DPTR MOVX  R1 A MOV  DPTR INC
        R3  DPL MOV  R2  DPH MOV
L: NEXT1
        DPL  R1 MOV  DPH  R0 MOV
        A @DPTR MOVX  S0H  A MOV  DPTR INC  A @DPTR MOVX
        DPL  A MOV  DPH S0H MOV  A CLR   @A+DPTR JMP
-->
```

```
FORTH

21
\ lit                                          \     09:34 01/28/86
FORTH DEFINITIONS
CODE LIT GET_IP LCALL
         A @DPTR MOVX  S0H  A MOV  ( get high byte of lit)
         DPTR INC  A @DPTR MOVX  ( get low byte of lit)
         SAVE_IP LCALL
         GET_SP LCALL
         @DPTR A MOVX   A  S0H MOV  APUSH SJMP
END-CODE
-->

22
\ enclose                                      \     14:31 03/31/86
CODE ENCLOSE GET_SP LCALL  DPTR INC  DPTR INC
     A @DPTR MOVX  S0L  A MOV  ( get delim)
     DPTR INC  A @DPTR MOVX  S1H  A MOV
     DPTR INC  A @DPTR MOVX  S1L  A MOV
     -DPTR LCALL  SAVE_SP LCALL
     DPL  S1L MOV  DPH  S1H MOV  ( DPTR <- adr, left on stk)
     A CLR  R0 A MOV  R1 A MOV  ( clr offset ctr)
1 $:   ( skip leading delimiter char(s)
     A @DPTR MOVX  A  S0L 3 $ CJNE  ( not delim ? )
     R1 INC  A R1 MOV 0= IF  R0 INC  THEN  ( incr offset ctr)
     DPTR INC  1 $ SJMP
3 $:   ( first non-delimiter)
     0= ( is first non-delimiter a null ?)
-->

23
\ enclose cont.                                \     09:41 04/01/86

     IF  GET_SP LCALL
         A R1 MOV  @DPTR A MOVX  -DPTR LCALL  A R0 MOV
         @DPTR A MOVX  -DPTR LCALL
         A R1 MOV  A INC  0= IF  R0 INC  THEN  R1 A MOV
         R1 A MOV  @DPTR A MOVX  -DPTR LCALL  A R0 MOV
         @DPTR A MOVX  -DPTR LCALL
         A R1 MOV  0= IF  R0 DEC  THEN  A DEC
         @DPTR A MOVX  -DPTR LCALL  A R0 MOV
         @DPTR A MOVX  4 $ SJMP
                                        ( push off to null 3x)
-->

24
\  enclose cont.                               \     09:34 01/28/86

         THEN
         A  DPL MOV  A R5 XCH  DPL  A MOV
         A  DPH MOV  A R4 XCH  DPH  A MOV  ( get sp)
         A R1 MOV  @DPTR A MOVX  -DPTR LCALL  A R0 MOV
         @DPTR A MOVX  -DPTR LCALL
         ( push offset to 1st non-delim)
         A  DPL MOV  A R5 XCH  DPL  A MOV
         A  DPH MOV  A R4 XCH  DPH  A MOV  ( get char adr)
-->

25
\ enclose cont.                                \     09:48 04/01/86

     2 $:   ( examine next char)
         R1 INC  A R1 MOV  0=
```

```
         IF  R0 INC  THEN  ( incr offset ctr)
         DPTR INC  A @DPTR MOVX  0= ( next char a null ?)
         IF  GET_SP LCALL
            A R1 MOV  @DPTR A MOVX  -DPTR LCALL  A R0 MOV
            @DPTR A MOVX  -DPTR LCALL
            A R1 MOV  @DPTR A MOVX  -DPTR LCALL  A R0 MOV
            @DPTR A MOVX  4 $ SJMP
                                         ( push off to null 2x)
         THEN  A  S0L 2 $ CJNE  ( not delim ?)
         GET_SP LCALL
         A R1 MOV  @DPTR A MOVX  -DPTR LCALL  A R0 MOV
   @DPTR A MOVX  -DPTR LCALL  --> ( push offset to 2nd delim)
26
\ enclose cont.                                   \     09:45 04/01/86

         R1 INC  A R1 MOV  0=
         IF  R0 INC  THEN  ( incr offset ctr)
         A R1 MOV  @DPTR A MOVX  -DPTR LCALL  A R0 MOV
         @DPTR A MOVX  ( push offset to 1st unexamined char)
    4 $:  SAVE_SP LCALL  NEXT LJMP
     END-CODE
-->

27
\ digit toggle                                          15:05 12/09/86
CODE DIGIT (S0) LCALL  DPTR INC  DPTR INC  A @DPTR MOVX
         C CLR  A # 30 SUBB  E7 2 $ JB   S1L  A MOV
         C CLR  A # 0A SUBB  E7 1 $ JB  A  S1L MOV
         C CLR  A # 11 SUBB  E7 2 $ JB
         A # 0A ADD   S1L A MOV
     1 $:  A  S1L MOV  C CLR  A  S0L SUBB  E7 2 $ JNB
         A S1L MOV  @DPTR A MOVX  -DPTR LCALL  A CLR
         @DPTR A MOVX  -DPTR LCALL  A # 1 MOV  A0PUSH LJMP
     2 $:  A CLR  A0PUSH LJMP END-CODE
CODE TOGGLE GET_SP LCALL  DPTR INC  DPTR INC
            A @DPTR MOVX  DPTR INC  R1 A MOV
            A @DPTR MOVX  DPTR INC  P2  A MOV
            A @DPTR MOVX  R0 A MOV   R4  DPH MOV  R5  DPL MOV
            A @R0 MOVX  A R1 XRL  @R0 A MOVX  NEXT LJMP
END-CODE -->
28
\ (find)                                          \     13:49 03/13/86

CODE (FIND) (S0) LCALL                       \ s0l,s0h=nfa
            (S1) LCALL                       \ s1h,s1l=string address
            R4  DPH MOV  R5  DPL MOV         \ save stack pointer
            D3 SETB                          \ reg bank #1
            R0  S0H MOV  R1  S0L MOV         \ R0,R1 = NFA
            R2  S1H MOV  R3  S1L MOV         \ R2,R3 = str adr
            DPL  R3 MOV  DPH  R2 MOV         \ dptr points to str adr
            A @DPTR MOVX                     \ count byte of str adr
            S2L  A MOV                       \ S2L = str len
-->

29
\ (find) continued                                \     14:15 03/13/86

\ check the string against this NF
   1 $:   DPH  R0 MOV  DPL  R1 MOV          \ point to nfa
          A @DPTR MOVX                      \ count byte to a
          S3L  A MOV                        \ save count byte in s3l
          A # 3F ANL                        \ mask precidence
          A S2L 3 $ CJNE                    \ jump lengths <>
          A # 1F ANL
```

```
          R6 A MOV                        \ length in r6
          A R3 MOV  R5 A MOV              \ R4,R5 = NFA
          A R2 MOV  R4 A MOV              \ and string ptrs
-->

30
\ (find) continued                             \     12:46 03/12/86

     2 $: A  DPH MOV  A R4 XCH  DPH  A MOV
          A  DPL MOV  A R5 XCH  DPL  A MOV
          DPTR INC  A @DPTR MOVX            \ string character
          S2H  A MOV                        \ save str char
          A  DPL MOV  A R5 XCH  DPL  A MOV
          A  DPH MOV  A R4 XCH  DPH  A MOV
          DPTR INC
          A @DPTR MOVX  A # 7F ANL          \ character
          A S2H 8 $ CJNE                    \ jump if <>
          R6 2 $ DJNZ                       \ compare again
-->

31
\ (find) continued                             \     10:10 02/28/86

          A  DPL MOV
          A # 5 ADD  CARRY
          IF  DPH INC  THEN
          S0H DPH MOV  S0L  A MOV         \ save PFA
          D3 CLR                          \ reg bank #0
          GET_SP LCALL                    \ get the stack pointer
          A  S0L MOV  @DPTR A MOVX  -DPTR LCALL
          A  S0H MOV  @DPTR A MOVX  -DPTR LCALL  \ stack PFA
          A  S3L MOV  @DPTR A MOVX  -DPTR LCALL
          A CLR  @DPTR A MOVX  -DPTR LCALL       \ stack count
          A # 1 MOV                              \ stack true
          A0PUSH LJMP
-->

32
\ (find) continued                             \     08:03 03/14/86

     8 $: A R6 MOV                       \ jump over <> char
          A DEC
     3 $: A # 1F ANL                     \ mask off precidence
          A DPL ADD                      \ jump over nfa
          DPL A MOV                      \ point at lfa
          CARRY IF DPH INC THEN
          DPTR INC                       \ skip to LFA
          A @DPTR MOVX  R0 A MOV
          DPTR INC  A @DPTR MOVX
          R1 A MOV
          7 $ JZ               \ jump if low byte of link is zero
          1 $ SJMP                       \ check this NF
-->

33
\ (find) continued                             \     13:28 03/12/86

     7 $: R0 # 00 1 $ CJNE               \ jump if not null link
          D3 CLR                         \ reg bank #0
          GET_SP LCALL  A CLR            \ false flag
          A0PUSH LJMP                    \ not found
          END-CODE -->

34
```

```
\ u*                                              10:02 03/03/89
CODE U* (S0) LCALL  (S1) LCALL  R4  DPH MOV  R5  DPL MOV
        D3 SETB  ( reg bank #1) R7  S0H MOV  R6  S0L MOV
        R5  S1H MOV  R4  S1L MOV
        F0 R6 MOV  A R4 MOV  AB MUL  S1L  A MOV  R1 F0 MOV
        A R5 MOV F0 R6 MOV  AB MUL  A R1 ADD  R1 A MOV
        A CLR  A F0 ADDC  R2 A MOV  A R4 MOV F0 R7 MOV
        AB MUL  A R1 ADD  S1H  A MOV  A F0 MOV  A R2 ADDC
        R2 A MOV  A CLR  A # 00 ADDC  R3 A MOV  A R5 MOV
        F0 R7 MOV  AB MUL  A R2 ADD  S0L  A MOV  A F0 MOV
        A R3 ADDC  S0H  A MOV
        D3 CLR  ( reg bank #0) GET_SP LCALL
        A  S1L MOV  @DPTR A MOVX  -DPTR LCALL  A  S1H MOV
        @DPTR A MOVX  -DPTR LCALL  A  S0L MOV  @DPTR A MOVX
        A  S0H MOV  APUSH LJMP
END-CODE -->
35
\ u/                                        \     14:30 02/26/86

\ double dividend\divisor --- remainder\quotient
CODE U/ DPH R4 MOV  DPL R5 MOV
        D3 SETB                            \ reg bank #1
        DPTR INC  A @DPTR MOVX  R5 A MOV \ high byte divisor
        DPTR INC  A @DPTR MOVX  R4 A MOV \ low  byte divisor
        DPTR INC  A @DPTR MOVX  R1 A MOV \ high high dividend
        DPTR INC  A @DPTR MOVX  R0 A MOV \ low  high dividend
        DPTR INC  A @DPTR MOVX  R7 A MOV \ high low  dividend
        DPTR INC  A @DPTR MOVX  R6 A MOV \ low  low  dividend
-->

36
\ u/ cont.                                  \     10:44 02/27/86

        C CLR
        A R1 MOV  A R5 SUBB       \ high dividend - divisor
        4 $ JC                    \ jump to shift dividend left
        2 $ JNZ                   \ jump to divide overflow
        A R0 MOV  A R4 SUBB       \ low dividend - divisor
        2 $ JNC                   \ jump to divide overflow
        4 $ SJMP                  \ shift and subtract
  2 $:  A # FF MOV  R1 A MOV      \ divide overflow
        R6 A MOV   R7 A MOV       \ set q and r to ffff
        7 $ SJMP                  \ jump to exit
  4 $:  R2 # 10 MOV               \ loop counter at 16
-->

37
\ u/ cont.                                  \     14:26 02/26/86
  3 $:  C CLR
        A R6 MOV  A RLC  R6 A MOV     \ shift dividend left one
        A R7 MOV  A RLC  R7 A MOV     \ leave room for quotient
        A R0 MOV  A RLC  R0 A MOV     \ bit
        A R1 MOV  A RLC  R1 A MOV     \
        C CLR
        A R1 MOV  A R5 SUBB           \ high dividend - divisor
        6 $ JC                        \ carry set jump taken
        5 $ JNZ                       \ carry clear
        A R0 MOV  A R4 SUBB           \ low dividend - divisor
        6 $ JC                        \ carry set jump taken
  5 $:  A R0 MOV  A R4 SUBB  R0 A MOV \ carry clear, q bit = 1
        A R1 MOV  A R5 SUBB  R1 A MOV \
        0E # 01 ORL                   \ set quotient bit
  6 $:  R2 3 $ DJNZ -->
38
```

```
\ u/ cont.                                      \      14:30 02/26/86

        A R0 MOV                        \ low byte remainder
  7 $:  @DPTR A MOVX  -DPTR LCALL
        A R1 MOV                        \ high byte remainder
        @DPTR A MOVX  -DPTR LCALL
        A R6 MOV                        \ low byte quotient
        @DPTR A MOVX
        A R7 MOV                        \ high byte quotient
        D3 CLR                          \ reg bank #0
        APUSH LJMP
        END-CODE -->

39
\ fill                                                 09:34 06/29/89

CODE FILL (S0) LCALL  (S1) LCALL  (S2) LCALL
          R4  DPH MOV   R5  DPL MOV
          A  S1L MOV  0<> IF  S1H INC  THEN
          DPH S2H MOV  DPL S2L MOV
          A  S0L MOV
       1 $:  @DPTR A MOVX  DPTR INC
          S1L 1 $ DJNZ   S1H 1 $ DJNZ
          NEXT LJMP
          END-CODE -->

40
\ cmove                                         \      14:05 03/31/86

CODE CMOVE (S0) LCALL  (S1) LCALL  (S2) LCALL  R4  DPH MOV
          R5  DPL MOV
          A  S0L MOV  0<> IF  S0H INC  THEN
          DPH  S2H MOV  DPL S2L MOV
       1 $:  A @DPTR MOVX  S3L  A MOV  DPTR INC
          A  DPH MOV  A  S1H XCH  DPH  A MOV
          A  DPL MOV  A  S1L XCH  DPL  A MOV
          A  S3L MOV  @DPTR A MOVX  DPTR INC
          A  DPH MOV  A  S1H XCH  DPH  A MOV
          A  DPL MOV  A  S1L XCH  DPL  A MOV
          S0L 1 $ DJNZ   S0H 1 $ DJNZ
          NEXT LJMP
END-CODE -->

41
\ + - < 0<                                      \      08:52 01/28/86

CODE + (S0) LCALL  (S1) LCALL  A  S0L ADD  @DPTR A MOVX
       A  S1H MOV  A  S0H ADDC  APUSH LJMP
END-CODE
CODE - (S0) LCALL  (S1) LCALL  C CLR  A  S1L MOV
       A  S0L SUBB  @DPTR A MOVX  A  S1H MOV
       A  S0H SUBB  APUSH LJMP
END-CODE
CODE < (S0) LCALL  (S1) LCALL  C CLR
       A  S0L SUBB  A  S1H MOV  A  S0H SUBB  C  E7 MOV
       A CLR  CARRY IF  A INC  THEN  A0PUSH LJMP
END-CODE
CODE 0< (S0) LCALL  A  S0H MOV  C  E7 MOV  A CLR  CARRY
        IF  A INC  THEN  A0PUSH LJMP
END-CODE -->
42
\ 0=                                            \      14:43 01/28/86

CODE 0=  GET_SP LCALL  DPTR INC  A @DPTR MOVX
```

```
        DPTR INC  S0H  A  MOV
        A @DPTR MOVX  A  S0H ORL  0=
        IF  A INC  ELSE  A CLR  THEN  A0PUSH LJMP
END-CODE
-->

43
\ minus dminus                                      12:55 12/09/86

CODE MINUS (S0) LCALL  A  S0H MOV  A CPL  S0H  A MOV
           A  S0L MOV  A CPL  A # 01 ADD  @DPTR A MOVX
           A  S0H MOV  CARRY IF  A INC  THEN  APUSH LJMP
END-CODE
CODE DMINUS (S0) LCALL  (S1) LCALL  C CLR
            A CLR  A S1L SUBB  S1L A MOV
            A CLR  A S1H SUBB  S1H A MOV
            A CLR  A S0L SUBB  S0L A MOV
            A CLR  A S0H SUBB  S0H A MOV
            A S1L MOV  @DPTR A MOVX  -DPTR LCALL
            A S1H MOV  @DPTR A MOVX  -DPTR LCALL
            A S0L MOV  @DPTR A MOVX
            A S0H MOV  APUSH LJMP  END-CODE -->

44
\ d+ s->d                                     \     08:52 01/28/86

CODE D+ (S0) LCALL  (S1) LCALL  (S2) LCALL  (S3) LCALL
        A  S1L MOV  A  S3L ADD  @DPTR A MOVX  -DPTR LCALL
        A  S1H MOV  A  S3H ADDC  @DPTR A MOVX  -DPTR LCALL
        A  S0L MOV  A  S2L ADDC  @DPTR A MOVX
        A  S0H MOV  A  S2H ADDC  APUSH LJMP
END-CODE

CODE S->D GET_SP LCALL  DPTR INC  A @DPTR MOVX  -DPTR LCALL
          C  E7 MOV  A CLR  CARRY IF  A # FF MOV  THEN
          @DPTR A MOVX  APUSH LJMP
END-CODE
-->

45
\ and or xor                                  \     08:52 01/28/86

CODE AND (S0) LCALL  (S1) LCALL  A  S0L ANL  @DPTR A MOVX
        A  S0H MOV  A  S1H ANL  APUSH LJMP
END-CODE

CODE OR  (S0) LCALL  (S1) LCALL  A  S0L ORL  @DPTR A MOVX
        A  S0H MOV  A  S1H ORL  APUSH LJMP
END-CODE

CODE XOR (S0) LCALL  (S1) LCALL  A  S0L XRL  @DPTR A MOVX
        A  S0H MOV  A  S1H XRL  APUSH LJMP
END-CODE
-->

46
\ sp@ sp! rp!                                 \     08:53 01/28/86

CODE SP@ GET_SP LCALL  A R5 MOV  @DPTR A MOVX  A R4 MOV
        APUSH LJMP
END-CODE

CODE SP! DPTR # SPP MOV  A @DPTR MOVX  R4 A MOV  DPTR INC
       A @DPTR MOVX  R5 A MOV  NEXT LJMP
```

```
END-CODE

CODE RP! DPTR # RPP MOV  A @DPTR MOVX  R6 A MOV  DPTR INC
       A @DPTR MOVX  R7 A MOV  NEXT LJMP
END-CODE
-->

47
\ >r r> i r                                    \     09:35 04/01/86
CODE >R (S0) LCALL  DPTR INC  SAVE_SP LCALL  GET_RP LCALL
        @DPTR A MOVX  -DPTR LCALL  A  S0H MOV  @DPTR A MOVX
        SAVE_RP LCALL  NEXT LJMP
END-CODE
CODE R> GET_RP LCALL  DPTR INC  A @DPTR MOVX  S0H  A MOV
        DPTR INC  A @DPTR MOVX  R7  DPL MOV
        R6  DPH MOV  DPL  R5 MOV  DPH  R4 MOV  @DPTR A MOVX
        A  S0H MOV  APUSH LJMP
END-CODE
CODE I L: I&R GET_RP LCALL  DPTR INC  A @DPTR MOVX
       S0H  A MOV  DPTR INC  A @DPTR MOVX  DPL  R5 MOV
       DPH  R4 MOV  @DPTR A MOVX  A  S0H MOV  APUSH LJMP
END-CODE
CODE R I&R SJMP
END-CODE -->
48
\ execute swap over drop                       \     08:53 01/28/86
CODE EXECUTE (S0) LCALL  R4  DPH MOV  R5  DPL MOV  R1  S0L MOV
             R0  S0H MOV  NEXT1 LJMP
END-CODE
CODE SWAP (S0) LCALL  (S1) LCALL  A  S0L MOV  @DPTR A MOVX
          -DPTR LCALL  A  S0H MOV  @DPTR A MOVX  -DPTR LCALL
          A  S1L MOV  @DPTR A MOVX  A  S1H MOV  APUSH LJMP
END-CODE
CODE OVER A R5 MOV  A # 3 ADD  DPL  A MOV  DPH  R4 MOV
          CARRY IF  DPH INC  THEN  A @DPTR MOVX  S0H  A MOV
          DPTR INC  A @DPTR MOVX  DPL  R5 MOV  DPH  R4 MOV
          @DPTR A MOVX  A  S0H MOV  APUSH LJMP
END-CODE
CODE DROP R5 INC  A R5 MOV  0= IF  R4 INC  THEN
          R5 INC  A R5 MOV  0= IF  R4 INC  THEN  NEXT LJMP
END-CODE -->
49
\ dup 2dup                                     \     15:04 01/28/86
CODE DUP GET_SP LCALL  DPTR INC  A @DPTR MOVX  S0H  A MOV
         DPTR INC  A @DPTR MOVX  DPH  R4 MOV  DPL  R5 MOV
         @DPTR A MOVX  A  S0H MOV  APUSH LJMP
END-CODE
CODE 2DUP      GET_SP LCALL   DPTR INC   A @DPTR MOVX
               S0H  A MOV   DPTR INC   A @DPTR MOVX
               S0L  A MOV   DPTR INC   A @DPTR MOVX
               S1H  A MOV   DPTR INC   A @DPTR MOVX
               GET_SP LCALL   @DPTR A MOVX   -DPTR LCALL
               A  S1H MOV  @DPTR A MOVX  -DPTR LCALL
               A  S0L MOV   @DPTR A MOVX
               A  S0H MOV  APUSH LJMP  END-CODE
-->

50
\ rot                                          \     08:53 01/28/86
CODE ROT GET_SP LCALL   DPTR INC
         A @DPTR MOVX   S0H  A MOV   DPTR INC
         A @DPTR MOVX   S0L  A MOV   DPTR INC
         A @DPTR MOVX   S1H  A MOV   DPTR INC
         A @DPTR MOVX   S1L  A MOV   DPTR INC
```

```
         A @DPTR MOVX   S2H  A MOV   DPTR INC
         A @DPTR MOVX   S2L  A MOV
         A  S1L MOV   @DPTR A MOVX   -DPTR LCALL
         A  S1H MOV   @DPTR A MOVX   -DPTR LCALL
         A  S0L MOV   @DPTR A MOVX   -DPTR LCALL
         A  S0H MOV   @DPTR A MOVX   -DPTR LCALL
         A  S2L MOV   @DPTR A MOVX   -DPTR LCALL
         A  S2H MOV   @DPTR A MOVX
         NEXT LJMP  END-CODE
-->
51
\ @ ! c@                                       \     12:41 01/28/86
CODE @ GET_SP LCALL  DPTR INC  A @DPTR MOVX  DPTR INC
       S0H  A MOV  A @DPTR MOVX  R4  DPH MOV  R5  DPL MOV
       DPL  A MOV  DPH    S0H MOV
       A @DPTR MOVX  DPTR INC  S0H  A MOV  A @DPTR MOVX
       DPH  R4 MOV  DPL  R5 MOV  @DPTR A MOVX  A  S0H MOV
       APUSH LJMP  END-CODE
CODE ! (S0) LCALL  (S1) LCALL  R4  DPH MOV  R5  DPL MOV
       DPH S0H MOV
       DPL S0L MOV  A  S1H MOV  @DPTR A MOVX  DPTR INC
       A  S1L MOV  @DPTR A MOVX  NEXT LJMP
END-CODE
CODE C@ GET_SP LCALL  DPTR INC  A @DPTR MOVX  DPTR INC
        P2  A MOV  A @DPTR MOVX  R0 A MOV  A @R0 MOVX
        A0PUSH LJMP
END-CODE -->
52
\                                              \     14:06 03/31/86

CODE PC@ GET_SP LCALL  DPTR INC  DPTR INC  A @DPTR MOVX
         R0 A MOV  A # 22 MOV  @DPTR A MOVX  -DPTR LCALL
         A R0 MOV  @DPTR A MOVX  -DPTR LCALL  A # E5 MOV
         @DPTR A MOVX  R0 # HERE 0A + FF AND MOV  00 PUSH
         R0 # HERE 06 + 0100 / MOV  00 PUSH  A CLR
         @A+DPTR JMP
         DPTR INC  DPTR INC
         A0PUSH LJMP  END-CODE
-->

53
\                                              \     08:53 01/28/86

CODE PC! GET_SP LCALL  DPTR INC  DPTR INC  A @DPTR MOVX
         R0 A MOV  DPTR INC  DPTR INC  A @DPTR MOVX  R1 A MOV
         A # 22 MOV  @DPTR A MOVX  -DPTR LCALL  A R1 MOV
         @DPTR A MOVX  -DPTR LCALL  A R0 MOV  @DPTR A MOVX
         -DPTR LCALL  A # 75 MOV  @DPTR A MOVX
         R0 # HERE  0A + FF AND MOV  00 PUSH
         R0 # HERE  06 + 0100 / FF AND MOV  00 PUSH
         A CLR  @A+DPTR JMP
         DPTR INC  DPTR INC  DPTR INC
         R4  DPH MOV  R5  DPL MOV  NEXT LJMP  END-CODE
-->

54
\                                              \     08:53 01/28/86

CODE IC@ GET_SP LCALL  DPTR INC  DPTR INC  A @DPTR MOVX
         R0 A MOV  A @R0 MOV  A0PUSH LJMP  END-CODE

CODE I@ GET_SP LCALL  DPTR INC  DPTR INC  A @DPTR MOVX
        R0 A MOV  A @R0 MOV  S0H  A MOV  R0 INC  A @R0 MOV
        @DPTR A MOVX  A  S0H MOV  APUSH LJMP  END-CODE
```

```
-->

55
\                                                  \     08:54 01/28/86

CODE IC! GET_SP LCALL  DPTR INC  DPTR INC  A @DPTR MOVX
         R0 A MOV  DPTR INC  DPTR INC  A @DPTR MOVX  @R0 A MOV
         R4  DPH MOV  R5  DPL MOV  NEXT LJMP  END-CODE

CODE I! GET_SP LCALL  DPTR INC  DPTR INC  A @DPTR MOVX
        R0 A MOV  DPTR INC  A @DPTR MOVX  @R0 A MOV  DPTR INC
        A @DPTR MOVX  R0 INC  @R0 A MOV
        R4  DPH MOV  R5  DPL MOV  NEXT LJMP  END-CODE
-->

56
\ C! +!                                            \     08:54 01/28/86

CODE C! GET_SP LCALL  DPTR INC  A @DPTR MOVX  P2  A MOV
        DPTR INC  A @DPTR MOVX  DPTR INC  DPTR INC  R0 A MOV
        DPTR INC  SAVE_SP LCALL  A @DPTR MOVX  @R0 A MOVX
        NEXT LJMP  END-CODE

CODE +! (S0) LCALL  (S1) LCALL  R4  DPH MOV  R5  DPL MOV
        DPH S0H MOV
        DPL S0L MOV  DPTR INC  A @DPTR MOVX  A  S1L ADD
        @DPTR A MOVX  -DPTR LCALL  A @DPTR MOVX  A  S1H ADDC
        @DPTR A MOVX  NEXT LJMP  END-CODE
-->

57
\ 2@ 2!                                            \     08:54 01/28/86
CODE 2@ GET_SP LCALL  DPTR INC  A @DPTR MOVX  DPTR INC
        S0H  A MOV  A @DPTR MOVX  R4  DPH MOV  R5  DPL MOV
        DPL  A MOV  DPH S0H MOV
        A @DPTR MOVX  DPTR INC  S0H  A MOV  A @DPTR MOVX
        DPTR INC  S0L  A MOV  A @DPTR MOVX  DPTR INC
        S1H  A MOV  A @DPTR MOVX  DPH  R4 MOV  DPL  R5 MOV
        @DPTR A MOVX  -DPTR LCALL  A  S1H MOV  @DPTR A MOVX
        -DPTR LCALL  A  S0L MOV  @DPTR A MOVX  A  S0H MOV
        APUSH LJMP  END-CODE
CODE 2! (S0) LCALL  (S1) LCALL  (S2) LCALL  R4  DPH MOV
        R5  DPL MOV  DPH S0H MOV  DPL S0L MOV
        A  S1H MOV  @DPTR A MOVX  DPTR INC  A  S1L MOV
        @DPTR A MOVX  DPTR INC  A  S2H MOV  @DPTR A MOVX
        DPTR INC  A  S2L MOV  @DPTR A MOVX  NEXT LJMP
END-CODE -->
58
\ rp@ branch 0branch                               \     08:54 01/28/86
CODE RP@ GET_SP LCALL  A R7 MOV  @DPTR A MOVX  A R6 MOV
         APUSH LJMP
END-CODE
CODE BRANCH L: BRAN DPH  R2 MOV  DPL  R3 MOV  A @DPTR MOVX
            S0H  A MOV  DPTR INC  A @DPTR MOVX  DPTR INC
            A R3 ADD  R3 A MOV  A  S0H MOV  A R2 ADDC
            R2 A MOV  NEXT LJMP
END-CODE
CODE 0BRANCH DPH  R4 MOV  DPL  R5 MOV  DPTR INC
             A @DPTR MOVX  DPTR INC
             S0H  A MOV  A @DPTR MOVX  A  S0H ORL
             R4  DPH MOV  R5  DPL MOV  0<>
             IF  A R3 MOV  A # 02 ADD  CARRY
                IF  R2 INC  THEN  R3 A MOV  NEXT LJMP
             THEN  BRAN SJMP  END-CODE -->
```

```
59
\ (loop  glenn russell's fix                  \      12:55 01/28/86
CODE (LOOP) DPH  R6 MOV  DPL  R7 MOV  DPTR INC
            A @DPTR MOVX  S0H  A MOV  DPTR INC
             R1  DPL MOV  R0  DPH MOV
            ( get index high )
            A @DPTR MOVX  A INC  ( get index low  inc index)
            0= IF  S0H INC  THEN  S0L  A MOV   S2H  # 00 MOV

   L: LOO1  DPTR INC  A @DPTR MOVX  S1H  A MOV  DPTR INC
            ( get limit high)
            A @DPTR MOVX  ( get limit low)
            C CLR  A  S0L SUBB  S1L  A MOV
            A  S1H MOV  A  S0H SUBB  S1H  A MOV
            C CLR  A  S2H MOV  E7 1 $ JNB  C SETB
            ( positive increment =no carry ) -->

60
\ (loop  glenn russell's fix                  \      09:48 04/01/86

            1 $:  A  S1H MOV  E7 2 $ JNB
                  4 $ JC
                  3 $ SJMP  ( negative result)
            2 $:  3 $ JC  ( positive result)
                  A  S1H MOV  A  S1L ORL  4 $ JNZ
            3 $:  R6  DPH MOV  R7  DPL MOV  ( exit loop )
                  A R3 MOV  A # 02 ADD  CARRY
                  IF  R2 INC  THEN  R3 A MOV  NEXT LJMP
-->

61
\ (loop cont.                                 \      14:12 03/31/86

            4 $:  DPL  R1 MOV  DPH  R0 MOV  A  S0L MOV
                  @DPTR A MOVX  A  DPL MOV  DPL DEC  0=
                  IF  DPH DEC  THEN  A  S0H MOV
                  @DPTR A MOVX  ( place new index)
                  DPH  R2 MOV  DPL  R3 MOV  A @DPTR MOVX
                  S0H  A MOV  DPTR INC  A @DPTR MOVX
                  DPTR INC  A R3 ADD  R3 A MOV  A  S0H MOV
                  A R2 ADDC R2 A MOV NEXT LJMP  ( branch)
                  END-CODE

-->

62
\ (+loop                                      \      15:37 01/28/86
CODE (+LOOP) DPH  R6 MOV  DPL  R7 MOV  DPTR INC
             A @DPTR MOVX  S0H  A MOV  DPTR INC
             ( get index high )
             A @DPTR MOVX  S0L  A MOV
             R1  DPL MOV  R0  DPH MOV
             DPH  R4 MOV  DPL  R5 MOV  ( get sp)
             DPTR INC  ( get index low )
             A @DPTR MOVX  S2H  A MOV  ( incr high)
             DPTR INC
             A @DPTR MOVX  ( incr low)
             R4  DPH MOV  R5  DPL MOV
             A  S0L ADD  S0L  A MOV  ( add incr low to index)
             A  S0H MOV  A  S2H ADDC  S0H  A MOV  ( + incr high)
             DPL  R1 MOV  DPH  R0 MOV
             LOO1 LJMP  END-CODE -->
63
\ (loop cont. (do ;s                          \      08:54 01/28/86
```

```
CODE (DO) (S0) LCALL  (S1) LCALL  R4  DPH MOV  R5  DPL MOV
          GET_RP LCALL  A  S1L MOV  @DPTR A MOVX
          -DPTR LCALL  A  S1H MOV  @DPTR A MOVX  -DPTR LCALL
          A  S0L MOV  @DPTR A MOVX  -DPTR LCALL
          A  S0H MOV  @DPTR A MOVX  SAVE_RP LCALL  NEXT LJMP
END-CODE

CODE ;S DPH  R6 MOV  DPL  R7 MOV  DPTR INC
        A @DPTR MOVX  R2 A MOV  DPTR INC
        A @DPTR MOVX  R3 A MOV  R6  DPH MOV
        R7  DPL MOV  NEXT LJMP
END-CODE
-->

64
\ leave 0 1 2                                  \      08:55 01/28/86

CODE LEAVE DPH  R6 MOV  DPL  R7 MOV  DPTR INC
           A @DPTR MOVX  S0H  A MOV  DPTR INC
           A @DPTR MOVX  S0L  A MOV  DPTR INC
           A  S0H MOV  @DPTR A MOVX  DPTR INC
           A  S0L MOV  @DPTR A MOVX  NEXT LJMP
END-CODE

CODE 0 DPH  R4 MOV  DPL  R5 MOV
       A # 0 MOV  A0PUSH LJMP  END-CODE
CODE 1 DPH  R4 MOV  DPL  R5 MOV
       A # 1 MOV  A0PUSH LJMP  END-CODE
CODE 2 DPH  R4 MOV  DPL  R5 MOV
       A # 2 MOV  A0PUSH LJMP  END-CODE
-->
65
\ 1+ 1-                                        \      08:55 01/28/86

CODE 1+ DPH  R4 MOV  DPL  R5 MOV  DPTR INC  DPTR INC
        A @DPTR MOVX  A INC  @DPTR A MOVX  0=
        IF  -DPTR LCALL
            A @DPTR MOVX  A INC  @DPTR A MOVX  THEN
        NEXT LJMP
END-CODE

CODE 1- DPH  R4 MOV  DPL  R5 MOV  DPTR INC  DPTR INC
        A @DPTR MOVX  A DEC
        @DPTR A MOVX  A INC  0=
        IF  -DPTR LCALL
            A @DPTR MOVX  A DEC  @DPTR A MOVX  THEN
        NEXT LJMP
END-CODE -->
66
\ 2+ 2-                                          WHP 09:59 05/21/86

CODE 2+ DPH  R4 MOV  DPL  R5 MOV  DPTR INC  DPTR INC
        A @DPTR MOVX  A # 02 ADD  @DPTR A MOVX  CARRY
        IF  -DPTR LCALL
            A @DPTR MOVX  A INC  @DPTR A MOVX  THEN
        NEXT LJMP
END-CODE

CODE 2- DPH  R4 MOV  DPL  R5 MOV  DPTR INC  DPTR INC
        A @DPTR MOVX  C CLR  A # 02 SUBB  @DPTR A MOVX  CARRY
        IF  -DPTR LCALL
            A @DPTR MOVX  A DEC  @DPTR A MOVX  THEN
        NEXT LJMP
```

```
END-CODE
-->
67
\ 2* 2/                                      \      08:55 01/28/86
CODE 2* DPH  R4 MOV  DPL  R5 MOV  DPTR INC  DPTR INC
        A @DPTR MOVX  C CLR  A RLC
        @DPTR A MOVX  -DPTR LCALL  A @DPTR MOVX  A RLC
        @DPTR A MOVX  NEXT LJMP
END-CODE
CODE 2/ DPH  R4 MOV  DPL  R5 MOV  DPTR INC
        A @DPTR MOVX  C CLR  A RRC
        @DPTR A MOVX  DPTR INC
        A @DPTR MOVX  A RRC  @DPTR A MOVX
        NEXT LJMP
END-CODE
-->

68
\       0>                                   \      14:13 03/31/86

CODE 0>         (S0) LCALL   A  S0H MOV   E7 1 $ JB
                A  S0L ORL   1 $ JZ
                A # 1 MOV  A0PUSH LJMP
          1 $:  A CLR  A0PUSH LJMP  END-CODE
-->

69
\ 2drop -dup                                 \      08:55 01/28/86

CODE 2DROP A R5 MOV  A # 4 ADD  R5 A MOV  CARRY
           IF  R4 INC  THEN  NEXT LJMP
END-CODE

CODE -DUP (S0) LCALL  A  S0L MOV  A  S0H ORL  0=
          IF  NEXT LJMP
          ELSE  GET_SP LCALL  A  S0L MOV  @DPTR A MOVX
               A  S0H MOV  APUSH LJMP
          THEN
END-CODE
-->

70
\ = <>                                       \      10:02 01/30/86

CODE = (S0) LCALL  (S1) LCALL  C CLR  A  S1L MOV
       A  S0L SUBB  S0L  A MOV  A  S1H MOV  A  S0H SUBB
       A  S0L ORL  0= IF  A INC  ELSE  A CLR  THEN
       A0PUSH LJMP
END-CODE

CODE <> (S0) LCALL  (S1) LCALL  C CLR  A  S1L MOV
        A  S0L SUBB  S0L  A MOV  A  S1H MOV
        A  S0H SUBB  A  S0L ORL  0<>
        IF  A # 1 MOV  THEN
        A0PUSH LJMP
END-CODE
-->

71
\ constant variable [romable]                \      08:55 01/28/86

: CONSTANT CREATE SMUDGE , ;CODE DPH  R0 MOV  DPL  R1 MOV
           DPTR INC  DPTR INC  A @DPTR MOVX  S0H  A MOV
           DPTR INC  A @DPTR MOVX  DPH  R4 MOV  DPL  R5 MOV
```

```
          @DPTR A MOVX  A  S0H MOV  APUSH LJMP  END-CODE

: VARIABLE CREATE SMUDGE HERE 2+ , , ;CODE DPH  R0 MOV
          DPL  R1 MOV  DPTR INC  DPTR INC  A @DPTR MOVX
          S0H  A MOV  DPTR INC  A @DPTR MOVX
          DPH  R4 MOV  DPL  R5 MOV
          @DPTR A MOVX  A  S0H MOV  APUSH LJMP  END-CODE
-->

72
\ : does>                                   \     08:55 01/28/86
: : ?EXEC !CSP CURRENT @ CONTEXT ! CREATE [COMPILE] ] ;CODE
   DPH  R6 MOV  DPL  R7 MOV  A R3 MOV  @DPTR A MOVX
   -DPTR LCALL  A R2 MOV  @DPTR A MOVX  -DPTR LCALL
   R6  DPH MOV  R7  DPL MOV  A R1 MOV  A # 2 ADD
   R3 A MOV  A R0 MOV  CARRY
   IF  A INC  THEN  R2 A MOV  NEXT LJMP  END-CODE
: DOES> R> LATEST PFA ! ;CODE DPH  R6 MOV  DPL  R7 MOV
      A R3 MOV  @DPTR A MOVX  -DPTR LCALL  A R2 MOV
      @DPTR A MOVX  -DPTR LCALL  R6  DPH MOV  R7  DPL MOV
      DPH  R0 MOV  DPL  R1 MOV  DPTR INC  DPTR INC
      A @DPTR MOVX  DPTR INC
      R2 A MOV  A @DPTR MOVX  DPTR INC  R3 A MOV
      S0H   DPH MOV  A  DPL MOV  DPH  R4 MOV  DPL  R5 MOV
      @DPTR A MOVX  A  S0H MOV  APUSH LJMP  END-CODE
-->
73
\ user vocabulary [romable] forth           \     08:56 01/28/86

: USER CONSTANT ;CODE DPH  R0 MOV  DPL  R1 MOV
          DPTR INC  DPTR INC  DPTR INC  A @DPTR MOVX
          S1L  A MOV  DPTR # UP MOV  A @DPTR MOVX  DPTR INC
          S0H  A MOV  A @DPTR MOVX  A  S1L ADD  DPH  R4 MOV
          DPL  R5 MOV  @DPTR A MOVX  A  S0H MOV
          CARRY IF  A INC  THEN  APUSH LJMP  END-CODE

: VOCABULARY            <BUILDS HERE 4 + ,
                        HERE VOC-LINK @ , VOC-LINK !
                        81A0 , CURRENT @ CFA ,
                        DOES> @ 2+ CONTEXT ! ;

VOCABULARY FORTH IMMEDIATE
-->
74
\ Stand-alone FORTH --- user-definitions    \     08:56 01/28/86
RPP CONSTANT RPP     UP CONSTANT UP
06 USER S0           08 USER R0              0A USER TIB
0C USER WIDTH        0E USER WARNING         10 USER FENCE
12 USER DP           14 USER VOC-LINK        16 USER BLK
18 USER IN           1A USER OUT             1C USER SCR
20 USER CONTEXT      22 USER CURRENT
24 USER STATE        26 USER BASE            28 USER DPL
2A USER FLD          2C USER CSP             2E USER R#
30 USER HLD
-->

75
\ Stand-alone FORTH   misc constants        \     15:07 01/28/86

3 CONSTANT 3
40 CONSTANT C/L
-->

76
```

```
\ Stand-alone FORTH    misc math and logica \     15:44 01/28/86

: M/MOD          >R 0 R U/ R> SWAP >R U/ R> ;
: D+-            0< IF DMINUS THEN  ;
: DABS           DUP D+- ;
: +-             0< IF MINUS THEN  ;
: ABS            DUP +- ;
: M/             OVER >R >R DABS R ABS U/ R> R XOR +-
                 SWAP R> +- SWAP ;
: /MOD           >R S->D R> M/ ;
: /              /MOD SWAP DROP ;
: MAX            2DUP < IF SWAP THEN  DROP ;
: MIN            2DUP > IF SWAP THEN  DROP ;
-->

77
\ Stand-alone FORTH    misc math and logic  \     08:56 01/28/86

: M*             2DUP XOR >R ABS SWAP ABS U* R> D+- ;
: *              M* DROP ;
: */MOD          >R M* R> M/ ;
: MOD            /MOD DROP ;

: >              SWAP < ;
: U<             2DUP XOR 0< IF DROP 0< 0= ELSE - 0< THEN ;
-->

78
\ Stand-alone FORTH --- +origin cfa here al \     08:56 01/28/86

: +ORIGIN        ORIGIN + ;
: CFA            2 - ;
: PFA            1 TRAVERSE 5 + ;
: NFA    5 - -1 TRAVERSE ;
: LFA    4 - ;
: TRAVERSE       SWAP BEGIN OVER + 07F OVER C@
                 < UNTIL SWAP DROP ;
: HERE           DP @ ;
: ALLOT          DP +! ;
: ,              HERE ! 2 ALLOT ;
: C,             HERE C! 1 ALLOT ;
-->

79
\ Stand-alone FORTH --- (type                     15:31 11/28/88
( address\length\delay count --- )
CODE (TYPE)      (S0) LCALL  (S1) LCALL  (S2) LCALL
                 R4  DPH MOV   R5  DPL MOV   A  S1L MOV
                 0<> IF  S1H INC  THEN
          1 $:   R0  S0L MOV  DPTR # TERMINAL 5 + MOV
                 BEGIN  A @DPTR MOVX   A # THRE ANL  0<> UNTIL
                 DPTR # TERMINAL 6 + MOV
                 BEGIN  A @DPTR MOVX  A # CTS ANL 0<> UNTIL
                 DPL  S2L MOV   DPH  S2H MOV
                 A @DPTR MOVX   A # 7F ANL
                 DPTR INC   S2H DPH MOV   S2L DPL MOV
                 DPTR # TERMINAL MOV   @DPTR A MOVX
          2 $:   R0  2 $ DJNZ
                 S1L 1 $ DJNZ   S1H 1 $ DJNZ
                 NEXT LJMP  END-CODE -->
80
\ Stand-alone FORTH --- count type pad hol  \     14:07 04/17/86

: TYPE           -DUP IF DUP OUT +! 01 (TYPE) ELSE DROP THEN ;
```

```
: COUNT          DUP 1+ SWAP C@ ;
: (.")           R COUNT DUP 1+ R> + >R TYPE ;
: (")            R DUP C@ 1+ R> + >R ;
: PAD            HERE 44 + ;
: #>             DROP DROP HLD @ PAD OVER - ;
: HOLD           -1 HLD +! HLD @ C! ;
: SIGN           ROT 0< IF 2D HOLD THEN ;
-->
: TYPE           -DUP IF OVER + SWAP DO I C@ 7F AND EMIT LOOP
                 ELSE DROP THEN ;
-->

81
\ Stand-alone FORTH --- m/mod # #s spaces   \     08:57 01/28/86

: #              BASE @ M/MOD ROT 9 OVER < IF 7 + THEN
                 30 + HOLD ;
: #S             BEGIN # 2DUP OR 0= UNTIL ;
: <#             PAD HLD ! ;              20 CONSTANT BL
: SPACE          BL EMIT ;
: SPACES         0 MAX -DUP IF 0 DO SPACE LOOP THEN ;
: BLANKS         BL FILL ;
: -TRAILING      DUP 0 DO OVER OVER + 1 - C@ BL - IF LEAVE
                 ELSE 1 - THEN LOOP ;
: ERASE          0 FILL ;
-->

82
\ Stand-alone FORTH --- d.r d. .cpu etc. )  \     09:37 01/28/86

: D.R            >R SWAP OVER DABS <# #S SIGN #> R>
                 OVER - SPACES TYPE ;
: D.             0 D.R SPACE ;
: .CPU           BASE @ 24 BASE ! CPU 2@ D. BASE ! ;
: .              S->D D. ;
: U.             0 D. ;
: ID.            PAD 20 5F FILL DUP PFA LFA OVER - PAD SWAP
                 CMOVE PAD COUNT 1F AND TYPE SPACE ;
: .R             >R S->D R> D.R ;
: ?              @ . ;
-->

83
\ Stand-alone FORTH --- terminal I/O              15:31 11/28/88

HEX
( send a character to an 8250 serial port )
( c --- )
CODE (EMIT)      DPTR # TERMINAL 6 + MOV
                 BEGIN  A @DPTR MOVX  A # CTS ANL 0<> UNTIL
                 DPTR # TERMINAL 5 + MOV
                 BEGIN  A @DPTR MOVX   A # THRE ANL  0<>  UNTIL
                 DPH  R4 MOV   DPL  R5 MOV
                 DPTR INC   DPTR INC  A @DPTR MOVX
                 R4  DPH MOV   R5  DPL MOV
                 DPTR # TERMINAL MOV   @DPTR A MOVX   NEXT LJMP
                 END-CODE
-->

84
\ Stand-alone FORTH --- terminal I/O        \     08:53 01/29/86

HEX
( send a character to the serial port, increment char count)
```

```
( c --- )
: EMIT          (EMIT) 1 OUT +! ;
( send carriage return and line feed to the serial port )
( and reset character count )
( stack effect:  --- )
: CR            0D EMIT 0A EMIT 0 OUT ! ;
-->
: EMIT          TERMINAL 5 +
                BEGIN DUP C@ TBR AND UNTIL 5 - C!
                1 OUT +! ;

85
\ Stand-alone FORTH --- terminal I/O               10:00 02/13/89
HEX ( leaves a flag on the stack )
( 0 if no character ready from keyboard )
( 1 if a character is waiting )
( this does not actually read in the character )
( --- flag )
CODE ?TERMINAL  DPTR # TERMINAL 5 + MOV
                A @DPTR MOVX   A # DR ANL  0<>
                IF  A # 1 MOV
                ELSE  DPTR # DISK 4 + MOV  A @DPTR MOVX
                  A # RTS ORL  @DPTR A MOVX
                  A # FF RTS - ANL  @DPTR A MOVX \ toggle rts
                  A CLR
                THEN DPH R4 MOV   DPL R5 MOV
                A0PUSH LJMP  END-CODE -->
: ?TERMINAL     TERMINAL 5 + C@ DR AND IF 1 ELSE 0 THEN ;
86
\ character flow control                            20:35 12/06/88
HEX -->
CODE (RTS)      DPTR # DISK 4 + MOV
                A @DPTR MOVX
                A # RTS ORL
                @DPTR A MOVX
                NEXT LJMP END-CODE
-->

87
\ character flow control                            15:26 11/28/88
HEX -->
CODE (-RTS)     DPTR # DISK 4 + MOV
                A @DPTR MOVX
                A # FF RTS - ANL
                @DPTR A MOVX
                NEXT LJMP END-CODE
-->

88
\ Stand-alone FORTH --- terminal I/O               20:49 01/31/89
HEX
( read a character from the 8250 terminal ace )
( --- c )
: @TERMINAL     TERMINAL C@ ;

( read a character from the serial port.  if none is ready )
( wait until a key is pushed )
( --- c )
: KEY          BEGIN ?TERMINAL
               UNTIL @TERMINAL ;
-->

89
\ 8085 FORTH --- disk interface              \     08:58 01/28/86
```

```
HEX

NBUF            CONSTANT #BUFF        ( number of disk buffers)
KBBUF BPS /     CONSTANT SEC/BLK      ( disk sectors per block)
400 KBBUF /     CONSTANT B/SCR        ( buffers per screen )
BUF1            CONSTANT FIRST        ( addr of 1st buffer)
EM              CONSTANT LIMIT        ( end of last buffer)
FIRST           VARIABLE USE          ( buffer to use next)
FIRST           VARIABLE PREV         ( buffer used last time)
0               VARIABLE REC          ( physical sector # )
0               VARIABLE DISK-ERROR   ( i/o error flag )
KBBUF           CONSTANT B/BUF        ( bytes per buffer)
-->

90
\ 8085 FORTH --- disk interface          \     08:58 01/28/86
HEX
( when SET-IO is called, USE contains the buffer address )
( and REC contains the logical sector number )
: SET-IO     0 DISK-ERROR ! ;
: DISKERROR  0 WARNING ! ERROR ;
-->
( modified by bill payne to a 1024 byte sector )
( performs a physical disk read of 128 byte sector )
( should set DISK-ERROR <> 0 if i/o error detected )
: SEC-READ ;

( performs physical disk write of 128 byte sector )
( should set DISK-ERROR <> 0 if i/o error detected )
: SEC-WRITE ;

91
\ RS-232 DISK I/O, bill payne                  10:35 10/20/88
DECIMAL
( --- )
: SEC-READ      REC @ READSEC SEC# 5 SENDBUF
                IF STX 5 RECVBUF
                  IF ACK SCREENRECV
                  THEN
                THEN ;
-->

92
\ RS-232 DISK I/O, bill payne            \     08:52 04/21/86
DECIMAL
( --- )
: SEC-WRITE       REC @ WRITESEC SEC# 5 SENDBUF
                  IF REC @ BLOCK 1024 CHECKSUM
                     STX SEC# 5 SENDBUF
                    IF SCREENSEND
                    THEN
                  THEN  ; -->

93
\ -ring for multiplexed i/o              \     10:21 04/28/86
HEX
CODE -RING      DPTR # DISK 5 + MOV
          1 $:  A @DPTR MOVX
                A # THRE TSRE OR ANL
                A # THRE TSRE OR XRL
                1 $ JNZ
                DPTR # DISK 4 + MOV
                A @DPTR MOVX
                A # 0FF OUT1 - ANL
```

```
                @DPTR A MOVX
                NEXT LJMP END-CODE
-->
clear ring indicator to identify terminal io

94
\ ring for multiplexed i/o                          \     10:19 04/28/86
HEX
CODE RING       DPTR # TERMINAL 5 + MOV
          1 $:  A @DPTR MOVX
                A # THRE TSRE OR ANL
                A # THRE TSRE OR XRL
                1 $ JNZ
                DPTR # DISK 4 + MOV
                A @DPTR MOVX
                A # OUT1 ORL
                @DPTR A MOVX
                NEXT LJMP END-CODE
-->
set ring indicator to identify disk io

95
\ 8085 FORTH --- disk interface                           18:20 12/06/88
HEX
: BUFFER        USE @ DUP >R BEGIN +BUF UNTIL
                USE ! R @ 0<
                IF R 2+ R @ 7FFF AND 0 R/W THEN
                R ! R PREV ! R> 2+ ;

: R/W           USE @ >R SWAP SEC/BLK * ROT USE !
                SEC/BLK 0 DO
                  OVER OVER REC ! SET-IO RING
                  IF SEC-READ ELSE SEC-WRITE THEN
                  -RING DISK-ERROR @ -DUP 0>
                  IF DISKERROR QUIT THEN
                  1+ BPS USE +! LOOP
                  2DROP R> USE ! ; -->

96
\ 8085 FORTH --- disk interface                     \     13:44 04/21/86
HEX
: +BUF          B/BUF 4 + + DUP LIMIT =
                IF DROP FIRST THEN
                DUP PREV @ - ;

: EMPTY-BUFFERS FIRST LIMIT OVER - ERASE
                LIMIT FIRST DO 07FFF I ! HDBT +LOOP ;

: UPDATE        PREV @ @ 8000 OR PREV @ ! ;
-->

97
\  revised flush                                    \     13:49 04/21/86
HEX
: FLUSH         LIMIT FIRST
                DO I @ 08000 AND
                  IF I @ 07FFF AND DUP I !
                    I 2+ SWAP 0 R/W
                  THEN B/BUF 4 +
                +LOOP ; -->
\ The fig flush below cause nulls to be sent to the file when
the sequence COLD 0 BLOCK UPDATE FLUSH is executed.  The problem
is in 0 BUFFER which apparently assigns a new USE value of a
buffer containing nulls.
```

```
: FLUSH          #BUFF 1+ 0
                 DO 0 BUFFER DROP LOOP
                 EMPTY-BUFFERS ;

98
\ 8085 FORTH --- disk interface              \      08:58 01/28/86
HEX
: BLOCK          0 DISK-ERROR !
                 >R PREV @ DUP @ R - DUP +
                 IF BEGIN +BUF 0=
                   IF DROP R BUFFER DUP R
                   1 R/W 2 - THEN
                 DUP @ R - DUP + 0= UNTIL
                 DUP PREV !
                 THEN
                 R> DROP 2+ ;
-->

99
\ 8085 FORTH --- disk interface              \      08:59 01/28/86
HEX
: LOAD           BLK @ >R IN @ >R 0 IN ! B/SCR * BLK !
                 INTERPRET R> IN ! R> BLK ! ;
: LIST           DECIMAL CR DUP SCR ! ." Screen # " . 10 0 DO
                 CR R 3 .R SPACE R SCR @ .LINE ?TERMINAL
                 IF LEAVE THEN  LOOP CR ;
: -->            ?LOADING 0 IN ! B/SCR BLK @ OVER MOD - BLK +! ;
                 IMMEDIATE
: INDEX          FFEED EMIT CR 1+ SWAP DO CR I 3 .R SPACE 0 I
                 .LINE ?TERMINAL IF LEAVE THEN  LOOP ;
: TRIAD          FFEED EMIT 3 / 3 * 3 OVER + SWAP DO CR I LIST
                 ?TERMINAL IF LEAVE THEN LOOP CR 0F MESSAGE CR ;
-->

100
\ 8085 FORTH  misc words                     \      08:59 01/28/86

: (LINE)         >R 40 B/BUF */MOD R> B/SCR * + BLOCK + 40 ;

: .LINE          (LINE) -TRAILING TYPE ;

: MESSAGE        WARNING @ IF -DUP IF 4 .LINE CR
                 SPACE THEN  ELSE ." Msg # " . THEN  ;

: THRU           1+ SWAP DO I LOAD LOOP ;
: SHOW-ERROR     BLK @ 0>
                 IF IN @ 2- 40 / BLK @ 2DUP
                 ." at screen " . ." line " . CR .LINE CR
                 IN @ 2- 40 MOD SPACES 5E EMIT CR CR
                 THEN QUIT ;
-->
101
\ 8085 FORTH misc wrds                       \      08:59 01/28/86

: J              RP@ 7 + @ ;  ( 8051 7 )
: EXIT           R> DROP ;
: PICK           SP@ SWAP 2* + 1+ @ ;  ( 8051 2* and 1+ )
: DEPTH          S0 @ SP@ - 2 - 2 / ;
: ROLL           DUP >R PICK R> 0 SWAP
                 DO SP@ 1+ I DUP + + DUP 2 - @ SWAP !
                 -1 +LOOP DROP ;  ( 8051 1+ )
: NOT            1 XOR ;
-->
```

```
102
\ Stand-alone FORTH --- message (abort erro \     08:59 01/28/86

: ERROR          WARNING @ 0< IF (ABORT) THEN HERE COUNT
                 ." Error: " 22 EMIT TYPE 22 EMIT 2 SPACES
                 MESSAGE SP! SHOW-ERROR ;
: ?ERROR         SWAP IF ERROR ELSE DROP THEN  ;
: ?COMP          STATE @ 0= 11 ?ERROR ;
: !CSP           SP@ CSP ! ;
: ?EXEC          STATE @ 12 ?ERROR ;
: ?STACK         SP@ S0 @ SWAP U< 1 ?ERROR
                 SP@ HERE 80 + U< 7 ?ERROR ;
: ?PAIRS         - 13 ?ERROR ;
: ?CSP           SP@ CSP @ - 14 ?ERROR ;
: ?LOADING       BLK @ 0= 16 ?ERROR ;
-->

103
\ Stand-alone FORTH --- number )             \     08:59 01/28/86

: (NUMBER)   BEGIN 1+ DUP >R C@ BASE @ DIGIT
             WHILE SWAP BASE @ U* DROP
                   ROT BASE @ U* D+ DPL @ 1+
                   IF 1 DPL +! THEN  R>
             REPEAT R> ;

: NUMBER     0 0 ROT DUP 1+ C@ 2D = DUP >R + -1
             BEGIN   DPL ! (NUMBER) DUP C@ BL -
             WHILE   DUP C@ 2E - 5 ?ERROR 0
             REPEAT  DROP R> IF DMINUS THEN  ;
-->

104
\ Stand-alone FORTH --- word -find null     \     10:53 02/28/86

: WORD         BLK @ IF BLK @ BLOCK ELSE TIB @ THEN
               IN @ + SWAP ENCLOSE HERE 22 BLANKS IN +! OVER -
               >R R HERE C! + HERE 1+ R> CMOVE ;

: -FIND          BL WORD HERE CONTEXT @ @ (FIND) DUP 0=
                 IF DROP HERE LATEST CONTEXT @ @ OVER -
                   IF (FIND) ELSE 2DROP 0 THEN THEN ;

: X              BLK @
                 IF 1 BLK +! 0 IN ! BLK @ B/SCR 1 - AND 0=
                   IF ?EXEC R> DROP THEN
                 ELSE R> DROP THEN  ; IMMEDIATE IS-X
-->

105
\ Stand-alone FORTH --- expect )                  08:56 10/18/88
HEX
: EXPECT OVER + OVER
         DO KEY DUP BSIN =
                IF DROP DUP I = DUP R> 2 - + >R
                     IF BELL
                     ELSE BSOUT EMIT BL EMIT BSOUT
                     THEN
                ELSE DUP 0D =
                     IF LEAVE DROP BL 0
                     ELSE DUP
                     THEN R C! 0 R 1+ !
                THEN EMIT
         LOOP DROP ;
```

```
-->

106
\ Stand-alone FORTH --- create )              \     09:00 01/28/86

: CREATE   -FIND
        IF   DROP NFA ID. 4 MESSAGE SPACE
        THEN HERE DUP C@ WIDTH @ MIN 1+ ALLOT
        DUP A0 TOGGLE HERE 1 - 80 TOGGLE
        LATEST , CURRENT @ ! HERE 2+ , ;
-->

107
\ Stand alone FORTH            interpret     \     09:00 01/28/86

: INTERPRET BEGIN -FIND
                  IF    STATE @ <
                        IF   CFA ,
                        ELSE CFA EXECUTE
                        THEN ?STACK
                  ELSE  HERE NUMBER DPL @ 1+
                        IF   [COMPILE] DLITERAL
                        ELSE DROP [COMPILE] LITERAL
                        THEN ?STACK
                  THEN
            AGAIN ;
-->

108
\ Stand-alone FORTH --- quit  abort           \     13:03 04/20/86

: QUIT            0 BLK ! [COMPILE] [  ." ok "
                  BEGIN CR RP! QUERY INTERPRET
                    STATE @ 0=
                    IF ." ok" THEN
                  AGAIN ;

: (ABORT)         ABORT ;          ( patched for user's abort )
-->

109
\ Stand-alone FORTH --- quit abort                  08:49 01/18/90

: ABORT           SP! DECIMAL ?STACK CR CR
                  .CPU ." series microcontroller" CR
                  ." ROMed DOS MC 2.2" CR
                  ." 19.2 kbs, rts, cts flow control" CR
                  ." Version 1.5 01/18/90 09:00" CR CR
                  [COMPILE] FORTH DEFINITIONS QUIT ;
-->

110
\ Stand-alone FORTH --- query definitions d \     09:00 01/28/86

: QUERY           TIB @ 50 EXPECT 0 IN ! ;
: [               0 STATE ! ; IMMEDIATE
: ]               C0 STATE ! ; IMMEDIATE
: DEFINITIONS     CONTEXT @ CURRENT ! ;
: LATEST          CURRENT @ @ ;
: DECIMAL         0A BASE ! ;
: HEX             10 BASE ! ;
: <BUILDS         0 CONSTANT ;
-->
```

```
111
\ Stand-alone FORTH --- structure words )   \     09:00 01/28/86

: BACK          HERE - , ;
: BEGIN         ?COMP HERE 1 ; IMMEDIATE
: THEN          ?COMP 2 ?PAIRS HERE OVER - SWAP ! ; IMMEDIATE
: DO            COMPILE (DO) HERE 3 ; IMMEDIATE
: LOOP          3 ?PAIRS COMPILE (LOOP) BACK ; IMMEDIATE
-->

112
\ Stand-alone FORTH --- structure words )   \     09:00 01/28/86

: +LOOP         3 ?PAIRS COMPILE (+LOOP) BACK ; IMMEDIATE
: UNTIL         1 ?PAIRS COMPILE 0BRANCH BACK ; IMMEDIATE
: END           [COMPILE] UNTIL ; IMMEDIATE
: AGAIN         1 ?PAIRS COMPILE BRANCH BACK ; IMMEDIATE
: REPEAT        >R >R [COMPILE] AGAIN R> R> 2 -
                [COMPILE] THEN  ; IMMEDIATE
: IF            COMPILE 0BRANCH HERE 0 , 2 ; IMMEDIATE
: ELSE          2 ?PAIRS COMPILE BRANCH HERE 0 , SWAP 2
                [COMPILE] THEN  2 ; IMMEDIATE
: WHILE         [COMPILE] IF 2+ ; IMMEDIATE
-->

113
\ Stand-alone FORTH --- ; smudge compile li \     09:00 01/28/86

: ;             ?CSP COMPILE ;S SMUDGE [COMPILE] [ ; IMMEDIATE
: SMUDGE        LATEST 20 TOGGLE ;
: COMPILE       ?COMP R> DUP 2+ >R @ , ;
: LITERAL       STATE @ IF COMPILE LIT , THEN  ; IMMEDIATE
: DLITERAL      STATE @ IF SWAP [COMPILE] LITERAL
                [COMPILE] LITERAL THEN  ; IMMEDIATE
: (;CODE)       R> LATEST PFA CFA ! ;
-->

114
\ Stand-alone FORTH --- ." warm immediate   \     14:06 04/17/86

: WARM1         CR ." Interrupt Ready" ( INT-ENABLE ) QUIT ;
: ."            22 STATE @
                IF COMPILE (.") WORD HERE C@ 1+ ALLOT
                ELSE WORD HERE COUNT TYPE THEN  ; IMMEDIATE
: "             22 STATE @ IF COMPILE (") THEN WORD HERE
                C@ 1+ ALLOT ; IMMEDIATE
: IMMEDIATE     LATEST 40 TOGGLE ;
: (             29 WORD ; IMMEDIATE
: [COMPILE]     -FIND 0= 0 ?ERROR DROP CFA , ; IMMEDIATE
: '             -FIND 0= 5 ?ERROR
                DROP [COMPILE] LITERAL ; IMMEDIATE
: WARM          EMPTY-BUFFERS SP! ?STACK
                [COMPILE] FORTH DEFINITIONS
                CR ." Ready" QUIT ; -->
115
\ Stand-alone FORTH --- forget )            \     15:33 02/20/86

: FORGET        CURRENT @ CONTEXT @ -
                18 ?ERROR
                [COMPILE] ' DUP
                FENCE @ U< 15 ?ERROR DUP NFA DP !
                LFA @ CURRENT @ ! ;

: \ IN @ 40 / 1+ 40 * IN ! ; IMMEDIATE
```

```
( address\address\length --- 0<>=,1= )
: S=            >R 1 ROT ROT R> 0
                DO OVER I + C@ OVER I + C@ XOR
                IF ROT DROP 0 ROT ROT LEAVE THEN LOOP 2DROP ;
-->

116
\ 8051 Stand Alone Forth  Vlist                    17:53 12/06/88
HEX
: VLIST         BASE @ >R HEX CR CR 0 OUT ! CONTEXT @ @
                BEGIN
                   DUP DUP 0 <# # # # # #> TYPE
                   SPACE ID. OUT @ 3C >
                   IF CR 0 OUT !
                   ELSE 14 OUT @ OVER MOD - SPACES
                   THEN PFA LFA @ DUP 0=
                   ?TERMINAL DUP IF KEY DROP THEN OR
                UNTIL
                DROP CR CR R> BASE ! ;
-->

117
\ 8051 Stand Alone Forth  .S              \        08:03 03/18/86
HEX
( I 1+ specific to 8051 series computers )
: .S            BASE @ >R  SP@ S0 @ =
                IF      CR ." <empty stack>" CR
                ELSE    SP@ S0 @ SWAP
                        DO CR I 1+ @ DUP DECIMAL 4 .R
                                HEX ."   ("  0 4 D.R  ." h)"
                        2 +LOOP CR
                THEN R> BASE !  ;
-->

118
\  peripheral initialization                       18:01 12/06/88

( ace base address --- )
: !ACE          DUP 3 + 80 SWAP C! ( dlab = 1 )
                DUP 6 SWAP C! DUP 1+ 0 SWAP C! ( 19.2 kbits )
                DUP 3 + 17 SWAP C! ( 8 data, 1 stop, no parity)
                4 + DTR RTS OR SWAP C! ; ( enable dtr, rts, )
               ( disable out1, out2=ring, and loop )
( --- )
: PINIT         TERMINAL !ACE DISK !ACE @TERMINAL1 DROP ;
-->

                DUP 2 SWAP C! DUP 1+ 0 SWAP C! ( 56 kbits )
                DUP 6 SWAP C! DUP 1+ 0 SWAP C! ( 19.2 kbits )

119
\ Stand-alone FORTH --- cold start                 13:09 02/03/90
HEX

: COLD          INIT-R0 RAM-START !
                INIT-RAM DUP >R 4 +
                  RAM-START 2+ R> @ 2 - CMOVE
                INIT-USERV S0 10 CMOVE
                INIT-FORTH @ ' FORTH 2+ @ 2+ !
                EMPTY-BUFFERS
                FIRST PREV !  FIRST USE !
                1 WARNING !
                400 0 DO LOOP PINIT \ 80c31 80c52 reset race
```

```
                ABORT ;
-->

120
\ CASE statement by Charles Eaker )          \     09:09 01/28/86
( from FORTH DIMENSIONS, II/3 page 37 )
FORTH DEFINITIONS DECIMAL

: CASE          ?COMP CSP @ !CSP 4 ; IMMEDIATE

: OF            4 ?PAIRS COMPILE OVER COMPILE = COMPILE
                0BRANCH HERE 0 , COMPILE DROP 5 ; IMMEDIATE

: ENDOF         5 ?PAIRS COMPILE BRANCH HERE 0 ,
                SWAP 2 [COMPILE] THEN  4 ; IMMEDIATE

: ENDCASE       4 ?PAIRS COMPILE DROP BEGIN SP@
                CSP @ = 0= WHILE 2 [COMPILE]
                THEN  REPEAT CSP ! ; IMMEDIATE
-->
121
\ Standalone 8085 FORTH  DUMP word           \     09:09 01/28/86
DECIMAL
: DUMP    ( addr  n  ---  )
  BASE @ >R HEX CR CR 5 SPACES
  16 0 DO I 3 .R LOOP 2 SPACES
  16 0 DO I 0 <# # #> TYPE LOOP CR
  OVER + SWAP DUP 15 AND XOR DO
  CR I 0 4 D.R SPACE
  I 16 + I 2DUP
    DO I C@ SPACE 0 <# # # #> TYPE LOOP
    2 SPACES
    DO I C@ DUP 32 < OVER 126 > OR IF DROP 46 THEN
    EMIT LOOP
  16 +LOOP CR R> BASE ! ;
-->

122
\ TVI 912C terminal cursor control function        10:48 10/11/89

: GOTOXY 27 EMIT 61 EMIT
  0 MAX 23 MIN 33 + EMIT 0 MAX 79 MIN 33 + EMIT ;
: CLS 26 EMIT ;
: -CURSOR 27 EMIT 46 EMIT 48 EMIT ;
: CURSOR 27 EMIT 46 EMIT 49 EMIT ;

-->

123
\ receive data from disk, bill payne                16:06 12/06/88
HEX
FFFF VARIABLE TIMEOUT
-->

(  --- character value\1 or 0 ; no character )
: ?KEY1         0 TIMEOUT @ 0 DO ?TERMINAL1
                IF DROP KEY1 1 LEAVE THEN LOOP ;

( address\max # to be received --- actual # received )
: EXPECT1       OVER + SWAP 0 ROT ROT
                DO ?KEY1 0= IF LEAVE
                ELSE I C! 1+ THEN LOOP ;

124
```

```
\ Stand-alone FORTH --- (type                           15:31 12/06/88
( address\length\delay count --- )
CODE (TYPE1)     (S0) LCALL  (S1) LCALL  (S2) LCALL
                 R4  DPH MOV   R5  DPL MOV   A  S1L MOV
                 0<> IF  S1H INC  THEN
           1 $:  R0  S0L MOV  DPTR # TERMINAL 5 + MOV
                 A @DPTR MOVX   A # THRE ANL  1 $ JZ
                 DPTR # DISK 6 + MOV
                 BEGIN  A @DPTR MOVX  A # CTS ANL 0<> UNTIL
                 DPL  S2L MOV   DPH  S2H MOV
                 A @DPTR MOVX
                 DPTR INC   S2H  DPH MOV   S2L  DPL MOV
                 DPTR # TERMINAL MOV   @DPTR A MOVX
-->

125
\ Stand-alone FORTH --- (type                           15:31 12/06/88

           2 $:  R0  2 $ DJNZ
                 S1L  1 $ DJNZ   S1H  1 $ DJNZ
                 NEXT LJMP  END-CODE
: TYPE1          -DUP IF DUP OUT +! 01 (TYPE1) ELSE DROP THEN ;
-->

126
\ code expect1                                          14:40 12/07/88
HEX
( address\length expected ---
  length expected - length received )
CODE (EXPECT1)   (S0) LCALL   (S1) LCALL
                 R4 DPH MOV   R5 DPL MOV
                 DPTR # DISK 4 + MOV  A @DPTR MOVX
                 A # RTS ORL  @DPTR A MOVX
                 DPTR # DISK 6 + MOV
                 BEGIN  A @DPTR MOVX  A # CTS ANL 0<> UNTIL
-->

127
\ code expect1                                          14:41 12/07/88

                 S2H # 00 MOV
           1 $:  S2L # 00 MOV
           2 $:  DPTR # DISK 5 + MOV   A @DPTR MOVX
                 A # DR ANL  0<>
                 IF  DPTR # DISK MOV   A @DPTR MOVX
                   DPH S1H MOV  DPL S1L MOV   @DPTR A MOVX
                   DPTR INC   S1H DPH MOV   S1L DPL MOV
                   S0L 1 $ DJNZ   A  S0H MOV  0=
                     IF  DPH R4 MOV   DPL R5 MOV
                       A0PUSH LJMP
                     ELSE  S0H DEC  1 $ SJMP
                     THEN
                 THEN  S2L 2 $ DJNZ
                 S2H 1 $ DJNZ -->
128
\ code expect1                                          14:38 12/07/88

                 DPTR # DISK 4 + MOV  A @DPTR MOVX
                 A # FF RTS - ANL  @DPTR A MOVX
                 DPH R4 MOV   DPL R5 MOV
                 A S0L MOV   @DPTR A MOVX   A S0H MOV
                 APUSH LJMP  END-CODE -->

129
```

```
\                                                         16:49 12/06/88
HEX
: EXPECT1        -DUP 0>
                 IF DUP >R (EXPECT1) R> SWAP -
                 ELSE DROP 0
                 THEN ;
( ---- character )
CODE @TERMINAL1 DPTR # DISK MOV  A @DPTR MOVX
                DPH R4 MOV  DPL R5 MOV  A0PUSH LJMP
                A0PUSH LJMP  END-CODE
-->

130
\                                                         16:51 12/06/88

\ --- character value\1 or 0 ; no character
: ?KEY1          TIMEOUT @
                 BEGIN 1- ?TERMINAL1 OVER 0= OR
                 UNTIL DROP ?TERMINAL1
                 IF @TERMINAL1 1 ELSE 0 THEN ; -->

131
\ RS-232 DISK I/O, bill payne                   \     12:30 04/17/86
HEX
02               CONSTANT STX
52               CONSTANT READSEC
53               CONSTANT WRITESEC
45               CONSTANT PC-EMPTYBUF
46               CONSTANT PC-FLUSH

: NAK            15 (EMIT1) ;
: ACK            06 (EMIT1) ;

DECIMAL
( two byte message\message type --- )
: SEC#           PAD SWAP OVER C!
                 1+ OVER 65535 XOR OVER 2+ ! ! ;
-->
132
\ RS-232 DISK I/O, bill payne                   \     14:20 03/31/86
DECIMAL
( start address\length --- checksum )
CODE CHECKSUM    (S0) LCALL   (S1) LCALL
                 R4  DPH MOV   R5   DPL MOV   S2H  # 00 MOV
                 S2L  # 00 MOV   DPH  S1H MOV   DPL  S1L MOV
                 A  S0L MOV  0<> IF  S0H INC  THEN
          1 $:   A @DPTR MOVX   A  S2L ADD   S2L  A MOV   CARRY
                 IF  S2H INC  THEN   DPTR INC
                 S0L  1 $ DJNZ   S0H  1 $ DJNZ
                 DPH  R4 MOV   DPL  R5 MOV   A  S2L MOV
                 @DPTR A MOVX   A  S2H MOV   APUSH LJMP
                 END-CODE
-->
: CHECKSUM       OVER + SWAP 0 ROT ROT DO I C@ + LOOP ;

133
\ RS-232 DISK I/O, bill payne                         17:10 12/06/88

( number of characters to be sent --- 1 okay 0 failed )
: SENDBUF        0 SWAP PAD SWAP TYPE1 ?KEY1
                 IF 06 =
                   IF DROP 1 ( CR ." ACK received)
                   ELSE NAK 09 DISK-ERROR !
                      ( CR ." NAK - NAK no ACK SENDBUF")
```

```
                  THEN
                ELSE NAK 08 DISK-ERROR !
                  ( CR ." NAK - timeout SENDBUF")
                THEN ;
-->

134
\ RS-232 DISK I/O, bill payne                        16:03 12/07/88
( 1st char expected\ # chars expected --- 1 okay or 0 failed )
: RECVBUF       0 ROT ROT DUP DUP PAD SWAP EXPECT1 =
                IF OVER PAD C@ =
                  IF PAD 1+ DUP @ SWAP 2+ @ 65535 XOR =
                    IF ( CR ." ACK -  okay recv")
                       2DROP 1 SWAP 0
                    ELSE NAK 10 DISK-ERROR !
                      ( CR ."  NAK - wrong complement")
                    THEN
                  ELSE NAK 11 DISK-ERROR !
                    ( CR ." NAK - wrong message")
                  THEN
                ELSE NAK 12 DISK-ERROR !
                  ( CR ." NAK - wrong # chars")
                THEN  2DROP ;  -->
135
\ RS-232 DISK I/O, bill payne                        21:41 12/05/88

( --- )
: SCREENRECV    1024 DUP USE @ SWAP EXPECT1 =
                IF USE @ 1024 CHECKSUM PAD 1+ @ <>
                  IF NAK 13 DISK-ERROR !
                    ( CR ." NAK - screen checksum")
                  ELSE ACK ( CR ." screen received okay")
                  THEN
                ELSE NAK 14 DISK-ERROR !
                  ( CR ." NAK - screen wrong character count")
                THEN ;
-->

136
\ RS-232 DISK I/O, bill payne                        21:41 12/05/88

( --- )
: SCREENSEND    REC @ BLOCK 1024 TYPE1 ?KEY1
                IF 06 <>
                  IF 15 DISK-ERROR !
                    ( CR ." no ack error 15")
                  THEN
                ELSE 16 DISK-ERROR !
                    ( CR ." Timeout on response")
                THEN ;
-->

137
\ Stand-alone FORTH --- disk     I/O                 15:32 12/06/88

HEX
( send a character to an 8250 serial port )
( c --- )
CODE (EMIT1)    DPTR # DISK 5 + MOV
                BEGIN  A @DPTR MOVX  A # THRE ANL  0<> UNTIL
                DPTR # DISK 6 + MOV
                BEGIN  A @DPTR MOVX  A # CTS ANL 0<> UNTIL
                DPH  R4 MOV   DPL  R5 MOV
                DPTR INC   DPTR INC  A @DPTR MOVX
```

```
                R4  DPH MOV   R5  DPL MOV
                DPTR # DISK MOV   @DPTR A MOVX   NEXT LJMP
                END-CODE
-->

138
\ Stand-alone FORTH --- DISK I/O            \      08:24 04/17/86
-->
HEX
( 8250 disk output, bill payne )
( send the lower eight bits of the word on top of the stack )
( to the disk ace )
( c --- )

: (EMIT1)       DISK 5 + BEGIN DUP C@ TBR AND UNTIL
                5 - C! ;

139
\ Stand-alone FORTH --- DISK I/O                   10:17 12/08/88
HEX ( leaves a flag on the stack )
( 0 if no character ready from disk )
( 1 if a character is waiting )
( this does not actually read in the character )
( --- flag )
CODE ?TERMINAL1 DPTR # DISK 5 + MOV
                A @DPTR MOVX   A # DR ANL  0<>
                IF  A # 1 MOV
                ELSE DPTR # DISK 4 + MOV  A @DPTR MOVX
                  A # RTS ORL  @DPTR A MOVX
                  A # FF RTS - ANL  @DPTR A MOVX \ toggle rts
                  A CLR
                THEN  DPH R4 MOV  DPL R5 MOV
                A0PUSH LJMP  END-CODE -->
: ?TERMINAL1    DISK 5 + C@ RDA AND IF 1 ELSE 0 THEN ;
140
\ Stand-alone FORTH --- disk I/O            \      21:36 04/16/86
-->
HEX
( read a character from the 8250 disk ace )
( --- c )
: @TERMINAL1    DISK C@ ;
-->

( read a character from the serial port.  if none is ready )
( wait until a key is pushed )
( stack effect:  --- c )
: KEY1          BEGIN ?TERMINAL1 UNTIL @TERMINAL1 ;
-->

141
\ PC empty-buffers and flush                \      13:50 04/21/86
DECIMAL
( address of PAD --- )
: BYE1          ." Started " RING 1+ 0 OVER !
                2+ 65535 SWAP ! 5 SENDBUF -RING
                IF ." ... completed."
                ELSE ." ... failed!"
                THEN CR ;

( --- )
: BYE           PAD PC-FLUSH OVER C! BYE1 ;

( --- )
: EMPTY-PCBUF   PAD PC-EMPTYBUF OVER C! BYE1 ;
```

```
-->

142
\  vectored execution case statement         \      09:14 01/28/86
HEX
( 0, 1, 2, ..., n --- )
: ONGOSUB         ?COMP COMPILE 2* COMPILE LIT HERE 0 ,
                  COMPILE 2DUP COMPILE OVER COMPILE 0<
                  COMPILE 0BRANCH HERE 0 , COMPILE SWAP
                  HERE OVER - SWAP ! COMPILE >
                  COMPILE 0BRANCH HERE 0 , COMPILE SWAP
                  HERE OVER - SWAP ! COMPILE DROP
                  COMPILE LIT HERE 0 , COMPILE + COMPILE @
                  COMPILE EXECUTE COMPILE BRANCH HERE 0 , SWAP
                  HERE SWAP ! HERE 6 ; IMMEDIATE

: ENDGOSUB        6 ?PAIRS HERE SWAP -  DUP 2 <
                  19 ?ERROR DUP 2+ ROT ! 2- SWAP ! ; IMMEDIATE
-->
143
\ Assembler local labels                     \      12:47 03/14/86
VOCABULARY ASSEMBLER IMMEDIATE
ASSEMBLER DEFINITIONS

0       CONSTANT REVSYM HERE DUP 2- ! " 02/27/86"
0       VARIABLE T0 2 ALLOT-RAM
0       VARIABLE TOP
0       VARIABLE CSP0
0       VARIABLE #$
20      CONSTANT MAX#$
0       VARIABLE $A MAX#$ 2- ALLOT-RAM

\ ---
: RESET           T0 4 ERASE 0 TOP ! DEPTH CSP0 ! ;
-->

144
\ assembler syntax tokens                    \      15:20 02/20/86
HEX
    00 CONSTANT NUL                00 CONSTANT DIRCT
    02 CONSTANT ADR16              03 CONSTANT DATA8
    04 CONSTANT DATA16             05 CONSTANT AREG
    06 CONSTANT RREG               07 CONSTANT @REG
    08 CONSTANT DPR                09 CONSTANT ABREG
    0A CONSTANT A+DPTR             0B CONSTANT @DP
    0C CONSTANT CBIT               0D CONSTANT BADDR
    0E CONSTANT A+PC               0F CONSTANT ADR11
    10 CONSTANT RELAD
: ?R0 FORTH       HERE 2+ - DUP DUP 07F > SWAP 0FF80 < OR ;
: ?R1             21 ?ERROR ;
: ?R              ?R0 ?R1 ;
-->

145
\ Assembler local labels                     \      08:37 04/01/86

\ label --- label
: $R              DUP 7FFC > OVER 0 < OR 22 ?ERROR ;
\ label\here --- adusted here
: $8051 FORTH     SWAP 0<
                  IF TOP @ 1 >
                    IF 1+
                    ELSE TOP @
                      IF 1+ THEN
```

```
                    TO C@ RREG =
                    IF 1- THEN
                  THEN
                THEN ; -->

146
\ local labels                                          13:40 10/12/86

\ label ---
: !$ FORTH      DUP #$ @
                IF $A #$ @ + $A
                  DO I @ 0=
                    IF DUP I ! HERE $8051 I 2+ !
                    DROP 0 LEAVE THEN
                  4 +LOOP
                THEN
                IF #$ @ DUP MAX#$ <
                  IF $A + OVER HERE $8051 OVER 2+ ! ! 4 #$ +!
                  ELSE 27 ?ERROR
                  THEN
                THEN ; -->

147
\ syntax table builder                                  15:49 10/13/86
DECIMAL
           ( VF = valid format )
           ( <destination>  <source> VF  )
        3 CONSTANT #VF

0       CONSTANT VFS HERE DUP 2- ! 0 , 41 2* ALLOT

\ transient module load
LATEST          \ save latest
HERE            \ save dp
SP@             \ check for balanced stack
10000 ALLOT     \ make room for tables
-->

148
\ syntax table builder                                  15:48 10/13/86
DECIMAL
( # processed\type0\type1\type2\type3 --- # processed + 1 )
: VF,           #VF 0 DO C, LOOP
                DUP 0 6 GOTOXY U. 1+ ;

( cummulative #\form # --- cummulative # )
: !VF#          VFS + OVER FORTH SWAP ! ;
ASSEMBLER

SP@ 2+ ?PAIRS   \ stack balanced?
DUP DP !        \ point to old here, end transient module
SP@             \ check for balanced stack
-->

149
\ syntax tables                                         14:52 10/13/86
DECIMAL
0 5 GOTOXY ." Loading syntax tables"

0       CONSTANT VF HERE DUP 2- !

0 ( start cumulative count of forms)
( A 2 hex 2 )
AREG  NUL NUL VF, \  1  A INC
```

```
2 !VF#

( direct 4 hex 4 )
DIRCT NUL NUL VF, \  2  17 DEC
4 !VF#
-->

150
\ syntax tables                                 \     09:15 01/28/86

( @Ri 6 hex 6 )
@REG NUL NUL VF,        \  3  @R0 DEC
6 !VF#

( Rn 8 hex 8 )
RREG NUL NUL VF,        \  4  R0 DEC
8 !VF#

( addr16 10 hex A )
ADR16 NUL NUL VF,       \  5  DEST LJMP
10 !VF#
-->

151
\ syntax tables                                 \     14:40 02/19/86

( bit,rel 12 hex C )
BADDR RELAD NUL VF, \ 6  17 1$ JBC
12 !VF#

( A,#data 14  hex E )
AREG DATA8 NUL VF,  \ 7  A # 51 ADD
14 !VF#

( A,Rn 16  hex 10 )
AREG RREG NUL VF,   \ 8  A @R0 ADD
16 !VF#
-->

152
\                                               \     09:15 01/28/86

( no operands 18 hex 12 )
NUL NUL NUL VF,           \  9  RETI
18 !VF#

( A,direct 20 hex 14 )
AREG DIRCT NUL VF,        \ 10  17 A ORL
20 !VF#

( direct,#data 22 hex 16 )
DIRCT DATA8 NUL VF,       \ 11  17 # 07 ORL
22 !VF#
-->

153
\                                               \     09:15 01/28/86
( bit,direct 24 hex 18 )
CBIT DIRCT NUL VF, \ 12  C 17 ORL
24 !VF#

( @A+DPTR 26 hex 1A )
A+DPTR NUL NUL VF, \ 13  @A+DPTR JMP
26 !VF#
```

```
( @Ri,#data 28 hex 1C )
@REG DATA8 NUL VF, \ 14  @R0 17 MOV
28 !VF#

( AB 30 hex 1E )
ABREG NUL NUL VF,  \ 15  AB MUL
30 !VF# -->
154
\ syntax tables                                    \      09:15 01/28/86

( Rn,#data 32 hex 20 )
RREG DATA8 NUL VF,  \ 16  R0 # 17 MOV
32 !VF#

( A,@A+PC 34 hex 22 )
AREG A+PC NUL VF,   \ 17  A @A+PC MOVC
34 !VF#

( direct,direct 36 hex 24 )
DIRCT DIRCT NUL VF, \ 18  17 S0 MOV
36 !VF#
-->

155
\ syntax tables                                    \      09:15 01/28/86

( direct,@Ri 38 hex 26 )
DIRCT @REG NUL VF,  \ 19  17 @R0 MOV
38 !VF#

( direct,C 40 hex 28 )
DIRCT CBIT NUL VF,  \ 20  2E C MOV
40 !VF#

( A,@A+DPTR 42 hex 2A )
AREG A+DPTR NUL VF, \ 21  A @A+DPTR MOVC
42 !VF#
-->

156
\                                                  \      09:16 01/28/86

( DPTR 44 hex 2C )
DPR NUL NUL VF,    \ 22  DPTR INC
44 !VF#

( @Ri,direct 46 hex 2E )
@REG DIRCT NUL VF, \ 23  @R0 # 17 MOV
46 !VF#

( bit 48 hex 30 )
BADDR NUL NUL VF,  \ 24  2E CLR
48 !VF#
-->

157
\                                                  \      09:16 01/28/86

( C 50 hex 32 )
CBIT NUL NUL VF,    \ 25  C CLR
50 !VF#

( CJNE operand forms 52 hex 34 )
```

```
AREG DATA8 RELAD VF, \ 26  A # 17 1 $ CJNE
AREG DIRCT RELAD VF, \ 27  A 17 1 $ CJNE
@REG DATA8 RELAD VF, \ 28  @R0 # 17 1 $ CJNE
RREG DATA8 RELAD VF, \ 29  R0 # 17 1 $ CJNE
52 !VF#
-->

158
\                                            \      12:28 02/19/86

( direct,rel or Rn,rel DJNZ 54 hex 36 )
DIRCT RELAD NUL VF,   \ 30  17 1 $ DJNZ
RREG  RELAD NUL VF,   \ 31  R0 1 $ DJNZ
54 !VF#

( A,@Ri 56 hex 38 )
AREG @REG NUL VF,     \ 32  A @R0 XCHD
56 !VF#
-->

159
\                                            \      09:16 01/28/86

( rel 58 hex 3A )
RELAD NUL NUL VF,    \ 33  1$ JC
58 !VF#

( A,@DPTR 60 hex 3C )
AREG @DP NUL VF,     \ 34  A @DPTR MOVX
60 !VF#

( DPTR,#data16 58 hex 3E )
DPR DATA8  NUL VF,   \ 35  DPTR # 12 MOV
DPR DATA16 NUL VF,   \ 36  DPTR # 1234 MOV
62 !VF#
-->

160
\                                            \      09:16 01/28/86

( addr11 64  hex 40 )
ADR11 NUL NUL VF,   \ 37  MYSUB ACALL
64 !VF#

( direct,A 66 hex 42 )
DIRCT AREG NUL VF,  \ 38  023 A ANL
66 !VF#

( C,bit 68 hex 44 )
CBIT BADDR NUL VF,  \ 39  C 023 ANL
68 !VF#
-->

161
\                                            \      09:16 01/28/86

( Rn,A 70 hex 46 )
RREG AREG NUL VF,  \ 40  R0 A MOV
70 !VF#

( @Ri,A 72 hex 48 )
@REG AREG NUL VF,  \ 41  @R0 A MOV
72 !VF#
```

```
( direct,Rn 74 hex 4A )
DIRCT RREG NUL VF, \ 42  17 R0 MOV
74 !VF#
-->

162
\                                              \      09:16 01/28/86

( Rn,direct 76 hex 4C )
RREG DIRCT NUL VF, \ 43  R0 # 17 MOV
76 !VF#

( @DPTR,A 78 hex 4E )
@DP AREG NUL VF,    \ 44  @DPTR A MOVX
78 !VF#
-->

163
\                                                     15:26 10/13/86

( @Ri,#data 80 hex 50 )
@REG DATA8 NUL VF,     \ 45  @R0 # 017 MOV
80 !VF#

( bit,C 82 hex 52 )
BADDR CBIT NUL VF,     \ 46  2E C MOV
82 !VF#
DROP

SP@ 2+ ?PAIRS   \ check for balanced stack
PFA LFA !       \ discard transient module
-->

164
\ attribute stack                                     07:26 10/12/89
HEX
( number ---  )
: ?TOP FORTH    3 > 24 ?ERROR ;
( --- )
: 1+TOP FORTH   TOP DUP @ DUP ?TOP 1+ SWAP ! ;

( opcode or operand type --- )
: !TOP          TO TOP @ + C! 1+TOP DEPTH CSP0 ! ;
-->

( stack attribute print diagnostic )
: .T FORTH      TO TOP @ DUP IF
                0 DO DUP I + C@ U. SPACE LOOP THEN DROP ;

165
\ stack check                                         13:35 10/12/86
HEX
: ?DISP FORTH   DEPTH CSP0 @ - -DUP 0>
                IF MINUS 0 SWAP
                  DO I ABS PICK DUP 0FF > SWAP FF00 < OR
                  IF 02 ELSE 01 THEN TO TOP @ 1- + C@ DATA16 =
                    IF 2+ TOP DUP @ 1- SWAP ! THEN !TOP
                      01 +LOOP
                THEN ;
-->

166
\ assembler code generator                     \      20:15 04/15/86
HEX
```

```
( diagnostic screen print of assembly )
: NDY           2A ERROR ;
-->
: ,             DUP , 0 <# # # # # #> TYPE ;
: C,            DUP C, 0 <# # # #> TYPE ;

167
\ code generation                                     13:36 10/12/86
HEX
: INVALID       25 ERROR ;

: T1            C, DROP ;          \  A INC
: T2            C, C, ;            \  17 DEC
: T3            OR C, ;            \  R0 DEC
: T4            C, T2 ;            \  17 19 MOV
: T5            OR C, DROP ;       \  A R0 ADD
: T6 FORTH      C, SWAP T2 ;       \  17 # 07 ORL
: T7            T2 DROP ;          \  A # 51 ADD
: T8            T2 C, ;            \  17 19 MOV
: T9            C, DROP C, ;       \  17 A MOV
: T10           ROT OR T2 ;        \  R0 17 MOV
: T11           C, 2DROP ;         \  A @A+DPTR
-->
168
\ code generation                                     11:27 01/31/89
HEX
: ?7F FORTH     DUP DUP 07F > SWAP FF80 < OR 21 ?ERROR ;
: REL,          HERE 1+ - ?7F C, ;

: T12 FORTH     SWAP >R SWAP >R OR C,
                R> R> SWAP C, REL, ;
: T13 FORTH     C, SWAP C, REL, ;           \  17 1 $ JB
: T14           OR T2 ;                     \  17 R0 MOV
: T15           04 OR T13 DROP ;            \  A # 17 1 $ CJNE
: T16           05 OR T13 DROP ;            \  A 17 1 $ CJNE
-->

169
\ code generation                                     16:15 01/30/89
HEX
: T17           08 OR T12 ;                  \  R0 # 17 1 $ CJNE
: T18           06 OR T12 ;                  \  @R0 # 17 1 $ CJNE
: T19           08 OR ROT OR C, REL, ;       \  R0 1 $ DJNZ
: T20           05 OR T13 ;                  \  17 1 $ DJNZ
: T21           C, REL, ;                    \  1 $ JC
: T22           C, , ;                       \  MYSUB LJMP
: T23           T22 DROP ;                   \  DPTR # 1234 MOV
: T24 FORTH     SWAP DROP OR C, ;            \  @R0 A MOV
: T25           >R DUP 0F800 AND HERE 2+ 0F800 AND -
                26 ?ERROR
                DUP 07FF AND 100 / 20 *
                R> OR T2 ;                   \  MYSUB AJMP
-->

170
\                                                     09:02 10/14/86
HEX
( index --- type )
: T0@           T0 + C@ ;

( index --- true or false )
: PNUL          T0@ NUL   = ;
: PDIRCT        T0@ DIRCT  = ;
: PADR16 FORTH  T0@ DUP DIRCT = SWAP ADR16 = OR ;
```

```
: PDATA8         T0@ DATA8  = ;
: PDATA16        T0@ DATA16 = ;
-->

171
\                                                  \      09:17 01/28/86
HEX
: PAREG          T0@ AREG   = ;
: PRREG          T0@ RREG   = ;
: P@REG          T0@ @REG   = ;
: PDP            T0@ DPR    = ;
: PABREG         T0@ ABREG  = ;
: PA+DPTR        T0@ A+DPTR = ;
: P@DP           T0@ @DP    = ;
: PCBIT          T0@ CBIT   = ;
: PBADDR         T0@ DIRCT  = ;
: PA+PC          T0@ A+PC   = ;
-->

172
\                                                         12:05 10/14/86
HEX
: PADR11 FORTH   T0@ DUP DIRCT = SWAP ADR16 = OR ;
: PRELAD FORTH   T0@ DUP RELAD = SWAP
                 DUP ADR16 = SWAP DIRCT = OR OR ;
: PINVALID       0 ;
-->

173
\                                                  \      09:17 01/28/86
HEX
( attribute table address --- true or false )
: ?= FORTH       FFFF SWAP #VF DUP
                   IF 0 DO DUP I DUP #VF SWAP - 1- ROT + C@
                     ONGOSUB
                     PNUL    PDIRCT     PADR16     PDATA8
                     PDATA16 PAREG      PRREG      P@REG
                     PDP     PABREG     PA+DPTR    P@DP
                     PCBIT   PBADDR     PA+PC      PADR11
                     PRELAD  PINVALID
                    ENDGOSUB ( ."   OUT OF ?= " DUP .)  0=
                    IF SWAP DROP 0 SWAP LEAVE THEN LOOP
                   THEN DROP ;
-->

174
\                                                  \      09:18 01/28/86

( form # --- 0=no match otherwise processing type )
: ?VF FORTH      0 SWAP VFS + DUP 2- @ #VF * SWAP @
                 #VF * OVER - OVER + SWAP
                 DO VF I + ?=
                 IF DROP I #VF / 1+ LEAVE THEN
                 #VF +LOOP ;
-->

175
\ valid operand forms                              \      11:16 02/05/86
HEX
: ASM,         (  .S KEY DROP) ONGOSUB INVALID
               (  1   2   3   4   5   6   7   8   9  10 )
                 T1  T2  T3  T3  T22 T13 T7  T5  C,  T7
               (  11  12  13  14  15  16  17  18  19  20 )
                 T6  T7  T1  T10 T1  T10 T11 T4  T14 T9
```

```
               (  21  22  23  24  25  26  27  28  29  30 )
                  T11 T1  T10 T2  T1  T15 T16 T18 T17 T20
               (  31  32  33  34  35  36  37  38  39  40 )
                  T19 T5  T21 T11 T23 T23 T25 T9  T7  T24
               (  41  42  43  44  45  46  47             )
                  T24 T14 T10 T11 T11 T9  T9 NDY
                  ENDGOSUB RESET ;
-->

176
\ opcode forms                               \     09:51 04/28/86
HEX
( form1\opcode1\...\formn\opcoden\2*n --- ;compile )
( --- byte opcode\form # found, 0 not found ;execute )
: 1MI FORTH       <BUILDS DUP C, 0 DO C, C, LOOP
                  DOES> >R ?DISP 0 R> DUP 1+ SWAP C@ 2 * OVER +
                  DO I 1- C@       \ DUP CR ." vf " .
                    ?VF -DUP
                  IF SWAP DROP I 2- C@ SWAP LEAVE THEN -2
                  +LOOP ASM, ;

: #       ?DISP  DATA16 !TOP ;
-->

177
\ symbolic bit addresses                           07:34 10/12/89
HEX
0E0 CONSTANT ACC               0F0 CONSTANT B
0D0 CONSTANT PSW               080 CONSTANT P0
090 CONSTANT P1                0A0 CONSTANT P2
0B0 CONSTANT P3                088 CONSTANT TCON
089 CONSTANT TMOD
0C8 CONSTANT T2CON             098 CONSTANT SCON
0B8 CONSTANT IP                0A8 CONSTANT IE
087 CONSTANT PCON              099 CONSTANT SBUF
08A CONSTANT TL0               08C CONSTANT TH0
08B CONSTANT TL1               08D CONSTANT TH1
0CC CONSTANT TL2               0CD CONSTANT TH2
0CA CONSTANT RCAP2L            0CB CONSTANT RCAP2H
083 CONSTANT DPH               082 CONSTANT DPL
-->
178
\ operand execution                          \     15:31 02/07/86
HEX
: R0     ?DISP 0 RREG !TOP ;      : R1     ?DISP 1 RREG !TOP ;
: R2     ?DISP 2 RREG !TOP ;      : R3     ?DISP 3 RREG !TOP ;
: R4     ?DISP 4 RREG !TOP ;      : R5     ?DISP 5 RREG !TOP ;
: R6     ?DISP 6 RREG !TOP ;      : R7     ?DISP 7 RREG !TOP ;

: @R0    ?DISP 0 @REG !TOP ;      : @R1    ?DISP 1 @REG !TOP ;

: DPTR   ?DISP 0 DPR  !TOP ;      : @DPTR ?DISP 0 @DP   !TOP ;
: A      ?DISP 0 AREG !TOP ;      : C      ?DISP 0 CBIT !TOP ;
: @A+PC ?DISP 0 A+PC !TOP ;

: AB     ?DISP 0 ABREG !TOP ;     : @A+DPTR ?DISP 0 A+DPTR !TOP ;

-->
179
\                                            \     09:18 01/28/86

                             040 011   01 1MI ACALL
010 028   014 025   038 026  00E 024   04 1MI ADD
010 038   014 035   038 036  00E 034   04 1MI ADDC
```

```
                                    040 001   01 1MI AJMP
010 058   014 055   038 056   00E 054
          042 052   016 053   044 082   07 1MI ANL
                                    044 0B0   01 1MI ANL/
                                    034 0B0   01 1MI CJNE
          002 0E4   032 0C3   030 0C2   03 1MI CLR
          002 0F4   032 0B3   030 0B2   03 1MI CPL
                                    002 0D4   01 1MI DA
 002 014 008 018   004 015   006 016   04 1MI DEC
-->

180
\                                                 \      09:18 01/28/86
                                          01E 084   01 1MI DIV
                                          036 0D0   01 1MI DJNZ
002 004   008 08   004 05   006 006   02C 0A3   05 1MI INC
                                          00C 020   01 1MI JB
                                          00C 010   01 1MI JBC
                                          03A 040   01 1MI JC
                                          01A 073   01 1MI JMP
                                          00C 030   01 1MI JNB
                                          03A 050   01 1MI JNC
                                          03A 070   01 1MI JNZ
                                          03A 060   01 1MI JZ
                                          00A 012   01 1MI LCALL
                                          00A 002   01 1MI LJMP
-->

181
\                                                 \      09:18 01/28/86

010 0E8   014 0E5   038 0E6
00E 074   046 0F8   04C 0A8
020 078   042 0F5   04A 088
024 085   026 086   016 075
048 0F6   02E 0A6   01C 076
044 0A2   052 092   03E 090   012 1MI MOV
-->

182
\                                                 \      09:18 01/28/86
                    02A 093   022 083   02 1MI MOVC
038 0E2   03C 0E0   048 0F2   04E 0F0   04 1MI MOVX
                              01E 0A4   01 1MI MUL
                              012 000   01 1MI NOP
010 048   014 045   038 046   00E 044
          042 042   016 043   044 072   07 1MI ORL
                              044 0A0   01 1MI ORL/
                              004 0D0   01 1MI POP
                              004 0C0   01 1MI PUSH
                              012 022   01 1MI RET
                              012 032   01 1MI RETI
                              002 023   01 1MI RL
                              002 033   01 1MI RLC
                              002 003   01 1MI RR
-->
183
\                                                 \      09:19 01/28/86

                              002 013   01 1MI RRC
                    030 0D2   032 0D3   02 1MI SETB
                              03A 080   01 1MI SJMP
010 098   014 095   038 096   00E 094   04 1MI SUBB
                              002 0C4   01 1MI SWAP
```

```
          010 0C8  014 0C5  038 0C6  03 1MI XCH
                            038 0D6  01 1MI XCHD
010 068   014 065  038 066  00E 064
                   042 062  016 063  06 1MI XRL
-->

184
\ 8051 asm high level control constructs    \     09:19 01/28/86
HEX
070   CONSTANT 0=        060     CONSTANT 0<>
050   CONSTANT CARRY     040     CONSTANT NOCARRY

: BIT             030 C, ;
: NOBIT           020 C, ;

: IF              C, HERE 00 C, DUP 1+ 07FFE RESET ;

: ELSE            07FFE ?PAIRS 080 C, HERE 0 C, ROT ROT
                  HERE FORTH SWAP ASSEMBLER - ?7F
                  FORTH SWAP ASSEMBLER C! DUP 1+ 07FFE RESET ;

: THEN            07FFE ?PAIRS HERE FORTH SWAP ASSEMBLER - ?7F
                  FORTH SWAP ASSEMBLER C! RESET ; -->
185
\ 8051 asm high level control constructs    \     12:27 01/29/86
HEX
: BEGIN           HERE 07FFF RESET ;

: UNTIL           FORTH SWAP 07FFF ?PAIRS C,
                  HERE 1+ - ?7F C, RESET ;

: WHILE           FORTH SWAP 07FFF ?PAIRS C, HERE 00 C,
                  07FFD RESET ;

: REPEAT          FORTH 07FFD ?PAIRS 080 C, SWAP
                  HERE 1+ - ?7F C, DUP HERE 1- SWAP
                  - ?7F SWAP C! RESET ;
-->

186
\ Assembler local labels                          09:58 10/14/86

\ ---
: BEGIN$         0 #$ ! ;

\ ---
: END$ FORTH      #$ @ IF $A #$ @ + $A DO I @ 0< 28 ?ERROR
                  4 +LOOP THEN ;
-->

187
\ Assembler local labels                          13:30 01/26/89
\ label --- address of backward reference
: $               >R ?DISP R> FORTH $R DUP #$ @
                  IF $A #$ @ + $A DO DUP I @ =
                    IF 2DROP I 2+ @ 0 LEAVE THEN
                    4 +LOOP
                  THEN
                  IF HERE SWAP MINUS !$ THEN RELAD !TOP ;
\ label ---
: $:              FORTH $R #$ @
                  IF $A #$ @ + $A DO DUP I @ OVER OVER =
                    23 ?ERROR MINUS =
                    IF I DUP 0 SWAP ! 2+ @ DUP ?R MINUS DUP 0>
```

```
                     IF 4 - SWAP 1+ C! THEN
                   THEN 4 +LOOP
                 THEN !$ RESET ; -->
188
\                                                          10:37 03/03/89
HEX
: X0L          S0L ;                    : X0H          S0H ;
: X1L          S1L ;                    : X1H          S1H ;
: X2L          S2L ;                    : X2H          S2H ;
: X3L          S3L ;                    : X3H          S3H ;

: GETSP,       GET_SP  12 C, , ;
: SAVESP,      SAVE_SP 12 C, , ;
: GETRP,       GET_RP  12 C, , ;
: SAVERP,      SAVE_RP 12 C, , ;
-->

189
\ macros                                                   10:37 03/03/89
HEX
: GETIP,       GET_IP  12 C, , ;
: SAVEIP,      SAVE_IP 12 C, , ;
: NEXT,        NEXT    02 C, , ;
: A0PUSH,      A0PUSH  02 C, , ;
: APUSH,       APUSH   02 C, , ;
: -DPTR,       -DPTR   12 C, , ;
: GETX0,       (S0)    12 C, , ;
: GETX1,       (S1)    12 C, , ;
: GETX2,       (S2)    12 C, , ;
: GETX3,       (S3)    12 C, , ;

: END-CODE     ASSEMBLER END$ FORTH
               ?EXEC ?CSP SMUDGE [COMPILE] FORTH ; IMMEDIATE
-->
190
\ CODE | ;CODE | END-CODE                                  13:23 10/12/86

ASSEMBLER ' RESET  NFA ' #     LFA !
ASSEMBLER ' REVSYM NFA ' RESET LFA !
FORTH DEFINITIONS

: CODE         ?EXEC !CSP CREATE [COMPILE] ASSEMBLER
               ASSEMBLER RESET BEGIN$ FORTH ; IMMEDIATE

: ;CODE        ?CSP COMPILE (;CODE)
               [COMPILE] [ [COMPILE] ASSEMBLER
               ASSEMBLER RESET BEGIN$ FORTH ; IMMEDIATE
-->

191
\ TVI 912C terminal cursor control function                10:49 10/11/89

VOCABULARY EDITOR IMMEDIATE
EDITOR DEFINITIONS
DECIMAL

: CLREOS 27 EMIT 89 EMIT ;
: CLREOL 27 EMIT 84 EMIT ;
-->

192
\ ANSI standard cursor controls - VT100, Bi \              09:09 01/28/86
--> ( The CLS         function must clear the CRT screen and
  leave the cursor in the upper left corner.  On some models
```

```
  this requires two separate escape sequences.
  The GOTOXY function is used as follows:  x y GOTOXY
  stack effect:  2 -> 0  X=0-79  Y=0-23 )
DECIMAL             27 CONSTANT Esc
: .num              0 <# # # #> TYPE ;
: CLS               Esc EMIT  ASCII [ EMIT  ASCII 2 EMIT
                    ASCII J EMIT CURHOM ;
: CURHOM            Esc EMIT ASCII [ EMIT 0 EMIT ASCII
                    ; EMIT 0 EMIT ASCII H EMIT ;
: GOTOXY            Esc EMIT  ASCII [ EMIT 2+ .num
                    ASCII ; EMIT 2+ .num    ASCII H EMIT ;
: CLREOL            Esc EMIT ASCII [ EMIT  ASCII K EMIT ;
: CLREOS            Esc EMIT ASCII [ EMIT  ASCII J EMIT ; -->
193
\ Mini Screen Editor for CRT's with cursor  \     10:32 04/19/86
HEX
0 VARIABLE CUR

05 CONSTANT ERASEFLAG    ( ctl/E )  02 CONSTANT HOME ( ctl/B )
15 CONSTANT UPCURSOR     ( ctl/U )  1A CONSTANT UNDO ( ctl/Z )
12 CONSTANT RIGHTCURSOR  ( ctl/R )  0E CONSTANT PGDN ( ctl/N )
04 CONSTANT DOWNCURSOR   ( ctl D )  10 CONSTANT PGUP ( ctl/P )
0C CONSTANT LEFTCURSOR   ( ctl/L )
1B CONSTANT EXITFLAG     ( Esc )
0D CONSTANT NEWLINE      ( CR )
09 CONSTANT HORIZTAB     ( ctl/I )
08 CONSTANT BACKSPACE
-->

194
\ Mini Screen Editor for CRT's with cursor        15:39 01/29/89
HEX

: .CUR CUR @ 40 /MOD 2+ SWAP 4 + SWAP GOTOXY ;
: !CUR 0 MAX 3FF MIN CUR ! ;
: +CUR CUR @ + !CUR ;
: +.CUR +CUR .CUR ;
: +LIN CUR @ 40 / + 40 * !CUR ;
: HOM 0 CUR ! .CUR ;
: !BLK SCR @ BLOCK CUR @ + C! UPDATE 1 +.CUR ;
-->
: .CUR CUR @ 40 /MOD 1 + SWAP 3 + SWAP GOTOXY ;

195
\ televideo 910 help frame                  \     10:21 04/19/86
-->
HEX
: EDITOR-INS
  0 11 GOTOXY CR
r down " CR  ." Ctl/E = erase screen    Ctl/R = cursor right
ESC   = exit editor " CR
cursor " CR  ." Ctl/Z = restore screen  Ctl/N = page down
Ctl/P = page up " CR ;
-->

196
\ ibm pc help frame                         \     10:25 04/19/86
DECIMAL
: EDITOR-INS
 0 18 GOTOXY 24 EMIT ."  cursor up"
 0 19 GOTOXY 25 EMIT ."  cursor down"
 0 20 GOTOXY 28 EMIT ."  cursor right" \ 28 is pc 26
24 18 GOTOXY 27 EMIT 27 EMIT ."  cursor left"
24 19 GOTOXY ." Home  start of screen"
```

```
24 20 GOTOXY ." ^Home  restore screen"
48 18 GOTOXY 17 EMIT 196 EMIT 217 EMIT ."  start of next line "
48 19 GOTOXY ." Del  backspace and delete"
48 20 GOTOXY ." PgDn  next screen"
 0 21 GOTOXY ." PgUp  previous screen"
24 21 GOTOXY  28 EMIT 221 EMIT  ."  tab right" \ 28 is pc 26
48 21 GOTOXY ." Esc  exit editor"
 0 22 GOTOXY ." ^End  erase screen" ; -->
197
\ Mini Screen Editor, continued                 \     09:42 04/14/86
HEX

: S.ERASE  SCR @ BLOCK 400 BLANKS
           CLS SCR @ LIST EDITOR-INS HOM ;

: CLHC     CLS LIST EDITOR-INS HOM .CUR ; -->

198
\ Mini Screen Editor, continued                 \     14:18 04/20/86
HEX
: EDIT    DECIMAL DEPTH 1 < 1 ?ERROR  CLS LIST
          HOM EDITOR-INS .CUR BEGIN KEY CASE
  ERASEFLAG      OF S.ERASE ENDOF
  EXITFLAG       OF 0 11 GOTOXY CLREOS CR QUIT ENDOF
  BACKSPACE      OF -1 +.CUR 20 DUP EMIT !BLK -1 +.CUR ENDOF
  DOWNCURSOR     OF 40 +.CUR ENDOF
                 7F OF -1 +.CUR ENDOF 5F OF -1 +.CUR ENDOF
  LEFTCURSOR     OF -1 +.CUR ENDOF
  HOME           OF HOM .CUR ENDOF
  PGUP           OF SCR @ 1- 0 MAX CLHC ENDOF
  PGDN           OF SCR @ 1+ CLHC ENDOF
  UNDO           OF 7FFF PREV @ ! SCR @ CLHC ENDOF
-->

199
\ Mini Screen Editor, continued                 \     08:43 02/27/86

  NEWLINE        OF 1 +LIN .CUR ENDOF
  UPCURSOR       OF -40 +.CUR ENDOF
  RIGHTCURSOR    OF 1 +.CUR ENDOF
  HORIZTAB       OF CUR @ 8 / 8 * 8 + !CUR .CUR ENDOF
  DUP 20 < IF 7 EMIT ELSE  DUP DUP EMIT !BLK THEN
  ENDCASE AGAIN ;

FORTH DEFINITIONS
: E EDITOR EDIT ;
-->

200
\ Stand-alone FORTH --- noop task                     12:48 10/13/86

0 VARIABLE EXTI0  THERE 2- 04 ! 1 ALLOT-RAM
0 VARIABLE TIMER0 THERE 2- 0C ! 1 ALLOT-RAM
0 VARIABLE EXTI1  THERE 2- 14 ! 1 ALLOT-RAM
0 VARIABLE TIMER1 THERE 2- 1C ! 1 ALLOT-RAM
0 VARIABLE SINT   THERE 2- 24 ! 1 ALLOT-RAM

: TASK ; IS-FENCE
FINIS

201
\                                                     12:02 12/28/88
Revsym                 Revision history
```

```
06/12/86 07:56  Formal release data of 8051 target.  Includes
                terminal flow control and ram interrupts.

10/14/86 12:03  Replaced TOF in P... with =. NMC 2.2 used, whp

12/06/86 10:54  07 changed to hex 11 in DIGIT to correct mis-
                identification of 3A thru 40 as valid digits.

                DMINUS rewritten to correct error which caused
                the double number hex 0 8000, and others, to be
                converted incorrectly, whp

202
\                                                 10:39 03/03/89
Revsym                  Revision history

12/28/88 10:30  Fixed .CUR to compensate for error found in
Rel 1.2         GOTOXY in terminal emulator.  Rel 1.0 was
                given to LANL.  1.1 fixed a flow control
                protocol error. whp

01/30/89 15:00  Changed .CUR to compensate for error found in
Rel 1.3         GOTOXY in terminal emulcation.  Fixed error
                checking for ACALL and AJMP in assembler. whp
03/03/89 10:00  Same as 1.3, whp
Rel 1.4

203
\                                                 13:09 02/03/90
Revsym                  Revision history

10/11/89        - Moved EDITOR vocabulary above ASSEMBLER
                  vocabulary as required by Meta-compiler.
                - Added ASSEMBLER invocation after FORTH
                  invocation in ASSEMBLER vocabulary
                - Changed assembler syntax
                  0 P2 -> P2 jfb

12/24/89        Added delay before PINIT to remove 80C31 80C52
                race condition at reset.  80C52 emerges from
                reset at 2v, 8031 at 2.5v, and 80C31 at 3.5v.
                whp

204
\ image.com dump                                  13:42 10/12/86
DECIMAL
: DUMP    ( addr  n  ---  )
  BASE @ >R HEX CR CR 5 SPACES
  16 0 DO I 3 .R LOOP 2 SPACES
  16 0 DO I 0 <# # #> TYPE LOOP CR
  OVER + SWAP DUP 15 AND XOR DO
  CR I 0 4 D.R SPACE
  I 16 + I 2DUP
    DO I 1024 /MOD BLOCK + C@ SPACE 0 <# # # #> TYPE LOOP
    2 SPACES
    DO I 1024 /MOD BLOCK + C@
            DUP 32 < OVER 126 > OR IF DROP 46 THEN
    EMIT LOOP
  16 +LOOP CR R> BASE ! ;
```

Appendix 10

ASCII Listing of the 8051 FORTH Operating System

The ASCII listing of the binary image created by metacompiling the 8051 FORTH operating system in Appendix 1 is given here. It runs on the 8051 hardware whose schematics are given in Chapter 1.

If you are unable to get a copy of IMAGE51.COM, the binary image from a participating vendor, then you can build an ASCII file of this listing using a word processor in nondocument mode. The BASIC program in Chapter 3 is used to convert it to a binary file. The contents of this binary file, when ROMed, run on the 8051 hardware shown in Chapter 1.

This list was reconverted to binary using the BASIC program listed in Chapter 3. The reconverted binary was compared with the original binary with the ICOMP utility shown in Chapter 3. The files compared equally with the exception of the last byte. This is the Ctrl Z inserted by BASIC. A solution to eliminating this last byte is to write an assembler subprogram to close the file. FORTH86, the source seen in Appendix 1, contains a BSAVE command, which saves a BASIC BLOAD format file. If you can discover which handle BASIC assigned to the output file, then it is easy to write an assembler subprogram similar to CLOSEHANDLE, which closes the output file without writing the unwanted hex 1A.

```
00
0200540280440000020000028047000002000002804A000002000002804D0000 038
0200000280500000020000020075010300 0E43FA0008F6B6F5B6F6B6F5B7001F 097
0000805380533E410005B2B5F5B6F6B6F6B6234C75812F90004CE0FCA3E0FD90 0FF
004EE0FEA3E0FF900052E582FBE583FA0200FC2058900073E582FBE583FA0200 119
FC7581317530757531 0032C58270021583C582158222 1200CAA3E0F520A3E0F5 0E5
2122A3E0F522A3E0F52322A3E0F524A3E0F52522A3E0F526A3E0F527228F828E 11F
832212008BAF82AE83228D828C832212008BAD82AC83228B828A8322A3AB82AA 0DD
8322F012008BE4F012008BAD82AC83800B12008BF012008BAD82AC838B828A83 0E2
E0F8A3E0F9A3AB82AA8389828883E0F520A3E0F582852083E473834C49D40000 12C
01221200D7E0F520A3E01200DC1200CAF0E52080BC87454E434C4F53C5011A01 0CA
411200CAA3A3E0F521A3E0F522A3E0F52312008B1200CF852382852283E4F8F9 103
E0B5210809E9700108A380F4702A1200CAE9F012008BE8F012008BE904700108 0D0
F9F9F012008BE8F012008BE970011814F012008BE8F08059E582CDF582E583CC 119
F583E9F012008BE8F012008BE582CDF582E583CCF58309E9700108A3E0701612 114
00CAE9F012008BE8F012008BE9F012008BE8F0801CB521DE1200CAE9F012008B 0FA
E8F012008B09E9700108E9F012008BE8F01200CF0200FC8544494749D4013502 0CB
01
01120096A3A3E0C3943020E72CF523C3940A20E70CE523C3941120E71C240AF5 0DC
23E523C3952130E710E523F012008BE4F012008B74010200E2E40200E286544F 0D1
47474CC501F702481200CAA3A3E0A3F9E0A3F5A0E0F8AC83AD82E269F20200FC 120
862846494E44A9023D026B1200961200A2AC83AD82D2D3A820A921AA22AB238B 0C3
828A83E0F52588838982E0F527543FB52558541FFEEBFDEAFCE583CCF583E582 13B
CDF582A3E0F524E582CDF582E583CCF583A3E0547FB52430DEDFE58224055002 133
0583858320F521C2D31200CAE521F012008BE520F012008BE527F012008BE4F0 0EC
12008B74010200E2EE14541F2582F58250020583A3E0F8A3E0F960028088B800 0D7
85C2D31200CAE40200E28255AA02600311 1200961200A2AC83AD82D2D3AF20AE 0D9
21AD22AC238EF0ECA4F523A9F0ED8EF0A429F9E435F0FAEC8FF0A429F522E5F0 14D
3AFAE43400FBED8FF0A42AF521E5F03BF520C2D31200CAE523F012008BE522F0 11B
12008BE521F0E5200200F18255AF030A03728C838D82D2D3A3E0FDA3E0FCA3E0 10D
F9A3E0F8A3E0FFA3E0FEC3E99D400F7006E89C5002800774FFF9FEFF80267A10 137
C3EE33FEEF33FFE833F8E933F9C3E99D400F7004E89C4009E89CF8E99DF9430E 135
01DADDE8F012008BE9F012008BEEF0EFC2D30200F18446494CCC036B03DE1200 0F8
961200A21200ABAC83AD82E52360020522852483852582E521F0A3D523FBD522 0DD
02
F80200FC85434D4F56C503D5040E1200961200A21200ABAC83AD82E521600205 0B4
20852483852582E0F527A3E583C522F583E582C523F582E527F0A3E583C522F5 128
83E582C523F582D521DDD520DA0200FC81AB04040456 1200961200A22521F0E5 0DE
2235200200F181AD0450046C1200961200A2C3E5239521F0E52295200200F181 0B5
BC046604851200961200A2C39521E5229520A2E7E45001040200E28230BC047F 0BD
04A2120096E520A2E7E45001040200E28230BD049B04B71200CAA3E0A3F520E0 0DB
45207003048001E40200E2854D494E55D304B004D5120096E520F4F520E521F4 0CF
2401F0E5205001040200F186444D494E55D304CB04F61200961200A2C3E49523 0BB
F523E49522F522E49521F521E49520F520E523F012008BE522F012008BE521F0 104
E5200200F18244AB04EB052C1200961200A21200AB1200B4E5232527F012008B 0A4
E5223526F012008BE5213525F0E52035240200F184532D3EC40525055D1200CA 0AF
A3E012008BA2E7E4500274FFF00200F183414EC405540578 1200961200A25521 0CB
F0E5205522 0200F1824FD20570058F1200961200A24521F0E5204522 0200F183 0B9
584FD2058805A71200961200A26521F0E5206522 0200F1835350C0059F05BF12 0B6
00CAEDF0EC0200F1835350A105B705D090004CE0FCA3E0FD0200FC835250A105 0FD
C805E390004EE0FEA3E0FF0200FC823ED205DB05F5120096A31200CF1200BDF0 0F4
03
12008BE520F01200C20200FC8252BE05EE06131200BDA3E0F520A3E0AF82AE83 0E4
8D828C83F0E5200200F181C9060C06301200BDA3E0F520A3E08D828C83F0E520 0F9
0200F181D2062A064980E587455845435554C506430657120096AC83AD82A921 0BB
A82002010A84535741D0064B066E1200961200A2E521F012008BE520F012008B 0A5
E523F0E5220200F1844F5645D206650691ED2403F5828C8350020583E0F520A3 0E4
E08D828C83F0E5200200F18444524FD0068806B40DED70010C0DED70010C0200 0C5
FC834455D006AB06C91200CAA3E0F520A3E08C838D82F0E5200200F184324455 0FB
D006C106E51200CAA3E0F520A3E0F521A3E0F522A3E01200CAF012008BE522F0 110
12008BE521F0E5200200F183524FD406DC07131200CAA3E0F520A3E0F521A3E0 0F0
F522A3E0F523A3E0F524A3E0F525E523F012008BE522F012008BE521F012008B 10A
```

```
E520F012008BE525F012008BE524F00200FC81C0070B07581200CAA3E0A3F520 0DE9
E0AC83AD82F582852083E0A3F520E08C838D82F0E5200200F181A10752077F12 106E
00961200A2AC83AD8285208385218 2E522F0A3E523F00200FC8243C0077907A0 0E34
1200CAA3E0A3F5A0E0F8E20200E2835043C0079907B61200CAA3A3E0F87422F0 10E8
12008BE8F012008B74E5F078D5C0007807C000E473A3A30200E2835043A107AE 0E94
07E21200CAA3A3E0F8A3A3E0F97422F012008BE9F012008BE8F012008B7475F0 10E9
04
780AC0007808C000E473A3A3A3AC83AD820200FC834943C007DA081C1200CAA3 0D71
A3E0F8E60200E28249C00814082E1200CAA3A3E0F8E6F52008E6F0E5200200F1 0FED
834943A1082708481200CAA3A3E0F8A3A3E0F6AC83AD820200FC8249A1084008 0E5D
511200CAA3A3E0F8A3E0F6A3E008F6AC83AD820200FC8243A1085A087D1200CA 0FDA
A3E0F5A0A3E0A3A3F8A31200CFE0F20200FC822BA10876089912009612 00A2AC 0FA2
83AD82852083852182A3E02523F012008BE03522F00200FC8232C0089208BF12 0D66
00CAA3E0A3F520E0AC83AD82F582852083E0A3F520E0A3F521E0A3F522E08C83 139C
8D82F012008BE522F012008BE521F0E5200200F18232A108B808FB1200961200 0CF0
A21200ABAC83AD82852083852182E522F0A3E523F0A3E524F0A3E525F00200FC 10D6
835250C008F409281200CAEFF0EE0200F1864252414E43C80920093C8A838B82 0CEA
E0F520A3E0A32BFBE5203AFA0200FC87304252414E43C80931095B8C838D82A3 0EBC
E0A3F520E04520AC83AD82600AEB240250010AFB0200FC80C386284C4F4F50A9 0DDE
094F09848E838F82A3E0F520A3A982A883E004700205 20F521752400A3E0F522 0E5C
A3E0C39521F523E5229520F522C3E52430E701D3E52230E704401880084006E5 0ECB
224523700EAE83AF82EB240250010AFB0200FC89828883E521F0E58215827002 0D4B
1583E520F08A838B82E0F520A3E0A32BFBE5203AFA0200FC87282B4C4F4F50A9 0FDC
05
09790A048E838F82A3E0F520A3E0F521A982A8838C838D82A3E0F524A3E0AC83 11A5
AD822521F521E5203524F5208982888302099C8428444FA909F80A3C12009612 0BA4
00A2AC83AD821200BDE523F012008BE522F012008BE521F012008BE520F01200 0D92
C20200FC823BD30A330A6B8E838F82A3E0FAA3E0FBAE83AF820200FC854C4541 0FD6
56C50A640A868E838F82A3E0F520A3E0F521A3E520F0A3E521F00200FC81B00A 10D6
7C0AA38C838D8274000200E281B10A9D0AB28C838D8274010200E281B20AAC0A 0C9E
C18C838D8274020200E28231AB0ABB0AD18C838D82A3A3E004F0700612008BE0 0E62
04F00200FC8231AD0ACA0AEC8C838D82A3A3E014F004700612008BE014F00200 0D61
FC8232AB0AE50B088C838D82A3A3E02402F0500612008BE004F00200FC8232AD 0DDD
0B010B248C838D82A3A3E0C39402F0500612008BE014F00200FC8232AA0B1D0B 0C2E
418C838D82A3A3E0C333F012008BE033F00200FC8232AF0B3A0B5B8C838D82A3 0ED8
E0C313F0A3E013F00200FC8230BE0B540B72120096E52020E709452160057401 0C73
0200E2E40200E2853244524FD00B6B0B91ED2404FD50010C0200FC842D4455D0 0BB1
0B870BA4120096E5214520700502 00FC800B1200CAE521F0E5200200F181BD0B 0B65
0B0BC31200961200A2C3E5239521F521E522952045217003048001E40200E282 0BC0
8CBE0BBD0BE61200961200A2C3E5239521F521E522952045216002740102 00E2 0B83
06
88434F4E5354414ED40BDF0C721C921FD71048204288838982A3A3E0F520A3E0 0E0C
8C838D82F0E5200200F1885641524941424CC50C000C721C921FD7102C0B0610 0ADF
48104820428883898 2A3A3E0F520A3E08C838D82F0E5200200F181BA0C2A0C72 0ECB
1A1119FF0DFC07560DEE077D1C921E3420428E838F82EBF012008BEAF012008B 0C9B
AE83AF82E92402FBE8500104FA0200FC85444F4553BE0C5A0C7206111E630FCA 0C64
077D20428E838F82EBF012008BEAF012008BAE83AF8288838982A3A3E0A3FAE0 1112
A3FB858320E5828C838D82F0E5200200F184555345D20C900C720C0B20428883 0E14
8982A3A3A3E0F523900050E0A3F520E025238C838D82F0E5205001040200F18A 0F71
564F434142554C4152D90CD10C721E9F102C01200004045410481 02C0DB90756 0800
10480DB9077D012081A010480DFC07560FBC10480C9807560B060DEE077D0A69 08C9
C5464F5254C80CFF0CA40D3680020000835250D00D400C15004E8255D00D500C 0A09
1500508253B00D5A0CDE00068252B00D630CDE0008835449C20D6C0CDE000A85 09FB
57494454C80D750CDE000C875741524E494EC70D7F0CDE000E8546454E43C50D 0A8C
8B0CDE00108244D00D990CDE001288564F432D4C494ECB0DA50CDE001483424C 0AC9
CB0DAE0CDE00168249CE0DBD0CDE0018834F55D40DC70CDE001A835343D20DD0 0C86
0CDE001C87434F4E544558D40DDA0CDE0020874355525 2454ED40DE40CDE0022 0B4A
07
8553544154C50DF20CDE002484424153C50E000CDE0026834450CC0E0C0CDE00 0AB7
2883464CC40E170CDE002A834353D00E210CDE002C8252A30E2B0CDE002E8348 09FB
4CC40E350CDE003081B30E3E0C15000383432FCC0E480C150040854D2F4D4FC4 08EA
0E500C7205F30AA1064703700611066C05F3037006110A6983442BAD0E5A0C72 0842
04A00959000404F40A6984444142D30E780C7206C70E7E0A69822BAD0E8A0C72 09D3
04A00959000404D30A69834142D30E990C7206C70E9E0A69824DAF0EAA0C7206 09F8
```

```
8F05F305F30E9106470EB003700611064705A50E9E066C06110E9E066C0A6984 08F4
2F4D4FC40EB80C7205F3055B06110EBD0A6981AF0EDF0C720EE6066C06B20A69 0AA
834D41D80EF20C7206E304830959000406 6C06B20A69834D49CE0F000C7206E3 0A3
0F7909590004066C06B20A69824DAA0F160C7206E305A505F30EB0066C0EB003 092
0F06110E7E0A6981AA0F2C0C720F3106B20A69852A2F4D4FC40F470C7205F30F 088
3106110EBD0A69834D4FC40F530C720EE606B20A6981BE0F670C72066C04830A 099
698255BC0F750C7206E305A504A00959000C06B204A004B5093A0006046A04A0 091
0A69872B4F52494749CE0F810C72012000004540A69834346C10FA20C720ABF 092
046A0A69835046C10FB60C720AB0100901200005045 40A69834E46C10FC40C72 08E
01200005046A0120FFFF10090A69834C46C10FD80C7201200004046A0A698854 085
08
524156455253C50FEE0C72066C068F04540120007F068F079E04830959FFF006 0A2
6C06B20A6984484552C50FFE0C720DAA07560A6985414C4C4FD410250C720DAA 0AB
08970A6981AC10340C72102C077D0ABF103C0A698243AC10440C72102C087B0A 085
B0103C0A69862854595045A9105410701200961200A21200ABAC83AD82E52360 0AC
020522A82190FFF5E0542060FB90FFF6E0541060FB85258285 2483E0547FA385 107
83248582 2590FFF0F0D8FED523D5D522D20200FC84545950C510650C720BA209 0F9
59001206C70DD6089701200001106E093A000406B20A6985434F554ED410B40C 082
7206C70ACF066C079E0A6984282E22A910D70C72064710DF06C70ACF06110454 09F
05F310BB0A69832822A910EB0C72064706C7079E0ACF0611045405F30A698350 0A6
41C411060C72102C0120004404540A698223BE111E0C7206B206B20E44075611 074
24068F046A0A6984484F4CC411300C720120FFFF0E4408970E440756087B0A69 093
84534947CE11470C72071104A00959000801200 02D114E0A6981A311600C720E 077
1307560E62071101200009068F048309590008012000070454012000300 45411 03E
4E0A698223D311790C72117D06E3058D04B50959FFF60A69823CA311A30C7211 0B7
240E44077D0A698242CC11B80C1500208553504143C511C70C7211CC134E0A69 097
865350414345D311D00C720AA10F060BA20959000C0AA10A3A11D80982FFFC0A 0A6
09
6986424C414E4BD311E00C7211CC03DC0A69892D545241494C494EC712010C72 0AE
06C70AA10A3A068F068F04540AB0046A079E11CC046A095900080A84093A0006 079
0AB0046A0982FFE00A69854552 4153C512120C720AA103DC0A6983442ED2124A 0B3
0C7205F3066C068F0E9111BD11A811671135061106 8F046A11E910BB0A698244 097
AE125A0C720AA1126011D80A69842E4350D5127E0C720E130756012000240E13 081
077D0120004808BD12830E13077D0A6981AE128D0C72055B12830A698255AE12 08A
B00C720AA112830A69834944AE12BC0C72112401200020012000 5F03DC06C70F 089
CA0FF4068F046A1124066C040C112410DF0120001F057610BB11D80A69822ED2 090
12C90C7205F3055B061112600A6981BF12FD0C72075612B40A698628454D4954 09E
A9130E132590FFF6E0541060FB90FFF5E0542060FB8C838D82A3A3E0AC83AD82 11F
90FFF0F00200FC84454D49D4131A0C7213230AB00DD608970A698243D213470C 0C2
720120000D134E0120000A134E0AA10DD6077D0A69893F5445524D494E41CC13 07C
5A138390FFF5E0540160047401800B90FFF4E04402F054FDF0E48C838D820200 0FE
E289405445524D494E41CC13750C720120FFF0079E0A69834B45D913A10C7213 0BE
810959FFFC13AD0A6985234255 46C613B70C150002875345432F424CCB13C90C 0B1
15000185422F5343D213D50C1500018546495253D413E30C15F6F6854C494D49 0AB
10
D413EF0C15FEFE835553C513FB0C45800684505245D614070C458008835245C3 0CD
14110C45800A8A4449534B2D4552524FD2141C0C45800C85422F4255C614260C 089
150400865345542D49CF14370C720AA11433077D0A6989444953 4B4552524FD2 094
14430C720AA10D95077D198F0A69885345432D524541C414560C721422075627 088
2A27850120000527F20959001 2271C01200005283A09590006277428BB0A6989 063
5345432D57524954C5146E0C72142207562739278501200005 27F20959001E14 078
220756168F0120040027AE271C27850120000527F20959000429140A69852D52 066
494EC7149F14E790FFF5E05460646070F990FFF4E054FBF00200FC8452494EC7 122
14DD150490FFF5E05460646070F990FFF4E04404F00200FC864255464645D214 0FB
FB0C72140D075606C705F315CA0959FFFC140D077D0647075604A00959001406 096
470B060647075601207FFF05760AA115670647077D06471418077D06110B060A 064
6983522FD715180C72140D075605F3066C13DF0F4B0711140D077D13DF0AA10A 088
3A068F068F1422077D144C150209590008147909 3A000414AB14E5143307560B 063
A20B70095900061462 1D350ACF01200400140D08970982FFCA0B8F0611140D07 073
7D0A69842B4255C615610C72143F01200004045404 5406C714030BC109590006 073
06B213F706C714180756046A0A698D454D5054592D42554646 4552D315C30C72 0A2
11
13F71403068F046A1252140313F70A3A01207FFF062E077D012004040A02FFF2 086
0A69865550444154C515EE0C721418075607560120800005 8D14180756077D0A 07E
```

```
985464C5553C816220C72140313F70A3A062E075601208000057609590001C06 073C
E075601207FFF057606C7062E077D062E0B06066C0AA11567143F0120000404 0684
40A02FFCE0A6985424C4F43CB16410C720AA11433077D05F31418075606C707 09B0
60647046A06C704540959003415CA04B50959001406B20647152106C706470A 0739
015670ABF046A06C707560647046A06C7045404B50959FFD606C71418077D06 09E0
106B20B060A69844C4F41C416870C720DC3075605F30DCC075605F30AA10DCC 0A63
77D13EB0F4B0DC3077D1CEA06110DCC077D06110DC3077D0A69844C4953D416 09DE
70C721E77135F06C70DE0077D10F20953637265656E20232012B4012000100A 0979
10A3A135F06470E4C130211D806470DE00756182C1381095900040A840982FF 07E9
4135F0A69C32D2DBE171A0C721A850AA10DCC077D13EB0DC30756068F0F6D04 0A3A
A0DC308970A6985494E4445D817650C720120000C134E135F0ACF066C0A3A13 0865
F062E0E4C130211D80AA1062E182C1381095900040A840982FFE60A69855452 08A4
941C417870C720120000C134E0E4C0EF60E4C0F4B0E4C068F0454066C0A3A13 071A
F062E17211381095900040A840982FFF0135F0120000F1840135F0A6986284C 07A6
2
94E45A917BD0C7205F301200040143F0F5B061113EB0F4B0454168F04540120 07D2
0400A69852E4C494EC517FD0C721806121E10BB0A69874D4553534147C51824 0974
C720D9507560959001 60BA20959000C01200004182C135F11D8093A000D10F2 0626
64D736720232012B40A6984544852D518360C720ACF066C0A3A062E16EE0982 092E
FFA0A698A53484F572D4552524FD2186B0C720DC307560B700959004B0DCC07 0AA4
60B22012000400EF60DC3075606E310F20A6174207363726565 6E2012B410F2 0A67
56C696E652012B4135F182C135F0DCC07560B22012000400F6D11E90120005E 0774
34E135F135F1D350A6981CA18840C720926012000070454075 60A6984455849 0758
418EA0C72061106B20A6984504943CB18FC0C7205BD066C0B3F04540ACF0756 0A5F
A69854445505 4C8190B0C720D68075605BD046A0ABF046A0ABF0EF60A698452 09DE
F4CCC19220C7206C705F3191206110AA1066C0A3A05BD0ACF062E06C7045404 0880
406C70ABF046A0756066C077D0120FFFF0A02FFE206B20A69834E4FD4193E0C 0B39
20AB005A50A69854552524FD219790C720D95075604A0095900041D6D102C10 08C7
F10F2074572726F723A2001200022134E10BB0120002213 4E0ABF11E9184005 087F
E18910A69863F4552524FD219870C72066C0959000819 8F093A000406B20A69 08CD
53F434F4DD019C50C720E08075604B50120001119CE0A6984214353D019E00C 0997
3
205BD0E31077D0A69853F455845C319F80C720E08075601200 01219CE0A6986 08E8
F53544143CB1A090C7205BD0D680756066C0F860AB019CE05BD102C01200080 08B1
4540F86012000071 9CE0A69863F50414952D31A1F0C72046A0120001319CE0A 077D
9843F4353D01A4C0C7205BD0E310756046A0120001419CE0A69883F4C4F4144 08B8
94EC71A610C720DC3075604B50120001619CE0A6988284E554D424552A91A7A 0984
C720ACF06C705F3079E0E13075601FF0959002C066C0E130756030F06B20711 079F
E130756030F052A0E1D07560ACF095900080AB00E1D08970611093AFFC60611 0644
A69864E554D4245D21A950C720AA10AA1071106C70ACF079E0120002D0BC106 0948
705F30454012 0FFFF0E1D077D1AA006C7079E11CC046A0959001806C7079E01 0A49
0002E046A0120000519CE0AA1093AFFDA06B20611095900040 4F40A6984574F 085A
2C41AE20C720DC307560959000C0DC30756168F093A00060D7B07560DCC0756 0861
454066C013F102C0120002212 0A0DCC0897068F046A05F30647102C087B0454 067C
02C0ACF0611040C0A69852D46494EC41B3D0C7211CC1B44102C0DEE07560756 0805
26906C704B50959002006B2102C1E630DEE07560756068F046A095900080269 0775
93A00060B8F0AA10A69C1801B8A0C720DC307560959002A0AB00DC308970AA1 08F2
DCC077D0DC3075613EB0AB0046A057604B5095900081A11061106B2093A0006 0791
4
61106B20A6986455850 4543D41BCA0C72068F0454068F0A3A13BD06C7012000 08F8
80BC10959003406B206C7062E0BC106C706110ABF046A045405F30959000A01 07C7
00007093A001001200008134E11CC134E01200008093A002806C70120000D0B 03DC
10959000E0A8406B211CC0AA1093A000406C70647087B0AA106470ACF077D13 084B
E0982FF9606B20A6986435245415 4C51C060C721B920959001006B20FDE12CF 0A98
1200004184011D8102C06C7079E0D8707560F1C0ACF103C06C7012000A00246 072B
02C0AB0046A0120008002461E6310480DFC0756077D102C0B0610480A698949 06FA
E544552505245D41C890C721B920959001E0E08075604830959000A0FBC1048 07CD
93A00060FBC06551A28093A001C102C1AEB0E1D07560ACF095900082026093A 05A5
00606B220091A28093AFFC20A6984515549D41CDE0C720AA10DC3077D1E2610 09B2
204206F6B20135F05E11E0E1CEA0E08075604B50959000710F2026F6B093AFF 094F
70A69872841424F5254A91D2E0C721D7B0A698541424F52D41D630C7205CE1E 0A6A
71A28135F135F129410F21673657269657 3206D6963726F636F6E74726F6C6C 0B8D
572135F10F210524F4D656420444F53204D4320322E32135F10F21F31392E32 08D7
06B62732C207274732C2063747320666C6F7720636F6E74726F6C135F10F21A 0B22
```

```
56657273696F6E20312E352030312F31382F39302030393A3030135F135F0D48 07A7
15
1E4E1D350A698551554552D91D730C720D7B0756012000501C0F0AA10DCC077D 0863
0A69C1DB1E060C720AA10E08077D0A69C1DD1E220C72012000C00E08077D0A69 08B3
8B444546494E4954494F4ED31E300C720DEE07560DFC077D0A69864C41544553 0A6A
D41E400C720DFC075607560A6987444543494D41CC1E5A0C720120000A0E1307 0825
7D0A69834845D81E6D0C72012000100E13077D0A69873C4255494C44D31E830C 08DD
720AA10C0B0A6984424143CB1E950C72102C046A10480A69C542454749CE1EA7 09D1
0C7219E8102C0AB00A69C4544845CE1EB80C7219E80ABF1A55102C068F046A06 0A2D
6C077D0A69C244CF1ECA0C721FED0A3A102C0E4C0A69C44C4F4FD01EE50C720E 0B04
4C1A551FED09821EAE0A69C52B4C4F4FD01EF60C720E4C1A551FED0A021EAE0A 0A84
69C5554E5449CC1F0B0C720AB01A551FED09591EAE0A69C3454EC41F210C721F 0AAF
290A69C541474149CE1F370C720AB01A551FED093A1EAE0A69C65245504541D4 0AD3
1F430C7205F305F31F4B061106110ABF046A1ED10A69C249C61F590C721FED09 09DD
59102C0AA110480ABF0A69C4454C53C51F760C720ABF1A551FED093A102C0AA1 09C2
1048066C0ABF1ED10ABF0A69C55748494CC51F8B0C721F7B0B060A69C1BB1FAC 0B09
0C721A681FED0A691FD71E260A6986534D554447C51FBC0C721E630120002002 0914
460A6987434F4D50494CC51FCE0C7219E8061106C70B0605F3075610480A69C7 0A11
16
4C4954455241CC1FE30C720E08075609590008 1FED012010480A69C8444C4954 08D7
455241CC1FFF0C720E080756095900008066C200920090A6987283B434F4445A9 0802
201B0C7206111E630FCA0FBC077D0A69855741524DB120380C72135F10F20F49 08FE
6E7465727275707420526564791D350A69C22EA220500C72012000220E0807 093F
56095900141FED10F21B44102C079E0ACF103C093A000A1B44102C10DF10BB0A 07EF
69C1A220720C72012000220E08075609590006 1FED110C1B44102C079E0ACF10 074C
3C0A6989494D4D4544494154C520A10C721E630120004002460A69C1A820C30C 097E
72012000291B440A69C95B434F4D50494C45DD20DB0C721B9204B50AA119CE06 0A0E
B20FBC10480A69C1A720E90C721B9204B50120000519CE06B220090A69845741 0A1A
52CD21070C7215FE05CE1A280D481E4E135F10F2055265616479 1D350A698646 09AD
4F524745D4211D0C720DFC07560DEE0756046A0120001819CE210B06C70DA107 08B7
560F860120001519CE06C70FDE0DAA077D0FF407560DFC0756077D0A69C1DC21 0A78
3E0C720DCC0756012000400EF60ACF012000400F4B0DCC077D0A698253BD217D 08EF
0C7205F30AB00711071106110AA10A3A068F062E0454079E068F062E0454079E 06F2
05A50959000E071106B20AA1071107110A840982FFDC0B8F0A6985564C4953D4 095D
219B0C720E13075605F31E89135F135F0AA10DD6077D0DEE0756075606C706C7 099C
17
0AA111BD117D117D117D117D113510BB11D812CF0DD6075601200003C0F790959 0913
000E135F0AA10DD6077D093A00120120001 40DD60756068F0F6D046A11E90FCA 07AE
0FF4075606C704B5138106C70959000613BD06B2058D0959FFA406B2135F135F 0A6A
06110E13077D0A69822ED321DA0C720E13075605F305BD0D6807560BC1095900 0863
1A135F10F20D3C656D707479207374616 36B3E135F093A003B05BD0D68075606 0904
6C0A3A135F062E0ACF075606C71E77012000041302 1E8910F2032020280AA101 06E8
200004126010F20268290ABF0A02FFD5135F06110E13077D0A6984214143C522 0885
680C7206C70E4C045401200080066C087B06C70120000 6066C087B06C70ACF0A 0794
A1066C087B06C70E4C045401200017066C087B01200004045401200001012000 0502
02058D066C087B0A698550494E49D422DA0C720120FFF022E10120FFF022E126 0C4F
D606B20A6984434F4CC423290C720120F6B601208000077D0120440506C705F3 0A12
0120000404540120800000B06061107560ABF046A040C012000380D6801200010 03E9
040C0120003207560120 0D4A0B0607560B06077D15FE13F71418077D13F7140D 0633
077D0AB00D95077D012004000AA10A3A0982FFFE23311D7B0A69C4434153C523 09E2
450C7219E80E31075619FF012000040A69C24FC623BA0C72012000041A551FED 08E2
068F1FED0BC11FED0959102C0AA110481FED06B2012000050A69C5454E444FC6 0A28
18
23D10C72012000051A551FED093A102C0AA11048066C0ABF1ED1012000040A69 0757
C7454E44434153C523FA0C72012000041A551FED06B205BD0E3107560BC104B5 0A10
0959000A0ABF1ED1093AFFEC0E31077D0A698444554DD024200C720E13075605 0907
F31E89135F135F0120000511E9012000100AA10A3A062E0E4C13020982FFF80A 07ED
BF11E9012000100AA10A3A062E0AA111BD117D113510BB0982FFF2135F068F04 09AC
54066C06C70120000F057605A50A3A135F062E0AA10120000 4126011D8062E01 0632
2000100454062E06E30A3A062E079E11D80AA111BD117D117D113510BB0982FF 08DE
EC0ABF11E90A3A062E079E06C701200020048306 8F0120007E0F79058D095900 0811
0806B20120002E134E0982FFDC012000100A02FF9C135F06110E13077D0A6986 07D5
474F544F58D924520C720120001B134E0120003D134E0AA10F06012000170F1C 05DD
012000210454134E0AA10F060120004F0F1C012000210454134E0A6983434CD3 05A9
```

```
251F0C720120001A134E0A69872D435552534FD2255C0C720120001B134E0120 06A0
902E134E01200030134E0A6986435552534FD2256C0C720120001B134E012000 0665
2E134E01200031134E0A698754494D454F55D4258C0C45800E87285459504531 0895
A925AB25C51200961200A21200ABAC83AD82E52360020522A82190FFF5E05420 0D0C
50F690FFF6E0541060FB85258285248 3E0A38583248582259 0FFF0F0D8FED523 12EA
19
07D522D40200FC8554595045B125B90C720BA20959001206C70DD60897012000 0B05
0125C3093A000406B20A6989284558504543543 1A92607263912009612 00A2AC 0843
33AD8290FFF4E04402F090FFF6E0541060FB75240075250090FFF5E054016026 10E1
90FFF0E0852283852382F0A3858322858223D521E0E52070098C838D820200E2 0FF0
3004152080CFD525CFD524C990FFF4E054FDF08C838D82E521F0E5200200F187 11CA
455850454354B1262B0C720BA20B700959001206C705F326370611066C046A09 0807
3A000606B20AA10A698A405445524D494E414CB1269F26D890FFF0E08C838D82 0D2D
0200E20200E2853F4B4559B126C90C7225B507560AEA2983068F04B5058D0959 0AAC
FFF406B22983095900 0A26D60AB0093A00040AA10A69835354D826E60C150002 0A0F
37524541445345C327160C150052885752495445534 5C327200C1500538B5043 08F5
2D454D5054594255C6272E0C1500458850432D464C5553C8273D0C150046834E 08BA
41CB274F0C720120001529520A69834143CB275E0C7201200006295 20A698453 07E5
4543A3276E0C721124066C068F087B0ACF068F0120FFFF05A5068F0B06077D07 0965
7D0A6988434845434B5355CD277E27B01200961200A2AC83AD82752400752500 0AB4
352283852382E52160020520E02525F52550020524A3D521F3D520F08C838D82 0D2F
E525F0E5240200F18753454E444255C627A30C720AA1066C1124066C260F26EE 0B59
20
0959002201200006 0BC10959000A06B20AB0093A000C2764012000091433077D 0524
093A000C276401200008143307 7D0A69875245435642 55C627E80C720AA10711 07A5
071106C706C71124066C26A90BC1095900500 68F1124079E0BC1095900361124 07AE
0ACF06C70756066C0B0607560120FFFF05A50BC10959000E0B8F0AB0066C0AA1 0959
093A000C27640120000A1433077D093A000C27640120000B1433077D093A000C 03F0
27640120000C1433077D0B8F0A698A53435245454E524543D628300C72012004 0785
0006C7140D0756066C26A90BC10959002C140D07560120040027AE11240ACF07 0673
560BE409590010276401200 00D1433077D093A00042774093A000C2764012000 0518
0E1433077D0A698A53435245454E53454EC428AE0C7214220756168F01200400 07F1
260F26EE095900180120000 60BE40959000A0120000F1433077D093A000A0120 04AE
00101433077D0A698728454D495431A92907295490FFF5E0542060FB90FFF6E0 0D4B
541060FB8C838D82A3A3E0AC83AD8290FFF0F00200FC8A3F5445524D494E414C 0FF3
312948298590FFF5E05401600474018 00B90FFF4E04402F054FDF0E48C838D82 10C9
0200E284425945B129760C7210F20853746172746564201502 0ACF0AA1068F07 0A4E
7D0B060120FFFF066C077D0120000527F214E50959001710F20E2E2E2E20636F 08E0
5D706C657465642E093A001010F20B2E2E2E206661696C656421135F0A698342 0953
21
59C529A30C721124275A068F087B29AA0A698B454D5054592D50434255C629FE 0ADA
0C721124274B068F087B29AA0A69C74F4E474F5355C22A120C7219E81FED0B3F 09F8
1FED0120102C0AA110481FED06E31FED068F1FED04A01FED0959102C0AA11048 0A5F
1FED066C102C068F046A066C077D1FED0F791FED0959102C0AA110481FED066C 0972
102C068F046A066C077D1FED06B21FED0120102C0AA110481FED04541FED0756 0932
1FED06551FED093A102C0AA11048066C102C066C077D102C012000060A69C845 077C
4E44474F5355C22A2E0C72012000061A55102C066C046A06C70ABF0483012000 0758
1919CE06C70B060711077D0B22066C077D0A69C9415353454D424C45D22ABE0C 08EB
A40D3680100D4E865245565359CD80020C152B140830322F32372F38368254B0 08C5
2B070C45801483543 0D02B1D0C4580188443535 0B02B260C45801A8223A42B30 0919
0C45801C854D415823A42B3B0C1500208224C12B440C45801E8552455345D42B 093E
070C722B220120000412520AA12B2C077D192A2B37077D0A69834E55CC2B590C 06FF
150000854449524 3D42B790C15000185414452 31B62B830C15000285444154 41 0809
382B8F0C15000386444154413 1B62B9B0C1500048441524 5C72BA70C15000584 08A7
525245C72BB40C1500068440524 5C72BBF0C15000783445 0D22BCA0C15000885 0976
41425245C72BD50C1500098641 2B445054D22BDF0C15000A834044D02BEB0C15 09FA
22
000B84434249D42BF80C15000C8542414444D22C020C15000D84412B50C32C0D 087B
0C15000E8541445231B12C190C15000F8552454C41C42C240C150010833F52B0 0794
2C300C72102C0B06046A06C706C70120007F0F79066C0120FF800483058D0A69 07F5
333F52B12C3C0C720120002119CE0A69823FD22C600C722C422C660A698224D2 09CF
2C700C7206C701207FFC0F79068F0AA10483058D0120002219CE0A6985243830 0912
35B12C7D0C72066C04A00959002C2B2C07560AB00F79095900080ACF093A001A 0747
2B2C0756095900040ACF2B22079E2BC60BC1095900040AEA0A698221A42C9C0C 088A
```

```
7206C72B40075609590036 2B552B40075604542B550A3A062E075604B5095900 06A
1806C7062E077D102C2CA4062E0B06077D06B20AA10A84012000040A02FFDA09 077
5900342B40075606C72B4C0483095900202B550454068F102C2CA4068F0B0607 06C
7D077D012000042B400897093A00080120002719CE0A69832356C62CDA0C1500 070
03835646D32D570C152D6B000000010002000300040005000600070008000900 035
0A000B000C000D000E000F0010001100120013001400150016001700180019 00 011
1D001F002000210022002400250026002700280029002A002B002C002D002E82 02E
56C62D610C152DC800000500000100000700000600000200100D000305000605 030
000000000105000301000 10C00000A000307000009000306000E050001010007 005
23
01000C01000A05000008000107000000D00000C1003051001051003071003060 0 00A
10010010060007050000100 00B050003080004080000 0F000501000D0C000506 00A
00050700060100010600050B000307000C0D843F5430D02DBF0C720E4C0F7901 04B
20002419CE0A6985312B5430D02E520C722B2C06C7075606C72E590ACF066C07 08F
7D0A6984215430D02E670C722B222B2C07560454087B2E6F192A2B37077D0A69 081
853F444953D02E830C72192A2B370756046A0BA20B700959005E04D30AA1066C 08E
0A3A062E0EB0191206C7012000FF0F79066C0120FF000483058D0959000A0120 070
0002093A000601200001 2B222B2C07560AEA0454079E2BB00BC1095900100B06 058
2B2C06C707560AEA066C077D2E8A012000010A02FFAE0A69834E44D92EA00C72 09A
0120002A198F0A6987494E56414C49C42F180C7201200025198F0A698254B12F 085
280C72105906B20A698254B22F3C0C72105910590A698254B32F490C72058D10 091
590A698254B42F560C7210592F4E0A698254B52F630C72058D105906B20A6982 09F
54B62F700C721059066C2F4E0A698254B72F7F0C722F4E06B20A698254B82F8E 0A9
0C722F4E10590A698254B92F9B0C72105906B210590A69835431B02FA80C7207 09B
11058D2F4E0A69835431B12FB70C7210590B8F0A69833F37C62FC70C7206C706 0A2
C70120007F0F79066C0120FF800483058D0120002119CE0A698452454CAC2FD5 09C
24
0C72102C0ACF046A2FDB10590A69835431B22FF90C72066C05F3066C05F3058D 0AA
105906110611066C105930000A69835431B3300E0C721059066C105930000A69 067
835431B4302E0C72058D2F4E0A69835431B530400C7201200004058D303406B2 089
0A69835431B6304E0C7201200005058D303406B20A69835431B730620C720120 086
0008058D30140A69835431B830760C7201200006058D30140A69835431B93088 081
0C7201200008058D0711058D105930000A69835432B0309A0C7201200005058D 06A
30340A69835432B130B20C72105930000A69835432B230C40C72105910480A69 095
835432B330D20C7230D806B20A69835432B430E00C72066C06B2058D10590A69 0B5
835432B530EE0C7205F306C70120F8000576102C0B060120F8000576046A0120 092
002619CE06C7012007FF057601200100 0EF6012000200F4B0611058D2F4E0A69 06D
835430C031000C722B220454079E0A6984504E55CC31400C7231462B7F0BC10A 095
69865044495243D431500C7231462B8B0BC10A69865041445231B631610C7231 0A7
4606C72B8B0BC1066C2B970BC1058D0A69865044415441B831740C7231462BA3 0AA
0BC10A69875044415441 31B631910C7231462BB00BC10A698550415245C731A4 0B3
0C7231462BBB0BC10A698550525245C731B80C7231462BC60BC10A6985504052 0B1
45C731CA0C7231462BD10BC10A69835044D031DC0C7231462BDB0BC10A698650 0C3
25
41425245C731EE0C7231462BE70BC10A698750412B445054D231FE0C7231462B 0B9
F40BC10A6984504044D032110C7231462BFE0BC10A698550434249D432250C72 0B4
31462C090BC10A69865042414444D232360C7231462B8B0BC10A698550412B50 098
C332480C7231462C200BC10A69865041445231B1325B0C72314606C72B8B0BC1 0A1
066C2B970BC1058D0A69865052454C41C4326D0C72314606C72C380BC1066C06 09C
C72B970BC1066C2B8B0BC1058D058D0A698850494E56414C49C4328A0C720AA1 0B2
0A69823FBD32B10C720120FFFF066C2D5D06C70959007C0AA10A3A06C7062E06 0A0
C72D5D066C046A0AEA07110454079E0B3F0120002206E3068F04A00959000406 075
6C0F7909590004066C06B2012033190454075606550 93A00263157316A317D31 066
9A31AE31C031D231E431F43207321B322C323E32513263327632933 2BC04B509 0B3
59000C066C06B20AA1066C0A840982FF8C06B20A69833F56C632C20C720AA106 0A7
6C2D67045406C70B2207562D5D0F4B066C07562D5D0F4B068F046A068F045406 073
6C0A3A2DC4062E045432C70959000E06B2062E2D5D0EF60ACF0A842D5D0A02FF 090
E40A698441534DAC33550C720B3F0120006006E3068F04A00959000 4066C0F79 08B
09590004066C06B2012033D6045407560655093A00642F322F412F4E2F5B2F5B 06D
30D830342F932F7510592F932F842F932F412FBD2F412FBD2FCD2F6830462FAD 0B0
26
2FCD2F412FBD2F4E2F4130543068308E307C30B830A02F7530CA2FCD30E630E6 0C4
31062FAD2F9330F430F430462FBD2FCD2FCD2FAD2FAD2F1E2B610A6983314DC9 0C4
33A30C721E9F06C710590AA10A3A105910590982FFFA0C9805F32EA80AA10611 0AC
```

```
6C70ACF066C079E0ABF0F4B068F04540A3A062E0AEA079E335B0BA209590010 088B
66C06B2062E0B22079E066C0A840120FFFE0A02FFDE33AA0A6981A32B590C72 0AAD
EA82BB02E8A0A69834143C3349A0C1500E081C234A80C1500F0835053D734B2 0C88
C1500D08250B034BA0C1500808250B134C40C1500908250B234CD0C1500A082 0AF6
0B334D60C1500B08454434FCE34DF0C15008884544D4FC434E80C1500898554 0BA9
2434FCE34F30C1500C88453434FCE34FE0C1500988249D0350A0C1500B88249 0B42
535150C1500A88450434FCE351E0C15008784534255C635270C15009983544C 0974
035320C15008A835448B0353D0C15008C83544CB135470C15008B835448B135 09B1
10C15008D83544CB2355B0C1500CC835448B235650C1500CD865243415032CC 0A54
56F0C1500CA865243415032C835790C1500CB834450C835860C150083834450 0A24
C35930C1500828252B0359D0C722EA80AA12BC62E8A0A698252B135A70C722E 0BB5
80AB02BC62E8A0A698252B235B80C722EA80ABF2BC62E8A0A698252B335C90C 0CBB
22EA80E4C2BC62E8A0A698252B435DA0C722EA8012000042BC62E8A0A698252 0ABE
7
535EB0C722EA8012000052BC62E8A0A698252B635FE0C722EA8012000062BC6 0A94
E8A0A698252B736110C722EA8012000072BC62E8A0A69834052B036240C722E 0960
80AA12BD12E8A0A69834052B136370C722EA80AB02BD12E8A0A6984445054D2 0C20
6490C722EA80AA12BDB2E8A0A698540445054D2365B0C722EA80AA12BFE2E8A 0B9F
A6981C1366E0C722EA80AA12BBB2E8A0A6981C336820C722EA80AA12C092E8A 0B51
A698540412B50C336920C722EA80AA12C202E8A0A698241C236A20C722EA80A 0AB0
12BE72E8A0A698740412B445054D236B60C722EA80AA12BF42E8A0A69854143 0C09
14CCC36C70CA43458011140834144C436DD0CA4345804240E26382514281084 0988
14444C336EC0CA4345804340E36383514381084414A4DD036FF0CA434580101 09CE
083414ECC37130CA4345807824453165242540E56385514581084414E4CAF37 0974
10CA4345801B04484434A4EC5373A0CA4345801B03483434CD237480CA43458 0AA7
3C230C332E402834350CC37560CA4345803B230B332F4028244C137670CA434 0C44
801D402834445C337780CA43458041606150418081402834449D637840CA434 08DD
801841E84444A4EDA37970CA4345801D03683494EC337A40CA4345805A32C06 0B14
605040808040282 4AC237B20CA4345801200C834A42C337C70CA4345801100C 082E
24AC337D30CA4345801403A834A4DD037E00CA4345801731A834A4EC237EC0C 0C27
8
4345801300C834A4EC337F90CA4345801503A834A4EDA38060CA4345801703A 0A5C
24ADA38130CA4345801603A854C43414CCC38200CA4345801120A844C4A4DD0 0A1D
82C0CA4345801020A834D4FD6383B0CA4345812903E9252A244761CA62EF648 0A9F
51686268524884AF5427820A84CF846740EE638E514E810844D4F56C338490C 0D0A
4345802832293 2A844D4F56D838780CA4345804F04EF248E03CE238834D55CC 0D71
8880CA4345801A41E834E4FD0389C0CA43458010012834F52CC38A90CA43458 0ADF
772444316424244 0E463845144810844F524CAF38B60CA4345801A04483504F 096C
038CF0CA4345801D00484505553C838DD0CA4345801C004835245D438EA0CA4 0D02
45801221284524554C938F80CA43458013212825 2CC39050CA4345801230283 096D
24CC339130CA43458013302825 2D2391F0CA43458010302835252C3392C0CA4 095E
4580113028453455 4C239380CA4345802D332D23084534A4DD039450CA43458 0A82
1803A84535542C239550CA4345804940E96389514981084535741D039630CA4 0B05
45801C402835843C839770CA4345803C638C514C81084584348C439850CA434 0BA4
801D638835852CC39960CA43458066316624264 0E663865146810823 0BD39A4 0ADB
C15007083303CBE39BB0C1500608543415252D939C40C150050874E4F434152 09A1
2D939CE0C150040834249D439DA0C72012000301059 0A69854E4F4249D439E8 0AD5
9
C72012000201059 0A698249C639F80C721059102C01200000105906C70ACF01 07B1
07FFE2B610A6984454C53C53A0A0C7201207FFE1A55012000801059102C0AA1 0989
05907110711102C066C046A2FDB066C087B06C70ACF01207FFE2B610A698454 08CF
845CE3A270C7201207FFE1A55102C066C046A2FDB066C087B2B610A69854245 096D
749CE3A5E0C72102C01207FFF2B610A6985554E5449CC3A7D0C72066C01207F 0A26
F1A551059102C0ACF046A2FDB10592B610A69855748494CC53A910C72066C01 0A06
07FFF1A551059102C012000001059 01207FFD2B610A69865245504541D43AB3 098C
C7201207FFD1A55012000801059066C102C0ACF046A2FDB105906C7102C0AEA 08F9
66C046A2FDB066C087B2B610A6986424547494EA43AD70C720AA12B40077D0A 09A0
984454E44A43B0E0C722B400756095900222B552B40075604542B550A3A062E 0713
75604A00120002819CE012000040A02FFEE0A6981A43B210C7205F32EA80611 08A6
C8206C72B400756095900 2E2B552B40075604542B550A3A06C7062E07560BC1 0761
959000E0B8F062E0B0607560AA10A84012000040A02FFE20959000A102C066C 0611
4D32CDF2C382E8A0A698224BA3B540C722C822B400756095900582B552B4007 0900
604542B550A3A06C7062E0756068F068F0BC10120002319CE04D30BC1095900 07F6
A062E06C70AA1066C077D0B06075606C72C7504D306C70B700959000E012000 0758
```

```
30
04046A066C0ACF087B012000040A02FFB82CDF2B610A69835830CC3BAA0C7201 096D
2000210A69835830C83C170C72012000200A69835831CC3C250C72012000230A 0711
69835831C83C330C72012000220A69835832CC3C410C72012000250A69835832 087A
C83C4F0C72012000240A69835833CC3C5D0C72012000270A69835833C83C6B0C 08BE
72012000260A69864745545350AC3C790C72012000CA0120001210591048OA69 0766
87534156455350AC3C870C72012000CF0120001210591048OA69864745545250 08A5
AC3CA00C72012000BD0120001210591048OA69875341564552 50AC3CBA0C7201 08C4
2000C20120001210591048OA69864745544950AC3CD30C72012000D701200012 07AC
1059104 80A69875341564549 50AC3CED0C72012000DC0120001210591048OA69 083A
854E455854AC3D060C72012000FC0120000210591048OA6987413050555348AC 0889
3D200C72012000E20120000210591048OA69864150555348AC3D380C72012000 06FC
F10120000210591048OA69862D44505452AC3D520C720120008B012000121059 0736
10480A69864745545830AC3D6B0C72012000960120001210591048OA69864745 07BE
545831AC3D840C72012000A20120001210591048OA69864745545832AC3D9D0C 0874
72012000AB0120001210591048OA69864745545833AC3DB60C72012000B40120 07A9
0012105910480A69C8454E442D434F44C53DCF0C723B281A111A681FD70D480A 089C
31
69C4434F44C52AF30C721A1119FF1C922AFF2B613B170A69C53B434F44C53E01 0BA8
0C721A681FED20421E262AFF2B613B170A69C6454449544FD23E180CA40D3680 0A02
3E2B0586434C52454FD380020C720120001B134E01200059134E0A6986434C52 078E
454FCC3E430C720120001B134E01200054134E0A69834355D23E5C0C45804289 0868
4552415345464C41C73E750C15000584484F4DC53E7F0C15000288555043555 2 0907
534FD23E8F0C15001584554E44CF3E9A0C15001A8B52494748544355552534FD2 0A2E
3EA90C15001284504744CE3EB40C15000E8A444F574E435552534FD23EC60C15 09AD
000484504755D03ED10C1500108A4C454654435552534FD23EE20C15000C8845 09B1
584954464C41C73EED0C15001B874E45574C494EC53EFE0C15000D88484F5249 0A33
5A5441C23F0D0C150009894241434B53504143C53F1B0C150008842E4355D23F 088E
2A0C723E7B0756012000400EE60B06066C012000040454066C25280A69842143 062D
55D23F3A0C720AA10F06012003FF0F1C3E7B077D0A69842B4355D23F5D0C723E 094D
7B075604543F640A69852B2E4355D23F760C723F7D3F410A69842B4C49CE3F89 0A4A
0C723E7B0756012000400EF60454012000400F4B3F640A6983484FCD3F990C72 085F
0AA13E7B077D3F410A698421424CCB3FB80C720DE00756168F3E7B0756045408 09B3
7B162B0AB03F910A698A454449544F522D494ED33FCA0C720AA1012000122528 0953
32
01200018134E10F20A20637572736F722075700AA1012000132528012000191 3 06E2
4E10F20C20637572736F7220646F776E0AA101200014252801200 01C134E10F2 08BF
0D20637572736F7220726967687401200018012000122528012000 1B134E0120 068C
001B134E10F20C20637572736F72206C6566740120001801200013252810F215 07E4
486F6D6520207374617274206F662073637265656E0120001801200014252810 0857
F2155E486F6D652020726573746F7265207363726565 6E0120003001200 01225 097E
2801200011134E012000C4134E012000D9134E10F2142073746172742 06F6620 07D5
6E657874206C696E65200120003001200013252810F21944656C20206261636B 087A
737061636520616E642064656C6574650120003001200014252810F211506744 08D3
6E20206E65787420736372656 56E0AA1012000152528 10F2155067557020 2070 097E
726576696F757320736372656 56E012000180120001525280120001C134E0120 0728
00DD134E10F20A207461622072696768740120003001200015252810F2104573 087D
632020657869742065646974 6F720AA101200016252810F2125E456E64202065 0961
726173652073637265656E0A6987532E45524153C53FE90C720DE00756168F01 0B4C
200400120A25620DE0075617213FF63FBE0A6984434C48C341AD0C7225621721 0937
3FF63FBE3F410A6984454449D441D30C721E77192A0AB004830AB019CE256217 0B39
33
213FBE3FF63F4113BD3E8B068F0BC10959000A06B241B7093A01943F09068F0B 09A9
C10959001606B20AA1012000112528 3E4C135F1D35093A01763F36068F0BC109 0702
59001E06B20120FFFF3F910120002006C7134E3FD10120FFFF3F91093A01503E 0A5E
DE068F0BC10959000E06B2012000403F91093A013A0120007F068F0BC1095900 0779
0E06B20120FFFF3F91093A01220120005F068F0BC10959000E06B20120FFFF3F 0982
91093A010A3EFA068F0BC10959000E06B20120FFFF3F91093A00F43E96068F0B 0A3A
C10959000C06B23FBE3F41093A00E03EE9068F0BC10959001406B20DE007560A 0991
EA0AA10F0641DA093A00C43ECD068F0BC10959001006B20DE007560ACF41DA09 0AA9
3A00AC3EB0068F0BC10959001806B201207FFF14180756077D0DE0075641DA09 0981
3A008C3F17068F0BC10959000E06B20AB03FA03F41093A00763EA5068F0BC109 08C4
59000E06B20120FFC03F91093A00603EC2068F0BC10959000C06B20AB03F9109 098C
3A004C3F26068F0BC10959002206B23E7B0756012000080EF6012000080F4B01 064F
```

```
0000804543F643F41093A002206C7012000200483095900OC01200007134E09 049D
A000A06C706C7134E3FD106B2093AFE580A6981C53E320C7241EF0A69854558 0B0C
449B043B30C4580448654494D4552B043BD0C4580478545585449B143C90C45 0BF4
04A8654494D4552B143D60C45804D8453494ED443E20C45805084544153CB43 0CBB
4
F0C720A690053202081A043FAF6F6F6F600000000FFFF81A03DE80000206700 0D74
0000000000006E20202020202020202020202020202020202020202020202020 036E
02020202081A041E80000000003500003100003000003900005 8 0411
```

Appendix 11

Symbol Map of the Binary of the FORTH 8051 Operating System

The FORTH 8051 Operating System source code, seen in Appendix 9, was metacompiled to a binary. This binary was converted to an ASCII file and listed in Appendix 10. The symbol table of the operating system, which points to the binary, is listed in this appendix.

After you convert the ASCII list in Appendix 10 to a binary, you can use the modified DUMP program at the end of the FORTH 8051 operating system in Appendix 9 to dump the binary and check to see that the symbol table list here matches Address in the binary.

The name of the symbol is followed by its Code Field Address in hexadecimal. The type of definition is listed next. The Y or N indicates whether or not the symbol is forward referenced. The block number and line number of the symbols definition is next. The number of times the symbol appears is listed just before the vocabulary in which it appears.

The symbol table file is in WordStar nondocument form. You can use the DOS SORT utility to sort it on the various fields.

```
HOM         3FBE :    N  194  8     4 EDITOR
HORIZTAB    3F26 CONS N  193 11     1 EDITOR
LEFTCURSOR  3EFA CONS N  193  8     1 EDITOR
PGUP        3EE9 CONS N  193  7     1 EDITOR
DOWNCURSOR  3EDE CONS N  193  7     1 EDITOR
PGDN        3ECD CONS N  193  6     1 EDITOR
HOME        3E96 CONS N  193  4     1 EDITOR
EDIT        41EF :    N  198  2     1 EDITOR
EDITOR-INS  3FF6 :    N  196  2     3 EDITOR
!BLK        3FD1 :    N  194  9     2 EDITOR
!CUR        3F64 :    N  194  4     3 EDITOR
EXITFLAG    3F09 CONS N  193  9     1 EDITOR
UNDO        3EB0 CONS N  193  5     1 EDITOR
UPCURSOR    3EA5 CONS N  193  5     1 EDITOR
ERASEFLAG   3E8B CONS N  193  4     1 EDITOR
BACKSPACE   3F36 CONS N  193 12     1 EDITOR
NEWLINE     3F17 CONS N  193 10     1 EDITOR
RIGHTCURSO  3EC2 CONS N  193  6     1 EDITOR
CLHC        41DA :    N  197  6     3 EDITOR
S.ERASE     41B7 :    N  197  3     1 EDITOR
+LIN        3FA0 :    N  194  7     1 EDITOR
+.CUR       3F91 :    N  194  6     9 EDITOR
+CUR        3F7D :    N  194  5     1 EDITOR
CUR         3E7B VARI N  193  2     7 EDITOR
CLREOL      3E65 :    N  191  7     0 EDITOR
CLREOS      3E4C :    N  191  6     1 EDITOR
X3H         3C7F :    N  188  5     0 ASSEMBLE
X3L         3C71 :    N  188  5     0 ASSEMBLE
X2H         3C63 :    N  188  4     0 ASSEMBLE
X2L         3C55 :    N  188  4     0 ASSEMBLE
X1H         3C47 :    N  188  3     0 ASSEMBLE
X1L         3C39 :    N  188  3     0 ASSEMBLE
X0H         3C2B :    N  188  2     0 ASSEMBLE
X0L         3C1D :    N  188  2     0 ASSEMBLE
PINVALID    32BC :    N  172  5     1 ASSEMBLE
PRELAD      3293 :    N  172  3     1 ASSEMBLE
PADR11      3276 :    N  172  2     1 ASSEMBLE
PA+PC       3263 :    N  171 11     1 ASSEMBLE
PBADDR      3251 :    N  171 10     1 ASSEMBLE
PCBIT       323E :    N  171  9     1 ASSEMBLE
P@DP        322C :    N  171  8     1 ASSEMBLE
PA+DPTR     321B :    N  171  7     1 ASSEMBLE
PABREG      3207 :    N  171  6     1 ASSEMBLE
PDP         31F4 :    N  171  5     1 ASSEMBLE
P@REG       31E4 :    N  171  4     1 ASSEMBLE
PRREG       31D2 :    N  171  3     1 ASSEMBLE
PAREG       31C0 :    N  171  2     1 ASSEMBLE
PDATA16     31AE :    N  170 10     1 ASSEMBLE
PDATA8      319A :    N  170  9     1 ASSEMBLE
PADR16      317D :    N  170  8     1 ASSEMBLE
PDIRCT      316A :    N  170  7     1 ASSEMBLE
PNUL        3157 :    N  170  6     1 ASSEMBLE
T0@         3146 :    N  170  3    17 ASSEMBLE
T25         3106 :    N  169 10     1 ASSEMBLE
T24         30F4 :    N  169  9     2 ASSEMBLE
T23         30E6 :    N  169  8     2 ASSEMBLE
T22         30D8 :    N  169  7     2 ASSEMBLE
T21         30CA :    N  169  6     1 ASSEMBLE
T20         30B8 :    N  169  5     1 ASSEMBLE
T19         30A0 :    N  169  4     1 ASSEMBLE
T18         308E :    N  169  3     1 ASSEMBLE
T17         307C :    N  169  2     1 ASSEMBLE
```

```
T16         3068 :     N  168 10     1 ASSEMBLE
T15         3054 :     N  168  9     1 ASSEMBLE
T14         3046 :     N  168  8     2 ASSEMBLE
T13         3034 :     N  168  7     4 ASSEMBLE
T12         3014 :     N  168  5     2 ASSEMBLE
T11         2FCD :     N  167 14     5 ASSEMBLE
T10         2FBD :     N  167 13     4 ASSEMBLE
T9          2FAD :     N  167 12     4 ASSEMBLE
T8          2FA0 :     N  167 11     0 ASSEMBLE
T7          2F93 :     N  167 10     4 ASSEMBLE
T6          2F84 :     N  167  9     1 ASSEMBLE
T5          2F75 :     N  167  8     2 ASSEMBLE
T4          2F68 :     N  167  7     1 ASSEMBLE
T3          2F5B :     N  167  6     2 ASSEMBLE
T2          2F4E :     N  167  5     9 ASSEMBLE
T1          2F41 :     N  167  4     5 ASSEMBLE
$8051       2CA4 :     N  145  5     2 ASSEMBLE
$R          2C82 :     N  145  3     2 ASSEMBLE
@DP         2BFE CONS  N  144  7     2 ASSEMBLE
DPR         2BDB CONS  N  144  6     2 ASSEMBLE
@REG        2BD1 CONS  N  144  5     3 ASSEMBLE
DATA16      2BB0 CONS  N  144  4     3 ASSEMBLE
DATA8       2BA3 CONS  N  144  3     1 ASSEMBLE
DIRCT       2B8B CONS  N  144  2     5 ASSEMBLE
$A          2B55 VARI  N  143 10     9 ASSEMBLE
TOP         2B2C VARI  N  143  6     7 ASSEMBLE
TO          2B22 VARI  N  143  5     5 ASSEMBLE
PSW         34C0 CONS  N  177  3     0 ASSEMBLE
P0          34C9 CONS  N  177  3     0 ASSEMBLE
P1          34D2 CONS  N  177  4     0 ASSEMBLE
P2          34DB CONS  N  177  4     0 ASSEMBLE
P3          34E4 CONS  N  177  5     0 ASSEMBLE
TCON        34EF CONS  N  177  5     0 ASSEMBLE
TMOD        34FA CONS  N  177  6     0 ASSEMBLE
T2CON       3506 CONS  N  177  7     0 ASSEMBLE
PCON        352E CONS  N  177  9     0 ASSEMBLE
TL0         3543 CONS  N  177 10     0 ASSEMBLE
TH0         354D CONS  N  177 10     0 ASSEMBLE
TL1         3557 CONS  N  177 11     0 ASSEMBLE
TH1         3561 CONS  N  177 11     0 ASSEMBLE
TL2         356B CONS  N  177 12     0 ASSEMBLE
TH2         3575 CONS  N  177 12     0 ASSEMBLE
DPH         3599 CONS  N  177 14     0 ASSEMBLE
DPL         35A3 CONS  N  177 14     0 ASSEMBLE
@R0         363D :     N  178  7     0 ASSEMBLE
@R1         364F :     N  178  7     0 ASSEMBLE
DPTR        3662 :     N  178  9     0 ASSEMBLE
@DPTR       3676 :     N  178  9     0 ASSEMBLE
@A+PC       36AA :     N  178 11     0 ASSEMBLE
@A+DPTR     36D1 :     N  178 13     0 ASSEMBLE
DA          377D HDF   N  179 12     0 ASSEMBLE
DEC         378A HDF   N  179 13     0 ASSEMBLE
DIV         379D HDF   N  180  1     0 ASSEMBLE
DJNZ        37AB HDF   N  180  2     0 ASSEMBLE
LCALL       3834 HDF   N  180 12     0 ASSEMBLE
LJMP        3842 HDF   N  180 13     0 ASSEMBLE
POP         38E3 HDF   N  182  8     0 ASSEMBLE
PUSH        38F1 HDF   N  182  9     0 ASSEMBLE
XCH         398B HDF   N  183  7     0 ASSEMBLE
XCHD        399D HDF   N  183  8     0 ASSEMBLE
XRL         39AA HDF   N  183 10     0 ASSEMBLE
0=          39C0 CONS  N  184  2     0 ASSEMBLE
0<>         39CA CONS  N  184  2     0 ASSEMBLE
THEN        3A65 :     N  184 14     0 ASSEMBLE
```

$	3B58	:	N	187	2	0	ASSEMBLE
$:	3BAF	:	N	187	9	0	ASSEMBLE
-DPTR,	3D74	:	N	189	7	0	ASSEMBLE
APUSH,	3D5B	:	N	189	6	0	ASSEMBLE
A0PUSH,	3D42	:	N	189	5	0	ASSEMBLE
1MI	3442	:	N	176	4	0	ASSEMBLE
ASM,	33AA	:	N	175	2	1	ASSEMBLE
INVALID	2F32	:	N	167	2	1	ASSEMBLE
!TOP	2E8A	:	N	164	8	20	ASSEMBLE
1+TOP	2E6F	:	N	164	5	1	ASSEMBLE
!VF#	54FA	:	N	148	7	0	ASSEMBLE
!$	2CDF	:	N	146	3	2	ASSEMBLE
ADR11	2C2C	CONS	N	144	9	0	ASSEMBLE
A+PC	2C20	CONS	N	144	9	2	ASSEMBLE
A+DPTR	2BF4	CONS	N	144	7	2	ASSEMBLE
ABREG	2BE7	CONS	N	144	6	2	ASSEMBLE
AREG	2BBB	CONS	N	144	4	2	ASSEMBLE
ADR16	2B97	CONS	N	144	3	3	ASSEMBLE
MAX#$	2B4C	CONS	N	143	9	1	ASSEMBLE
END$	3B28	:	N	186	6	1	ASSEMBLE
ACC	34AE	CONS	N	177	2	0	ASSEMBLE
IP	351A	CONS	N	177	8	0	ASSEMBLE
IE	3523	CONS	N	177	8	0	ASSEMBLE
A	3686	:	N	178	10	0	ASSEMBLE
AB	36BB	:	N	178	13	0	ASSEMBLE
ACALL	36E5	HDF	N	179	2	0	ASSEMBLE
ADD	36F2	HDF	N	179	3	0	ASSEMBLE
ADDC	3706	HDF	N	179	4	0	ASSEMBLE
AJMP	371A	HDF	N	179	5	0	ASSEMBLE
ANL	3727	HDF	N	179	7	0	ASSEMBLE
ANL/	3741	HDF	N	179	8	0	ASSEMBLE
INC	37B8	HDF	N	180	3	0	ASSEMBLE
MOV	384F	HDF	N	181	7	0	ASSEMBLE
MOVC	387F	HDF	N	182	1	0	ASSEMBLE
MOVX	388F	HDF	N	182	2	0	ASSEMBLE
MUL	38A2	HDF	N	182	3	0	ASSEMBLE
IF	3A0F	:	N	184	8	0	ASSEMBLE
ELSE	3A2E	:	N	184	10	0	ASSEMBLE
UNTIL	3A99	:	N	185	4	0	ASSEMBLE
NEXT,	3D28	:	N	189	4	0	ASSEMBLE
REL,	3000	:	N	168	3	4	ASSEMBLE
NDY	2F1E	:	N	166	3	1	ASSEMBLE
VF	2DC4	CONS	N	149	4	1	ASSEMBLE
VF,	54D5	:	N	148	3	0	ASSEMBLE
VFS	2D67	CONS	N	147	6	2	ASSEMBLE
RELAD	2C38	CONS	N	144	10	2	ASSEMBLE
BADDR	2C15	CONS	N	144	8	0	ASSEMBLE
RREG	2BC6	CONS	N	144	5	10	ASSEMBLE
NUL	2B7F	CONS	N	144	2	1	ASSEMBLE
REVSYM	2B10	CONS	N	143	4	0	ASSEMBLE
RESET	2B61	:	N	143	13	11	ASSEMBLE
BEGIN$	3B17	:	N	186	3	2	ASSEMBLE
B	34B6	CONS	N	177	2	0	ASSEMBLE
RCAP2L	3582	CONS	N	177	13	0	ASSEMBLE
RCAP2H	358F	CONS	N	177	13	0	ASSEMBLE
R0	35AC	:	N	178	2	0	ASSEMBLE
R1	35BD	:	N	178	2	0	ASSEMBLE
R2	35CE	:	N	178	3	0	ASSEMBLE
R3	35DF	:	N	178	3	0	ASSEMBLE
R4	35F0	:	N	178	4	0	ASSEMBLE
R5	3603	:	N	178	4	0	ASSEMBLE
R6	3616	:	N	178	5	0	ASSEMBLE
R7	3629	:	N	178	5	0	ASSEMBLE
JB	37CC	HDF	N	180	4	0	ASSEMBLE

```
JBC         37D9 HDF  N  180  5      0 ASSEMBLE
JC          37E5 HDF  N  180  6      0 ASSEMBLE
JMP         37F2 HDF  N  180  7      0 ASSEMBLE
JNB         37FF HDF  N  180  8      0 ASSEMBLE
JNC         380C HDF  N  180  9      0 ASSEMBLE
JNZ         3819 HDF  N  180 10      0 ASSEMBLE
JZ          3825 HDF  N  180 11      0 ASSEMBLE
NOP         38AF HDF  N  182  4      0 ASSEMBLE
RET         38FE HDF  N  182 10      0 ASSEMBLE
RETI        390C HDF  N  182 11      0 ASSEMBLE
RL          3918 HDF  N  182 12      0 ASSEMBLE
RLC         3925 HDF  N  182 13      0 ASSEMBLE
RR          3931 HDF  N  182 14      0 ASSEMBLE
RRC         393E HDF  N  183  2      0 ASSEMBLE
NOCARRY     39E4 CONS N  184  3      0 ASSEMBLE
BIT         39EE :    N  184  5      0 ASSEMBLE
NOBIT       3A00 :    N  184  6      0 ASSEMBLE
BEGIN       3A85 :    N  185  2      0 ASSEMBLE
REPEAT      3AE0 :    N  185 10      0 ASSEMBLE
GETX3,      3DD8 :    N  189 11      0 ASSEMBLE
GETX2,      3DBF :    N  189 10      0 ASSEMBLE
GETX1,      3DA6 :    N  189  9      0 ASSEMBLE
GETX0,      3D8D :    N  189  8      0 ASSEMBLE
SAVEIP,     3D10 :    N  189  3      0 ASSEMBLE
GETIP,      3CF6 :    N  189  2      0 ASSEMBLE
SAVERP,     3CDD :    N  188 10      0 ASSEMBLE
GETRP,      3CC3 :    N  188  9      0 ASSEMBLE
SAVESP,     3CAA :    N  188  8      0 ASSEMBLE
GETSP,      3C90 :    N  188  7      0 ASSEMBLE
?VF         335B :    N  174  3      1 ASSEMBLE
?=          32C7 :    N  173  3      1 ASSEMBLE
?7F         2FDB :    N  168  2      6 ASSEMBLE
?DISP       2EA8 :    N  165  2     20 ASSEMBLE
?TOP        2E59 :    N  164  3      1 ASSEMBLE
#VF         2D5D CONS N  147  4      7 ASSEMBLE
?R          2C75 :    N  144 13      1 ASSEMBLE
?R1         2C66 :    N  144 12      1 ASSEMBLE
?R0         2C42 :    N  144 11      1 ASSEMBLE
CBIT        2C09 CONS N  144  8      2 ASSEMBLE
#$          2B40 VARI N  143  8     11 ASSEMBLE
CSP0        2B37 VARI N  143  7      3 ASSEMBLE
SCON        3511 CONS N  177  7      0 ASSEMBLE
SBUF        3539 CONS N  177  9      0 ASSEMBLE
C           3696 :    N  178 10      0 ASSEMBLE
#           349E :    N  176 11      0 ASSEMBLE
CJNE        374F HDF  N  179  9      0 ASSEMBLE
CLR         375C HDF  N  179 10      0 ASSEMBLE
CPL         376D HDF  N  179 11      0 ASSEMBLE
ORL         38BC HDF  N  182  6      0 ASSEMBLE
ORL/        38D6 HDF  N  182  7      0 ASSEMBLE
SETB        394C HDF  N  183  3      0 ASSEMBLE
SJMP        395C HDF  N  183  4      0 ASSEMBLE
SUBB        396A HDF  N  183  5      0 ASSEMBLE
SWAP        397E HDF  N  183  6      0 ASSEMBLE
CARRY       39D6 CONS N  184  3      0 ASSEMBLE
WHILE       3ABB :    N  185  7      0 ASSEMBLE
TASK        4401 :    N  200  8      0 FORTH
TIMER1      43EB VARI N  200  5      0 FORTH
TIMER0      43D2 VARI N  200  3      0 FORTH
(EMIT1)     2952 CODE Y  137  5      2 FORTH
PC-FLUSH    275A CONS N  131  6      1 FORTH
PC-EMPTYBU  274B CONS N  131  5      1 FORTH
(EXPECT1)   2637 CODE N  126  4      1 FORTH
TYPE1       260F :    N  125  5      2 FORTH
```

(TYPE1)	25C3	CODE	N	124	2	1	FORTH
TIMEOUT	25B5	VARI	N	123	2	1	FORTH
DUMP	2459	:	N	121	2	0	FORTH
@TERMINAL1	26D6	CODE	Y	129	7	2	FORTH
PINIT	2331	:	N	118	9	1	FORTH
(NUMBER)	1AA0	:	N	103	2	1	FORTH
(ABORT)	1D6D	:	Y	108	8	1	FORTH
DEPTH	192A	:	N	101	5	4	FORTH
PICK	1912	:	N	101	4	2	FORTH
TRIAD	17C5	:	N	99	11	0	FORTH
DISKERROR	1462	:	N	90	5	1	FORTH
DISK-ERROR	1433	VARI	N	89	11	12	FORTH
PREV	1418	VARI	N	89	9	8	FORTH
LIMIT	1403	CONS	N	89	7	4	FORTH
@TERMINAL	13AD	:	N	88	4	1	FORTH
(EMIT)	1323	CODE	N	83	5	1	FORTH
D.R	1260	:	N	82	2	4	FORTH
(")	110C	:	N	80	5	1	FORTH
(TYPE)	106E	CODE	N	79	2	1	FORTH
<>	BE4	CODE	N	70	8	2	FORTH
LOO1	99C	LABE	N	59	8	0	FORTH
PC!	7E0	CODE	N	53	2	0	FORTH
PC@	7B4	CODE	N	52	2	0	FORTH
(FIND)	269	CODE	N	28	2	2	FORTH
DIGIT	1FF	CODE	N	27	1	1	FORTH
(S3)	B4	LABE	N	14	4	0	FORTH
(S2)	AB	LABE	N	13	4	0	FORTH
(S1)	A2	LABE	N	12	4	0	FORTH
(S0)	96	LABE	N	11	3	0	FORTH
DTR	1	EQUA	N	4	9	0	FORTH
TSRE	40	EQUA	N	4	7	0	FORTH
THRE	20	EQUA	N	4	6	0	FORTH
DR	1	EQUA	N	4	5	0	FORTH
DISK	FFF0	EQUA	N	4	4	0	FORTH
TERMINAL	FFF0	EQUA	N	4	3	0	FORTH
HDBT	404	EQUA	N	3	2	0	FORTH
DBT	2	EQUA	N	2	13	0	FORTH
DBH	2	EQUA	N	2	12	0	FORTH
LF	A	EQUA	N	2	9	0	FORTH
DLE	10	EQUA	N	2	9	0	FORTH
X	1BCE	:	N	104	10	0	FORTH
@	756	CODE	N	51	1	142	FORTH
TIB	D7B	USER	N	74	2	2	FORTH
DP	DAA	USER	N	74	4	3	FORTH
DPL	E1D	USER	N	74	7	4	FORTH
HLD	E44	USER	N	74	9	4	FORTH
HERE	102C	:	Y	78	9	53	FORTH
,	1048	:	Y	78	11	38	FORTH
TOGGLE	246	CODE	N	27	10	4	FORTH
DECIMAL	1E77	:	Y	110	7	4	FORTH
HEX	1E89	:	N	110	8	3	FORTH
TYPE	10BB	:	N	80	2	9	FORTH
(LINE)	1806	:	N	100	2	1	FORTH
(	20DF	:	N	114	9	0	FORTH
\	2181	:	N	115	8	0	FORTH
PAD	1124	:	N	80	6	13	FORTH
HOLD	114E	:	N	80	8	2	FORTH
<#	11BD	:	N	81	5	4	FORTH
LFA	FF4	:	N	78	6	3	FORTH
TRAVERSE	1009	:	Y	78	7	2	FORTH
PFA	FCA	:	Y	78	4	4	FORTH
LATEST	1E63	:	Y	110	6	6	FORTH
0>	B70	CODE	N	68	2	5	FORTH
0<	4A0	CODE	N	41	13	13	FORTH

```
0=            4B5 CODE N   42  2    16 FORTH
<             483 CODE N   41  9    14 FORTH
D+            52A CODE N   44  2     1 FORTH
D+-           E7E :    N   76  3     2 FORTH
DABS          E91 :    N   76  4     2 FORTH
DMINUS        4F4 CODE N   43  6     2 FORTH
DROP          6B2 CODE N   48 13    71 FORTH
DUP           6C7 CODE N   49  1    96 FORTH
XOR           5A5 CODE N   45 10     8 FORTH
LIT           120 CODE N   21  2   321 FORTH
LITERAL      2009 :    Y  113  5     4 FORTH
DLITERAL     2026 :    Y  113  6     1 FORTH
0             AA1 CODE N   64  9     0 FORTH
DEFINITION   1E4E :    Y  110  5     2 FORTH
(.")         10F2 :    N   80  4    33 FORTH
(DO)          A3A CODE N   63  2    30 FORTH
LEAVE         A84 CODE N   64  2    11 FORTH
0BRANCH       959 CODE N   58  9   123 FORTH
(+LOOP)       A02 CODE N   62  1    13 FORTH
(LOOP)        982 CODE N   59  1    18 FORTH
DO           1EEA :    N  111  5     0 FORTH
THEN         1ED1 :    N  111  4     4 FORTH
LOOP         1EFD :    N  111  6     0 FORTH
D.           1283 :    N   82  4     3 FORTH
<BUILDS      1E9F :    Y  110  9     2 FORTH
DOES>         C98 :    N   72  7     2 FORTH
(;CODE)      2042 :    Y  113  8     6 FORTH
LOAD         16EE :    N   99  2     1 FORTH
THRU         1872 :    N  100  9     0 FORTH
LIST         1721 :    N   99  4     4 FORTH
EXTI1        43DE VARI N  200  4     0 FORTH
EXTI0        43C5 VARI N  200  2     0 FORTH
E            43B7 :    N  199 10     0 FORTH
EDITOR       3E3B VOCA N  191  2     0 FORTH
ENDGOSUB     2AC9 :    N  142 13     0 FORTH
EMPTY-PCBU   2A20 :    N  141 13     0 FORTH
EXPECT1      26A9 :    N  129  2     2 FORTH
-CURSOR      2576 :    N  122  5     0 FORTH
ENDCASE      242A :    N  120 12     0 FORTH
ENDOF        2402 :    N  120  9     0 FORTH
!ACE         22E1 :    N  118  3     2 FORTH
END          1F3D :    N  112  4     0 FORTH
ABORT        1D7B :    Y  109  2     2 FORTH
EXIT         1903 :    N  101  3     0 FORTH
INDEX        178F :    N   99  9     0 FORTH
INTERPRET    1CEA :    Y  107  2     2 FORTH
QUIT         1D35 :    Y  108  2     6 FORTH
-RING        14E5 CODE N   93  2     2 FORTH
ACK          2774 :    Y  131  9     2 FORTH
USE          140D VARI N   89  8     9 FORTH
ID.          12CF :    N   82  8     2 FORTH
U<            F86 :    N   77  9     3 FORTH
M/MOD         E62 :    N   76  2     1 FORTH
UP            D5F CONS N   74  1     0 FORTH
I!            85F CODE N   55  7     0 FORTH
IC!           846 CODE N   55  2     0 FORTH
I@            82C CODE N   54  5     0 FORTH
IC@           81A CODE N   54  2     0 FORTH
EXECUTE       655 CODE N   48  1     4 FORTH
I&R           630 LABE N   47 10     0 FORTH
APUSH          F1 LABE N   19  4     0 FORTH
A0PUSH         E2 LABE N   18  4     0 FORTH
-DPTR          8B LABE N    9  3     0 FORTH
UP             50 LABE N    6 13     0 FORTH
```

```
INIT-WARNI    40 LABE N     6  6     0 FORTH
INIT-USERV    38 LABE N     6  5     0 FORTH
INIT-S0     F5B6 EQUA N     3 11     0 FORTH
INIT-R0     F6B6 EQUA N     3 10     0 FORTH
US            40 EQUA N     3  6     0 FORTH
ADOT          2E EQUA N     2  8     0 FORTH
ACR            D EQUA N     2  8     0 FORTH
ABL           20 EQUA N     2  7     0 FORTH
USRVER         0 EQUA N     2  7     0 FORTH
INIT-RAM    4405 LABE Y     0  0     1 FORTH
INIT-FENCE    42 LABE N     6  7     0 FORTH
INIT-DP       44 LABE N     6  8     0 FORTH
INIT-VOC-L    46 LABE N     6  9     0 FORTH
INIT-FORTH    32 LABE N     6  3     0 FORTH
ENCLOSE      13F CODE N    22  1     1 FORTH
!            77D CODE N    51  7    90 FORTH
IN           DCC USER N    74  5    12 FORTH
ALLOT       103C :    N    78 10     5 FORTH
ERASE       1252 :    N    81 11     2 FORTH
EMPTY-BUFF  15FE :    N    96  6     2 FORTH
UPDATE      162B :    N    96  9     1 FORTH
-TRAILING   121E :    N    81  9     1 FORTH
MESSAGE     1840 :    Y   100  6     3 FORTH
ERROR       198F :    Y   102  2     4 FORTH
!CSP        19FF :    Y   102  7     3 FORTH
I            62E CODE N    47 10    35 FORTH
IMMEDIATE   20CF :    N   114  8     0 FORTH
]           1E34 :    Y   110  4     1 FORTH
-FIND       1B92 :    N   104  6     4 FORTH
-            46A CODE N    41  5    50 FORTH
-DUP         BA2 CODE N    69  6     8 FORTH
1+           ACF CODE N    65  2    37 FORTH
1-           AEA CODE N    65  9     8 FORTH
=            BC1 CODE N    70  2    54 FORTH
ABS          EB0 :    N    76  6     4 FORTH
AND          576 CODE N    45  2     9 FORTH
M*           F31 :    N    77  3     2 FORTH
M/           EBD :    N    76  7     2 FORTH
MAX          F06 :    N    76 11     5 FORTH
MIN          F1C :    N    76 12     4 FORTH
MINUS        4D3 CODE N    43  2     5 FORTH
MOD          F6D :    N    77  6     3 FORTH
U*           30F CODE N    34  1     3 FORTH
U/           370 CODE N    35  3     3 FORTH
EMIT        134E :    Y    84  5    40 FORTH
1            AB0 CODE N    64 11     0 FORTH
USER         CD8 :    N    73  2     0 FORTH
AGAIN       1F4B :    N   112  5     1 FORTH
ELSE        1F92 :    N   112  9     0 FORTH
IF          1F7B :    N   112  8     1 FORTH
UNTIL       1F29 :    N   112  3     1 FORTH
U.          12C1 :    N    82  7     1 FORTH
EXPECT      1C0F :    N   105  2     1 FORTH
QUERY       1E0E :    Y   110  2     1 FORTH
ASSEMBLER   2AFF VOCA N   143  1     2 FORTH
END-CODE    3DF3 :    N   189 13     0 FORTH
-->         176B :    N    99  7     0 FORTH
EM          FEFE EQUA N     2  5     0 FORTH
BYE         2A04 :    N   141 10     0 FORTH
BYE1        29AA :    N   141  3     2 FORTH
NAK         2764 :    N   131  8     7 FORTH
VLIST       21E2 :    N   116  2     0 FORTH
FORGET      2147 :    N   115  2     0 FORTH
"           20A5 :    N   114  6     0 FORTH
```

```
NUMBER       1AEB :      N  103  8     1 FORTH
NOT          197F :      N  101  9     0 FORTH
ROLL         1945 :      N  101  6     0 FORTH
J            18EE :      N  101  2     0 FORTH
FLUSH        1649 :      N   97  2     0 FORTH
RING         1502 CODE N   94  2     2 FORTH
RECVBUF      283A :      Y  134  2     1 FORTH
READSEC      272A CONS Y  131  3     1 FORTH
B/BUF        143F CONS N   89 12     3 FORTH
REC          1422 VARI N   89 10     5 FORTH
FIRST        13F7 CONS N   89  6     6 FORTH
B/SCR        13EB CONS N   89  5     4 FORTH
RPP           D56 CONS N   74  1     0 FORTH
2DROP         B8F CODE N   69  2     7 FORTH
2/            B59 CODE N   67  6     0 FORTH
BRAN          93C LABE N   58  4     0 FORTH
RP@           926 CODE N   58  1     1 FORTH
2!            8F9 CODE N   57 10     0 FORTH
2@            8BD CODE N   57  1     1 FORTH
2DUP          6E3 CODE N   49  5    10 FORTH
NEXT1         10A LABE N   20  7     0 FORTH
FORTHINT       81 LABE N    8  9     0 FORTH
NEXT           FC LABE Y   20  4     3 FORTH
RPP            4E LABE N    6 12     0 FORTH
RTS             2 EQUA N    4 10     0 FORTH
RTS           100 EQUA N    3  7     0 FORTH
BUF1         F6F6 EQUA N    3  4     0 FORTH
NBUF            2 EQUA N    3  3     0 FORTH
NSCR            2 EQUA N    2 15     0 FORTH
BPS           400 EQUA N    2 11     0 FORTH
FFEED           C EQUA N    2  9     0 FORTH
BSOUT           8 EQUA N    2  9     0 FORTH
BSIN            8 EQUA N    2  8     0 FORTH
BELL            7 EQUA N    2  8     0 FORTH
FIGVER          3 EQUA N    2  7     0 FORTH
FIGREL          1 EQUA N    2  7     0 FORTH
RAM-START    8000 LABE Y    0  0     2 FORTH
VARIABLE      C35 :      N   71  7     0 FORTH
VOCABULARY    D0C :      N   73  9     0 FORTH
R0            D71 USER N   74  2     0 FORTH
FENCE         DA1 USER N   74  3     1 FORTH
VOC-LINK      DB9 USER Y   74  4     2 FORTH
BLK           DC3 USER N   74  4    14 FORTH
BASE          E13 USER N   74  7    15 FORTH
FLD           E27 USER N   74  8     0 FORTH
R#            E3A USER N   74  8     0 FORTH
FILL          3DC CODE N   39  2     3 FORTH
BLANKS       120A :      N   81  8     2 FORTH
R/W          1567 :      Y   95  7     3 FORTH
BUFFER       1521 :      N   95  2     1 FORTH
BLOCK        168F :      Y   98  2     6 FORTH
RP!           5E1 CODE N   46 10     1 FORTH
>R            5F3 CODE N   47  1    36 FORTH
R>            611 CODE N   47  5    42 FORTH
R             647 CODE N   47 14    19 FORTH
NFA           FDE :      N   78  5     2 FORTH
*             F4B :      N   77  4    11 FORTH
*/MOD         F5B :      N   77  5     1 FORTH
2*            B3F CODE N   67  1     4 FORTH
2+            B06 CODE N   66  2    24 FORTH
2-            B22 CODE N   66  9     5 FORTH
>             F79 :      Y   77  8    12 FORTH
BL           11CC CONS N   81  5     7 FORTH
ROT           711 CODE N   50  1    18 FORTH
```

```
2             ABF CODE N   64 13      0 FORTH
:             C5E :    N   72  1      0 FORTH
BACK         1EAE :    N  111  2      4 FORTH
BRANCH        93A CODE N   58  4     61 FORTH
BEGIN        1EC0 :    N  111  3      0 FORTH
REPEAT       1F62 :    N  112  6      0 FORTH
FORTH         D48 VOCA N   73 14      3 FORTH
SINT         43F6 VARI N  200  6      0 FORTH
ONGOSUB      2A38 :    N  142  3      0 FORTH
?TERMINAL1   2983 CODE Y  139  6      2 FORTH
?KEY1        26EE :    N  130  3      2 FORTH
CURSOR       2595 :    N  122  6      0 FORTH
OF           23D6 :    N  120  6      0 FORTH
CASE         23C1 :    N  120  4      0 FORTH
S=           21A0 :    N  115 11      0 FORTH
WARM         2124 :    N  114 13      0 FORTH
SCREENSEND   2914 :    Y  136  3      1 FORTH
CHECKSUM     27AE CODE Y  132  3      2 FORTH
WRITESEC     2739 CONS Y  131  4      1 FORTH
SCREENRECV   28BB :    Y  135  3      1 FORTH
STX          271C CONS Y  131  2      2 FORTH
SENDBUF      27F2 :    Y  133  3      4 FORTH
SEC#         2785 :    Y  131 13      3 FORTH
SEC/BLK      13DF CONS N   89  4      2 FORTH
#BUFF        13D1 CONS N   89  3      0 FORTH
C/L           E56 CONS N   75  3      0 FORTH
SAVE_IP        DC LABE N   17  8      0 FORTH
GET_IP         D7 LABE N   17  4      0 FORTH
SAVE_SP        CF LABE N   16  8      0 FORTH
SAVE_RP        C2 LABE N   15  8      0 FORTH
GET_RP         BD LABE N   15  4      0 FORTH
GET_SP         CA LABE Y   16  4      1 FORTH
S3L            27 EQUA N   10  5      0 FORTH
S3H            26 EQUA N   10  5      0 FORTH
S2L            25 EQUA N   10  4      0 FORTH
S2H            24 EQUA N   10  4      0 FORTH
S1L            23 EQUA N   10  3      0 FORTH
S1H            22 EQUA N   10  3      0 FORTH
S0L            21 EQUA N   10  2      0 FORTH
S0H            20 EQUA N   10  2      0 FORTH
WARM1        2058 :    Y  114  2      1 FORTH
WRM1           73 LABE N    8  2      0 FORTH
COLD         234C :    Y  119  3      1 FORTH
CLD1           52 LABE N    7  2      0 FORTH
SPP            4C LABE N    6 11      0 FORTH
CPU            48 LABE N    6 10      0 FORTH
WRM            75 LABE Y    8  6      1 FORTH
CLD            54 LABE Y    7  6      1 FORTH
OUT1            4 EQUA N    4 11      0 FORTH
CTS            10 EQUA N    4  8      0 FORTH
KBBUF         400 EQUA N    2 14      0 FORTH
ORIGIN          0 LABE N    0  0      0 FORTH
S0            D68 USER N   74  2      5 FORTH
WIDTH         D87 USER N   74  3      1 FORTH
WARNING       D95 USER N   74  3      4 FORTH
OUT           DD6 USER N   74  5      8 FORTH
SCR           DE0 USER N   74  5      8 FORTH
CONTEXT       DEE USER Y   74  6      7 FORTH
CURRENT       DFC USER Y   74  6      7 FORTH
STATE         E08 USER N   74  7     10 FORTH
CSP           E31 USER N   74  8      5 FORTH
C!            87B CODE N   56  2     18 FORTH
C@            79E CODE N   51 12     24 FORTH
+!            897 CODE N   56  7     11 FORTH
```

```
C,          1059 :    N   78 12    51 FORTH
CMOVE        40C CODE N   40  2     4 FORTH
COUNT       10DF :    N   80  3     4 FORTH
SEC-READ    1479 :    N   91  3     1 FORTH
SEC-WRITE   14AB :    N   92  3     1 FORTH
SET-IO      144C :    N   90  4     1 FORTH
+BUF        15CA :    Y   96  2     2 FORTH
WORD        1B44 :    N  104  2     5 FORTH
#           117D :    N   81  2     8 FORTH
#S          11A8 :    N   81  4     1 FORTH
#>          1135 :    N   80  7     4 FORTH
SIGN        1167 :    N   80  9     1 FORTH
SHOW-ERROR  1891 :    N  100 10     1 FORTH
?ERROR      19CE :    N  102  5    22 FORTH
?COMP       19E8 :    N  102  6     5 FORTH
?EXEC       1A11 :    Y  102  8     4 FORTH
?LOADING    1A85 :    Y  102 13     1 FORTH
?STACK      1A28 :    N  102  9     4 FORTH
?CSP        1A68 :    N  102 12     3 FORTH
CFA          FBC :    Y   78  3     5 FORTH
SMUDGE      1FD7 :    Y  113  3     4 FORTH
[           1E26 :    Y  110  3     3 FORTH
CREATE      1C92 :    Y  106  2     4 FORTH
+            454 CODE N   41  2    60 FORTH
+-           E9E :    N   76  5     3 FORTH
/            EF6 :    N   76 10     8 FORTH
/MOD         EE6 :    N   76  9     3 FORTH
?TERMINAL   1381 CODE N   85  6     5 FORTH
CR          135F :    N   84  9    39 FORTH
GOTOXY      2528 :    N  122  2    16 FORTH
OR           58D CODE N   45  6    28 FORTH
OVER         68F CODE N   48  8    63 FORTH
S->D         55B CODE N   44  9     3 FORTH
SP!          5CE CODE N   46  6     3 FORTH
SP@          5BD CODE N   46  2    10 FORTH
SPACE       11D8 :    N   81  6    10 FORTH
SPACES      11E9 :    N   81  7     7 FORTH
SWAP         66C CODE N   48  4    99 FORTH
KEY         13BD :    N   88  9     3 FORTH
CLS         2562 :    N  122  4     3 FORTH
COMPILE     1FED :    Y  113  4    34 FORTH
[COMPILE]   20F5 :    N  114 10     0 FORTH
'           210B :    N  114 11     1 FORTH
3            E4C CONS N   75  2     0 FORTH
;S           A69 CODE N   63  9   306 FORTH
;           1FC0 :    N  113  2     0 FORTH
CONSTANT     C0B :    N   71  2     2 FORTH
?PAIRS      1A55 :    N  102 11    15 FORTH
+LOOP       1F13 :    N  112  2     0 FORTH
WHILE       1FB4 :    N  112 11     0 FORTH
?           1312 :    N   82 11     0 FORTH
CODE        3E08 :    N  190  6     0 FORTH
;CODE       3E20 :    N  190  9     0 FORTH
+ORIGIN      FAC :    N   78  2     0 FORTH
```

Appendix 12

8051 Cross Disassembler to Screen

This 8051 table-driven disassembler is run on the FORTH86 operating system listed in Appendix 1. The disassembler disassembles to screen only. The secondary file points to the image to be disassembled.

```
0
\ Intel 8051 microprocessor disassembler          15:13 08/21/86

Intel 8051 series microcontroller disassembler

Written by Bill Payne
Division 2311
Sandia Labs
PO Box 5800
Albuquerque, NM 87185

1
\                                                  08:42 08/21/86
FORTH DEFINITIONS DECIMAL HERE
: TASK ;
0 VARIABLE REVSYM -2 ALLOT " 08/13/86"
: CASE          ?COMP CSP @ !CSP 4 ; IMMEDIATE

: OF            4 ?PAIRS COMPILE OVER COMPILE = COMPILE
                0BRANCH HERE 0 , COMPILE DROP 5 ; IMMEDIATE

: ENDOF         5 ?PAIRS COMPILE BRANCH HERE 0 ,
                SWAP 2 [COMPILE] THEN 4 ; IMMEDIATE

: ENDCASE       4 ?PAIRS COMPILE DROP BEGIN SP@
                CSP @ = 0= WHILE 2 [COMPILE]
                THEN REPEAT CSP ! ; IMMEDIATE
-->
2
\ 8031/51/32/52 8731 opcodes                       12:31 08/13/86
DECIMAL

CLS ." Compiling 8051 series disassembler " REVSYM COUNT TYPE
-CURSOR

      0 VARIABLE NAMEWIDTH

( # opnames processed --- # opnames processed + 1 )
: OPNAME        1+ BL WORD NAMEWIDTH @ ALLOT ; -->

3
\ 8051 series opcodes                              12:31 08/13/86

0     VARIABLE #OPCODES      6 CONSTANT OPCODELENGTH
OPCODELENGTH NAMEWIDTH !     0 VARIABLE OPCODETABLE -2 ALLOT
0   OPNAME ACALL  OPNAME ADD    OPNAME ADDC    OPNAME AJMP
    OPNAME ANL    OPNAME CJNE   OPNAME CLR     OPNAME CPL
    OPNAME DA     OPNAME DEC    OPNAME DIV     OPNAME DJNZ
    OPNAME INC    OPNAME JB     OPNAME JBC     OPNAME JC
    OPNAME JMP    OPNAME JNB    OPNAME JNC     OPNAME JNZ
    OPNAME JZ     OPNAME LCALL  OPNAME LJMP    OPNAME MOV
    OPNAME MOVC   OPNAME MOVX   OPNAME MUL     OPNAME ORL
    OPNAME NOP    OPNAME POP    OPNAME PUSH    OPNAME RET
    OPNAME RETI   OPNAME RL     OPNAME RLC     OPNAME RR
    OPNAME RRC    OPNAME SETB   OPNAME SJMP    OPNAME SUBB
    OPNAME SWAP   OPNAME XCH    OPNAME XCHD    OPNAME XRL
    OPNAME resvd  DUP #OPCODES ! CR . ." opcodes " -->
4
( operand mnemonics                         WHP 09:15 12/19/84 )

      8 CONSTANT OPERANDLENGTH  OPERANDLENGTH NAMEWIDTH !
      0 VARIABLE #OPERANDS      0 VARIABLE SPECIALOPS1
```

```
      0 VARIABLE OPERANDTABLE -2 ALLOT
0    OPNAME A          OPNAME AB         OPNAME C
     OPNAME DPTR       OPNAME @DPTR      OPNAME @A+DPTR
     OPNAME @A+PC      OPNAME @R0        OPNAME @R1
     OPNAME R0         OPNAME R1         OPNAME R2
     OPNAME R3         OPNAME R4         OPNAME R5
     OPNAME R6         OPNAME R7         DUP SPECIALOPS1 !
     OPNAME DIRECT     OPNAME BIT        OPNAME #DATA8
     OPNAME #DATA16    OPNAME REL        OPNAME ADDR11
     OPNAME ADDR16     DUP #OPERANDS !
CR . ." operands " -->
5
( assembler tables                              WHP 09:15 12/19/84 )
DECIMAL

    0 VARIABLE ERROR
    0 VARIABLE BYTEVALUE
    0 VARIABLE TABLE#
    0 VARIABLE #CHECKED
    0 VARIABLE OPCODE   254 ALLOT OPCODE   256 ERASE
    0 VARIABLE OPERAND1 254 ALLOT OPERAND1 256 ERASE
    0 VARIABLE OPERAND2 254 ALLOT OPERAND2 256 ERASE
    0 VARIABLE OPERAND3 254 ALLOT OPERAND3 256 ERASE -->

6
( table of assembler tables                     WHP 09:15 12/19/84 )

    0 VARIABLE TABLE -2 ALLOT
      OPCODETABLE  , OPCODELENGTH  , #OPCODES  @ , OPCODE   ,
      OPERANDTABLE , OPERANDLENGTH , #OPERANDS @ , OPERAND1 ,
      OPERANDTABLE , OPERANDLENGTH , #OPERANDS @ , OPERAND2 ,
      OPERANDTABLE , OPERANDLENGTH , #OPERANDS @ , OPERAND3 ,

( field# --- address )
: TABLE@        2* TABLE# @ 8 * + TABLE + @ ; -->

7
\ store positions valid opcodes                        11:05 08/21/86

: OVERLAY ;

( address of counted string --- see error )
: !OPS          0 ERROR ! 0 #CHECKED !
                BEGIN DUP #CHECKED @ 1 TABLE@ * 0 TABLE@ + DUP
                  C@ 1+ S=
                  IF #CHECKED @ 1+ 3 TABLE@ BYTEVALUE C@ + C!
                    2 TABLE@ 1+ #CHECKED ! 0 ERROR !
                  ELSE 1 ERROR !
                  THEN  1 #CHECKED +! #CHECKED @ 2 TABLE@ < 0=
                UNTIL DROP ; -->

8
( process assembler forms                       WHP 09:22 12/19/84 )

( byte value --- )
: MNEOPS        BYTEVALUE C! 0 ERROR ! 0 TABLE# !
                BEGIN HERE BL WORD DUP " END" DUP C@ 1+ S= 0=
                WHILE DUP !OPS ERROR @ 0>
                  IF CR ." Couldn't find " COUNT TYPE QUIT THEN
                  0 4 GOTOXY ."          "
                  0 4 GOTOXY COUNT TYPE
                  1 TABLE# +!
                REPEAT DROP ;
```

```
CR 0 3 GOTOXY ." Loading                                   " -->

9
(  operand forms                                WHP 08:23 12/19/84 )
HEX
00   MNEOPS NOP            END      0E   MNEOPS INC   R6 END
01   MNEOPS AJMP   ADDR11 END      0F   MNEOPS INC   R7 END
02   MNEOPS LJMP   ADDR16 END
03   MNEOPS RR     A      END
04   MNEOPS INC    A      END
05   MNEOPS INC    DIRECT END
06   MNEOPS INC    @R0    END
07   MNEOPS INC    @R1    END
08   MNEOPS INC    R0     END
09   MNEOPS INC    R1     END
0A   MNEOPS INC    R2     END
0B   MNEOPS INC    R3     END
0C   MNEOPS INC    R4     END
0D   MNEOPS INC    R5     END -->
10
(  operand forms                                WHP 08:24 12/19/84 )
HEX
10   MNEOPS JBC    BIT REL END          1E   MNEOPS DEC   R5 END
11   MNEOPS ACALL  ADDR11  END          1F   MNEOPS DEC   R6 END
12   MNEOPS LCALL  ADDR16  END
13   MNEOPS RRC    A       END
14   MNEOPS DEC    A       END
15   MNEOPS DEC    DIRECT  END
16   MNEOPS DEC    @R0     END
17   MNEOPS DEC    @R1     END
18   MNEOPS DEC    R0      END
19   MNEOPS DEC    R1      END
1A   MNEOPS DEC    R2      END
1B   MNEOPS DEC    R3      END
1C   MNEOPS DEC    R4      END
1D   MNEOPS DEC    R5      END -->
11
(  operand forms                                WHP 08:24 12/19/84 )
HEX
20   MNEOPS JB    BIT REL  END       2E   MNEOPS ADD   A R6 END
21   MNEOPS AJMP  ADDR11   END       2F   MNEOPS ADD   A R7 END
22   MNEOPS RET            END
23   MNEOPS RL    A        END
24   MNEOPS ADD   A #DATA8 END
25   MNEOPS ADD   A DIRECT END
26   MNEOPS ADD   A @R0    END
27   MNEOPS ADD   A @R1    END
28   MNEOPS ADD   A R0     END
29   MNEOPS ADD   A R1     END
2A   MNEOPS ADD   A R2     END
2B   MNEOPS ADD   A R3     END
2C   MNEOPS ADD   A R4     END
2D   MNEOPS ADD   A R5     END -->
12
(  operand forms                                WHP 08:24 12/19/84 )
HEX
30   MNEOPS JNB    BIT REL  END       3E   MNEOPS ADDC   A R6 END
31   MNEOPS ACALL  ADDR11   END       3F   MNEOPS ADDC   A R7 END
32   MNEOPS RETI            END
33   MNEOPS RLC    A        END
34   MNEOPS ADDC   A #DATA8 END
35   MNEOPS ADDC   A DIRECT END
36   MNEOPS ADDC   A @R0    END
```

```
37  MNEOPS ADDC  A @R1     END
38  MNEOPS ADDC  A R0      END
39  MNEOPS ADDC  A R1      END
3A  MNEOPS ADDC  A R2      END
3B  MNEOPS ADDC  A R3      END
3C  MNEOPS ADDC  A R4      END
3D  MNEOPS ADDC  A R5      END -->
13
(  operand forms                             WHP 08:24 12/19/84 )
HEX
40  MNEOPS JC    REL            END    4E  MNEOPS ORL  A R6 END
41  MNEOPS AJMP  ADDR11         END    4F  MNEOPS ORL  A R7 END
42  MNEOPS ORL   DIRECT A       END
43  MNEOPS ORL   DIRECT #DATA8  END
44  MNEOPS ORL   A #DATA8       END
45  MNEOPS ORL   A DIRECT       END
46  MNEOPS ORL   A @R0          END
47  MNEOPS ORL   A @R1          END
48  MNEOPS ORL   A R0           END
49  MNEOPS ORL   A R1           END
4A  MNEOPS ORL   A R2           END
4B  MNEOPS ORL   A R3           END
4C  MNEOPS ORL   A R4           END
4D  MNEOPS ORL   A R5           END -->
14
(  operand forms                             WHP 08:24 12/19/84 )
HEX
50  MNEOPS JNC    REL            END   5E  MNEOPS ANL  A R6 END
51  MNEOPS ACALL  ADDR11         END   5F  MNEOPS ANL  A R7 END
52  MNEOPS ANL    DIRECT A       END
53  MNEOPS ANL    DIRECT #DATA8  END
54  MNEOPS ANL    A #DATA8       END
55  MNEOPS ANL    A DIRECT       END
56  MNEOPS ANL    A @R0          END
57  MNEOPS ANL    A @R1          END
58  MNEOPS ANL    A R0           END
59  MNEOPS ANL    A R1           END
5A  MNEOPS ANL    A R2           END
5B  MNEOPS ANL    A R3           END
5C  MNEOPS ANL    A R4           END
5D  MNEOPS ANL    A R5           END -->
15
(  operand forms                             WHP 08:24 12/19/84 )
HEX
60  MNEOPS JZ   REL            END     6E  MNEOPS XRL  A R6 END
61  MNEOPS AJMP ADDR11         END     6F  MNEOPS XRL  A R7 END
62  MNEOPS XRL  DIRECT A       END
63  MNEOPS XRL  DIRECT #DATA8  END
64  MNEOPS XRL  A #DATA8       END
65  MNEOPS XRL  A DIRECT       END
66  MNEOPS XRL  A @R0          END
67  MNEOPS XRL  A @R1          END
68  MNEOPS XRL  A R0           END
69  MNEOPS XRL  A R1           END
6A  MNEOPS XRL  A R2           END
6B  MNEOPS XRL  A R3           END
6C  MNEOPS XRL  A R4           END
6D  MNEOPS XRL  A R5           END -->
16
(  operand forms                             WHP 08:24 12/19/84 )
HEX
70  MNEOPS JNZ    REL            END 7E  MNEOPS MOV R6 #DATA8 END
71  MNEOPS ACALL  ADDR11         END 7F  MNEOPS MOV R7 #DATA8 END
72  MNEOPS ORL    C BIT          END
```

```
73  MNEOPS JMP    @A+DPTR       END
74  MNEOPS MOV   A #DATA8       END
75  MNEOPS MOV   DIRECT #DATA8 END
76  MNEOPS MOV   @R0 #DATA8     END
77  MNEOPS MOV   @R1 #DATA8     END
78  MNEOPS MOV   R0 #DATA8      END
79  MNEOPS MOV   R1 #DATA8      END
7A  MNEOPS MOV   R2 #DATA8      END
7B  MNEOPS MOV   R3 #DATA8      END
7C  MNEOPS MOV   R4 #DATA8      END
7D  MNEOPS MOV   R5 #DATA8      END -->
17
\  operand forms                                   09:56 10/17/86
HEX
80  MNEOPS SJMP  REL           END 8E  MNEOPS MOV   DIRECT R6 END
81  MNEOPS AJMP  ADDR11        END 8F  MNEOPS MOV   DIRECT R7 END
82  MNEOPS ANL   C BIT          END
83  MNEOPS MOVC  A @A+PC        END
84  MNEOPS DIV   AB             END
85  MNEOPS MOV   DIRECT DIRECT END
86  MNEOPS MOV   DIRECT @R0     END
87  MNEOPS MOV   DIRECT @R0     END
88  MNEOPS MOV   DIRECT R0      END
89  MNEOPS MOV   DIRECT R1      END
8A  MNEOPS MOV   DIRECT R2      END
8B  MNEOPS MOV   DIRECT R3      END
8C  MNEOPS MOV   DIRECT R4      END
8D  MNEOPS MOV   DIRECT R5      END -->
18
(  operand forms                              WHP 08:24 12/19/84 )
HEX
90  MNEOPS MOV    DPTR #DATA16 END     9E  MNEOPS SUBB  A R6 END
91  MNEOPS ACALL  ADDR11       END     9F  MNEOPS SUBB  A R7 END
92  MNEOPS MOV    BIT C        END
93  MNEOPS MOVC   A @A+DPTR    END
94  MNEOPS SUBB   A #DATA8     END
95  MNEOPS SUBB   A DIRECT     END
96  MNEOPS SUBB   A @R0        END
97  MNEOPS SUBB   A @R1        END
98  MNEOPS SUBB   A R0         END
99  MNEOPS SUBB   A R1         END
9A  MNEOPS SUBB   A R2         END
9B  MNEOPS SUBB   A R3         END
9C  MNEOPS SUBB   A R4         END
9D  MNEOPS SUBB   A R5         END -->
19
\  operand forms                                   08:49 08/21/86
HEX
0A0   MNEOPS ORL   C BIT       END 0AE  MNEOPS MOV   R6 DIRECT END
0A1   MNEOPS AJMP  ADDR11      END 0AF  MNEOPS MOV   R7 DIRECT END
0A2   MNEOPS MOV   C BIT       END
0A3   MNEOPS INC   DPTR        END
0A4   MNEOPS MUL   AB          END
0A5   MNEOPS resvd             END (  A5  reserved )
0A6   MNEOPS MOV   @R0 DIRECT END
0A7   MNEOPS MOV   @R1 DIRECT END
0A8   MNEOPS MOV   R0 DIRECT   END
0A9   MNEOPS MOV   R1 DIRECT   END
0AA   MNEOPS MOV   R2 DIRECT   END
0AB   MNEOPS MOV   R3 DIRECT   END
0AC   MNEOPS MOV   R4 DIRECT   END
0AD   MNEOPS MOV   R5 DIRECT   END -->
20
\  operand forms                                   08:49 08/21/86
```

```
HEX
0B0  MNEOPS ANL    C BIT   END 0BE MNEOPS CJNE  R6 #DATA8 REL END
0B1  MNEOPS ACALL ADDR11 END 0BF MNEOPS CJNE  R7 #DATA8 REL END
0B2  MNEOPS CPL    BIT             END
0B3  MNEOPS CPL    C               END
0B4  MNEOPS CJNE   A #DATA8 REL    END
0B5  MNEOPS CJNE   A DIRECT REL    END
0B6  MNEOPS CJNE   @R0 #DATA8 REL  END
0B7  MNEOPS CJNE   @R1 #DATA8 REL  END
0B8  MNEOPS CJNE   R0 #DATA8 REL   END
0B9  MNEOPS CJNE   R1 #DATA8 REL   END
0BA  MNEOPS CJNE   R2 #DATA8 REL   END
0BB  MNEOPS CJNE   R3 #DATA8 REL   END
0BC  MNEOPS CJNE   R4 #DATA8 REL   END
0BD  MNEOPS CJNE   R5 #DATA8 REL   END -->
21
\  operand forms                                  08:50 08/21/86
HEX
0C0  MNEOPS PUSH             END      0CE  MNEOPS XCH   A R6 END
0C1  MNEOPS AJMP  ADDR11     END      0CF  MNEOPS XCH   A R7 END
0C2  MNEOPS CLR   BIT        END
0C3  MNEOPS CLR   C          END
0C4  MNEOPS SWAP             END
0C5  MNEOPS XCH   A DIRECT   END
0C6  MNEOPS XCH   A @R0      END
0C7  MNEOPS XCH   A @R1      END
0C8  MNEOPS XCH   A R0       END
0C9  MNEOPS XCH   A R1       END
0CA  MNEOPS XCH   A R2       END
0CB  MNEOPS XCH   A R3       END
0CC  MNEOPS XCH   A R4       END
0CD  MNEOPS XCH   A R5       END -->
22
\  operand forms                                  08:50 08/21/86
HEX
0D0  MNEOPS POP                  END   0DE  MNEOPS DJNZ  R6 REL END
0D1  MNEOPS ACALL ADDR11         END   0DF  MNEOPS DJNZ  R7 REL END
0D2  MNEOPS SETB  BIT            END
0D3  MNEOPS SETB  C              END
0D4  MNEOPS DA    A              END
0D5  MNEOPS DJNZ  DIRECT REL     END
0D6  MNEOPS XCHD  A @R0          END
0D7  MNEOPS XCHD  A @R1          END
0D8  MNEOPS DJNZ  R0 REL         END
0D9  MNEOPS DJNZ  R1 REL         END
0DA  MNEOPS DJNZ  R2 REL         END
0DB  MNEOPS DJNZ  R3 REL         END
0DC  MNEOPS DJNZ  R4 REL         END
0DD  MNEOPS DJNZ  R5 REL         END -->
23
\  operand forms                                  08:50 08/21/86
HEX
0E0  MNEOPS MOVX  A @DPTR   END     0EE  MNEOPS MOV   A R6 END
0E1  MNEOPS AJMP  ADDR11    END     0EF  MNEOPS MOV   A R7 END
0E2  MNEOPS MOVX  A @R0     END
0E3  MNEOPS MOVX  A @R1     END
0E4  MNEOPS CLR   A         END
0E5  MNEOPS MOV   A DIRECT  END
0E6  MNEOPS MOV   A @R0     END
0E7  MNEOPS MOV   A @R1     END
0E8  MNEOPS MOV   A R0      END
0E9  MNEOPS MOV   A R1      END
0EA  MNEOPS MOV   A R2      END
0EB  MNEOPS MOV   A R3      END
```

```
0EC  MNEOPS MOV   A R4      END
0ED  MNEOPS MOV   A R5      END -->
24
\  operand forms                                        08:46 08/21/86
HEX
0F0  MNEOPS MOVX  @DPTR A   END       0FE  MNEOPS MOV  R6 A END
0F1  MNEOPS ACALL ADDR11    END       0FF  MNEOPS MOV  R7 A END
0F2  MNEOPS MOVX  @R0 A     END
0F3  MNEOPS MOVX  @R1 A     END
0F4  MNEOPS CPL   A         END
0F5  MNEOPS MOV   DIRECT A  END
0F6  MNEOPS MOV   @R0 A     END
0F7  MNEOPS MOV   @R1 A     END
0F8  MNEOPS MOV   R0 A      END
0F9  MNEOPS MOV   R1 A      END
0FA  MNEOPS MOV   R2 A      END
0FB  MNEOPS MOV   R3 A      END
0FC  MNEOPS MOV   R4 A      END
0FD  MNEOPS MOV   R5 A END FORGET OVERLAY CR ." Compiling" -->
25
\ location counter management                           08:46 08/21/86

      0 VARIABLE LOCATION
( --- address )
: DISK@           LOCATION @ 400 /MOD SBLOCK + ;

( --- byte )
: LC@             DISK@ C@ ;
( --- word )
: L@              DISK@ @ ;
( --- )
: 1+L             1 LOCATION +! ;
( --- )
: 2+L             2 LOCATION +! ; -->

26
( operand print formats                           WHP 10:49 01/16/85 )
HEX

: .2HEX           0 <# # # #> TYPE ;
: .WHICH2HEX      CASE
            E0    OF ." ACC"  ENDOF    F0   OF ." B"       ENDOF
            D0    OF ." PSW"  ENDOF    81   OF ." SP"      ENDOF
            83    OF ." DPH"  ENDOF    82   OF ." DPL"     ENDOF
            80    OF ." P0 "  ENDOF    90   OF ." P1"      ENDOF
            A0    OF ." P2"   ENDOF    B0   OF ." P3"      ENDOF
            B8    OF ." IP"   ENDOF    A8   OF ." IE"      ENDOF
            89    OF ." TMOD" ENDOF    88   OF ." T2CON"   ENDOF
            C8    OF ." TCON" ENDOF    8C   OF ." TH0"     ENDOF
            8A    OF ." TL0"  ENDOF    8D   OF ." TH1"     ENDOF
            8B    OF ." TL1"  ENDOF    CD   OF ." TH2"     ENDOF
-->
27
( operand print formats                           WHP 10:51 01/16/85 )

            CC    OF ." TL2"     ENDOF   CB   OF ." RCAP2H" ENDOF
            CA    OF ." RCAP2L"  ENDOF   98   OF ." SCON"   ENDOF
            99    OF ." SBUF"    ENDOF   97   OF ." PCON"   ENDOF
                  DUP .2HEX ENDCASE ; -->

28
( operand print formats                           WHP 17:07 01/29/85 )
HEX
```

```
: .DIRECT        LC@ .WHICH2HEX 1+L ;
: .#DATA8        LC@ 23 EMIT .2HEX 1+L ;
: .BIT           .DIRECT ;

: .4HEX          0 <# # # # # #> TYPE ;
: .ADDR16        L@ >< .4HEX 2+L ;
: .#DATA16       L@ >< 23 EMIT .4HEX 2+L ;
: .REL           LC@ >< 100 / LOCATION @ 1+ + .4HEX 1+L ;
: .ADDR11        DUP 10 / 2/  >< LC@ + .4HEX 1+L ; -->

29
\ opcode/operand print scheduler                    12:26 08/13/86
HEX

: .,             TABLE# @ 1 > IF 2C EMIT THEN ;

( first byte --- ) HEX
: .OPS           DUP 3 TABLE@ + C@ -DUP 0>
                 IF DUP SPECIALOPS1 @ > 0= TABLE# @ 0= OR
                   IF 1- 1 TABLE@ * 0 TABLE@ + COUNT ., TYPE
                   ELSE ., SPECIALOPS1 @ -  1-
                     ONGOSUB .DIRECT  .BIT     .#DATA8  .#DATA16
                             .REL     .ADDR11  .ADDR16
                     ENDGOSUB
                   THEN
                 THEN DROP ; -->

30
\ object code printer, assembler format             15:18 08/13/86
HEX

      0 VARIABLE STARTLOCATION
( --- )
: @OBJ           0400 /MOD SBLOCK + C@ ;

( byte --- )
: .OBJCODE       0D EMIT
                 STARTLOCATION @ DUP .4HEX 2 SPACES
                 LOCATION @ SWAP
                 DO I @OBJ 0 <# # # #> TYPE LOOP ;

: OP             CR 0 OUT ! 18 SPACES 1+L ;
: OP1            21 OUT @ - SPACES ; -->

31
\ disasssembler main format                         08:51 08/21/86
        4 CONSTANT #FIELDS
HEX
( start address of disassembly --- )
: DIS            CR ." Key space to proceed; esc to stop "
                 HEX LOCATION !
                 BEGIN LOCATION @ STARTLOCATION !
                   LC@ #FIELDS 0
                   DO I ONGOSUB OP OP1 ENDGOSUB
                      I TABLE# ! DUP .OPS
                   LOOP .OBJCODE DROP KEY 1B =
                 UNTIL CR ;
DECIMAL CR HERE SWAP - U. ."   bytes used by disassembler."
CR ." Type <address> DIS to disassemble an 8051 program."
CURSOR

32
\  ongosub endgosub                          \      15:02 01/27/86
```

```
( 0, 1, 2, ..., n <- n is else case --- )
: ONGOSUB       ?COMP COMPILE 2* COMPILE LIT HERE 0 ,
                COMPILE 2DUP COMPILE OVER COMPILE 0<
                COMPILE 0BRANCH HERE 0 , COMPILE SWAP
                HERE OVER - SWAP ! COMPILE >
                COMPILE 0BRANCH HERE 0 , COMPILE SWAP
                HERE OVER - SWAP ! COMPILE DROP
                COMPILE LIT HERE 0 , COMPILE + COMPILE @
                COMPILE EXECUTE COMPILE BRANCH HERE 0 , SWAP
                HERE SWAP ! HERE 6 ; IMMEDIATE

: ENDGOSUB      6 ?PAIRS HERE SWAP -  DUP 2 <
                13 ?ERROR DUP 2+ ROT ! 2- SWAP ! ; IMMEDIATE
-->
33
\ disasssembler main format                          15:12 08/13/86
        4 CONSTANT #FIELDS
HEX
( start address of disassembly --- )
: DIS           CR ." Key space to proceed; esc to stop "
                HEX LOCATION ! ( WHICHSEGMENT ) F400 SEGMENT !
                BEGIN LOCATION @ STARTLOCATION !
                  LC@ #FIELDS 0
                  DO I ONGOSUB OP OP1 ENDGOSUB
                     I TABLE# ! DUP .OPS
                  LOOP .OBJCODE DROP KEY 1B =
                UNTIL CR ;
DECIMAL CR SP@ HERE - U. ."   bytes remaining in dictionary."
CR ." Type <address> DIS to disassemble an 8051 program."
CURSOR
```

Appendix 13

The 8051 FORTH Operating System PC Terminal and Disk Emulator

The 8051 FORTH operating system listed in Appendix 9, which runs on the hardware described in Chapter 2, uses this code to communicate to the terminal and PC disk. The primary file is the disk file accessed by the 8051 FORTH system.

The code is set to use COM1. The COM constant must be changed if you switch COM ports. This code must be recompiled and saved with the SAVE code seen on screen number 3 of the system file, SYSTEM.SCR.

This code is written partially in 8086 family assembler. The assembler listed in Appendix 6 must be loaded with the FORTH86 operating system or loaded as a transient module. This procedure is explained in Chapter 4.

The FORTH word BEGINIDS (Begin—Initialize Development System) must be issued before the 8051 FORTH operating system is accessed. This code initializes the videor mode and prints the emulator's logo.

Type IDS to initialize the PC's serial interrupts and 82C50, if necessary, and log onto the 8051 FORTH operating system. Keying Ctrl A gets you back to the PC's FORTH system.

If you inadvertently key an Esc, hex 1B, or decimal 27, you need to key Ctrl Break, then IDS and key Return. Escape sequences are used in the protocol.

```
0
\ history                                             21:52 10/12/89

DISKIO was originally written by Joseph Flores.
The 8250 communcations routines, interrupt driven
SECREAD and SECWRITE, terminal emulation was written by
Bill Payne.
DISKIO was modified by Bill Payne.
Code clean up by Jerry Boutelle

1
\ setup and load ids                                  22:11 10/12/89
 DECIMAL FORTH
 ?DEF REVSYM
 #IF ' REVSYM NFA FENCE ! FORGET REVSYM
 #THEN

 ?DEF ASSEMBLER 0=
 #IF CR ." The 8086 assembler is required for loading"
     SP! QUIT
 #THEN

 FORTH DEFINITIONS
 0 VARIABLE REVSYM -2 ALLOT " 10/12/89  22:11"
  -->

2
\ define case statement                               21:54 10/12/89
?DEF CASE 0=
#IF
: CASE          ?COMP CSP @ !CSP 4 ; IMMEDIATE

: OF            4 ?PAIRS COMPILE OVER COMPILE = COMPILE
                OBRANCH HERE 0 , COMPILE DROP 5 ; IMMEDIATE

: ENDOF         5 ?PAIRS COMPILE BRANCH HERE 0 ,
                SWAP 2 [COMPILE] THEN 4 ; IMMEDIATE

: ENDCASE       4 ?PAIRS COMPILE DROP BEGIN SP@
                CSP @ = 0= WHILE 2 [COMPILE]
                THEN REPEAT CSP ! ; IMMEDIATE
#THEN
  -->
3
\ set comm port                                       21:55 10/12/89
1 CONSTANT COM1                \ symbolic name of com1:
2 CONSTANT COM2                \ symbolic name of com2:

COM1 CONSTANT COM-PORT         \ 1 for com1: or 2 for com2:

\ insure the com port is specified correctly before loading
COM-PORT COM1 =
COM-PORT COM2 = OR 0=
#IF CR  ." Invalid com port number: " COM-PORT .
   SP! QUIT
#THEN
  -->

4
\ tell user which com port will be used               21:55 10/12/89
\ ---
: COMPORT?       ." com"
```

```
                    COM-PORT COM1 =
                    IF ." 1:"
                    ELSE ." 2:"
                    THEN SPACE ;

CR ." Using com port: " COMPORT?
  -->

5
\ specify a hex number                                21:55 10/12/89
\ --- n
: H#          BASE @ >R          \ save current numeric base
              HEX                \ convert number in hex base
              BL WORD            \ get next token from input
              HERE               \ get address of token
              NUMBER DROP        \ convert token to single number
              [COMPILE] LITERAL \ compile number if required
              R> BASE ! ;        \ restore the numeric base
              IMMEDIATE
  -->

6
\ define 8250 base port address                  JFB 07:32 05/22/89

 COM-PORT COM1 =
 #IF   H# 3F8 CONSTANT COM-PORT-BASE \ com1: base port address
 #ELSE H# 2F8 CONSTANT COM-PORT-BASE \ com2: base port address
 #THEN
  -->

7
\ define symbolic 8250 register names            JFB 12:48 05/22/89

 0 COM-PORT-BASE + CONSTANT COM-DATA   \ rcv\xmit data
 0 COM-PORT-BASE + CONSTANT COM-BAUD0 \ baud rate low byte
 1 COM-PORT-BASE + CONSTANT COM-IER    \ interrupt id reg
 1 COM-PORT-BASE + CONSTANT COM-BAUD1 \ baud rate high byte
 2 COM-PORT-BASE + CONSTANT COM-IID    \ interrupt id reg
 3 COM-PORT-BASE + CONSTANT COM-LCR    \ line control reg
 4 COM-PORT-BASE + CONSTANT COM-MCR    \ modem control reg
 5 COM-PORT-BASE + CONSTANT COM-LSR    \ line status reg
 6 COM-PORT-BASE + CONSTANT COM-MSR    \ modem status reg
  -->

8
\ define symbolic 8259 registers & constants  JFB 12:45 05/22/89

 H# 20 CONSTANT PIC-CTL      \ interrupt control reg
 H# 21 CONSTANT PIC-MASK     \ interrupt mask reg

 H# 20 CONSTANT PIC-EOI-CMD \ end of interrupt command
  -->

9
\ define interrupt mask and interrupt number  JFB 07:46 05/22/89

 COM-PORT COM1 =
 #IF   H# 0EF CONSTANT COM-INT-MASK
       H#  0C CONSTANT COM-INT-NUMB
 #ELSE H# 0F7 CONSTANT COM-INT-MASK
       H#  0B CONSTANT COM-INT-NUMB
 #THEN
  -->
```

```
10
\ storage to hold the old interrupt vector    JFB 08:18 05/22/89

 0 VARIABLE OLD-INT-VEC 0 ,
  -->

11
\ convert baud rate to divisor bytes                 21:55 10/12/89
\ baud-rate --- msb lsb
 : BAUD-RATE>DIVISOR-BYTES  SP@ >R   \ save stack for check
                            DUP   110 = IF H# 17 H# 04 ROT THEN
                            DUP   150 = IF H# 00 H# 03 ROT THEN
                            DUP   300 = IF H# 80 H# 01 ROT THEN
                            DUP   600 = IF H# C0 H# 00 ROT THEN
                            DUP  1200 = IF H# 60 H# 00 ROT THEN
                            DUP  2400 = IF H# 30 H# 00 ROT THEN
                            DUP  4800 = IF H# 18 H# 00 ROT THEN
                            DUP  9600 = IF H# 0C H# 00 ROT THEN
                            DUP 19200 = IF H# 06 H# 00 ROT THEN
                            DUP 38400 = IF H# 03 H# 00 ROT THEN
                            DUP 56000 = IF H# 02 H# 00 ROT THEN
  -->

12
\ convert baud rate to divisor bytes cont.           21:55 10/12/89
                            R> SP@ - 6 <> \ check for params
                            IF CR ." Invalid baud rate: " .
                               SP! QUIT
                            ELSE DROP
                            THEN ;
  -->

13
\ validate char size                                 21:56 10/12/89
\ char-size ---
: VALIDATE-CHAR-SIZE DUP  5  =
                     OVER 6 = OR
                     OVER 7 = OR
                     OVER 8 = OR  0=
                     IF CR ." Invalid character size: " .
                        SP! QUIT
                     THEN DROP  ;
  -->

14
\ validate stop bits                                 21:56 10/12/89
\ stop-bits
: VALIDATE-STOP-BITS DUP  1 =
                     OVER 2 = OR  0=
                     IF CR ." Invalid number of stop bits: " .
                        SP! QUIT
                     THEN DROP ;
  -->

15
\ validate parity                                    21:56 10/12/89
\ parity ---
: VALIDATE-PARITY   DUP  0 =
                    OVER 1 = OR
                    OVER 2 = OR  0=
                    IF CR ." Invalid parity: " .
                       SP! QUIT
                    THEN DROP ;
  -->
```

```
16
\ configure com port                               21:56 10/12/89
\ baud-rate parity stop-bits char-size --
\ baud-rate: 110-9600, see BAUD-RATE>DIVISOR-BYTES
\ parity:    0 for none, 1 for odd or 2 for even
\ stop bits: 1 or 2
\ char size: 5, 6, 7 or 8
: CONFIG-COM-PORT   DUP VALIDATE-CHAR-SIZE
                    5 - SWAP
                    DUP VALIDATE-STOP-BITS
                    2- 0=                    \ set word length
                    IF 4  OR                 \ set stop bits
                    THEN SWAP
                    DUP VALIDATE-PARITY
  -->

17
\ configure com port cont.                         21:56 10/12/89
                         -DUP 0>
                       IF SWAP 8 OR
                          SWAP 2- 0=              \ enable parity
                          IF H# 10 OR             \ even parity
                          THEN
                      THEN SWAP BAUD-RATE>DIVISOR-BYTES
                      3 PICK H# 80 OR \ set divisor latch bit
                      COM-LCR PC!            \ set divisor latch
                      COM-BAUD1 PC!
                      COM-BAUD0 PC!          \ store baud rate
                      COM-LCR PC! ;          \ clear divisor latch
  -->

18
\ get an interrupt vector                          21:56 10/12/89
\ int-numb --- int-seg int-offset
CODE GET-INT         CX ES MOV       \ preserve ES:
                     AX POP          \ get interrupt number
                     AH # H# 35 MOV
                     H# 21 INT       \ get interrupt vector from DOS
                     ES PUSH         \ push interrupt segment
                     BX PUSH         \ push interrupt offset
                     ES CX MOV       \ restore ES:
                     NEXT, END-CODE
  -->

19
\ set an interrupt vector                          21:56 10/12/89
\ int-seg int-off int-numb ---
CODE SET-INT    AX POP          \ get interrupt number
                DX POP          \ get interrupt offset
                BX DS MOV       \ preserve DS:
                DS POP          \ get interrupt segment
                AH # H# 25 MOV
                H# 21 INT       \ have DOS install the vector
               DS BX MOV        \ restore DS:
               NEXT, END-CODE
  -->

  The interrupt routine is assumed to be in the code segment

20
\ clear the 8250                                   21:56 10/12/89
\ ---
: CLEAR-8250      7 0
```

```
                    DO COM-PORT-BASE I +
                       PC@          \ read all registers to clear
                       DROP
                    LOOP ;
  -->

21
\ disable com interrupts                                 21:56 10/12/89
\ ---
: DISABLE-COM-INTS    COM-MCR PC@  \ get the modem control reg
                      H# 0F7 AND   \ clear GPO2 to disable ints
                      COM-MCR PC!
                      0 COM-IER PC! ; \ disable all 8250 ints
  -->

22
\ enable com interrupts                                  21:56 10/12/89
\ ---
: ENABLE-COM-INTS    1 COM-IER PC! \ enable reciever interrupts
                     COM-MCR PC@   \ get the modem control reg
                     8 OR  \ set GPO2 to enable interrupts
                    COM-MCR PC! ;
  -->

23
\ unmask com ints in pic                                 21:56 10/12/89
\ ---
: UNMASK-COM-IN-PIC    PIC-MASK PC@      \ get the pic int mask
                       COM-INT-MASK AND  \ clear com mask bit
                       PIC-MASK
                       PC! ;     \ store the pic interrupt mask
  -->

24
\ mask com in pic                                        21:56 10/12/89
\ ---
: MASK-COM-IN-PIC  PIC-MASK PC@       \ get the pic int mask
                   COM-INT-MASK H# 0FF
                   XOR                \ isolate com bit in pic
                   OR                 \ set the com mask bit
                   PIC-MASK PC! ; \ store the pic interrupt mask
  -->

25
\ @status @modem @ints                                   21:56 10/12/89

\ --- 1=data ready, 2=buffer overrun,
\ 4=parity error, 8=framing error, 10=break received,
\ 20=transmitter holding register empty, 40=transmitter empty
: @STATUS       COM-LSR PC@ ;
  -->

26
\ @com !com key-com emit-com                             21:56 10/12/89

\ byte ---
: !COM          COM-DATA PC! ;

\ byte ---
: EMIT-COM      BEGIN @STATUS H# 20 AND 0> UNTIL !COM ;
  -->

27
\ set video mode                                         21:57 10/12/89
```

```
0 VARIABLE &VMODE

\ ---
: BW           0 &VMODE ! ;

\ ---
: CO           1 &VMODE ! ;

\ ---
: INIT-VMODE    ?MODE ONGOSUB BW CO BW CO CO CO CO BW CO
                      ENDGOSUB 2DROP ;
  -->

28
\ low level cursor fetch                              21:57 10/12/89
0 VARIABLE (@CURSOR) -2 ALLOT ASSEMBLER RESET
                AX &VMODE MOV                      \ video mode
                AX # 0 CMP =                       \ is it zero?
                IF DX # H# 3B4 MOV                 \ black and white
                  AL # H# 0E MOV  DX AL OUT
                  DX # H# 3B5 MOV AL DX IN         \ cursor high
                  AH AL MOV
                  DX # H# 3B4 MOV
                  AL # H# 0F MOV  DX AL OUT
                  DX # H# 3B5 MOV  AL DX IN        \ cursor low
                  RET
  -->

29
\ low level cursor fetch cont.                        21:58 10/12/89
                ELSE DX # H# 3D4 MOV               \ color
                  AL # H# 0E MOV  DX AL OUT
                  DX # H# 3D5 MOV  AL DX IN        \ cursor high
                  AH AL MOV
                  DX # H# 3D4 MOV
                  AL # H# 0F MOV  DX AL OUT
                  DX # H# 3D5 MOV  AL DX IN        \ cursor low
                  RET                            \
                THEN FORTH

\ --- cursor-position
CODE @CURSOR    (@CURSOR) CALL  AX PUSH  NEXT, END-CODE
  -->

30
\ low level cursor store                              21:58 10/12/89
\ cursor position in bx
0 VARIABLE (!CURSOR) -2 ALLOT ASSEMBLER RESET
                AX &VMODE MOV                     \ video mode
                AX # 0 CMP =                      \ is it zero?
                IF
                  DX # H# 3B4 MOV                 \ black and white
                  AL # H# 0E MOV  DX AL OUT
                  AL BH MOV
                  DX # H# 3B5 MOV DX AL OUT \ cursor high
                  DX # H# 3B4 MOV
                  AL # H# 0F MOV  DX AL OUT
                  AL BL MOV
                  DX # H# 3B5 MOV  DX AL OUT \ cursor low
                  RET
  -->
31
\ low level cursor store cont.                        21:58 10/12/89
                ELSE
```

```
              DX # H# 3D4 MOV              \ color
              AL # H# 0E MOV  DX AL OUT
              AL BH MOV
              DX # H# 3D5 MOV  DX AL OUT \ cursor high
              DX # H# 3D4 MOV
              AL # H# 0F MOV  DX AL OUT
              AL BL MOV
              DX # H# 3D5 MOV  DX AL OUT \ cursor low
              RET
            THEN FORTH
  -->

32
\ scroll up screen subroutine                          21:58 10/12/89
0 VARIABLE (SCROLLUP) -2 ALLOT ASSEMBLER RESET
            AX # H# 601 MOV  CX # 0 MOV
            DX # H# 184F MOV
            BH VIDEO MOV  H# 10 INT    \ scroll up
            RET FORTH
  -->

33
\ fast emit                                            21:58 10/12/89
\ character ---
CODE FEMIT  CX POP                  \ character
            SI PUSH  CX PUSH        \ save forth ip
            (@CURSOR) CALL          \ get cursor position
            AX # H# 07CF CMP U>     \ end of screen?
            IF (SCROLLUP) CALL      \ yes, scroll screen up
              AX # H# 0780 MOV      \ column 0 of line 25
            THEN
            AX 1 SHL                \ convert to word position

  -->

34
\ fast typet                                           21:58 10/12/89
            DI AX MOV             \ point di to video offset
            AX 1 SHR              \ cursor to byte position
            AX INC  BX AX MOV     \ increment cursor
            (!CURSOR) CALL        \ store cursor
            CX POP
            AX &VMODE MOV         \ video mode
            AX # 0 CMP =          \ is it zero?
          IF
            AX # H# B000 MOV      \ bw80
            ES AX MOV             \ point es at video buffer
            AH VIDEO MOV          \ black and white video write
            AL CL MOV             \ character/attribute in ax
            WORD STOS
  -->

35
\ fast typet                                           21:58 10/12/89
          ELSE
            AX # H# B800 MOV        \ co80 segment
            ES AX MOV               \ point es at video buffer
            AH VIDEO MOV            \ color attribute
            DX # H# 3DA MOV         \ video adapter status
            CLI                     \ interrupts off
      3 $:  AL DX IN AL # 1 AND     \ snow?
            3 $ JZ                  \ wait for snow to clear
            AL CL MOV  WORD STOS    \ write character
            STI                     \ interrupts on
```

```
              THEN
                SI POP                \ restore forth ip
                NEXT, END-CODE
  -->

36
\ determine if clear to send is active          21:59 10/12/89
\ --- 0=cts or delta cts not asserted, 1=asserted
CODE (?CTS)     DX # COM-MSR MOV
                AL DX IN
                AL # H# 11 AND 0<>
                IF AX # 1 MOV
                ELSE AX AX SUB
                THEN AX PUSH
                NEXT, END-CODE

\ --- 0=cts or delta cts not asserted, 1=asserted
: ?CTS  BEGIN (?CTS) UNTIL ;
  -->

37
\ set any bit in a com port                     21:59 10/12/89
\ bit\com port ---
CODE COMBIT     DX POP            \ select com port
                AX DX IN          \ read it
                BX POP            \ get bit
                AX BX OR          \ set bit
                DX AL OUT         \ write result
                NEXT, END-CODE
  -->

38
\ clear any bit in a com port                   21:59 10/12/89
\ bit\com port ---
CODE -COMBIT    DX POP            \ select com port
                AX DX IN          \ read it
                BX # H# 0FF MOV   \ get a mask template
                CX POP            \ get bit
                BX CX SUB         \ make the mask
                AX BX AND         \ clear bit
                DX AL OUT         \ write result
                NEXT, END-CODE
  -->

39
\ display sign on and sign off logos            22:00 10/12/89
\ ---
: LOGO      CLS ." 8051 televideo 910 terminal emulator" CR ;

\ ---
: PCLOGO    ." Forth 86" CR CR ;
  -->

40
\ set and clear request to send                 22:01 10/12/89
\ ---
: RTS       2 COM-MCR COMBIT ;
\ ---
: -RTS      2 COM-MCR -COMBIT ;
  -->

41
\ emit a char after checking clear to send      22:01 10/12/89
\ ---
```

```
: EMIT1     ?CTS EMIT-COM ;
  -->

42
\ com1 interrupt set up                                22:02 10/12/89
\ rbuf1_size must be a power of 2
  4096  CONSTANT RBUF1_SIZE
    0   VARIABLE RBUF1 RBUF1_SIZE 6 + ALLOT

\ ---
: ERBUF1          RBUF1 RBUF1_SIZE 6 + ERASE
                  RBUF1_SIZE 1- RBUF1 ! ;
ERBUF1
  -->
data structure
bytes 0-1  com1_read_buffer_size 1-
      2-3  pointer to byte to store in buffer
      4-5  pointer to byte to get from buffer
      6-rbuf1_size+6  com1 read buffer

43
\ com1 interrupt set up                                22:02 10/12/89
\ dbuf1_size must be a power of 2
  2048  CONSTANT DBUF1_SIZE
    0   VARIABLE DBUF1 DBUF1_SIZE 6 + ALLOT

\ ---
: EDBUF1          DBUF1 DBUF1_SIZE 6 + ERASE
                  DBUF1_SIZE 1- DBUF1 ! ;
EDBUF1
  -->
data structure
bytes 0-1  com1_disk_buffer_size - 1
      2-3  pointer to byte to store in buffer
      4-5  pointer to byte to get from buffer
      6-rbuf1_size+6  com1 disk buffer

44
\ com interrupt service routine                        22:02 10/12/89
0 VARIABLE RPUT1 -2 ALLOT ASSEMBLER RESET
                STI
                DI PUSH              \ save registers
                DX PUSH
                BX PUSH
                AX PUSH
                DS PUSH
                AX CS MOV            \ establish ds addressability
                DS AX MOV
                DX # COM-DATA MOV    \ com1
                AL DX IN             \ read byte from com1
                AH AL MOV            \ read byte in ah
                CLI                  \ interrupts off
  -->

45
\ com interrupt service routine cont.                  22:02 10/12/89
                DX # COM-MSR MOV
                AL DX IN              \ read modem status reg
                BL AL MOV
                BL # H# 0A AND        \ ddsr or ddcd
                1 $ JNZ               \ discard char if reset
                AL # H# 40 AND 0=
                IF BX # RBUF1 MOV     \ point to com1 read buffer
                ELSE BX # DBUF1 MOV \ point to com1 disk buffer
```

```
                THEN
                DI 2 [BX] MOV        \ put pointer in di
                6 [BX+DI] AH MOV     \ store received char
                DI INC               \ increment put pointer
                DI [BX] AND          \ mod buffer size
                2 [BX] DI MOV        \ update put pointer
  -->
46
\ com interrupt service routine cont.              22:02 10/12/89
                DI 4 [BX] SUB NOSIGN \ put - get pointer
                IF DI [BX] SUB THEN  \ add in buffer size - 1
                DI NEG
                DI # H# 10 CMP U<
                IF DX # COM-MCR MOV  \ possible buffer over run
                  AL DX IN           \ turn off guest cts
                  AL # H# OFF 02 - AND
                  DX AL OUT
                THEN
  -->

47
\ com interrupt service routine cont.              22:02 10/12/89
          1 $:  AL # PIC-EOI-CMD MOV
                PIC-CTL AL OUT        \ acknowledge interrupt
                STI
                DS POP                \ restore registers
                AX POP
                BX POP
                DX POP
                DI POP
                IRET                  \ return from interrupt
                FORTH
  -->

48
\ install the com interrupt service routine        22:03 10/12/89
\ ---
: INSTALL-COM-INT   COM-INT-NUMB GET-INT \ get current int vec
                    ?CS: ' RPUT1
                    D= NOT         \ is interrupt not installed
                    IF DISABLE-COM-INTS
                       CLEAR-8250
                       COM-INT-NUMB GET-INT
                       OLD-INT-VEC 2!    \ save the old int vec
                       ?CS: ' RPUT1
                       COM-INT-NUMB SET-INT  \ set our int svc
                       UNMASK-COM-IN-PIC
                       ENABLE-COM-INTS
                   THEN ;
  -->

49
\ remove the com interrupt service routine         22:03 10/12/89
\ ---
: REMOVE-COM-INT   COM-INT-NUMB GET-INT \ get current int vec
                   ?CS: ' RPUT1
                   D=            \ is our int vec installed ?
                   IF DISABLE-COM-INTS \ disable com ints
                      MASK-COM-IN-PIC  \ mask ints in pic
                      OLD-INT-VEC 2@   \ get the old int vec
                      COM-INT-NUMB
                      SET-INT     \ restore the int svc routine
                   THEN ;
  -->
```

```
50
\ is a char in the receive ring                        22:03 10/12/89
\ --- 0=no,1=yes
CODE ?COM1R      AX RBUF1 2+ MOV        \ put offset
                 AX RBUF1 4 + CMP =     \ get offset=put offset
                 IF AX # 0 MOV          \ yes, no character
                 ELSE AX # 01 MOV       \ no, character
                 THEN  AX PUSH          \ show result
                 NEXT, END-CODE
  -->

51
\ get a char from the receive ring                     22:04 10/12/89
\ --- character
CODE @COM1R      BX # RBUF1 6 + MOV              \ start of buffer
                 DI RBUF1 4 + MOV                \ get offset
                 AH AH SUB                       \ clear high byte
                 AL [BX+DI] MOV                  \ get character
                 AX PUSH                         \ return character
                 RBUF1 4 + WORD INC              \ increment get
                 RBUF1 4 + # RBUF1_SIZE 1- AND \ mod buf1 size
  -->

52
\ get a char from the receive ring cont.               22:04 10/12/89
                 DI RBUF1 2+ MOV            \ put pointer in di
                 DI RBUF1 4 + SUB  NOSIGN  \ put - get pointer
                 IF DI RBUF1 SUB THEN    \ add in buffer size - 1
                 DI NEG
                 DI # H# 10 CMP U>
                 IF DX # COM-MCR MOV    \ possible buffer over run
                   AL DX IN             \ turn on guest cts
                   AL # 02 OR
                   DX AL OUT
                 THEN
                 NEXT, END-CODE
  -->

53
\ is a char in the disk ring                           22:04 10/12/89
\ --- 0=no,1=yes
CODE ?COM1D      AX DBUF1 2+ MOV        \ put offset
                 AX DBUF1 4 + CMP =     \ get offset=put offset
                 IF AX # 0 MOV          \ yes, no character
                 ELSE AX # 01 MOV       \ no, character
                 THEN  AX PUSH          \ show result
                 NEXT, END-CODE
  -->

54
\ get a char from the disk ring                        22:05 10/12/89
\ --- character
CODE @COM1D      BX # DBUF1 6 + MOV       \ start of buffer
                 DI DBUF1 4 + MOV         \ get offset
                 AH AH SUB                \ clear high byte
                 AL [BX+DI] MOV           \ get character
                 AX PUSH                  \ return character
                 AX DBUF1 2+ MOV          \ put offset
                 AX DBUF1 4 + CMP <>      \ put offset=get offset?
                 IF DBUF1 4 + WORD INC    \ no, increment get
                    DBUF1 4 + # DBUF1_SIZE 1- AND \ mod buf1 size
                 THEN  NEXT, END-CODE
  -->
```

```
55
\ display blanks on the screen                        22:05 10/12/89
\ cursor\number of blanks
CODE !BLANKS     CX POP              \ character
                 1 $ JCXZ
                 DI POP              \ get cursor position
                 DI 1 SHL            \ end of screen?
                 AX &VMODE MOV       \ video mode
                 AX # 0 CMP =        \ is it zero?
               IF
                 AX # H# B000 MOV    \ bw80
                 ES AX MOV           \ point es at video buffer
                 AH VIDEO MOV        \ black and white video write
                 AL # H# 20 MOV      \ a blank
                 REP WORD STOS
  -->

56
\ display blanks on the screen cont.                  22:05 10/12/89
               ELSE
                 AX # H# B800 MOV      \ co80 segment
                 ES AX MOV             \ point es at video buffer
                 AH VIDEO MOV          \ color attribute
                 DX # H# 3DA MOV       \ video adapter status
                 CLI                   \ interrupts off
           3 $:  AL DX IN AL # 1 AND   \ snow?
                 3 $ JZ                \ wait for snow to clear
                 AL # H# 20 MOV  WORD STOS \ write character
                 STI  3 $ LOOP           \ interrupts on
               THEN
           1 $:  NEXT, END-CODE
  -->

57
\  set the cursor position                            22:05 10/12/89
\ x y ---
CODE SETCURPOS   AX POP
                 DH AL MOV
                 AX POP
                 DL AL MOV
                 BH BH SUB
                 AX # H# 0200 MOV
                 H# 10 INT
                 NEXT, END-CODE
\ 08 ---
: BACKSPACE      @CURSOR 0 80 U/ SETCURPOS EMIT ;
  -->

58
\ set and clear data terminal ready                   22:06 10/12/89
\ ---
: DTR            1 COM-MCR COMBIT ;
\ ---
: -DTR           1 COM-MCR -COMBIT ;
  -->

59
\ return to host mode                                 22:06 10/12/89
\ ---
: 8051ABORT      &VMODE @
                 IF YELLOW FOREGROUND
                 THEN CLS PCLOGO -RTS
                 ERBUF1 EDBUF1
```

```
                 REMOVE-COM-INT
                 SP! QUIT ;
\ ---
: HOST           DROP 8051ABORT ;

\ ---
: CLS1           DROP CLS ;
  -->

60
\ screen primatives                                      22:06 10/12/89
\ ---
: HOME           DROP 1 1 GOTOXY ;

\ ---
: CLREOL         @CURSOR DUP 80 MOD 80 SWAP - !BLANKS ;

\ ---
: CLREOS         @CURSOR 2000 OVER - !BLANKS ;

\ ---
: LEFTARROW      DROP 26 EMIT ;
  -->

61
\ guest escape processing                                22:06 10/12/89
\ --- key
: COM1KEY        BEGIN ?COM1R UNTIL @COM1R ;
\ 01B ---
: ESCAPE         DROP COM1KEY CASE
                 61 OF COM1KEY 33 - COM1KEY 33 -
                       SWAP GOTOXY ENDOF
                 46 OF COM1KEY 48 =
                       IF -CURSOR
                       ELSE CURSOR
                       THEN  ENDOF
                 89 OF CLREOS ENDOF
                 84 OF CLREOL ENDOF
                 27 OF 27 FEMIT ENDOF
                 CR ." Bad esc " DUP U. ENDCASE ;
  -->
62
\ initialize i/o parameters                              22:07 10/12/89
65535 VARIABLE TIMEOUT

\ program control variables
0 VARIABLE FINI
0 VARIABLE STOP

\ i/o buffer variables
0 VARIABLE RESP
0 VARIABLE SNUM
0 VARIABLE SUM
0 VARIABLE OUTB  3 ALLOT
0 VARIABLE INBUF 3 ALLOT
  -->

63
\ ack and nack guest                                     22:07 10/12/89
\ ---
: NAK            21 EMIT1 ;

\ ---
: ACK             6 EMIT1 ;
```

```
  -->

64
\ error messages                                    22:07 10/12/89
\ ---
: CNTR1        ." ERROR IN COMMAND      "   1 STOP ! CR ;

\ ---
: CNTR2        ." COMPLEMENT TEST FAILS "   1 STOP ! CR ;

\ ---
: CNTR3        ." T/O IN CMND FROM HOST "            CR ;

\ ---
: CNTR4        ." BAD STX FROM HOST     "   1 STOP ! CR ;

\ ---
: CNTR5        ." T/O IN CKSM FROM HOST "   1 STOP ! CR ;
  -->
65
\ error messages cont.                              22:07 10/12/89
\ ---
: CNTR6        ." CHECKSUM ERROR        "   1 STOP ! CR ;

\ ---
: CNTR7        ." T/O IN DATA FROM HOST "   1 STOP ! CR ;

\ ---
: CNTR8        ." NAK OR BADACK FROM GUEST" 1 STOP ! CR ;

\ ---
: CNTR9        ." ACK TIMEOUT FROM GUEST"   1 STOP ! CR ;
  -->

66
\ send chars to guest                               22:07 10/12/89
\ --- character value\1 or 0 ; no character
: ?KEY1D        RTS BEGIN ?COM1D
                UNTIL -RTS ?COM1D
                IF @COM1D 1 ELSE 0 THEN ;

\ start address\length ---
: TYPE1         -DUP  RTS
                IF OVER + SWAP DO I C@ EMIT1 LOOP -RTS
                ELSE DROP
                THEN ;
  -->

67
\ get chars from guest                              22:08 10/12/89
\ address\max # to be received --- actual # received
: EXPECT1       OVER + SWAP 0 ROT ROT
                DO ?KEY1D
                  IF I C! 1+
                  ELSE LEAVE
                  THEN
                LOOP ;
  -->

68
\ determing if guest has acked                      22:08 10/12/89
\ ---
: TESTACK       0 ?KEY1D
                IF DUP 06 =
```

```
                  IF 2DROP 1
                  ELSE CNTR8 U.
                  THEN
                ELSE CNTR9
                THEN ;
  -->

69
\ check input message buffer                    22:08 10/12/89

\ ---
: LOADBUF >< DUP OUTB 1+ ! 65535 XOR OUTB 3 + ! 2 OUTB C! ;

\ --- 1=passed,0=failed
: COMPTEST INBUF 1+ @ INBUF 3 + @ 65535 XOR =   ;
  -->

70
\ checksum a disk block                         22:08 10/12/89
\ --- checksum
CODE CHECKSUM   CX POP
                BX POP
                AX AX SUB
           1 $: AL [BX] ADD
                CARRY IF AH INC THEN
                BX INC
                1 $ LOOP
                AX PUSH
                NEXT, END-CODE
  -->

71
\ get a message from the guest                  22:09 10/12/89
\ --- 1=got right number, 0=no
: GETMESS       INBUF 5 EXPECT1 5 = ;
  -->

72
\ send a block to the guest                     22:09 10/12/89
\ ---
: SENDDATA
     BEGIN                           \ loop until finish or stop
       SNUM @ BLOCK 1024 TYPE1       \ fetch scr again and send
       TESTACK FINI !                \ test for ack message
       FINI @ STOP @ OR
     UNTIL ;
  -->

73
\ send a block to the guest                     22:09 10/12/89
\ ---
: SEND
    BEGIN                             \ loop until finish or stop
      SNUM @ BLOCK  1024 CHECKSUM     \ fetch scr and checksum
      LOADBUF OUTB 5 TYPE1            \ transmit cs to host
      TESTACK                         \ test for ack
      IF SENDDATA THEN                \ ack, then send data
      FINI @ STOP @ OR
    UNTIL ;
  -->

74
\ receive a block from the guest                22:09 10/12/89
\ ---
```

```
: RECDATA
     BEGIN SNUM @ BLOCK 1024 EXPECT1 1024 =
       IF SNUM @ BLOCK 1024 CHECKSUM INBUF 1+ @ >< =
         IF ACK 1 FINI !                    \ finish receiving data
         UPDATE                             \ update block
         ELSE CNTR6
         THEN
       ELSE CNTR7
       THEN FINI @ STOP @ OR UNTIL ;
  -->

75
\ receive a block from the guest                          22:09 10/12/89
\ ---
: RECV
    BEGIN GETMESS                   \ get the message
      IF COMPTEST ACK               \ complement test
        IF RECDATA                  \ passed, ack & receive data
        ELSE CNTR4                  \ bad components
        THEN
      ELSE CNTR5                    \ mess t/o
      THEN FINI @ STOP @ OR
    UNTIL ;
  -->

76
\ disk block primatives                                   22:10 10/12/89
\ ---
: FLSH          FLUSH ;                 \ flush all screens

\ ---
: EMPTY         EMPTY-BUFFERS ;         \ empty all screens

\ ---
: CLEAR-END-MARKS 0 FINI ! 0 STOP ! ;
  -->

77
\ do disk functions                                       22:10 10/12/89
\ ---
: DO-DISK-FUNCTION   INBUF C@
                     CASE 83 OF RECV   ENDOF
                     82 OF SEND        ENDOF
                     70 OF FLSH        ENDOF
                     69 OF EMPTY       ENDOF
                            CNTR1      ENDCASE ;
  -->

78
\ disk i/o                                                22:10 10/12/89
\ --- command
: DISKIO        RTS GETMESS ACK -RTS
                IF INBUF 1+ @ >< SNUM ! COMPTEST
                   IF DO-DISK-FUNCTION
                   ELSE CNTR2
                  THEN  RTS
               ELSE CNTR3 EDBUF1
               THEN STOP @
               IF 8051ABORT
               THEN ;
  -->

79
\ filter keys from the host                               22:10 10/12/89
```

```
\ key ---  filtered-key
: FILTERKEY      DUP H# 0FF >
                 IF CASE
                    H# 0175    OF H# 05 ENDOF      \ ^end
                    H# 0148    OF H# 15 ENDOF      \ up arrow
                    H# 014D    OF H# 12 ENDOF      \ right arrow
                    H# 0150    OF H# 04 ENDOF      \ down arrow
                    H# 014B    OF H# 0C ENDOF      \ left arrow
                    H# 0149    OF H# 10 ENDOF      \ page up
                    H# 0151    OF H# 0E ENDOF      \ page down
                    H# 0177    OF H# 1A ENDOF      \ undo
                    H# 0147    OF H# 02 ENDOF      \ home
                    0 SWAP ENDCASE
                 THEN ;
  -->
80
\ main loop                                         22:10 10/12/89
\ ---
: MAIN  BEGIN ?COM1D IF DISKIO THEN ?COM1R
          IF @COM1R DUP ONGOSUB
             DROP  DROP  DROP   DROP        DROP
             DROP  DROP  EMIT   BACKSPACE   DROP
             EMIT  DROP  DROP   EMIT        DROP
             DROP  DROP  FEMIT  DROP        DROP
             DROP  DROP  DROP   DROP,       FEMIT
             FEMIT CLS1  ESCAPE LEFTARROW   DROP
             HOME  FEMIT
             ENDGOSUB
          THEN
  -->

81
\ main loop cont.                                   22:11 10/12/89
          ?TERMINAL
          IF KEY DUP 01 =
            IF HOST THEN FILTERKEY EMIT-COM
          THEN
        AGAIN ;
  -->

82
\ ids, the top word                                 22:11 10/12/89
\ ---
: IDS            INIT-VMODE
                 &VMODE @
                 IF CYAN FOREGROUND
                 THEN LOGO CR
                 19200 0 1 8 CONFIG-COM-PORT
                 INSTALL-COM-INT
                 ERBUF1 EDBUF1
                 8 COM-MCR PC!         \ dsr on all else off
                 DTR RTS               \ dtr and rts on
                 CLEAR-END-MARKS
                 MAIN ;
  -->

83
\ beginids, the initilization word                  22:11 10/12/89
\ ---
: IDSLOGO        LOGO
                 REVSYM COUNT TYPE
                 CR ." Type IDS to run emulator"
                 CR ." Type ^A to return to Forth 86"
                 CR PCLOGO ;
```

```
\ ---
: BEGINIDS      &VMODE @
                IF YELLOW FOREGROUND
                THEN IDSLOGO ;

BEGINIDS

84
\ revision history                                  22:11 10/12/89

date            revision

10/12/89        Cleaned up the code and named the file DS4
```

Appendix 14
Nautilus 2 Metacompiler Base

The Nautilus Metacompiler requires the word defined in the screen for its compilation. The base includes 8086 family assembler CODE definitions. The 8086 family assembler given in Appendix 6 is loaded as a transient module. Joe Barnhart's transient module code is used. The transient module code listed in Chapter 5 was adapted from Barnhart's code. The Chapter 5 method uses the FORTH interpreter to save and restore data so no transient module code is retained in the dictionary.

The assembler must be called ASM86.SCR, otherwise screen 4 must be edited to reflect a name change.

```
1
\                                               07:53 10/12/89
-->

Joe Barnhart's transient module load
Bill Payne's voc-link modification

2
\                                           JFB 15:02 05/07/88
FORTH DEFINITIONS DECIMAL
0 VARIABLE LINKS 4 ALLOT    \ storage of dp, nfa, and voc-link
\ nnnn ---
: BEGIN.MOD      HERE LINKS !              \ save old dp
                 LATEST LINKS 2+ !        \ and nfa of latest word
                 VOC-LINK @ LINKS 4 + !   \ and voc-link
                 S0 @ SWAP 168 + - DP ! ; \ space for pad and
                                          \ stack

: END.MOD        LINKS @ DP !              \ restore old dp
                 LINKS 4 + @ VOC-LINK ! ; \ restore voc-link

: FORGET.MOD     LINKS 2+ @            \ nfa of "old" latest word
                 LINKS @ PFA LFA ! ;   \ lfa of most recent word
-->
3
\                                               14:51 07/16/86
-->
1.      Type nnnn BEGIN.MOD to reserve nnnn bytes for the
        transient module.

2.      Load the mode.  If you get a "stack space" error you
        didn't reserve enough space.

3.      Type END.MOD to finish the transient module.

4.      Use the module until you're through (defining CODE
        words for example).

5.      Type FORGET.MOD to reclaim the space used by the
        transient module.  Your new difinitions are retained.

4
\                                         \ JFB 12:55 01/05/89
DECIMAL 13000 BEGIN.MOD
SFILE ASM86 \ bring in the assembler
1 SLOAD
END.MOD
SECF CLOSEHANDLE
-->

5
\ QUAN                                      JFB 07:33 05/28/88
HEX
\ XXX QUAN NAME tocfa atcfa
CODE DOTO        AX POP BX DEC BX DEC [BX] AX MOV
                 NEXT, END-CODE

CODE DOAT
                 BX DEC BX DEC BX DEC BX DEC
                 BX PUSH NEXT, END-CODE

: QUAN           ( - )
```

```
                 0 CONSTANT
                 ' DOTO ,
                 ' DOAT , ;
-->

6
\ AT TO                                           JFB 07:34 05/28/88

: TO -FIND 0= 0 ?ERROR DROP 2+ STATE @
     IF , ELSE EXECUTE THEN ; IMMEDIATE

: AT -FIND 0= 0 ?ERROR DROP 4 + STATE @
     IF , ELSE EXECUTE THEN ; IMMEDIATE
-->

7
\ ASCII NIP 0!                                        13:32 07/11/86

: ASCII ( - ; ascii char follows )
        BL WORD HERE 1+ C@ [COMPILE] LITERAL ; IMMEDIATE

CODE NIP    ( value2 \ value1 - value1 )
           AX POP  BX POP  AX PUSH  NEXT, END-CODE

CODE 0!      BX POP  AX AX XOR  [BX] AX MOV
             NEXT, END-CODE
-->

8
\ 4+ 4* TRUE FALSE                                    13:32 07/11/86

CODE 4*   AX POP  AX 1 SAL   AX 1 SAL
          AX PUSH  NEXT, END-CODE

CODE 4+   ( value - value + 4 )
          AX POP AX # 4 ADD  AX PUSH  NEXT,  END-CODE

CODE TRUE AX #  1 MOV  AX PUSH  NEXT, END-CODE

CODE FALSE AX AX SUB  AX PUSH NEXT,  END-CODE
-->

9
\ 3DROP 4DROP NOT NOOP SYM.FOUND >BODY          JFB 07:08 05/07/88
CODE 3DROP   ( value to be dropped - )
            AX POP  AX POP  AX POP NEXT, END-CODE

CODE 4DROP  ( double value to be dropped - )
            AX POP  AX POP
            AX POP  AX POP
            NEXT, END-CODE
CODE NOT  AX POP  AX AX OR  AX # 1 MOV  1 $ JZ
          AX DEC  1 $:  AX PUSH  NEXT,  END-CODE
CODE NOOP NEXT,  END-CODE
QUAN SYM.FOUND
: >BODY 2+ ;
-->

10
\ !BIT @BIT                                     JFB 08:07 05/07/88
: !BITS ( value \ address \ mask - ) ROT OVER
   BEGIN DUP 1 AND 0=
   WHILE 2/ SWAP 2* SWAP \ shift value to mask
   REPEAT DROP OVER AND \ mask value
```

```
   SWAP ROT DUP >R @ SWAP
   0FFFF XOR AND \ clear (address) of mask bits
   OR R> ! ; \ place new bits
: @BITS ( address \ mask - value ) SWAP @ OVER AND SWAP
   BEGIN DUP 1 AND 0=
   WHILE 2/ SWAP 2/ 07FFF AND SWAP
   REPEAT DROP ;
-->

11
\ segment definitions                          JFB 22:12 05/23/88
QUAN SCR.SEG \ holds segment of the screen storage
QUAN TRG.SEG \ holds segemnt of the the target image
QUAN SYM.SEG \ holds segment of the symbol table
QUAN SEG \ holds either the video or screen buffer segment
\ Note: the user variable R# is used to determine if the
\ segments above are allocated. bit 0 = SCR.SEG,
\ bit 1 = TRG.SEG and bit 2 = SYM.SEG
: GOT.SCR.SEG  ( - bool )   R# 1 @BITS ;
: GOT.SCR.SEG! ( - )      1 R# 1 !BITS ;
: GOT.TRG.SEG  ( - bool )   R# 2 @BITS ;
: GOT.TRG.SEG! ( - )      1 R# 2 !BITS ;
: GOT.SYM.SEG  ( - bool )   R# 4 @BITS ;
: GOT.SYM.SEG! ( - )      1 R# 4 !BITS ;
  -->

12
\ <FIND(H>                                           07:08 10/12/89

CODE <FIND(H> ( string address \ NFA - CFA of host \ length byte
              \ true flag OR string address \ NFA - false flag )
                AX ' TRG.SEG MOV
                ES AX MOV       \ es = target segment
                AX ' SYM.SEG MOV
                DS AX MOV       \ ds = symbol segment
                AX SI MOV       \ forth ip to ax
                SI POP          \ nfa pointer
                BX POP          \ save string count address
                AX PUSH         \ save forth ip
           1 $: DL [SI] MOV     \ save nfa count
                DI BX MOV       \ di points to string count
-->

13
\ <FIND(H> cont.                               \ JFB16:48 03/10/86

                BYTE LODS       \ nfa count byte to al
                AL # 3F AND     \ leave only smudge and count
                BYTE SCAS       \ compare to string count
                4 $ JNZ         \ <> jump
                AX # 1F AND     \ leave count byte in ax
                AX DEC          \ only search n-1 bytes
                CX AX MOV       \ cx is the scan count
                2 $ JCXZ        \ jump if count is zero
                REPE BYTE CMPS  \ are the first n-1 bytes =
                2 $ JZ          \ jump =
                SI CX ADD       \ <>, then point si to lfa
                SI INC          \ jump over last byte
                5 $ JMP         \ report <>
-->
14
\ <FIND(H> cont.                                     07:08 10/12/89

           2 $: BYTE LODS       \ last byte
```

```
                AL # 7F AND        \ nfa byte - 80
                BYTE SCAS          \ is it = last string byte?
                3 $ JZ             \ jump if =
                5 $ JMP            \ report <>
           3 $: AX POP             \ forth ip to ax & report =
                SI # 4 ADD         \ point at pfa
                CS: ' SYM.FOUND SI MOV
                SI # 2 SUB
                BX [SI] MOV        \ fetch host CFA
                BX PUSH            \ return CFA
-->

15
\ <FIND(H> cont.                                    13:38 07/11/86

                SI AX MOV          \ forth ip to si
                DX # 040 AND
                DX PUSH            \ return presidence bit
                AX # 01 MOV        \ set true flag
                AX PUSH            \ return true flag
                AX CS MOV
                DS AX MOV          \ restore data seg
                NEXT,
           4 $: AX # 1F AND       \ leave count
                SI AX ADD         \ move to lfa & report <>
-->

16
\ <FIND(H> cont.                                    09:46 07/16/86

           5 $: SI [SI] MOV        \ move from lfa to nfa
                SI # 0 CMP         \ compare lfa to zero
                1 $ JNE            \ jump if lfa <> 0, try again
                SI POP             \ restore forth ip
                AX AX SUB          \ false flag
                CS: ' SYM.FOUND AX MOV \ clear SYM.FOUND
                AX PUSH            \ return false flag
                AX CS MOV
                DS AX MOV          \ restore data seg
                NEXT, END-CODE
-->

17
\ ENCLOSEx                                          09:46 07/16/86
VOCABULARY WORDSx IMMEDIATE WORDSx DEFINITIONS
CODE ENCLOSEx   CLD
                AX ' TRG.SEG MOV
                ES AX MOV              \ es = target segment
                DS AX MOV              \ ds = target segment
                AX POP                 \ delimiter
                DI POP                 \ start address of string
                DI PUSH                \ start address of string
                AH AH SUB              \ null in ah
                CX # -1 MOV            \ maximum repeat count
                REPE BYTE SCAS         \ look for 1st nondelimiter
                DX # -2 MOV            \ start to calc offset
                DX CX SUB              \ offset to 1st nondelimite
                DX PUSH                \ offset of string start
-->
18
\ ENCLOSEx cont.                                    13:39 07/11/86

                AH -1 [DI] CMP         \ is it a null?
                1 $ JNZ           \ jump if it is not
```

```
                AX DX MOV          \ offset of unexamined character
                AX INC AX PUSH     \ push offset of null
                DX PUSH
                AX CS MOV
                DS AX MOV
                NEXT,
           1 $: SI DI XCHG         \ save forth ip
                BX AX MOV          \ null and delimiter to bx
           2 $: BYTE LODS          \ character to examine
                AL BL CMP          \ is it a delimiter?
                3 $ JZ             \ jump if it is
-->
19
\ ENCLOSEx cont.                                      13:34 07/11/86

                AL BH CMP          \ is it a null?
                2 $ LOOPNZ         \ jump if it is not
                DX # -2 MOV
                DX CX SUB          \ offset to null
                DX PUSH
                DX PUSH
                SI DI XCHG         \ restore forth ip
                AX CS MOV
                DS AX MOV
                NEXT,
-->

20
\ ENCLOSEx cont.                                      13:34 07/11/86

           3 $: DX # -1 MOV
                DX CX SUB      \ offset to delimiter
                DX PUSH
                DX INC         \ offset of unexamined charater
                DX PUSH
                SI DI XCHG     \ restore forth ip
                AX CS MOV
                DS AX MOV
                NEXT,
                END-CODE
FORTH DEFINITIONS
-->

21
\ DUMPL.HEAD DUMPL.LINE                               13:42 07/11/86
0 CONSTANT DUMPSEG
: DUMPL.HEAD ( address - )
            CR DUP 0B SPACES 10 0
            DO DUP 0F AND 1 .R 2 SPACES 1+ LOOP
            DROP SPACE 10 0
            DO DUP 0F AND 1 .R 1+ LOOP DROP ;

: DUMPL.LINE ( address - )
              DUMPSEG 0 4 D.R ." :"
              DUP 0 4 D.R SPACE 10 OVER + SWAP 2DUP
              DO DUMPSEG I C@L 2 .R SPACE
              LOOP SPACE ." /"
              DO DUMPSEG I C@L DUP 1A > OVER 7B < AND 0=
                 IF DROP 7F THEN EMIT
              LOOP ." /" CR ; -->
22
\ DUMPL                                               14:17 07/16/86
: DUMPL ( segment \ address \ count - )
        BASE @ >R HEX ROT ' DUMPSEG !
```

```
        OVER DUMPL.HEAD CR OVER + SWAP
        DO I DUMPL.LINE ?TERMINAL
           IF LEAVE THEN 10
        +LOOP R> BASE ! ;
  -->

23
\ XY>                                             JFB 16:40 06/04/88

\ --- X\Y
CODE XY>        AH # 3 MOV
                BH # 0 MOV
SI PUSH BP PUSH 10 INT BP POP SI POP
                AH # 0 MOV
                AL DL MOV
                AX PUSH
                AL DH MOV
                AX PUSH
                NEXT, END-CODE
  -->

24
\ ?NOMEM                                          JFB 08:34 05/01/88
: ?NOMEM ( b - ) IF CR ." Not enough memory" QUIT THEN DROP ;
  -->

25
\ Notes about use of display screen              JFB 11:17 05/30/88
-->
The display screen is written directly, and snow is ignored !
VID.SEG defines the base address for the video ram:
B800 for color text.

26
\ data storage for compiler screen               JFB 17:36 05/30/88
B800 CONSTANT VID.SEG \ segment address for color text
QUAN ?SCR \ screen switch, 0 = forth scr visible 1 = compiler
QUAN S0.OFF \ cursor position in forth screen
QUAN S1.OFF \ cursor position in compiler screen
QUAN S0.BORDER \ border color for forth screen
QUAN S1.BORDER \ border color for compiler screen
QUAN ?S0.CURSOR \ true if S0 cursor is visable
QUAN ?S1.CURSOR \ true if S1 cursor is visable
  -->

27
\ CMOVEWL FILLWL                                  JFB 11:09 05/07/88
CODE CMOVEWL ( from seg, from off, to seg to off, word count - )
  BX SI MOV CX POP DI POP AX POP ES AX MOV SI POP AX POP
  DS AX MOV CX>0 IF CLD REP WORD MOVS THEN SI BX MOV AX CS MOV
  DS AX MOV NEXT, END-CODE
CODE FILLWL ( seg, off, count, word - )
  AX POP CX POP DI POP BX POP ES BX MOV CLD REP WORD STOS NEXT,
  END-CODE
-->

28
\ Scroll S0                                       JFB 16:12 06/04/88
: ?SCROLL-S0 ( - )
   S0.OFF 7CF >
   IF SEG A0 SEG 0 780 CMOVEWL \ scroll screen
      SEG F00 50 VIDEO @ 100 * 20 + FILLWL \ clr 1st line
      780 TO S0.OFF \ cursor to last line
   THEN ;
```

```
  -->

29
\ S0 emit primatives                              JFB 16:41 06/04/88
: S0CURSOR! ( - ) S0.OFF 0 50 U/ (GOTOXY) (CURSOR) ;
: (S0-EMIT) ( char - )
   ?SCROLL-S0 SEG S0.OFF 2* C!L 1 AT S0.OFF +!
   ?S0.CURSOR ?SCR 0= AND IF S0CURSOR! THEN ;
: S0-BE-EMIT ( bell - ) (EMIT) ; \ let dos handle this one
: S0-BS-EMIT ( backspace - ) DROP S0.OFF 1- 0 MAX
  TO S0.OFF ;
: S0-LF-EMIT ( line feed - ) DROP S0.OFF 50 / 1+ 50 *
   TO S0.OFF ;
: S0-CR-EMIT ( carriage return - ) DROP S0.OFF 50 / 50 * 1+
   TO S0.OFF ;
  -->

30
\ S0 emit primatives                              JFB 16:41 06/04/88
' (S0-EMIT) CFA
0 VARIABLE S0.CONTROL.VEC -2 ALLOT
\ 0     1     2     3
  DUP , DUP , DUP , DUP ,
\ 4     5     6     7
  DUP , DUP , DUP , ' S0-BE-EMIT CFA ,
\ 8                 9     10                   11
  ' S0-BS-EMIT CFA , DUP , ' S0-LF-EMIT CFA , DUP ,
\ 12    13                      14    15
  DUP , ' S0-CR-EMIT CFA , DUP , DUP ,
\ 16    17    18    19
  DUP , DUP , DUP , DUP ,
\ 20    21    22    23
  DUP , DUP , DUP , DUP ,
  -->
31
\ S0 emit primatives                              JFB 16:41 06/04/88
\ 24    25    26    27
  DUP , DUP , DUP , DUP ,
\ 28    29    30    31
  DUP , DUP , DUP ,       ,
  -->

32
\ S0 emit                                         JFB 16:41 06/04/88
: S0-EMIT ( char - ) ?SCR IF SCR.SEG ELSE VID.SEG THEN TO SEG
   DUP 20 <
   IF DUP 2* S0.CONTROL.VEC + @ EXECUTE
   ELSE (S0-EMIT)
   THEN ;
  -->

33
\ Scroll and wrap S1                              JFB 16:42 06/04/88
: ?SCROLL-S1 ( - )
   S1.OFF 72E >
   IF SEG 640 SEG 5A0 410 CMOVEWL \ scroll screen
      SEG DC2 4E VIDEO @ 100 * 20 + FILLWL \ clr 1st line
      6E1 TO S1.OFF \ cursor to last line
   THEN ;
: ?WRAP-S1 ( - ) S1.OFF 0 50 U/ DROP 4F =
   IF 2 AT S1.OFF +! THEN ;
  -->

34
```

```
\ S1 emit primatives                                07:42 10/12/89
: (S1-EMIT) ( char - )
   ?SCROLL-S1 ?WRAP-S1 SEG S1.OFF 2* C!L 1 AT S1.OFF +! ;
: S1-BE-EMIT ( bell - ) (EMIT) ; \ let dos handle this one
: S1-BS-EMIT ( backspace - ) DROP S1.OFF 0 50 U/ DROP 1 =
  IF -3 ELSE -1 THEN S1.OFF + 02D1 MAX TO S1.OFF ;
: S1-LF-EMIT ( line feed - ) DROP S1.OFF 50 / 1+ 50 * 1+
   TO S1.OFF ?SCROLL-S1 ;
: S1-CR-EMIT ( carriage return - ) DROP S1.OFF 50 / 50 * 1+
   TO S1.OFF ?SCROLL-S1 ;
  -->

35
\ S1 emit primatives                            JFB 16:42 06/04/88
' (S1-EMIT) CFA
0 VARIABLE S1.CONTROL.VEC -2 ALLOT
\ 0     1     2     3
  DUP , DUP , DUP , DUP ,
\ 4     5     6     7
  DUP , DUP , DUP , ' S1-BE-EMIT CFA ,
\ 8                   9     10                  11
  ' S1-BS-EMIT CFA , DUP , ' S1-LF-EMIT CFA , DUP ,
\ 12    13                 14    15
  DUP , ' S1-CR-EMIT CFA , DUP , DUP ,
\ 16    17    18    19
  DUP , DUP , DUP , DUP ,
\ 20    21    22    23
  DUP , DUP , DUP , DUP ,
  -->
36
\ S1 emit primatives                            JFB 16:42 06/04/88
\ 24    25    26    27
  DUP , DUP , DUP , DUP ,
\ 28    29    30    31
  DUP , DUP , DUP ,     ,
  -->

37
\ S1 emit                                       JFB 16:42 06/04/88
: S1-EMIT ( char - ) ?SCR IF VID.SEG ELSE SCR.SEG THEN TO SEG
   DUP 20 <
   IF DUP 2* S1.CONTROL.VEC + @ EXECUTE
   ELSE (S1-EMIT)
   THEN ;
  -->

38
\ fast S1 ( compiler screen ) emit              JFB 09:53 05/28/88
: FAST-S1-EMIT ( char - ) ?SCR IF VID.SEG ELSE SCR.SEG THEN
   S1.OFF 2* C!L 1 AT S1.OFF +! ;
  -->

39
\ forth and compiler screens GOTOXY             JFB 17:55 05/08/88
: S0-GOTOXY ( x, y - ) 50 * + TO S0.OFF ;
: S1-GOTOXY ( x, y - ) 50 * + TO S1.OFF ;
  -->

40
\ forth and compiler screens BORDER             JFB 17:40 05/30/88
: S0-BORDER ( color - ) DUP TO S0.BORDER ?SCR
   IF DROP
   ELSE (BORDER)
   THEN ;
```

```
: S1-BORDER ( color - ) DUP TO S1.BORDER ?SCR
   IF (BORDER)
   ELSE DROP
   THEN ;
  -->

41
\ forth and compiler screens CLS                 JFB 17:38 05/30/88
: CLS.SCR ( - ) SCR.SEG 0 7D0 VIDEO @ 100 * 20 + FILLWL ;
: S0-CLS ( - ) ?SCR
  IF CLS.SCR
  ELSE (CLS) VIDEO @ 10 / DUP TO S0.BORDER (BORDER)
  THEN 0 TO S0.OFF ;
: S1-CLS ( - ) ?SCR
  IF (CLS) S1.BORDER (BORDER)
  ELSE CLS.SCR
  THEN 0 TO S1.OFF ;
  -->

42
\ compiler TYPE                                  JFB 15:52 05/07/88
: COMPILER-TYPE    -DUP IF OVER + SWAP DO I C@ EMIT LOOP
                   ELSE DROP THEN ;

' COMPILER-TYPE CFA ' TYPE 6 + !
  -->

43
\ FILP-SCR                                       JFB 15:30 05/07/88
CODE FLIP-SCR ( - )
 BP PUSH DX SI MOV
 AX ' VID.SEG MOV ES AX MOV \ es:di video screen
 AX ' SCR.SEG MOV DS AX MOV \ ds:si screen buffer
 AX AX XOR DI AX MOV SI AX MOV CX # 07D0 MOV CLD
 1 $: ES: BX [DI] MOV \ get a video char
 AX [SI] MOV \ get a buffer char
 WORD STOS \ put buffer char in video
 [SI] BX MOV \ put video char in buffer
 SI INC SI INC CX DEC 1 $ JNZ
 SI DX MOV BP POP AX CS MOV DS AX MOV NEXT, END-CODE
 -->

44
\ save system                                        07:53 10/12/89

FORGET.MOD

HEX
LATEST      0C +ORIGIN !   \ top NFA
HERE        1C +ORIGIN !   \ FENCE
HERE        1E +ORIGIN !   \ DP
VOC-LINK @ 20 +ORIGIN !   \ vocabulary list

SAVE NCC2BASE.COM
CR ." For Nautilus Meta-compiler version 2.5 10/12/89 07:24
"  CR

45
\ revision history                                   07:48 10/12/89
Revsym                Revision history

10/12/89         - Added printing version to match Meta-compiler
                 - Made comment changes in <FIND(H> indicating
                   this word returns a host CFA.
                 - Corrected error in S0-BS-EMIT and S1-BS-EMIT
```

Appendix 15

The Nautilus Version 2 Metacompiler

The Nautilus Version 2.5 source code is listed here. After the Nautilus base code listed in Appendix 14 is loaded on FORTH86, the compiler can be compiled. FORTH86 must be the minimum size. There is not enough room for the editor or assembler. The ASCII listing of the minimum sized FORTH86 code is given in Appendix 2.

The metacompiler is declared as the primary file compiled by typing:

```
PFILE MC 1 LOAD
```

After it is loaded, you can save just the compiler without a metaassembler loaded, by typing Y in response to its asking whether you want to save MCNOASM.COM. This saves it in the file MCNOASM.COM.

The compiler is not usable until either the 8086 or 8051 metaassembler is loaded. These are listed in appendices 16 and 17, respectively.

```
0
\                                                    10:37 02/26/88

Nautilus Forth Metacompiler
Written by: Jerry Boutelle
            542 Blackjack Lane
            Santa Cruz, CA 95062
            408-462-9461

1
\ print title and version                            07:24 10/12/89
: .TITLE ." Nautilus Forth Meta-compiler " ;
: .VERSION ." 2.5 10/12/89 07:24" ;
CR ." Loading " .TITLE ." Version " .VERSION CR
: --> BASE @  >R DECIMAL  BLK @ 1+ .  ( .S) R> BASE !
   [COMPILE] --> ; IMMEDIATE
HEX \ load it all in HEX
-->

2
\ vector defining word and vectors               JFB 21:17 05/07/88
: VECTOR ( - ) CREATE SMUDGE
   BB C, [ ' QUIT CFA ] LITERAL , \ BX # ' QUIT MOV
   FF C, 27 C, ;                  \ WORD [BX] JMP

WORDSx DEFINITIONS
VECTOR SWAP-BYTESx     VECTOR @x            VECTOR !x
VECTOR VARIABLEx       VECTOR VOCABULARYx

FORTH DEFINITIONS
VECTOR DOINTERPRET(H   VECTOR DO?ERRORx      VECTOR DOASMINIT
VECTOR DOASMCODE       VECTOR DOASMEND-CODE  VECTOR DO.TARGET
VECTOR DOASMFWD        VECTOR DOASMTYPE1     VECTOR DOASMTYPE2
VECTOR DO?UNCONS       VECTOR DOASMRESET     VECTOR DO.PROGRESS
VECTOR DO.SYMBOL.TABLE VECTOR DOASMVERSION
   -->
3
\ numeric constants                            \ JFB 10:49 05/11/86
  1F CONSTANT $1F                  1A CONSTANT $1A
  20 CONSTANT $20                  24 CONSTANT $24
  40 CONSTANT $40                  50 CONSTANT $50
  7F CONSTANT $7F                  80 CONSTANT $80
  81 CONSTANT $81                 0A0 CONSTANT $A0
 0FF CONSTANT $FF                 400 CONSTANT $400
 404 CONSTANT $404               1000 CONSTANT $1000
2000 CONSTANT $2000              3C00 CONSTANT $3C00
3D00 CONSTANT $3D00              3E00 CONSTANT $3E00
3F00 CONSTANT $3F00              4000 CONSTANT $4000
4200 CONSTANT $4200              4202 CONSTANT $4202
7FFF CONSTANT $7FFF              8000 CONSTANT $8000
A081 CONSTANT $A081              F000 CONSTANT $F000
FFFF CONSTANT $FFFF
   -->
4
\ constants                                      JFB 13:15 05/08/88
          0 CONSTANT ASM.STATE(H \ host assemble state value
          1 CONSTANT INTP.STATE(H \ host interpret state value
          2 CONSTANT COMP.STATE(H \ host compile state value
          0 CONSTANT INTP.STATE(T \ target interpret state value
        0C0 CONSTANT COMP.STATE(T \ target compile state value
          4 CONSTANT #VOC.THREADS \ number threads in sym voc
        100 CONSTANT CFA.HASH.TBL.SIZE \ words in CFA hash table
```

```
' HEX CFA @ CONSTANT DO:(H \ address of host's do :
        13E CONSTANT F4KEY \ F4 key code returned from ?KEY
         1B CONSTANT ESCKEY \ ESC key code returned from ?KEY
-->

5
\ forward reference type codes              \ JFB 10:42 03/14/86
0 CONSTANT CF.REF \ code field reference code
1 CONSTANT CFA.REF \ code field address reference code
2 CONSTANT PFA.REF \ PFA reference code
3 CONSTANT HLP.REF \ high level pointer reference code
4 CONSTANT ABS.ASM.REF \ absolute assembler reference code
5 CONSTANT ASMTYPE1 \ assembler reference type 1
6 CONSTANT ASMTYPE2 \ assembler reference tyep 2
-->

6
\ variables                                 \ JFB 10:42 03/14/86
0 VARIABLE DP(S \ symbol dictionary pointer
0 VARIABLE DP-RAM(T \ target ram dictionary pointer
0 VARIABLE CONTEXT(S   \ pointer to symbol context pointer
0 VARIABLE CURRENT(S   \ pointer to symbol current pointer
0 VARIABLE VOC-LINK(S \ links all symbol table vocs
0 VARIABLE COMPILE(T.LINK \ links all COMPILE(T words
  -->

7
\ quans                                     \ JFB 21:00 06/30/86
QUAN NOT.DONE? \ not done with compilation flag
QUAN POP? \ flag to exit inner interpreter
QUAN ROMING? \ true if making a ROMable image
QUAN LATEST(S \ NFA of latest symbol table entry
QUAN LATEST(T(S \ NFA of symbol table entry for LATEST(T
QUAN LATEST(T(S.PFA(S  \ PFA of symbol table entry for LATEST(T
QUAN VOC.HASH# \ last voc hash
QUAN WRD.STR  \ pointer to a word start
QUAN STATE(H  \ host is: interpreting, assembling or compiling
QUAN R0(H \ initial simulated target return stack address
QUAN RP(H \ simulated target return stack pointer
QUAN IP(H \ simulated target interpreter pointer
QUAN MAP.HANDLE \ holds handle of the map file
  -->

8
\ quans cont.                               \ JFB 07:54 05/28/86
QUAN PACKET.HEAD \ pointer to head of free packet list
QUAN PACKET.BASE \ pointer to the current packet
QUAN PACKET.HERE \ pointer to bottom of packet dictionary
QUAN DEF.SYM.FOUND \ holds symbol PFA of the defining symbol
QUAN TRACE1 \ first trace point, in WORDx
QUAN TRACE2 \ second trace point, in <INTERPRET(H>
QUAN TRACE3 \ third trace point, in INTERPRET(H
QUAN .STACK? \ true to print stack between screens
QUAN 'GET.TRG.PFA \ GET.TRG.PFA adr, identifies a host def word
QUAN TARGET.ORG \ holds lowest address used in target image
QUAN EM(H \ holds the targets end of memory address
 -->

9
\ quans cont.                                 JFB 13:35 05/08/88
QUAN FORTH.SYM.FOUND \ PFA of FORTH in sym tab
QUAN DOES>.SYM.FOUND \ PFA of DOES> in sym tab
QUAN X.SYM.FOUND \ PFA of X ( i.e. null) in sym tab
QUAN INIT-FORTH.SYM.FOUND \ PFA of INIT-FORTH in sym tab
```

```
QUAN INIT-VOC-LINK.SYM.FOUND \ PFA of INIT-VOC-LINK in sym tab
QUAN INIT-DP.SYM.FOUND \ PFA of INIT-DP in sym tab
QUAN INIT-FENCE.SYM.FOUND \ PFA of INIT-FENCE in sym tab
QUAN INIT-RAM.SYM.FOUND \ PFA of INIT-RAM in sym tab
QUAN RAM-START.SYM.FOUND \ PFA of RAM-START in sym tab
QUAN ORIGIN.SYM.FOUND \ PFA of ORIGIN in sym tab
QUAN VOC.NFA(S \ hold voc nfa during printing of symbol tab
QUAN ?.FILE \ display file name flag
QUAN +-REF \ up/down counter of unresolved references
  -->

10
\ symbol type constants                        \ JFB 08:49 03/10/86
 0 CONSTANT UNK.TYPE  \ unknow type
 1 CONSTANT CODE.TYPE \ code type
 2 CONSTANT :.TYPE    \ colon type
 3 CONSTANT CON.TYPE  \ constant type
 4 CONSTANT VAR.TYPE  \ variable type
 5 CONSTANT USR.TYPE  \ user type
 6 CONSTANT VOC.TYPE  \ vocabulary type
 7 CONSTANT LAB.TYPE  \ label type
 8 CONSTANT EQU.TYPE  \ equate type
 9 CONSTANT HDF.TYPE  \ high level defining word type
0A CONSTANT LDF.TYPE  \ low level defining word type
-->

11
\ symbol table addresses                       \ JFB 11:15 03/23/86
    0 DUP CONSTANT HOLD.CONTEXT(S \ CONTEXT for symbol table
   2+ DUP CONSTANT HOLD.CURRENT(S \ CURRENT for symbol table
   2+ DUP CONSTANT HOLD.VOC-LINK(S \ VOC-LINK for symbol table
   2+ DUP CONSTANT HOLD.CONTEXT(T \ CONTEXT for target
   2+ DUP CONSTANT HOLD.CURRENT(T \ CURRENT for target
   2+ DUP CONSTANT HOLD.VOC-LINK(T \ VOC-LINK for target
   2+ DUP CONSTANT HOLD.TARGET.ORG \ holds lowest target adr
   2+ DUP CONSTANT HOLD.ROMING? \ holds flag if target is rom
   2+ DUP CONSTANT HOLD.RAM.AREA \ holds adr of ram area in trg
   2+ DUP CONSTANT HOLD.RAM.START \ start of ram in rom target
   2+ DUP CONSTANT PACKET.PTR \ ptr to saved packets
   2+ DUP CONSTANT HOLD.PACKET.HERE \ holds packet address
   2+ DUP CONSTANT HOLD.PACKET.HEAD \ holds ptr to free packets
   2+ DUP CONSTANT HOLD.PACKET.SIZE \ length of saved packets
-->
12
\ symbol table addresses cont.                 \ JFB 11:15 03/23/86
   2+ DUP CONSTANT CFA.HASH.TBL \ hash table for CFA's
CFA.HASH.TBL.SIZE 2* +
      DUP CONSTANT FORTH.THREAD \ FORTH voc threads
#VOC.THREADS 4* +
      DUP CONSTANT ASM.THREAD \ ASSEMBLER voc threads
#VOC.THREADS 4* +
          CONSTANT INIT-DP(S \ first usable symbol address
  -->

13
\ symbol table field definitions               \ JFB 15:37 03/12/86
\ NOTE: the first two fields must be contiqeous to the CF
 0 DUP CONSTANT TRG.CFA.LINKS \ linkage to all target CFA's
2+ DUP CONSTANT TRG.CFA \ target code field address
2+ DUP CONSTANT SYM.IN \ offset to symbol
   DUP CONSTANT SYM.TYPE \ word type
   DUP CONSTANT FORWARD \ word is forward referenced
2+ DUP CONSTANT SYM.BLK \ block of symbol
   DUP CONSTANT FILE \ pointer to file table
```

```
   DUP CONSTANT DEFINED \ word is defined
2+ DUP CONSTANT REF.CTR \ reference counter
2+ DUP CONSTANT EXTEND.PTR \ pointer to extend area
2+     CONSTANT SYM.LEN \ length of symbol table parameter field
-->

14
\ symbol table extend field definition      \ JFB 10:04 03/17/86
\ NOTE: the following field must be first in the extend area
 0 DUP CONSTANT DOCODE.PTR \ adr code after ;CODE
   DUP CONSTANT DOES>HL.PTR \ adr of high level after DOES>
\ NOTE: the following fields are present only for vocs
\ NOTE: the following three fields must be contigeous
2+ DUP CONSTANT VOC.THREAD.PTR \ pointer to voc threads
2+ DUP CONSTANT SYM.VOC.LINK \ links symbol table vocs
2+ DUP CONSTANT EXTEND.BACK.PTR \ PFA of extended entry
2+     CONSTANT EXTEND.SIZE \ size of extend area
-->

15
\ symbol table masks                        \ JFB 16:35 03/18/86
FFC0 CONSTANT SYM.IN.MASK
  3C CONSTANT SYM.TYPE.MASK
   1 CONSTANT FORWARD.MASK

FFC0 CONSTANT SYM.BLK.MASK
  3C CONSTANT FILE.MASK
   2 CONSTANT DEFINED.MASK
-->

16
\ packet field definition                   \ JFB 11:02 03/23/86
\ NOTE: the first two fields must be contigeous
 0 DUP CONSTANT PACKET.LINK  \ link to next packet
2+ DUP CONSTANT PACKET.HOST.ADR \ host address
2+ DUP CONSTANT PACKET.TRG.ADR \ target address
2+ DUP CONSTANT PACKET.FILE \ file of reference
   DUP CONSTANT PACKET.IN \ offset of reference
2+ DUP CONSTANT PACKET.REF.TYPE \ type of reference
   DUP CONSTANT PACKET.BLK \ block of reference
2+     CONSTANT PACKET.SIZE \ size of packet
-->

17
\ packet masks                              \ JFB 08:50 03/10/86
F000 CONSTANT PACKET.FILE.MASK
 3FF CONSTANT PACKET.IN.MASK

   7 CONSTANT PACKET.REF.TYPE.MASK
FFC0 CONSTANT PACKET.BLK.MASK
-->

18
\ define target memory and disk param       \ JFB 08:42 03/15/86
               F000 CONSTANT INIT-TIB(T
INIT-TIB(T 50 + DUP CONSTANT NULL.VOC(T
                 2+ CONSTANT UP(T
        UP(T 100 + CONSTANT FIRST(T
     FIRST(T 808 + CONSTANT LIMIT(T
                400 CONSTANT B/BUF(T
                  1 CONSTANT B/SCR(T
                400 CONSTANT BPS(T
                 1 CONSTANT SEC/BLK(T
```

```
                    0 VARIABLE USE(T
                    0 VARIABLE PREV(T
                    0 VARIABLE REC(T
                    0 VARIABLE DISK-ERROR(T
  -->
19
\ vocabulary definitions                         \ JFB 10:04 03/10/86
VOCABULARY ASSEMBLER IMMEDIATE

: ?ATVOC ( nfa - next link \ bool; t=at the voc end )
   PFA LFA @  DUP @ $A081 = ; \ at the voc ?
-->

20
\ target user variable defining word             \ JFB 23:49 03/12/86
: USER(T ( offset - )
   <BUILDS 2* ,
   DOES> @ UP(T + ;
-->

21
\ target user variables                          \ JFB 17:40 03/18/86
WORDSx DEFINITIONS
 1 USER(T S0x         \ initial stack pointer
 2 USER(T R0x         \ initial return stack pointer
 3 USER(T TIBx        \ terminal input buffer
 4 USER(T WIDTHx      \ holds maximum target head width
 5 USER(T WARNINGx    \ holds error report mode
 6 USER(T FENCEx      \ holds NFA of top word in protected dict
 7 USER(T DPx         \ target dictionary pointer
 8 USER(T VOC-LINKx   \ links vocabularies together
 9 USER(T BLKx        \ holds block # being loaded
0A USER(T INx         \ input pointer
0B USER(T OUTx        \ display cursor position
0C USER(T SCRx        \ holds the last screen # listed
  -->

22
\ target user variables cont.                    \ JFB 17:40 03/18/86
0D USER(T OFFSETx     \ offset to disk block
0E USER(T CONTEXTx    \ pointer to target context pointer
0F USER(T CURRENTx    \ pointer to target current pointer
10 USER(T STATEx      \ interpreting, assembling or compiling
11 USER(T BASEx       \ numeric base for number i/o
12 USER(T DPLx        \ holds the number of decimal places
13 USER(T FLDx        \ output field width
14 USER(T CSPx        \ holds stack pointer
15 USER(T R#x         \ cursor position during editing
16 USER(T HLDx        \ points to last character held in pad
FORTH DEFINITIONS
  -->

23
\ .FILE                                            JFB 14:00 05/28/88

: .FILE ( - ) WORDSx ?.FILE
   IF 148 TO S1.OFF 28 SPACES
      BLKx @x -DUP
      IF 148 TO S1.OFF 0F000 AND    DUP    0=
         IF PRIF COUNT TYPE THEN DUP 2000 =
         IF SECF COUNT TYPE THEN DUP 4000 =
         IF AUXF COUNT TYPE THEN     6000 =
         IF SYSF COUNT TYPE THEN
      THEN 0 TO ?.FILE
```

```
   THEN ;
  -->

24
\ .BLOCK&LINE                                    JFB 10:51 05/08/88

: .BLOCK&LINE ( - ) WORDSx BASE @ DECIMAL
   BLKx @x -DUP
   IF 0FFF AND 19A TO S1.OFF 3 .R
      INx @x 40 / 1A6 TO S1.OFF 2 .R
   ELSE 19A TO S1.OFF 3 SPACES 1A6 TO S1.OFF 2 SPACES
   THEN BASE ! ;
  -->

25
\ target memory reference                        JFB 13:36 05/08/88
: !(T      TRG.SEG SWAP !L ;
' !(T CFA WORDSx ' !x 1+ !
: @(T      TRG.SEG SWAP @L ;
' @(T CFA WORDSx ' @x 1+ !
: ><!(T SWAP >< SWAP !(T ;
: ><@(T @(T >< ;
WORDSx DEFINITIONS
: C!x      TRG.SEG SWAP C!L ;
: C@x      TRG.SEG SWAP C@L ;
: HEREx    DPx @x ;
: +!x      DUP >R @x + R> !x ;
: ,x       HEREx !x 2 DPx +!x ;
: C,x      HEREx C!x 1 DPx +!x ;
: ALLOTx    DPx +!x ;
: TOGGLEx OVER C@x XOR SWAP C!x ;  -->
26
\ target memory reference                      \ JFB 09:12 11/04/88
: THEREx     DP-RAM(T @ ;
: ,(R)x      THEREx !x 2 DP-RAM(T +! ;
: C,(R)x     THEREx C!x 1 DP-RAM(T +! ;
: ALLOT-RAMx DP-RAM(T +! ;
FORTH DEFINITIONS
: TARGET.ORG! ( adr - adr )
  DUP TARGET.ORG U<
  IF DUP TO TARGET.ORG
  THEN ;
-->

27
\ state referenceing                           \ JFB 15:43 03/12/86
: ASSEMBLING? ( - bool; t=assembling )
   STATE(H ASM.STATE(H = ;
: INTERPRETING? ( - bool; t=interpreting)
   STATE(H INTP.STATE(H = ;
: COMPILING? ( - bool; t=compiling )
   STATE(H COMP.STATE(H = ;
: ASSEMBLING! ( - ) WORDSx ASM.STATE(H TO STATE(H
   INTP.STATE(T STATEx !x ;
: INTERPRETING! ( - ) WORDSx INTP.STATE(H TO STATE(H
   INTP.STATE(T STATEx !x ;
: COMPILING! ( - ) WORDSx COMP.STATE(H TO STATE(H
   COMP.STATE(T STATEx !x ;
-->

28
\ BASEx! RESTORE(H DECIMALx HEXx                 JFB 18:25 05/30/88
: BASEx! ( - ) WORDSx BASEx @x BASE ! ;
: INHERIT WORDSx BASEx! BLKx @x BLK ! INx @x IN ! ;
```

```
  -->

29
\ screen cursors                                   JFB 16:44 06/04/88
: S0-CURSOR ( - ) 1 TO ?S0.CURSOR ?SCR 0=
   IF ?SCROLL-S0 S0.OFF 0 50 U/ (GOTOXY) (CURSOR)
   THEN ;
: S1-CURSOR ( - ) 1 TO ?S1.CURSOR ?SCR
   IF S1.OFF 0 50 U/ (GOTOXY) (CURSOR)
   THEN ;
: S0--CURSOR ( - ) 0 TO ?S0.CURSOR ?SCR 0=
  IF (-CURSOR)
  THEN ;
: S1--CURSOR ( - ) 0 TO ?S1.CURSOR ?SCR
  IF (-CURSOR)
  THEN ;
  -->

30
\ show forth screen                                JFB 16:20 06/04/88
: SHOW-S0 ( - ) ?SCR
  IF ?SCROLL-S0
     0 TO ?SCR
     FLIP-SCR
     ?S0.CURSOR
     IF S0.OFF 0 50 U/ (GOTOXY) (CURSOR)
     ELSE (-CURSOR)
     THEN
     S0.BORDER (BORDER)
  THEN ;
  -->

31
\ show compiler screen                             JFB 18:38 06/04/88
: SHOW-S1 ( - ) ?SCR 0=
  IF ?SCROLL-S1
     1 TO ?SCR
     FLIP-SCR
     S1.BORDER (BORDER)
     ?S1.CURSOR
     IF S1.OFF 0 50 U/ (GOTOXY) (CURSOR)
     ELSE (-CURSOR)
     THEN
   THEN ;
: S1! ?SCR 0= IF SHOW-S1 THEN ;
  -->

32
\  key check                                       JFB 16:44 06/04/88
: DO>(S0) NOOP ;
: (KEYCHECK) ( key - )
  DUP F4KEY  = IF ?SCR IF SHOW-S0 ELSE SHOW-S1 THEN THEN
      ESCKEY = IF INHERIT DO>(S0) SHOW-S0 S0CURSOR!
                  SP! QUIT THEN ;
  -->

33
\ S0 and S1 KEY                                    JFB 16:46 06/04/88
: S0-KEY S0-CURSOR
  BEGIN ?KEY DUP (KEYCHECK) DUP F4KEY =
    IF DROP 0
    THEN -DUP
  UNTIL S0--CURSOR ;
: S1-KEY S1-CURSOR
```

```
  BEGIN ?KEY DUP (KEYCHECK) DUP F4KEY =
    IF DROP 0
    THEN -DUP
  UNTIL S1--CURSOR ;
  -->

34
\ switch output vectors                           JFB 18:37 05/30/88
: >(S0) ( - ) [ ' (EMIT) CFA ] LITERAL ' EMIT !
      [ ' (GOTOXY) CFA ] LITERAL ' GOTOXY !
      [ ' (CLS) CFA ] LITERAL ' CLS !
      [ ' (BORDER) CFA ] LITERAL ' BORDER !
      [ ' (KEY) CFA ] LITERAL ' KEY !
      [ ' (CURSOR) CFA ] LITERAL ' CURSOR !
      [ ' (-CURSOR) CFA ] LITERAL ' -CURSOR ! ;
' >(S0) CFA ' DO>(S0) !
  -->

35
\ switch output vectors                           JFB 18:36 05/30/88
: >S0 ( - ) [ ' S0-EMIT CFA ] LITERAL ' EMIT !
      [ ' S0-GOTOXY CFA ] LITERAL ' GOTOXY !
      [ ' S0-CLS CFA ] LITERAL ' CLS !
      [ ' S0-BORDER CFA ] LITERAL ' BORDER !
      [ ' S0-KEY CFA ] LITERAL ' KEY !
      [ ' S0-CURSOR CFA ] LITERAL ' CURSOR !
      [ ' S0--CURSOR CFA ] LITERAL ' -CURSOR ! ;
: >S1 ( - ) [ ' S1-EMIT CFA ] LITERAL ' EMIT !
      [ ' S1-GOTOXY CFA ] LITERAL ' GOTOXY !
      [ ' S1-CLS CFA ] LITERAL ' CLS !
      [ ' S1-BORDER CFA ] LITERAL ' BORDER !
      [ ' S1-KEY CFA ] LITERAL ' KEY !
      [ ' S1-CURSOR CFA ] LITERAL ' CURSOR !
      [ ' S1--CURSOR CFA ] LITERAL ' -CURSOR ! ;
  -->
36
\ draw lines on the compiler screen               JFB 06:57 05/08/88
: .COMPILER-LINES ( - )
0C4  9E   2 DO DUP SCR.SEG I C!L 2 +LOOP DROP \ horiz line top
0C4 59E 502 DO DUP SCR.SEG I C!L 2 +LOOP DROP \ horiz line mid
0C4 EFE E62 DO DUP SCR.SEG I C!L 2 +LOOP DROP \ horiz line bot
0B3 EC0  A0 DO DUP SCR.SEG I C!L A0 +LOOP DROP \ ver line lft
0B3 F52 13E DO DUP SCR.SEG I C!L A0 +LOOP DROP \ ver line lft
0DA SCR.SEG   0 C!L \ upper left corner
0BF SCR.SEG  9E C!L \ upper right corner
0C0 SCR.SEG E60 C!L \ lower left corner
0D9 SCR.SEG EFE C!L \ lower right corner
0C3 SCR.SEG 500 C!L \ left bar side
0B4 SCR.SEG 59E C!L \ right bar side
;
  -->

37
\ place boiler plate text on compiler screen  JFB 08:48 05/28/88
: .COMPILER-TEXT ( - ) >S1 2 1 GOTOXY ." Compiler version:"
  2 2 GOTOXY ." Assembler version:"
  2 4 GOTOXY ." File:"
  2 5 GOTOXY ." Screen:       Line:"
  2 6 GOTOXY ." State:"
  2 7 GOTOXY ." Undefined references:"
  [ ' FAST-S1-EMIT CFA ] LITERAL ' EMIT ! \ no scroll
  2 18 GOTOXY ." F4 - Switch screen  ESC - Quit"
  >S0 ;
  -->
```

```
38
\ initialize compiler screen                        JFB 19:45 05/30/88
: INIT-SCR ( - ) XY> 50 * + TO S0.OFF 0 TO S1.OFF
   GOT.SCR.SEG NOT
   IF ?CS: 0 0 0FA 4800 21INT5 \ get memory for scr buffer
      ?NOMEM TO SCR.SEG GOT.SCR.SEG! \ define screen seg
   THEN 0 TO ?SCR \ forth screen is visible
   VIDEO @ 10 / DUP TO S0.BORDER \ inherit forth border color
                    TO S1.BORDER
   1 TO ?S0.CURSOR 0 TO ?S1.CURSOR \ init cursors
   CLS.SCR \ clr scr buffer
   ' EMIT @ [ ' FAST-S1-EMIT CFA ] LITERAL ' EMIT !
   .COMPILER-LINES \ draw boxes on the compiler screen
   .COMPILER-TEXT \ place text on the compiler screen
   ' EMIT ! >S0 ;
  -->

39
\ FILLx ERASEx CMOVEx                               JFB 18:25 05/30/88
WORDSx DEFINITIONS
: DECIMALx ( - ) 0A BASEx !x BASEx! ;
: HEXx ( - ) 10 BASEx !x BASEx! ;
: FILLx ( target address \ count \ char - ) SWAP DUP 1 <
   IF DROP
   ELSE >R SWAP R> 0
     DO 2DUP I + C!x
     LOOP
   THEN 2DROP ;
: ERASEx ( target address \ count - ) 0 FILLx ;
: BLANKSx BL FILLx ;
: CMOVEx 0
  DO OVER I + C@x OVER I + C!x
  LOOP 2DROP ;
  -->
40
\ COUNTx TYPEx                                      JFB 09:55 06/04/88
: COUNTx  ( string address - text address \ character count )
   DUP 1+ SWAP C@x ;
: TYPEx  ( address \ count - ) -DUP
   IF OVER + SWAP
      DO I C@x EMIT
      LOOP
   ELSE DROP
   THEN ;
-->

41
\ symbol memory reference                         \ JFB 01:05 03/15/86
FORTH DEFINITIONS
: HERE(S   DP(S @ ;
: !(S      SYM.SEG SWAP !L ;
: @(S      SYM.SEG SWAP @L ;
: +!(S     DUP >R @(S + R> !(S ;
: C!(S     SYM.SEG SWAP C!L ;
: C@(S     SYM.SEG SWAP C@L ;
: ,(S      HERE(S !(S 2 DP(S +! ;
: C,(S     HERE(S C!(S 1 DP(S +! ;
: ALLOT(S DP(S +! ;
: TOGGLE(S OVER C@(S XOR SWAP C!(S ;
-->

42
\ !BIT(S @BIT(S                                   \ JFB 08:18 03/21/86
```

```
: !BITS(S ( value \ address \ mask - ) ROT OVER
   BEGIN DUP 1 AND 0=
   WHILE 2/ SWAP 2* SWAP \ shift value to mask
   REPEAT DROP OVER AND \ mask value
   SWAP ROT DUP >R @(S SWAP
   $FFFF XOR AND \ clear (address) of mask bits
   OR R> !(S ; \ place new bits
: @BITS(S ( address \ mask - value ) SWAP @(S OVER AND SWAP
   BEGIN DUP 1 AND 0=
   WHILE 2/ SWAP 2/ $7FFF AND SWAP
   REPEAT DROP ;
-->

43
\ symbol table dictionary                    \ JFB 01:07 03/15/86
: CFA(S ( symbol PFA - symbol CFA ) 2- ;
: TRAVERSE(S ( address \ direction flag - address ) SWAP
   BEGIN OVER + $7F OVER C@(S <
   UNTIL NIP ;
: PFA(S ( symbol NFA - symbol PFA ) 1 TRAVERSE(S 5 + ;
: NFA(S ( symbol PFA - symbol NFA ) 5 - -1 TRAVERSE(S ;
: >BODY(S ( symbol CFA - symbol PFA ) 2+ ;
-->

44
\ print stack for meta-compilation trace    \ JFB 10:09 04/14/86
-1 CONSTANT .SS(NOCR
: .S(NOCR ." [" BASE @ >R HEX DEPTH
    IF .SS(NOCR
       IF SP@ 2- S0 @ 2-
       ELSE SP@ S0 @ SWAP
       THEN
       DO I @ U. 2 .SS(NOCR +-
       +LOOP
    ELSE ." empty stack "
    THEN R> BASE ! 8 EMIT ." ] " ;
  -->

45
\ print stack and check keys                   JFB 18:13 05/30/88
: PRINT-STACK? .STACK? IF >S1 .S(NOCR >S0 THEN ;
: CR0> S1.OFF 50 MOD 1 <>
   IF CR THEN ;
  -->

46
\ ask y/n ? and stop compilation             \ JFB 10:32 11/03/88
: Y/N? ( - bool ; t= 'Y' or 'y' entered )
   >S1 S1! ."  ? " S1-KEY DUP S1-EMIT SPACE DUP ASCII y = SWAP
   ASCII Y = OR >S0 ;
: STOPIT ( - )
      >S1 S1! CR0> ." Press any key to continue" S1-KEY DROP
      INHERIT >(S0) SHOW-S0 S0CURSOR! SP!
      [COMPILE] FORTH DEFINITIONS QUIT ;
  -->

47
\ print names for meta-compilation trace    \ JFB 10:33 04/14/86
: ID.(S ( symbol NFA - ) DUP 1+ SWAP C@(S 01F AND 0
   DO DUP I + C@(S $7F AND EMIT
   LOOP DROP ;
: .{NAME}  ( CFA - ) >BODY DUP @ 'GET.TRG.PFA =
   IF LFA @ ." {do " \ a host defining word
   ELSE NFA ." {"
```

```
   THEN ID. 8 EMIT ." } " ;
: .(NAME) ( CFA - ) >BODY DUP @ 'GET.TRG.PFA =
   IF LFA @ ." (do " \ a host defining word
   ELSE NFA ." ("
   THEN ID. 8 EMIT ." ) " ;
  -->

48
\ trace meta-compilation cont.                    JFB 20:43 05/30/88
: TRACE.WORDx ( - ) WORDSx >S1 .S(NOCR
  ASCII " EMIT HEREx @x 1 =
  IF ." null"
  ELSE HEREx COUNTx TYPEx
  THEN ASCII " EMIT SPACE >S0 ;
: KEY.TRACE.WORDx ( - ) TRACE.WORDx >S1 S1-KEY >S0 DROP ;
: TRACE.<I(H> ( CFA - CFA ) WORDSx >S1 >R .S(NOCR R> DUP .{NAME}
  >S0 ;
: KEY.TRACE.<I(H> ( CFA - CFA ) TRACE.<I(H> >S1 S1-KEY >S0
  DROP ;
: TRACE.I(H ( CFA - CFA ) WORDSx >R >S1 .S(NOCR R> DUP .(NAME)
   >S0 ;
: KEY.TRACE.I(H ( CFA - CFA ) >S1 TRACE.I(H S1-KEY DROP >S0 ;
-->

49
\ SEC-READx SEC-WRITEx                            JFB 15:16 05/28/88
WORDSx DEFINITIONS
: SEC-READx ( - ) TRG.SEG USE(T @ BPS(T
   REC(T @ GETHANDLE $3F00 21INT5 NIP
   IF DUP DISK-ERROR(T ! >S1 S1! ." Disk read error # " . >S0
   STOPIT THEN DUP $400 <>
   IF DUP USE(T @ + OVER $400 SWAP - ERASEx
   THEN DROP ;
: SEC-WRITEx ( - ) TRG.SEG USE(T @ BPS(T
   REC(T @ GETHANDLE $4000 21INT5 NIP
   IF DUP DISK-ERROR(T ! >S1 S1! ." Disk write error # " . >S0
      STOPIT
   THEN $400 <>
   IF  >S1 S1! ." Disk full" >S0 STOPIT
   THEN ;
  -->
50
\ SET-IOx R/Wx                                  \ JFB 16:29 04/21/86
: SET-IOx ( - ) REC(T @ DUP GETHANDLE SWAP 1FFF AND $400 M*
   SEEK+ -DUP IF CR >S1 S1! ." Seek error " . >S0
   STOPIT THEN ;
: R/Wx ( buffer address \ block # \ 0=write, 1=read - )
       USE(T @ >R SWAP SEC/BLK(T * ROT USE(T ! SEC/BLK(T 0
       DO OVER OVER REC(T ! SET-IOx
          IF SEC-READx ELSE SEC-WRITEx
          THEN 1+ BPS(T USE(T +!
       LOOP 2DROP R> USE(T ! ;
  -->

51
\ +BUFx BUFFERx UPDATEx                         \ JFB 22:45 07/01/86
: +BUFx ( buffer address - next buffer address \ PREV flag )
   B/BUF(T 4 + + DUP LIMIT(T =
   IF DROP FIRST(T THEN DUP PREV(T @ - ;
: BUFFERx ( block number - address ) USE(T @ DUP >R
   BEGIN +BUFx
   UNTIL USE(T ! R @x 0<
   IF R 2+ R @x $7FFF AND 0 R/Wx
   THEN R !x R PREV(T ! R> 2+ ;
```

```
: EMPTY-BUFFERSx FIRST(T LIMIT(T OVER - ERASEx
   LIMIT(T FIRST(T
   DO $7FFF I !x B/BUF(T 4+
   +LOOP ;
: UPDATEx PREV(T @ @x $8000 OR PREV(T @ !x ;
  -->

52
\ BLOCKx                                        \ JFB 16:30 04/21/86
: BLOCKx  DUP GETHANDLE 0= DOSERR 5F + DO?ERRORx
   DISK-ERROR(T 0!
   >R PREV(T @ DUP @ R - DUP +
   IF
      BEGIN +BUFx 0=
         IF DROP R BUFFERx DUP R
            DISK-ERROR(T 0! 1 R/Wx 2 -
         THEN DUP @x R - DUP + 0=
      UNTIL
      DUP PREV(T ! DISK-ERROR(T @
      IF UPDATEx
      THEN
   THEN R> DROP 2+ ;
  -->

53
\ WORDx                                         \ JFB 14:43 04/14/86
WORDSx DEFINITIONS
: WORDx ( char - )
   BLKx @x
   IF BLKx @x BLOCKx
   ELSE TIBx @x
   THEN INx @x + SWAP ENCLOSEx HEREx 22 BLANKSx
   INx +!x INx @x TO WRD.STR
   OVER - >R R HEREx C!x + HEREx 1+ R> CMOVEx
   [ HERE TO TRACE1 ] NOOP ;
-->

54
\ -TRAILINGx (LINE)x .LINEx (x \x               \ JFB 23:11 06/27/86
: -TRAILINGx DUP 0
   DO OVER OVER + 1- C@x BL -
      IF LEAVE
      ELSE 1-
      THEN
   LOOP ;
: (LINE)x >R $40 B/BUF(T */MOD R> B/SCR(T * + BLOCKx
  + $40 ;
: .LINEx (LINE)x -TRAILINGx TYPEx ;
: (x ASCII ) WORDx ; IMMEDIATE
: (! ASCII ) WORDx ; IMMEDIATE
: \x INx @x $40 / 1+ $40 * INx !x ; IMMEDIATE
: \Fx [COMPILE] \x ; IMMEDIATE
: \Mx ; IMMEDIATE
-->
55
\ numeric formatting                            \ JFB 17:36 03/18/86
: PADx ( - buffer address ) HEREx 44 + ;
: HOLDx ( character - ) -1 HLDx +!x HLDx @x C!x ;
: <#x ( - ) PADx HLDx !x ;
: #x ( unsigned double value - unsigned double value ) BASEx @x
   M/MOD ROT 9 OVER <
   IF 7 +
   THEN 30 + HOLDx ;
: #Sx ( unsigned double value - 0 \ 0 )
```

```
   BEGIN #x 2DUP OR 0=
   UNTIL ;
: #>x ( unsigned double value - address \ count ) 2DROP HLDx @x
  PADx OVER - ;
: SIGNx ( sign flag \ double value - double value ) ROT 0<
        IF ASCII - HOLDx
        THEN ;  -->
56
\ fig-Forth messages                                JFB 21:27 05/30/88
FORTH DEFINITIONS
: MSG0 ." ?" ;
: MSG1 ." Empty Stack" ;
: MSG4 ." Redefined" ;
: MSG7 ." Stack overflow" ;
: MSG11 ." Compilation only" ;
: MSG12 ." Execution only" ;
: MSG13 ." Conditionals not paired" ;
: MSG14 ." Definition not finished" ;
: MSG15 ." In protected dictionary" ;
: MSG16 ." Use only when loading" ;
: MSG18 ." Declare vocabulary" ;
  -->

57
\ Meta-compiler messages                            JFB 21:33 05/30/88
: MSG30 ." Forward reference to LABEL in colon definition" ;
: MSG31 ." Can't do" ;
: MSG32 ." Forward reference to EQU" ;
: MSG33 ." Origin not defined :" ;
: MSG34 ." To many references" ;
: MSG35 ." Unconsumed forward reference" ;
  -->

58
\ ', MESSAGE-ARRAY                                  JFB 21:25 05/30/88
: ', -FIND 0= 5 ?ERROR DROP CFA , ;
: MESSAGE-ARRAY <BUILDS
             DOES> OVER 2* + @ -DUP
                IF EXECUTE DROP SPACE
                ELSE ." Msg # " .
                THEN ;
  -->

59
\ MESSAGES                                          JFB 21:30 05/30/88
MESSAGE-ARRAY MESSAGES
\ fig-Forth messages
\       0        1        2        3        4        5        6
 ', MSG0  ', MSG1       0 ,      0 , ', MSG4       0 ,      0 ,
\       7        8        9        A        B        C        D
 ', MSG7       0 ,      0 ,      0 ,      0 ,      0 ,      0 ,
\       E        F       10       11       12       13       14
     0 ,      0 ,      0 , ', MSG11 ', MSG12 ', MSG13 ', MSG14
\      15       16       17       18
 ', MSG15 ', MSG16      0 , ', MSG18
  -->

60
\ MESSAGES cont.                                    JFB 21:34 05/30/88
\ Meta-Assembler messages
HERE 2E 2DUP DUP ALLOT ERASE
\ Meta-compiler messages
\      30       31       32       33       34       35
 ', MSG30 ', MSG31 ', MSG32 ', MSG33 ', MSG34 ', MSG35
```

```
CONSTANT ASMMSGSIZ \ size of assembler messages
CONSTANT 'ASMMSG   \ address of assembler messages
  -->

61
\ >MESSAGES                                     \ JFB 11:31 05/12/86
: >MESSAGES ( adr \ n - ) 2* ' MESSAGES 2+ \ over high lvl ptr
   + ! ;
  -->

62
\ MESSAGEx                                        JFB 15:50 06/04/88
WORDSx DEFINITIONS
: MESSAGEx  ( message # - ) >S1 S1! WARNINGx @x
   IF MESSAGES
   ELSE ." Msg # " .
   THEN >S0 ;
: SHOW-ERRORx ( - ) BLKx @x
   IF INx @x 2- 40 / BLKx @x
      CR .LINEx CR INx @x 2- 40 MOD SPACES 18 EMIT CR
   THEN ;
  -->

63
\ SHOW-ERRORx ERRORx ?ERRORx ?COMPx               JFB 16:47 06/04/88
: ERRORx >S1 S1! DECIMAL HEREx COUNTx
  CR0> ." Error: " 22 EMIT TYPEx 22 EMIT 2 SPACES
   MESSAGEx SHOW-ERRORx STOPIT ;
: ?ERRORx SWAP IF ERRORx ELSE DROP THEN ;
' ?ERRORx CFA ' DO?ERRORx 1+ !
: ?COMPx COMPILING? NOT 11 ?ERRORx ;
: ?EXECx ( - ) COMPILING? 12 ?ERRORx ;
: ?LOADINGx BLKx @x 0= 16 ?ERRORx ;
  -->

64
\ ?STACKx ?CSPx !CSPx                           \ JFB 13:34 03/14/86
: ?STACKx SP@ S0 @ SWAP U< 1 ?ERRORx
          SP@ HERE 80 + U< 7 ?ERRORx ;
: ?CSPx SP@ CSPx @x - 14 ?ERRORx ;
: !CSPx SP@ CSPx !x ;
FORTH DEFINITIONS
  -->

65
\ simulated return stack management             \ JFB 13:08 03/14/86
40 ALLOT \ target simulated return stack
HERE 2- TO R0(H
WORDSx DEFINITIONS
: RP!x ( - ) R0(H TO RP(H ;
: >Rx ( n - ) RP(H  DUP 2-  TO RP(H  ! ;
: R>x ( - n ) RP(H  2+ DUP  TO RP(H  @ ;
: Rx ( - n ) RP(H 2+ @ ;
: Ix ( - n ) RP(H 2+ @ ;
FORTH DEFINITIONS
: IP(H.PUSH ( - ) WORDSx IP(H >Rx ;
: IP(H.POP  ( - ) WORDSx R>x TO IP(H ;
-->

66
\ FILL(S                                        \ JFB 15:59 03/12/86
: FILL(S  ( symbol address \ count \ char - ) SWAP DUP 1 <
   IF DROP
   ELSE >R SWAP R> 0
```

```
     DO 2DUP I + C!(S
     LOOP
  THEN 2DROP ;
-->

67
\ CMOVET>S CMOVES>T HEAD(S>T                    \ JFB 15:40 03/11/86
: CMOVET>S ( target address \ symbol address \ count - )
   WORDSx 0
   DO OVER I + C@x OVER I + C!(S
   LOOP 2DROP ;
: CMOVES>T ( symbol address \ target address \ count - )
   WORDSx 0
   DO OVER I + C@(S OVER I + C!x
   LOOP 2DROP ;
: HEAD(S>T ( symbol NFA - ) WORDSx
   DUP C@(S $1F AND DUP >R HEREx C!x \ count
   DUP 1+ HEREx 1+ R> 0
   DO OVER I + C@(S $7F AND OVER I + C!x
   LOOP 2DROP ;
 -->

68
\ CMOVEH>T CMOVET>H CMOVE(S                     \ JFB 18:56 03/18/86
: CMOVEH>T ( address \ target address \ count - ) WORDSx 0
   DO OVER I + C@ OVER I + C!x
   LOOP 2DROP ;
:  CMOVET>H ( target address \ address \ count - )
   WORDSx 0
   DO OVER I + C@x OVER I + C!
   LOOP 2DROP ;
:  CMOVE(S ( symbol address \ symbol address \ count - )
   WORDSx 0
   DO OVER I + C@(S OVER I + C!(S
   LOOP 2DROP ;
-->

69
\ packet references                             \ JFB 10:44 03/14/86
: +PACKET.BASE ( offset - address ) PACKET.BASE + ;

: PACKET.LINK! ( address - ) PACKET.LINK +PACKET.BASE !(S ;
: PACKET.TRG.ADR! ( target address - ) PACKET.TRG.ADR
   +PACKET.BASE !(S ;
: PACKET.HOST.ADR! ( host address - ) PACKET.HOST.ADR
   +PACKET.BASE !(S ;
: PACKET.REF.TYPE! ( type - ) PACKET.REF.TYPE +PACKET.BASE
   PACKET.REF.TYPE.MASK !BITS(S ;
: PACKET.FILE! ( file code - ) PACKET.FILE +PACKET.BASE
   PACKET.FILE.MASK !BITS(S ;
: PACKET.BLK! ( - ) WORDSx BLKx @x PACKET.BLK +PACKET.BASE
   PACKET.BLK.MASK !BITS(S ;
: PACKET.IN! ( in - ) WRD.STR PACKET.IN +PACKET.BASE
   PACKET.IN.MASK !BITS(S ; -->
70
\ packet references cont.                       \ JFB 08:19 03/11/86
: PACKET.LINK@ ( - address ) PACKET.LINK +PACKET.BASE @(S ;
: PACKET.TRG.ADR@ ( - target address ) PACKET.TRG.ADR
   +PACKET.BASE @(S ;
: PACKET.HOST.ADR@ ( - host address ) PACKET.HOST.ADR
   +PACKET.BASE @(S ;
: PACKET.REF.TYPE@ ( - type ) PACKET.REF.TYPE +PACKET.BASE
   PACKET.REF.TYPE.MASK @BITS(S ;
: PACKET.FILE@ ( - file code ) PACKET.FILE +PACKET.BASE
```

```
   PACKET.FILE.MASK @BITS(S ;
: PACKET.BLK@ ( - blk ) PACKET.BLK +PACKET.BASE PACKET.BLK.MASK
   @BITS(S ;
: PACKET.IN@ ( - in ) PACKET.IN +PACKET.BASE PACKET.IN.MASK
   @BITS(S ;
-->

71
\ packet list                               JFB 13:59 05/08/88
: PACKET.LIST@ ( - )
   PACKET.HEAD -DUP
   IF DUP @(S TO PACKET.HEAD \ use packet from free list
   ELSE PACKET.HERE PACKET.SIZE -
      DUP TO PACKET.HERE \ create new packet
   THEN TO PACKET.BASE 1 AT +-REF +! ;
: PACKET.LIST! ( - ) PACKET.HEAD PACKET.LINK!
   PACKET.BASE TO PACKET.HEAD -1 AT +-REF +! ;
: NEXT.PACKET ( - ) PACKET.LINK@ PACKET.LIST! TO PACKET.BASE ;
-->

72
\ target dictionary                       \ JFB 13:04 03/14/86
WORDSx DEFINITIONS
: CFAx ( target PFA - target CFA ) 2- ;
: LFAx 4 - ;
: TRAVERSEx ( adr \ dir - adr ) SWAP
   BEGIN OVER + $7F OVER C@x < UNTIL NIP ;
: PFAx 1 TRAVERSEx 5 + ;
: NFAx 5 - -1 TRAVERSEx ;
FORTH DEFINITIONS
: >BODY(T ( target CFA - target PFA ) 2+ ;
: NOT.NULL? ( - bool; t=not a null ) WORDSx
  HEREx 1+ C@x 0= NOT ;
-->

73
\ access to target LATEST                 \ JFB 20:18 03/10/86
: +LATEST(T(S.PFA(S ( symbol field off - symbol field of LATEST)
   LATEST(T(S.PFA(S + ;
: LATEST(T.CFA(T ( - CFA of LATEST) TRG.CFA +LATEST(T(S.PFA(S
  @(S ;
WORDSx DEFINITIONS
: LATESTx ( - target NFA ) CURRENTx @x @x ;
FORTH DEFINITIONS
: LATEST(T(S.CFA(S! ( host execution address - )
   LATEST(T(S.PFA(S CFA(S @(S
   IF DROP \ don't store if there is an address there
   ELSE LATEST(T(S.PFA(S CFA(S !(S
   THEN ;
-->

74
\ target and symbol IMMEDIATE and SMUDGE    \ JFB 10:04 05/10/86
: SMUDGE(S ( - ) LATEST(S $20 TOGGLE(S ;
: SMUDGE(T ( - ) WORDSx LATESTx $20 TOGGLEx ;
: SMUDGE(T(S ( - ) LATEST(T(S $20 TOGGLE(S ;
: IMMEDIATE(T(S LATEST(T(S DUP C@(S $40 OR SWAP C!(S ;
: IMMEDIATE(S LATEST(S DUP C@(S $40 OR SWAP C!(S ;
WORDSx DEFINITIONS
: IMMEDIATEx ( - ) LATESTx $40 TOGGLEx IMMEDIATE(T(S ;
: SMUDGEx ( - ) SMUDGE(T SMUDGE(T(S
   DEFINED +LATEST(T(S.PFA(S DEFINED.MASK 2DUP @BITS(S
   0= ROT ROT !BITS(S ; \ toggle is defined bit
FORTH DEFINITIONS
```

```
-->

75
\ symbol table field access                    \ JFB 21:53 03/13/86
: +SYM.FOUND ( offset - address ) SYM.FOUND + ;

: TRG.CFA.LINKS.FOUND ( - target CFA link address )
   SYM.FOUND ; \ NOTE: assumes its first !!
: TRG.CFA.FOUND ( - target CFA address ) TRG.CFA +SYM.FOUND ;
: REF.CTR.FOUND ( - ref counter address ) REF.CTR +SYM.FOUND ;
: EXTEND.PTR.FOUND ( - extend pointer address )
  EXTEND.PTR +SYM.FOUND ;
: EXTEND.PTR.FOUND@ ( - extend pointer ) EXTEND.PTR.FOUND @(S ;
: EXTEND.BACK.PTR.FOUND ( - address of back pointer )
   EXTEND.PTR.FOUND@ EXTEND.BACK.PTR + ;
: SYM.VOC.LINK.FOUND ( - address of symbol voc link )
   EXTEND.PTR.FOUND@ SYM.VOC.LINK + ;
  -->

76
\ symbol table field access cont.              \ JFB 11:02 03/13/86
: VOC.THREAD.PTR.FOUND ( - address of symbol voc link )
   EXTEND.PTR.FOUND@ VOC.THREAD.PTR + ;
: TRG.CFA.LINKS.FOUND! ( value - )
   SYM.FOUND !(S ; \ assumes its first
: TYPE.FOUND! ( type - ) SYM.TYPE +SYM.FOUND SYM.TYPE.MASK
   !BITS(S ;
: EXTEND.PTR.FOUND! ( extend pointer - ) EXTEND.PTR.FOUND !(S ;
: VOC.THREAD.PTR.FOUND! ( voc thread - ) VOC.THREAD.PTR.FOUND
   !(S ;
: SYM.VOC.LINK.FOUND! ( symbol voc link - ) SYM.VOC.LINK.FOUND
   !(S ;
: EXTEND.BACK.PTR.FOUND! ( - ) SYM.FOUND EXTEND.BACK.PTR.FOUND
   !(S ;
  -->

77
\ symbol table field access cont.              \ JFB 07:30 03/21/86
: VOC.THREAD.PTR.FOUND@ ( voc thread - )
   VOC.THREAD.PTR.FOUND @(S ;
: TRG.CFA.FOUND@ ( - value ) TRG.CFA.FOUND @(S ;
: TYPE.FOUND@ ( - type ) SYM.TYPE +SYM.FOUND SYM.TYPE.MASK
   @BITS(S ;
: SYM.BLK.FOUND@ ( - blk ) SYM.BLK +SYM.FOUND SYM.BLK.MASK
   @BITS(S ;
: SYM.IN.FOUND@ ( - in ) SYM.IN +SYM.FOUND SYM.IN.MASK
  @BITS(S ;
: GET.TRG.PFA ( - target pfa ) TRG.CFA.FOUND@ >BODY(T ;
' GET.TRG.PFA CFA TO 'GET.TRG.PFA
: SYM.BLK! ( - ) WORDSx BLKx @x SYM.BLK +SYM.FOUND
   SYM.BLK.MASK !BITS(S ;
: SYM.IN! ( in - ) WRD.STR SYM.IN +SYM.FOUND
   SYM.IN.MASK !BITS(S ; -->
78
\ symbol table field access cont.              \ JFB 07:28 03/21/86
: DEF.DOCODE.PTR.FOUND ( - symbol table address )
   DEF.SYM.FOUND EXTEND.PTR + @(S -DUP NOT
   IF HERE(S 0 ,(S DUP DEF.SYM.FOUND EXTEND.PTR + !(S
   THEN ;
: DEF.DOES>HL.PTR.FOUND ( - symbol table address )
   DEF.SYM.FOUND EXTEND.PTR + @(S -DUP NOT
   IF HERE(S 0 ,(S DUP DEF.SYM.FOUND EXTEND.PTR + !(S
   THEN ;
: LAT.DOES>HL.PTR.FOUND ( - symbol table address )
```

```
   EXTEND.PTR +LATEST(T(S.PFA(S @(S -DUP NOT
   IF HERE(S 0 ,(S DUP EXTEND.PTR +LATEST(T(S.PFA(S !(S
   THEN ;
: DEF.SYM.FOUND! SYM.FOUND TO DEF.SYM.FOUND ;
  -->

79
\ symbol table bit flags access              \ JFB 23:44 03/24/86
: DEFINED! ( - ) TRUE  DEFINED +SYM.FOUND DEFINED.MASK
   !BITS(S ;
: IS.FORWARD ( - ) TRUE  FORWARD +SYM.FOUND FORWARD.MASK
   !BITS(S ;
-->

80
\ word defined and simulating tests          \ JFB 07:23 03/21/86
: DEFINED? ( - bool; t=defined ) DEFINED +SYM.FOUND
   DEFINED.MASK  @BITS(S ;
: DEF.DEFINED? ( - bool; t=defining word defined ) DEFINED
  DEF.SYM.FOUND + DEFINED.MASK  @BITS(S ;
: FORWARD? ( - bool; t=word forward referenced ) FORWARD
  +SYM.FOUND FORWARD.MASK  @BITS(S ;
: SIMULATING? ( - bool; t=simulating ) R0(H RP(H - ;
: LABEL? ( symbol pfa - bool; t = a defined label )
   TO SYM.FOUND DEFINED? TYPE.FOUND@ LAB.TYPE = AND ;
  -->

81
\ hashing                                    \ JFB 16:07 03/11/86
: VOC.HASH ( - lfa ) WORDSx HEREx 1+ C@x 3 AND 4* 2+ DUP
   TO VOC.HASH# ; \ save hash number
: HASH-CFA ( - )
   TRG.CFA.LINKS.FOUND
   TRG.CFA.FOUND@ $FF AND 2* CFA.HASH.TBL + DUP @(S
   TRG.CFA.LINKS.FOUND! !(S ;
-->

82
\ set BLKx and INx for error                 \ JFB 15:18 05/10/86
: SET.PACKET.BLK&IN ( - ) WORDSx PACKET.BLK@ -DUP
   IF BLKx !x PACKET.IN@ INx !x \ symbol was typed
   THEN PACKET.HOST.ADR@ NFA(S HEAD(S>T ;
: SET.SYM.BLK&IN ( - ) WORDSx SYM.BLK.FOUND@ -DUP
   IF BLKx !x SYM.IN.FOUND@ INx !x
   THEN SYM.FOUND NFA(S HEAD(S>T ;
  -->

83
\ find words in symbol table                 \ JFB 09:33 03/13/86
: -FIND(H  ( - host CFA \ precedence flag \ true OR false )
   WORDSx HEREx
   CONTEXT(S @  VOC.HASH + @(S  <FIND(H> \ in context ?
   IF TRUE
   ELSE CONTEXT(S @ CURRENT(S @ =
      IF FALSE
      ELSE HEREx  CURRENT(S @  VOC.HASH# + @(S
         <FIND(H> \ no, search current
      THEN
   THEN ; \ NOTE: word at target here
          \ side effect: <FIND(H> sets SYM.FOUND
-->

84
\ target word creation                       \ JFB 09:02 05/08/86
```

```
: CREATE(T ( - ) WORDSx WIDTHx @x
   IF HEREx DUP  C@x  WIDTHx @x  MIN  1+ ALLOTx
      DUP $A0 TOGGLEx  HEREx 1- $80 TOGGLEx
      LATESTx ,x  CURRENTx @x !x
   THEN HEREx 2+ ,x ;
-->

85
\ symbol table word creation                      \ JFB 08:37 03/25/86
: <CREATE(S> ( - ) WORDSx HERE(S HEREx C@x DUP WIDTH @ MIN
    >R $A0 OR C,(S \ count
    HEREx 1+ HERE(S R CMOVET>S R> ALLOT(S \ move name
    HERE(S 1- $80 TOGGLE(S \ set high bit of last char
    CURRENT(S @ VOC.HASH + @(S ,(S \ place link
    DUP TO LATEST(S
    CURRENT(S @ VOC.HASH# + !(S \ update latest
    0 ,(S \ place code field
    HERE(S DUP  TO SYM.FOUND \ save pfa
    SYM.LEN 0 FILL(S  SYM.LEN ALLOT(S ; \ 0 parameter field
-->

86
\ symbol table word creation cont.                \ JFB 10:30 11/03/88
: CREATE(S ( - ) WORDSx
   -FIND(H \ is this name in the symbol table ?
   IF 2DROP DEFINED?
      IF >S1 S1! HEREx COUNTx TYPEx SPACE >S0
         4 MESSAGEx \ yes, shout
         <CREATE(S> \ make a new one
      ELSE SYM.FOUND NFA(S TO LATEST(S
         SMUDGE(S \ hide old one
      THEN
   ELSE <CREATE(S> \ no, make it
   THEN SYM.BLK! SYM.IN! ;
-->

87
\ address resolution                              \ JFB 21:22 06/30/86
: RESOLVE.CF ( value \ address - ) WORDSx !x ;
: RESOLVE.CFA ( value \ address - ) WORDSx
  TYPE.FOUND@ LAB.TYPE = DEFINED? AND
  IF SET.PACKET.BLK&IN 30 ERRORx
  THEN !x ;
: RESOLVE.PFA ( value \ address - ) WORDSx SWAP >BODY(T
  SWAP !x ;
: RESOLVE.HLP ( value \ address - ) WORDSx !x ;
: RESOLVE.ABS.ASM ( value \ address - ) WORDSx !x ;
  -->

88
\ address resolution cont.                        \ JFB 18:58 11/04/88
0 VARIABLE RESOLVE.VECTOR      -2 ALLOT
' RESOLVE.CF  CFA , ' RESOLVE.CFA     CFA , ' RESOLVE.PFA CFA ,
' RESOLVE.HLP CFA , ' RESOLVE.ABS.ASM CFA , ' DOASMTYPE1  CFA ,
' DOASMTYPE2  CFA ,
: RESOLVE ( value \ pointer to reference link - ) DUP @(S
  TO PACKET.BASE OVER SWAP !(S \ place value
   BEGIN PACKET.BASE
   WHILE DUP PACKET.TRG.ADR@  PACKET.REF.TYPE@ 2*
      RESOLVE.VECTOR + @ EXECUTE NEXT.PACKET \ -1 AT +-REF +!
   REPEAT DROP ;
-->

89
```

```
\ address compilation cont.                   \ JFB 15:48 03/18/86
: COMPILE-DOCODE.PTR ( target address \ docode ptr - ) WORDSx
   DEF.DEFINED? \ is this defining word defined ?
   IF @(S SWAP !x \ yes, use it
   ELSE PACKET.LIST@ DUP @(S PACKET.LINK! \ no, forward ref it
      PACKET.BASE SWAP !(S \ link it in
      PACKET.TRG.ADR! \ place target address
      CF.REF PACKET.REF.TYPE!
      PACKET.BLK! PACKET.IN!
   THEN ;
\ compiles a DOCODE address into a code field
  -->

90
\ address compilation cont.                    JFB 13:55 05/08/88
: COMPILE-DOES>HL.PTR ( target address - ) WORDSx
   DEF.DOES>HL.PTR.FOUND \ address of defining word DOCODE field
   DEF.DEFINED? \ is this defining word defined ?
   IF @(S SWAP !x \ yes, use it
   ELSE PACKET.LIST@ DUP @(S PACKET.LINK! \ no, forward ref it
      PACKET.BASE SWAP !(S \ link it in
      PACKET.TRG.ADR! \ place target address
      CF.REF PACKET.REF.TYPE!
      PACKET.BLK! PACKET.IN!
   THEN ;
\ compiles a high level code address into the PFA of a
\ defining word
  -->

91
\ address compilation cont.                   \ JFB 11:19 03/22/86
: COMPILE.CFA.FOUND ( - ) WORDSx DEFINED? NOT
   IF IS.FORWARD
      PACKET.LIST@ TRG.CFA.FOUND DUP @(S PACKET.LINK!
      PACKET.BASE SWAP !(S \ link it in
      HEREx PACKET.TRG.ADR! \ place target address
      SYM.FOUND PACKET.HOST.ADR!
      CFA.REF PACKET.REF.TYPE!
      PACKET.BLK! PACKET.IN!
   THEN 1 REF.CTR.FOUND +!(S TRG.CFA.FOUND@ ,x ;
: COMPILE.FWD.CFA ( - ) CREATE(S SMUDGE(S
   COMPILE.CFA.FOUND ;
  -->

92
\ address compilation cont.                   \ JFB 15:49 03/18/86
: <COMPILE(T> WORDSx ?COMPx R @ -DUP
   IF TO SYM.FOUND COMPILE.CFA.FOUND
   ELSE R 4+ DUP C@ 1+ HEREx SWAP CMOVEH>T
     HEREx CURRENT(S @ VOC.HASH + @(S
     <FIND(H> \ found in current ?
     IF 2DROP COMPILE.CFA.FOUND
     ELSE COMPILE.FWD.CFA
     THEN SYM.FOUND R !
  THEN R> 4+ DUP C@ + 1+ >R ;
: COMPILE(T COMPILE <COMPILE(T> 0 ,
   HERE COMPILE(T.LINK @ , COMPILE(T.LINK !
   BL WORD HERE C@ 1+ ALLOT ; IMMEDIATE
  -->

93
\ host ;CODE                                  \ JFB 09:56 04/14/86
: <;CODE(H> ( DO;CODE(H CFA - )
  LATEST(T(S.CFA(S! \ put symbol CF
```

```
  LATEST(T.CFA(T DEF.DOCODE.PTR.FOUND
  COMPILE-DOCODE.PTR ; \ put target CF
: ;CODE(H ( - symbol PFA )
  HERE 0A + [COMPILE] LITERAL \ address of DO:(H
  COMPILE <;CODE(H> COMPILE ;S
  LATEST , \ leave latest for trace
  DO:(H , COMPILE GET.TRG.PFA ; IMMEDIATE
-->

94
\ [x ]x CREATEx                              \ JFB 09:56 05/12/86
WORDSx DEFINITIONS
: [x ( - ) INTERPRETING! ; IMMEDIATE
: ]x ( - ) COMPILING! ; IMMEDIATE
: CREATEx ( - ) BL WORDx CREATE(S CREATE(T
  SYM.FOUND DUP TO LATEST(T(S.PFA(S \ save symbol PFA
  NFA(S TO LATEST(T(S \ save symbol NFA
  HEREx CFAx TRG.CFA.FOUND RESOLVE \ resolve refs to this CFA
  HASH-CFA ; \ link this CFA to the hash table
: -FINDx BL WORDx -FIND(H DEFINED?
    IF >R 2DROP TRG.CFA.FOUND@ >BODY(T DUP NFAx C@x R>
    ELSE IF 2DROP
         THEN 0
    THEN ;
FORTH DEFINITIONS
  -->
95
\ host <BUILDS DOES>                         \ JFB 09:49 04/14/86
: <BUILDS(H ( - ) WORDSx CREATEx SMUDGEx HEREx 0 ,x
   COMPILE-DOES>HL.PTR ; \ put high level ptr
: <DOES>(H> ( DODOES>(H CFA - ) WORDSx
   LATEST(T(S.CFA(S! \ put symbol CF
   LATEST(T.CFA(T
   DOES>.SYM.FOUND TO DEF.SYM.FOUND DEF.DOCODE.PTR.FOUND
   COMPILE-DOCODE.PTR ; \ put target dodoes CF
: DOES>(H ( - symbol PFA )
   HERE 0A + [COMPILE] LITERAL \ address of DO:(H
   COMPILE <DOES>(H>  COMPILE ;S
   LATEST , \ leave latest for trace
   DO:(H , COMPILE GET.TRG.PFA COMPILE 2+ ; IMMEDIATE
-->

96
\ locate target addresses                    \ JFB 19:29 03/12/86
: GET.CF ( target CFA - host CFA \ FALSE
                      - TRUE;  t=host CFA is 0 )
  WORDSx HEREx OVER U<
   IF 2+ @(S DUP TO SYM.FOUND
   ELSE DUP >R $FF AND 2* CFA.HASH.TBL + @(S
     BEGIN DUP 2+ @(S R =
        IF TO SYM.FOUND 1 \ found it leave
        ELSE -DUP
           IF @(S 0 \ get next
           ELSE 0 TO SYM.FOUND 1 \ end, leave FALSE
           THEN
        THEN
     UNTIL R> DROP SYM.FOUND
   THEN 2- @(S -DUP 0= ; -->

97
\ locate target addresses cont.                JFB 16:48 06/04/88
: CAN'T.DO.ERROR WORDSx 31 ERRORx ;
: CAN'T.DO SET.SYM.BLK&IN CAN'T.DO.ERROR ;
: CAN'T.DO! LATEST(T(S.PFA(S CFA(S @(S 0=
```

```
   IF [ ' CAN'T.DO CFA ] LITERAL
      LATEST(T(S.PFA(S CFA(S !(S \ can't do one of these
   THEN ;
: GET.HOST.CFA ( target CFA - host CFA ) WORDSx GET.CF
   IF HEREx IP(H 2- @x U< \ a packet reference ?
      IF IP(H 2- @x TO PACKET.BASE SET.PACKET.BLK&IN
      ELSE SET.SYM.BLK&IN
      THEN CAN'T.DO.ERROR
   THEN ;  -->

98
\ alias host words                               \ JFB 21:18 03/26/86
: ALIAS ( - ) BL WORD HERE LATEST (FIND) NOT 5 ?ERROR
   DROP CFA ASCII x HERE DUP C@ + 1+ C!
   HERE DUP C@ 1+ SWAP C!
   HERE CURRENT @ @ (FIND)
   IF DROP NFA CR ID. 4 MESSAGE SPACE
   THEN HERE DUP C@ WIDTH @ MIN 1+ ALLOT
   DUP $A0 TOGGLE HERE 1- $80 TOGGLE
   LATEST , CURRENT @ ! HERE 2+ ,
   BB C, , \ BX # ' name MOV
   FF C, 27 C, \ WORD [BX] JMP
   SMUDGE ;
-->

99
\ alias definitions                                JFB 07:13 06/30/89
WORDSx DEFINITIONS            ALIAS 0>
ALIAS     *   ALIAS      */   ALIAS */MOD   ALIAS          +
ALIAS    +-   ALIAS       -   ALIAS  -DUP   ALIAS          /
ALIAS  /MOD   ALIAS      0<   ALIAS    0=   ALIAS         1+
ALIAS    1-   ALIAS      2*   ALIAS    2+   ALIAS         2-
ALIAS     <   ALIAS       =   ALIAS     >   ALIAS ?TERMINAL
ALIAS   ABS   ALIAS     AND   ALIAS    BL   ALIAS   CONSOLE
ALIAS    CR   ALIAS      D+   ALIAS   D+-   ALIAS       D2/
ALIAS  DABS   ALIAS  DMINUS   ALIAS  DROP   ALIAS       DUP
ALIAS GOTOXY  ALIAS      M*   ALIAS    M/   ALIAS       MAX
ALIAS   MIN   ALIAS   MINUS   ALIAS   MOD   ALIAS        OR
ALIAS  OVER   ALIAS PRINTER   ALIAS   ROT   ALIAS      S->D
ALIAS   SP!   ALIAS     SP@   ALIAS SPACE   ALIAS    SPACES
ALIAS  SWAP   ALIAS      U*   ALIAS    U/   ALIAS       XOR
ALIAS   KEY   ALIAS    EMIT   ALIAS   CLS -->
100
\ COMPILEx [COMPILE]x                              JFB 20:53 05/30/88
: COMPILEx ( - ) IP(H DUP 2+ TO IP(H @x
   GET.CF 0= IF DROP THEN COMPILE.CFA.FOUND ;
: [COMPILE]x BL WORDx -FIND(H
   IF 2DROP COMPILE.CFA.FOUND
   ELSE COMPILE.FWD.CFA
   THEN ; IMMEDIATE
  -->

101
\ LITx LITERALx DLITERALx                        \ JFB 10:07 05/10/86
: LITx IP(H DUP 2+ TO IP(H @x ;
: LITERALx ( number - number; if not compiling )
   COMPILING? ( SIMULATING? NOT AND)
   IF COMPILE(T LIT ,x
   THEN ; IMMEDIATE
: DLITERALx ( double number - number ; if not compiling )
  COMPILING?
  IF SWAP [COMPILE] LITERALx [COMPILE] LITERALx
  THEN ; IMMEDIATE
  -->
```

```
102
\ 'x                                         \ JFB 15:14 06/30/86
: 'x COMPILING?
   IF COMPILE(T LIT BL WORDx -FIND(H DUP
      IF NIP NIP
      THEN DEFINED? AND
      IF TRG.CFA.FOUND@ >BODY(T ,x
      ELSE COMPILE.FWD.CFA PFA.REF PACKET.REF.TYPE!
      THEN
   ELSE BL WORDx -FIND(H NOT DEFINED? NOT OR
      IF ASSEMBLING?
         IF DOASMFWD PFA.REF PACKET.REF.TYPE!
         ELSE 5 ERRORx
         THEN
      ELSE 2DROP TRG.CFA.FOUND@ >BODY(T
      THEN
   THEN ; IMMEDIATE  -->
103
\ target numeric constants                   \ JFB 09:28 07/02/86
FORTH DEFINITIONS
: "NUMBER" WORDSx COMPILING? DEFINED? AND SIMULATING? NOT AND
   IF DROP TRG.CFA.FOUND@ ,x
   ELSE COMPILING? SIMULATING? NOT AND
      IF COMPILE(T LIT ,x
      THEN
   THEN ;
WORDSx DEFINITIONS
: 0x 0 "NUMBER" ; IMMEDIATE
: 1x 1 "NUMBER" ; IMMEDIATE
: 2x 2 "NUMBER" ; IMMEDIATE
: 3x 3 "NUMBER" ; IMMEDIATE
: -1x -1 "NUMBER" ; IMMEDIATE
: -2x -2 "NUMBER" ; IMMEDIATE
  -->
104
\ host inner interpreter                     \ JFB 09:58 04/14/86
FORTH DEFINITIONS
: <INTERPRET(H> ( interpreter pointer - ) WORDSx
  DEF.SYM.FOUND! IP(H.PUSH TO IP(H
      BEGIN IP(H DUP 2+ TO IP(H @x
         GET.HOST.CFA
         [ HERE TO TRACE2 ] NOOP
         EXECUTE POP?
      UNTIL FALSE TO POP? ;
  -->

105
\ :x                                               07:18 10/12/89
WORDSx DEFINITIONS
: :x  ( - ) DEF.SYM.FOUND!
   ?EXECx !CSPx CURRENT(S @ CONTEXT(S !
   CURRENTx @x CONTEXTx !x
   CREATEx :.TYPE TYPE.FOUND!
   [COMPILE] ]x
   ;CODE(H <INTERPRET(H> ;
  -->

106
\ ;Sx ;x ;!                                  \ JFB 16:15 03/18/86
: ;Sx ( - ) SIMULATING?
      IF IP(H.POP TRUE TO POP?
      ELSE $400 INx !x
      THEN ;
```

```
: ;x ( - ) ?CSPx COMPILE(T ;S SMUDGEx
   [COMPILE] [x ;
   IMMEDIATE
: ;! ( - ) ?CSPx COMPILE(T ;S SMUDGEx
   [COMPILE] [x ;
   IMMEDIATE
  -->

107
\ USERx CONSTANTx                              \ JFB 09:39 03/25/86
: USERx ( value - ) DEF.SYM.FOUND!
   CREATEx USR.TYPE TYPE.FOUND!
      ,x \ place offset value
   SMUDGEx \ make it visible
   ;CODE(H @x ; \ get constant value
: CONSTANTx ( value - ) DEF.SYM.FOUND!
   CREATEx CON.TYPE TYPE.FOUND!
   SMUDGEx \ make it visible
     ,x \ place constant value
   ;CODE(H @x ; \ get constant value
  -->

108
\ ram and rom variables                        \ JFB 10:53 04/06/86
FORTH DEFINITIONS
: VARIABLE-RAM ( value - ) WORDSx DEF.SYM.FOUND!
   CREATEx VAR.TYPE TYPE.FOUND!
   SMUDGEx \ make it visible
      ,x \ place value
   ;CODE(H ; \ leave variable address
' VARIABLE-RAM CFA WORDSx ' VARIABLEx 1+ ! FORTH
: VARIABLE-ROM ( value - ) WORDSx DEF.SYM.FOUND!
   CREATEx VAR.TYPE TYPE.FOUND!
   SMUDGEx \ make it visible
      THEREx ,x \ point to ram
      ,(R)x \ place variable value
   ;CODE(H @x ; \ get variable address
  -->

109
\ extend a vocabulary                          \ JFB 16:17 03/18/86
: EXTEND-VOC ( - ) HERE(S DUP EXTEND.SIZE 0 FILL(S
   EXTEND.SIZE ALLOT(S \ extend VOC
   EXTEND.PTR.FOUND! EXTEND.BACK.PTR.FOUND! \ point it
   VOC-LINK(S @ SYM.VOC.LINK.FOUND! \ link to prev voc
   SYM.VOC.LINK.FOUND VOC-LINK(S ! \ save this link
   HERE(S DUP #VOC.THREADS 4*
   DUP >R 0 FILL(S R> ALLOT(S \ make voc threads
   DUP VOC.THREAD.PTR.FOUND! #VOC.THREADS 0
   DO $A081 OVER I 4* + !(S \ blank name
      CURRENT(S @ I 4* + \ link to CURRENT voc
      OVER I 4* + 2+ !(S
   LOOP DROP ;
  -->

110
\ ram vocabularies                             \ JFB 18:33 03/25/86
: VOCABULARY-RAM ( - ) WORDSx DEF.SYM.FOUND!
   <BUILDS(H VOC.TYPE TYPE.FOUND!
      $81 C,x $A0 C,x CURRENTx @x NULL.VOC(T =
      IF HEREx CURRENTx !x NULL.VOC(T @x ,x
      ELSE CURRENTx @x 2- ,x
      THEN HEREx VOC-LINKx @x ,x VOC-LINKx !x
      EXTEND.PTR.FOUND@ NOT \ an undefined voc ?
```

```
      IF EXTEND-VOC
      THEN
   DOES>(H 2+ CONTEXTx !x VOC.THREAD.PTR.FOUND@ CONTEXT(S ! ;
FORTH  DEFINITIONS
' VOCABULARY-RAM CFA WORDSx ' VOCABULARYx 1+ ! FORTH
  -->

111
\ rom vocabularies                               \ JFB 09:03 04/06/86
: VOCABULARY-ROM ( - ) WORDSx DEF.SYM.FOUND!
   <BUILDS(H VOC.TYPE TYPE.FOUND!
      THEREx ,x $81 C,(R)x $A0 C,(R)x CURRENTx @x
      NULL.VOC(T =
      IF THEREx CURRENTx !x NULL.VOC(T @x ,(R)x
      ELSE CURRENTx @x 2- ,(R)x
      THEN HEREx VOC-LINKx @x ,x VOC-LINKx !x
      EXTEND.PTR.FOUND@ NOT \ an undefined voc ?
      IF EXTEND-VOC
      THEN
   DOES>(H @x 2+ CONTEXTx !x
   VOC.THREAD.PTR.FOUND@ CONTEXT(S ! ;
  -->

112
\ DEFINITIONSx <VALUE>                           \ JFB 08:35 04/06/86
WORDSx DEFINITIONS
: DEFINITIONSx CONTEXT(S @ CURRENT(S !
   CONTEXTx @x CURRENTx !x ;
FORTH DEFINITIONS
: <VALUE> ( - value; if interpreting ) WORDSx
   ASSEMBLING? DEFINED? NOT AND
   IF DOASMFWD
   ELSE COMPILING? DEFINED? NOT AND
      IF SYM.FOUND COMPILE(T LIT TO SYM.FOUND COMPILE.CFA.FOUND
      ELSE INTERPRETING? DEFINED? NOT AND 5 ?ERRORx
         TRG.CFA.FOUND@ [COMPILE] LITERALx
      THEN
   THEN ;
WORDSx DEFINITIONS
  -->
113
\ LABELx L:x EQUx                                \ JFB 17:18 05/12/86
: LABELx ( value - ) BL WORDx CREATE(S SMUDGE(S \ make it
   [ ' <VALUE> CFA ] LITERAL SYM.FOUND CFA(S !(S \ put CF
   LAB.TYPE TYPE.FOUND! DEFINED!
   TRG.CFA.FOUND RESOLVE \ save value
   IMMEDIATE(S ;
: L:x ( - ) HEREx LABELx ;
: EQUx ( value - ) BL WORDx CREATE(S SMUDGE(S
   FORWARD?
   IF SET.SYM.BLK&IN 32 ERRORx
   THEN [ ' <VALUE> CFA ] LITERAL SYM.FOUND CFA(S !(S
   TRG.CFA.FOUND !(S \ save value
   EQU.TYPE TYPE.FOUND!
   DEFINED! IMMEDIATE(S ;
  -->

114
\ (.")x ."x                                      \ JFB 16:10 03/12/86
: (.")x ( - ) IP(H COUNTx DUP 1+ IP(H + TO IP(H TYPEx ;
: ."x ( - ) ASCII " COMPILING?
   IF COMPILE(T (.") WORDx HEREx C@x 1+ ALLOTx
   ELSE WORDx HEREx COUNTx TYPEx
   THEN ;  IMMEDIATE
```

```
  -->

115
\ BACKx (DO)x LEAVEx BRANCHx 0BRANCHx        \ JFB 14:56 03/12/86
: BACKx ( address - ) HEREx - ,x ;
: (DO)x ( - ) SWAP >Rx >Rx ;
: LEAVEx  ( - ) R>x DROP R>x DUP >Rx >Rx ;
: BRANCHx ( - ) IP(H DUP @x + TO IP(H ;
: 0BRANCHx  ( bool - ) IF IP(H 2+ TO IP(H
  ELSE BRANCHx
  THEN  ;
: ?PAIRSx - 13 ?ERRORx ;
  -->

116
\ (+LOOP)x (LOOP)x +LOOPx AGAINx BEGINx      \ JFB 10:09 03/12/86
: (+LOOP)x ( increment - ) R>x OVER + R>x 2DUP
  >Rx >Rx ROT 0<
  IF SWAP
  THEN  <
  IF BRANCHx
  ELSE  R>x R>x 2DROP
    IP(H 2+ TO IP(H
  THEN  ;
: (LOOP)x ( - ) 1 (+LOOP)x ;
: +LOOPx ( loop address \ 3 - ) 3 ?PAIRSx COMPILE(T (+LOOP)
   BACKx ; IMMEDIATE
: AGAINx ( loop address \ 1 - ) 1 ?PAIRSx COMPILE(T BRANCH
   BACKx ; IMMEDIATE
: BEGINx ( - loop address \ 1 ) ?COMPx HEREx 1 ; IMMEDIATE
  -->
117
\ DOx THENx ENDIFx ELSEx                     \ JFB 15:42 03/12/86
: DOx ( - loop address \ 3 ) COMPILE(T (DO) HEREx 3 ;
  IMMEDIATE
: THENx ( offset address \ 2 - ) ?COMPx 2 ?PAIRSx HEREx OVER
  - SWAP !x ; IMMEDIATE
: ENDIFx  [COMPILE] THENx ; IMMEDIATE
: ELSEx ( offset address \ 2 - offset address \ 2 )
   2 ?PAIRSx COMPILE(T BRANCH HEREx 0 ,x SWAP 2
   [COMPILE] THENx
   2 ; IMMEDIATE
  -->

118
\ IFx LOOPx REPEATx UNTILx WHILEx            \ JFB 09:16 11/01/88
: IFx ( - offset address \ 2 - ) COMPILE(T 0BRANCH
    HEREx 0 ,x 2 ; IMMEDIATE
: LOOPx ( loop address \ 3 - ) 3 ?PAIRSx COMPILE(T (LOOP)
   BACKx ; IMMEDIATE
: REPEATx ( loop address \ 1 \ offset address \ 4 - )
   >R >R [COMPILE] AGAINx R> R>
   2- [COMPILE] THENx ;
   IMMEDIATE
: UNTILx ( loop address \ 1 - ) 1 ?PAIRSx COMPILE(T 0BRANCH
   BACKx ; IMMEDIATE
: WHILEx ( loop address \ 1 - loop address \ 1 \ offset address
         \ 4 ) [COMPILE] IFx 2+ ; IMMEDIATE
  -->

119
\ .x ?x .Sx U.x D.x                          \ JFB 12:04 03/15/86
: .x ( value - ) BASEx! . ;
: ?x ( address - ) @x .x ;
```

```
: .Sx ( - ) BASEx! .S ;
: U.x ( value - ) BASEx! U. ;
: D.x ( d - ) BASEx! 0 D.R SPACE ;
  -->

120
\ EXPECTx                                JFB 20:34 05/30/88
: EXPECTx OVER + OVER
   DO KEY DUP 0E +ORIGIN @ =
      IF DROP DUP I = DUP R> 2- + >R
         IF 7 ( BELL)
         ELSE 8 ( BSOUT) EMIT BL EMIT 8 ( BSOUT)
         THEN
      ELSE DUP 0D =
      IF LEAVE DROP BL 0
      ELSE DUP
      THEN R C!x 0 R 1+ !x
      THEN EMIT
   LOOP DROP ;
  -->

121
\ QUERYx                               \ JFB 16:15 05/10/86
: QUERYx BLKx @x 0=
   IF TIBx @x 50 EXPECTx 0 INx !x
   ELSE INx @x $400 =
      IF FALSE TO NOT.DONE?
      THEN
  THEN ;
  -->

122
\ <BUILDSx DOES>x                      \ JFB 11:48 03/22/86
FORTH DEFINITIONS
: DODOES>(H ( - ) WORDSx TRG.CFA.FOUND@
   >BODY(T DUP 2+ \ leave "PFA"
   SWAP @x \ get high level pointer
   <INTERPRET(H> ;
WORDSx DEFINITIONS
: <BUILDSx CREATEx SMUDGEx HEREx 0 ,x
    COMPILE-DOES>HL.PTR \ put high level ptr
    HDF.TYPE TYPE.FOUND! [ ' DODOES>(H CFA ] LITERAL
    LATEST(T(S.CFA(S! ; \ put symbol CF
: DOES>x
   LATEST(T.CFA(T
   DOES>.SYM.FOUND TO DEF.SYM.FOUND DEF.DOCODE.PTR.FOUND
   COMPILE-DOCODE.PTR \ put target dodoes CF
   IP(H.POP TRUE TO POP? ;  -->
123
\ FORTHx                               \ JFB 10:52 07/17/86
: FORTHx FORTH.THREAD CONTEXT(S ! DEFINED?
   IF TRG.CFA.FOUND@ ROMING?
      IF 4+ @x 2+
      ELSE 6 +
      THEN CONTEXTx !x
   ELSE NULL.VOC(T CONTEXTx !x
   THEN ASSEMBLING?
   IF INTERPRETING!
   THEN ; IMMEDIATE
  -->

124
\ ASSEMBLERx                           \ JFB 11:43 07/17/86
: ASSEMBLERx ASM.THREAD CONTEXT(S ! DEFINED?
```

```
   IF TRG.CFA.FOUND@ ROMING?
      IF 4+ @x 2+
      ELSE 6 +
      THEN CONTEXTx !x
   ELSE NULL.VOC(T CONTEXTx !x
   THEN INTERPRETING?
   IF ASSEMBLING! DOASMRESET
   THEN ; IMMEDIATE
  -->

125
\ CODEx END-CODEx ;CODEx                              12:30 07/25/86
: CODEx CREATEx CODE.TYPE TYPE.FOUND! CAN'T.DO!
   ?EXEC !CSPx [COMPILE] ASSEMBLERx DOASMCODE ;
: END-CODEx DO?UNCONS ?CSPx SMUDGEx
   [COMPILE] FORTHx DOASMEND-CODE ;
: (;CODE)x [ ' CAN'T.DO CFA ] LITERAL
   LATEST(T(S.PFA(S CFA(S !(S \ can't do one of these
   LDF.TYPE SYM.TYPE +LATEST(T(S.PFA(S SYM.TYPE.MASK !BITS(S
   IP(H LATEST(T.CFA(T !x \ store CF
   IP(H.POP TRUE TO POP? ;
: ;CODEx ?CSPx COMPILE(T (;CODE) HEREx
   LATEST(T(S.PFA(S TO DEF.SYM.FOUND DEF.DOCODE.PTR.FOUND
   RESOLVE [COMPILE] [x [COMPILE] ASSEMBLERx DOASMCODE
   ; IMMEDIATE
  -->

126
\ file and extent names                          \ JFB 12:32 05/14/86
FORTH DEFINITIONS
: ASCII"  0 VARIABLE -2 ALLOT 22 WORD HERE C@ 1+ ALLOT ;
: ASCIIZ" 0 VARIABLE -2 ALLOT HERE 1- DUP >R C@ >R
   -1 ALLOT 22 WORD HERE C@ 1+ ALLOT R> R> C! 0 C, ;
ASCII" IMAGE" IMAGE"
ASCIIZ" DEFAULT.SYM DEFAULT.SYM"
ASCIIZ" COM-EXT .COM"
ASCIIZ" SYM-EXT .SYM"
ASCIIZ" MAP-EXT .MAP"
ASCIIZ" RES-EXT .RES"
  -->

127
\ USINGx PFILEx SFILEx AFILEx                      JFB 13:38 05/08/88
WORDSx DEFINITIONS
: USINGx DUP CLOSEHANDLE DUP BL WORDx HEREx SWAP
   OVER C@x 1+ DUP $40 > $1A ?ERROR
   CMOVET>H DUP ?.SCR
   DUP COUNT + 3 ERASE OPENHANDLE 1 TO ?.FILE ;
: PFILEx PRIF USINGx ;
: SFILEx SECF USINGx ;
: AFILEx AUXF USINGx ;
  -->

128
\ LOADx -->x THRUx LISTx                           JFB 16:39 06/04/88
: LOADx PRINT-STACK?
   BLKx @x >R INx @x >R 0 INx !x B/SCR(T * BLKx !x
   DOINTERPRET(H R> INx !x R> BLKx !x ;
: -->x ?LOADINGx
   PRINT-STACK? 0 INx !x B/SCR(T BLKx @x OVER MOD - BLKx +!x ;
   IMMEDIATE
: THRUx DECIMAL 1+ SWAP DO I LOADx LOOP ;
: .STACKx >S1 S1! CR0> ." Print stack between screens" Y/N? >S0
  IF TRUE TO .STACK?
```

```
  THEN ;
: NO.STACK?x FALSE TO .STACK? ;
: LISTx >S1 S1! CR0> DUP SCRx !x ." Screen # " 1FF AND . 10 0
   DO CR R 3 .R SPACE R SCRx @x WORDSx .LINEx
   LOOP CR >S0 ;
  -->
129
\ TRACEx KEYTRACEx NOTRACEx                         JFB 15:12 05/22/88
: TRACEx >S1 S1! CR0> ." Trace" Y/N? >S0
   IF [ ' TRACE.WORDx CFA ] LITERAL TRACE1 !
      [ ' TRACE.<I(H> CFA ] LITERAL TRACE2 !
      [ ' TRACE.I(H CFA ] LITERAL TRACE3 !
   THEN ; IMMEDIATE
: KEYTRACEx >S1 S1! CR0> ." Key trace" Y/N? >S0
   IF [ ' KEY.TRACE.WORDx CFA ] LITERAL TRACE1 !
      [ ' KEY.TRACE.<I(H> CFA ] LITERAL TRACE2 !
      [ ' KEY.TRACE.I(H CFA ] LITERAL TRACE3 !
   THEN ; IMMEDIATE
: NOTRACEx [ ' NOOP CFA ] LITERAL DUP TRACE1 ! DUP TRACE2 !
  TRACE3 ! ; IMMEDIATE
  -->

130
\ RAM-ORIGINx ROM/RAMx FORTH-ORIGINx         \ JFB 18:10 04/21/86
: RAM-ORIGINx ( starting address of RAM - )
   TRUE TO ROMING?
   [ ' VARIABLE-ROM CFA ] LITERAL
   [ ' VARIABLEx 1+ ] LITERAL !
   [ ' VOCABULARY-ROM CFA ] LITERAL
   [ ' VOCABULARYx 1+ ] LITERAL !
   DUP HOLD.RAM.START !(S DP-RAM(T ! ;
: ROM/RAMx DROP RAM-ORIGINx ; \ V1.0
: FORTH-ORIGINx DUP DPx !x TARGET.ORG! ORIGIN.SYM.FOUND
   TO SYM.FOUND TRG.CFA.FOUND RESOLVE DEFINED! ;
: ORG/DBx DROP FORTH-ORIGINx ; \ V1.0
: ORG/IMGx DROP FORTH-ORIGINx ; \ V1.0
  -->

131
\ ORIGINx +ORIGINx EMx MEM-ENDx BASE-36x    \ JFB 07:30 07/11/86
: ORGx TARGET.ORG! DPx !x ;
: +ORIGINx ORIGIN.SYM.FOUND TO SYM.FOUND DEFINED?
   IF TRG.CFA.FOUND@ +
   ELSE 33 ERRORx
   THEN ;
: EMx EM(H [COMPILE] LITERALx ; IMMEDIATE
: MEM-ENDx ' EM(H ! ;
: BASE-36x $24 BASEx !x ; \ V1.0
: IS-Xx ; \ V1.0
: IS-FENCEx LATESTx FENCEx !x ;
: TARGET-WIDTHx WIDTHx !x ; \ V1.0
  -->

132
\ set up meta-compiler to swap target bytes \ JFB 08:46 03/19/86
FORTH DEFINITIONS
: SWAP-BYTES(H WORDSx FIRST(T NULL.VOC(T - 1+ 0
   DO NULL.VOC(T I + DUP
      @x >< SWAP !x 2 \ swap all user vars ect.
   +LOOP LIMIT(T FIRST(T
   DO I @x >< I !x $404 \ swap all blk #'s
   +LOOP [ ' ><!(T CFA ] LITERAL [ ' !x 1+ ] LITERAL !
   [ ' ><@(T CFA ] LITERAL [ ' @x 1+ ] LITERAL !
   [ ' NOOP CFA ]  LITERAL
```

```
   [ ' SWAP-BYTESx 1+ ] LITERAL ! ; \ ignore a second time
' SWAP-BYTES(H CFA ' SWAP-BYTESx 1+ !
  -->

133
\ add an extent to a file name                    JFB 09:08 04/23/88
: EXTENT(H ( extent string address - )
   0 PAD 2- ! \ clear for 1 char names
   >R 1 PAD DUP C@ + 4 0
   DO DUP I - C@ 2E =
      IF NIP 0 SWAP LEAVE
      THEN
   LOOP DROP
   IF R PAD DUP C@ + 1+ 5 CMOVE
      PAD C@ 4 + PAD C! ELSE 0 PAD DUP C@ + 1+ C!
   THEN R> DROP ;
  -->

134
\ check for dos file error                        JFB 09:43 05/30/88
: DOSERR? ( ax \ dx \ bool \ fun - ax \ dx; t=dos error occured)
   SWAP
   IF >S1 S1! CR0> ." File error, function: " BASE @ >R HEX U.
      8 EMIT ." , error: " SWAP . ." file: " PAD COUNT TYPE
      R> BASE ! >S0 STOPIT
   ELSE DROP
   THEN ;
  -->

135
\ save the symbol table                               10:00 09/29/86
: SAVE-IMAGE.SYM ( - )
   0 PAD DUP C@ 4 - DUP >R OVER C! R> + 1+ C! SYM-EXT
   EXTENT(H ?CS: PAD 1+ 0 0 $3C00 21INT5 \ create handle
   $3C00 DOSERR? DROP
   >R SYM.SEG 0 HERE(S R $4000 21INT5 \ write file
   $4000 DOSERR? 2DROP
   ?CS: 0 0 R> $3E00 21INT5 \ close file handle
   $3E00 DOSERR? 2DROP
   >S1 ." Symbols placed in file: " PAD COUNT TYPE SPACE >S0 ;
  -->

136
\ save the target image                         \ JFB 08:58 05/08/86
: SAVE-IMAGE.COM ( - )
   WORDSx COM-EXT EXTENT(H ?CS: PAD 1+ 0 0 $3C00 21INT5
   $3C00 DOSERR? DROP
   >R TRG.SEG TARGET.ORG HEREx OVER - R $4000 21INT5
   $4000 DOSERR? 2DROP
   ?CS: 0 0 R> $3E00 21INT5
   $3E00 DOSERR? 2DROP
   >S1 CR0> ." Image placed in file: " PAD COUNT TYPE SPACE
   >S0 ;
  -->

137
\ finish up the target                          \ JFB 08:25 04/14/86
: FINIS-TARGET ( - ) WORDSx ROMING? HOLD.ROMING? !(S
   INIT-FENCE.SYM.FOUND LABEL?
   IF FENCEx @x
      IF FENCEx @x
      ELSE HEREx
      THEN TRG.CFA.FOUND@ !x
   THEN INIT-VOC-LINK.SYM.FOUND LABEL?
```

```
   IF VOC-LINKx @x TRG.CFA.FOUND@ !x
   THEN INIT-FORTH.SYM.FOUND LABEL?
   IF TRG.CFA.FOUND@ FORTH.SYM.FOUND TO SYM.FOUND
      TRG.CFA.FOUND@ 6 + @x SWAP !x
   THEN INIT-DP.SYM.FOUND LABEL?
   IF HEREx TRG.CFA.FOUND@ !x
   THEN  -->

138
\ finish up the target cont.                  \ JFB 12:06 04/06/86
   X.SYM.FOUND TO SYM.FOUND DEFINED?
   IF $80 TRG.CFA.FOUND@ >BODY(T NFAx 1+ C!x
   THEN ;
  -->

139
\ finish up a rom target                      \ JFB 17:57 04/21/86
: FINIS-ROM-TARGET ( - ) WORDSx ROMING? HOLD.ROMING? !(S
   INIT-FENCE.SYM.FOUND LABEL?
   IF THEREx TRG.CFA.FOUND@ !x
   THEN INIT-VOC-LINK.SYM.FOUND LABEL?
   IF VOC-LINKx @x TRG.CFA.FOUND@ !x
   THEN INIT-FORTH.SYM.FOUND LABEL?
   IF TRG.CFA.FOUND@ FORTH.SYM.FOUND TO SYM.FOUND
      TRG.CFA.FOUND@ 4+ @x 2+ @x  SWAP !x
   THEN INIT-DP.SYM.FOUND LABEL?
   IF THEREx TRG.CFA.FOUND@ !x
   THEN HEREx HOLD.RAM.AREA !(S
   INIT-RAM.SYM.FOUND TO SYM.FOUND
   HEREx TRG.CFA.FOUND RESOLVE DEFINED!
   THEREx HOLD.RAM.START @(S - DUP >R ,x \ save length
  -->
140
\ finish up a rom target cont.                \ JFB 17:56 04/21/86
   HOLD.RAM.START @(S HEREx R CMOVEx \ move initialized area
   R> ALLOTx RAM-START.SYM.FOUND TO SYM.FOUND
   HOLD.RAM.START @(S TRG.CFA.FOUND RESOLVE DEFINED!
   X.SYM.FOUND TO SYM.FOUND DEFINED?
   IF $80 TRG.CFA.FOUND@ >BODY(T NFAx 1+ C!x
   THEN ;
  -->

141
\ finish up the symbol table                  \ JFB 16:03 03/19/86
: FINIS-SYMBOL ( - ) WORDSx CONTEXT(S @ HOLD.CONTEXT(S !(S
   CURRENT(S @ HOLD.CURRENT(S !(S
   VOC-LINK(S @ HOLD.VOC-LINK(S !(S
   CONTEXTx @x HOLD.CONTEXT(T !(S CURRENTx @x
   HOLD.CURRENT(T !(S VOC-LINKx @x HOLD.VOC-LINK(T !(S
   TARGET.ORG HOLD.TARGET.ORG !(S ;
  -->

142
\ finish up packets                           \ JFB 19:02 03/19/86
: FINIS-PACKETS ( - ) PACKET.HERE
   IF PACKET.HERE HOLD.PACKET.HERE !(S HERE(S PACKET.PTR !(S
      PACKET.HERE HERE(S 0 PACKET.HERE - DUP
      HOLD.PACKET.SIZE !(S DUP >R CMOVE(S
      R> ALLOT(S PACKET.HEAD HOLD.PACKET.HEAD !(S
   THEN ;
  -->

143
\ word on line                                \ JFB 21:19 11/04/88
```

```
: WOL ( - bool ; t=word at here, f=no word) WORDSx
      BLKx @x
      IF INx @x >R BL WORDx R 40 / 1+ 40 * INx @x >
         HEREx @x 1 = NOT AND
      ELSE INx @x >R BL WORDx HEREx @x 0100 =
                              HEREx @x 1 = OR NOT
      THEN R> OVER
      IF DROP
      ELSE INx !x
      THEN ;
  -->

144
\ FINISx                                        \ JFB 19:59 11/04/88
WORDSx DEFINITIONS
: FINISx ( - ) XY> DROP 5 =
   IF OD S1-EMIT
   THEN WOL \ is there a word on this line ?
   IF HEREx DUP C@x 1+ PAD SWAP CMOVET>H \ yes, use it
   ELSE IMAGE" PAD 6 CMOVE \ use default name "IMAGE"
   THEN ROMING?
   IF FINIS-ROM-TARGET
   ELSE FINIS-TARGET
   THEN FINIS-PACKETS FINIS-SYMBOL SAVE-IMAGE.COM SAVE-IMAGE.SYM
   FALSE TO NOT.DONE? DO.PROGRESS >S1 S1! CR0>
   ." Compilation complete, press any key to continue" CR
   S1-KEY DROP INHERIT
   >(S0) SHOW-S0 S0CURSOR!
   BLK @ 0= IF SP! QUIT THEN ; -->
145
\ STOPx                                           JFB 21:10 05/30/88
: STOPx ( - ) FALSE TO NOT.DONE? INHERIT >(S0) SHOW-S0 S0CURSOR!
  SP! QUIT ;
  -->

146
\ host compiler                                 \ JFB 08:49 03/18/86
FORTH DEFINITIONS
: COMPILE.IT ( - ) WORDSx COMPILE.CFA.FOUND
   SYM.FOUND DOES>.SYM.FOUND =
   IF HEREx LAT.DOES>HL.PTR.FOUND RESOLVE
   THEN ;
  -->

147
\ host number and forward referencing           \ JFB 18:26 03/24/86
: FORWARD.EXIT ( - ) WORDSx COMPILING?
   IF COMPILE.FWD.CFA
   ELSE DOASMFWD
   THEN R> DROP ; \ exit NUMBER(H
: <NUMBER(H> WORDSx
   BEGIN   1+ DUP >R C@x BASEx @x DIGIT
   WHILE   SWAP BASEx @x U* DROP ROT
      BASEx @x U* D+  DPLx @x 1+
      IF   1 DPLx +!x
      THEN R>
   REPEAT  R> ;  -->

148
\ host number processing                        \ JFB 19:03 03/25/86
: NUMBER(H ( - double number ) WORDSx
   HEREx 0 0 ROT DUP 1+ C@x 2D = DUP >R + -1
   BEGIN DPLx !x <NUMBER(H> DUP C@x BL -
   WHILE DUP C@x 2E -
```

```
      IF R> 4DROP FORWARD.EXIT \ fwd ref and exit
      THEN 0
   REPEAT DROP R>
   IF DMINUS
   THEN DPLx @x 1+
   IF [COMPILE] DLITERALx
   ELSE DROP [COMPILE] LITERALx
   THEN ;
  -->

149
\ show progress of meta compilation          \ JFB 19:52 11/04/88
: .PROGRESS ( - ) >S1 [ ' FAST-S1-EMIT CFA ] LITERAL
   ' EMIT ! S1.OFF .FILE .BLOCK&LINE
   1E9 TO S1.OFF STATE(H INTP.STATE(H  =
   IF     ." Interpreting"
   ELSE STATE(H ASM.STATE(H =
     IF   ." Assembling  "
     ELSE ." Compiling   "
     THEN
   THEN 248 TO S1.OFF BASE @ DECIMAL +-REF 4 .R BASE !
   TO S1.OFF >S0 ;
' .PROGRESS CFA ' DO.PROGRESS 1+ !
  -->

150
\ key checker                                  JFB 17:06 05/22/88
: KEYCHECK ( - )
  ?KEY -DUP
  IF (KEYCHECK)
  THEN ;
  -->

151
\ host outer interpreter                     \ JFB 19:51 11/04/88
: INTERPRET(H ( - ) WORDSx
   BEGIN BL WORDx NOT.NULL? NOT.DONE? AND
   WHILE -FIND(H
      IF 0= COMPILING? AND   \ not immediate and comp
         IF DROP COMPILE.IT
         ELSE [ HERE TO TRACE3 ] NOOP EXECUTE
         THEN
      ELSE NUMBER(H
      THEN .PROGRESS KEYCHECK ?STACKx
   REPEAT ;
' INTERPRET(H CFA ' DOINTERPRET(H 1+ !
-->

152
\ EXTENT                                       JFB 21:35 06/04/88
: EXTENT ( extent string address - )
         0 PAD 2- ! \ clear for 1 char names
         >R 1 PAD DUP C@ + 4 0
         DO DUP I - C@ ASCII . =
            IF NIP 0 SWAP LEAVE
            THEN
         LOOP DROP
         IF R> PAD DUP C@ + DUP >R 2+ 3 CMOVE
            ASCII . R 1+ C!
            PAD C@ 4 + PAD C!
         THEN R> DROP 0 PAD DUP C@ + 1+ C! ;
  -->

153
```

```
\ make the symbol table                              JFB 12:37 06/05/88
: MAKE-SYMBOL-TABLE ( - ) WORDSx >S1 S1!
   ." Generating default symbol table, please wait"
   DO.SYMBOL.TABLE CR ." Enter the file name for the compiler: "
   BEGIN HEREx 31 EXPECTx HEREx @x
   DUP 0= IF 8 EMIT THEN UNTIL \ wait for something
   HEREx HERE 1+ 31 CMOVET>H 31 31 0 DO HERE 1+ I + C@ 0=
   IF DROP I LEAVE THEN LOOP HERE C! \ count the file name
   HERE DUP C@ 1+ PAD SWAP CMOVE S0 [ 12 +ORIGIN ]
   LITERAL 10 CMOVE [ ' FORTH 4 + ] LITERAL @
   [ 0C +ORIGIN ] LITERAL !  >(S0) \ forth vectors
   COM-EXT 1+ EXTENT ?CS: PAD 1+ 0 0 3C00 21INT5 2DROP >R
   ?CS: 0 +ORIGIN HERE OVER - R 4000 21INT5
   2DROP DROP ?CS: 0 0 R> 3E00 21INT5 2DROP DROP >S1 S1!
   CR ." Compiler placed in file: " PAD COUNT TYPE SPACE >S0 ;
  -->
154
\ get the default symbol table                       JFB 12:36 06/05/88
: GET-DEFAULT.SYM ( - ) DEFAULT.SYM PAD 1+ 0B CMOVE 0B PAD C!
   ?CS: DEFAULT.SYM 0 0 $3D00 21INT5 3 PICK 2 = \ no file ?
   IF DROP 2DROP MAKE-SYMBOL-TABLE
   ELSE $3D00 DOSERR? DROP >R \ create handle
     ?CS: 0 0 R $4202 21INT5
     $4202 DOSERR? DROP DUP DP(S ! \ size it
     ?CS: 0 0 R $4200 21INT5
     $4200 DOSERR? 2DROP \ pos to begin
     SYM.SEG 0 ROT R $3F00 21INT5
     $3F00 DOSERR? 2DROP \ read it
     ?CS: 0 0 R> $3E00 21INT5 \ close file handle
     $3E00 DOSERR? 2DROP
   THEN ;
  -->

155
\ get the image symbol table                       \ JFB 11:43 03/19/86
: GET-IMAGE.SYM ( - ) WORDSx SYM-EXT EXTENT(H ?CS: PAD 1+
   0 0 $3D00 21INT5
   $3D00 DOSERR? DROP >R \ create handle
   ?CS: 0 0 R $4202 21INT5
   $4202 DOSERR? DROP DUP DP(S ! \ size it
   ?CS: 0 0 R $4200 21INT5
   $4200 DOSERR? 2DROP \ pos to begin
   SYM.SEG 0 ROT R $3F00 21INT5
   $3F00 DOSERR? 2DROP \ read it
   ?CS: 0 0 R> $3E00 21INT5
   $3E00 DOSERR? 2DROP ; \ close file handle
  -->

156
\ get the target image                             \ JFB 09:01 05/08/86
: GET-IMAGE.COM ( - ) WORDSx 0 PAD DUP C@ 4 - DUP >R OVER C!
   R> + 1+ C! COM-EXT EXTENT(H
   ?CS: PAD 1+ 0 0 $3D00 21INT5
   $3D00 DOSERR? DROP >R \ create handle
   ?CS: 0 0 R $4202 21INT5
   $4202 DOSERR? DROP DUP TARGET.ORG + DPx !x \ size it
   ?CS: 0 0 R $4200 21INT5
   $4200 DOSERR? 2DROP \ pos to begin
   TRG.SEG TARGET.ORG ROT R $3F00 21INT5
   $3F00 DOSERR? 2DROP \ read it
   ?CS: 0 0 R> $3E00 21INT5
   $3E00 DOSERR? 2DROP ; \ close file handle
  -->
```

```
157
\ set target and symbol table segemnts          JFB 21:24 06/04/88
: SET.SYM.SEG GOT.SYM.SEG NOT
  IF ?CS: 0 0 1000 4800 21INT5
  ?NOMEM TO SYM.SEG GOT.SYM.SEG!
  THEN ; \ define symbol seg
: SET.TRG.SEG GOT.TRG.SEG NOT
  IF ?CS: 0 0 1000 4800 21INT5
  ?NOMEM TO TRG.SEG GOT.TRG.SEG!
  THEN ; \ define target seg
  -->

158
\ initialize the target                         JFB 18:19 05/08/88
: INIT-TARGET-INPUT ( - ) WORDSx
   0 INIT-TIB(T DUP TIBx !x !x RP!x BLK @
   IF BLK @ IN @
   ELSE 0 IN @ TIB @ TIBx @x $50 CMOVEH>T
   THEN INx !x BLKx !x ;
: <INIT-TARGET> ( - ) WORDSx SET.TRG.SEG INIT-TARGET-INPUT
   FIRST(T DUP PREV(T ! USE(T ! EMPTY-BUFFERSx
   0 FENCEx !x 0 OFFSETx !x 1 WARNINGx !x
   $1F WIDTHx !x DECIMALx ;
: INIT-TARGET ( - ) WORDSx <INIT-TARGET> NULL.VOC(T DUP
   CONTEXTx !x CURRENTx !x 0 NULL.VOC(T !x 0 DPx !x
   0 VOC-LINKx !x $FFFF TO TARGET.ORG ;
  -->

159
\ initialize the meta-compiler                  JFB 08:43 06/05/88
: INIT-SYMBOL ( - ) SYM.SEG 0= SET.SYM.SEG
   IF MAKE-SYMBOL-TABLE \ Make the symbol table
   ELSE GET-DEFAULT.SYM
   THEN FORTH.THREAD DUP
   CONTEXT(S ! CURRENT(S ! 0 TO PACKET.HERE 0 TO PACKET.HEAD ;
: CLEAR-COMPILE(T.LINK ( - ) COMPILE(T.LINK
   BEGIN @ -DUP
   WHILE 0 OVER 2- !
   REPEAT ;
  -->

160
\ initialize the compiler screen              \ JFB 19:44 11/04/88
: INIT-SHOW ( - )
   INIT-SCR >S1 17 0 GOTOXY SPACE .TITLE
   14 1 GOTOXY .VERSION
   15 2 GOTOXY DOASMVERSION
    2 3 GOTOXY DO.TARGET
   1 TO ?.FILE .FILE .BLOCK&LINE
   9 6 GOTOXY ." Interpreting"
   0 TO +-REF 18 7 GOTOXY 0 4 .R
   >S0 2D1 TO S1.OFF SHOW-S1 ;
  -->

161
\ initialize the meta-compiler                      09:30 10/12/89
: INIT-HOST ( - ) WORDSx CLEAR-COMPILE(T.LINK DOASMINIT
   TRUE TO NOT.DONE? FALSE TO ROMING?
   FALSE TO POP? [COMPILE] NOTRACEx INTERPRETING!
   FALSE TO .STACK?
   ?MODE >R 2DROP R> 7 =
   IF 0B000 ' VID.SEG ! \ support output to Monochrome monitor
   THEN ;
: INIT-META-COMPILE ( - ) INIT-HOST INIT-TARGET INIT-SHOW
```

```
   INIT-SYMBOL ;
  -->

162
\ initialize for meta-compiler restart       \ JFB 18:04 06/05/86
: RESTART-SYMBOL ( - ) SET.SYM.SEG GET-IMAGE.SYM
   HOLD.CONTEXT(S @(S CONTEXT(S ! HOLD.CURRENT(S @(S CURRENT(S !
   HOLD.VOC-LINK(S @(S VOC-LINK(S ! PACKET.PTR @(S
   IF HOLD.PACKET.HEAD @(S TO PACKET.HEAD PACKET.PTR @(S
      HOLD.PACKET.HERE @(S DUP TO PACKET.HERE HOLD.PACKET.SIZE
      @(S DUP >R CMOVE(S R> MINUS DP(S +!
   ELSE 0 TO PACKET.HERE 0 TO PACKET.HEAD
   THEN ;
  -->

163
\ restart the target image                      JFB 21:32 06/04/88
: RESTART-TARGET ( - ) WORDSx HOLD.TARGET.ORG @(S TO TARGET.ORG
   GET-IMAGE.COM CR0> ." Restarting " PAD COUNT TYPE SPACE
   HOLD.VOC-LINK(T @(S VOC-LINKx !x
   HOLD.CONTEXT(T @(S CONTEXTx !x HOLD.CURRENT(T
   @(S CURRENTx !x HOLD.ROMING? @(S DUP TO ROMING?
   IF HOLD.RAM.AREA @(S 2+ HOLD.RAM.START @(S HOLD.RAM.AREA @(S
      @x DUP >R CMOVEx \ move the ram area
      R> HOLD.RAM.START @(S + DP-RAM(T ! \ init ram dp
      HOLD.RAM.AREA @(S DPx !x \ init rom dp
   THEN ;
  -->

164
\ envoke meta-compilation                       JFB 09:47 06/04/88
: <META-COMPILE> ( - ) WORDSx
   BEGIN NOT.DONE?
   WHILE COMPILING? NOT BLKx @x 0= AND
     IF ." Ok" CR
     THEN WORDSx QUERYx INTERPRET(H
   REPEAT ;
: CROSS-COMPILE ( - ) INIT-META-COMPILE <META-COMPILE>
  >(S0) SHOW-S0 S0CURSOR! ;
: RESUME ( - ) ( - ) INIT-HOST INIT-TARGET-INPUT
  <META-COMPILE> >(S0) SHOW-S0 S0CURSOR! ;
-->

165
\ restart meta-compilation                      JFB 21:20 06/04/88
: RESTART ( - ) WORDSx <INIT-TARGET>
   WOL \ is there a word on this line ?
   IF HEREx DUP C@x 1+ PAD SWAP CMOVET>H \ yes, use it
   ELSE IMAGE" PAD 6 CMOVE \ use default name "IMAGE"
   THEN INIT-HOST RESTART-SYMBOL RESTART-TARGET INIT-SHOW
   <META-COMPILE> >(S0) SHOW-S0 S0CURSOR! ;
  -->

166
\  "print" spaces and numbers                 \ JFB 11:21 11/04/88
\ WORDSx DEFINITIONS
\ : C,x EMIT ;
\ FORTH DEFINITIONS
\ : CMOVEH>T SWAP DROP 0 DO DUP I + C@ EMIT LOOP DROP ;
: SPACE(T WORDSx BL C,x ;
: SPACES(T DUP 0 >
   IF 0 DO SPACE(T LOOP ELSE DROP THEN ;
: U.Rx ( value \ field width - ) WORDSx 0 SWAP >R SWAP OVER
   DABS <# #S SIGN #> R> OVER - SPACES(T
```

```
   DUP >R HEREx SWAP CMOVEH>T R> ALLOTx SPACE(T ;
  -->

167
\ "print" strings                              \ JFB 08:40 03/22/86
: CLEAR.HIGH ( - ) WORDSx HEREx 1- DUP C@x $7F AND SWAP C!x ;
: .MAP(S ( width \ symbol table adr - ) WORDSx DUP C@(S $1F AND
   ROT DUP >R MIN >R  1+ HEREx R CMOVES>T R ALLOTx CLEAR.HIGH
    R> R> SWAP - SPACES(T SPACE(T ;
: .MAP ( width \ host adr - ) WORDSx DUP C@ $1F AND
   ROT DUP >R MIN >R  1+ HEREx R CMOVEH>T R ALLOTx CLEAR.HIGH
   R> R> SWAP - SPACES(T SPACE(T ;
: .MAP" ( width \ host adr - ) WORDSx DUP C@ $1F AND 1-
   ROT DUP >R MIN >R  1+ HEREx R CMOVEH>T R ALLOTx CLEAR.HIGH
   R> R> SWAP - SPACES(T SPACE(T ;
: MAP.LIT ( width - )
   <BUILDS LATEST ,
   DOES> @ .MAP" ;
  -->

168
\ record field widths                          \ JFB 21:14 06/30/86
 0A CONSTANT NAME.WIDTH
  4 CONSTANT TYPE.WIDTH
  1 CONSTANT FORWARD.WIDTH
  8 CONSTANT VOC.WIDTH
  4 CONSTANT CFA.WIDTH
  4 CONSTANT SYM.FILE.WIDTH
  4 CONSTANT SYM.BLK.WIDTH
  2 CONSTANT LINE.WIDTH
  5 CONSTANT REF.CTR.WIDTH
\ change these numbers to widen or shorten a field
  -->

169
\ "print" the symbol name                      \ JFB 08:41 03/22/86
: .NAME ( - ) NAME.WIDTH SYM.FOUND NFA(S .MAP(S ;
  -->

170
\ symbol type literals                         \ JFB 08:41 03/22/86
MAP.LIT UNKNOWN"
MAP.LIT CODE"
MAP.LIT :"
MAP.LIT CONSTANT"
MAP.LIT VARIABLE"
MAP.LIT USER"
MAP.LIT VOCABULARY"
MAP.LIT LABEL"
MAP.LIT EQUATE"
MAP.LIT HDF"
MAP.LIT LDF"
  -->

171
\ "print" the symbol type                      \ JFB 08:41 03/22/86
0 VARIABLE TYPE.VEC -2 ALLOT
' UNKNOWN"    CFA , ' CODE"     CFA , ' :"       CFA ,
' CONSTANT"   CFA , ' VARIABLE" CFA , ' USER"    CFA ,
' VOCABULARY" CFA , ' LABEL"    CFA , ' EQUATE" CFA ,
' HDF"        CFA , ' LDF"      CFA ,
: .TYPE ( - ) TYPE.WIDTH TYPE.FOUND@ 2* TYPE.VEC + @ EXECUTE ;
  -->
```

```
172
\ "print" if a symbol has been forward ref  \ JFB 08:42 03/22/86
MAP.LIT YES"
MAP.LIT NO"
: .FORWARD ( - ) FORWARD.WIDTH FORWARD? IF YES" ELSE NO" THEN ;
  -->

173
\ "print" the voc of the symbol             \ JFB 08:42 03/22/86
: .VOC ( - ) VOC.WIDTH VOC.NFA(S .MAP(S ;
  -->

174
\ "print" the cfa of the symbol             \ JFB 08:43 03/22/86
: .CFA ( - ) TRG.CFA.FOUND@ CFA.WIDTH HEX U.Rx ;
\ Note: this is also used to "print" the value of a LABEL or
\       EQUATE
  -->

175
\ "print" the line number of the symbol     \ JFB 10:16 06/10/86
: .LINE# ( - ) SYM.IN.FOUND@
   40 / LINE.WIDTH DECIMAL U.Rx ;
  -->

176
\ "print" the number of symbol references   \ JFB 22:13 06/09/86
: REF.CTR.FOUND@ REF.CTR +SYM.FOUND @(S ;
: .REF.CTR ( - ) REF.CTR.FOUND@
   REF.CTR.WIDTH DECIMAL U.Rx ;
  -->

177
\ "print" the block of the symbol
: .SYM.BLK ( - ) SYM.BLK.FOUND@
   SYM.BLK.WIDTH DECIMAL U.Rx ;
  -->

178
\ "print" a CR and LF                       \ JFB 08:50 03/22/86
: .CRLF WORDSx 0D C,x 0A C,x ;
  -->

179
\ "print" a record for a symbol             \ JFB 20:49 06/30/86
: WRITE.MAP WORDSx TRG.SEG TARGET.ORG HEREx OVER -
   MAP.HANDLE $4000 21INT5
   $4000 DOSERR? 2DROP 0 DPx !x ;
: .RECORD ( - ) WORDSx DEFINED?
  IF HEREx 2800 >
     IF WRITE.MAP
     THEN
     .NAME
     .CFA .TYPE .FORWARD
     .SYM.BLK .LINE#
     .REF.CTR .VOC .CRLF
  THEN ;
  -->

180
\ test for end of a thread                  \ JFB 09:51 03/22/86
: LFA(S 4 - ;
: ?ATVOC(S ( symbol NFA - symbol NFA \ bool, t= end of thread)
   PFA(S LFA(S @(S DUP @(S $A081 = OVER 0= OR ;
```

```
  -->

181
\ "print" a vocabulary thread                    \ JFB 10:04 03/22/86
: .THREAD ( symbol NFA - )
   BEGIN DUP PFA(S TO SYM.FOUND .RECORD ?ATVOC(S
   UNTIL DROP ;
  -->

182
\ "print" an entire vocabulary                   \ JFB 11:10 03/22/86
: .VOC-MAP ( - ) CONTEXT(S @ #VOC.THREADS 0
   DO DUP I 4* + 2+ @(S DUP 0= OVER @(S $A081 = OR
      IF DROP
      ELSE .THREAD
      THEN
   LOOP DROP ;
  -->

183
\ initialize for map printing                    \ JFB 09:46 07/02/86
: INIT-MAP ( - ) WORDSx <INIT-TARGET>
   WOL \ is there a word on this line ?
   IF INx @x IN !
      HEREx DUP C@x 1+ PAD SWAP CMOVET>H \ yes, use it
   ELSE IMAGE" PAD 6 CMOVE \ use default name "IMAGE"
   THEN RESTART-SYMBOL
   0 DPx !x 0 TO TARGET.ORG
   0 PAD DUP C@ 4 - DUP >R OVER C! R> + 1+ C! MAP-EXT
   EXTENT(H•?CS: PAD 1+ 0 0 $3C00 21INT5
   $3C00 DOSERR? DROP TO MAP.HANDLE ; \ create handle
  -->

184
\ "print" the map                                  JFB 13:59 05/08/88
: .TARGET-MAP ( - ) INIT-MAP VOC-LINK(S @
   BEGIN -DUP
   WHILE DUP 2+ @(S NFA(S TO VOC.NFA(S \ get name of voc
      DUP 2- @(S CONTEXT(S ! \ get voc thread
      .VOC-MAP \ "print" this voc
      @(S \ get next voc
   REPEAT WRITE.MAP
   ?CS: 0 0 MAP.HANDLE $3E00 21INT5
   $4000 DOSERR? 2DROP
   CR ." Map placed in file: " PAD COUNT TYPE SPACE ;
  -->

185
\ resolve record field widths                    \ JFB 08:42 06/05/86
 8 CONSTANT NAME.WIDTH-RESOLVE
 4 CONSTANT TARGET.ADR.WIDTH-RESOLVE
 4 CONSTANT SYM.FILE.WIDTH-RESOLVE
 4 CONSTANT SYM.BLK.WIDTH-RESOLVE
 2 CONSTANT LINE.WIDTH-RESOLVE
  -->

186
\ "print" the resolve symbol name                \ JFB 09:20 03/23/86
: .NAME-RESOLVE ( - ) NAME.WIDTH-RESOLVE  SYM.FOUND NFA(S
   .MAP(S ;
  -->

187
\ "print" the resolve target address             \ JFB 09:03 03/23/86
```

```
: .TARGET.ADR-RESOLVE ( - ) PACKET.TRG.ADR@
   TARGET.ADR.WIDTH-RESOLVE HEX U.Rx ;
  -->

188
\ "print" the block of the resolve symbol   \ JFB 23:00 07/01/86
: .SYM.BLK-RESOLVE ( - ) PACKET.BLK@
   IF PACKET.BLK@ SYM.BLK.WIDTH-RESOLVE DECIMAL U.Rx
   ELSE SYM.BLK.WIDTH-RESOLVE 1+ SPACES(T
   THEN ;
  -->

189
\ "print" the line number of the resolve sy \ JFB 09:07 03/23/86
: .LINE#-RESOLVE ( - ) PACKET.IN@
   IF PACKET.IN@ 40 / LINE.WIDTH-RESOLVE DECIMAL U.Rx
   ELSE LINE.WIDTH-RESOLVE 1+ SPACES(T
   THEN ;
  -->

190
\ "print" a packet                          \ JFB 20:52 06/30/86
: .PACKET ( - ) .TARGET.ADR-RESOLVE
   .SYM.BLK-RESOLVE .LINE#-RESOLVE SPACE(T ;
  -->

191
\ compute the number of entries per line    \ JFB 09:30 07/02/86
: ENTRIES/LINE ( - n ) 50 NAME.WIDTH-RESOLVE 1+ -
   TARGET.ADR.WIDTH-RESOLVE SYM.BLK.WIDTH-RESOLVE
   LINE.WIDTH-RESOLVE + + 4+ / ;
  -->

192
\ "print" the unresolved packets            \ JFB 11:05 03/23/86
: .PACKETS ( - )
    BEGIN PACKET.BASE
    WHILE .NAME-RESOLVE ENTRIES/LINE 0
       DO .PACKET NEXT.PACKET PACKET.BASE 0=
          IF LEAVE
          THEN
       LOOP PACKET.BASE IF .CRLF THEN
    REPEAT .CRLF ;
  -->

193
\ "print" a resolve record for a symbol     \ JFB 09:23 03/23/86
: .RECORD-RESOLVE ( - ) DEFINED? NOT
  IF TRG.CFA.FOUND@
     IF TRG.CFA.FOUND@ TO PACKET.BASE
        .PACKETS
        EXTEND.PTR.FOUND@
        IF EXTEND.PTR.FOUND@ @(S TO PACKET.BASE
           .PACKETS
        THEN
     THEN
  THEN ;
  -->

194
\ "print" resolve for a vocabulary thread   \ JFB 09:48 04/13/86
: .THREAD-RESOLVE ( symbol NFA - ) WORDSx
   BEGIN DUP PFA(S TO SYM.FOUND .RECORD-RESOLVE ?ATVOC(S
    $F000 HEREx U< OR
```

```
   UNTIL DROP ;
  -->

195
\ "print" resolve for an entire vocabulary  \ JFB 08:33 03/23/86
: .VOC-MAP-RESOLVE ( - ) CONTEXT(S @ #VOC.THREADS 0
   DO DUP I 4* + 2+ @(S DUP 0= OVER @(S $A081 = OR
      IF DROP
      ELSE .THREAD-RESOLVE
      THEN
   LOOP DROP ;
  -->

196
\ save the map                                     09:44 10/13/86
: SAVE-IMAGE.RES ( - ) WORDSx
   0 PAD DUP C@ 4 - DUP >R OVER C! R> + 1+ C! RES-EXT
   EXTENT(H ?CS: PAD 1+ 0 0 $3C00 21INT5 \ create handle
   $3C00 DOSERR? DROP
   >R TRG.SEG TARGET.ORG HEREx OVER - R $4000 21INT5
   $4000 DOSERR? 2DROP
   ?CS: 0 0 R> $3E00 21INT5
   $3E00 DOSERR? 2DROP
   CR ." Resolve map placed in file: " PAD COUNT TYPE SPACE ;
  -->

197
\ "print" the resolve map                    \ JFB 11:21 11/04/88
: .TARGET-RESOLVE ( - ) INIT-MAP VOC-LINK(S @
  BEGIN -DUP
  WHILE DUP 2+ @(S NFA(S TO VOC.NFA(S \ get name of voc
     DUP 2- @(S CONTEXT(S ! \ get voc thread
     .VOC-MAP-RESOLVE \ "print" this voc
     @(S \ get next voc
  REPEAT SAVE-IMAGE.RES ;
\ WORDSx ' C,x NFA 020 TOGGLE
\ FORTH ' CMOVEH>T NFA 020 TOGGLE
  -->

198
\ initialize for symbol table creation       JFB 22:44 05/01/88
: INIT-SYMBOL.TABLE ( - )
   INIT-DP(S DP(S ! \ init sym dict ptr
   FORTH.THREAD DUP CONTEXT(S !
   CURRENT(S ! \ init sym context and current
   CFA.HASH.TBL CFA.HASH.TBL.SIZE
   2* 0 FILL(S ; \ 0 the CFA hash table
-->

199
\ make vocabulary threads                    \ JFB 13:29 03/16/86
: MAKE-VOC.THREADS ( - ) #VOC.THREADS 0
   DO $A081 FORTH.THREAD I 4* + !(S \ blank name
      0 FORTH.THREAD I 4* + 2+ !(S \ link for FORTH
   LOOP #VOC.THREADS 0
   DO $A081 ASM.THREAD I 4* + !(S \ blank name
      FORTH.THREAD I 4* + \ link to FORTH
      ASM.THREAD I 4* + 2+ !(S \ link for asm
   LOOP ;
-->

200
\ make compiler words                        \ JFB 11:03 03/14/86
: MAKE-WORDSx ( - ) WORDSx [COMPILE] WORDSx CONTEXT @ @ 0
```

```
   BEGIN NOT
   WHILE DUP C@ $1F AND 1- DUP >R HEREx C!x \ count
      DUP 1+ HEREx 1+ R> CMOVEH>T \ name minus "x"
      <CREATE(S> SMUDGE(S \ make symbol table entry
      DUP C@ $40 AND LATEST(S DUP >R C@(S OR
      R> C!(S \ move presidence bit
      DUP PFA CFA
      LATEST(S PFA(S CFA(S !(S \ place execution address
      ?ATVOC
   REPEAT DROP ;
-->

201
\ make assembler words                      \ JFB 08:32 03/25/86
: MAKE-ASM ( - ) WORDSx ASM.THREAD CURRENT(S ! \ assembler voc
   [COMPILE] ASSEMBLER CONTEXT @ @ 0
   BEGIN NOT
   WHILE DUP C@ $1F AND DUP >R HEREx C!x \ count
      DUP 1+ HEREx 1+ R> CMOVEH>T
      HEREx DUP C@x + $80 TOGGLEx \ clear high bit
      <CREATE(S> SMUDGE(S \ make symbol table entry
      DUP C@ $40 AND LATEST(S DUP >R C@(S OR
      R> C!(S \ move presidence bit
      DUP PFA CFA
      LATEST(S PFA(S CFA(S !(S \ place execution address
      ?ATVOC
   REPEAT DROP ;
-->

202
\ find names in symbol table                \ JFB 11:59 04/06/86
: 'NAME(S ( - ; 'name, at compile
             - SYM.FOUND; on execution ) WORDSx
        <BUILDS LATEST ,
        DOES> @ DUP C@ $1F AND 1- DUP >R HEREx C!x
           2+ HEREx 1+ R CMOVEH>T R 1+ ALLOTx
           HEREx 1- $80 TOGGLEx R> 1+ MINUS ALLOTx
           HEREx CONTEXT(S @ VOC.HASH + @(S <FIND(H>
           IF 2DROP
           ELSE <CREATE(S> SMUDGE(S \ not found, make it
           THEN SYM.FOUND ;
  -->

203
\ symbol table names of interest            \ JFB 12:00 04/06/86

'NAME(S 'FORTH
'NAME(S 'ASSEMBLER
'NAME(S 'DOES>
'NAME(S 'INIT-FORTH
'NAME(S 'INIT-VOC-LINK
'NAME(S 'INIT-DP
'NAME(S 'INIT-FENCE
'NAME(S 'INIT-RAM
'NAME(S 'RAM-START
'NAME(S 'ORIGIN
'NAME(S 'X
  -->

204
\ extent the resident vocabularies          \ JFB 12:55 03/15/86
: EXTEND-VOCS
   'FORTH DUP TO FORTH.SYM.FOUND TO SYM.FOUND
   HERE(S DUP EXTEND.SIZE 0 FILL(S
```

```
   EXTEND.SIZE ALLOT(S \ extend FORTH
   EXTEND.PTR.FOUND! EXTEND.BACK.PTR.FOUND! \ point it
   FORTH.THREAD VOC.THREAD.PTR.FOUND! \ point to thread
   SYM.VOC.LINK.FOUND \ save link
   'ASSEMBLER TO SYM.FOUND
   HERE(S DUP EXTEND.SIZE 0 FILL(S
   EXTEND.SIZE ALLOT(S \ extend ASSEMBLER
   EXTEND.PTR.FOUND! EXTEND.BACK.PTR.FOUND! \ point it
   ASM.THREAD VOC.THREAD.PTR.FOUND! \ point to thread
   SYM.VOC.LINK.FOUND! \ link back to FORTH
   SYM.VOC.LINK.FOUND VOC-LINK(S ! ; \ save link
  -->
205
\ find DOES> symbol table                      \ JFB 18:00 04/14/86
: FIND-SYM.DOES> ( - ) FORTH.THREAD CURRENT(S !
   'DOES> TO DOES>.SYM.FOUND ;
  -->

206
\ find labels in the symbol table              \ JFB 23:15 04/14/86
: FIND-LABELS ( - ) FORTH.THREAD CURRENT(S !
   'INIT-FORTH TO INIT-FORTH.SYM.FOUND IMMEDIATE(S
   [ ' <VALUE> CFA ] LITERAL SYM.FOUND CFA(S !(S \ put CF
   LAB.TYPE TYPE.FOUND!
   'INIT-VOC-LINK TO INIT-VOC-LINK.SYM.FOUND IMMEDIATE(S
   [ ' <VALUE> CFA ] LITERAL SYM.FOUND CFA(S !(S \ put CF
   LAB.TYPE TYPE.FOUND!
   'INIT-DP TO INIT-DP.SYM.FOUND IMMEDIATE(S
   [ ' <VALUE> CFA ] LITERAL SYM.FOUND CFA(S !(S \ put CF
   LAB.TYPE TYPE.FOUND!
   'INIT-FENCE TO INIT-FENCE.SYM.FOUND IMMEDIATE(S
   [ ' <VALUE> CFA ] LITERAL SYM.FOUND CFA(S !(S \ put CF
   LAB.TYPE TYPE.FOUND!
  -->

207
\ find labels in the symbol table cont.        \ JFB 12:03 04/21/86
   'INIT-RAM TO INIT-RAM.SYM.FOUND IMMEDIATE(S
   [ ' <VALUE> CFA ] LITERAL SYM.FOUND CFA(S !(S \ put CF
   LAB.TYPE TYPE.FOUND!
   'RAM-START TO RAM-START.SYM.FOUND IMMEDIATE(S
   [ ' <VALUE> CFA ] LITERAL SYM.FOUND CFA(S !(S
   LAB.TYPE TYPE.FOUND!
   'ORIGIN TO ORIGIN.SYM.FOUND IMMEDIATE(S
   [ ' <VALUE> CFA ] LITERAL SYM.FOUND CFA(S !(S
   LAB.TYPE TYPE.FOUND! ;
  -->

208
\ save the default symbol table                  JFB 06:42 05/07/88
: FIND-SYM.X ( - ) FORTH.THREAD CURRENT(S !
   'X TO X.SYM.FOUND ;
: SAVE-DEF.SYM ( - ) ?CS: DEFAULT.SYM 0 0 $3C00 21INT5 2DROP >R
   SYM.SEG 0 HERE(S R $4000 21INT5 3DROP
   ?CS: 0 0 R> $3E00 21INT5 3DROP ;
-->

209
\ create the default symbol table              \ JFB 20:32 11/04/88
: (SYMBOL.TABLE) ( - )
   INIT-SYMBOL.TABLE \ init for making the default symbol table
   MAKE-VOC.THREADS \ make vocabulary threads
   MAKE-WORDSx \ make the "x" words
   MAKE-ASM \ make the assembler words
```

```
   FIND-SYM.DOES>
   FIND-SYM.X
   FIND-LABELS
   EXTEND-VOCS
   SAVE-DEF.SYM
   [COMPILE] FORTH ;
' (SYMBOL.TABLE) CFA ' DO.SYMBOL.TABLE 1+ !
: SYMBOL.TABLE SET.TRG.SEG SET.SYM.SEG (SYMBOL.TABLE) ;
   -->

210
\ print loaded message                           09:10 10/12/89

DECIMAL
CR0> .TITLE .VERSION ."  loaded " CR
HERE ' .TITLE NFA - U. ." bytes used" CR

HEX
LATEST     0C +ORIGIN !  \ top NFA
HERE       1C +ORIGIN !  \ FENCE
HERE       1E +ORIGIN !  \ DP
VOC-LINK @ 20 +ORIGIN !  \ vocabulary list

SAVE MCNOASM.COM
CR

211
\                                            JFB 11:23 04/23/88
                       Revsion History

09/29/86 09:58         $400 changed to $3E00 screen 122 line 8,
                       for jb by whp

10/13/86 09:42         $400 changed to $3E00 screen 176 line 8,
                       for jb by whp

                       TRACE changed to KEY.TRACE screen 116
                       line 9 for jb by whp.

04/23/88               Modified EXTENT(H work correctly with
                       with one character names.

212
\ revision history                         \ JFB 20:32 11/04/88

date            revision

05/01/88        Made symbol table generation automatic

05/05/88        Updated compiler version to 2.3

11/03/88        - Added [COMPILE] FORTH DEFINITIONS, to
                  STOPIT.
                - Modified CREATE(S to print redefined word
                  on the compiler screen.

213
\ revision history                               09:09 10/12/89

11/04/88        - Added .PROGRESS printing to FINISx
                - Added GOT.SYM.SEG! to GOT.SYM.SEG
                - Added GOT.TRG.SEG! to GOT.TRG.SEG
                - Modified WOL to correctly deal with
                  null.
```

- Updated compiler version to 2.4.

11/12/89
- Corrected error in :x
- Added support for Monochrome adapters in INIT-HOST
- Added auto-save of MCNOASM.COM
- Updated compiler version to 2.5.

Appendix 16
The 8086 Family Metaassembler

The 8086 family metaasembler is listed here. Once the metacompiler base listed in Appendix 14 and the metacompiler listed Appendix 16 are loaded, then the 8086 family metaassembler listed in this appendix is compiled. You type:

```
PFILE MA8086 1 LOAD
```

The file name for this metaassembler is MA8086.SCR. When the metassembler compilation is complete, then type

```
SYMBOL.TABLE
```

This creates a required symbol table for the compiler. The symbol table is specific to the target machine.

At this point you can save the metacompiler and 8086 family metaassembler together with the commands

```
3 SYSLOAD SAVE MC86.COM
```

MC86 can be loaded at a future time and executed without going through the preceding steps.

Keep the 8051 and 8086 metacompilation files in separate directories. When the symbol table generation is complete, then to metacompile the 8086 family FORTH type

```
PFILE FORTH86 1 LOAD
```

where FORTH86 is the code listed in Appendix 1. At the conclusion of the metacompilation, the binary of the ASCII listing seen in Appendix 2 is generated and placed in a file called IMAGE.COM.

Type

```
.TARGET-RESOLVE IMAGE
```

Check for unresolved references. The output of this routine is a WordStar nondocument file called IMAGE.RES. This file should be empty if no unresolved references are left.

Type

```
.TARGET-MAP IMAGE
```

to generate the 8086 version of the 8051 symbol table seen in Appendix 11. This symbol table is in WordStar nondocument format.

```
0
\                                               JFB 10:14 05/08/88

1
\ Nautilus 8086 meta-assembler                  JFB 11:58 02/27/88

CR ." Loading 8086 meta-assembler "

ASSEMBLER DEFINITIONS

QUAN REF1

HEX \ load it all in HEX
  -->

2
\ assembler messages                            JFB 21:34 05/30/88
: MSG21 ." Branch out of Range" ;
: MSG22 ." Illegal label" ;
: MSG24 ." To many operands" ;
: MSG25 ." Invalid opcode/operand form" ;
: MSG26 ." CS illegal" ;
: MSG27 ." Local label table full" ;
: MSG28 ." Unresolved local label" ;
  -->

3
\ initialize asembler                           JFB 21:34 05/30/88
: INITASM 'ASMMSG ASMMSGSIZ ERASE \ clear old messages
   [ ' MSG21 CFA ] LITERAL 21 >MESSAGES
   [ ' MSG22 CFA ] LITERAL 22 >MESSAGES
   [ ' MSG24 CFA ] LITERAL 24 >MESSAGES
   [ ' MSG25 CFA ] LITERAL 25 >MESSAGES
   [ ' MSG26 CFA ] LITERAL 26 >MESSAGES
   [ ' MSG27 CFA ] LITERAL 27 >MESSAGES
   [ ' MSG28 CFA ] LITERAL 28 >MESSAGES
   0 TO REF1 ;
' INITASM CFA ' DOASMINIT 1+ !  -->

4
\ check references                              JFB 21:35 05/30/88
: ?REFS ( - ) WORDSx
   REF1
   IF SHOW-ERRORx \ show current unknown
      REF1 TO PACKET.BASE SET.PACKET.BLK&IN
      34 ERRORx
   THEN ;
  -->

5
\ Nautilus 8086 mata-assembler                \ JFB 22:21 04/14/86
: ASMFWD(H ( - pseudo adr ) WORDSx ASSEMBLING? NOT 5 ?ERRORx
   1 REF.CTR.FOUND +!(S
   PACKET.LIST@ TRG.CFA.FOUND DUP @(S PACKET.LINK!
   PACKET.BASE SWAP !(S \ link it in
   HEREx 1+ PACKET.TRG.ADR! \ place target address
   SYM.FOUND PACKET.HOST.ADR!
   ABS.ASM.REF PACKET.REF.TYPE!
   PACKET.BLK! PACKET.IN! ?REFS
   PACKET.BASE TO REF1 HEREx ;
  -->
```

```
6
\ Nautilus 8086 meta-assembler                   \ JFB 10:18 04/09/86
: ASMFWD ( - pseudo adr )
   CREATE(S SMUDGE(S IS.FORWARD
   SYM.FOUND CFA(S @(S 0=
   IF [ ' ASMFWD(H CFA ] LITERAL SYM.FOUND CFA(S !(S \ put CF
   THEN ASMFWD(H ;
' ASMFWD CFA ' DOASMFWD 1+ !
  -->

7
\ RESOLVE.OFF8 RESOLVE.OFF16                     \ JFB 11:50 03/27/86
: RESOLVE.OFF8 WORDSx SWAP OVER 1+ - DUP
  ABS $7F > \ 8 bit off
   21 ?ERRORx SWAP C!x ;
' RESOLVE.OFF8 CFA ' DOASMTYPE1 1+ !
: RESOLVE.OFF16 WORDSx SWAP OVER 2+ - SWAP !x ;
' RESOLVE.OFF16 CFA ' DOASMTYPE2 1+ !
  -->

8
\ address resolution                             \ JFB 10:31 07/06/86
: ABSOLUTE WORDSx REF1
   IF REF1 TO PACKET.BASE HEREx PACKET.TRG.ADR!
      PACKET.REF.TYPE@ PFA.REF -
      IF ABS.ASM.REF PACKET.REF.TYPE!
      THEN 0 TO REF1
   THEN ,x ;
: OFF8 WORDSx REF1
   IF REF1 TO PACKET.BASE HEREx PACKET.TRG.ADR!
      ASMTYPE1 PACKET.REF.TYPE! 0 TO REF1
  THEN C,x ;
: OFF16 WORDSx REF1
   IF REF1 TO PACKET.BASE HEREx PACKET.TRG.ADR!
      ASMTYPE2 PACKET.REF.TYPE! 0 TO REF1
  THEN ,x ;
  -->
9
\ ?UNCONS                                          JFB 21:41 05/30/88
: ?UNCONS ( - ) WORDSx REF1
   IF REF1 TO PACKET.BASE SET.PACKET.BLK&IN
      35 ERRORx
   THEN ;
' ?UNCONS CFA ' DO?UNCONS 1+ !
  -->

10
\ print the target processor                     \ JFB 12:43 07/13/86
: .TARGET ." Target: 8086" ;
' .TARGET CFA ' DO.TARGET 1+ !
  -->

11
\ product logo copyright notice                    JFB 21:36 05/30/88

CR  ." PC/ASSEMBLER " ." TM "
CR ." Intel 8086/87/88/186/188/286/287"
CR ." NEC   V20/30 uPD70108/70116  processors"
CR ." Copyright 1985, 1986, 1987 by"
CR ." Computer Systems Documentation"
CR
-->

12
```

```
\ Assembler local labels                        \ JFB 15:27 01/05/89

: MA86REVSYM ." 2.1 01/05/89 15:29" ; MA86REVSYM
' MA86REVSYM CFA ' DOASMVERSION 1+ !
      " Copyright, P. L. Payne, CSD, 1985,86,87"
     0  VARIABLE T0 3 ALLOT
     0  VARIABLE TOP
     0  VARIABLE CSP0
     0 VARIABLE #$
    20 CONSTANT MAX#$
     0  VARIABLE $A -2 ALLOT MAX#$ 4 * ALLOT
     0 VARIABLE WF

( --- )
: RESET         ?UNCONS T0 4 ERASE TOP 0! DEPTH CSP0 ! ;
-->
13
\                                               \ JFB 13:41 01/05/89
-->
MA86REVSYM  Revision symbol of release
T0          Operand attribute stack
TOP         Pointer to top of operand stack
CSP0        Assembler compiler stack pointer used to detect
            numbers placed on the parameter stack not by the
            assembler.
#$          Number of local labels or forward references
            times 4.
MAX#$       Maximum number of local labels plus forward
            references permitted.
$A          Array containing the local labels, forward
            references, and their addresses.
WF          XX8087 wait flag

14
\ Assembler local labels                        \ JFB 12:36 03/27/86

\ ---
: BEGIN$        #$ 0! ;

\ ---
: END$          #$ @ IF $A #$ @ + $A DO I @ 0< 28 DO?ERRORx
                4 +LOOP THEN ;

-->

15
\ CODE END-CODE                                 JFB 08:07 02/27/88
: ASMCODE RESET BEGIN$ -1 WF ! ;
' ASMCODE CFA ' DOASMCODE 1+ !

: ASMRESET RESET -1 WF ! ;
' ASMRESET CFA ' DOASMRESET 1+ !

: ASMEND-CODE END$ ;
' ASMEND-CODE CFA ' DOASMEND-CODE 1+ !

-->

16
\ Check relative jumps                          JFB 08:14 02/27/88
\ address --- relative address\0=range okay,1=out of range
: ?R0 WORDSx    HEREx 2+ - DUP DUP 07F > SWAP 0FF80 < OR ;
\ Check whether short jump is within +127 to -128 bytes and
\ return relative address.
```

```
\ 0=range okay,1=out of range ---
: ?R1           21 DO?ERRORx ; \ error on rel branch range ??
\ branch address --- relative address
: ?R            ?R0 ?R1 ;

-->
```

```
17
\ Assembler local labels                        JFB 08:15 02/27/88
\ label --- label
: $R            DUP 7FFC > OVER 0 < OR 22 DO?ERRORx ;
-->
```

Check whether local label value is greater than 0 and less than 32764. Zero indicates that there is no local label stored in the table. The local label table has the structure

```
        0 offset 2 offset
        label    address
```

Local labels (like 1 $:) are stored as a negative value. Forward references (like 1 $) are stored as a positive value. Local label code checks for forward references, immediately resolve them, and deletes the entry from the table. Backward references are immediately resolved.

```
18
\ Assembler local labels                        JFB 08:20 02/27/88
\ label ---
: !$ WORDSx     DUP     \ make a copy of label
                #$ @    \ get number of labels * 4.
                IF      \ if there are any labels
                  $A #$ @ + $A  \ scan table
                  DO I @ 0=     \ look for a vacant space
                    IF          \ space is found
                      I !       \ store the label
                      HEREx I 2+ !   \ and its address
                      DROP 0 LEAVE  \ discard label and leave 0
                    THEN
                  4 +LOOP  \ keep scanning or leave
                THEN  \ 0 indicates label is stored, >0 no space
                      \ available to reclaim
-->
19
\ Assembler local labels                        JFB 08:19 02/27/88
                IF \ space not reclaimed, try to in new space
                  #$ @ DUP \ get number of labels * 4
                  4 /      \ number of labels
                  MAX#$ <  \ is there room?
                  IF                \ yes,
                    $A +            \ get table address
                    HEREx OVER 2+ ! \ store address
                    !               \ store label
                    4 #$ +!         \ more label space used
                  ELSE 27 DO?ERRORx \ table size exceeded
                  THEN
                THEN ; -->
```

"Store label" stores a local label in the local label table. Error 27 is issued if no space remains in local label table.

```
20
\ syntax tokens                                       09:54 09/25/86

    00 CONSTANT NUL                 \ null token
    01 CONSTANT DISP=LO             \ eight bit displacement
    02 CONSTANT DISP=LOHI           \ 16 bit displacement
```

```
    03 CONSTANT DATA8              \ eight bit data
    04 CONSTANT DATA16             \ 16 bit data
    05 CONSTANT ALREG              \ AL register
    06 CONSTANT AXREG              \ AX register
    07 CONSTANT BREG               \ byte register
    08 CONSTANT WREG               \ word register
    09 CONSTANT SREG               \ segment register
    0A CONSTANT R/M                \ r/m memory reference
    0B CONSTANT BYT8               \ BYTE modifier
-->

21
\ syntax tokens                                       09:56 09/25/86

    0C CONSTANT WO16               \ WORD modifier
    0D CONSTANT STX                \ ST0 ... ST7
    0E CONSTANT ST0                \ ST0
    0F CONSTANT ST1                \ ST1
    10 CONSTANT FI/R               \ SHORTREAL, SHORTINTEGER, ...
    11 CONSTANT FQTB               \ TEMPORARYREAL, LONGINTEGER, ..
    12 CONSTANT CLREG              \ CL register
    13 CONSTANT ONE                \ 1
    14 CONSTANT PT                 \ PTR modifier
    15 CONSTANT FR                 \ FAR modifier
    16 CONSTANT DXREG              \ DX register
    17 CONSTANT PKD                \ BCD modifier
-->

22
\ syntax table builder                            JFB 08:39 02/27/88
DECIMAL
     58 CONSTANT #VFS      \ number of valid forms
      0 VARIABLE VFS       \ Number of syntax types and boundaries
                           \ to the attribute forms
        #VFS 2* ALLOT      \ space for the boundary pointers
        VFS 0!             \ number of syntax types

-->

23
\ syntax table builder                            JFB 08:40 02/27/88

\ # processed\type0\type1\type2\type3 --- # proceesed + 1
: VF,           >< OR ROT ROT >< OR , ,
                DUP 0 4 D.R 4 0 DO 8 EMIT LOOP 1+ ;

\ cummulative #\form # --- cummulative #
: !VF#          VFS + OVER SWAP ! ;
-->
```

VF, compiles valid operand form attrbiute tables into memory. The boundaries of each set of valid operand is stored into VFS. The attribute stack, T0, is compared to each valid operand form to check syntax for an opcode. If attribute stack does not match any of the valid syntax forms, then the operand for that opcode is invalid.

```
24
\ syntax tables                                   JFB 08:48 02/27/88

      0 VARIABLE VF -2 ALLOT
( register to register 2 hex 2 )
0 ( start cumulative count of forms)
BREG BREG NUL NUL VF, \ 1  CL DL MOV
WREG WREG NUL NUL VF, \ 2  CX DX MOV
```

```
2 !VF# -->

25
( syntax tables                                PLP 19:04 03/10/85 )

( memory to register 4 hex 4 )
BREG DISP=LO   NUL NUL VF, \  3   CL 12 MOV
BREG DISP=LO   R/M NUL VF, \  4   CL 12 [BX] MOV
BREG DISP=LOHI NUL NUL VF, \  5   CL 1234 MOV
BREG DISP=LOHI R/M NUL VF, \  6   CL 1234 [BX] MOV
BREG R/M       NUL NUL VF, \  7   CL [BX] MOV
WREG DISP=LO   NUL NUL VF, \  8   CX 12 MOV
WREG DISP=LO   R/M NUL VF, \  9   CX 12 [BX] MOV
WREG DISP=LOHI NUL NUL VF, \ 10   CX 1234 MOV
WREG DISP=LOHI R/M NUL VF, \ 11   CX 1234 [BX] MOV
WREG R/M       NUL NUL VF, \ 12   CX [BX] MOV
4 !VF# -->

26
( syntax tables                                PLP 19:04 03/10/85 )

( register to memory 6 hex 6 )
DISP=LO   BREG NUL  NUL VF, \ 13  12 CL MOV
DISP=LO   R/M  BREG NUL VF, \ 14  12 [BX] CL MOV
DISP=LOHI BREG NUL  NUL VF, \ 15  1234 CL MOV
DISP=LOHI R/M  BREG NUL VF, \ 16  1234 [BX] CL MOV
R/M       BREG NUL  NUL VF, \ 17  [BX] CL MOV
DISP=LO   WREG NUL  NUL VF, \ 18  12 CX MOV
DISP=LO   R/M  WREG NUL VF, \ 19  12 [BX] CX MOV
DISP=LOHI WREG NUL  NUL VF, \ 20  1234 CX MOV
DISP=LOHI R/M  WREG NUL VF, \ 21  1234 [BX] CX MOV
R/M       WREG NUL  NUL VF, \ 22  [BX] CX MOV
6 !VF#  -->

27
\ syntax tables                                   \     20:09 02/15/86

( data to reg 8 hex 8 )
BREG DATA8  NUL  NUL  VF,       \ 23  CL # 12 ADC
WREG DATA8  NUL  NUL  VF,       \ 24  CX # 12 ADC
WREG DATA16 NUL  NUL  VF,       \ 25  CX # 1234 ADC
8 !VF#

( data to memory 10 hex A )
DISP=LO   DATA8  BYT8  NUL  VF, \ 26  12 # 34 BYTE ADC
DISP=LOHI DATA8  BYT8  NUL  VF, \ 27  1234 # 56 BYTE ADC
DISP=LO   DATA8  NUL   NUL  VF, \ 28  12 # 34 ADC
DISP=LOHI DATA8  NUL   NUL  VF, \ 29  1234 # 56 ADC
DISP=LO   DATA16 NUL   NUL  VF, \ 30  12 # 3456 ADC
DISP=LOHI DATA16 NUL   NUL  VF, \ 31  1234 # 5678 ADC
-->
28
\ syntax tables                                   \     20:09 02/15/86

( data to memory, continued )
DISP=LO   R/M    DATA8  BYT8 VF, \ 32  12 [BX] # 34 BYTE ADC
DISP=LOHI R/M    DATA8  BYT8 VF, \ 33  1234 [BX] # 56 BYTE ADC
DISP=LO   R/M    DATA8  NUL  VF, \ 34  12 [BX] # 34 ADC
DISP=LOHI R/M    DATA8  NUL  VF, \ 35  1234 [BX] # 56 ADC
DISP=LO   R/M    DATA16 NUL  VF, \ 36  12 [BX] # 3456 ADC
DISP=LOHI R/M    DATA16 NUL  VF, \ 37  1234 [BX] # 5678 ADC
R/M       DATA8  BYT8   NUL  VF, \ 38  [BX] # 12 BYTE ADC
R/M       DATA8  NUL    NUL  VF, \ 39  [BX] # 12 ADC
R/M       DATA16 NUL    NUL  VF, \ 40  [BX] # 1234 ADC
```

```
10 !VF# -->

29
( syntax tables                              PLP 21:55 06/23/85 )

( accumulator to memory 12 hex C )
DISP=LO   ALREG NUL NUL VF,      \ 41  12 AL MOV
DISP=LOHI ALREG NUL NUL VF,      \ 42  1234 AL MOV
DISP=LO   AXREG NUL NUL VF,      \ 43  12 AX MOV
DISP=LOHI AXREG NUL NUL VF,      \ 44  1234 AX MOV
12 !VF#

( memory to accumulator 14  hex E )
ALREG DISP=LO   NUL NUL VF,      \ 45  AL 12 MOV
ALREG DISP=LOHI NUL NUL VF,      \ 46  AL 1234 MOV
AXREG DISP=LO   NUL NUL VF,      \ 47  AX 12 MOV
AXREG DISP=LOHI NUL NUL VF,      \ 48  AX 1234 MOV
14 !VF#
-->
30
( syntax tables                              PLP 21:34 06/23/85 )

( data to accumulator 16  hex 10 )
ALREG DATA8  NUL  NUL  VF, \ 49  AL # 12 ADD
AXREG DATA8  NUL  NUL  VF, \ 50  AX # 12 ADD
AXREG DATA16 NUL  NUL  VF, \ 51  AX # 1234 ADD
16 !VF# -->

31
(                                            PLP 21:34 06/23/85 )

( memory or register to segment register not cs 18 hex 12 )
SREG WREG      NUL NUL VF, \ 52  ES AX MOV
SREG DISP=LO   NUL NUL VF, \ 53  ES 12 MOV
SREG DISP=LOHI NUL NUL VF, \ 54  ES 1234 MOV
SREG DISP=LO   R/M NUL VF, \ 55  ES 12 [BX] MOV
SREG DISP=LOHI R/M NUL VF, \ 56  ES 1234 [BX] MOV
SREG R/M       NUL NUL VF, \ 57  ES [BX] MOV
18 !VF# -->

32
(                                            PLP 21:34 06/23/85 )

( segment register to memory or register 20 hex 14 )
WREG      SREG NUL NUL VF, \ 58  CX ES MOV
DISP=LO   SREG NUL NUL VF, \ 59  12 ES MOV
DISP=LOHI SREG NUL NUL VF, \ 60  1234 ES MOV
DISP=LO   R/M SREG NUL VF, \ 61  12 [BX] ES MOV
DISP=LOHI R/M SREG NUL VF, \ 62  1234 [BX] ES MOV
R/M       SREG NUL NUL VF, \ 63  [BX] ES MOV
20 !VF# -->

33
(                                            PLP 10:36 06/24/85 )

( cl rotates 22 hex 16 )
BREG      CLREG NUL   NUL   VF, \ 64  BL CL RCL
WREG      CLREG NUL   NUL   VF, \ 65  BX CL RCL
DISP=LO   CLREG BYT8  NUL   VF, \ 66  12 CL BYTE RCL
DISP=LO   R/M   CLREG BYT8  VF, \ 67  12 [BX] CL BYTE RCL
DISP=LOHI CLREG BYT8  NUL   VF, \ 68  1234 CL BYTE RCL
DISP=LOHI R/M   CLREG BYT8  VF, \ 69  1234 [BX] CL BYTE RCL
R/M       CLREG BYT8  NUL   VF, \ 70  [BX] CL BYTE RCL
DISP=LO   CLREG WO16  NUL   VF, \ 71  12 CL WORD RCL
```

```
DISP=LOHI CLREG WO16   NUL   VF, \ 72  1234 CL WORD RCL
DISP=LO   R/M   CLREG  WO16  VF, \ 73  12 [BX] CL WORD RCL
DISP=LOHI R/M   CLREG  WO16  VF, \ 74  1234 [BX] CL WORD RCL
R/M       CLREG WO16   NUL   VF, \ 75  [BX] CL WORD RCL
22 !VF# -->
34
(                                           PLP 13:46 06/24/85 )

( 1 rotates 24 hex 18 )
BREG      ONE  NUL  NUL  VF, \ 76  BL 1 RCL
WREG      ONE  NUL  NUL  VF, \ 77  BX 1 RCL
DISP=LO   ONE  BYT8 NUL  VF, \ 78  12 1 BYTE RCL
DISP=LO   R/M  ONE  BYT8 VF, \ 79  12 [BX] 1 BYTE RCL
DISP=LOHI ONE  BYT8 NUL  VF, \ 80  1234 1 BYTE RCL
DISP=LOHI R/M  ONE  BYT8 VF, \ 81  1234 [BX] 1 BYTE RCL
R/M       ONE  BYT8 NUL  VF, \ 82  [BX] 1 BYTE RCL
DISP=LO   ONE  WO16 NUL  VF, \ 83  12 1 WORD RCL
DISP=LOHI ONE  WO16 NUL  VF, \ 84  1234 1 WORD RCL
DISP=LO   R/M  ONE  WO16 VF, \ 85  12 [BX] 1 WORD RCL
DISP=LOHI R/M  ONE  WO16 VF, \ 86  1234 [BX] 1 WORD RCL
R/M       ONE  WO16 NUL  VF, \ 87  [BX] 1 WORD RCL
24 !VF# -->
35
(                                           PLP 10:36 06/24/85 )
( segment register, not cs 26 hex 1A )
SREG NUL NUL NUL VF,      \ 88  SS POP
26 !VF#

( segment register, 28 hex 1C )
SREG NUL NUL NUL VF,      \ 89  CS PUSH
28 !VF#

( memory word operand  30 hex 1E )
DISP=LO   NUL NUL NUL VF, \ 90  12 PUSH
DISP=LO   R/M NUL NUL VF, \ 91  12 [BX] PUSH
DISP=LOHI NUL NUL NUL VF, \ 92  1234 PUSH
DISP=LOHI R/M NUL NUL VF, \ 93  1234 [BX] PUSH
R/M       NUL NUL NUL VF, \ 94  [BX] PUSH
30 !VF# -->
36
( syntax tables                             PLP 10:37 06/24/85 )

( indirect 32 hex 20 )
DISP=LO   PT  NUL NUL VF, \ 95  12 PTR JMP
DISP=LOHI PT  NUL NUL VF, \ 96  1234 PTR JMP
DISP=LO   R/M NUL NUL VF, \ 97  12 [BX] JMP
DISP=LOHI R/M NUL NUL VF, \ 98  1234 [BX] JMP
R/M       NUL NUL NUL VF, \ 99  [BX] JMP
WREG      NUL NUL NUL VF, \ 100 CX JMP
32 !VF# -->

37
( syntax tables                             PLP 10:37 06/24/85 )

( far indirect 34 hex 22 )
DISP=LO   PT  FR  NUL VF, \ 101  12 PTR FAR JMP
DISP=LOHI PT  FR  NUL VF, \ 102  1234 PTR FAR JMP
DISP=LO   R/M FR  NUL VF, \ 103  12 [BX] FAR JMP
DISP=LOHI R/M FR  NUL VF, \ 104  1234 [BX] FAR JMP
R/M       FR  NUL NUL VF, \ 105  [BX] FAR JMP
WREG      FR  NUL NUL VF, \ 106  CX FAR JMP
34 !VF#

( data to register 36 hex 24 )
```

```
BREG DATA8  NUL NUL VF,    \ 107  BL # 12 MOV
WREG DATA8  NUL NUL VF,    \ 108  BX # 12 MOV
WREG DATA16 NUL NUL VF,    \ 109  BX # 1234 MOV
36 !VF# -->
38
( syntax tables                                PLP 10:37 06/24/85 )

( word or byte 38 hex 26 )
NUL  NUL NUL NUL VF,    \ 110  LODS
BYT8 NUL NUL NUL VF,    \ 111  BYTE LODS
WO16 NUL NUL NUL VF,    \ 112  WORD LODS
38 !VF#

( word register only 40 hex 28 )
WREG NUL NUL NUL VF,    \ 113  BX DEC or AX PUSH
40 !VF# -->

39
( syntax tables                                PLP 18:45 07/03/85 )

( intrasegment relative or direct 42 hex 2A )
DISP=LO   NUL NUL NUL VF,       \ 114  012 JMP
DISP=LOHI NUL NUL NUL VF,       \ 115  1234 JMP
42 !VF#

( intersegment direct 44 hex 2C )
DISP=LO   DISP=LO   FR  NUL VF, \ 116  12 34 FAR CALL
DISP=LO   DISP=LOHI FR  NUL VF, \ 117  12 3456 FAR CALL
DISP=LOHI DISP=LO   FR  NUL VF, \ 118  1234 56 FAR CALL
DISP=LOHI DISP=LOHI FR  NUL VF, \ 119  1234 5678 FAR CALL
44 !VF#
-->

40
( syntax tables                                WHP 08:43 09/02/85 )

( relative jump 46 hex 2E )
DISP=LO   NUL NUL NUL VF,    \ 120  12 JNE
DISP=LOHI NUL NUL NUL VF,    \ 121  1234 JNE
46 !VF#

( fixed input port 48 hex 30 )
ALREG DISP=LO NUL NUL VF,    \ 122  AL 12 IN
AXREG DISP=LO NUL NUL VF,    \ 123  AX 12 IN
48 !VF#
-->

41
( syntax tables                                PLP 10:19 08/20/85 )

( variable port 50 hex 32 )
BREG DXREG NUL NUL VF,     \ 124  AL DX IN
WREG DXREG NUL NUL VF,     \ 125  AX DX IN
50 !VF#

( interrupts 52 hex 34 )
DISP=LO NUL NUL NUL VF,    \ 126  67 INT or 3 INT
52 !VF#
-->

42
( syntax tables                                PLP 15:44 07/05/85 )

( byte or word memory operand 54 hex 36 )
```

```
DISP=LO   BYT8 NUL  NUL VF, \ 127  12 BYTE DEC
DISP=LO   R/M  BYT8 NUL VF, \ 128  12 [BX] BYTE DEC
DISP=LOHI BYT8 NUL  NUL VF, \ 129  1234 BYTE DEC
DISP=LOHI R/M  BYT8 NUL VF, \ 130  1234 [BX] BYTE DEC
R/M       BYT8 NUL  NUL VF, \ 131  [BX] BYTE DEC
DISP=LO   WO16 NUL  NUL VF, \ 132  12 WORD DEC
DISP=LO   R/M  WO16 NUL VF, \ 133  12 [BX] WORD DEC
DISP=LOHI WO16 NUL  NUL VF, \ 134  1234 WORD DEC
DISP=LOHI R/M  WO16 NUL VF, \ 135  1234 [BX] WORD DEC
R/M       WO16 NUL  NUL VF, \ 136  [BX] WORD DEC
BREG      NUL  NUL  NUL VF, \ 137  BL DEC
WREG      NUL  NUL  NUL VF, \ 138  BX DEC
54 !VF#  -->
43
( syntax tables                              PLP 15:44 07/05/85 )
( mod reg r/m not mod=11 56 hex 38 )
WREG DISP=LO   NUL NUL VF, \ 139  CX 12 LES
WREG DISP=LO   R/M NUL VF, \ 140  CX 12 [BX] LES
WREG DISP=LOHI NUL NUL VF, \ 141  CX 1234 LES
WREG DISP=LOHI R/M NUL VF, \ 142  CX 1234 [BX] LES
WREG R/M       NUL NUL VF, \ 143  CX [BX] LES
56 !VF#
( returns 58 hex 3A )
NUL       NUL NUL NUL VF,  \ 144  RET
DISP=LO   NUL NUL NUL VF,  \ 145  12 RET
DISP=LOHI NUL NUL NUL VF,  \ 146  1234 RET
FR        NUL NUL NUL VF,  \ 147  FAR RET
DISP=LO   FR  NUL NUL VF,  \ 148  12 FAR RET
DISP=LOHI FR  NUL NUL VF,  \ 149  1234 FAR RET
58 !VF# -->
44
( syntax tables                              PLP 18:45 07/03/85 )
( intrasegment direct 60 hex 3C )
DISP=LO   NUL NUL NUL VF, \ 150  12 CALL
DISP=LOHI NUL NUL NUL VF, \ 151  1234 CALL
60 !VF#

( null byte 62 hex 3E )
NUL NUL NUL NUL VF,       \ 152  AAA
62 !VF#

( null word 64 hex 40 )
NUL NUL NUL NUL VF,       \ 153  AAD
64 !VF#
-->

45
( 8087 syntax tables                         PLP 15:44 07/05/85 )
( stx to st0 66 hex 42 )
ST0 STX NUL NUL VF,  \ 154  ST0 ST2 FLD
66 !VF#

( st0 to stx 68  hex 44 )
STX ST0 NUL NUL VF,  \ 155  ST2 ST0 FST
68 !VF#

( st0 70 hex 46 )
ST0 NUL NUL NUL VF,  \ 156  ST0 FTST
70 !VF#

( st0 and st1 72 hex 48 )
ST0 ST1 NUL NUL VF,  \ 157  ST0 ST1 FCOMPP
72 !VF# -->
46
```

```
\ 8087 syntax tables                        P      09:48 09/25/86

( integer/real memory to st0 74 hex 4A )
ST0 DISP=LO   FI/R NUL  VF, \ 158  ST0 12 SHORTREAL FLD
ST0 DISP=LO   R/M  FI/R VF, \ 159  ST0 12 [BX] SHORTREAL FLD
ST0 DISP=LOHI FI/R NUL  VF, \ 160  ST0 1234 SHORTREAL FLD
ST0 DISP=LOHI R/M  FI/R VF, \ 161  ST0 1234 [BX] SHORTREAL FLD
ST0 R/M       FI/R NUL  VF, \ 162  ST0 [BX] SHORTREAL FLD
ST0 WREG      FI/R NUL  VF, \ 163  ST0 AX SHORTREAL FLD
74 !VF# -->

47
( 8087 syntax tables                        PLP 15:43 07/05/85 )

( integer/real st0 to memory 76 hex 4C )
DISP=LO   ST0  FI/R NUL  VF, \ 164  12 ST0 SHORTREAL FST
DISP=LO   R/M  ST0  FI/R VF, \ 165  12 [BX] ST0 SHORTREAL FST
DISP=LOHI ST0  FI/R NUL  VF, \ 166  1234 ST0 SHORTREAL FST
DISP=LOHI R/M  ST0  FI/R VF, \ 167  1234 [BX] ST SHORTREAL FST
R/M       ST0  FI/R NUL  VF, \ 168  [BX] ST0 SHORTREAL FST
WREG      ST0  FI/R NUL  VF, \ 169  AX ST0 SHORTREAL FLD
76 !VF# -->

48
\ 8087 syntax tables                        P      09:50 09/25/86

( other ftype memory to st0 78 hex 4E )
ST0 DISP=LO   FQTB NUL  VF, \ 170  ST0 12 PACKED FLD
ST0 DISP=LO   R/M  FQTB VF, \ 171  ST0 12 [BX] PACKED FLD
ST0 DISP=LOHI FQTB NUL  VF, \ 172  ST0 1234 PACKED FLD
ST0 DISP=LOHI R/M  FQTB VF, \ 173  ST0 1234 [BX] PACKED FLD
ST0 R/M       FQTB NUL  VF, \ 174  ST0 [BX] PACKED FLD
ST0 WREG      FQTB NUL  VF, \ 175  ST0 AX PACKED FLD
78 !VF#
-->

49
( 8087 syntax tables                        PLP 15:43 07/05/85 )

( integer/real st0 to memory 80 hex 50 )
DISP=LO   ST0  FQTB NUL  VF, \ 176  12 ST0 PACKED FSTP
DISP=LO   R/M  ST0  FQTB VF, \ 177  12 [BX] ST0 PACKED FSTP
DISP=LOHI ST0  FQTB NUL  VF, \ 178  1234 ST0 PACKED FSTP
DISP=LOHI R/M  ST0  FQTB VF, \ 179  1234 [BX] ST0 PACKED FSTP
R/M       ST0  FQTB NUL  VF, \ 180  [BX] ST0 PACKED FSTP
WREG      ST0  FQTB NUL  VF, \ 181  AX ST0 PACKED FSTP
80 !VF#

( stx 82 hex 52 )
STX       NUL  NUL  NUL  VF, \ 182  ST2 FFREE
82 !VF#
-->

50
( 8087 syntax tables                        PLP 18:46 07/03/85 )

( to/from  memory 84 hex 54 )
DISP=LO   NUL NUL NUL  VF, \ 183  12 FSTENV
DISP=LO   R/M NUL NUL  VF, \ 184  12 [BX] FSTENV
DISP=LOHI NUL NUL NUL  VF, \ 185  1234 FSTEVN
DISP=LOHI R/M NUL NUL  VF, \ 186  1234 [BX] FSTENV
R/M       NUL NUL NUL  VF, \ 187  [BX] FSTENV
WREG      NUL NUL NUL  VF, \ 188  AX FSTENV
84 !VF#
```

```
-->

51
( 80186/80286 insructions                    PLP 11:03 07/03/85 )

( push immediate 86  hex 56 )
DATA8  NUL NUL  NUL  VF,        \ 189  # 12 PUSH
DATA16 NUL NUL  NUL  VF,        \ 190  # 1234 PUSH
86 !VF#

( immediate data word 88 hex 58 )
WREG  WREG       DATA8  NUL  VF, \ 191  CX DX # 12 IMUL
WREG  WREG       DATA16 NUL  VF, \ 192  CX DX # 1234 IMUL
WREG  DISP=LO    DATA8  NUL  VF, \ 193  CX 12 # 34 IMUL
WREG  DISP=LOHI DATA8  NUL  VF, \ 194  CX 1234 # 56 IMUL
-->

52
( 80186/80286 insructions                    PLP 15:39 07/05/85 )

( immediate data word continued )
WREG DISP=LO   DATA16 NUL    VF, \ 195  CX 12 # 3456 IMUL
WREG DISP=LOHI DATA16 NUL    VF, \ 196  CX 1234 # 5678 IMUL
WREG DISP=LO   R/M    DATA8  VF, \ 197  CX 12 [BX] # 34 IMUL
WREG DISP=LOHI R/M    DATA8  VF, \ 198  CX 1234 [BX] # 56 IMUL
WREG DISP=LO   R/M    DATA16 VF, \ 199  CX 12 [BX] # 3456 IMUL
WREG DISP=LOHI R/M    DATA16 VF, \ 200  CX 1234 [BX] # 5678 IMUL
WREG R/M       DATA8  NUL    VF, \ 201  CX [BX] # 12 IMUL
WREG R/M       DATA16 NUL    VF, \ 202  CX [BX] # 1234 IMUL
88 !VF# -->

53
( 80186/80286 insructions                    PLP 13:12 07/03/85 )

( immediate rotates 90 hex 5A )
BREG      DISP=LO NUL     NUL   VF, \ 203  BL 7 RCL
WREG      DISP=LO NUL     NUL   VF, \ 204  BX 7 RCL
DISP=LO   DISP=LO BYT8    NUL   VF, \ 205  12 7 BYTE RCL
DISP=LO   R/M     DISP=LO BYT8  VF, \ 206  12 [BX] 7 BYTE RCL
DISP=LOHI DISP=LO BYT8    NUL   VF, \ 207  1234 7 BYTE RCL
DISP=LOHI R/M     DISP=LO BYT8  VF, \ 208  1234 [BX] 7 BYTE RCL
R/M       DISP=LO BYT8    NUL   VF, \ 209  [BX] 7 BYTE RCL
DISP=LO   DISP=LO WO16    NUL   VF, \ 210  12 7 WORD RCL
DISP=LOHI DISP=LO WO16    NUL   VF, \ 211  1234 7 WORD RCL
DISP=LO   R/M     DISP=LO WO16  VF, \ 212  12 [BX] 7 WORD RCL
DISP=LOHI R/M     DISP=LO WO16  VF, \ 213  1234 [BX] 7 WORD RCL
R/M       DISP=LO WO16    NUL   VF, \ 214  [BX] 7 WORD RCL
90 !VF# -->
54
( 80186/80286 insructions                    PLP 14:37 07/03/85 )

( enter 92 hex 5C )
DISP=LO   DISP=LO NUL NUL  VF, \ 215  12 34 ENTER
DISP=LOHI DISP=LO NUL NUL  VF, \ 216  1234 56 ENTER
92 !VF#

( word register to register 94 hex 5E )
WREG NUL NUL NUL VF,            \ 217  CX DX LTR
94 !VF# -->

55
( 80186/80286 insructions                    PLP 18:46 07/03/85 )

( memory to word register 96 hex 60 )
```

```
WREG DISP=LO   NUL NUL VF, \ 218  CX 12 or 1234 BOUND
WREG DISP=LO   R/M NUL VF, \ 219  CX 12 [BX] BOUND
WREG DISP=LOHI NUL NUL VF, \ 220  CX 1234 BOUND
WREG DISP=LOHI R/M NUL VF, \ 221  CX 1234 [BX] BOUND
WREG R/M       NUL NUL VF, \ 222  CX [BX] BOUND
96 !VF# -->

56
( 80186/80286 insructions                  PLP 18:47 07/03/85 )

( memory or word register to word register 98 hex 62 )
WREG WREG      NUL NUL VF, \ 223  CX DX LTR
WREG DISP=LO   NUL NUL VF, \ 224  CX 12 LTR
WREG DISP=LO   R/M NUL VF, \ 225  CX 12 [BX] LTR
WREG DISP=LOHI NUL NUL VF, \ 226  CX 1234 LTR
WREG DISP=LOHI R/M NUL VF, \ 227  CX 1234 [BX] LTR
WREG R/M       NUL NUL VF, \ 228  CX [BX] LTR
98 !VF# -->

57
( 80186/80286 insructions                  PLP 10:05 08/20/85 )

( memory operand protection 100  hex 64 )
DISP=LO   NUL NUL NUL VF,  \ 229  12 LGDT
DISP=LO   R/M NUL NUL VF,  \ 230  12 [BX] LGDT
DISP=LOHI NUL NUL NUL VF,  \ 231  1234 LGDT
DISP=LOHI R/M NUL NUL VF,  \ 232  1234 [BX] LGDT
R/M       NUL NUL NUL VF,  \ 233  [BX] LGDT
100 !VF#

( xchg ax with register 102 hex 66 )
AXREG WREG NUL NUL VF,     \ 234  AX BX XCHG
102 !VF#
-->

58
\                                             plp 08:06 06/05/86

( fixed output port 104 hex 68 )
DISP=LO ALREG NUL NUL VF,    \ 235  # 12 AL OUT
DISP=LO AXREG NUL NUL VF,    \ 236  # 12 AX OUT
104 !VF#

( variable output port 106 hex 6A )
DXREG BREG NUL NUL VF,     \ 237  DX AL OUT
DXREG WREG NUL NUL VF,     \ 238  DX AX OUT
106 !VF#
-->

59
\                                                 07:03 06/11/86

( NEC V20/30 lods stos 108 hex 6C )
BREG BREG    NUL NUL VF,     \ 239  DL CL LODS      V20/30
108 !VF#

( NEC V20/30 lods stos 110 hex 6E )
BREG DISP=LO NUL NUL VF,     \ 240  DL 3 LODS       V20/30
110 !VF#

( NEC V20/30 bcd add sub cmp 112 hex 70 )
PKD  NUL     NUL NUL VF,     \ 241  BCD CMP         V20/30
112 !VF#
-->
```

```
60
\                                                  JFB 08:50 02/27/88
( NEC V20/30 bcd rotates 114 hex 72 )
BREG      PKD NUL NUL VF, \ 242  BL BCD ROL          V20/30
DISP=LO   PKD NUL NUL VF, \ 243  12 BCD ROL
DISP=LO   R/M PKD NUL VF, \ 244  12 [BX] BCD ROL
DISP=LOHI PKD NUL NUL VF, \ 245  1234 BCD ROL
DISP=LOHI R/M PKD NUL VF, \ 246  1234 [BX] BCD ROL
R/M       PKD NUL NUL VF, \ 247  [BX] BCD ROL
114 !VF#

( NEC V20/30 brkem 116 hex 74 )
DISP=LO   NUL NUL NUL VF, \ 248  12 BRKEM            V20/30
116 !VF#
DROP   \ drop the cumulative count
-->

61
\ attribute vector                                 JFB 08:54 02/27/88
HEX
( number ---  )
: ?TOP          3 > 24 DO?ERRORx ; \ too many operands?
( --- )
: 1+TOP         TOP DUP @ DUP ?TOP 1+ SWAP ! ; \ increment TOP

( opcode or operand type --- )
: !TOP          TO TOP @ + C!    \ push the attribute on the
                1+TOP            \ stack.  Increment stack ptr
                DEPTH CSP0 !     \ reset assembler compiler
;                                \ stack pointer
-->

62
\ stack check                                      JFB 11:58 02/27/88
HEX
: ?DISP         DEPTH CSP0 @ - -DUP 0>
                IF MINUS 0 SWAP
                  DO I ABS PICK DUP 0FF > SWAP FF00 < OR
                  IF 02 ELSE 01 THEN TO TOP @ 1- + C@ DATA16 =
                    IF 2+ TOP DUP @ 1- SWAP ! THEN !TOP
                  LOOP
                THEN ;
-->
```

?DISP checks to see if any number has been palced on the stack since the last opcode or operand was processed. If one or more number appeared, then their attributes are correctly added to the attribute stack. Eight or 16 bit displacements are distinguished from 8 and 16 bit data.

```
63
\ assembler code generator                         JFB 08:56 02/27/88
-->
```

The assembler code generator is documented by example of representative instructions processed by each routine.

```
64
\ assembler code generator                         JFB 10:15 05/08/88
: INVALID WORDSx 25 ERRORx ;

: L0            0100 OR ; \ set word operands
: L7            0200 OR ; \ set sign extended data
: PL            0006 OR ; \ effective address = disp-high:low
: PM            0040 OR ; \ disp-low sign extended
```

```
: PN             0080 OR ; \ disp-high:disp-low
: PO             00C0 OR ; \ r/m treated as "reg" field

: LV WORDSx      >< ,x ;
: PK             OR LV ;   \ [BX]
: L3 WORDSx      OR C,x ;  \  BX POP or CX INC
: QO WORDSx      LV C,x ;  \ 12 BRKEM
-->

65
\ assembler code generator                    JFB 09:07 02/27/88
: L4             SWAP 8 * PK ;
: JT             OR L4 ;
: L1             PO JT ;    \ DL CL
: L2             L0 L1 ;    \ CX DX

: PQ WORDSx      C,x C,x ;
: NZ WORDSx      C,x ,x ;   \ 1234 RET
: PJ             01 OR ;
: KC             02 OR ;
-->

66
\ assembler code generator                    JFB 09:07 02/27/88

: L5             PL L4 ABSOLUTE ; \ 12 or 1234 CL
: L6 WORDSx      PM ROT JT C,x ;  \ 12 [BX] CL
: L8 WORDSx      PN ROT JT ,x ;   \ 1234 [BX] CL
: L9 WORDSx      ROT DUP 06 =
                 IF PM JT 0 C,x   \ 0 [BP] CL
                 ELSE JT
                 THEN ;           \ [BX] CL

: LA             L0 L5 ;          \ 12 or 1234 CX
: LB             L0 L6 ;          \ 12 [BX] LX
: LD             L0 L8 ;          \ 1234 [BX] CX
: LE             L0 L9 ;          \ [BX] CX
-->

67
\ assembler code generator                  \ JFB 10:47 03/27/86

: LF             >R SWAP R> ;
: LG             >R ROT R> ;
: JU             OR LF ;

: LH             LF L5 ;     \ CL 12 or 1234
: LI             LG L6 ;     \ CL 12 [BX]
: LK             LG L8 ;     \ CL 1234 [BX]
: LL             LF L9 ;     \ CL [BX]

: LM             L0 LF LA ; \ CX 12 or 1234
: LN             L0 LG LB ; \ CX 12 [BX]
: LP             L0 LG LD ; \ CX 1234 [BX]
: LQ             L0 LF LE ; \ CX [BX]
-->
68
\ assembler code generator                  \ JFB 21:58 03/27/86

: PF             OR ROT PK ;

: LS WORDSx      02C0 PF C,x ;          \ CL # 12 ADC
: QF WORDSx      03C0 PF C,x ;          \ CX # 12 ADC
: PE WORDSx      01C0 PF ,x ;           \ CX # 1234 ADC
```

```
: LT              DUP C000 U>
                  IF PE
                  ELSE DUP 038 AND 8 /   \ is sign extended?
                  ONGOSUB QF PE QF QF    \ or an AND, OR,or XOR
                          PE QF PE QF    \ which cannot be sign
                  ENDGOSUB               \ extended.
                  THEN ;
-->

69
\ assembler code generator                       JFB 09:09 02/27/88

: PH              SWAP DROP ;
: PR WORDSx       ABSOLUTE C,x ;
: PS WORDSx       ,x ABSOLUTE ;
: LX              PH PL LF LV PR ;   \ 1234 # 56 BYTE 12 # 34 BYTE
: LY              0306 JU LV PR ;    \ 12 # 34 ACD
: LZ              0106 JU LV PS ;    \ 1234 # 56 AND
: LW              DUP C000 U>
                  IF LZ                  \ MOV and TEST
                  ELSE DUP 038 AND 8 /   \ is sign extended?
                  ONGOSUB LY LZ LY LY    \ or an AND, OR,or XOR
                          LZ LY LZ LY    \ which cannot be sign
                  ENDGOSUB               \ extended.
                  THEN ;
-->
70
\ assembler code generator                       JFB 09:09 02/27/88

: PI              >R ROT ROT R> ;
: PG              PI OR LV ;

: M2              PH PM PG PQ ;          \ 12 [BX] # 34 BYTE
: M3              PH PN PG PR ;          \ 1234 [BX] # 56 BYTE
: QA              0140 OR PG NZ ;        \ 12 [BX] # 34 AND
: M4              0340 OR PG PQ ;        \ 12 [BX] # 34 ACD
: Q9              DUP C000 U>
                  IF QA                  \ MOV and TEST
                  DUP 038 AND 8 /        \ is sign extended?
                  ONGOSUB M4 QA M4 M4    \ or an AND, OR,or XOR
                          QA M4 QA M4    \ which cannot be sign
                  ENDGOSUB               \ extended.
                  THEN ; -->
71
\ assembler code generator                       JFB 09:10 02/27/88

: QB              0180 OR PG PS ;         \ 1234 [BX] # 56 AND
: M5              0380 OR PG PR ;         \ 1234 [BX] # 56 ADC
: QC              DUP C000 U>
                  IF QB                   \ MOV and TEST
                  ELSE DUP 038 AND 8 /    \ is sign extended?
                  ONGOSUB M5 QB M5 M5     \ or an AND, OR,or XOR
                          QB M5 QB M5     \ which cannot be sign
                  ENDGOSUB                \ extended.
                  THEN ;
: M6              0140 OR PI OR LV NZ ;  \ 12   [BX] # 3456
: M7              0180 OR PI OR LV PS  ; \ 1234 [BX] # 5678
: M8 WORDSx       PH LF OR QO ;           \ [BX] # 12 BYTE
  -->
72
\ assembler code generator                       JFB 09:15 02/27/88

: MB WORDSx       C,x PH ABSOLUTE ;   \ AL 1234
: MC              PJ MB ;             \ AX 1234
```

```
: MD WORDSx      C,x DROP ABSOLUTE ; \ 1234 AL
: ME             PJ MD ;             \ 1234 AX

: MK             PQ DROP ;           \ AL # 12
: ML WORDSx      PJ NZ DROP ;        \ AX # 1234

: MN             0006 PK ABSOLUTE ;  \ 12 or 1234
: MP WORDSx      PM PK C,x ;         \ 12 [BX]
: MQ WORDSx      PN PK ,x ;          \ 1234 [BX]
: MR             PO PK ;             \ CL or CX
-->
73
\ assembler code generator                      \ JFB 22:05 03/27/86

: QE WORDSx      0100 JU OR LV ,x ;      \ [BX] # 12 AND
: M9 WORDSx      0300 JU OR QO ;         \ [BX] # 12 ADC
: QD             DUP C000 U>
                 IF QE
                 ELSE DUP 038 AND 8 /    \ is sign extended?
                 ONGOSUB M9 QE M9 M9     \ or an AND, OR,or XOR
                         QE M9 QE M9     \ which cannot be sign
                 ENDGOSUB                \ extended.
                 THEN ;
: MA WORDSx      L0 LF OR LV ,x ;         \ [BX] # 1234

-->

74
\ assembler code generator                      JFB 09:19 02/27/88

: MS    PH PH ;
: MT    MS 0006 PK ABSOLUTE ; \ 12 or 1234 1 BYTE RCL
: MU    L0 MT ;               \ 12 or 1234 1 WORD RCL
: MV    MS PK ;               \ [BX] 1 BYTE RCL
: MW    L0 MV ;               \ [BX] 1 WORD RCL
: MX WORDSx   MS PM PK C,x ;  \ 12 [BX] 1 BYTE RCL
: MY    L0 MX ;               \ 12 [BX] 1 WORD RCL
: MZ WORDSx   MS PN PK ,x ;   \ 1234 [BX] 1 BYTE RCL
: N0    L0 MZ ;               \ 1234 [BX] 1 WORD RCL
: N1    PH PO PK ;            \ CL 1 RCL
: N3    L0 N1 ;               \ CX 1 RCL
-->

75
\ assembler code generator                      JFB 09:18 02/27/88

: N2             26 DO?ERRORx ;
: N4             SWAP 08 * L3 ;       \ CS PUSH
: N5             OVER 01 = N2 N4 ;    \ SS POP
: N6             LF L3 ;
: N7 WORDSx      N6 C,x ;             \ DL # 12 MOV
: N8             08 OR N6 ABSOLUTE ;  \ DL # 1234 MOV
: N9 WORDSx      C,x DROP ;           \ BYTE LODS
: NA             01 L3 ;              \ LODS
: LJ             PH NA ;              \ WORD LODS
: NB WORDSx      PH C,x SWAP PS  ;    \ OFFSET SEGAD FAR JMP
-->

76
\ assembler code generator                      JFB 09:28 02/27/88

: NE WORDSx      SWAP ?R SWAP C,x OFF8 ; \ 1$ JZ
: NF             PQ DROP ;               \ AL 12 IN
: NG             1 OR NF ;               \ AX 12 IN
```

```
: NH WORDSx      C,x 2DROP ;              \ AL DX IN
: NI             PJ NH ;                  \ AX DX IN
: Q4             LF NF ;                  \ 12 AL OUT
: Q5             LF NG ;                  \ 12 AX OUT
: Q6             LF NH ;                  \ DX AL OUT
: Q7             LF NI ;                  \ DX AX OUT

: NJ WORDSx      SWAP DUP 3 =
                 IF DROP C,x
                 ELSE SWAP PJ PQ THEN ;   \ 67 INT
-->
77
\ assembler code generator                          JFB 09:28 02/27/88

: NK             PH 0006 PK ABSOLUTE ; \ 12 or 1234 BYTE DEC
: NL WORDSx      PH PM SWAP PK C,x ;   \ 12 [BX] BYTE DEC
: NM WORDSx      PH PN SWAP PK ,x ;    \ 1234 [BX]
: NO             PH PK ;               \ [BX]
: NP             L0 NK ;               \ 12 WORD DEC
: NQ             L0 NL ;               \ 12 [BX] WORD DEC
: NR             L0 NM ;               \ 1234 [BX] WORD DEC
: NS             L0 NO ;               \ [BX] WORD DEC
: NT             PO PK ;               \ BL DEC
: NU             L0 NT ;               \ BX DIV
-->

78
\ assembler code generator                          JFB 09:28 02/27/88

: NV             PL ROT 8 * PK ABSOLUTE ; \ CX 12 or 1234 LES
: NW WORDSx      PM OR ROT 8 * PK C,x ;   \ CX 12 [BX] LES
: NX WORDSx      PN OR ROT 8 * PK ,x ;    \ CX 12 [BX] LES
: NY             OR L4 ;                  \ CX [BX] LES

: O0 WORDSx      PJ  C,x ;                \ RET
: O1             PH 08 OR O0 ;            \ FAR RET
: O2             PH 08 OR NZ ;            \ 1234 FAR RET
-->

79
\ assembler code generator                          JFB 09:29 02/27/88

: O4             PICK 01 = N2 ;
: O5             3 O4 L1 ;   \ ES CX MOV
: O6             3 O4 LH ;   \ ES 12 CX MOV
: O7             3 O4 LH ;   \ ES 1234 CX MOV
: O8             4 O4 LI ;   \ ES 12 [BX] MOV
: O9             4 O4 LK ;   \ ES 1234 [BX] MOV
: OA             3 O4 LL ;   \ ES [BX] MOV
: OB             LF L1 ;     \ CX ES MOV
-->

80
\ assembler code generator                          JFB 09:31 02/27/88

: OI WORDSx      OR C,x DROP ;            \ AX DX XCHG

: OJ             PH MN ;                  \ 12 or 1234 PTR JMP
: OK             PH MP ;                  \ 12 [BX] FAR JMP
: OL             PH MQ ;                  \ 1234 [BX] FAR JMP
: OM             PH PK ;                  \ [BX] FAR JMP
: PC             PH MR ;                  \ CX FAR JMP
: OO             MS MN ;                  \ 12 or 1234 PTR FAR JMP
```

```
: OP WORDSx      SWAP ?R0
                 IF SWAP C,x 1- OFF16
                 ELSE SWAP KC C,x OFF8
                 THEN ;                  \ 1$ JMP
-->
81
\ assembler code generator                      JFB 09:32 02/27/88

: OQ             PK DROP ;               \ ST ST(2) FLD
: OS             LV DROP ;               \ ST FTST
: OT             PH PK ;                 \ ST(2) ST FST
: OV             LV 2DROP ;              \ ST ST(1) FTST
: OW             >R LF R> ;
: OX             >R PI R> ;
: OY             PL OR >< PS DROP ;  \ ST 12 or 1234 SHORTREAL
: OZ WORDSx      PM OR PK C,x DROP ; \ ST 12 [BX] SHORTREAL
: P0 WORDSx      PN OR PK ,x DROP ;  \ ST 1234 [BX] SHORTREAL
: P1             OR PK DROP ;            \ ST [BX] SHORTREAL
-->

82
\ assembler code generator                      JFB 09:33 02/27/88

: P2             OR P0 OR OS ; \ ST AX SHORTREAL
: P3             OW OY ;       \ ST 12 SHORTREAL
: P4             OX OZ ;       \ ST 12 [BX] SHORTREAL
: P5             OX P0 ;       \ ST 1234 [BX] SHORTREAL
: P6             OW P1 ;       \ ST [BX] SHORTREAL
: P7             OW P2 ;       \ ST AX SHORTREAL

: K0             KC PQ ;       \ # 12 PUSH

: K1             PI OR PO L4 ;
: K2 WORDSx      L7 K1 C,x ;   \ CX DX # 12 IMUL
: K3 WORDSx      K1 ,x ;       \ CX DX # 1234 IMUL
-->

83
\ assembler code generator                      JFB 09:34 02/27/88

: K4            L7 PL LG L4 SWAP PR ; \ CX 12 or 1234 # 56 IMUL
: K5            PL LG L4 SWAP PS ;    \ CX 12 or 1234 # 5678 IMUL
: K6 WORDSx     L7 PM SWAP >R JU
                L4 C,x R> C,x ;       \ CX 12 [BX] # 34 IMUL
: K7 WORDSx     L7 PN SWAP >R JU
                L4 ,x R> C,x ;        \ CX 1234 [BX] # 56 IMUL
: K8 WORDSx     PM SWAP >R JU
                L4 C,x R> ,x ;        \ CX 12 [BX] # 3456 IMUL
: K9 WORDSx     PN SWAP >R JU
                L4 ,x R> ,x ;         \ CX 1234 [BX] # 5678 IMU
: KA WORDSx     L7 PI JT C,x ;        \ CX [BX] # 12 IMUL
: KB WORDSx     PI JT ,x ;            \ CX [BX] # 1234 IMUL
-->

84
\ assembler code generator                      JFB 09:34 02/27/88

: J9            03 PICK ;

: KD WORDSx     02 PICK >R N1 R> C,x  ; \ BL 7 RCL
: KE            L0 KD ;                 \ BX 7 RCL
: KF WORDSx     J9 >R MT R> C,x ;       \ 12 or 1234 7 BYTE RCL
: KH WORDSx     J9 >R MX R> C,x ;       \ 12 [BX] 7 BYTE RCL
: KI WORDSx     J9 >R MZ R> C,x ;       \ 1234 [BX] 7 BYTE RCL
```

```
: KK WORDSx      J9 >R MV R> C,x ;          \ [BX] 7 BYTE RCL
: KL             L0 KF ;                    \ 12 or 1234 7 WORD RCL
: KM             L0 KH ;                    \ 12 [BX] 7 WORD RCL
: KN             L0 KI ;                    \ 1234 [BX] 7 WORD RCL
: KO             L0 KK ;                    \ [BX] 7 WORD RCL
-->

85
\ assembler code generator                              JFB 09:34 02/27/88

: KR WORDSx      PL LF L4 ,x ;  \  CX 12 or 1234 BOUND
: KS WORDSx      PM JU L4 C,x ; \  CX 12 [BX] BOUND
: KT WORDSx      PN JU L4 ,x ;  \  CX 1234 [BX] BOUND

: J0 WORDSx      0F C,x ;
: J1             DUP 6300 <>
                 IF J0 THEN ;
: KV             J1 PO JT ;     \  CX DX LAR
: KW             J1 KR ;        \  CX 12 or 1234 LAR
: KX             J1 KS ;        \  CX 12 [BX] LAR
: KY             J1 KT ;        \  CX 1234 [BX] LAR
: KZ             J1 JT ;        \  CX [BX] LAR
-->

86
\ assembler code generator                              JFB 09:36 02/27/88

: KQ             J0 PO PK ;                 \ CX LTR

: J2 WORDSx      J0 PL LV ,x ;              \ 12 or 1234 LGDT
: J3 WORDSx      J0 PM PK C,x ;             \ 12 [BX] LGDT
: J5 WORDSx      J0 PN PK ,x ;              \ 1234 [BX] LGDT
: J6             J0 PK ;                    \ [BX] LGDT

: PD WORDSx      C,x HEREx 2+ - OFF16 ; \ FREESUB CALL
: Q3 WORDSx      C,x ;                      \ for printing

-->

87
\                                                       JFB 09:37 02/27/88

: QN             LV 8 * 0C0
                 OR OR C, ;        \ DL CL LODS or STOS V20/30

: QG             LV SWAP 0C0       \ DL 9 LODS              V20/30
                 OR C, C, ;

: QI             OS C0 OR C, ;     \ DL BCD ROL             V20/30
: QJ             OS 06 C, , ;      \ 12 or 1234 BCD ROL
: QK             OS 40 OR C, C, ; \ 12 [BX] BCD ROL
: QL             OS 80 OR C, ,  ; \ 1234 [BX] BCD ROL
: QM             OS C, ;           \ [BX] BCD ROL
: QR             C, SWAP , C, ;    \ 1234 56 ENTER
-->

88
\ assembler code generator                              JFB 11:58 02/27/88

: ?WAIT WORDSx   0F800 AND 0D800 = \ need an ndp wait?
                 IF WF @           \ yes, is wait flag set
                   IF 09B C,x      \ assemble a wait
                   THEN 1 WF !     \ set wait flag
                 THEN ;
```

```
-->

89
\ attribute analyzer                                 11:02 09/25/86
-->
The attribute analyzer compares each value on the attribute
stack to each value in the valid operand syntax table.

90
\ attribute analyzer                             \ JFB 10:47 03/27/86

( index --- type )
: T0@            T0 + C@ ;

( index --- true or false )
: PNUL           T0@ NUL       = ;
: PDISP=LO       T0@ DISP=LO   = ;
: PDISP=LOHI     T0@ DISP=LOHI = ;
: PDATA8         T0@ DATA8     = ;
: PDATA16        T0@ DATA16    = ;
: ?REG           = SWAP TOP @ 1- SWAP - DEPTH CSP0 @ - SWAP +
                    PICK ;
-->

91
\ attribute analyzer                             \ JFB 10:47 03/27/86

: JV             ?REG 0 = AND ;
: JW             ?REG 1 = AND ;
: PALREG         DUP T0@ BREG JV ;
: PAXREG         DUP T0@ WREG JV ;
: PBREG          T0@ BREG = ;
: PWREG          T0@ WREG = ;
: PSREG          T0@ SREG = ;
: PR/M           T0@ R/M  = ;
: PBYTE          T0@ BYT8 = ;
: PWORD          T0@ WO16 = ;
: PSTX           T0@ STX  = ;
: PST0           DUP T0@  STX JV ;
-->

92
\ attribute analyzer                               JFB 11:58 02/27/88

: PST1           DUP T0@ STX JW ;
: PFI/R          T0@ FI/R = ;
: PFQTB          T0@ FQTB = ;
: PCLREG         DUP T0@ BREG JW ;
: PONE           DUP T0@ DISP=LO JW ;
: PPT            T0@ PT = ;
: PFR            T0@ FR = ;
: PDXREG         DUP T0@ WREG ?REG 2 = AND ;
: PBCD           T0@ PKD = ;
: PINVALID       0 ;
-->

93
\ attribute analyzer                               JFB 11:59 02/27/88

( attribute table address --- true or false )
: ?=             FFFF SWAP 4 0
                 DO DUP I DUP ROT + C@ ONGOSUB
                    PNUL    PDISP=LO    PDISP=LOHI PDATA8
                    PDATA16 PALREG      PAXREG     PBREG
```

```
               PWREG    PSREG        PR/M         PBYTE
               PWORD    PSTX         PST0         PST1
               PFI/R    PFQTB        PCLREG       PONE
               PPT      PFR          PDXREG       PBCD
               PINVALID
               ENDGOSUB 0=
            IF SWAP DROP 0 SWAP LEAVE THEN
            LOOP DROP ; -->
```

94
```
\ attribute analyzer                         JFB 11:59 02/27/88

( form # --- 0=no match otherwise processing type )
: ?VF       0 SWAP VFS + DUP 2-
            @ 4 * SWAP @ 4 * OVER - OVER + SWAP
            DO VF I + ?=
              IF DROP I 4 / 1+ LEAVE THEN
            4 +LOOP ;
-->
```

Main loop of attribute analyzer.

95
```
\ code generator vector                    \ JFB 21:56 03/27/86

: ASM,      OVER ?WAIT ONGOSUB
            INVALID L1     L2      LH      LI      \ 0
            LH      LK     LL      LM      LN      \ 5
            LM      LP     LQ      L5      L6      \ 10
            L5      L8     L9      LA      LB      \ 15
            LA      LD     LE      LS      LT      \ 20
            PE      LX     LX      LW      LW      \ 25
            PK      LZ     M2      M3      Q9      \ 30
            QC      M6     M7      M8      QD      \ 35
            MA      MD     MD      ME      ME      \ 40
            MB      MB     MC      MC      MK      \ 45
            ML      ML     O5      O6      O7      \ 50
            O8      O9     OA      OB      L5      \ 55
-->
```

96
```
\ code generator vector                    \ JFB 10:47 03/27/86

            L5      L6     L8      L9      N1      \  60
            N3      MT     MX      MT      MZ      \  65
            MV      MU     MU      MY      NO      \  70
            MW      N1     N3      MT      MX      \  75
            MT      MZ     MV      MU      MU      \  80
            MY      NO     MW      N5      N4      \  85
            MN      MP     MN      MQ      PK      \  90
            OJ      OJ     MP      MQ      PK      \  95
            MR      OO     OO      OK      OL      \ 100
            OM      PC     N7      N8      N8      \ 105

-->
```

97
```
\ code generator vector                    \ JFB 10:47 03/27/86

            NA      N9     LJ      L3      OP      \ 110
            OP      NB     NB      NB      NB      \ 115
            NE      NE     NF      NG      NH      \ 120
            NI      NJ     NK      NL      NK      \ 125
            NM      NO     NP      NQ      NP      \ 130
            NR      NS     NT      NU      NV      \ 135
            NW      NV     NX      NY      O0      \ 140
```

```
                NZ       NZ       O1       O2       O2        \ 145
                PD       PD       Q3       LV       OQ        \ 150
-->

98
\ code generator vector                          \ JFB 10:47 03/27/86

                OT       OS       OV       OY       OZ        \ 155
                OY       P0       P1       P2       P3        \ 160
                P4       P3       P5       P6       P7        \ 165
                OY       OZ       OY       P0       P1        \ 170
                P2       P3       P4       P3       P5        \ 175
                P6       P7       PK       MN       MP        \ 180
                MN       MQ       PK       MR       K0        \ 185
-->

99
\ code generator vector                            JFB 11:59 02/27/88
                NZ       K2       K3       K4       K4        \ 190
                K5       K5       K6       K7       K8        \ 195
                K9       KA       KB       KD       KE        \ 200
                KF       KH       KF       KI       KK        \ 205
                KL       KL       KM       KN       KO        \ 210
                QR       QR       KQ       KR       KS        \ 215
                KR       KT       JT       KV       KW        \ 220
                KX       KW       KY       KZ       J2        \ 225
                J3       J2       J5       J6       OI        \ 230
                Q4       Q5       Q6       Q7                 \ 235
                ENDGOSUB RESET ;
-->

100
\ opcode forms                                         14:05 09/25/86
-->
1MI compiles in the valid form types of each instruction and the
generic opcode for each valid form.  The opcodes execute 1MI to
search the syntax tables for the first encountered valid form.
1MI returns the code generation index if a match of the
attribute stack and syntax tables is found.  Otherwise a 0 is
returned.  The code generation index is passed to the code
generator.  The code generator issues the invalid opcode/operand
error message if it receives a zero index.

101
\ opcode forms                                     JFB 11:59 02/27/88

( form1\opcode1\...\formn\opcoden\2*n --- ;compile )
( --- word opcode\form # found, 0 not found ;execute )
: 1MI           <BUILDS DUP C, 0 DO , C, LOOP
                DOES> >R ?DISP 0 R> DUP 1+ SWAP C@ 3 * OVER +
                DO I 1- C@               \  DUP CR ." VF " .
                  ?VF -DUP
                  IF SWAP DROP I 3 - @ SWAP LEAVE THEN -3
                +LOOP ASM, ;

: JX            STX !TOP ;
: JY            BREG !TOP ;
: Q8            WREG !TOP ;
: Q0            R/M !TOP ;
-->
102
\ attribute vector modifiers                       JFB 12:09 02/27/88
HEX
( --- )
```

```
: BYTE            ?DISP 0 BYT8 !TOP ;
: WORD            ?DISP 0 WO16 !TOP ;
: PTR             ?DISP 0 PT   !TOP ;
: FAR             ?DISP 0 FR   !TOP ;
: BCD             ?DISP 0 PKD  !TOP ;
: #               ?DISP DATA16  !TOP ;
: SHORTREAL       ?DISP    0 FI/R !TOP ;
: SHORTINTEGER    ?DISP 0200 FI/R !TOP ;
: LONGREAL        ?DISP 0400 FI/R !TOP ;
: WORDINTEGER     ?DISP 0600 FI/R !TOP ;
: TEMPORARYREAL   ?DISP 0228 FQTB !TOP ;
: LONGINTEGER     ?DISP 0628 FQTB !TOP ;
: PACKED          ?DISP 0620 FQTB !TOP ; -->
103
\ operand execution                                JFB 11:59 02/27/88
HEX
: ABSOLUTE        REF1 IF DROP 7FFF THEN ;
: REL16 WORDSx    REF1 IF DROP HEREx 82 + THEN ;
: REL8 ;

: ST        ?DISP 0 JX ;
: ST0       ?DISP 0 JX ;
: ST1       ?DISP 1 JX ;
: ST2       ?DISP 2 JX ;
: ST3       ?DISP 3 JX ;
: ST4       ?DISP 4 JX ;
: ST5       ?DISP 5 JX ;
: ST6       ?DISP 6 JX ;
: ST7       ?DISP 7 JX ;
-->
104
\ operand execution                                    08:53 09/26/86
HEX

: AL    ?DISP 0 JY ;       : CL    ?DISP 1 JY ;
: DL    ?DISP 2 JY ;       : BL    ?DISP 3 JY ;
: AH    ?DISP 4 JY ;       : CH    ?DISP 5 JY ;
: DH    ?DISP 6 JY ;       : BH    ?DISP 7 JY ;

: AX    ?DISP 0 Q8 ;       : CX    ?DISP 1 Q8 ;
: DX    ?DISP 2 Q8 ;       : BX    ?DISP 3 Q8 ;
: SP    ?DISP 4 Q8 ;       : BP    ?DISP 5 Q8 ;
: SI    ?DISP 6 Q8 ;       : DI    ?DISP 7 Q8 ;
-->

105
\ operand execution                                    08:53 09/26/86
HEX

: [BX+SI]   ?DISP 0 Q0 ; : [BX+DI]   ?DISP 1 Q0 ;
: [BP+SI]   ?DISP 2 Q0 ; : [BP+DI]   ?DISP 3 Q0 ;
: [SI]      ?DISP 4 Q0 ; : [DI]      ?DISP 5 Q0 ;
: [BP]      ?DISP 6 Q0 ; : [BX]      ?DISP 7 Q0 ;

: ES        ?DISP 0 SREG !TOP ;
: CS        ?DISP 1 SREG !TOP ;
: SS        ?DISP 2 SREG !TOP ;
: DS        ?DISP 3 SREG !TOP ;
-->

106
\ syntax forms                                         14:11 09/25/86
-->
Syntax forms given in the following screens define the search
```

order within each generic opcode. The form is followed by a generic opcode.

```
107
\ syntax forms                                          plp 09:21 06/05/86
HEX
                   3E 0037 01 1MI AAA
                   40 D50A 01 1MI AAD
                   40 D40A 01 1MI AAM
                   3E 003F 01 1MI AAS
 02 1200  04 1200  06 1000
 10 0014  08 8010  0A 8010 06 1MI ADC
                   02 0200
 04 0200  06 0000  10 0004
 08 8000  0A 8000  70 0F20 07 1MI ADD
 02 2200  04 2200  06 2000
 10 0024  08 8020  0A 8020 06 1MI AND
 3C 00E8  20 FF10  2C 009A
                   22 FF18 04 1MI CALL
                   60 6200 01 1MI BOUND -->
108
\ syntax forms                                          PLP 10:50 06/08/86
HEX
                   74 0FFF 01 1MI BRKEM
                   3E 0098 01 1MI CBW
                   3E 00F8 01 1MI CLC
                   3E 00FC 01 1MI CLD
                   3E 00FA 01 1MI CLI
          16 1200  5A 1A00 02 1MI CLRB
: CLRB 0F C, CLRB ; ' CLI NFA ' CLRB LFA !
                   3E 00F5 01 1MI CMC
                   02 3A00
 04 3A00  06 3800  10 003C
 08 8038  0A 8038  70 0F26 07 1MI CMP
                   26 00A6 01 1MI CMPS
                   3E 0099 01 1MI CWD
                   3E 0027 01 1MI DAA -->
109
\ syntax forms                                              15:58 01/20/87
HEX
                   3E 002F 01 1MI DAS
          28 0048  36 FE08 02 1MI DEC
                   36 F630 01 1MI DIV
                   5C 00C8 01 1MI ENTER
                   3E 00F4 01 1MI HLT
                   36 F638 01 1MI IDIV
          36 F628  58 6900 02 1MI IMUL
          30 00E4  32 00EC 02 1MI IN
          28 0040  36 FE00 02 1MI INC
                   26 006C 01 1MI INS
                   34 00CC 01 1MI INT
                   3E 00CE 01 1MI INTO
                   3E 00CF 01 1MI IRET
-->
110
( syntax forms                                       PLP 19:16 07/03/85 )
HEX
 2E 0077 01 1MI JA
 2E 0077 01 1MI JNBE
 2E 0073 01 1MI JAE
 2E 0073 01 1MI JNB
 2E 0072 01 1MI JB
 2E 0072 01 1MI JNAE
 2E 0076 01 1MI JBE
```

```
 2E 0076 01 1MI JNA
 2E 0072 01 1MI JC
 2E 00E3 01 1MI JCXZ
 2E 0074 01 1MI JE
 2E 0074 01 1MI JZ
 2E 007F 01 1MI JG
-->
111
( syntax forms                                 PLP 19:16 07/03/85 )
HEX
                    2E 007F 01 1MI JNLE
                    2E 007D 01 1MI JGE
                    2E 007D 01 1MI JNL
                    2E 007C 01 1MI JL
                    2E 007C 01 1MI JNGE
                    2E 007E 01 1MI JLE
                    2E 007E 01 1MI JNG
  2A 00E9  20 FF20  2C 00EA
                    22 FF28 04 1MI JMP
                    2E 0073 01 1MI JNC
                    2E 0075 01 1MI JNE
                    2E 0075 01 1MI JNZ
-->

112
( syntax forms                                 PLP 19:16 07/03/85 )
HEX
 2E 0071 01 1MI JNO
 2E 0079 01 1MI JNS
 2E 007B 01 1MI JNP
 2E 007B 01 1MI JPO
 2E 0070 01 1MI JO
 2E 007A 01 1MI JP
 2E 007A 01 1MI JPE
 2E 0078 01 1MI JS
 3E 009F 01 1MI LAHF
 38 C500 01 1MI LDS
 38 8D00 01 1MI LEA
 3E 00C9 01 1MI LEAVE
 38 C400 01 1MI LES
-->
113
\ syntax forms                                       08:00 06/11/86
HEX
                    3E 00F0 01 1MI LOCK
 26 00AC  6C 0F33   6E 0F3B 03 1MI LODS
                    2E 00E2 01 1MI LOOP
                    2E 00E1 01 1MI LOOPE
                    2E 00E1 01 1MI LOOPZ
                    2E 00E0 01 1MI LOOPNZ
                    2E 00E0 01 1MI LOOPNE
 02 8A00  24 00B0   0E 00A0
 0C 00A2  04 8A00   06 8800
 0A C600  12 8E00   14 8C00 09 1MI MOV
                    26 00A4 01 1MI MOVS
                    36 F620 01 1MI MUL
                    36 F618 01 1MI NEG
                    3E 0090 01 1MI NOP -->
114
\ syntax forms                                   PLP 10:50 06/08/86
HEX
                    36 F610 01 1MI NOT
          16 1600   5A 1E00 02 1MI NOTB
: NOTB OF C, NOTB ; ' NOT NFA ' NOTB LFA !
```

```
 02 0A00   04 0A00   06 0800
 10 000C   08 8008   0A 8008 06 1MI OR
           68 00E6   6A 00EE 02 1MI OUT
                     26 006E 01 1MI OUTS
 28 0058   1A 0007   1E 8F00 03 1MI POP
                     3E 0061 01 1MI POPA
                     3E 009D 01 1MI POPF
 28 0050   1C 0006   1E FF30
                     56 0068 04 1MI PUSH
                     3E 0060 01 1MI PUSHA
                     3E 009C 01 1MI PUSHF -->
115
\ syntax forms                                      JFB 08:21 04/23/88
HEX
 18 D010   16 D210   5A C010 03 1MI RCL
 18 D018   16 D218   5A C018 03 1MI RCR
                     3E 00F2 01 1MI REP
                     3E 0065 01 1MI REPC
                     3E 00F3 01 1MI REPE
                     3E 00F3 01 1MI REPZ
                     3E 0064 01 1MI REPNC
                     3E 00F2 01 1MI REPNE
                     3E 00F2 01 1MI REPNZ
                     3A 00C2 01 1MI RET
                     18 D000
 16 D200   5A C000   72 0F28 04 1MI ROL
                     18 D008
 16 D208   5A C008   72 0F2A 04 1MI ROR -->
116
\ syntax forms                                      PLP 10:50 06/08/86
HEX
                     3E 009E 01 1MI SAHF
 18 D020   16 D220   5A C020 03 1MI SAL
 18 D020   16 D220   5A C020 03 1MI SHL
 18 D038   16 D238   5A C038 03 1MI SAR
 02 1A00   04 1A00   06 1800
 10 001C   08 8018   0A 8018 06 1MI SBB
                     26 00AE 01 1MI SCAS
           16 1400   5A 1C00 02 1MI SETB
: SETB 0F C, SETB ; ' SCAS NFA ' SETB LFA !
 18 D028   16 D228   5A C028 03 1MI SHR
                     3E 00F9 01 1MI STC
                     3E 00FD 01 1MI STD
                     3E 00FB 01 1MI STI -->

117
\                                                       08:00 06/11/86
HEX
 26 00AA   6C 0F31   6E 0F39 03 1MI STOS
                     02 2A00
 04 2A00   06 2800   10 002C
 08 8028   0A 8028   70 0F22 07 1MI SUB
 02 8400   04 8400   06 8400
 10 00A8   08 F600   0A F600 06 1MI TEST
           16 1000   5A 1800 02 1MI TESTB
: TESTB 0F C, TESTB ; ' TEST NFA ' TESTB LFA !
-->

118
\ syntax forms                                      plp 11:47 06/06/86
HEX
                     3E 009B 01 1MI WAIT
 66 0090
 02 8600   04 8600 06 8600   04 1MI XCHG
```

```
                   3E 00D7 01 1MI XLAT
 02 3200  04 3200  06 3000
 10 0034  08 8030  0A 8030 06 1MI XOR
                   3E 0036 01 1MI SS:
                   3E 0026 01 1MI ES:
                   3E 003E 01 1MI DS:
                   3E 002E 01 1MI CS:  -->

119
( 8087 syntax forms                      PLP 19:17 07/03/85 )
HEX
                   46 D9E1 01 1MI FABS
 42 D8C0  44 DCC0  4A D800 03 1MI FADD
          44 DEC0  42 DAC0 02 1MI FADDP
                   46 D9E0 01 1MI FCHS
                   40 DBE2 01 1MI FCLEX
                            ( FNCLEX )
          42 D8D0  4A D810 02 1MI FCOM
          42 D8D8  4A D818 02 1MI FCOMP
                   48 DED9 01 1MI FCOMPP
                   40 D9F6 01 1MI FDECSTP
                   40 DBE1 01 1MI FDISI
                            ( FNDISI )
-->

120
( 8087 syntax forms                      PLP 19:17 07/03/85 )
HEX
 42 D8F0  44 DCF0  4A D830 03 1MI FDIV
          44 DEF0  42 DAF0 02 1MI FDIVP
 42 D8F8  44 DCF8  4A D838 03 1MI FDIVR
          42 DAF8  44 DEF8 02 1MI FDIVRP
                   40 DBE0 01 1MI FENI
                            ( FNENI )
                   52 DDC0 01 1MI FFREE
                   40 D9F7 01 1MI FINCSTP
                   40 DBE3 01 1MI FINIT
                            ( FNINIT )
 42 D9C0  4A D900  4E D900 03 1MI FLD
                   54 D928 01 1MI FLDCW
-->

121
\ 8087 syntax forms                      P       10:18 01/01/80
HEX
                   54 D920 01 1MI FLDENV
                   46 D9EC 01 1MI FLDLG2
                   46 D9ED 01 1MI FLDLN2
                   46 D9EA 01 1MI FLDL2E
                   46 D9E9 01 1MI FLDL2T
                   46 D9EB 01 1MI FLDPI
                   46 D9EE 01 1MI FLDZ
                   46 D9E8 01 1MI FLD1
 42 D8C8  44 DCC8  4A D808 03 1MI FMUL
          44 DEC8  42 DAC8 02 1MI FMULP
                   40 D9D0 01 1MI FNOP
                   48 D9F3 01 1MI FPATAN
-->

122
( 8087 syntax forms                      PLP 19:17 07/03/85 )
HEX
          48 D9F8 01 1MI FPREM
          46 D9F2 01 1MI FPTAN
```

```
          46 D9FC 01 1MI FRNDINT
          54 DD20 01 1MI FRSTOR
          54 DD30 01 1MI FSAVE
                       ( FNSAVE )
          48 D9FD 01 1MI FSCALE
          46 D9FA 01 1MI FSQRT
 44 DDD0  4C D910 02 1MI FST
          54 D938 01 1MI FSTCW
                       ( FNSTCW )
-->

123
\ 8087 syntax forms                            P      15:58 01/01/80
HEX
                   54 D930  1 1MI FSTENV
                                ( FNSTENV )
 44 DDD8  4C D918  50 D910 03 1MI FSTP
                   54 DD38 01 1MI FSTSW
                                ( FNSTSW )
 42 D8E0  44 DCE0  4A D820 03 1MI FSUB
          44 DEE0  42 DAE0 02 1MI FSUBP
 42 D8E8  44 DCE8  4A D828 03 1MI FSUBR
          42 DAE8  44 DEE8 02 1MI FSUBRP
                   46 D9E4 01 1MI FTST
                ( 40 009B 01 1MI FWAIT )
                   46 D9E5 01 1MI FXAM
-->

124
( 8087 syntax forms and 80286 priviledged  PLP 09:11 07/06/85 )
HEX
 42 D9C8 01 1MI FXCH
 46 D9F4 01 1MI FXTRACT
 48 D9F1 01 1MI FYL2X
 48 D9F9 01 1MI FYL2XP1
 46 D9F0 01 1MI F2XM1

 64 0110 01 1MI LGDT
 64 0100 01 1MI SGDT
 64 0118 01 1MI LIDT
 64 0108 01 1MI SIDT
-->

125
( 80286 priviledged                        PLP 09:11 07/06/85 )
HEX

 5E 0010 64 0010 02 1MI LLDT
 5E 0000 64 0000 02 1MI SLDT
 5E 0018 64 0018 02 1MI LTR
 5E 0008 64 0008 02 1MI STR
 5E 0130 64 0130 02 1MI LMSW
 5E 0120 64 0120 02 1MI SMSW
 5E 0020 64 0020 02 1MI VERR
 5E 0028 64 0028 02 1MI VERW
         62 0200 01 1MI LAR
         62 0300 01 1MI LSL
         62 6300 01 1MI ARPL
         40 0F06 01 1MI CLTS
-->
126
\ macros                                     \ JFB 10:47 03/27/86

: NEXT,        WORD LODS  BX AX MOV  [BX] JMP ;
```

```
: NOWAIT        WF 0! ;

: FNCLEX        NOWAIT FCLEX  ;
: FNDISI        NOWAIT FDISI  ;
: FNENI         NOWAIT FENI   ;
: FNINIT        NOWAIT FINIT  ;
: FNSAVE        NOWAIT FSAVE  ;
: FNSTCW        NOWAIT FSTCW  ;
: FNSTENV       NOWAIT FSTENV ;
: FNSTSW        NOWAIT FSTSW  ;
-->
```

```
127
\  structured assembler constructs          JFB 12:00 02/27/88

74 CONSTANT 0<>            75 CONSTANT 0=
74 CONSTANT <>             75 CONSTANT =
73 CONSTANT U<             72 CONSTANT U>=
77 CONSTANT U<=            76 CONSTANT U>
7E CONSTANT >              7F CONSTANT <=
7D CONSTANT <              7C CONSTANT >=
79 CONSTANT SIGN           78 CONSTANT NOSIGN
72 CONSTANT NOCARRY        73 CONSTANT CARRY
71 CONSTANT OVERFLOW       70 CONSTANT NOOVERFLOW
7B CONSTANT EVENPARITY     7A CONSTANT ODDPARITY
E3 CONSTANT CX>0           E2 CONSTANT CX0=
-->
```

The opcodes opcodes for the high-level constructs are defined by these constants

```
128
\ Assembler local labels                    JFB 12:00 02/27/88
\ label --- address of backward reference
: $             FORTH $R DUP #$ @
                IF $A #$ @ + $A DO DUP I @ =
                  IF 2DROP I 2+ @ 0 LEAVE THEN
                  4 +LOOP THEN
                IF WORDSx HEREx FORTH SWAP MINUS !$ THEN ;
-->
```

The local label table is searched for a label matching the candidate forward or backward reference. If the label is found, then the reference is backward and it is resolved by placing the address on the stack. If the label is not found, then it is an unresolved forward reference. The label is negated and placed in the local label table.

```
129
\ Assembler local labels                    JFB 12:00 02/27/88
\ label ---
: $:            FORTH $R #$ @
                IF $A #$ @ + $A
                DO DUP I @ OVER OVER = 21 WORDSx ?ERRORx FORTH
                  MINUS =
                  IF I DUP 0! 2+ @ DUP ?R MINUS DUP 0>
                    IF 4 - SWAP 1+ WORDSx C!x FORTH THEN
                  THEN 4 +LOOP THEN !$ ;
-->
```

The local label table is searched to check for a duplicate label. If one is found, then error message 23 is issued. The local label table is searched to resolve any forward references to it. It is then stored in the table.

```
130
\  structured assembler constructs          JFB 12:00 02/27/88
```

```
: IF WORDSx      RESET C,x HEREx
                 0 C,x HEREx 2+ 7FFE RESET ;
: ELSE WORDSx    7FFE ?PAIRS 0EB C,x 0 C,x ?R MINUS SWAP
                 C!x HEREx 1- HEREx 2+ 7FFE RESET ;
: THEN WORDSx    7FFE ?PAIRS ?R MINUS SWAP C!x RESET ;
: BEGIN WORDSx   HEREx 7FFF RESET ;
: UNTIL WORDSx   SWAP 7FFF ?PAIRS C,x ?R 1+ C,x RESET ;
: WHILE WORDSx   SWAP 7FFF ?PAIRS C,x HEREx
                 DUP 0 C,x 7FFD RESET ;
: REPEAT WORDSx 7FFD ?PAIRS 0EB C,x ?R 2+ MINUS SWAP C!x
                 ?R 1+ C,x RESET ;
-->

131
\ print meta-assembler size                    \ JFB 11:01 07/17/86

HERE ' REF1 - DECIMAL
CR U. ." bytes used by meta-assembler"
CR
' REF1 LFA @ ' RESET LFA !
' RESET NFA   ' BEGIN$ LFA !
' END$ NFA  ' BYTE LFA ! \ hide defining words

FORTH DEFINITIONS

132
\ Revision history                             \ JFB 13:48 01/05/89

date                  revision
02/27/88              Added the latest changes from CSD.

01/05/88              Renamed ASMREVSYM to MA86REVSYM
```

Appendix 17
8051 FORTH Metaassembler

The Nautilus base listed in Appendix 14 and the Nautilus Version 2 metacompiler listed in Appendix 15 are compiled and assembled on the minimum sized version of FORTH86. Once this is done, then the 8051 FORTH metaassembler listed in this Appendix is compiled. You type

```
PFILE MA8051 1 LOAD
```

to compile the 8051 metaassembler on top of the compiler. When compilation is complete, then type

```
SYMBOL.TABLE
```

This creates a metacompiler symbol table specific to the 8051. The version 2.5 metacompiler automatically creates the symbol table, DEFAULT.SYM, if you forget to explicitly type the command.

Keep 8051 metacompiler files in a separate directory from the 8086 files. The metacompiler cannot distinguish 8051 and 8086 symbol tables.

The metacompiler combined with the 8051 assembler can be saved by typing

```
3 SYSLOAD SAVE MC51.COM
```

MC51.COM can be invoked at a later time without recompiling the metaassembler or regenerating the compiler symbol tables.

```
1
\ Nautilus 8051 meta-assembler                        07:37 10/12/89

CR ." Loading 8051 meta-assembler "

: ASMREVSYM ." 10/12/89 07:37" ; ASMREVSYM

' ASMREVSYM CFA ' DOASMVERSION 1+ !

ASSEMBLER DEFINITIONS

QUAN REF1
QUAN REF2

HEX \ load it all in HEX
  -->

2
\ assembler messages                          \ JFB 07:12 08/06/88
: MSG19 ." Illegal label" ;
: MSG20 ." Local label table full" ;
: MSG21 ." Unbalanced operand stack" ;
: MSG22 ." To many operands for opcode" ;
: MSG23 ." Invalid operand type" ;
: MSG25 ." Relative branch outside of 7f hex range" ;
: MSG26 ." ACALL or AJMP outside 2k window" ;
: MSG27 ." Bit pointer out of range" ;
: MSG28 ." Unresolved local label" ;
  -->

3
\ initial the assembler                       \ JFB 18:42 05/12/86
: INITASM 'ASMMSG ASMMSGSIZ ERASE \ clear old messages
   [ ' MSG21 CFA ] LITERAL 21 >MESSAGES
   [ ' MSG22 CFA ] LITERAL 22 >MESSAGES
   [ ' MSG23 CFA ] LITERAL 23 >MESSAGES
   [ ' MSG25 CFA ] LITERAL 25 >MESSAGES
   [ ' MSG26 CFA ] LITERAL 26 >MESSAGES
   [ ' MSG27 CFA ] LITERAL 27 >MESSAGES
   [ ' MSG28 CFA ] LITERAL 28 >MESSAGES
   0 TO REF1 0 TO REF2 ;
' INITASM CFA ' DOASMINIT 1+ !
  -->

4
\ check references                            \ JFB 05:57 08/06/88
: ?REFS ( - ) WORDSx
   REF1 0= NOT REF2 0= NOT AND
   IF SHOW-ERRORx \ show current unknown
      REF1 TO PACKET.BASE SET.PACKET.BLK&IN SHOW-ERRORx
      REF2 TO PACKET.BASE SET.PACKET.BLK&IN
      34 ERRORx
   THEN ;
  -->

5
\ Nautilus 8051 meta-assembler                \ JFB 11:27 04/14/86
: ASMFWD(H ( - pseudo adr ) WORDSx ASSEMBLING? NOT 5 ?ERRORx
   1 REF.CTR.FOUND +!(S
   PACKET.LIST@ TRG.CFA.FOUND DUP @(S PACKET.LINK!
   PACKET.BASE SWAP !(S \ link it in
   HEREx 1+ PACKET.TRG.ADR! \ place target address
```

```
   SYM.FOUND PACKET.HOST.ADR!
   ABS.ASM.REF PACKET.REF.TYPE!
   PACKET.BLK! PACKET.IN! ?REFS REF1
   IF PACKET.BASE TO REF2
   ELSE PACKET.BASE TO REF1
   THEN HEREx ;
  -->

6
\ Nautilus 8051 meta-assembler                 \ JFB 10:18 04/09/86
: ASMFWD ( - pseudo adr )
   CREATE(S SMUDGE(S IS.FORWARD
   SYM.FOUND CFA(S @(S 0=
   IF [ ' ASMFWD(H CFA ] LITERAL SYM.FOUND CFA(S !(S \ put CF
   THEN ASMFWD(H ;
' ASMFWD CFA ' DOASMFWD 1+ !
  -->

7
\ RESOLVE.OFF8 RESOLVE.11BIT                   \ JFB 09:29 11/04/88
: RESOLVE.OFF8 WORDSx SWAP OVER 1+ - DUP ABS 7F > \ 8 bit off
  25 ?ERRORx SWAP C!x ;
' RESOLVE.OFF8 CFA ' DOASMTYPE1 1+ !
: RESOLVE.11BIT WORDSx 2DUP 2+ - ABS 800 / 26 ?ERRORx
   >R DUP 0700 AND >< 20 * R C@x 1F AND OR R C!x
   R> 1+ C!x ;
' RESOLVE.11BIT CFA ' DOASMTYPE2 1+ !
  -->

8
\ address resolution                           \ JFB 07:43 08/07/88
: ABSOLUTE WORDSx REF1 REF2 OR
   IF REF1 -DUP
      IF 0 TO REF1
      ELSE REF2 0 TO REF2
      THEN TO PACKET.BASE HEREx PACKET.TRG.ADR!
      PACKET.REF.TYPE@ PFA.REF -
      IF ABS.ASM.REF PACKET.REF.TYPE!
      THEN
   THEN ,x ;
  -->

9
\ address resolution                           \ JFB 08:14 11/01/88
: ?7F WORDSx    DUP DUP 07F > SWAP FF80 < OR
  25 ?ERRORx ;
: OFF8 WORDSx REF1 REF2 OR
   IF REF1 -DUP
      IF 0 TO REF1
      ELSE REF2 0 TO REF2
      THEN TO PACKET.BASE HEREx PACKET.TRG.ADR!
      ASMTYPE1 PACKET.REF.TYPE!
  ELSE ?7F
  THEN C,x ;
  -->

10
\ address resolution                           \ JFB 07:43 08/07/88
: 11BIT WORDSx REF1 REF2 OR
   IF REF1 -DUP
      IF 0 TO REF1
      ELSE REF2 0 TO REF2
      THEN TO PACKET.BASE HEREx PACKET.TRG.ADR!
      ASMTYPE2 PACKET.REF.TYPE!
```

```
   THEN C,x C,x ;
  -->

11
\ ?UNCONS                                        \ JFB 06:01 08/06/88
: ?UNCONS  ( - ) WORDSx REF1
   IF REF1 TO PACKET.BASE SET.PACKET.BLK&IN
      35 ERRORx
   THEN REF2
   IF REF2 TO PACKET.BASE SET.PACKET.BLK&IN
      35 ERRORx
   THEN ;
' ?UNCONS CFA ' DO?UNCONS 1+ !
  -->

12
\ print the target processor                     \ JFB 15:23 07/06/86
: .TARGET ." Target: 8051" ;
' .TARGET CFA ' DO.TARGET 1+ !
  -->

13
\ product logo copyright notice                      10:21 10/13/86

CR ." PC/ASSEMBLER technology assembler"
CR ." Intel 8051 family processors"
CR
-->

14
\ Operand stack and local labels                 \ JFB 07:34 08/06/88
HEX

     0  VARIABLE T0 2 ALLOT
     0  VARIABLE TOP
     0  VARIABLE CSP0
     0 VARIABLE #$
    20 CONSTANT MAX#$
     0 VARIABLE $A -2 ALLOT MAX#$ 4* ALLOT

( --- )
: RESET         ?UNCONS T0 4 ERASE TOP 0! DEPTH CSP0 ! ;

-->

15
\ Operand stack and local labels                 \ JFB 07:34 08/06/88
-->
T0      Operand attribute stack
TOP     Pointer to top of operand stack
CSP0    Assembler compiler stack pointer used to detect numbers
        placed on the parameter stack not by the assembler.
#$      Number of local labels or forward references times 4.
MAX#$   Maximum number of local labels plus forward references
        permitted.

16
\ Operand stack and local labels                 \ JFB 07:51 08/06/88
-->
$A      Array containing the local labels, forward references,
        and their addresses.
        The local label table has the structure
        0 offset 2 offset
        label    address
```

Local labels (like 1 $:) are stored as a negative value. Forward references (like 1 $) are stored as a positive value. Local label code checks for forward references, immediately resolve them, and deletes the entry from the table. Backward references are immediately resolved. Zero indicates that there is no local label stored in the table.

```
17
\ BEGIN$ END$                                  \ JFB 09:47 03/28/86

\ ---
: BEGIN$          #$ 0! ;

\ ---
: END$ WORDSx     #$ @ IF $A #$ @ + $A DO I @ 0< 28 ?ERRORx
                  4 +LOOP THEN ;

-->

18
\ ASMCODE ASMEND-CODE                          \ JFB 12:03 07/17/86
: ASMCODE RESET BEGIN$ ;
' ASMCODE CFA ' DOASMCODE 1+ !
: ASMRESET RESET ;
' ASMRESET CFA ' DOASMRESET 1+ !
: ASMEND-CODE END$ ;
' ASMEND-CODE CFA ' DOASMEND-CODE 1+ !
  -->

19
\ ?R0 ?R1 ?R                                         07:36 10/12/89
\ address --- relative address\0=range okay,1=out of range
: ?R0 WORDSx     HEREx 2+ - DUP DUP 07F > SWAP 0FF80 < OR ;
\ Check whether short jump is within +127 to -128 bytes and
\ return relative address.

\ 0=range okay,1=out of range ---
: ?R1 WORDSx   25 ?ERRORx ;

\ branch address --- relative address
: ?R              ?R0 ?R1 ;
  -->

20
\ $R                                           \ JFB 07:52 08/06/88
\ label --- label
: $R              DUP 7FFC > OVER 0 < OR 22 DO?ERRORx ;
-->
```

Check whether local label value is greater than 0 and less than 32764.

```
21
\ assembler syntax tokens                      \ JFB 06:29 08/06/88

    00 CONSTANT NUL              01 CONSTANT DIRCT
    02 CONSTANT ADR16            03 CONSTANT DATA8
    04 CONSTANT DATA16           05 CONSTANT AREG
    06 CONSTANT RREG             07 CONSTANT @REG
    08 CONSTANT DPR              09 CONSTANT ABREG
    0A CONSTANT A+DPTR           0B CONSTANT @DP
    0C CONSTANT CBIT             0D CONSTANT BADDR
    0E CONSTANT A+PC             0F CONSTANT ADR11
    10 CONSTANT RELAD
```

```
-->

22
\ $8051                                   \ JFB 06:37 08/06/88
: $8051 FORTH SWAP 0<
    IF TOP @ 1 >
      IF 1+
      ELSE TOP @
        IF 1+
         THEN TO C@ RREG =
         IF 1-
         THEN
      THEN
    THEN ;  -->

23
\ Assembler local labels                  \ JFB 08:51 11/02/88
\ label ---
: !$ WORDSx     DUP      \ make a copy of label
                #$ @     \ get number of labels * 4.
                IF       \ if there are any labels
                  $A #$ @ + $A  \ scan table
                  DO I @ 0=     \ look for a vacant space
                    IF          \ space is found
                      DUP I !   \ store the label
                      HEREx $8051 I 2+ !   \ and its address
                      DROP 0 LEAVE  \ discard label and leave 0
                    THEN
                  4 +LOOP  \ keep scanning or leave
                THEN  \ 0, label is stored; <> 0, no space
                      \ available to reclaim
-->
24
\ Assembler local labels                  \ JFB 10:18 11/03/88
                IF \ space not reclaimed, try to in new space
                  #$ @ DUP \ get number of labels * 4
                  4 /      \ number of labels
                  MAX#$ <  \ is there room?
                  IF              \ yes,
                    $A +          \ get table address
                    OVER HEREx $8051
                    OVER 2+ ! \ store address
                    !              \ store label
                    4 #$ +!        \ more label space used
                  ELSE 27 DO?ERRORx \ table size exceeded
                  THEN
                THEN ; -->
"Store label" stores a local label in the local label table.
Error 27 is issued if no space remains in local label table.
25
\ syntax table builder                    \ JFB 06:49 08/06/88
DECIMAL
           ( VF = valid format )
           ( <destination>  <source> VF  )
        3 CONSTANT #VF

 ( # processed\type0\type1\type2\type3 --- # processed + 1 )
 : VF,          #VF 0 DO C, LOOP
                DUP 0 4 D.R 4 0 DO 8 EMIT LOOP 1+ ;
     41 CONSTANT #VFS
      0 VARIABLE VFS #VFS 2* ALLOT 0 VFS !

 ( cummulative #\form # --- cummulative # )
 : !VF#         VFS + OVER SWAP ! ;
```

```
-->

26
\ syntax tables                                \ JFB 07:10 08/07/88
DECIMAL

0       CONSTANT VF HERE DUP 2- !

0 ( start cumulative count of forms)
( A 2 hex 2 )
AREG  NUL NUL VF, \  1  A INC
2  !VF#

( direct 4 hex 4 )
DIRCT NUL NUL VF, \  2  17 DEC
4  !VF#
-->

27
\ syntax tables                                \      09:15 01/28/86

( @Ri 6 hex 6 )
@REG NUL NUL VF,        \  3  @R0 DEC
6  !VF#

( Rn 8 hex 8 )
RREG NUL NUL VF,        \  4  R0 DEC
8  !VF#

( addr16 10 hex A )
ADR16 NUL NUL VF,       \  5  DEST LJMP
10  !VF#
-->

28
\ syntax tables                                \      14:40 02/19/86

( bit,rel 12 hex C )
BADDR RELAD NUL VF, \ 6  17 1$ JBC
12  !VF#

( A,#data 14  hex E )
AREG DATA8 NUL VF,  \ 7  A # 51 ADD
14  !VF#

( A,Rn 16  hex 10 )
AREG RREG NUL VF,   \ 8  A @R0 ADD
16  !VF#
-->

29
\                                              \      09:15 01/28/86

( no operands 18 hex 12 )
NUL NUL NUL VF,          \  9  RETI
18  !VF#

( A,direct 20 hex 14 )
AREG DIRCT NUL VF,       \ 10  17 A ORL
20  !VF#

( direct,#data 22 hex 16 )
DIRCT DATA8 NUL VF,      \ 11  17 # 07 ORL
22  !VF#
```

```
-->

30
\                                                      09:15 01/28/86
( bit,direct 24 hex 18 )
CBIT DIRCT NUL VF, \ 12  C 17 ORL
24  !VF#

( @A+DPTR 26 hex 1A )
A+DPTR NUL NUL VF, \ 13  @A+DPTR JMP
26  !VF#

( @Ri,#data 28 hex 1C )
@REG DATA8 NUL VF, \ 14  @R0 17 MOV
28  !VF#

( AB 30 hex 1E )
ABREG NUL NUL VF,  \ 15  AB MUL
30  !VF# -->
31
\ syntax tables                              \        09:15 01/28/86

( Rn,#data 32 hex 20 )
RREG DATA8 NUL VF,  \ 16  R0 # 17 MOV
32  !VF#

( A,@A+PC 34 hex 22 )
AREG A+PC NUL VF,   \ 17  A @A+PC MOVC
34  !VF#

( direct,direct 36 hex 24 )
DIRCT DIRCT NUL VF, \ 18  17 S0 MOV
36  !VF#
-->

32
\ syntax tables                              \        09:15 01/28/86

( direct,@Ri 38 hex 26 )
DIRCT @REG NUL VF,  \ 19  17 @R0 MOV
38  !VF#

( direct,C 40 hex 28 )
DIRCT CBIT NUL VF,  \ 20  2E C MOV
40  !VF#

( A,@A+DPTR 42 hex 2A )
AREG A+DPTR NUL VF, \ 21  A @A+DPTR MOVC
42  !VF#
-->

33
\                                            \        09:16 01/28/86

( DPTR 44 hex 2C )
DPR NUL NUL VF,     \ 22  DPTR INC
44  !VF#

( @Ri,direct 46 hex 2E )
@REG DIRCT NUL VF, \ 23  @R0 # 17 MOV
46  !VF#

( bit 48 hex 30 )
BADDR NUL NUL VF,  \ 24  2E CLR
```

```
48  !VF#
-->

34
\                                          \     09:16 01/28/86

( C 50 hex 32 )
CBIT NUL NUL VF,      \ 25  C CLR
50  !VF#

( CJNE operand forms 52 hex 34 )
AREG DATA8 RELAD VF, \ 26  A # 17 1 $ CJNE
AREG DIRCT RELAD VF, \ 27  A 17 1 $ CJNE
@REG DATA8 RELAD VF, \ 28  @R0 # 17 1 $ CJNE
RREG DATA8 RELAD VF, \ 29  R0 # 17 1 $ CJNE
52  !VF#
-->

35
\                                          \     12:28 02/19/86

( direct,rel or Rn,rel DJNZ 54 hex 36 )
DIRCT RELAD NUL VF,   \ 30  17 1 $ DJNZ
RREG  RELAD NUL VF,   \ 31  R0 1 $ DJNZ
54  !VF#

( A,@Ri 56 hex 38 )
AREG @REG NUL VF,     \ 32  A @R0 XCHD
56  !VF#
-->

36
\                                          \     09:16 01/28/86

( rel 58 hex 3A )
RELAD NUL NUL VF,     \ 33  1$ JC
58  !VF#

( A,@DPTR 60 hex 3C )
AREG @DP NUL VF,      \ 34  A @DPTR MOVX
60  !VF#

( DPTR,#data16 58 hex 3E )
DPR DATA8  NUL VF,    \ 35  DPTR # 12 MOV
DPR DATA16 NUL VF,    \ 36  DPTR # 1234 MOV
62  !VF#
-->

37
\                                          \     09:16 01/28/86

( addr11 64  hex 40 )
ADR11 NUL NUL VF,    \ 37  MYSUB ACALL
64  !VF#

( direct,A 66 hex 42 )
DIRCT AREG NUL VF,  \ 38  023 A ANL
66  !VF#

( C,bit 68 hex 44 )
CBIT BADDR NUL VF,  \ 39  C 023 ANL
68  !VF#
-->
```

```
38
\                                            \     09:16 01/28/86

( Rn,A 70 hex 46 )
RREG AREG NUL VF,  \ 40  R0 A MOV
70  !VF#

( @Ri,A 72 hex 48 )
@REG AREG NUL VF,  \ 41  @R0 A MOV
72  !VF#

( direct,Rn 74 hex 4A )
DIRCT RREG NUL VF, \ 42  17 R0 MOV
74  !VF#
-->

39
\                                            \     09:16 01/28/86

( Rn,direct 76 hex 4C )
RREG DIRCT NUL VF, \ 43  R0 # 17 MOV
76  !VF#

( @DPTR,A 78 hex 4E )
@DP AREG NUL VF,    \ 44  @DPTR A MOVX
78  !VF#
-->

40
\                                                  13:05 08/27/86

( @Ri,#data 80 hex 50 )
@REG DATA8 NUL VF,      \ 45  @R0 # 017 MOV
80  !VF#

( bit,C 82 hex 52 )
BADDR CBIT NUL VF,      \ 46  2E C MOV
82  !VF#
DROP
-->

41
\ attribute stack                            \ JFB 07:12 08/07/88
HEX
( number ---  )
: ?TOP WORDSx   3 > 22 ?ERRORx ; \ to many operands ?

( --- )
: 1+TOP         TOP DUP @ DUP ?TOP 1+ SWAP ! ; \ increment TOP

( opcode or operand type --- )
: !TOP          TO TOP @ + C! \ push the attribute on the
                1+TOP         \ stack. Increment the stack ptr
                DEPTH CSP0 !  \ reset assembler
;                             \ stack pointer
-->

42
\ stack check                                \ JFB 07:12 08/07/88
: ?DISP         DEPTH CSP0 @ - -DUP 0>
                IF MINUS 0 SWAP
                  DO I ABS PICK DUP 0FF > SWAP 0FF00 < OR
                     IF 02 ELSE 01 THEN
                     TO TOP @ 1- + C@ DATA16 =
```

```
                        IF 2+ TOP DUP @ 1- SWAP !
                        THEN !TOP
                     01 +LOOP
                   THEN ;
 -->
```

?DISP checks to see if any number has been palced on the stack since the last opcode or operand was processed. If one or more number appeared, then their attributes are correctly added to the attribute stack. Eight or 16 bit displacements are distinguished from 8 and 16 bit data.

```
43
( assembler code generator                    EAD 08:44 09/12/85 )
HEX
:  NDY WORDSx    23 ERRORx ;
-->

44
\ code generation                             \ JFB 08:17 11/01/88
HEX
: INVALID WORDSx 23 ERRORx ;

: T1 WORDSx     C,x DROP ;         \  A INC
: T2 WORDSx     C,x C,x ;           \  17 DEC
: T3 WORDSx     OR C,x ;           \  R0 DEC
: T4 WORDSx     C,x T2 ;     \  17 # 19 ANL
: T5 WORDSx     OR C,x DROP ;      \  A R0 ADD
: T6 WORDSx     C,x SWAP T2 ;      \  17 # 07 ORL
: T7            T2 DROP ;         \  A # 51 ADD
: T8 WORDSx     T2 C,x ;           \  17 19 MOV
: T9 WORDSx     C,x DROP C,x ;      \  17 A MOV
: T10           ROT OR T2 ;       \  R0 17 MOV
: T11 WORDSx    C,x 2DROP ;        \  A @A+DPTR
-->
45
\ code generation                             \ JFB 10:22 11/03/88
HEX

: REL, WORDSx   HEREx 1+ - OFF8 ;

: T12 WORDSx    SWAP >R SWAP >R OR C,x R> R> SWAP C,x REL, ;
: T13 WORDSx    C,x SWAP C,x REL, ;        \  17 1 $ JB
: T14           OR T2 ;                     \  17 R0 MOV
: T15           04 OR T13 DROP ;       \  A # 17 1 $ CJNE
: T16           05 OR T13 DROP ;       \  A 17 1 $ CJNE
-->

46
\ code generation                             \ JFB 09:30 11/04/88
HEX
: T17           08 OR T12 ;               \  R0 # 17 1 $ CJNE
: T18           06 OR T12 ;               \  @R0 # 17 1 $ CJNE
: T19 WORDSx    08 OR ROT OR C,x REL, ;      \  R0 1 $ DJNZ
: T20           05 OR T13 ; \  1 $ 17 DJNZ
: T21 WORDSx    C,x REL, ;                   \  1 $ JC
: T22 WORDSx    C,x ABSOLUTE ;              \  MYSUB LJMP
: T23 WORDSx    C,x ,x DROP ;                \  DPTR # 1234 MOV
: T24 WORDSx    SWAP DROP OR C,x ;            \  @R0 A MOV
: T25 WORDSx    >R 0F800 AND
                26 ?ERRORx
                DUP 0FF AND SWAP 100 / 20 *
                R> OR 11BIT ;                  \  MYSUB AJMP
-->

47
```

```
(                                              \ JFB 10:56 04/05/86
HEX
( index --- type )
: T0@            T0 + C@ ;

( index --- true or false )
: PNUL           T0@ NUL    = ;
: PDIRCT         T0@ DIRCT  = ;
: PADR16         T0@ DUP ADR16 = SWAP DIRCT = OR ;
: PDATA8         T0@ DATA8  = ;
: PDATA16        T0@ DATA16 = ;
-->

48
(                                              WHP 10:42 10/02/85 )
HEX
: PAREG          T0@ AREG   = ;
: PRREG          T0@ RREG   = ;
: P@REG          T0@ @REG   = ;
: PDP            T0@ DPR    = ;
: PABREG         T0@ ABREG  = ;
: PA+DPTR        T0@ A+DPTR = ;
: P@DP           T0@ @DP    = ;
: PCBIT          T0@ CBIT   = ;
: PBADDR         T0@ DIRCT  = ;
: PA+PC          T0@ A+PC   = ;
-->

49
\ PADR11 PRELAD PINVALID                              10:38 10/14/86
HEX
: PADR11         T0@ DUP DIRCT = SWAP ADR16 = OR ;
: PRELAD T0@ DUP RELAD = SWAP DUP
       ADR16 = SWAP DIRCT = OR OR ;
: PINVALID       0 ;
-->

50
(                                              WHP 10:43 10/02/85 )
HEX
( attribute table address --- true or false )
: ?=             FFFF SWAP #VF DUP
                   IF 0 DO DUP I DUP #VF SWAP - 1- ROT + C@
                     ONGOSUB
                     PNUL    PDIRCT      PADR16      PDATA8
                     PDATA16 PAREG       PRREG       P@REG
                     PDP     PABREG      PA+DPTR     P@DP
                     PCBIT   PBADDR      PA+PC       PADR11
                     PRELAD  PINVALID
                     ENDGOSUB 0=
                    IF SWAP DROP 0 SWAP LEAVE THEN LOOP
                   THEN DROP ;
-->

51
(                                              \ JFB 15:33 07/06/86

( form # --- 0=no match otherwise processing type )
: ?VF            0 SWAP VFS + DUP 2- @ #VF * SWAP @
                 #VF * OVER - OVER + SWAP
                 DO VF I + ?=
                 IF DROP I #VF / 1+ LEAVE THEN
                 #VF +LOOP ;
-->
```

```
52
\ valid operand forms                          \ JFB 08:16 11/01/88
HEX

: ASM, WORDSx ONGOSUB INVALID
             (  1   2   3   4   5   6   7   8   9  10 )
               T1  T2  T3  T3  T22 T13 T7  T5  C,x   T7
             ( 11  12  13  14  15  16  17  18  19  20 )
               T6  T7  T1  T10 T1  T10 T11 T4  T14 T9
             ( 21  22  23  24  25  26  27  28  29  30 )
               T11 T1  T10 T2  T1  T15 T16 T18 T17 T20
             ( 31  32  33  34  35  36  37  38  39  40 )
               T19 T5  T21 T11 T23 T23 T25 T9  T7  T24
             ( 41  42  43  44  45  46  47              )
               T24 T14 T10 T11 T11 T9  T9 NDY
               ENDGOSUB RESET ;
-->
53
\ opcode forms                                 \ JFB 16:26 04/04/86
HEX
( form1\opcode1\...\formn\opcoden\2*n --- ;compile )
( --- byte opcode\form # found, 0 not found ;execute )
: 1MI          <BUILDS DUP C, 0 DO C, C, LOOP
               DOES> >R ?DISP 0 R> DUP 1+ SWAP C@ 2* OVER +
               DO I 1- C@ ?VF -DUP
               IF SWAP DROP I 2- C@ SWAP LEAVE THEN -2
               +LOOP ASM, ;
-->

54
\ symbolic bit addresses                       W      07:38 10/12/89
HEX
0E0 CONSTANT ACC              0F0 CONSTANT B
0D0 CONSTANT PSW              080 CONSTANT P0
090 CONSTANT P1               0A0 CONSTANT P2
0B0 CONSTANT P3               088 CONSTANT TCON
089 CONSTANT TMOD
0C8 CONSTANT T2CON            098 CONSTANT SCON
0B8 CONSTANT IP               0A8 CONSTANT IE
087 CONSTANT PCON             099 CONSTANT SBUF
08A CONSTANT TL0              08C CONSTANT TH0
08B CONSTANT TL1              08D CONSTANT TH1
0CC CONSTANT TL2              0CD CONSTANT TH2
0CA CONSTANT RCAP2L           0CB CONSTANT RCAP2H
083 CONSTANT DPH              082 CONSTANT DPL
-->
55
( operand execution                            WHP 10:43 10/02/85 )
HEX
: R0     ?DISP 0 RREG !TOP ;      : R1     ?DISP 1 RREG !TOP ;
: R2     ?DISP 2 RREG !TOP ;      : R3     ?DISP 3 RREG !TOP ;
: R4     ?DISP 4 RREG !TOP ;      : R5     ?DISP 5 RREG !TOP ;
: R6     ?DISP 6 RREG !TOP ;      : R7     ?DISP 7 RREG !TOP ;

: @R0    ?DISP 0 @REG !TOP ;      : @R1    ?DISP 1 @REG !TOP ;

: DPTR   ?DISP 0 DPR  !TOP ;      : @DPTR ?DISP 0 @DP  !TOP ;
: A      ?DISP 0 AREG !TOP ;      : C      ?DISP 0 CBIT !TOP ;
: @A+PC ?DISP 0 A+PC !TOP ;

: AB     ?DISP 0 ABREG !TOP ;     : @A+DPTR ?DISP 0 A+DPTR !TOP ;

: #      ?DISP  DATA16 !TOP ; -->
```

```
56
(                                          WHP 10:43 10/02/85 )
                           040 011  01 1MI ACALL
010 028  014 025  038 026  00E 024  04 1MI ADD
010 038  014 035  038 036  00E 034  04 1MI ADDC
                           040 001  01 1MI AJMP
010 058  014 055  038 056  00E 054
         042 052  016 053  044 082  07 1MI ANL
                           044 0B0  01 1MI ANL/
                           034 0B0  01 1MI CJNE
         002 0E4  032 0C3  030 0C2  03 1MI CLR
         002 0F4  032 0B3  030 0B2  03 1MI CPL
                           002 0D4  01 1MI DA
 002 014 008 018  004 015  006 016  04 1MI DEC
-->

57
(                                          WHP 10:43 10/02/85 )
                                  01E 084  01 1MI DIV
                                  036 0D0  01 1MI DJNZ
002 004  008 08  004 05  006 006  02C 0A3  05 1MI INC
                                  00C 020  01 1MI JB
                                  00C 010  01 1MI JBC
                                  03A 040  01 1MI JC
                                  01A 073  01 1MI JMP
                                  00C 030  01 1MI JNB
                                  03A 050  01 1MI JNC
                                  03A 070  01 1MI JNZ
                                  03A 060  01 1MI JZ
                                  00A 012  01 1MI LCALL
                                  00A 002  01 1MI LJMP
-->

58
(                                          WHP 10:44 10/02/85 )

010 0E8  014 0E5  038 0E6
00E 074  046 0F8  04C 0A8
020 078  042 0F5  04A 088
024 085  026 086  016 075
048 0F6  02E 0A6  01C 076
044 0A2  052 092  03E 090  012 1MI MOV
-->

59
(                                          WHP 10:44 10/02/85 )
                  02A 093  022 083  02 1MI MOVC
038 0E2  03C 0E0  048 0F2  04E 0F0  04 1MI MOVX
                           01E 0A4  01 1MI MUL
                           012 000  01 1MI NOP
010 048  014 045  038 046  00E 044
         042 042  016 043  044 072  07 1MI ORL
                           044 0A0  01 1MI ORL/
                           004 0D0  01 1MI POP
                           004 0C0  01 1MI PUSH
                           012 022  01 1MI RET
                           012 032  01 1MI RETI
                           002 023  01 1MI RL
                           002 033  01 1MI RLC
                           002 003  01 1MI RR
-->
60
(                                          WHP 10:44 10/02/85 )
```

```
                        002 013   01 1MI RRC
               030 0D2  032 0D3   02 1MI SETB
                        03A 080   01 1MI SJMP
010 098  014 095  038 096  00E 094   04 1MI SUBB
                        002 0C4   01 1MI SWAP
         010 0C8  014 0C5  038 0C6   03 1MI XCH
                        038 0D6   01 1MI XCHD
010 068  014 065  038 066  00E 064
               042 062  016 063   06 1MI XRL
-->

61
( 8051 asm high level control constructs   WHP 10:44 10/02/85 )
HEX
070   CONSTANT 0=       060     CONSTANT 0<>
050   CONSTANT CARRY    040     CONSTANT NOCARRY

: BIT WORDSx     030 C,x ;
: NOBIT WORDSx   020 C,x ;

: IF WORDSx      C,x HEREx 00 C,x DUP 1+ 07FFE RESET ;

: ELSE WORDSx    07FFE ?PAIRSx 080 C,x HEREx 0 C,x ROT ROT
                 HEREx FORTH SWAP - ?7F
                 FORTH SWAP WORDSx C!x DUP 1+ 07FFE RESET ;

: THEN WORDSx    07FFE ?PAIRSx HEREx FORTH SWAP - ?7F
                 FORTH SWAP WORDSx C!x RESET ; -->
62
\ 8051 asm high level control constructs    \ JFB 09:19 11/01/88
HEX
: BEGIN WORDSx   HEREx 07FFF RESET ;

: UNTIL          FORTH SWAP 07FFF WORDSx ?PAIRSx C,x
                 HEREx 1+ - ?7F C,x RESET ;

: WHILE WORDSx   FORTH SWAP WORDSx 07FFF ?PAIRSx C,x
                 HEREx 00 C,x 07FFD RESET ;

: REPEAT WORDSx 07FFD ?PAIRSx 080 C,x FORTH SWAP WORDSx
                 HEREx 1+ - ?7F C,x DUP HEREx 1- FORTH SWAP
                 - ?7F SWAP WORDSx C!x
                 RESET ;
-->

63
\ Assembler local labels                    \ JFB 11:17 11/03/88
\ label --- address of backward reference
: $ WORDSx       >R ?DISP R> $R DUP #$ @
                 IF $A #$ @ + $A DO DUP I @ =
                   IF 2DROP I 2+ @ 0 LEAVE THEN
                   4 +LOOP THEN
                 IF HEREx SWAP MINUS !$ THEN
                 RELAD !TOP ;
\ label ---
: $: WORDSx      $R #$ @
                 IF $A #$ @ + $A
                 DO DUP I @ OVER OVER = 25 ?ERRORx
                   MINUS =
                   IF I DUP 0! 2+ @ DUP ?R MINUS DUP 0>
                     IF 4 - SWAP 1+ C!x THEN
                   THEN 4 +LOOP THEN !$ RESET ; -->
64
```

```
\ print meta-assembler size                    \ JFB 12:00 07/17/86

HERE ' REF1 - DECIMAL
CR U. ." bytes used by meta-assembler"
CR
' REF1 LFA @ ' RESET LFA !
' RESET NFA   ' BEGIN$ LFA !
' END$ NFA  ' ACC LFA ! \ hide defining words

FORTH DEFINITIONS

65
\                                                  07:39 10/12/89
Rev Sym                 Revison history

10/14/86  10:36         Replaced tof with = in the P... checker,
                        whp

11/12/89                - Corrected check of rel branch in ?R0
                        - Changed syntax of Direct registers
                          0 PSW -> PSW
```

Appendix 18

The DIS FORTH Decompiler

The decompiler included here was written and distributed by Ray Duncan. It works on the 8051 FORTH operating system. C/L, which equals 64, is not understood on the 8086 family FORTH operating system. The decompiler must be modified to work on this system.

```
7
\ FORTH Decompiler)                                   16:05 09/30/90

CR ." Wait ... loading Decompiler " CR

FORTH DEFINITIONS DECIMAL

: TASK ;

( 13 LOAD )  ( CASE statement )

0   VARIABLE     QUIT.FLAG
0   VARIABLE     WORD.PTR

: N.     DUP DECIMAL . SPACE HEX 0 ."  (" D. ." h) "
         DECIMAL ;
-->
8
\ FORTH Decompiler, continued )                       15:59 09/30/90

( find addresses of all special runtime routines )
' (LOOP)        2 - CONSTANT     LOOP.ADR
' LIT           2 - CONSTANT     LIT.ADR
' :             2 - @ CONSTANT   DOCOL.ADR
' 0BRANCH       2 - CONSTANT     0BRANCH.ADR
' BRANCH        2 - CONSTANT     BRANCH.ADR
' (+LOOP)       2 - CONSTANT     PLOOP.ADR
' (.")          2 - CONSTANT     PDOTQ.ADR
' C/L           2 - @ CONSTANT   CONST.ADR
' BASE          2 - @ CONSTANT   USERV.ADR
' USE           2 - @ CONSTANT   VAR.ADR
' (;CODE)       2 - CONSTANT     PSCODE.ADR
-->

9
( FORTH Decompiler, continued )
: PDOTQ.DSP     WORD.PTR @ 2+ DUP >R DUP C@ + 1- WORD.PTR !
                R> COUNT TYPE ;
: WORD.DSP      3 - -1 TRAVERSE DUP 1+ C@ 59 =
                IF 1 QUIT.FLAG ! THEN  DUP C@ 160 AND 128 =
                IF ID. ELSE 1 QUIT.FLAG ! DROP THEN ;
: BRANCH.DSP    ." to "  WORD.PTR @ 2+ DUP WORD.PTR ! DUP @
                + 0 HEX D. DECIMAL ;
: USERV.DSP     ." User variable, current value = "
                WORD.PTR @ 2+ C@ 38 +ORIGIN @ + @ N.
                1 QUIT.FLAG ! ;
: VAR.DSP       ." Variable, current value = "
                WORD.PTR @ 2+ @ N. 1 QUIT.FLAG ! ;
: CONST.DSP     ." Constant, current value = "
                WORD.PTR @ 2+ @ N. 1 QUIT.FLAG ! ;
-->
10
( FORTH Decompiler, continued )

: DIS
  -FIND 0=
  IF 3 SPACES ." ? not in glossary " CR
  ELSE DROP DUP DUP 2- @ =
  IF 3 SPACES ." <primitive>" CR
  ELSE 0 QUIT.FLAG ! 2- WORD.PTR ! CR CR
  BEGIN
  WORD.PTR @ DUP 0 HEX D. SPACE DECIMAL
```

```
  @ CASE
  LIT.ADR OF    WORD.PTR @ 2+ DUP WORD.PTR ! @ N. ENDOF
  DOCOL.ADR OF  ." : " ENDOF
  0BRANCH.ADR OF  ." Branch if zero " BRANCH.DSP ENDOF
  BRANCH.ADR OF  ." Branch " BRANCH.DSP ENDOF
-->
11
( FORTH Decompiler, continued )
  LOOP.ADR OF   ." Loop " BRANCH.DSP ENDOF
  PLOOP.ADR OF  ." +Loop " BRANCH.DSP ENDOF
  PDOTQ.ADR OF  ." Print text: " PDOTQ.DSP ENDOF
  USERV.ADR OF  USERV.DSP ENDOF
  VAR.ADR OF VAR.DSP ENDOF
  CONST.ADR OF CONST.DSP ENDOF
  PSCODE.ADR OF WORD.PTR @ @ WORD.DSP 1 QUIT.FLAG ! ENDOF
  DUP WORD.DSP
  ENDCASE CR
  2 WORD.PTR +!
  QUIT.FLAG @ ?TERMINAL OR
  UNTIL THEN THEN CR ;
CR  ." To decompile word xxx type: DIS xxx <return> " CR
```

Appendix 19

The SEE FORTH Decompiler

The SEE FORTH decompiler was written by Mike Perry. It works on both the 8051 and 8086 FORTH operating systems.

The THRU on screen 1 is not needed since the loading of the screens was changed to -->. Screen 1 was authored by Mr. Perry. It is left as it was submitted for your appreciation.

```
1
\ Load Screen for Decompiler                       \     03:53 10/01/86
: THRU   1+ SWAP DO I LOAD LOOP ;
   2 12 THRU   CR ." Decompiler Loaded "   ;S
```

A Forth decompiler is a utility program that translates executable forth code back into source code. Normally this is impossible, since traditional compilers produce more object code than source, but in Forth it is quite easy. The decompiler is almost one to one, failing only to correctly decompile the various Forth control stuctures and special compiling words. It was written with modifiability in mind, so if you add your own special compiling words, it will be easy to change the decompiler to include them. This code is highly implementation dependant, and will NOT work on other Forth systems. To invoke the decompiler, use the word SEE <name> where <name> is the name of a Forth word.

```
2
3
4
( System messages )                                \     09:47 02/19/86
empty stack
dictionary full
has incorrect address mode
is redefined
is undefined
disk address out of range
stack overflow
disk error
line 4 09
line 4 10
line 4 11
line 4 12
BASE must be DECIMAL
missing decimal point
line 4 15
5
( System messages )                                \     09:48 02/19/86
compilation only, use in definition
execution only
conditionals not paired
definition not finished
in protected dictionary
use only when loading
off current editing screen
declare vocabulary
no case body
line 5 10
line 5 11
line 5 12
line 5 13
line 5 14
line 5 15
6
( 8051 assembler messages )                        \     13:15 02/19/86
relative address out of range
illegal label
duplicate label
too many operands
invalid opcode/operand form
11 bit address out of range
local label table full
```

```
unresolved local label
illegal bit address designation
command form not implemented
line 6 12
line 6 13
line 6 14
line 6 15
line 6 16
7
\ Positional case defining word                    10:21 12/03/86
: CR   CR  0 OUT !  ;
: NID.   ( apf -- )   OUT @ 72 > IF CR THEN  NFA ID.  ;

( Subscripts start FROM 0 )
: BAD-INDEX   ( # adf -- ) ( report out of range error )
   CR  ." Subscript out of range on "  DUP 2- NID.
   ."    Max is " ?   ."    tried " .  QUIT   ;
: MAP  ( # adf -- a ) ( convert subscript # to address a )
   2DUP @  U< IF   2+ SWAP 2* +   ELSE   BAD-INDEX  THEN   ;

: CASE:   ( n --  ) ( define positional case defining word )
   <BUILDS  ,  !CSP  SMUDGE  [COMPILE] ]  \ for immediate ]
   DOES>   ( #subscript -- ) ( executes #'th word )
     MAP @ EXECUTE  ;
-->
8
\ ASSOCIATIVE:                Table Lookup         15:39 12/02/86

: ASSOCIATIVE:   ( n -- )
   <BUILDS  ,
   DOES>          ( N -- INDEX )
      DUP @ ( N PFA CNT )   ROT ROT DUP @ 0 ( CNT N PFA CNT 0 )
      DO   2+   2DUP @ = ( CNT N PFA' BOOL )
         IF 2DROP DROP   I 0 0   LEAVE   THEN
            ( CLEAR STACK AND RETURN INDEX THAT MATCHED )
      LOOP   2DROP   ;
-->

9
\ Decompile each type of word                       15:39 12/02/86
0 VARIABLE 'SEE
: (SEE)   'SEE @ EXECUTE  ;

: .WORD        ( IP -- IP' )
   DUP @ 2+ NID.   2+    ;
: .INLINE      ( IP -- IP' )
   2+   DUP @ U.   2+    ;
: .BRANCH      ( IP -- IP' )
   .WORD   DUP @ U.   2+    ;
: .QUOTE       ( IP -- IP' )
   .WORD   .WORD    ;
-->

10
\ Decompile each type of word                       15:39 12/02/86
: .STRING      ( IP -- IP' )
   .WORD   COUNT 2DUP TYPE SPACE  +  ;
: .(;CODE)     ( IP -- IP' )
   .WORD   DROP 0  ;
: .UNNEST      ( IP -- IP' )
   ." ; "   DROP   0   ;
: .FINISH      ( IP -- IP' )
   .WORD   DROP   0   ;
-->
```

```
11
\ Classify each word in a definition                    08:17 12/03/86
 9 ASSOCIATIVE: EXECUTION-CLASS
   ( 0 ) '   LIT       CFA ,        ( 1 ) '   0BRANCH  CFA ,
   ( 2 ) '   BRANCH    CFA ,        ( 3 ) '   (LOOP)   CFA ,
   ( 4 ) '   (+LOOP)   CFA ,        ( 5 ) '   COMPILE  CFA ,
   ( 6 ) '   (;CODE)   CFA ,        ( 7 ) '   (.")     CFA ,
   ( 8 ) '   ;S        CFA ,
-->

12
\ Classify each word in a definition                    09:16 12/03/86
10 CASE: .EXECUTION-CLASS
   ( 0 )      .INLINE               ( 1 )      .BRANCH
   ( 2 )      .BRANCH               ( 3 )      .BRANCH
   ( 4 )      .BRANCH               ( 6 )      .QUOTE
   ( 6 )      .(;CODE)              ( 7 )      .STRING
   ( 8 )      .UNNEST               ( 9 )      .WORD       ;
-->

13
\ Decompile a : definition                              15:39 12/02/86
: .PFA   ( apf -- )
   BEGIN   DUP @ EXECUTION-CLASS .EXECUTION-CLASS
      DUP 0= ?TERMINAL OR
   UNTIL   DROP   ;
: .IMMEDIATE   ( apf -- )
   NFA C@ 64 AND IF   ." IMMEDIATE "   THEN   ;
-->

14
\ Display category of word                              15:40 12/02/86
: .CONSTANT     ( apf -- )
   DUP @ U.    ." CONSTANT "   NID.   ;
: .VARIABLE     ( apf -- )
   DUP @ U.    ." VARIABLE "   DUP NID.  ;
: .:            ( apf -- )
   ." : "  DUP NID. 2 SPACES  .PFA   ;
: .USER-VARIABLE    ( apf -- )
   DUP @ U.    ." USER "   DUP NID.
   ."   Value = "   @ 38 +ORIGIN @ + @ U.   ;
-->

15
\ Display category of word                              15:40 12/02/86
: >PARENT    ( apf -- parent-apf )
   BEGIN  1- DUP @ [ ' : CFA @ ] LITERAL = UNTIL  2+  ;
: .DOES>          ( apf -- )
   DUP @ >PARENT  DUP NID.  SWAP NID.  (SEE)  ;
: .OTHER    ( apf -- )
   DUP NID.   ." is "
   DUP CFA @ = ( cf points to the pf in code words )
   IF   ." code"   ELSE   ." unknown type"   THEN   SPACE  ;
-->

16
\ Classify a word based on its code field               09:16 12/03/86
5 ASSOCIATIVE: DEFINITION-CLASS
   ( 0 )    ' QUIT  CFA @ ,    ( 1 )    ' FIRST CFA @ ,
   ( 2 )    ' USE   CFA @ ,    ( 3 )    ' BASE  CFA @ ,
   ( 4 )    ' FORTH CFA @ ,

6 CASE:   .DEFINITION-CLASS
```

```
   ( 0 )     .:                   ( 1 )     .CONSTANT
   ( 2 )     .VARIABLE            ( 3 )     .USER-VARIABLE
   ( 4 )     .DOES>               ( 5 )     .OTHER       ;
-->

17
\ Top level of the Decompiler SEE           \     03:53 10/01/86
: ((SEE))   ( apf -- )
   CR  DUP  DUP CFA @   DEFINITION-CLASS .DEFINITION-CLASS
   .IMMEDIATE   ;   ' ((SEE)) CFA 'SEE !

: SEE   ( -- )   [COMPILE] ' (SEE)  ;
```

Index

SYMBOLS

!, 148, 298
!CSP, 159, 310
!DATE, 166
!L, 166
!TIME, 166
″, 159, 312
#, 153, 305
#>, 153, 305
#BUFF, 307
#IF, 167
#S, 153, 305
#THEN, 167
$, 329
$:, 329
′, 312
(, 160, 312
(″), 153, 305
(+LOOP), 149, 300
(−CURSOR), 151
(−RTS), 306
(.″), 153, 305
(;CODE), 159, 312
(ABORT), 157, 311
(BORDER), 152
(CLS), 154
(CURSOR), 151
(DO), 149, 301
(EMIT), 305
(EMIT1), 317, 318
(FIND), 145, 292
(GOTOXY), 154
(KEY), 155
(LINE), 154, 309
(LOOP), 149, 300
(NUMBER), 158, 310
(RTS), 306
(S0), 288
(S1), 288
(S3), 289
(TYPE), 153, 304
*, 146, 304
*/MOD, 304
+, 146, 295
+!, 148, 299
+−, 148, 304
+BUF, 156, 308
+LOOP, 159, 312
+ORIGIN, 150, 304
,, 150, 160, 304
-, 146, 295
-->, 160, 309

−1, 146
−2, 146
−3, 146
-BLINK, 151
-CURSOR, 151, 314
-DPTR, 98, 288
-DPTR, 273
-DUP, 147, 302
-FIND, 158, 310
-INTENSITY, 151
-REVERSE, 151
-RING, 307
-TRAILING, 154, 305
-UNDERLINE, 151
/, 157, 304
/MOD, 157, 304
0, 146, 301
0<, 147, 295
0=, 147, 295
0>, 147, 302
0BRANCH, 149, 299
0DIV, 143
1, 146, 301
1+, 146, 301
1−, 146, 301
2, 146, 301
2!, 148, 299
2!L, 166
2*, 146, 302
2+, 146, 301
2−, 146, 301
2/, 146, 302
21INT, 154
21INT5, 149
2@, 148, 299
2@L, 166
2DROP, 148, 302
2DUP, 148, 297
3, 146
80286 privileged, 257
8051 asm high level control constructs, 329
8051 Cross Disassembler, 359
8051 Family Bus, 35
8051 family FORTH, 78
8051 FORTH Cross Assembler, 261
8051 FORTH Metaassembler, 479
8051 FORTH Operating System, 109, 285
8086 Family FORTH Nucleus, 141
8086 Family Metaassembler, 445
8086/186/286, 73
8087 syntax forms, 256
8087/287, 73
8250 ACE, 43
:, 150, 303
;, 159, 312
;CODE, 259, 273, 330
;S, 149, 301
<, 147, 295
<#, 153, 305
<>, 146, 302
<BUILDS, 159, 311
=, 147, 302
>, 147, 304
><, 148
>R, 147, 297
?, 153, 305
?COMP, 157, 310
?CS:, 166
?CSP, 157, 310
?DEF, 167
?DEPTH, 157
?ERROR, 157, 310
?EXEC, 157, 310
?GOSUBW, 167
?KEY, 155
?LOADING, 157, 310
?MODE, 151
?PAIRS, 157, 310
?STACK, 157, 310
?TERMINAL, 155, 306
@, 148, 298
@DATE, 166
@L, 166
@TERMINAL, 306
@TIME, 166
[, 159, 311
[COMPILE], 159, 312
], 159, 311

A

A0PUSH, 98, 290
A0PUSH,, 273
ABL, 142
ABLOCK, 164
ABORT, 163, 311
ABS, 148, 304
ACR, 142

ADIOS, 160
AFILE, 162
AGAIN, 159, 312
ALIST, 165
allocation of ROM, RAM, and I/O, 24
ALLOT, 150, 304
ALOAD, 164
AND, 146, 296
APUSH, 98, 143, 290
APUSH,, 273
ASCII Listing 8051 FORTH, 335
ASCIITOSCR, 66, 189
assembler, 78
assembler code, 93, 103
Assembler local labels, 258, 319, 329
assembler programming, 77
assembler syntax forms, 78
assembler syntax tokens, 319
AUX, 162
AUXF, 160
AUXILIARY, 162

B

B/BUF, 307
B/SCR, 307
BACK, 159, 312
BACKGROUND, 152
BASE, 150, 303
BEGIN, 62, 159, 259, 272, 312, 329
BEGIN$, 329
BELL, 142
bit addresses, 6
BLACK, 152
BLANKS, 148, 305
BLINK, 151
BLK, 303
BLOCK, 156, 309
BLOSAVE, 164
BLUE, 152
Boutelle, Jerry, 542
BPS, 142
BRANCH, 149, 299
BRKEY, 143
BROWN, 152
BSIN, 142
BTOASCII, 59
BUFFER, 156, 308
bussed 8051 microcontroller, 36
BW320, 151
BW40, 151
BW640, 151
BW80, 151
BWCURSOR, 151
BYE, 163

C

C, 139
C!, 148, 299
C!L, 166
C, 150, 304
C/L, 303
C@, 148, 298
C@L, 104, 166
CASE, 63, 314, 360, 370
CASE statement, 64
CFA, 89, 91, 150, 304
CHECKSUM, 316, 384
Chronological, 92
CLOSEH, 161
CLOSEHANDLE, 161
CLOSEMESS, 161
CLS, 154, 314
CMOVE, 148, 295
CMOVE>, 149
CMOVEL, 166
CO320, 151
CO40, 151
CO80, 151
CODE, 259, 273, 330
CODE and DATA memory, 9
Code Field, 91
CODE memory, 2
COLD, 117, 143, 163, 287, 313
COLORCURSOR, 151
com interrupt service routine, 378
COMPILE, 159, 312
COMSAVE, 164
CONSOLE, 155
CONSTANT, 149, 302
CONTEXT, 91, 150, 303
CONTEXT @, 118
conversion, 62
COUNT, 153
CR, 306
CREATE, 158, 311
CREATEHANDLE, 161

cross assembler, 83
CSP, 150, 303
Ctrl Break interrupt, 76
CURRENT, 91, 150, 303
CURRENT U., 118
CURSOR, 314
CYAN, 152

D

D+, 146, 296
D+−, 148, 304
D−, 146
D., 153, 305
D.R, 153, 305
D2/, 146
D<, 147
D=, 147
D>, 147
DABS, 148, 304
DATA memory, 3
DBT, 142
debugging strategies, 10
DECIMAL, 150, 311
decoding, 25
decompiler, 133, 134, 135, 495, 499
DEFINITIONS, 159, 311
DEPTH, 148, 309
DIGIT, 144, 292
DIS, 367, 368
disassembler, 104, 360
disassembler main format, 367, 368
disassembly, 103
DISKERROR, 307
DISK-ERROR, 307
disk system, 119
DLE, 142
DLITERAL, 159, 312
DMINUS, 148, 296
DO, 159, 312
DOCTOSCR.DOC, 188
DOES>, 150, 303
DOSERR, 155
DOSFCB, 142
DOSVER, 160
DP, 113, 150, 303
DPL, 150, 303
DPUSH, 143
DROP, 147, 297
DUMP, 85, 87, 116, 117, 165, 314, 333
Duncan, Ray, 495
DUP, 147, 297

E

ELSE, 82, 159, 259, 271, 312, 329
embedded controller, 1
EMIT, 155, 306
EMPTY-BUFFERS, 156, 308
ENCLOSE, 143, 144, 291
END, 159, 312
ENDCASE, 63, 314, 360, 370
END-CODE, 259, 272, 330
ENDGOSUB, 151, 319, 368
ENDOF, 63, 314, 360, 370
ERASE, 148, 305
ERROR, 157, 310
EWRM, 143
EXECUTE, 147, 297
EXIT, 159, 309
EXPECT, 158, 310

F

FENCE, 303
Fig FORTH, 138
FIG-REL, 142
FIG-VER, 142
FILL, 148, 295
FILP-SCR, 398
FIRST, 113, 307
FLD, 303
FLUSH, 156, 308, 309
FOREGROUND, 152
FORGET, 160, 312
FORTH86, 141, 171
FORTH ASSEMBLER, 73, 229
FORTH operating system, 40
Four File FORTH System, 54
full screen editor, 70

G

GETHANDLE, 155
GETX0,, 273
GETX1,, 273
GETX2,, 273
GETX3,, 273

GET_IP, 97, 290
GET_RP, 97, 289
GET_SP, 97, 289
glitch, 21, 22
GOTOXY, 154, 314
GRAY, 152
GREEN, 152

H

HANDLE, 161
Harris RTX 2000 chip, 110
HERE, 150, 304
HEX, 150, 311
HLD, 303
HOLD, 153, 305

I

I, 147, 297
I!, 299
I@, 298
IBM PC/XT bus pin assignments, 34
IC!, 299
IC@, 298
ID., 154, 305
IF, 82, 159, 259, 271, 312, 329
image.com dump, 333
IMAGE.DOC to IMAGE.COM, 61
IMMEDIATE, 159, 312
IN, 150, 303
INDEX, 309
INTENSITY, 151
internal RAM, 4
INTERPRET, 158, 311
IS-X, 158, 310

J

J, 147, 309

K

KBBUF, 142
KEY, 155, 306

L

LATEST, 94, 159, 311
Laxen Full Screen Editor, 191
LEAVE, 149, 301
LF, 142
LFA, 89, 150, 304
LIGHTBLUE, 152
LIGHTCYAN, 152
LIGHTGRAY, 152
LIGHTGREEN, 152
LIGHTMAGENTA, 152
LIGHTRED, 152
LIMIT, 113, 307
Link Field, 91, 92
LIST, 309
LIT, 149, 291
LITERAL, 159, 312
LOAD, 160, 309
local labels, 81, 231, 262, 272
LOOP, 159, 312
LPFLAG, 151

M

M*, 146, 304
M/, 157, 304
M/MOD, 157, 304
macros, 95, 98, 272
MAGENTA, 152
MASM, 102
MAX, 148, 304
memory space, 1, 2
MESSAGE, 157, 309
metaassembler, 128, 445
metacompiler, 123, 130, 399
Metacompiler Base, 389
metacompiling, 129
MIN, 148, 304
Mini Screen Editor, 331
MINUS, 148, 296
MOD, 157, 304
ModMemAloc, 162
Moore, Charles, 140
motherboard, 36, 46

N

Name Field, 91
National 82C50 Asynchronous Communications Element (ACE), 47, 49, 50

Nautilus FORTH Metacompiler, 400
Nautilus Metacompiler, 389
Nautilus Version 2 Metacompiler, 399
NEC V20/30, 73
NEXT, 98, 143, 290
NEXT,, 273
NEXT1, 98, 143, 290
NFA, 89, 150, 304
NFA=, 167
NOT, 147, 309
NSCR, 142
nulls, 114
NUMBER, 158, 310

O

OF, 63, 314, 360, 370
ONGOSUB, 150, 319, 368
OPENH, 161
OPENHANDLE, 162
OR, 147, 296
ORG/DB, 142
OUT, 150, 303
OVER, 147, 297

P

P!, 149
P@, 149
PAD, 153, 305
pad master, 47
PC!, 149, 298
PC/ASSEMBLER, 229
PC@, 149, 298
PCKEY, 155
Perry, Mike, 499
PFA, 89, 150, 304
PFILE, 162
PICK, 148, 309
PINIT, 313
porting, 138
porting FORTH, 137
PREV, 307
PRI, 162
PRIF, 160
PRINTER, 155
Pseudo Name Field, 92

Q

QUERY, 159, 311
QUIT, 159, 311

R

R, 147, 297
R#, 150, 303
R/W, 156, 308
R0, 113, 150, 303
R>, 147, 297
READ, 155
REC, 307
RECVBUF, 317
RED, 152
REPEAT, 83, 159, 259, 272, 312, 329
reset, 28, 29
RESINTS, 161
REVERSE, 151
reverse software engineering, 103
RING, 308
ROLL, 157, 309
ROT, 148, 297
RP, 113
RP!, 147, 297
RP@, 147, 299
RPP, 303

S

S→D, 146, 296
S0, 113, 150, 303
S0H, 288
S1H, 288
S2H, 288
S3H, 288
S=, 166, 313
save, 398
SAVE, 163
save system, 181
SAVE_IP, 98, 290
SAVE_RP, 97, 289
SAVE_SP, 97, 289
SBLOCK, 164
schematics, 15
SCR, 303
SCREENRECV, 317
SCREENSEND, 317
SCROLLD, 154
SCROLLU, 154
SCRTOASCII, 60, 141
SEC, 162
SECF, 160
SECONDARY, 162
SEC-READ, 156, 307
SEC-WRITE, 156

SEC/BLK, 307
SEC_WRITE, 307
SEE, 503
SEEK+, 155
SEEK+−, 155
SEEK−, 155
SENDBUF, 316
SET-IO, 155
SETCURSOR, 151
SETINTS, 160
SFILE, 162
SHOW, 165
SHOWVOCS, 92
SHOW-ERROR, 157, 309
SIGN, 153, 305
single board, 30
SLIST, 165
SLOAD, 164
SMUDGE, 159, 312
SP, 113
SP!, 147, 296
SP@, 147, 296
SPACE, 153, 305
SPACES, 153, 305
Special Function Registers, 7, 8
STATE, 303
storage locations, 96
structured assembler constructs, 258
SWAP, 147, 297
symbolic bit addresses, 327
Symbol Map of FORTH 8051 Operating System, 347
Syntax Tables 8051 FORTH Assembler, 275
SYS, 162
SYSBLOCK, 164
SYSERR, 150
SYSF, 160
SYSLIST, 165
SYSLOAD, 164
SYSMESS, 150
SYSTEM.SCR, 179

T

table-driven assembler, 73
Terminal and Disk Emulator, 369
terminal emulator, 119
THEN, 82, 159, 259, 271, 312, 329
THRU, 309
TIB, 303
timing diagram, 19, 20, 23
TOGGLE, 145, 292
tools, 12
transient modules, 88, 94
TRAVERSE, 149, 304
TRIAD, 165, 309
Turbo Assembler, 102
TVI 912C terminal cursor control function, 330
TYPE, 153, 304, 305

U

U*, 146, 294
U., 153, 305
U/, 146, 294
U<, 147, 304
U>, 147
UNDERLINE, 151
UNIX-like, 57
UNTIL, 82, 159, 259, 272, 312, 329
UP, 113, 303
UPDATE, 156, 308
US, 142
USE, 307
USER, 149, 303
USING, 162

V

VARIABLE, 150, 303
VIDEO, 151
VLIST, 165, 313
VOCABULARY, 150, 303
VOC-LINK, 150, 303

W

WARM, 163, 312
WARM1, 287, 312
WARNING, 150, 303
WHILE, 82, 159, 259, 272, 312, 329
WHITE, 152
WIDTH, 150, 303
WORD, 158, 310
WRITE, 155

X

X, 158, 310
XOR, 147, 296

Y

YELLOW, 152